ALSO BY JONATHAN ALLEN & AMIE PARNES

HRC: State Secrets and the Rebirth of Hillary Clinton
Shattered: Inside Hillary Clinton's Doomed Campaign

LUCKY

LUCKY

• • •

How Joe Biden Barely Won the Presidency

Jonathan Allen
& Amie Parnes

CROWN
NEW YORK

Published in the United States by Crown, an imprint of Random House, a division of Penguin Random House LLC, New York.

CROWN and the Crown colophon are registered trademarks of Penguin Random House LLC.

Hardback ISBN 978-0-525-57422-4
Ebook ISBN 978-0-525-57424-8

Printed in the United States of America on acid-free paper

crownpublishing.com

2 4 6 8 9 7 5 3 1

FIRST EDITION

For Stephanie, Asher, and Emma;
Ira and Marin; and Amanda

—JA

For Remy,
who makes me the absolute luckiest

—AP

CONTENTS

•

AUTHORS' NOTE

THE DAY BEFORE WE FINISHED WORK ON THIS BOOK, PRESIDENT DONald Trump incited his followers to march to the Capitol, storm into the people's house, and commit acts of terrorism against the United States of America. We were enraged and heartbroken over the meaningless violence, the desecration of the Capitol Building—where we have spent years reporting on Congress—and the attempt to defile our democracy.

As the meeting place of the first branch of American government—the branch closest to the citizenry—the Capitol is both the heart of our republic and the most recognizable symbol of democracy across the globe. Any attack on it is an assault on our liberty, our popular sovereignty, our culture, and our way of life. Sadly, the president found aid and comfort in the voices and votes of a shocking number of Republican lawmakers willing to support his delusional and dangerous attempt to overturn the will of the electorate.

He was not robbed. There was no fraud. He tried to deny the American people their sacred right to self-governance by every means available to him. We have no doubt that barrels of ink will be spilled on Trump's failed effort to subvert democracy and cling to power in contravention of the rule of law. Likewise, journalists and historians will have their hands full examining the abnormalities and perversities of Trump's presidency, right through a lame-duck period defined by desperation and denial.

This book is about the reality of the 2020 election. It is about Joe Biden's victory over Trump. We believe that the health of our republic rests on an informed citizenry having as much accurate information as possible, and this book takes readers behind the scenes of the Biden campaign, the Trump campaign, and the campaigns of several of Biden's Democratic primary rivals.

It is the story of a candidate whose life, politics, and message best met the moment, as judged by the collective wisdom of the 155 million-plus Americans who cast ballots. Biden's victory was conclusive, but, at the same time, it was also very, very close—closer than Democrats or independent prognosticators expected.

While it is valuable to look at the popular vote totals to gauge national sentiment—Biden's 81 million-plus votes were a record—presidential elections are decided by the electoral college. Candidates and their aides steer campaigns with that in mind, competing almost exclusively in a handful of swing states that effectively determine the winner. That system is unjust in the eyes of many Americans, but it is enshrined in the Constitution and cannot be changed without two-thirds votes in each chamber of Congress and ratification by three-quarters of the states. Not only is the Electoral College here to stay for the foreseeable future, but Biden won, without any doubt, under its rules.

He did that by articulating a rationale for his candidacy that focused on what he was uniquely positioned to deliver for the American people. It was premised not on a complex set of policy initiatives, but on a simple promise to restore "the soul of this nation." In his third bid for the presidency, he bet that voters would turn away from the trend of electing outsider candidates vowing to change the system and toward an insider who could improve their lives by applying his experience and values to that system. Biden presented himself as a man of character, compassion, and competence—traits he portrayed as absent in Trump—and he stuck to his story through both a brutal Democratic primary that almost knocked him out and a general election that unfolded against the backdrop of a plague and societal upheaval over systemic racial injustice.

But all along the way, Biden caught breaks—at the Iowa caucuses, in the pivotal South Carolina primary, and from an incumbent president who mishandled the major crisis he faced. Those breaks, which he capitalized on, contributed to his victory. But after all the votes were counted, Biden was hardly alone in finding himself fortunate. During the election, and in its aftermath, the nation's institutions and its democratic values were put under extreme duress. The Founding Fathers fashioned a republic that could keep power dispersed, meet the exigencies of any moment, and withstand enormous pressures by bending without breaking. Their glorious architecture held firm to ensure the transfer of power to a duly elected president.

Luck, it has been said, is the residue of design. It was for Joe Biden, and for the republic.

—Jonathan Allen & Amie Parnes,
January 2021

PROLOGUE

TWO YEARS AFTER HILLARY CLINTON'S DEFEAT AT THE HANDS OF DON-
ald Trump, the remnants of her political team gathered in the spar-
tan conference room of her office high above Forty-fifth Street in
Midtown Manhattan. What had been a billion-dollar, thousand-
person operation had since been downsized to little more than half
a dozen longtime aides with experience in fundraising, grassroots
organizing, communications, and tending to Clinton's personal
needs.

But even this group of ride-or-die Hillary loyalists wasn't ready
for what the leader of their little pack was about to unload on
them. It was December 5, 2018, and, with the Democratic victory
in the midterm elections now in the rearview mirror, they expected
the discussion that day to focus on how Hillary could help the party's candidates. They assumed she wouldn't make a third bid for
the presidency.

Her defeat in 2016 had been so devastating, so shocking, and
so close. Donald Trump had won the electoral college by capturing three Rust Belt bastions of the Democratic "blue wall"—
Pennsylvania, Michigan, and Wisconsin—by a grand total of
77,736 votes. Her fans believed she'd been robbed of the presidency,
and her detractors blamed her for Trump's victory. Two years later,
some of her aides were already fielding recruiting calls from prospective Democratic presidential campaigns, and that created a
tension point that Huma Abedin, Hillary's closest adviser, wanted
to put out in the open.

Hillary was absent from the meeting because she had been called away that morning to attend the funeral service of President George H. W. Bush at Washington National Cathedral alongside her husband, President Bill Clinton, the other living presidents and first ladies, and just about every other current and former federal official of note in the nation's capital. But there was important business to discuss, and the meeting went on without her—in fact, the most pressing matter might have best been talked about without Hillary in the room.

Departing from the scripted agenda at the start, Abedin made a special point of noting that one of their colleagues, Adam Parkhomenko, had promoted the presidential ambitions of Michael Avenatti, a lawyer and tormentor of Trump who had rocketed to fame by representing porn star Stormy Daniels and leveling a string of allegations against the president that gave him nearly round-the-clock access to twenty-four-hour cable television for months. It was also well known among the group that Emmy Ruiz, an expert in field organizing who had developed a reputation as a star operative on Hillary's two bids for president, was taking calls from several presidential campaigns interested in acquiring her services for the 2020 campaign.

Parkhomenko and Ruiz had become trusted advisers to Hillary over more than a decade of service to her. While they had taken on other political projects around her runs for office, they had grown up in her operation and were among a small set of her personal favorites. The fact that they were looking at new ventures for 2020 was a sign of just how far Hillary was from the center of the political game two years after her loss. It made sense that they would seek new opportunities given that Hillary had told her advisers in the wee hours after election night 2016 that she would not run again and had said the same thing publicly repeatedly.

That's why Abedin's next words stunned the room.

"In her mind," Abedin said, "she is running."

The forty-two-year-old Clinton family courtier who had earned her savvy through the public tribulations of her bosses and her ex-husband, former congressman Anthony Weiner, knew instantly that she'd gone too far. After two decades at Hillary's side, she could read a room, and this one was not excited by what she had just said. She began to backtrack immediately.

There was still a chance, she said, that Hillary might run. The option had not been entirely foreclosed. The point was that a discussion should be had about whether to delay decisions on working with other candidates out of deference to Hillary.

It would be hard to find a focus group in the world where Hillary's best interests were a higher priority than this one, and her own advisers didn't think it was a good idea. They weren't even certain, at first, if Abedin was serious.

"We all went in there thinking the door was closed," one participant said. "It was a little shocking to everybody that she hadn't ruled out running for president again."

If anyone thought it was appropriate to wait for Hillary, no one said that. The group agreed that each member could continue to work on Clinton's political projects and pursue work with other 2020 candidates at the same time. Her diehards were ready to walk away quietly, confident that was the right decision for them and for her.

But Hillary was hardly the only political player who thought she might have another run in her. Aside from the friends who whispered in her ear that she could take the reins of the Democratic Party again—and she heard from them frequently in private conversations—one of Trump's top 2016 campaign aides constantly referred to Hillary as "the vampire in the bullpen" who might shake up the 2020 race, either as a late entrant into the primary or, more likely, as a consensus choice at a brokered convention. The thinking was simple enough: A rerun of the 2016 campaign with a Democratic base as energized as it was during the 2018 midterms could turn the electoral map in Democrats' favor.

Trump had framed the 306 electoral votes he won as a "landslide." His spin, designed to bolster his legitimacy and credibility, was absurd. He had squeezed into the White House, winning Pennsylvania, Michigan, and Wisconsin by 77,736 votes combined—or about half a percent of ballots cast in the pivotal battlegrounds. Those states accounted for 46 electoral votes, meaning Clinton would have been president if she had won those states. It could have been a closer shave for Trump, but not by much. The math was clear. For Hillary, though, the calculus involved a heavy helping of vindication on a timetable she couldn't predict. She hoped that special counsel Robert Mueller, who was deep into an investigation of

Trump's ties to Russia, would report to the Justice Department and the American public that the president had conspired with Moscow to cheat when he beat her and then obstructed justice to cover it up.

If more of the public could see what she saw—that she and the country had been deprived of a fair election—then the prospects of another bid for the presidency would be much brighter. But there was perhaps another, more important, factor in her thinking. The field of Democratic hopefuls, in her estimation, was weak.

"She did not think any of these people could beat Donald Trump," said one confidant. That included former vice president Joe Biden, whom she had boxed out of a run in 2016.

As her advisers absorbed the news that she was still thinking about running, and hammered out the ground rules for working on 2020 campaigns while they continued to assist her, they periodically glanced at their phones to watch clips of the funeral in Washington.

Like the elder Bush president himself, the National Cathedral is a pillar of Washington's high society; it has long provided shelter and comfort to establishment political leaders of both parties, a refuge from the city's various nonpartisan and highly political institutions. On the morning of Bush's funeral service, metal detectors and camera positions were set up early on the front lawn outside the towering ecumenical sanctuary, ready to receive a stream of dressed-and-painted luminaries from D.C.—as well as the biggest-name TV anchors from New York—for a sad-to-be-seen and seen-to-be-sad farewell.

Shortly before eleven A.M., under soaring limestone arches and stained glass windows, the pews filled with Bushes, members of Congress, foreign dignitaries, former vice presidents, high-ranking national security officials and their predecessors, and, of course, plainclothes Secret Service and other law-enforcement agents who were distinctive only for the coiled wires that jutted out from their collars and looped around and into their ears.

Aside from George W. Bush—the eldest son of George H. W. Bush—the living former presidents of the United States and their first ladies made their way into the stately nave, with seats reserved for Jimmy and Rosalynn Carter, Bill and Hillary Clinton, and Barack and Michelle Obama in the front left pew and a space next to the Obamas left open for the arrival of President Trump and First Lady Melania Trump.

Donald Trump's imminent appearance at George H. W. Bush's funeral would be, at best, a momentary pause in the hostilities of an existential war over American values and political power. Trump had buried Bush's Republican Party and the Clinton dynasty at the ballot box in 2016, and he was in the midst of overturning as much of Obama's legacy as he could. He'd tarnished the Bush family, the Clintons, and the Obamas with his rhetoric, his behavior, his electoral victories, and the power of his office. He would walk into a den full of his political enemies, knowing they would perceive him as the villain in the morality play of eulogies to the last Greatest Generation president, and hold his chin out, as he always did, defiant in his pride. He didn't have to make a scene to know he'd won. He just had to be there. The man who'd vandalized the establishment would be granted the seat of honor—front row, right on the aisle—in the hallowed cathedral used to pay tribute to its great statesmen.

As Trump strode toward the front pew and handed his overcoat to a young Marine attendant in dress uniform with a blood-red stripe down his blue pants leg, Melania shook hands with the Obamas and with Bill Clinton. Her husband sat down, leaned to his side, and shook hands with the Obamas. Hillary never broke eye contact with the middle distance in front of her, staring icily ahead and refusing to acknowledge Trump's existence.

Back in Manhattan, in her Midtown conference room, this was the Hillary her aides adored. Without a word, without so much as a shift in her body or the movement of a muscle in her face, she had spoken for the Democratic mainstream, the never-Trump Republicans, the liberal Western order, and anyone whose values clashed with those of a president who had treated a victory delivered by a minority of the electorate with the assistance of a foreign power as a mandate to crush the pillars of republican governance.

The Bushes were constrained by the wishes of their patriarch—to honor him with unfailing grace—and the other former presidents were held in check by the unwritten code of their small fraternity, as well as the risk of tainting their own legacies by continuing to engage in the polarizing arena of partisan politics.

Hillary's powerful silent rebuke of Trump was also a sign that nearly halfway through Trump's presidency there was still no new leader of the Democratic Party who could occupy the same stage as The Donald and not flinch.

Biden sat a row behind them and off to the side with his wife, Jill. Having just turned seventy-six, he was already deep in the planning stages for a third run for the presidency, holding regular meetings with top advisers at a rental house in the Washington suburb of McLean, Virginia. Biden wouldn't make a final call on a race until he had a chance to consult his family over the Christmas holiday, but he had given thought to two of the people in the row in front of him. "I never thought she was a great candidate," Biden had said of Hillary in early 2017, lamenting his choice not to take her on. "I thought I was a great candidate." Ever since her defeat, he had been talking to his inner circle about how he would approach a campaign against Trump and what Hillary had done wrong. She had used her platform to try to define Trump, but everyone already knew Trump's flaws, Biden thought. If you're going to take on Trump, he told confidants, people want to know *what you're for*. She didn't have a message, he thought.

Hillary was a "terrible candidate," he had said privately in 2016. That year, he advised Bernie Sanders on how to better match up against Clinton. Brush up on your foreign policy, he had told Sanders, and make a bigger deal out of refusing to take the political action committee donations that she receives.

As the Clinton-Sanders race heated up, Biden remarked to one ally that he couldn't believe how bad Hillary's trustworthiness numbers were—he could cite them from memory—and said that, while he hoped she would not get indicted, he wasn't sure. He added that the trust issue could be politically fatal for her. But, of course, he said, he was rooting for her to win the presidency.

Since Trump's election, the Democratic Party's most visible leaders were figures on the left. Sanders, the Vermont independent who had fought Hillary through the primary in 2016 and who remained irritated that some of her loyalists blamed him for her loss to Trump, was lining up another bid for the presidency. In a sign of the strength of his faction within the party, his introduction of a "Medicare for All" single-payer health insurance bill a few months earlier had secured co-sponsorship from Senators Kamala Harris of California, Kirsten Gillibrand of New York, Cory Booker of New Jersey, and Elizabeth Warren of Massachusetts, all of whom were also gearing up to run. Trump derided the plan as a socialist takeover of American healthcare—the same terminology used by opponents of Obamacare—and he would be joined in that framing by the health insurance industry and some moderate Democrats. Warren, a liberal lion in her own right who had passed up a 2016 run, had become iconic in a floor fight over Trump's nomination of Jeff Sessions to be attorney general and was also gearing up to seek the nomination.

Sanders and Warren represented a one-two punch for a progressive wing of the party that had become far more politically sophisticated in response to both the rise of the Tea Party and what they viewed as Obama's timidity in office. Even in the House of Representatives, where Democrats had won control with moderates defeating Republicans in swing districts, the freshest voice of the freshman class belonged to Alexandria Ocasio-Cortez, a Sanders acolyte who had won her seat in an ultraliberal Queens-and-Bronx district by beating Clinton pal Joe Crowley in a Democratic primary.

This is what the Clintons had warned DNC chairman Tom Perez about in early 2017 after he'd narrowly won his job over the more progressive candidate, Keith Ellison. Unimpressed with Perez's presentation on how he planned to restructure the party and raise $100 million, Bill told the new DNC chairman the one thing that mattered over the course of the next few years.

"This is *not* going to be the party of Bernie," Bill said.

But Perez was too weak to rebuff the organized and energized progressives. If he couldn't beat Sanders, he could join him for a little while. They toured the country together over the ensuing weeks as a show of solidarity. A Unity Reform Commission formed to rewrite the party's presidential nominating rules—at Bernie's insistence and with Hillary's acquiescence in 2016—ended up removing party leaders, so-called superdelegates, from the first round of balloting at the 2020 party convention, and the DNC bowed to pressure from the left in rejecting contributions from donors with ties to the fossil fuel industry. At the national level, the Democratic Party was marching left. Its narrowly focused campaign against Trump's push to repeal Obamacare had worked to flip competitive House districts, but that message would hardly be enough for a presidential campaign.

Deep divisions within the Democratic Party had been glazed

over with scar tissue from the injuries of the Trump era, but toxic distrust festered beneath the surface. On one side stood establishment Democrats who firmly believed that a return toward Obama's course was the right salve for the nation. Biden was first among them. They saw the hard left as an obstacle to reclaiming power and a scary bunch who, if given enough authority, would take too much from the haves and give too much to the have-nots.

On the other side stood progressives who saw Trump's victory as a misguided reaction to legitimate distrust of the establishment. In their view, voters were right to believe they had been boondoggled by elites in Washington and New York who had spilled blood and treasure in foreign wars, paid no penalty for a financial crisis that hamstrung ordinary Americans, and built Byzantine healthcare, investment, education, telecommunications, and transportation systems to benefit the wealthy at the expense of everyone else. It's just that Trump was, in their estimation, not just a false prophet but a con man who had appropriated their language to make it all worse.

In her own way, as she sat staring forward at the Bush funeral, Hillary could see it all. Handing the party over to Bernie meant defeat—and she knew, from personal experience, there wasn't much political upside to that. But she, more than anyone, viewed The Donald as a cheap swindler, a thief, and a traitor. He had lied to the American people about who he was, what he represented, and what he had done, she believed. He'd asked Russia for help, taken emails stolen from her friends and used them against her in a political campaign, won power and used it to reward himself and his allies while punishing adversaries. She hoped that Mueller would shine a light on some of his acts. As for where Bernie and his ilk wanted to take the country on policy, she felt that the platform she'd ended up with in 2016 had been far more progressive than that of her husband or even of Obama. If she wasn't the giant leap leftward that Bernie promised, she remained what she'd called herself a few years earlier—a pragmatic progressive.

But the most important thing she could see was that the Democratic Party, at that moment, had no challenger who could defeat Trump. In two years, no next-generation candidate had risen from nowhere like Obama, come to reclaim lost family glory like a Clinton or Bush, or gained such nonpartisan renown in business or entertainment that he or she could gather together the broken remnants of the Democratic Party and join with the never-Trump Republicans to cast Trump back into the private sector—and perhaps into the hands of federal or state authorities. Alongside the party's most powerful figures of the recent past that day at the cathedral, she was certain there was no other Trumpslayer in their midst. If she could have shouted that from a mountaintop, it's unlikely she would have been heeded. She had been told, repeatedly, by talking heads, op-ed writers, and Twitter pundits, to go home and stop talking.

If she was right that there was no one better than her to take on Trump, Hillary's role in 2020 might be that of Cassandra—the tragic Greek heroine who could see perfectly into the future but whom the gods cursed by ensuring that no one would believe her prophecies.

Even at the height of anti-Trump fervor, one aspect of 2020 that was clear to Hillary should have been obvious to everyone else: Democratic voters were nowhere near settling on a direction or a leader as they prepared for what they all viewed as a war for the very soul of the nation. To win, they would need that candidate, that direction, and, perhaps, a little bit of good fortune.

LUCKY

CHAPTER 1

•

"You *Know* Me"

INSIDE THE MAYFLOWER HOTEL'S GRAND BALLROOM, A HISTORIC ten-thousand-square-foot hall lined with gold-splashed columns, arches, and verandas just half a mile from the White House, a full complement of civil rights activists waited to hear from Joe Biden. But there was only one person the former vice president really needed to talk to. He pulled Reverend Al Sharpton into a backstage greenroom so they could speak privately. Left alone, the two men perched on ballroom chairs so close together that their suit-covered knobby knees almost touched. Biden leaned in, the porcelain veneers of his trademark smile just inches away from Sharpton's mustache.

Man, he's in my face, Sharpton thought.

"I'm Joe," Biden started, fixing his eyes on Sharpton's as he spoke. "You *know* me."

It was January 21, 2019, more than three years after Biden had taken a pass on running to succeed Barack Obama as president. That would have been his third bid for the job. He had run for the 1988 and 2008 Democratic nominations, and he had flirted with campaigns dating back to 1980, when he was first old enough to seek the presidency. Now seventy-six, his skin blotched with age and his white mane, sustained by decades-old hair implants, grown wispy, Biden was six years past the age of the oldest man ever sworn into the job for the first time. The telltale signs of experience were the price he'd paid for his unique place in an emerging Democratic presidential field: He'd served thirty-six years in the Senate and eight years in the vice presidency and had generally built enduring goodwill within the party.

Democrats' positive sentiments about Biden ran deep. Over the course of more than four decades in the public eye, he'd endured the car-crash deaths of his first wife and a daughter just before he was sworn in for his first Senate term, run twice with Obama, covered the president's flank for two terms, and lost his eldest son, Beau, who succumbed to brain cancer in 2015. It was easy to find Democrats who could take issue with elements of Biden's record; it was hard to find members of the party who did not view him with sympathy. Polls suggested he was broadly liked but that no more than three in ten Democratic voters would pick him first in a growing field of primary hopefuls.

If he was finally going to win that most elusive of prizes and fulfill the ambition that had driven him for so long, he had to suck it up and ask men and women with lesser credentials for their blessings, their cash, and their endorsements. He hated seeking favors, detested raising money, and abhorred the prospect of rejection. Or, as one of his top aides put it bluntly in 2019, "He doesn't like to kiss ass."

At the same time, Biden put a lot of faith in his own charm as a tool for bridging personal differences and substantive divides. In nearly half a century in politics, he'd learned he could make law with northern liberals and southern segregationists, fashion foreign policy with hawks and doves, and form friendships with democrats and dictators.

But now the elder statesman found himself as a supplicant once again, eager to earn the help of a man whose politics had diverged from his own on countless occasions.

If Biden had remade himself politically over the years, from conservative opponent of school busing and abortion to standard-issue Obama-administration Democrat, Sharpton had polished his own brand in different ways. Once a chubby, tracksuit-wearing acolyte of Jesse Jackson who was dismissed by much of white America as a loud-mouthed agitator, the slimmed-down sixty-four-year-old Sharpton now ate dry toast, sipped tea, and puffed cigars at Manhattan's Grand Havana Room alongside onetime targets of his protests, like former New York mayor Rudy Giuliani. The silver streaks in his hair and a mustache turned almost completely white gave Sharpton a more regal bearing than he'd had in his younger days, and they helped sell the political and social transformation of his image.

In the rarified air of Democratic presidential politics, the veteran organizer, broadcaster, and preacher, who hosted a television show on MSNBC and who had run for president himself in 2004, was one of the last remaining civil rights leaders with real clout among the various Black communities across the nation. He could instantaneously reach into the homes of Black voters who were rich or poor, focused on criminal justice issues or climate change, or leaning toward any one of the various Democratic presidential hopefuls.

If Biden was concerned that aligning too closely with Sharpton could hurt him with white swing voters in a general election, he didn't betray it. Sharpton had been half Sherpa and half flak jacket for Obama in the Black community, both during the 2008 campaign and for eight years in the White House. In Biden's mind, Sharpton could play a similar role for him. But with two Black candidates seeking the presidency—Senator Kamala Harris of California had announced her bid that morning and Senator Cory Booker of New Jersey was expected to follow soon—it was not a given that Biden could get that kind of help. Biden's plan for winning the nomination rested heavily on the idea that he could run up the score with Black voters. He and his advisers knew that Harris and Booker represented potential threats to that strategy. They could siphon Black support from Biden, or, in a worst-case scenario, one or both of them could rob him almost completely of Black voters. If Sharpton endorsed one of them, it would hurt Joe. If he endorsed Joe over both of them, it would be a coup for the former vice president.

Reverend Al's ring needed to be kissed, and it had to be kissed just right.

For the better part of thirty minutes, Biden solicited Sharpton's thoughts. In theory, this was an exercise in giving Sharpton the impression that his views mattered. In practice, Biden occasionally let Sharpton speak before answering his own questions. But the thrust was clear enough. Sharpton was supposed to help convince him to run and offer advice on an array of tactical decisions.

"What happens if I say I'm only going to be there four years?" Biden asked, openly toying with the idea of appealing to voters by taking a radically un-politician-like vow to limit himself to just a single presidential term. Biden would turn eighty-two before the inauguration following the 2024 election, and concerns about his age might be allayed by such a promise, he thought.

"I think Trump will use that to kill you," Sharpton replied.

"Where do you think my vulnerabilities are?" Biden queried.

"You're going to have to deal with the crime bill," Sharpton said, referring to Biden's authorship of a 1994 law that stocked America's prisons for a generation with its stiffer sentencing guidelines and financial incentives for states and cities to build more jails. "And you're going to have to deal with Anita Hill." Biden had been criticized heavily for his treatment of Hill, a Black woman who'd accused Clarence Thomas of sexual harassment during Thomas's 1991 Supreme Court confirmation hearings.

Biden didn't need Sharpton to tell him where he had potential problems with Black voters. He could pick up an iPad and click on any news app to find out that the crime bill, Hill, and his ardent opposition to school busing in the 1970s were a minefield—particularly with activists who were too young to remember any of those politically complicated fights themselves. But he was methodically building up to a big ask—the one Sharpton knew was coming. All the rest was foreplay.

Now, as they neared the time when they would move from the greenroom to the stage, with Sharpton set to introduce Biden to an audience of several hundred activists gathered to commemorate Martin Luther King, Jr.'s birthday, the former vice president cut to the chase. If he ran—and the entirety of the conversation indicated that he would—he wanted Sharpton's backing.

"Al, where you go is going to matter," Biden said. "It's not only your megaphone. You were the guy that was the civil rights guy in the Obama-Biden era." Biden wanted Sharpton, needed him, as a crucial piece of his coalition. He couldn't campaign as effectively as the natural heir to Obama—literally the guardian and extender of the "Obama-Biden" legacy—if Obama's validator in the civil rights arena was on a rival's team. Sharpton heard the appeal for what it was: *Please endorse me, and, good God, man, at least don't endorse anyone else.*

Biden again recounted the Obama administration's efforts on various civil rights matters, leaning on Sharpton harder.

"Yeah," Sharpton said, "but that doesn't mean that I'm not going to judge everybody fairly."

"You gotta be fair, but you gotta deal with the history," Biden said. "We were there every step of the way with you."

There it is again, Sharpton thought. *"We." This guy's laying it on thick. Obama wasn't going to endorse him last time. He's not going to endorse him now. There's no way Obama will push me to do it.*

And that's how Sharpton decided to let Biden down, delivering precisely the kind of disappointing message Biden was hearing often as he prepared to launch his campaign.

"Well, if you decide to run, Mr. Vice President," Sharpton said, "I'll surely check in with Obama."

Biden's failed attempt to bring Sharpton on board hinted at a broader problem for his prospective candidacy. He believed he was uniquely situated to defeat Bernie Sanders in the Democratic primary and President Donald Trump in the general election. But he couldn't count on Obama, or most of the former president's allies, to help him clear the rest of the primary field.

It had stung Biden badly in 2015 when Obama made clear his preference for Hillary Clinton. Adding insult to injury, Obama's advisers told Biden aides back then that they didn't think he could beat Clinton. They pressured him to get out of her way. This time around, Biden knew, the former president would remain neutral. Obama was meeting with other hopefuls and wanted to preserve his ability to play the role of party unifier after the primary fight. If he was going to win a nomination that he hadn't sniffed in two previous bids, Biden would have to crush a cattle call of candidates without the backing of the president he'd campaigned for and worked with for more than eight years.

Because he didn't have Obama on his wing, winning endorsements from elite players like Sharpton was all the more important. And for that reason, it was all the more crushing when they told him no. The same went for heavy-hitting donors, many of whom declined to get on board with Biden early. But the rejections Biden received from prominent Black political figures were most devastating. They could give him cover when, inevitably, his record on race was thrown in his face, and they could help him win over the Black voters central to his campaign strategy.

At a time when Trump's racist rants and policies had divided Americans and fortified white supremacists, Biden thought he could mobilize Black voters and appeal to swing-voting whites in battleground states—a group that included people who harbored some level of racial resentment but were turned off by Trump's extremist tendencies. The counterintuitive concept had roots in Biden's experience navigating the burning shoals of Delaware's racially charged politics early in his career, and it was aimed squarely at demographic groups vital to both a primary victory and Democrats' chances of winning the White House. It also tied tightly into the message Biden wanted to deliver about his reason for seeking the presidency.

Biden was just twenty years old in May 1963, when Bull Connor, the public safety commissioner in Birmingham, Alabama, ordered police to turn dogs and high-pressure water hoses on Black children protesting segregation. The images that ran in newspapers and on broadcasts across the country struck a nerve with whites outside the Deep South, helping turn the tide of the civil rights movement. There was little record of political activism on Biden's part, but he would clearly come to understand the power of that moment to bring much of white America to the defense of the nation's Black minority. "My soul raged on seeing Bull Connor and his dogs," Biden would say at a political convention in the early 1980s.

Fifty-four years after Birmingham, in August 2017, a violent white supremacist demonstration in Charlottesville, Virginia, provided a narrative touchstone for his reentry into the political arena. Along with the rest of America, Biden watched white supremacists gather with tiki torches at the University of Virginia in Charlottesville, chanting "Jews will not replace us" as they marched. He saw video clips of a murderer plowing a car into a crowd of counterprotesters. And he heard Trump equivocate in assessing blame for the violence. There were "very fine people on both sides," Trump said, infuriating Democrats and many Republicans.

Biden's friends and advisers said the clash in Charlottesville and

Trump's response flipped a switch for the former vice president. Before that, he had avoided criticizing the president publicly, and he spoke little of Trump privately, preferring to focus his energy on building new centers named for him at the University of Pennsylvania and the University of Delaware. But that all changed quickly, according to the coterie of confidants who spent time with Biden in the summer of 2017.

"That day really stuck with the vice president in his mind—that this was much larger than Donald Trump and the presidency, a shift in the attitude and the nation," one of them said.

Suddenly, Biden started talking about Trump and Charlottesville incessantly when advisers met with him at his rental house in the Washington suburb of McLean, Virginia. Sitting in a chair reserved for him, with aides fanned out on two couches in a basement-level living room, the former vice president was still getting the equivalent of policy briefings from former high-ranking public officials. That was one dead giveaway that, even before Charlottesville, he was contemplating a comeback. Another had occurred a few months earlier when his aides registered a political action committee called American Possibilities to collect and distribute campaign money on Biden's behalf.

No matter how genuine Biden's moral indignation, Charlottesville lined up perfectly with his frame for a campaign. "If it wasn't clear before, it's clear now," he wrote in *The Atlantic* magazine, "we are living through a battle for the soul of this nation." One close adviser to Biden told an ally at the time that Charlottesville had shifted Bidenworld from playing fantasy politics onto the footing of realistically mounting a campaign.

"He ran in part because he has very real concerns about what happens to our form of democracy if Donald Trump serves two terms," the ally said later. But that same ally also noted that Biden, like other multi-campaign candidates, had never really stopped running for president. "Once they get in their head that they might want to be president, that never, never goes away."

Unlike Trump, who used race to define his political tribe, Biden had used it as a fulcrum. During his career, he had sided with southern segregationists to resist federal school-integration orders and written a crime bill, supported by some Black lawmakers, that ushered in an era of mass incarceration. He also had been a force in renewing civil rights law and had been picked to balance the ticket of the first Black president. At each turn, Biden had been on the side of majority opinion. That is, Biden grasped the capacity of white America to cast race aside. But he also knew the limits of its ability to do so, depending on the issue and the political tides. And having represented a state where a large share of his vote came from the Black electorate, he believed he had a good feel for its needs and concerns.

Trump had revealed himself to the country, and moderate whites had recoiled at the reflection cast upon them by racists. Frightened by Trump's victory, many people of color had come to the conclusion that their best chance to take down the president might lie with a white candidate. Older Black voters in particular could tell the difference between a white guy who talked like Archie Bunker and governed like George Wallace and one who talked like Archie Bunker and governed like Lyndon Johnson.

Biden thought that the time had come for the political middle to reject Trump's extremism and the white supremacy Trump emboldened. He thought he could lead a coalition of voters to push the pendulum of American politics back to its proper track. He could do that, in part, because he wasn't asking whites to be "woke" or to do more than cast a ballot to register their feelings. And, he thought, he could do that because Black voters liked and trusted him. After all, he'd been Obama's reliable sidekick for eight years, and he'd never let anyone forget that.

Though Biden wasn't explicit about his thinking, longtime aides began to take the prospects of another presidential run much more seriously in the late summer and early fall of 2017. Greg Schultz, tasked with running the American Possibilities PAC, and Kate Bedingfield, the former vice president's top communications adviser, both concluded that they were responsible for positioning their boss—through campaign events for other candidates and a book tour for *Promise Me, Dad*—to be ready to run.

In his midthirties at the time, with prematurely graying black hair and an easy smile, Schultz had flown onto Biden's political radar in 2012 when he ran Obama's successful reelection operation in Ohio. The son of two retired special education teachers, and a native of the far southern suburbs of Cleveland's Cuyahoga County, Schultz took a job as a senior adviser to Biden in the White House during the vice president's second term. Loyal and humble—perhaps too nonthreatening for his own good—Schultz was well liked in a Bidenworld that prized those traits in staffers.

But he wasn't fully looped into the long-term plan early on. When he was first directed to create a political committee for Biden in the spring of 2017, for example, Schultz wanted to build a "dark money" organization that could engage in lobbying on issues and spend independently on political campaigns without disclosing its donors. Schultz told Biden about that option, and Biden shot it down, preferring a traditional political action committee. That would allow Biden to cut checks directly to candidates and build up favors, but it would restrict him from raising unlimited sums from anonymous donors. Democratic activists hate dark money committees, and it would be hard for Biden to run in a Democratic primary if he had used one to set up for a presidential run. Biden traveled the country to make appearances on behalf of candidates in 2018 in a familiar pre-campaign ritual that built up his own profile and political credits to be paid later.

Through it all, Biden was publicly noncommittal on running for president, but the chants of "Run, Joe, Run" that greeted him at stops for Senate and House candidates rang in his ears. The siren song of the campaign trail was calling to him, and his barnstorming tour during the midterms added to his advisers' belief that he would run. On a flight home late that year, with three aides huddled around him, Biden let slip just how much thought he'd already given to his presidency.

"If I were to run, there's a lot of good women out there for VP," he said.

By January 2019, with the perfunctory holiday-season family sign-off out of the way, Biden brought his old band of top political advisers back together at the house in McLean. It was a short trip for his top aide, Steve Ricchetti, who had served as chief of staff in the vice president's office, and lived about a mile away. They were joined for a series of pre-launch meetings by Mike Donilon—"Mike D."—who started out with Biden in 1981 and was closer to the candidate than anyone not named Biden. The Washington power couple Anita Dunn, former White House communications director and now managing director of a major public relations firm, and Bob Bauer, former White House counsel, provided strategic and legal advice. Biden's sister, Valerie Biden Owens, who had run all of his Senate campaigns, assisted in the planning, as did Bedingfield and Schultz, who stood out for being a generation or two younger than the rest of the group.

Sitting on couches around a coffee table in the basement of Biden's sparsely decorated rental house was a reminder to this team—the same set of people—who just four years earlier, and less than ten miles away, had been planning Biden's 2016 presidential run in a far more ornate setting. Back in 2015, as Biden deliberated, these advisers had drawn up a campaign blueprint at the vice president's residence, the Naval Observatory. The cream-colored house, set back behind the gates of a Navy compound three miles northwest of the White House by car, was the perfect location for secret meetings because it was out of the way and only invited guests had access to it.

From the observatory, Biden had called donors and greeted potential political allies, including Massachusetts senator Elizabeth Warren, who had opted against running. In August 2015, as he was still trying to figure out how he could defeat Clinton in a primary, Biden invited Warren to sit on the porch and talk politics. It was a much more serene setting than the hearing room in the Dirksen Senate Office Building where they had clashed a decade earlier over a bankruptcy bill. Back then, Warren had lit into Biden for defending lenders. "You're very good, professor," Biden had told her at the time. Now, he wanted something from her, and he was willing to give a bit to get it.

For Biden to win the Democratic nomination in 2016, he had to beat Bernie Sanders, a progressive, and Clinton, a woman. As a progressive woman, Warren's backing might be able to help Biden draw votes from both camps. At the very least, she could provide political cover from attacks by progressives and women.

If I run, he told Warren, I would ask you to be on my ticket.

It was a big offer, but an oddly conditional one. It sounded like Biden was ready to run, and at the same time he was asking her to commit to a campaign that he wasn't fully committed to yet. There was no reason for Warren to think that she wouldn't get consideration from either Clinton or Sanders, both of whom were actually running, and there was no reason at that point to think that Biden, who had flamed out twice before in presidential bids, would win Iowa or the nomination. A little too earnest for her own good when she first arrived in Washington a few years earlier, Warren was now wary of flattery.

She politely declined to make any commitments.

Warren was barely out of the gates of the Naval Observatory when Biden's team leaked the news of her visit to the media. At the time, it was characterized as a two-hour discussion about economics. But the real intention was to bring Warren on board. "He was explicit about VP," said one person familiar with the meeting. Biden would later say privately that had he run and won the nomination in 2016, Warren would have been his pick for the second slot on the ticket and that Hillary should have chosen her for the spot. Biden kept Warren close throughout the 2016 election. They had breakfast at the observatory in April, during the height of primary season—and they spoke often on the phone about their shared concern for the direction of Hillary's campaign and about policy matters.

The Biden-Warren ticket never came to be in 2016, but the seeds of a strategy for winning the Democratic nomination took root in the Naval Observatory in that summer of 2015. In their own private conclaves, Biden's advisers identified a path to the nomination that relied heavily on the vice president performing well in South Carolina, where Black voters might make up a majority of the primary vote and moderate whites would constitute a big chunk of the remainder. They believed that Iowa and New Hampshire, with their liberal caucus and primary electorates, respectively, didn't line up well for him at all.

So it was devastating when the most powerful Black Democrat in South Carolina, Representative Jim Clyburn, told *The Huffington Post* on October 19 of that year, "If I were advising him, I would advise him not to get in." Clyburn's remark was a surprise to Biden, who had known him for many years and had been counting on his support. Two days after that, Biden gathered the national media in the Rose Garden of the White House to announce he wouldn't run.

Nearly four years later, as Biden looked around his living room at the same faces that had made up his kitchen cabinet in the observatory house, not much had changed. His leadership style was the same. A dealmaker by nature, he sought consensus, but within his own team, he wanted a consensus based on his view. Biden didn't like to be questioned, and he could let what he described as his "Irish temper" get the better of him. It wasn't unusual for him to let out a well-placed F-bomb. Those closest to him conspicuously avoided confrontation. In meetings, Dunn tended to agree with Biden, sometimes even if when she had espoused an opposite view before the meeting. Ricchetti refused to take a hard line on anything, mimicking Biden's tendency toward consensus. Like Donilon, who was generally risk averse, he had a direct line to Biden and could always weigh in privately later on. It was the younger two, Schultz and Bedingfield, who were most likely to get their ears boxed for pushing back on Biden's ideas, and Bedingfield was a little more delicate than Schultz. "No, well, sir . . . ," the red-haired Atlantan and former aide to Obama and John Edwards would start when she wanted to guide him in a different direction.

In one meeting in early 2019, Biden unloaded on Schultz. The political operative had told the former vice president that he needed to adjust his tone with younger voters. Biden had a tendency to talk down to them when he defended his record against charges that his generation had failed to solve major national problems, and Schultz was worried that Biden's tone only reinforced the generational divide.

Biden became visibly irritated as the conversation unfolded. He didn't think his tone was a problem. In fact, truth be told, he was pretty sure he knew more about natural political skills than his young adviser.

Schultz pointed out that Biden was getting upset, which only made Biden angrier. "Don't be a horse's tail!" he hollered at Schultz. As if to prove Schultz's point, he had lost his temper at a man half his age over the question of whether he responded poorly to criticism from younger people. Later, Valerie Biden Owens and Ted Kaufman, a former Biden chief of staff who had been appointed to the Senate to succeed Biden in 2009, told Schultz not to take the dressing-down too hard. It was a sign, they said, that Biden felt comfortable around him and trusted him.

Biden's temper, and his willingness to unleash it in small group settings, was one reason the people closest to him often avoided pushing him too hard to change his ways or take a particular course of action. Meetings often ended with no clear outcome. Decisions languished.

In the early months of 2019, as other campaigns launched, snapped up staff, and locked in donors, Biden and his troops muddled toward their rollout. In one early internal battle, Biden insisted on anchoring the campaign in his hometown of Wilmington, Delaware. Schultz thought Philadelphia was a better spot; Wilmington didn't have the amenities necessary for a big campaign. He secured agreement from his colleagues before the matter came up in a meeting with Biden. But when they all sat down together, Schultz found himself on an island.

It's going to be in Wilmington, said Biden, who preferred the ease of having an office in his hometown.

We can't recruit staff, Schultz countered. We can't find short-term housing or public transportation. Let's prepare for a general election and think about having five hundred staff, he said.

Biden stared him down. Schultz expected to get backup from the other aides, who had agreed to Philadelphia beforehand. None came. Biden was ticked off at him, and him alone. Eventually, Schultz's logic would win out—the campaign put down roots in Philadelphia over Biden's initial objections—but he'd been left isolated by the older generation of Biden confidants. The unwillingness of anyone else to confront Biden just led to an unnecessary delay. Even the decision to hire Schultz as campaign manager was never officially made—or, at least, no one ever told him he had been hired. He first found out about it from the media.

Over pizza, or sometimes sandwiches from a deli down the street, Biden and his advisers knocked around countless ideas for tactics, like announcing he would run for just one term or that he would pick a woman as his running mate. Often, he had to be disabused of bad instincts gingerly and indirectly. In two previous runs, he had flamed out badly. One recurring problem was that he had never figured out how to raise the kind of money needed for a serious bid, and his views on campaign fundraising were not in line with what he would have to do this time around. He often didn't listen to the advice he got from people directly involved with the campaign.

Sometimes, it took voices from outside the inner circle—

particularly those belonging to fellow politicians or people who were highly successful in other walks of life—to sway him.

In mid-January, Mark Gilbert, the former U.S. ambassador to New Zealand and a heavyweight money bundler, paid a visit to Biden. Still lean and athletic at sixty-two, Gilbert had played in seven games as an outfielder for Hall of Fame manager Tony LaRussa's Chicago White Sox in 1985. Now, he was the vice chairman for private wealth management at UBS and an occasional golf partner of Barack Obama. During the 2012 election, he had helped the vice president raise money for the reelection campaign, and he was on board to organize donors this time around.

Biden wanted to pick Gilbert's brain about the developing plans for the campaign, and Biden's advisers thought it would be good for their boss to hear from someone else with experience in fundraising and other aspects of building a modern presidential campaign. Biden, his sister, Ricchetti, Schultz, and Gilbert gathered in Biden's den, where a centerpiece desk sat in front of a window. Sometimes, Biden would hold forth from behind the desk. But for this occasion, he sat with his guest and his advisers in chairs arranged in a horseshoe pattern in front of the desk. The intention was clear: Gilbert was meant to feel like an equal, not a servant.

Ricchetti led what amounted to a presentation of the campaign plan to Gilbert, including a basket of ideas that were left over from the planning for a 2016 bid. Biden chimed in on some of the matters about which he felt strongly. He talked about who he would hire for the campaign, noting that his staff in the White House had been diverse, including people of color, women, and members of the LGBTQ community. But as he listed the people he had identified for top campaign slots—mostly familiar Bidenworld stalwarts—diversity wasn't reflected at all.

"Sir, with all due respect," Gilbert said, "and, I'll throw myself in there, everyone you've named is an old white guy. You can't launch a campaign with all white guys. You'll be dead."

Biden abruptly turned to Ricchetti.

"We have to get her on board today," he said, referring to Symone Sanders, the onetime Bernie Sanders spokeswoman. Scoring Symone Sanders, who is Black, would be a coup for Biden not only because she was a talented operative and deeply devoted surrogate but because of the signal that it would send to the rest of the Democratic Party that she was placing her bet with Biden. If Symone Sanders leaped from Bernie Sanders to Biden, it would be impossible for primary voters to miss the implicit judgment from her that her old boss shouldn't or couldn't be president.

"You should [also] have a woman of color who is your traveling aide," Gilbert said. He meant that it should be visually clear to voters that representation mattered to Biden.

Biden was also wrestling with the question of how much to use Obama in his campaign. Later, Biden would say publicly that he had told Obama he didn't want the former president's endorsement—a conversation that was impossible to pinpoint in time because, according to one person very close to Obama, it never happened. Obama, like much of his brain trust, seemed to be enamored with a former Texas congressman, Beto O'Rourke. While Biden expected Obama to officially stay out of the primary, there was a risk in overplaying his ties to the former president only to get pushed back in place by key Obama advisers who preferred other candidates—or, worse yet, by Obama himself.

"I don't think he wanted to put Obama in that position," said one Biden adviser.

There was also an unspoken danger for the general election that Biden might alienate some of the white swing voters key to his strategy by binding himself too closely to the former president. After all, Trump had won more than two hundred counties that had favored Obama in both 2008 and 2012. But Biden was also reluctant to hook his star to Obama's for the most natural reason for any presidential candidate: He believed in his own merit.

"These guys have egos," the adviser said.

Schultz had previously explained to Biden that he thought it was a mistake not to lean on the one aspect of Biden's candidacy that was truly unique and gave him instant credibility with Democrats across ideological, geographic, and racial lines.

Gilbert echoed that sentiment. The key, he said again, was visual evidence.

"You must have hundreds of thousands of photos with Barack Obama and with world leaders and Supreme Court justices," he said. "Show pictures of you and Barack Obama laughing or of you and Barack Obama working. You have something that no one else has. You have to build this on social media. This is where young people and people who don't know you will get to know you. Of course, the biggest advantage you have is that Barack Obama is the most popular Democrat there is, and you probably have a picture with Barack Obama for every occasion."

As Gilbert spoke, the advisers listened. Valerie Biden Owens, seldom shy to offer her insights, quietly nodded her assent. Biden sprang up from his chair at one point to grab a pen and a legal pad from his desk so that he could write down what Gilbert was saying.

Another conundrum that bedeviled the Biden camp revolved around the difficulty he would have countering attacks from Bernie, Warren, and other Democrats that he was too closely tied to big-money interests and establishment power centers. For two years, Biden had watched as the most prominent voices in his party had pulled its brand in a more populist direction. Without Obama in the White House or Hillary as the heir apparent, the party's de facto leaders had been the handful of figures who had been able to briefly seize national attention from Trump with behavior or policy proposals outlandish enough to draw scorn. The new New York congresswoman Alexandria Ocasio-Cortez, for example, had made abolishing the U.S. Immigration and Customs Enforcement agency a central part of her campaign, leading several prospective Democratic presidential candidates to follow suit.

Biden worried that if AOC was the future of the Democratic Party, maybe the party had left him. *I can beat Trump in a general election, no doubt,* he thought. *But can I get through this Democratic Party's primary?* He often asked his advisers: Did I miss my window? His gut told him that the progressives were more vocal and visible than ascendant. The mainstream of the country would want someone who could resist the extremes of both Trump and the left, he thought—or at least hoped. To get through the primary without being pulled too far to the left, he wanted to find ways to signal to progressives that he shared values with them.

Campaign finance was an area where Biden thought he might be able to show a progressive streak without compromising substantive ground on policy. Many progressives were zealous in the view that policy decisions all led back to campaign contributions, and it was already clear there would be a lot of pressure on candidates to reject money from various sources deemed to be impure by the political left.

He was also confident that he could raise money from all the people who had told him in recent years that they would support him. Biden took them at their word, but flattery flowed more freely than cash. He didn't seem to understand that only a fraction of the wealthy donors who encouraged him to run would actually be standing by ready to help raise money for him. He didn't like the act of fundraising. He hated the obsequiousness of political panhandling. And yet there were only so many ways to raise the hundreds of millions of dollars it might take to compete in an extended primary.

Biden told Gilbert he was planning to limit contributions to the campaign to $200 and refuse money from Wall Street. He also wanted to launch the campaign in the third quarter of the year, in defiance of aides' advice that he open up in the second quarter instead.

Even a former ambassador couldn't muster a diplomatic response to how awful the proposal to cap contributions was for a candidate who would need big checks to supplement his grassroots fundraising. Without those big checks, "if you start in the third quarter, you'll be done by the fourth quarter," Gilbert replied flatly.

Biden raised his eyebrows, quizzically, as if to ask for a deeper explanation.

Look, Gilbert said, Sanders and Warren have been building grassroots fundraising lists for years. They can live off the land and raise tens of millions of dollars a month, he said. Biden would need $2,800 maximum-donation checks—and a lot of them—to fund his campaign, particularly at the start. The staff he wanted to hire, including many of the names he'd just listed, would require serious salaries. Besides, Gilbert argued, Warren wasn't clean on big money. She'd raised it before the presidential campaign, and most voters didn't care if someone who worked at Goldman Sachs wrote a $2,800 check. Very few people would think that kind of money bought influence.

The alternative was to ask allies to put together huge numbers of relatively small donations. But the math on that didn't work particularly well. "It's hard for a bundler to raise $50,000 in the primaries," said one person familiar with the fundraising discussions. "That's a lot of $200 checks." Indeed, raising $50,000 in max-out contributions requires a wealthy bundler to get seventeen or eighteen friends to contribute $2,800, or to find 250 people to give $200. It was one thing to ask a rich guy to write a check or hold a small fundraising dinner. It was another thing entirely—a fantasy—to think he could find an army of bundlers to become grassroots-fundraising machines. Biden's expectations for raising money were simply out of line with reality.

None of the issues were fully resolved by the time Gilbert left that day—save for trying to hire Symone Sanders—but Biden had effectively been given a powerful push to do some key things: bring in more diverse staff at senior levels, which would necessarily mean younger aides who were not part of his longtime brain trust; embrace Obama; and buckrake from big-time donors. Yet it wasn't at all clear Biden would heed the advice. His resistance to new blood and his hesitation about Obama reflected a core tension between Biden's political instincts and those of the small set of younger aides who had cracked into his inner circle. His assumption that he would win the votes and contributions of every person who encouraged him to run left a dangerous gap between reality and his perceptions of how easy it would be to raise money, win endorsements, and take the nomination.

At the time, there were other centrists champing at the bit to get into the race. Former Virginia governor Terry McAuliffe had tapped Michael Halle, a former Clinton aide, to run his operation. But McAuliffe was unsure of what Biden would do. Likewise, New York governor Andrew Cuomo and New Orleans mayor Mitch Landrieu were contemplating bids.

Biden tried to neutralize his competition with what his advisers referred to as "the Anzo Deck." At some point while in conversation with one or another of his potential rivals, Biden would slowly pull a few folded pieces of paper out of his pocket, as though he were sharing the Dead Sea Scrolls. In reality, they were numbers from pollster John Anzalone—"Anzo"—showing Biden's popularity. But these weren't secret internal surveys. They were just a series of public polls compiled by Anzalone.

"Biden showed that thing to everyone," said one Democratic insider who marveled at Biden's exuberance over early public polls. "It clearly was enough for Biden."

McAuliffe, who also lived in McLean, got a look at the deck, and Biden confided that he was in the final stages of making a decision. McAuliffe walked away convinced that Biden was in. That didn't knock McAuliffe out—there were other considerations for him—but it made his path much harder.

The public polls didn't really dissuade the other centrists, but Biden brandished them in Trumpian fashion. "No matter where he was, he would always have some tattered copy," one of his advisers said. "He loved that deck." The numbers suited Biden's relentless belief in himself. He believed he was the right guy for this moment. At the very least, the numbers felt like evidence that this time a presidential run might end at the White House instead of in the wilderness. He was convinced, but he needed others to believe it, too.

In that way, Biden's confidence was, at once, a great strength and a weakness that could leave him sounding a little self-delusional. It was certainly contagious. He had sold himself and an orbit of friends, family, and advisers on the prospects of a Biden presidency for forty years. In most of the elections over that time, he had at least considered running.

If the public polling had reassured Biden of his viability in a Democratic primary, he became equally enamored of the "pendulum" theory of general elections for president. Often credited to Obama adviser David Axelrod, it basically held that voters would often choose a new president who was in some clear way the opposite of the incumbent. Donilon subscribed to the idea, and he sold Biden on it. Biden saw his character and compassion as antidotes to Trump's loutish behavior and self-interest. He viewed Trump as a con man who had made people believe he served their interests, and himself as someone who actually did. Of course, as he planned a presidential campaign for at least the seventh time in his life, it could not be said of Biden that he lacked ego or personal ambition—just, perhaps, that they were not the only forces that motivated him.

For four long years, Biden had also wrestled with the what-if of the campaign he didn't run in 2016. So many people had told him he would have defeated Trump had he won the Democratic nomination that year. He thought so, too. He believed in his own appeal. He thought he was more "likable" than Hillary. He told confidants he wasn't even worried about winning the general election in 2020.

"There was never a doubt whether he could take on the president," one of them said of Biden's thinking.

Biden and Donilon had been talking privately for as long as anyone could remember about the rationale for a presidential campaign. Described by friends as having a "dark Irish" side that made it hard to tell whether he was at peace or gloomy, Donilon was the Biden whisperer. He had been working for Biden since the year Schultz was born, and the other aides liked to needle him about how long he'd been fleshing out this raison d'être for Biden. Was it 2019? 2015? 1981?

Donilon had practical experience as a pollster and campaign operative. Biden trusted his political instincts and relied on him to translate the Biden narrative into prose. Part keeper of that Biden brand and part speechwriter, Donilon spoke for Biden. If he approved of a junior aide's request, it was as good as getting a blessing from Biden. Balding, with bushy white eyebrows and round glasses, he was also one of the few advisers truly capable of changing Biden's thinking on any given matter. He and Biden had been talking privately about how to frame a centrist campaign that could win in the primary and the general election at a time when rising populism and base-focused politics seemed to be all the rage.

One day in late January or February, Biden called an important meeting of his advisers in the basement of the McLean house. One tipoff of the significance of the agenda was the presence of his wife, Jill Biden, who didn't waste her time at planning sessions that could drag on. When she participated, she sat in a chair next to her husband, with the aides arrayed on the couches in front of them. Her top aide, Anthony Bernal, accompanied her to this meeting. Valerie Biden Owens, Ricchetti, Donilon, Schultz, and Bedingfield, were also in attendance.

But it was really the Donilon show. Exhibiting deference to Biden, Donilon looked up at his boss and said, "Sir, this is what you and I talked about." Then, he proceeded to lay out for the rest of the group what he called the three pillars of Biden's campaign. They were Biden's battle for "the soul of this nation," fighting for the "ramrod" middle class of America, and bringing the country together. "Ramrod" would later be changed to "backbone" because "ramrod" didn't sound quite right. The pillars set up further discussion of a fleshed-out launch speech and, later on, how the campaign would roll out. Notably, the pillars were all reactions—pendulum swings—based on Biden's perceptions of where the president, his party, or both were getting things wrong. These themes weren't really up for discussion. Biden, with Donilon's help, had decided. This is what his campaign would be about, and Donilon was informing the rest of the group.

Biden had talked about Trump and the soul of the nation after Charlottesville, and any number of Trump's demagogic behaviors and authoritarian actions could fit in that bucket. Biden believed Trump had won the votes of so many working-class whites in part because Democrats talked down to them. He came from working-class roots, he was proud of that, and he believed he could appeal to many Trump voters with his background, his message, and his center-left policies. Trump's presidency, he thought, wasn't serving them as much as Trump would have them believe—or as much as it was serving the wealthiest Americans—and he thought he could swing things back in their direction. And by not going too far left, while highlighting his record of bipartisan work in the Senate, he thought he could credibly claim to be a uniter at a time when the nation was badly polarized.

In those early months of 2019, Biden encountered a pair of paradoxes. He was at once the leading Democrat in the field and the one least likely to draw attention from the media. There were spurts of interest around Elizabeth Warren, Bernie Sanders, Kamala Harris, Cory Booker, and Amy Klobuchar—mostly surrounding their campaign launches—and an outright media-palooza around Beto O'Rourke. Seemingly out of nowhere, the little-known mayor of South Bend, Indiana, Pete Buttigieg, was raising money like gangbusters, receiving glowing profiles in major news outlets and landing himself on prime-time television. For Biden, will-he-or-won't-he speculation drove some coverage, but the stories often included long distillations of the concerns his own advisers had about a potential candidacy—including how he would react to Trump attacks on members of his family.

The other paradox for Biden was the difference in reception he got from voters and from political insiders. On the campaign trail during the midterms, on his book tour, and at events in the early months of 2019, he'd felt a strong bond with voters who encouraged him to run. Their support seemed to explain why he was running ahead of the other candidates. Many pundits theorized that his numbers would drop if he jumped into the race, but it wasn't clear whether he was in the lead despite, because of, or regardless of the fact that he was still on the sidelines.

Amid the growing field of Democratic contestants, Biden most resembled the establishment, and the establishment had reacted to him by turning up its nose. It was painful, and embarrassing, that even when he led in the polls, Democratic insiders did not seem to believe in him. For months on end, in discussions with elected officials, mega-donors, top operatives, and various influencers within the Democratic Party, Biden heard variations of the same tepid response he'd gotten from Sharpton. He wasn't lining up big money. The top campaign talent—the A-team operatives—was going to other campaigns or sitting on the sidelines. Obamaworld figures, with a couple of notable exceptions, were nowhere to be found. In his last, best chance to win the presidency, Biden wasn't able to call in a lifetime of political favors. Almost no one thought he could win.

Biden had not been able to scare off all the rivals who positioned themselves as cures for the party's problem with working-class white voters in the Rust Belt. Most worrisome, prominent Black political figures, like Obama and Sharpton, were not willing to commit to him. They weren't going to waste political capital pushing him on voters. The best he could hope for is that they would keep their powder dry in case he won the nomination on his own.

Even if the rest of the party couldn't see what he saw, Biden knew he was the right guy for the job. He was going to have to prove himself. Rather than deterring him, the polite rejections redoubled his determination. He was a childhood stutterer who grew up to filibuster on the Senate floor. He was a working-class kid who ended up working in the West Wing as the vice president of the United States. To his core, he believed that his life, his values, and his conduct as a public servant reflected what his party preached—but didn't always practice—and provided a black-and-white contrast with the silver-spoon president.

In mid-March, as he began to signal more publicly that an an-

nouncement of his campaign was imminent, Biden invited Stacey
Abrams, the former Georgia House of Representatives minority
leader, to his home in Virginia. Abrams, who was considering her
own bid for the presidency, had built a political operation outside
the traditional Atlanta machine and had nearly become the nation's first Black woman governor in a razor-thin defeat in 2018.
During her run, she had become an overnight sensation in the
Democratic political world, winning help from Oprah among other
luminaries.

By the time Biden sat down with Abrams at his kitchen table,
she had already met with more than half a dozen presidential-
hopeful suitors, from Kamala Harris to Pete Buttigieg to Washington governor Jay Inslee. Biden was a late addition to her dance
card.

"Turkey or chicken?" Biden asked, referring to the two sandwiches on the table.

"Turkey," Abrams replied.

As they dug in, Biden laid out his concerns about the emerging
field of candidates and its race to the left, and why he might run.
He asked Abrams about Fair Fight, the voting-rights organization
she had set up in the wake of her defeat. They also talked about the
potential for Abrams to make a presidential run.

Abrams moved to preempt the main question she anticipated.
Biden hadn't yet asked for her endorsement, and she wanted to
avoid having to answer it directly.

"I'm happy to do whatever I can to be helpful," Abrams said.
"But I'm not going to take a position in the race." Before they finished lunch, Abrams told Biden she worried about a myopic focus
in the Democratic Party on swing voters.

Swing voters are the unicorns of presidential elections, she
thought. *It's hard to find them and persuade them.* The point was
that Democrats, in her view, spent way too much time and money
trying to convert working-class white swing voters in Rust Belt suburbs when it was easier and cheaper to find nonvoters who agreed
with the Democrats already, register them to vote, and turn them
out to the polls. Abrams thought some money and attention should
go to swing voters, but that the focus on them was way out of
whack. If swing voters comprise 5 percent of your electorate, they
should not account for 75 percent of your investment, she told him.

She was firmly coming down on one side of a raging battle within the Democratic Party over whether winning presidential elections required them to mobilize Black and brown voters or try to sway persuadable whites. One of the main reasons Biden thought he could win the presidency was his belief that he could appeal effectively to both.

In an important way, Abrams was Biden's new Elizabeth Warren. She had barely left his house when his team leaked the idea that he was considering her as a running mate.

This time, though, he tripped over his own feet. In 2015, Warren had already announced she was not running. Now, the Biden team's move undercut Abrams at a time when she was still publicly undecided about a campaign. The suggestion that she might make a good No. 2 came as a surprise to her, and it was taken by some as a slight to two Black women: It knocked Abrams down a peg, and it threatened to peel away support for Kamala Harris by offering Democrats a way to back a Black woman without voting for Harris. The daughter of a Jamaican father and an Indian mother, Harris was expected to compete with Biden for the support of Black voters and the caches of delegates they could deliver. Biden would later apologize to Abrams for "any discomfort" he might have caused her. But he had gotten what he needed out of the publicity surrounding the meeting.

Even if Democratic elites weren't going to fall in love with him on the first date, Biden could accept a little bit of rejection in pursuit of lasting goodwill. Likability was going to be his calling card, and all he needed in a crowded field of lesser-known candidates was to be one of the top two or three choices for both the power players and the voters. To the extent that it hurt a bit to be the process-of-elimination candidate in a party he'd proudly served for forty-four years in the Senate and the vice presidency, Biden wouldn't show it.

Left unspoken in the awkward rituals—a courtship-era candidate operating in a Tinder world—was the hard truth that no one wanted to hurt Biden's feelings. No one who rejected his advances wanted to tell him that his best days on the stump were behind him. The winter version of this lion read his speeches off of video screens, and he often struggled to do that smoothly. It seemed clear that he didn't have the hand speed to box with Trump, who lived for the instant gratification of slinging political mud at his enemies in relentless barrages of tweets, offhand remarks to reporters, and call-ins on Fox News. The president was geared to the punch communication of the digital age, while Biden thought out loud in long, circular patterns, finally arriving at his destination. Some people who spent time with him insisted in private conversations that he rambled and repeated himself more than he had in his younger days—when he also had a knack for rambling and repeating himself. Others said he might be a little older but that he was not diminished. Video recordings of Biden in his forties, fifties, and sixties showed a more lively force.

For many Democrats, Biden simply seemed unsuited for a modern campaign. Obama's allies sometimes explained the former president's reluctance to bless Biden's candidacy as fear that Biden would dishonor himself with a bad campaign. In the early months of 2019, it could be argued that Biden had both the best chance of beating Trump and the best chance of falling flat on his face.

CHAPTER 2

•

"We Avoided That Misstep, But Not All of Them"

IN A SMALL WEWORK OFFICE NEAR THE CORNER OF FOURTEENTH Street and Florida Avenue in Northwest Washington, Greg Schultz and a small but growing coterie of Biden 2020 operatives spent March and early April 2019 building a campaign operation.

For all the hesitance on the part of fellow Democrats to unify behind him, Biden came into the race with some significant advantages. Because everyone in the country knew his name, he didn't have to jump in early and spend heavily to raise his profile the way that most of the rest of the field did. Senators, House members, and governors might be household names for Washington insiders and cable news junkies, but they weren't familiar to the vast majority of Iowa caucus-goers and New Hampshire primary voters. He could afford to sit back on his polling lead and let the other candidates face harsh presidential-level media scrutiny.

But he also paid a price for waiting.

In the office, Schultz and his top deputy, Pete Kavanaugh, kept a whiteboard with the names of top potential staff hires in the first four states on the primary calendar. It looked like an NFL draft board. But Biden wasn't ready to make any picks, or to have it leak out that he was hiring staff. He denied Schultz the authority to extend offers.

"It was frustrating," said one person who watched names come off the board as other campaigns hired them. "There's a bunch of top staff in Iowa, New Hampshire, South Carolina, where we had talked to the staff and they would have gone with Joe Biden but we didn't have a job to offer them."

Elizabeth Warren had hired some of the best talent in Iowa right out of the gate, including Janice Rottenberg, who had been the state Democratic party's coordinated campaign director in 2018, and Emily Parcell, who had been Obama's political director in the state in 2008 when he shocked the country by beating John Edwards and Hillary Clinton handily.

By the end of March, a dozen candidates had entered the race. Most were hiring at least in Iowa and New Hampshire. It was quickly becoming clear that Biden would be lucky to patch together a JV team in some of the early states. His overarching plan was to follow the path blazed by Obama and Hillary in their primary triumphs by becoming the exclusive favorite of Black voters in South Carolina, the rest of the Deep South, and in delegate-rich cities in northern states. But each of them had first won Iowa, and neither of them had to contend with such a crowded field.

Iowa, the first state on the calendar, was still the same bedeviling problem for Biden that it had always been. The caucuses tended to be filled with liberal activists, and Biden was not one of them. If anything, his politics could be defined as reactive centrist. Over the years, he had considered and shot down the idea of skipping the Iowa caucuses altogether. He'd gotten 1 percent there in 2008. He'd had no path in Iowa when he chose not to run in 2015. Iowa was just not part of his plan for winning the Democratic nomination and the presidency, even though it was obvious to any political historian that the state was the graveyard of presidential ambitions. Biden's 1988 and 2008 campaigns had headstones there.

"No one is ever excited about Iowa," one Biden aide said of the team's sentiment about the state heading into the campaign.

While the preternaturally cautious Biden was in no rush to actually announce his candidacy—and most of his gray-haired advisers felt the same—there was a younger cohort in his circle who believed that he was letting valuable time slip by and affording opportunity to the other candidates to build their fundraising and get-out-the-vote operations.

The timing and buildup to Biden's launch would be the first of many contentious issues that would divide these camps within his campaign. The older group would come to be known by some internally as the pooh-bahs. It included Donilon; Dunn and her husband, Bauer; former deputy national security adviser Tony Blinken; Biden's former chiefs of staff Ricchetti, Ron Klain, and Bruce Reed; and, in the role of grand pooh-bah, former senator Ted Kaufman, who had been Biden's top aide on Capitol Hill before being appointed to a temporary job succeeding him in the chamber in 2009. Jill Biden and Valerie Biden Owens counted as both family and pooh-bahs. They had all been in Biden's orbit for decades, they knew his record and his instincts, and they tended to reflect his thinking as much as they shaped it.

Along with Donilon, the most influential pooh-bahs were Ricchetti and Dunn. Ricchetti, a balding revolving-door operator in his early sixties who had lobbied for insurance, drug, and telecommunications companies between stints in government, shared Biden's political outlook and style. Like Biden, he was drawn to the action of the political game. He wanted back inside the government, and, as the owner of a $4.5 million home close to Biden's Virginia rental, he didn't need a salary from the campaign.

Dunn, one of the few Obamaworld luminaries to sign on with Biden, had built one of the top public relations shops in Washington. Recognizable for her above-the-shoulder silver-blond hair and warm blue eyes, the sixty-one-year-old had navigated through Washington's old boy network from the time she got her start as an intern in Jimmy Carter's White House. Calm in any crisis—her manner inspired loyalty from subordinates and Biden—the Bethesda, Maryland, native brought management skills along with her media acumen.

Biden felt most secure with the pooh-bahs, but he also understood at some level that donors, surrogates, and voters would want his campaign to reflect the diversity of the Democratic Party. It had taken outsiders like Gilbert to convince him that he couldn't just have an all-white, mostly old, mostly male team around him. If he did, he would inevitably wander into political minefields within the primary that could easily be avoided with good advice from a diverse array of counselors.

Biden slowly hired a younger group to join the campaign's leadership table. In addition to Schultz and Bedingfield, he added Symone Sanders; Brandon English, a Black veteran of the Democratic Congressional Campaign Committee; and Cristóbal Alex, who had been deputy director of voter outreach for Hillary in 2016 and ran a group called Latino Victory.

It had taken two and a half months for Biden to hire Sanders after he'd first directed Ricchetti to get her on board. The courting ritual began with Schultz reaching out in January. Sanders, who was fielding calls from several campaigns, rescheduled their discussion three times before finally connecting with Schultz. She asked Dunn, a mentor to many political communicators, what she should do. Dunn told her to sit down with Biden. "You'll know if it's a good fit when you meet him," she said.

In early March, Sanders went to Biden's house in McLean for what she expected would be a thirty-minute meeting. It lasted two hours, as Biden gave her a tour of the house, talked to her about his dogs, and recounted how Jill Biden rejected his marriage proposals repeatedly before saying "I do." In many ways Sanders was in a similar position. The former VP was building up to an offer, but she wasn't ready to commit. She was playing hard to get—and she wanted to keep him interested while retaining her other options.

When they sat down after the tour, Sanders asked Biden why he wanted to run for president. Biden answered with a now-well-rehearsed answer. She asked about Anita Hill. Biden had developed a response to that, too. Sanders liked what she heard, and she liked Biden. It was going well. Then he pressed her to sign on.

"I need you to work for me," he said.

Sanders demurred. She wasn't going to make any decisions before an upcoming trip, she told him. He followed up with her by phone and said he would get his staff to send her a list of touristy things she could do while she had a layover in Ireland. At the end of March, Kamala Harris's campaign circled back with Sanders, but they couldn't strike a deal. Sanders was still intrigued by the former vice president. She couldn't shake the feeling that she liked him. Like Dunn had said, meeting him was key. She agreed to join the Biden campaign, a decision that was leaked to the media before she was ready to have her job change made public.

Sanders, more than the others, was a known quantity to the media and to television audiences from her time working for Bernie Sanders in the 2016 campaign. But she was just one of several senior advisers and aides who were specifically hired to make Biden's campaign younger and more diverse.

"There was a decision, very intentional, that they couldn't do what they did in the past, which was just to have the old school around him, because they wouldn't have success if they did that," one top Biden adviser said during the summer of 2019. "There's a couple of folks who come from a different space, and I think that's where the tension started to show a little bit." The question was whether the expansion of Biden's campaign cabinet was mostly for show.

At the same time, Obama's fears about Biden and his team ran deep—deeper than defeat. Obama worried that his former vice president would embarrass himself on the campaign trail and that the people around him would not be able to prevent a belly-flop. The former president invited Biden aides to his office in Washington's West End in March so that he could get a briefing on the imminent campaign. He wasn't so much interested in strategy, tactics, or which person would be placed in which job. He didn't care how Biden would answer a question about the crime bill or climate change. He wanted reassurance that Biden's legacy would be protected, that his staff would not let him become a tragicomic caricature of an aging politician having his last hurrah. This concern was mostly about looking out for his friend, but Obama's name was also inextricably tied to Biden's.

"Obama wanted to make sure that Joe's long-term reputation wasn't going to be endangered," said one person who participated in the meeting. "He certainly wasn't confident Joe was going to win. No one was." But win or lose, Obama looked at the coming primary as the Wild West of politics, a lawless and unpredictable melee that could leave Biden not just beaten but permanently scarred.

When Biden's aides left, Obama felt better about the prospects of Biden being protected from himself. The two men looked at each other like a mentor and mentee, according to sources close to them, but it was never clear that they agreed on which of them was in which role.

Meanwhile, friction within Biden's camp continued to grow as he dawdled. The younger set argued for an earlier kickoff in part because waiting made Biden look like he wasn't sure he wanted to run—that he didn't have what political insiders call the "fire in the belly" needed to mount a winning campaign. And even without a formal launch, they thought, there were a million ways for Biden to make absolutely clear that he felt something stronger than the modest urgency of meh. Most Democrats looked at Donald Trump as an existential threat to the republic. Could Biden credibly represent them if he needed to be coaxed into running? In that way, he had created his own negative media myth: He had decided to run, but he was treated as indecisive because he wouldn't say it.

"There was all this debate going on in terms of when do we fucking launch the damn campaign," said one Biden insider. "We get all the narrative of him dragging his feet and we were already getting heat for it when we got hit with the Lucy Flores thing."

One evening in late March, Kate Bedingfield dialed Biden from the campaign's WeWork office to tell him that he was the subject of breaking bad news. Writing in *New York* magazine's "The Cut" on March 29, 2019, Lucy Flores, the 2014 Nevada Democratic nominee for lieutenant governor, revealed that "an awkward kiss changed how I saw Joe Biden." In the midst of the #MeToo movement, a reckoning for powerful men who abused their positions to take sexual advantage of women, Flores's allegation threatened to turn the avuncular former vice president into Creepy Uncle Joe with the speed of an Internet click.

Flores accused him of standing behind her, sniffing her unwashed hair, and planting a kiss on the back of her head before endorsing her at a campaign event.

As Bedingfield relayed the allegation, Biden listened silently.

My God, he thought. *I didn't do that—not like that.*

At first, he said nothing. Bedingfield and Schultz, who was right beside her, exchanged glances as they waited for the boss to say something. A few seconds felt like an hour. They both knew Biden was a toucher by nature. He embraced women and men. He draped his arm over shoulders and wrapped his fingers around waists. Sometimes he bowed forward to touch foreheads with an acquaintance. Because they knew him—had seen him draw people in close without a hint of sexuality—they were more concerned about the public reaction than the reality.

"I thought I was doing the opposite," Biden said, processing the shock. "I've always tried to support women."

He didn't think he'd done anything wrong, and he was having a hard time understanding how his actions might have been interpreted differently than they were meant. Already, aides were compiling a list of women who had been around Biden for a long time who could vouch for him. Bedingfield and Schultz recommended releasing a statement in response to the Flores column.

Biden didn't want to apologize. It took two days for him to put out the statement, which focused on his tendency to offer gestures of physical support on the campaign trail. "Not once—never—did I believe I acted inappropriately," he said. "If it is suggested I did so, I will listen respectfully. But it was never my intention."

By that time, videos of Biden awkwardly touching, hugging, or kissing other women had flooded social media. A full-on examination of his record on issues affecting women, which was mixed enough to include both the Anita Hill saga and writing the federal law designed to protect women from domestic abusers, was under way. Elizabeth Warren, Kamala Harris, and Julian Castro, three of his rivals for the Democratic nomination, had already said publicly that they believed Flores or soon would. Some Democrats questioned whether he could continue a campaign that hadn't even launched yet. The story was spiraling out of control.

Outside the campaign, it was clear that Biden needed to do more to stop the bleeding. But he was reluctant to go any further. The internal debate matched him and the pooh-bahs against the younger aides, with the Gen X and millennial set telling the baby boomers—and Biden, who was born a few years before the boom—that he needed to issue an apology quickly.

Depending on the debate, pooh-bahs and newbies might cross generational lines, but in this case, alarm bells rang much louder for the kids than for Biden and the graybeards. He was not going to apologize. "Joe Biden doesn't do anything Joe Biden doesn't want to do," said one person very close to him.

"I don't think he understood it on some level," said a longtime ally involved in the discussions. "He constantly thought 'Yeah, so what? What's the big deal?' He needed a lot of convincing. Every time someone flagged that it was a problem, it went right over his head."

Biden simply refused to say he was sorry. "He won't apologize because he thinks he did nothing wrong," said one adviser. "He's told us this repeatedly. And if he does apologize everyone will hold this over him from now until the end of the campaign." That was one of the ways in which Biden's political instincts weren't so different from Trump's. It was difficult for his younger aides to understand why a guy who would often apologize privately if he'd wronged them in some way couldn't bring himself to say he was sorry in public.

Eventually, grudgingly, he came part of the way around. Biden released a face-to-camera video, filmed at his home in Wilmington, five days after Flores's column and three days after his initial statement. In it, he reiterated that he believed he hadn't acted improperly, but promised to be more cognizant of women's personal space in the future. Then he joked about it all at his next public event, further demonstrating that he was out of touch.

"Dude won't apologize. He just won't do it—even when he should," said one frustrated campaign official. "When we did the Lucy Flores pushback after days of getting the shit kicked out of us and we finally got him on camera, I thought that was fine. But there's a difference between 'I'm sorry' and 'I'm sorry you felt that way.'"

What his newer aides were absorbing was a maxim that had been burned into the psyches of generations of their predecessors: You quickly learn in Bidenworld that you can change some things, but you can't change anything quickly.

A series of unforeseen events, including the Flores allegations and Biden's selection to deliver a eulogy at former senator Fritz Hollings's funeral in South Carolina, made it impossible to launch in the first few weeks of April. He had lined up enough high-dollar donors to get a campaign off the ground. Comcast senior executive vice president David Cohen, who'd served as chief of staff to former governor Ed Rendell of Pennsylvania, would host the first major fundraising event for the former vice president in Philadelphia in late April, and Dreamworks co-founder Jeffrey Katzenberg agreed to co-host a similar shindig in Los Angeles in early May. But the wasted time meant that Biden would have a shorter window to collect before the next deadline for reporting fundraising tallies—a measure used by the media and political insiders to gauge the relative strength of each campaign.

Behind the scenes, Biden and his top aides circulated word to allies and other politicians that a launch was imminent. During one such round of calls, Biden settled in behind the big desk in the den at his McLean house. He dialed Warren. When she answered, he went from zero to buddy-buddy in a heartbeat.

"Listen, Elizabeth, I think you're doing great, keep it up," he said. "I want you to know I'm going to enter this race." He went on to tell her why he was running—a spiel he'd been giving to friends and donors for a while—but made sure to tell her that his decision wasn't about a lack of faith in her.

"I trust you," he said. "I believe in you."

Warren wasn't surprised he was running, but she didn't quite know what to say. Just four years earlier, he'd invited her over to the Naval Observatory to float the running-mate idea. Despite the advancement of their relationship, it hadn't changed her fundamental view of Biden. She saw him as the worst kind of politician: one who would fully reverse his position—even revise his record—when it suited his needs. She'd seen him do it on the bankruptcy bill. Where he'd once been proud to own his defense of his home-state credit card industry, he now disowned it. He hadn't just favored that bill, he'd been the author.

One person close to Warren described her take on him this way: "He has a very— What's the word for making history up?"

As Biden talked her up and told her about his plans, Warren said little in response. He wanted more from her, maybe just a touch of warmth.

"She was very cold on the phone," said a Biden aide familiar with the discussion. "Like the opposite of him on the phone."

It was a little hard for Warren to swallow Biden's claim that he wasn't running against her. She found the whole charade pompous, patronizing, and a little ridiculous. What they had in common could be boiled down to three things: blue-collar-to-Senate-pin backgrounds, the desire to be president, and the belief that Hillary had blown it in 2016. Nonplussed, she said good-bye and hung up the phone.

As Biden's staff slowly grew, so did the tension between the pooh-bahs and the young guns hired to inject new blood—and new thinking—into the operation. The junior set of senior advisers brought a different sensibility of modern politics to internal discussions than the grizzled group who had known Biden for decades. Specifically, as was the case with the allegations of inappropriate touching by Biden, they felt his sensitivity on matters of race, gender, and ethnicity—really any issue of intersectionality—could feel outdated to progressives, and they worked to massage this wherever possible.

The younger crew's reasons for joining up with Biden varied, but the most compelling and common one was that they thought he stood the best chance of winning. This pragmatism, common on any campaign for an establishment candidate leading in the polls, contrasted starkly with the idealism of aides who signed on with longer-shot candidates who more closely reflected their own values but had less chance of ending up in the White House. But Biden's younger aides also saw in him a politician of basic decency, humanity, and empathy. He asked about their families, he consoled them in times of personal crisis, and, aside from losing his temper from time to time, he treated them with dignity. When he was vice president, incoming aides received a memo from him in their "welcome packet." This is an important job, the memo said. But family is more important. If I find out you're missing soccer games, birthdays, or weddings because of work, Biden wrote, I'm going to be really upset. I don't want to hear that you're missing family time for work. "He meant that one thousand percent," one longtime aide said. It wasn't surprising that a former vice president could attract campaign aides for his presidential run; it was shocking that more top talent hadn't jockeyed for jobs with him.

But if the loose structure of the campaign leadership was designed to give voice to a younger and more diverse set of advisers, it wasn't built to give them power. Even Schultz, the campaign manager, found himself operating more as a wrangler of the pooh-bahs than as a decision maker. Ultimately, Biden made his own decisions, and he got cranky when they were made for him. Nobody wanted to suffer one of his epic tongue-lashings. For everyone, pooh-bahs and youngsters alike, managing the candidate was its own delicate dance.

Alliances within the campaign staff could shift around a bit depending on the day or the issue, but generally speaking, the younger group was more attuned to the rhythms of a self-perpetuating news cycle—anxious to jump into the fray quickly and to cripple negative story lines before they could grow legs. But the pooh-bahs, several of whom had worked in the White House, tended to be more reserved and glacial. Like Biden, they waited for politics to come to them. Rather than racing to the nearest fire extinguisher and blasting it in every direction, they were content to wait a couple of news cycles to see if an attack on Biden or a gaffe flamed out on its own.

And, of course, they knew that's how Biden preferred to deal with things. It would take the newcomers a little longer to figure out that, even if the advice was good, there was often little use in giving it to the boss. Biden delivered decisions through Ricchetti, Donilon, or Dunn and seldom adjusted course based on the counsel he received from others. After nearly half a century in national politics—and now running in his fourth presidential election cycle—he didn't believe there was much anyone could tell him about the game he was playing.

All of these dynamics came to a head on the eve of Biden's actual launch. He and his longer-serving advisers had been happy to nurse what was a substantial lead in the polls. From the beginning of the campaign, the Biden team saw a path to the presidency that was more about playing expert defense than going on offense—up to, and including, limiting the candidate's exposure to public exchanges that might highlight his famous lack of message discipline. Getting in, according to most of the punditry, would only cause him to look more partisan and lose favor. His approval would sink, his lead would shrivel. Plus, as the spring had worn on, it had become increasingly clear that it made sense for him to wait for April so that he didn't give a huge public relations advantage to other campaigns by posting a weak first-quarter fundraising total based on a few weeks of donations rather than the months the others had spent dialing for dollars.

But even with that proviso—that he would wait for April—Schultz, Kavanaugh, and other younger aides wanted to get going as soon as possible. He was wasting valuable time that could be spent campaigning in early states, openly building relationships with political heavyweights, attending major fundraising events, and creating field operations on the ground across the country. Finally, the date was set for April 24.

And then, just as quickly, it was unset.

There were thousands of reasons not to pick April 24, and most of them were women of color. These women would assemble for the She the People presidential forum in Houston, an event intended to elevate relevant issues. Not everyone on the campaign innately grasped the lose-lose construct of Biden announcing his candidacy on the same day. He would either distract from the conference or the conference would distract from him. Even if he managed to outshine the forum, he would be seen as stealing the spotlight from women of color—the most loyal voting bloc in the Democratic Party—at a time when he had just been accused of kissing and sniffing the hair of a Latina candidate. In the best-case scenario, Biden would tell the country he was running because of Trump's reaction to Charlottesville while sending the message that Black and brown women were invisible to him.

Cristóbal Alex reached for the emergency brake.

"For legal purposes, this thing was moving and everybody was on board and there was a significant number of staff, and this train was moving, and [Cristóbal] said we're going to have to fucking stop the train," one member of Biden's team recalled of a tense private email exchange among the top advisers.

Dunn pushed back on him. She the People would be in the morning. Biden could hold off on his launch for a few hours and do it in the afternoon, she argued. Biden wouldn't want to hold off, though it was not clear to many of the participants in the discussion whether he had actually been consulted yet. Symone Sanders, breaking generational ranks but holding firm with the fellow communications specialist who had helped bring her in, lined up with Dunn.

Alex couldn't believe what he was reading.

"We're going to get murdered," he argued. "If you want a clean launch, and you want to hit it out of the park," he tried to explain, "you will not have it on the same day."

There was another problem bubbling up at the makeshift precampaign headquarters. Even with the launch date set, Biden hadn't given anyone the authority to spend money—on vendors or staff hires—until the day before the launch, which was making the rollout a logistical nightmare. Schultz and Kavanaugh piped in to let Donilon and Ricchetti know that "we just aren't there," as one participant in the conversation recalled.

Biden had dithered for months, and now, on the eve of his campaign launch, he had left his team unable to prepare adequately.
The wait-and-hurry-up culture of his operation was catching up to
him. Between the rush job to put launch events together and the
negligence of picking the day of the She the People conference,
Biden had set his campaign up to blow what promised to be his best
news day in years.

Biden's aides went back and forth for a bit, both over email and
on the phone, with others joining in. Ricchetti held his fire until the
group heard from Mike Donilon. It was a bit of a surprise when
Donilon—definitely in the camp of longtime Biden hands with
White House experience—jumped in to say the launch should be
moved back. He was taking up for the younger crowd, and showing
deference to the event for women of color. Both could be blind
spots for the older, all-white circle of Biden's most trusted advisers.

As he often did in senior staff debates at the time, Ricchetti had
the last word.

Fine, he said, move it back a fucking day.

"I'm so glad now we didn't do it," one Biden aide confided later.
"It would have been part of this record—one more piece of evidence in this long record—of him not respecting or understanding
the community or really getting it."

Still, the aide added, "We avoided that misstep, but not all of
them."

CHAPTER 3

•

Reform or Revolution?

BERNIE SANDERS ARRIVED AT ELIZABETH WARREN'S SWANKY condo in Washington's Penn Quarter neighborhood after a long day at the Capitol on December 12, 2018. It was 9:45 P.M. by the time the Senate's two most prominent progressives sat down to eat a takeout dinner from the Italian chain Vapiano and talk politics. Like boxers feeling each other out in the early rounds of a prize fight, they eased into a discussion of the national landscape heading into the 2020 election. Both of them had sent strong public signals that they might run. But Sanders knew that he had been summoned so that Warren could smoke out his intentions.

In 2016, she had passed up a bid. Sanders, wanting to ensure that Hillary Clinton didn't coast into the party's nomination that year without being challenged from her left flank, had jumped in. And then he had taken off. He came up short of the nomination, but the surprising competitiveness of his campaign turned him into the 800-pound gorilla of the political left. He had been successful enough to put a deep scare into the party establishment, highlight populist issues in ways that Trump later echoed in the upper Midwest, and force subsequent changes to Democratic nominating rules.

The Rust Belt was the region of the country on Bernie's mind as he and Warren sat down to dinner. From his perspective, the political world had shifted considerably in four years. Back then, Trump wasn't a player. No one knew that he was going to remake the landscape by mounting what Sanders thought of as a phony populist campaign—or that he would ride the rage of anti-establishment, anti-trade white rural and suburban voters in Michigan, Wisconsin, and Pennsylvania to the presidency.

Sanders thought Democrats couldn't afford to counter Trump with a culture-signaling candidate like Joe Biden—aviator sunglasses and a Corvette wouldn't cut it—or even a watered-down version of himself like Warren. Sure, he and Warren voted alike most of the time in the Senate. They both railed about corporate greed and inequalities in wealth and income. But she fundamentally believed in the system. She didn't call for a revolution. She called for a reformation. He had spent years bashing the Democratic Party and cementing his image as an independent. She was a former Republican who embraced the party with the zeal of a convert. She wanted to change it from the inside. He wanted to blow it up from the outside in a hostile takeover. They were aligned, but they weren't the same.

Sanders thought he had proved himself in the fires of 2016 and that he had a right to continue on the path that Warren had forgone four years earlier. He had taken the risk of running when she had not. He had a big national following, and now he was positioned to build on that.

Warren had a different perspective on the history of his first campaign. If she competed this time, she thought, it followed that Sanders didn't have to run to promote the progressive agenda. He had taken his shot and lost. A lot of Democrats blamed him for Clinton's defeat, citing Trump's repetition of criticism Sanders had leveled at her and lackluster support for her from his backers in the general election.

Together, Sanders and Warren had more early backing than Biden, according to a series of public polls. But Biden led the pack, with Sanders trailing close behind. Despite Warren's fame in her home state of Massachusetts and in Washington—notoriety, to some of her fellow Democrats—the sixty-nine-year-old former professor wasn't particularly well known to voters across the country. Bernie Sanders, the iconic, establishment-bashing seventy-seven-year-old from Vermont, had become a household name. It was obvious that if only one of them ran in the midst of a crowded field, progressives would likely unify behind that candidate. If both ran, policy-minded progressives would split, and Biden or another centrist would have a much easier path to the nomination.

Warren wanted to know not only whether Sanders was going to run, but why. What was his rationale, given that he had cited her absence from the 2016 race as his reason for campaigning? But rather than press him, the former Harvard law professor coaxed her witness gingerly.

I think a woman can win the presidency, she said, inviting Bernie to give his thoughts on a topic that had consumed Democratic politicians and operatives since Clinton's defeat two years earlier. Sanders had been accused of promoting—or at least tolerating— misogynistic "Bernie Bro" supporters during that year's primary. It was not a well-kept secret that toxic masculinity permeated his campaign operation. The political question of whether America was ready for a woman to be president—and, as important, whether any of the women who were looking at running could be that woman—came down more to a matter of instinct than empirical evidence. It could be argued that Clinton had proved, by winning a popular-vote majority and losing the electoral college by a margin of just 77,736 votes over three states, that a woman could win. But it could also be argued that, regardless of whether it was fair, Trump had effectively stoked latent sexist reactions to Clinton and would do the same with any other woman. For that matter, his history suggested that he would play to conscious and subconscious prejudices against candidates of color, too. Few in the Democratic Party wanted to spell it out, but the posttraumatic stress of Trump's election and presidency had left a lot of primary voters convinced that Democrats needed a white man at the top of their ticket.

Sanders danced around the edges of that case.

"Trump's a sexist, a racist, and a liar," he replied impassively, his brown eyes unflickering behind trademark wire-rimmed glasses. He will weaponize anything at his disposal to win, he said, offering what he considered to be an objective and inoffensive observation.

Warren did not hear it the way Sanders thought he said it. Now, at least, she believed she knew what he was thinking. He was going to run, all right, and he would try to take advantage of Democrats' fear that nominating a woman for a second consecutive election would produce another term for Trump.

Indeed, Sanders's camp was increasingly confident that Warren would be a weak candidate, but not because of her gender. It was because of her claims about her ethnic makeup.

For years, Trump had been taunting Warren, by calling her "Pocahontas" and then "Faux-cahontas," to highlight the claim she had made earlier in her career that she was a descendant of Native Americans. There had been a long-running battle among her top aides and advisers about whether and when to address an issue that had lingered since her first run for office. It intensified over the summer months of 2018, and Warren put an end to the internal back-and-forth by releasing results of a DNA test in mid-October. Her ancestry was almost entirely European.

For Sanders's camp, it didn't matter whether she had Native heritage or not. Taking Trump's bait—and then releasing a DNA test that weakened her case rather than strengthening it—amounted to political malpractice. Sanders's advisers couldn't believe how she handled it.

"It showed to a lot of us that her team was just not up to the game," said one Sanders ally. "If you're going to respond every time Trump taunts you, you're really going to be playing on his field and not yours." If that's how Warren and her team would respond to the pressure of a presidential campaign, she wouldn't be long for the race, they concluded.

Sanders and Warren referred to each other as friends, but their bond was more professional than personal. Sanders didn't have many friends in Washington. He was a loner. He didn't slap backs. He didn't talk about his personal life, and he didn't inquire about those of his peers.

Warren knew what it was like to be on the outside looking in, too. She had broken a lot of pillars of the establishment in her quests to rewrite bankruptcy law, oversee the financial system bailout, and build the Consumer Financial Protection Bureau. She had a knack for alienating allies when she disagreed with them, even when that included the most important person in the Democratic Party, President Barack Obama. She had fought him tooth and nail on the Trans-Pacific Partnership trade deal and tanked one of his Treasury Department nominees, Antonio Weiss, who had worked at a Wall Street firm that executed corporate inversions.

The tension between Warren and Obama had peaked in 2017. She was touring to promote her bestselling book when she was asked about the former president getting paid $400,000 to speak to Wall Street investors. "I was troubled by that," she said on an April episode of the SiriusXM radio show *Alter Family Politics*. The influence of money is "a snake that slithers through Washington and it shows up in so many different ways," she continued.

The remark, picked up by virtually every news outlet in America, infuriated Obama. The former president, who had run on lobbying and earmark reforms, didn't much care for the characterization that he was a serpent in the D.C. "swamp."

Later in the spring, Warren asked to meet with Obama at his West End postpresidential office. When she arrived at his relatively new daytime digs, she could see the American flag hanging in the reception and a collection of mementos given to the former president sprinkled throughout the T-shaped space. Heading down a hallway with light wood floors and darker wood paneling, Warren turned into Obama's private office. She didn't realize she would be there for almost two hours.

Warren talked about Trump, how he had done "so much damage" in just five or six months in office, according to a person familiar with the meeting. Obama, who was trying to keep a low public profile when it came to the new president, indulged Warren's topic of choice behind closed doors. But he wanted to talk about something else.

Obama mentioned her commentary on his speaking fee.

Warren took the opportunity to explain herself. She was on a book tour. She was asked a question. She hadn't given it any deep thought. She didn't mean to suggest he was corrupt.

It didn't really matter what she said. Obama's point had been made. He didn't have to be explicit about the consequences of crossing him again.

Warren's book was widely viewed as a stepping-stone for a presidential run, and if she wanted his help—even if she wanted him to remain neutral toward her—she couldn't go around tarnishing his reputation just months after he departed the Oval Office. Even Sanders, who had once suggested that Obama needed a primary challenge from his left in 2012, had maintained a good relationship with the former president in the years since. Making herself look righteous at Obama's expense might serve Warren in the short term—and it might be her honest opinion—but it didn't serve the

Democratic Party or its progressive wing to make Obama look crooked. It was Trump talk. Warren got the message.

As Warren and Sanders wrapped up their dinner around midnight, one thing was clear: The progressive movement could split during a death match with the establishment wing. The ambitions of two millionaire populist U.S. senators, colliding in a posh two-bedroom pied-à-terre in the nation's capital, could imperil the chances of a progressive victory.

Warren and Sanders both knew how much was at stake for their shared worldview. They both saw Biden as a picture-perfect representation of how compromising with Republicans led Democrats to compromise the public interest. They both believed that Democrats stood a better chance of winning with a progressive nominee. And if Biden or another moderate managed to win the presidency, that would mean the appointment of centrist, corporate-background Democrats—and probably at least a few Republicans—to the cabinet and other high-ranking administration jobs. Personnel is policy, Warren liked to say.

The two senators came to an informal understanding that night that they would try to avoid letting the establishment wing pit them against each other, according to people familiar with their parley. It was less a nonaggression pact and more acknowledgment of the mutually assured destruction that would ensue if they turned on each other.

Warren, obsessed with details and trained as a lawyer, created a record of the conversation after Sanders left, according to one friend. Sanders tended to synthesize his political interactions, recalling his overall impressions but seldom the blow-by-blow. "He's not a good reporter in terms of reading out meetings," said one Sanders aide. He told an associate afterward that he had gleaned just one thing from the dinner. "Yeah," he said, "she's running."

Almost a year earlier, in January 2018, Bernie's top advisers had gathered around him at senior Senate aide Ari Rabin-Havt's condo in Washington's Adams Morgan neighborhood, named for the white and Black elementary schools that merged the year after the Supreme Court's 1954 desegregation decision and known for bars with live bands and cheap late-night pizza. They picked the spot to avoid being detected by the press. This first meeting to discuss a possible second Sanders bid for the presidency was meant to be secretive.

The leader of the pack, Jeff Weaver, had run Bernie's 2016 campaign. Chuck Rocha, a talented Texas political operative once convicted of embezzling union money, had signed on for a senior role if Bernie ran. Nothing important happened for Sanders without Tim Tagaris and the monster online moneymaking machine he had developed. A handful of other familiar Bernieworld consultants and confidants packed into the room, and Jane Sanders, the senator's wife, joined the conclave by phone.

For Washington, it was a motley crew of Democratic Party outcasts and rabble-rousers. Among the Bernie crowd, this was the legit set of political professionals. Bernie wanted to know if he could actually make a serious bid for the party's nomination in 2020. He believed he could beat Trump, but he wanted to be certain that he was the Democrat best situated to do it. Like Biden, Sanders worried about whether he could get through the primary. Weaver and former Ohio state senator Nina Turner, who was also present, had just served on a party commission that recommended dramatically reducing the influence of superdelegates in the nominating process. The rules, which still had to be finalized by the Democratic National Committee, were moving in Bernie's direction—or at least in a way that was less stacked against an insurgent candidate. But that didn't mean Sanders could or would win in a fair fight.

He had come to Adams Morgan to play the part of skeptic while his advisers presented him with the case for running. Weaver was the most forward leaning of the bunch. He wanted Sanders to run, and he made no secret of it. One by one, the advisers mapped out fundraising, polling, and what they believed was a plausible path to victory. Sanders held up a cellphone and pointed it at each aide who spoke, as if that would help Jane, on the other end of the line, hear better. At intervals, smokers stepped onto the balcony, into the crisp winter air, to get a break from what amounted to a pep rally.

"It was a meeting to make him feel better about making the decision," said one person who participated.

The basic theme was to show Bernie how he could repeat what

he'd done right in 2016 and use additional time, money, and experience to improve on his weaknesses in 2020. As always, Sanders was obsessed with how he would raise the money he would need to compete and spend it more wisely this time. Tagaris, the online fundraising expert behind the 2016 campaign's grassroots cash explosion, assured him that money would come in buckets.

Ben Tulchin, a San Francisco–based pollster in his midforties, talked about the loyalty of Sanders's political base. The advisers already envisioned a long fight for the nomination among a bunched-up set of contenders. In that scenario, Sanders could amass a delegate lead heading into the Democratic convention by winning state after state with 25 percent or 30 percent of the vote. Tulchin explained that surveys showed Bernie's core backers were rock-solid and would provide that kind of support. They also demonstrated that the vast majority of Democratic voters viewed Sanders favorably.

The flip side, and it was obvious to everyone in the room, was that 25 or 30 percent was a lot less than he'd had in the 2016 primary, and it was a losing proposition in a head-to-head race. The plan required Sanders to either expand his base significantly or rely on the rest of the field remaining large enough and at relative parity for long enough.

If it consolidates down to him and one other person, we don't have a shot, one of the advisers thought. *Because no one will ever be as hated as Hillary Clinton.*

Bernie listened politely and asked questions. But before he left, he wanted everyone assembled to understand one thing: "If we do this, I don't want to do it just to make a point," he said. "I want to do it to win."

He didn't make a decision that day, but it was clear he was inclined to run. It took an uncommon combination of ambition, ego, and faith in his own abilities to assess the battlefield in front of him and see victory. Without Hillary, he was demonstrably—numerically—the favorite of far fewer party voters than he had been in 2016. But the likelihood of a crowded primary, the party rules he was working to change, the lessons he'd learned from his first run, and his ability to filter national debates through a progressive lens all contributed to his sense that he might be able to win with a committed base and the tolerance of the rest.

That's how Trump had done it in the Republican primary in 2016. The two parties differed in the way they awarded delegates— Democratic delegates were won proportionally in each state and congressional district—making it harder but not impossible to effectively replicate what Trump did with a plurality of GOP voters. The main difference is that it was unlikely that a drawn-out, multi-candidate primary would result in Bernie walking into the convention with a majority of Democratic delegates in his fold. For him to win, he would have to win more delegates than anyone else during the primaries *and* force the party to nominate him. The latter was contingent on the former: If he had a lead, denying him the nomination would put the party at risk of imploding at Trump's feet. There just wasn't a feasible way for him to become president without first taking the Democratic Party hostage, and Sanders and his advisers knew that from the start.

There was another truth at play, according to people close to Sanders. He was hooked on the game. He reveled in the idea that he was leading a movement. He loved the adulation. As he considered another run, he asked confidants whether they thought people would show up to see him again now that the novelty had worn off. "Whether he says it or not, he and his wife absolutely thrive on these crowds—particularly Jane," said one longtime Sanders ally. "I call it 'candidate addiction.'"

Sanders would spend a good part of 2018 campaigning on behalf of progressive candidates, promoting bills and causes that put pressure on potential rivals to move to the left, and plotting to make a more sophisticated second bid. Like Biden, he had never really stopped running for president. Even early on, he saw Biden as a double-edged sword: either the man who would take him down or a key spoiler who would deprive other Democrats of the delegates they needed to beat him.

While Bernie kept hope alive for the left on the stump and in the Senate, his advisers mostly waited on the official word that he would run. In the fall, worried that they were losing valuable time, Weaver, Rocha, and a few others began to build a campaign-in-waiting on weekends in the offices of consultants Mark Long-abaugh and Julian Mulvey near the bustling corner of Fourteenth and U streets in Northwest Washington. Rocha, who associated the neighborhood with since-closed Stetson's, a landmark Tex-Mex bar that served Shiner Bock on tap, rode his bike down from Capitol Hill. Later on, as Rocha took on more responsibility for building out the campaign, he'd coax Weaver to meet at his row house, where his English bulldog Apache sat under a table farting up enough of a storm that it offended the senses and sensibilities of Weaver.

"Good God Almighty, you've got to do something about that," Weaver said at one meeting.

As the Washington air grew colder and the presidential campaign preseason heated up, the two men modeled a campaign designed to take advantage of both the brand Sanders had built and the lessons they had learned from his last run. Weaver was adamant that the leadership team they built had to depart from the Bernie Bro reputation the senator's operation had acquired. The inclusion of Rocha at a senior level—Bernie and Weaver asked him to run the campaign, but he declined, citing his felony conviction and tendency to shoot from the hip—reflected that. A fast-talking operative with an East Texas drawl and a penchant for profane neologisms that would make James Carville jealous, Rocha instead put himself to work looking for a Black or brown campaign manager and women or minorities to run every department under that manager. He and Weaver would retain control over big decisions, but someone else would be the day-to-day manager and the face of the operation.

Coming from the progressive wing of the party, Sanders had a more developed grasp of the concept of representation—that it required people from a diverse set of backgrounds to form and sell policies that reflected the values of minority communities—than Biden. In that way, the move to diversify his campaign leadership reflected a lesson learned from 2016. It wasn't just about showing Democrats he was more inclusive. He was also going to make a major play for Latino voters of all ages and for younger voters of all colors. Among the politicians who shared elements of his agenda were the four incoming first-term House members in a group that would be known as "The Squad": Representatives Alexandria Ocasio-Cortez of New York, Ayanna Pressley of Massachusetts, Rashida Tlaib of Michigan, and Ilhan Omar of Minnesota—two of whom are Muslim, two of whom are Black, and one of whom is Latina. At least in theory, empowering people of color within his campaign would help him reach out to a broader coalition of voters this time around.

Even as the campaign foundation was built under his feet, Bernie hesitated to commit. He knew he was taking a lot of risks in running. He told friends he was worried that voters might see him as too old. He feared he might embarrass himself, and the progressive movement, if he flamed out. In the fall of 2018, if ever so briefly, his feet looked a little cold to friends.

"He really wanted to take his time and be absolute about it," said one adviser.

Weaver applied gentle pressure.

"If we're going to do this, we should do this," he told Bernie. "You have to decide by October fifteenth."

Sanders blew right through that deadline.

On November 8, 2016, Elizabeth Warren watched election returns roll in just like most Democrats across the country. She knew calls for her to run for president would come fast and furious. But there was an important prelude to a possible campaign. The grassroots had to be rallied around a common purpose. *I want to protect the country from Donald Trump,* she thought. *I want to find a way to create and harness a force to push back on whatever he does.* Before Hillary Clinton had even conceded, Elizabeth Warren was envisioning a resistance.

At that moment, there were two major projects on her calendar: finishing her latest book, which would have to be rewritten to reflect the surprise ending of the election, and building her campaign for a second Senate term—the one she would be two years into if she eventually sought and won the presidency in 2020.

In a way, the Senate reelection campaign was a major gift, and she recognized it for that. Unlike candidates in competitive states, Warren could be fairly confident that Republicans wouldn't be able to field a serious challenger to her in Massachusetts. She could raise tons of money from donors in her home state and across the country in 2017 and 2018 for her Senate campaign—giving some of it out to other Democratic candidates—and transfer any leftover funds to a presidential account later. And she could road test her barnstorming skills and campaign tactics at a time when most of her potential competitors for the presidency were assiduously avoiding questions about whether they would seek the Oval Office.

All the while, Warren would build her case for systemic change. She had watched Hillary fail to tell the American people why she was running for president in a way that convinced them it was about their lives, and she had watched Trump succeed at that. She thought Trump was a big fraud—and that he proved it more each day, from the very moment he took the oath of office. He was playing directly into the argument she was constructing, she thought.

In the spring of 2017, after she had all but signed off on the logistics of what would be a series of thirty-eight town hall meetings as part of her Senate reelection campaign, Warren inquired about a detail that her campaign manager, Roger Lau, considered to be insignificant at first.

"Why do we do the rope lines?" she asked Lau, who had worked assiduously to coordinate an airtight plan.

What the fuck? Lau thought. Warren herself had insisted on making town hall meetings the centerpiece of her campaign. It was one of a handful of items that were on her list of must-dos in what everyone around her understood was a dry run for a potential presidential bid. The point was to have direct contact with voters—the kind that Hillary didn't have much of in 2016 and that politicians had increasingly avoided over the years—and the rope line was the key element of a town hall–style event that showed a candidate actually wanted to be face-to-face with constituents. Now, she seemed to be questioning the purpose of her own demand.

"What do you mean?" Lau asked, hoping that maybe he'd misheard her.

"Why do we do the rope lines?" she repeated.

Lau fought the urge to condescend. *Okay,* he thought, *I'll entertain this.*

First, he said, voters want the connection—the handshake, the hug, the photo. Two, people will take selfies with you in the background and post it online and it goes mini-viral within their own personal networks. That, he said, would give her appearances amplification and personal validation from supporters, which could be more valuable than anything potential voters received through a traditional media filter. And third, he explained, the press would give better coverage to a candidate who interacted with the public directly. "For them, it shows energy, but they also want to see the conflict," he said. If someone yelled at her in a rope line, there was an authenticity to the exchange. "That's why I love you doing it," he said, hoping the step-by-step analysis would satisfy the professor.

It didn't.

"Huh," she half-grunted in familiar fashion. "Are we sure if those are three worthy goals, and if that's what we are trying to accomplish—and I agree with that—are we sure that we're doing it in the best possible way?"

What other fucking way is there to do this? Lau wondered.

Warren explained her concern with the setup: When she did it his way, she would give a speech, take questions from the audience, and then walk off the stage to meet with the public. But the first people she ran into would be the elected officials and VIPs who had already met with her backstage. The most motivated and aggressive voters might make their way to the front of the line, too. Warren didn't feel like she was getting enough contact with everyone else.

"I don't see little girls," she said. "I don't see older people. I don't see people who are disabled. Are you sure we're doing this the right way?"

"Well," Lau said, acknowledging in the softening of his tone that she had a point but a difficult one to address. "How else would we do it?"

"Roger, what if we invited every single person who wants to say 'hello,' has a question, wants to take a selfie," she said, "what if we invited them to come onstage and we just run through it."

The question hung for a moment.

"It will be quick," she assured him.

He was not so sure. "It will take forever," he said. "We can't do that."

Warren loved the word *can't*. It was a special challenge to do the thing she was being told not to do. She asked how long it would take.

"A long time," a now-belligerent Lau replied. He did the math. He told her she wouldn't be out of her events until eleven P.M.

They had the same conversation several times with the same impasse. The night before the first town hall, Warren emailed Lau.

"This is great," she said of the plan, adding a few notes of praise for her staff. "The one thing I would say is, I don't care how many people come, I don't care how good the coverage is, if there's a single person who came to the event who wanted to say 'hello,' who wanted to take a selfie who doesn't get an opportunity to do so, I will consider this event a failure."

Fuck it, Lau thought as he resigned himself to the goddamned selfie line. *She'll fucking hate it and we'll never have to do it again.*

After a year and a half and several dozen "selfie" lines—she actually just posed for regular pictures with voters—Warren won reelection handily in the 2018 midterms, which saw Democrats flood to the polls to register their hatred of Donald Trump and deliver their party to majority power in the House of Representatives. The photos she took with little girls enabled her to reap the political upside of being a role model for ambitious women without paying the price Hillary and others have for talking about it. In a move that foreshadowed her plans to run for president, Warren husbanded about $10 million of the more than $30 million she had raised for the Senate race.

If Hillary had proved anything in Warren's mind, it was that a woman running the right campaign could win. It just wasn't a tough decision to run. She knew if she lost, she would still have her Senate seat and a larger platform than she'd started with for her efforts to reform the nation's political and economic systems. If she won, she believed, she had the best chance to actually implement what she called "big, structural changes" to the landscape of American life. Bernie was a dreamer with a sketch; she was a builder with a detailed blueprint.

Truth seldom mattered as much as political reality. If Sanders ran, she knew, she would have to fight for the support of the progressive activists who would be a force. And she knew, from advisers, the biggest regret of every candidate who lost a close race in Iowa: that there wasn't another week or two to build their operation. If she could have started the day after the 2018 midterms, she might have.

"We were reading the room on how early we could start," said one of her top advisers. "It was 'How early can we get away with going?' What you're getting with each day is another incremental day before Iowa. Every day matters."

Warren's day was New Year's Eve 2018. That would give her nearly four hundred days to campaign before the Iowa caucuses. She quickly lined up her first hires, and by Friday, January 4, 2019, she was speaking to hundreds of Iowans at a bowling alley in Council Bluffs, Iowa.

"This is how it starts," she said. "Person to person. Town to town. Across Iowa and then across America."

Though Warren got out of the gate first, she would get off to a frustratingly slow start—particularly when it came to raising the money necessary to run a long campaign. There were going to be a lot of candidates competing for the attention of top donors, and she had alienated much of Wall Street with her anti-corporate rhetoric over the years. On the other hand, Bernie was the favorite of grassroots givers who signed up to have their credit cards charged on a revolving basis every month for ten or twenty bucks a pop. The money challenge spoke to the larger political dilemma—and opportunity—facing Warren: Done right, a toned-down version of Bernie-ism could harness populism in the party and give a more palatable alternative to the establishment. Maybe there was a kind of conscientious capitalism that appealed to both working-class families in need of real change and guilt-ridden elites. It would be a thinner tightrope to walk than it looked like from the ground. Between Biden and Sanders, who were both likely to run, there was a sweet spot of Democrats who didn't subscribe to either of the ideological poles within the party and who were open to a third choice. But the field competing for them would be crowded.

In late December 2018, around the time of Bernie's meeting with Warren, more than two dozen men and women who had worked for him wrote a letter seeking a meeting to address complaints of sexual violence and harassment on his 2016 campaign. At the time, Hollywood producer Harvey Weinstein was in court for pretrial hearings in New York surrounding allegations of sexual misconduct. In a few months, Lucy Flores would accuse Biden of having caused her discomfort by kissing her neck and smelling her hair.

On the cusp of launching his campaign, Bernie was suddenly thrust into the most highly charged social issue of the time. The obvious political move was to take the meeting, admit error, and move on as quickly as possible. But like those of Trump and Biden, Bernie's political persona was unapologetic. They all saw public apologies as signs that voters would take as weakness. Powerful white men seldom said they were sorry, even as society increasingly demanded contrition from them. Now, culture was crossing into politics. The tipping point for when it became more politically advantageous to apologize than to play defense was not always obvious.

For a candidate like Sanders, who presented himself as iron willed and incorruptible, there was never a good time to back down. That was part of his appeal. He stood his ground. Even when he was wrong. Even when he presented his own record or that of a rival misleadingly. But in the #MeToo moment of early 2019, and amid the backlash against Trump within the Democratic Party, he had little choice. The risk of ignoring #MeToo, of permanently alienating large swaths of the party and of nonvoters he hoped to recruit into his campaign, was too great.

This first crisis created a test of whether he was running another white-male-dominated Bernie Bro campaign from the get-go. In 2016, Bernie's inner circle was full of white men. His base of supporters tilted heavily white, male, working-class, and young. It was a lively and aggressive bunch, and it often tended to be harshly misogynistic in social media interactions with Hillary supporters. Bernie did little to control even the most vituperative activity, and Hillary's camp believed he encouraged ugly behavior from his backers and his staff.

When the harassment claims arose, they threatened to demonstrate that Bernie had a deeper problem. Even worse, if he didn't handle the situation right, it would look like he couldn't change or that he was uninterested in social progressivism. On January 10, 2019, he issued a long statement thanking the staffers for coming forward, apologizing, and calling for a "cultural revolution" in workplace "attitudes and behavior" in the United States. He and a set of his top advisers, including Jane and at least two women who had taken on senior roles in his operation since the 2016 campaign, met with the group six days later at a hotel in Washington.

Consistency was Bernie's greatest strength—voters knew what they were getting from his uncompromising fight for an agenda so progressive it harkened back to a liberalism that was last ascendant before most of them were born—but he knew he needed to change the culture around him, and the signals it sent to voters about his values, to build a winning coalition.

He recognized the value in putting a new face on his campaign to help blunt the complaints about his last bid and the excitement surrounding fresher candidates.

The solution was something of a hybrid in which much of the original team remained heavily involved while a new set took on high-ranking official roles on the campaign. Bernie hired Faiz Shakir, a second-baseman in his collegiate days at Harvard, to run the campaign. Shakir, the five-foot-nine son of Pakistani immigrants, had not yet turned forty and had never run a political campaign. But he had made a name for himself in progressive circles by masterminding innovative online organizing tools and as an aide at the ACLU, the Center for American Progress, and in congressional leadership offices. The quick-witted and soft-spoken Shakir offered a lot to a presidential candidate looking to straddle generational, ideological, and cultural divides without losing the essence of his brand.

Sanders and Shakir drew an amusing contrast. Bernie was an old Jewish democratic socialist from Brooklyn who bounced between gloomy prognostication of failure and fantastical visions of remaking an entire nation's future. He often looked as if he'd just sought shelter from a tornado of his own thoughts. Shakir was a young, Catholic-school-educated Muslim progressive from Melbourne, Florida, whom Bernie described as the "Prozac" of his campaign. Clean-cut and meticulous, Shakir usually looked as if he'd just finished posing for wedding photos. Sanders described himself as "mediocre" in college; Shakir had been one of the nation's elite students.

What joined them would be at the heart of the story Bernie wanted to tell in bringing Democrats together before turning to Trump in a general election. It was a story that was hard for him to talk about. He didn't like opening up personally. But he had come to understand the importance of making a personal connection to voters, and Shakir shared an experience that Bernie felt made them like many other Americans—particularly those who could make a difference in expanding his coalition.

Like Shakir, Bernie's story started with immigration. His father was born in a part of Austria-Hungary that is in modern-day Poland. His mother, born in New York, was the daughter of Eastern European immigrants. While Bernie had focused so much of his 2016 campaign on economic issues and what he described as the "endless" wars in Iraq and Afghanistan—and he would do so again—immigration would play a much bigger role in a new campaign.

The immigration story line gave Sanders a way to introduce himself to the constituency he most wanted to court in a second campaign: Hispanic voters. Trump had called Mexicans rapists and murderers, he was in the process of trying to build a wall between the United States and Mexico, and he'd tried to discourage illegal immigration by separating undocumented immigrant parents from their children. The president, who often spoke in derogatory terms about minorities, was also a harsh critic of Obama's executive order protecting a class of undocumented immigrants—known as "Dreamers"—who had been brought to the country illegally by their parents and grown up in the United States. It all amounted to a massive assault on a segment of society that was virtually powerless. While the targets of Trump's push to crack down on both legal and illegal immigration from Mexico couldn't vote, their U.S.-citizen friends and family members could. Moreover, as the son of an immigrant, Sanders was making the argument that voters, regardless of their backgrounds, should rally in defense of immigrants. He viewed Trump's policies and rhetoric toward immigrants, the otherization of whole groups of people, as echoing the anti-Semitism that had wiped away much of his own family in Europe.

"It was very upsetting to him, given his family's history," said one Sanders confidant. "He was growing up in a community where people had tattoos on their arms" from Nazi concentration camps.

Telling his own biography would add another layer of authenticity to Sanders's narrative, and putting it in the frame of immigration would give him a ready contrast against Trump that he believed would work in both the primary and a general election. Bernie believed that Trump had co-opted part of his message to defeat Hillary in 2016. Trump talked about endless wars and bad trade deals. But Sanders despised Trump. They were both born in New York—

Trump to a wealthy real estate developer father and Bernie to poor parents from an immigrant community. In Bernie's estimation, Trump cared about workers only to the extent that they could benefit him, financially or politically.

With Shakir out front and in charge of day-to-day national campaign operations, Weaver and Rocha would maintain control over major portions of the campaign behind the scenes, including ad spending and building teams in the key early states. When Bernie was finally ready to roll out the campaign, he set up a series of January and early February planning calls with the team that had met in Rabin-Havt's condo a year earlier, plus a handful of additions. Warren was already in the race. Former San Antonio mayor Julián Castro; South Bend, Indiana, mayor Pete Buttigieg; California senator Kamala Harris; and New Jersey senator Cory Booker were all clearly about to jump in.

The biggest battle wasn't over strategy or policy. It was over where to start, literally.

Let's do it in Burlington, Bernie said. That was where Jane Sanders wanted to hold the launch.

Josh Orton, who had joined the operation to head up communications, policy, and law, pushed back on behalf of the whole team of advisers.

Vermont is lovely, Orton said, but it doesn't hold much political value. You'll win the primary there by a landslide like you did in 2016. It might make more sense to go back to your real roots, he offered, in Brooklyn. You'll have a shot at winning the New York primary this time around, and you can pick a spot in your old neighborhood that speaks to people of more modest means. You will draw a compelling contrast with the high-dollar fundraising events everyone else is holding in ritzy Manhattan condos.

In that way, Brooklyn was a shorthand to remind Sanders that the plan was for him to speak more about his personal narrative this time around.

Bernie, who had tried and failed to launch his 2016 bid at the DNC headquarters before choosing a little patch of grass known as the Senate "Swamp" outside the Capitol, was a little reluctant to give in on Jane's priority. But Orton persisted. This will force the conversation about your bio and where you come from, he explained.

Ultimately, the logic appealed to Bernie, who was still trying to get comfortable with the idea that he would be talking more about himself on the campaign trail. If he was going to get into a cold pool, there was no reason to just dip a toe in.

After announcing in mid-February that he would run, Bernie went to Brooklyn College, where he had attended classes for a year. It wasn't far from the rent-controlled apartment he grew up in, and he drew on that experience to tell the roaring crowd a little bit about the man who would be president.

"I am not going to tell you that I grew up in a home of desperate poverty," he said. "That would not be true. But what I will tell you is that coming from a lower-middle-class family, I will never forget how money—or, really, lack of money—was always a point of stress in our family." The iconoclastic Bernie Sanders, so long proud to stand apart from the crowd and insist that others come to him, had a new message on March 2, 2019: We're alike, and, because of that, we can work together.

There was good reason for the Democratic establishment to be skeptical. The face of the Sanders campaign was kinder, gentler, and more about broadening its coalition. But the strategy and tactics were still very much fire at will.

Even before Sanders jumped into the race, his legions of social media supporters began unloading political attacks on potential rivals for the Democratic nomination. The most visible ringleader was communications specialist David Sirota, an over-the-top political reactionary who spent much of his time on Twitter attacking fellow Democrats to help clear a path for his candidate. Sanders routinely denied involvement in social media campaigns, led by his staff and his supporters, to destroy other candidates, but these campaigns showed no sign of slowing. Even as Sanders was dealing with the complaint from former aides, Sirota and other minions were actively engaged in an all-out war against former Texas congressman Beto O'Rourke. The Sanders campaign looked at O'Rourke as a threat to win over young white progressive men and Hispanics, and his fans led a charge to portray O'Rourke as a corporate elitist by highlighting a couple of House votes on which he had sided with businesses. If anything, O'Rourke's full voting record stood out for not standing out from the Democratic Caucus.

Throughout the campaign, Sanders's other aides would pretend that Sirota wasn't really involved. "He's just out there in Colorado retweeting himself," one Sanders aide said dismissively. But he wasn't just retweeting himself. He was like a cheer captain with his bullhorn piped into the collective conscience of Bernie's digital armies. He had spent years in Washington pumping out opposition research on President George W. Bush's administration. In 2016, he'd led an online onslaught against Hillary Clinton. Now, with Sanders ready to run again, he trained his fire on Democrats. He went after Harris's record as a prosecutor—even though it seemed laughable that Sirota cared more about systemic injustice against people of color than Harris. He trashed Booker, too. He was a useful weapon for Sanders, who often publicly denounced negative campaigning while his allies—paid and unpaid—sprayed suppressive fire at his rivals. When Sirota identified a target, hundreds or thousands of Sanders supporters would be sure to follow his lead. In the 2016 campaign, federal prosecutors found, some of the social media accounts that jumped on the Sanders bandwagon were Russian bots.

Sanders was aware enough of the backlash all of this engendered that he sent a message to his supporters when he entered the race admonishing them that he condemned "bullying and harassment of any kind and in any space." It simply wasn't true. He was secretly taking counsel from Sirota, who had been a journalist. Eventually, Sanders would hire the online warrior as a senior adviser and speechwriter and pay him more than $150,000 in campaign funds. Sirota wasn't just on the campaign; he was one of its higher-paid employees. Sanders's tough talk against bullying distracted attention from the Internet mob that was helping him destroy the reputations of his opponents. Bernie knew only one way to campaign and it was as common to high-level candidates as it was duplicitous: Everyone but the candidate slashes and burns. Only Donald Trump violated that rule consistently and won. Still, few politicians had Sanders-level chutzpah when it came to declaring their own hands clean.

With the cover of the candidate's disavowal of negative campaigning, legions of "Sandernistas"—nicknamed for the Nicaraguan socialist Sandinista Party Sanders had supported in the 1980s—could beat down other candidates in an effort to make them unpalatable to Democratic voters.

If anything, Sanders felt like he had pulled some of his punches in 2016. He hadn't gone after Hillary as hard as he could have in the primary. His team had worked with her team to shut down protests at the Democratic convention. He'd campaigned with her. But there was no gratitude, no reward for what he saw as playing the good soldier. He got nothing but resistance from the establishment, insults from her, and endless allegations from her world that he had cost her the election. Politics was war. This time, he would take no prisoners, make no exchanges, give nothing to the enemy. He would build up his base, like Trump, crush his opponents on the political battlefield, and then force the Democratic Party into submission.

That is, if he wasn't taken out by a glass shower door first.

In mid-March, during a campaign swing through South Carolina, Sanders gashed his forehead open in the bathroom and went to a walk-in clinic to get stitches. The mishap unnerved him because he knew that it would be taken by the public as a sign of his aging, according to a friend. More septuagenarians than presidential candidates injure themselves seriously in bathroom accidents.

Sanders chose not to cancel his events, though, and brushed off aides who suggested he could cover the stitches with makeup.

"No, that's not me," he said. Instead, he appeared at events with a large white bandage over his left eye. Though his staff insisted that he had neither slipped nor fallen to the ground, he had managed to remind voters that he was old enough to have problems with his balance.

It was balance that Warren believed she could provide as a candidate—progressive but not socialist, reformer but not revolutionary, uncompromised but not uncompromising. There was a tendency among candidates, political operatives, and the media to think about the contrast between candidates along the lines of ideological lanes. Without Sanders in the race, it seemed, she could have her base and most of his, too. With him running, she and a lot of other candidates would have to compete for the slight majority of primary voters who weren't sold on Sanders or Biden.

But voters didn't cram themselves into neat ideological boxes to choose among candidates. Many of them couldn't precisely articulate why they preferred, or detested, one over the others. Ingredients of style, judgment, messaging, policy, race, and gender all went into the mix. But for the vast majority of Democrats, the most important question wasn't about which candidate had the most plausible healthcare plan or the cleanest record. It was all about who was the least likely to lose to Donald Trump.

CHAPTER 4

•

"This Is Just a Bunch of Bullshit!"

JOE BIDEN'S OBJECTIVE IN THE FIRST PRIMARY DEBATE MATCHED the unofficial mission of his campaign: Don't fuck up.

Biden knew he was going to be rusty. It had been almost seven years since he'd gone head-to-head with Paul Ryan in 2012. He also knew that he had to cram to get up to speed on issues that had changed since he was last in office. On top of all of that, his advisers knew his penchant for gaffes and other slips of the tongue became noticeably more pronounced later in the day, and the debate in Miami would be held at nine P.M. With President Trump leading Republicans in an all-out assault on Biden's mental fitness, the bar was low and the stakes were high for a credible showing. A few weeks before the debate, Trump had gone on an extended rant about Biden in comparison to the rest of the Democratic field. Gesturing to his own head, Trump said, "I think he is the weakest up here." The best retort, Biden's aides knew, was for the candidate to show it wasn't true. The fear among many Biden-leaning Democrats was that, for whatever reason, he might not look steady on stage.

For a stronger front-runner, the first debate might have been an opportunity to blow the rest of the competition out of the water. Come out with shock and awe, pummel the munchkins for a couple of hours, and answer the doubts of Democrats. For Biden, it was more a matter of playing defense—of surviving and advancing with his lead intact. He was better known than the other candidates, which meant he wouldn't have to fight for a breakout moment to garner attention from voters and donors. The less memorable the debate, the better for him, some of his aides thought. But the format was a challenge. He liked to give twenty-minute discourses in response to yes-or-no questions, and here he would be limited to one-minute answers and thirty-second rebuttals. He just wasn't built for the clapback speed of a modern debate.

In June, he hunkered down with top advisers for debate camp. With Jill sipping fine wine while staffers emptied pizza boxes, Biden spent several days and nights running through rigorous drills. In a spacious first-floor room, podiums were arranged side by side so he could engage in mock competitions with stand-in foes. Ron Klain, the Democratic Party's most prominent debate-prep guru, and Anita Dunn ran the show. Biden also pored over briefing books to get up to speed on the complexities of issues that had changed since he left the White House. That's how he preferred to get ready.

But there was only so much he could do in cram sessions. Most of the other candidates had been fully engaged in daily political wars for the past few years or longer, and Biden knew deep down that one of them—or maybe several of them—would be coming after him. He might be walking into an ambush. He even had a pretty good idea what the progressives would attack him on. They would try to rip him apart on race: the crime bill, Anita Hill, his recent recollections of working amicably with segregationists, and, almost assuredly, leading the fight against school busing in the 1970s.

In Biden's early years in the Senate, federal courts and the presidential administrations of Nixon, Ford, and Carter were still trying to implement the *Brown v. Board of Education* ruling that was supposed to desegregate schools. School districts in the North and South had found ever more innovative ways to stop integration. Similarly, in the Senate, segregationists invented new means to help these districts by blocking courts and the executive branch. Biden, whose border state mirrored many southern states with its history of slavery, its white majority, and its sizable Black minority, not only joined the segregationists but led them on some of their most audacious attempts to block Black students from attending white schools. His language, like that of his contemporaries, was typically cloaked in one legal principle or another, but the point was clear enough for voters without law degrees to understand: He would fight to prevent the federal government from requiring schools to integrate.

The issue was reduced to one word—"busing"—which represented federal courts' orders that districts bus kids across communities to ensure desegregation. But some of the efforts by Biden and others went much further. One amendment Biden won adoption of on the Senate floor would have allowed schools to have white classrooms and Black classrooms without fear of losing federal funding. Biden only reversed course and pushed for his provision to be killed after *The New York Times* accused him of wiping away decades of progress on civil rights. Senate majority leader Robert Byrd, a Democrat from West Virginia who'd once been a member of the Ku Klux Klan, would note Biden's aggressive posture on busing in his own autobiography.

Biden and his aides were confident that race would come up in the debate, so they devoted extra time to prepackaging a defense. Yet when Biden began workshopping responses in the living room, some of his younger advisers were disturbed by what they heard.

Look, Biden said, I was in favor of *voluntary* busing. It's not right to force parents to bus their kids an hour, two hours to go to school. If there's de jure segregation—if a state has a law supporting segregation—the courts have a responsibility to step in, he argued. But they shouldn't write busing plans for local school districts if the laws aren't discriminatory. I had support from white parents and Black parents on this.

From a political standpoint, the back end was a pretty good answer. White and Black parents in Delaware agreed with him at the time. Many moderate-to-conservative white parents, and more than a few who might describe themselves as liberals, didn't want Black kids in their schools. A larger share didn't want to bus their kids to schools in Black neighborhoods. Some Black parents were worried about putting their kids on buses to go into hostile territory in white neighborhoods. Biden was also a supporter of increased education funding for schools in poorer areas throughout his career. He believed in allowing parents to move their kids from a bad school to a good school, but he drew a line at busing students to effect racial balance. The combination of positions created a separate-but-equal kind of policy solution to the desegregation fight, in which Black-majority schools in poorer areas would get extra funding but remain segregated.

At the debate prep session Biden simply wanted to explain his thinking, which had not changed. Done right, it would put him on the side of the majority of the country, and the party, against the "woke" left. "Forced busing" hadn't been an issue at the federal level since Ronald Reagan won office. It was over. The liberals had lost. Biden could now casually place himself between progressives of all colors and Trump on race—just where he wanted to be to appeal to white suburban swing voters.

But to his younger aides, his language was cringeworthy. The argument about de jure and de facto segregation was a segregation-ist talking point from another era. At best, it was senator-speak. His whole frame gave too much insight into his thinking at the time, which wouldn't play well now with the left. The world had changed. Even if his position was defensible by either era's standards, there was little upside in talking about race in the terms of the 1970s.

"When you're explaining de jure and de facto segregation, you're not in a good place," said one person who participated in the debate prep sessions.

The splits between old and young on his campaign, and between white and non-white, were intensifying. Klain had focused on fill-ing Biden's head with specifics of the old fight, and some of the younger advisers thought their boss was getting a little stuck in a morass of information overload. They didn't want him to give a blow-by-blow of the busing fight or any of the other issues that touched on race. There was no upside to that. Even if most Ameri-cans agreed with him—even if most Democrats did—there was no reason to agitate progressive voters. Instead, they pushed for Biden to hit the high points of his civil rights record. That, they thought, would be a shield on busing and similar topics.

Just pivot to what you've done since then, they argued.

Biden was frustrated. His aversion to apology reared up. His position back then was popular at home in Delaware, and he wanted to clarify that. I was where everybody was, he said. But he gradually began to accept that there were other points of view.

"We were moving him back toward values and 'your long his-tory'" of supporting civil rights, one adviser said.

By the end, the cautious, consensus-driven campaign had Biden down to a pretty pat response that reflected a little bit of his own instincts and a lot of what the younger set preferred: *It was a complicated time, but I was supportive of voluntary busing. I fought against segregation and for voting rights and civil rights for my entire career.*

Like an athlete returning to full-speed play after a rehab assignment, Biden would try to avoid getting hurt in his first debate. But to the extent that he might get hit from the left on race—and busing, specifically—he and his aides felt his negotiated script put him on firm political ground.

Just across the Potomac River, around the same time, Kamala Harris holed up with her top advisers in the second-floor offices of GMMB, one of Washington's all-purpose media and political consulting firms. In a cylindrical conference room overlooking the Georgetown waterfront, Harris could see the John F. Kennedy Center for the Performing Arts through one side of the room-spanning windows, and a panorama of the river, its banks, and suburban Virginia on the other. Crew teams rowed on the river below and jets departing from and arriving at Reagan National Airport flew overhead, approximating the course of the water to limit noise over the heart of the capital city. Occasionally, a military chopper could be seen cutting through the sky in the distance.

Inside, Harris zeroed in on her target—Biden—whom she wanted to strike with military precision. Her early debate prep meetings resembled a writers' room for a television show, informal bull sessions about how to approach various topics that might come up.

But after Biden waxed nostalgic about working with segregationist senators James Eastland and Herman Talmadge during a fundraiser in mid-June, Harris and her aides began to map out what she might say in response if a reporter caught her in the halls of the Capitol before the debate. New Jersey senator Cory Booker called on Biden to apologize, which prompted Biden to demand an apology from Booker, who "should know better" than to attack him on civil rights.

Harris said she was "deeply" troubled. "If those men had their way, I wouldn't be in the United States Senate and on this elevator right now," she said in just the kind of ad hoc Capitol interaction that her team had anticipated.

Now that a fight had broken open between the two Black senators and Biden on race, there was a stronger likelihood that the topic would be raised at the debate. That created a unique opportunity for Harris to grab the spotlight for the first time since the earliest days of her campaign.

Four months after an electrifying campaign launch in Oakland, which had drawn roughly twenty thousand people and set the standard for the field, the California senator was looking for a way to recapture that kind of enthusiasm for her candidacy. In just a couple of weeks, Harris had put together a rally that would help springboard her from the mid-single digits in polling to a clear third place behind Biden and Sanders at about 12 percent by the end of February. She raised $1.5 million in her first twenty-four hours as a candidate, and there was good reason to think she might ride that momentum into a three-way fight for the nomination. The combination of her California constituency and her potential to reach Black voters set up an opening for Harris to rack up delegates on Super Tuesday. That is, if she could get to Super Tuesday, and if she could navigate to the top of a mass of candidates who trailed Biden and Sanders in the polls and fell between them on the ideological spectrum.

At the same time, Harris was caught in the cultural crosscurrents of a country and a party obsessed with race and identity. On the one hand, Barack Obama's presidency and Hillary Clinton's near miss had paved the way for the rising-star, first-term-senator daughter of a Jamaican-born father and an Indian-born mother to be seen immediately as a contender for the Democratic nomination. On the other, many Democrats viewed Donald Trump's election as a backlash to Obama and Clinton and worried that nominating a woman, a person of color, or both would be a disadvantage. From the start, Harris was determined to show that she could provide a new definition of a central-casting commander in chief.

"She wanted to look strong, wanted to look presidential," said one adviser who worked on the launch. "Nobody like her had seriously contended."

The Oakland rally served that purpose to a tee. Even Trump

was impressed with the optics, calling it "the best opening so far." But, as longtime associates of Harris observed even before she got into the race, she was great at hitting her marks in big moments and terrible at following through afterward. She was often better at playing the part than living it—*The West Wing* writer's dream and the West Wing aide's nightmare.

"There was a very clear plan to launch the campaign; there wasn't a very clear plan to win the campaign," one top adviser said of the early months. It took a long time to hire staff and build a hybrid fundraising operation that mixed big-bucks donors with grassroots online givers. Maya Harris, the candidate's sister and campaign chairwoman, clashed with the campaign manager, Juan Rodriguez, over policy and political strategy. At times that spring, aides felt like they were standing around doing nothing, waiting to see if an instruction they got would be reversed. Maya Harris and Rodriguez seemed like "two heads" of the same campaign, said one official. "It was just frustrating to be a part of that because we wanted to know the direction we were going," said one aide.

Even the basic theory of the campaign—that Harris could bridge a divide in a party split between Hillary supporters and Bernie backers—proved quickly to be the application of old fault lines to a new race. It was, in many ways, the same bet Elizabeth Warren was making, and they competed for many of the same voters. From the end of February through late May, Harris faded as both Warren and Pete Buttigieg ate into her base of support. They, too, appealed to educated progressives. It was traditionally a high-value, trend-setting set within Democratic primaries—one Warren adviser theorized that the Democratic nominee was always the candidate voters thought had read the most books—but there were a lot of candidates courting its votes.

The truly key groups in Democratic primaries—Black voters, and Black women in particular—were the ones Harris expected would develop a natural affinity with her. So far, they hadn't. She was an Alpha Kappa Alpha from Howard University, the first Greek-letter Black sorority in the nation, and Black voters still liked the old white guy better. Actually, they liked two old white guys better.

In early June, the Black Economic Alliance commissioned a poll that found 76 percent of Black Democrats were enthusiastic about or comfortable with the idea of Biden being the nominee, followed by Sanders at 64 percent. Harris barely broke into majority territory with 53 percent saying the same of her. If she was going to win the nomination, she was going to have to turn those numbers around. The silver lining in the survey's findings: Almost everyone knew Biden and Sanders, but one in five Black Democrats had never heard her name. She needed to change that in a hurry.

Sitting at a round table at GMMB headquarters in Washington, Harris and her advisers brainstormed what one of them called "moments of friction" she could create with Biden. School busing was at the top of the list. It wasn't something she had discussed much publicly, but she'd deposited a political time bomb in her pre-campaign book, *These Truths We Hold: An American Journey,* when she wrote that she had been part of the second integrated class at her Oakland elementary school.

When CNN's Jake Tapper asked her about her personal experience in January 2019, and noted Biden's opposition to busing, Harris brushed him off. "I didn't know that," she said. If she didn't, it was because she hadn't studied up much on the front-runner for the nomination she was about to seek. If she did, it was a sign that she wasn't ready to light a fuse.

Now, though, Harris's advisers saw an opportunity to accomplish a second goal by going after Biden on busing, specifically. They knew she needed to establish a better emotional connection to a larger number of Black voters and white progressives. Even before she started running, critics tried to undermine her with Black voters by portraying her as too tough on people of color when she was a district attorney in San Francisco and as California's attorney general. She also faced the same *bullshit* insinuations that she wasn't *really Black* or Black *enough* that Obama heard when he first ran for president. "Jamaica is not America," CNN host Don Lemon said in February as he wondered aloud whether Harris could rightfully identify as African American after she had said she was born Black and would die Black in an interview with the radio host Charlamagne Tha God. "Jamaica did not come out of Jim Crow. I'm just saying." But riding the bus to integrate a school placed her squarely in the experience of Black Americans and on the side of having to overcome oppression.

The issue framed Biden—at least the Biden of the 1970s—as a

conductor of that oppression. In the run-up to the debate, he gave it more immediate salience by talking about his personal relationships with segregationist Democrats, whom he inaccurately described as being in the other party. The point Biden was trying to make was that he could get things done in Washington because of his ability to work with people across ideological divides. "At least there was some civility," he said of his bond with the two senators. "We didn't agree on much of anything." What Biden did agree with them on was busing.

Whether intentionally or not, Biden was leaning into a fight on race. His younger advisers, who had been working to spin his busing position forward, were horrified at what they saw as a blunder.

Watching it all unfold, Harris thought it was pretty ugly. Her advisers Ace Smith, Lily Adams, and Jim Margolis pressed her to hammer Biden on busing. At the time, her argument to voters was that she was the candidate most capable of prosecuting the Democratic case against Trump in the general election. The whole primary was about who could beat Trump. The busing issue, long dead for many voters, was just a way into that battle. What better way to show voters her strength than a public takedown of the front-runner for the nomination?

Beyond that, Harris was running a campaign based on diversity and inclusion, while Biden had already established a broader coalition among Black voters and conservative Democratic whites. Some voters of color were attracted to him because of the affinity conservative white Democrats had for him, not despite it. The chance that white voters in swing states would pick Biden over Trump—backed up by polls showing Biden defeating Trump head-to-head—appealed to many Black Democrats who were more concerned with a Democrat winning the presidency than which Democrat did it. Harris, who was never going to be the candidate of conservative white voters in the primary, had to drive a wedge between the pillars of Biden's coalition to try to peel away Black voters.

Still, it wasn't an easy decision.

The first six months of 2019 had been an unusual time in the Democratic universe. Trump's election and presidency had taken a heavy psychic toll on party insiders and voters. In many ways, that was even more true for establishment types than it was for a progressive movement that capitalized on the backlash to Trump by yanking the party to the left. When he announced an aggressive policy cracking down on immigration, threatening health insurance benefits, or banning trans people from military service, liberal activists could count on the reaction to it pulling more establishment Democratic sentiment, and even some centrist Republicans, toward their camp.

At least two major factors drove most of the party's presidential hopefuls and elite political leaders to bend over backward in playing nice with one another. The first was the belief in the establishment, spurred on by Hillary, that disaffected Bernie voters had cost her the election—along with Russia, Jim Comey, and a variety of other forces that boiled down to "not me."

"It was fueled by the idea that the nastiness of 2016 caused the loss in the general, and that weakening the nominee was a bad idea," said one prominent Democrat who maintained relationships with most of the candidates.

But Trump's polarization of the country also played a role in the way Democratic candidates treated one another. While he drove people apart on policy, his behavior was even more divisive. It was repugnant to Democratic voters across the ideological spectrum, as well as to many independents and Republicans. That created an incentive, many Democratic candidates thought, to show respect to one another as a way of demonstrating a contrast to Trump.

Trump used his Twitter account to trash his political rivals. Almost all of the Democratic candidates used social media to praise opponents; some of them sent supportive text messages to each other—letting that be known to members of the media—and avoided criticizing each other in television town halls and other public venues. When they went on the attack, it was exclusively against Republicans, and they were rewarded for that in contributions and polling.

Violating the existing norm of collegiality created one risk for Harris in terms of her chances of winning the nomination. The other risk involved her prospects of becoming the Democratic vice presidential candidate if her campaign failed. She was the most oft-mentioned potential running mate for Biden. She had to choose between her ambition for the presidency and her viability for the vice presidency. But the more Harris talked with advisers—and the more she heard from Biden about segregationists—the more convinced she became that attacking the former vice president was the right tack.

"I'm not running for second place," she told her aides in one debate prep session. "I'm running to win."

She just wanted to make sure, in her own mind, that she wasn't taking a cheap shot.

If it's righteous, she thought, *I'll do it.*

In a conference room at the luxurious Fontainebleau Miami Beach hotel a couple of days before the debate, she started toying with the phrasing of her attack. Standing at a podium set up in front of a window framing the Miami skyline, with press aide Ian Sams standing in for Biden and Ace Smith playing Sanders, Harris practiced talking about diversity, inclusion, and riding the bus as a child. Aides pulled the curtains closed so they could stay focused on their boss.

"This was a new speed for her," one aide who participated in the sessions said of Harris talking about her childhood. At first, her delivery was unnatural. Her aides coaxed her by emphasizing that she really needed to make a connection with Black voters.

"I get it," Harris said. "I have to *demonstrate* who I am."

She was talking about her "lived experience," but she might as well have been assessing the whole decision to attempt a takedown. And even as she became increasingly convinced that it was the right move, there were other aspects of the construct that gave her pause.

Yes, it was about her. But it was about Biden, too. And whether or not it was a fair shot, there was no doubt about the explosiveness of placing Biden in front of the schoolhouse. The message was that he was racist, or at least intolerant. There was no getting around that. It was the point of what she was saying: They had different values and hers were better for Black voters.

Jim Margolis, the GMMB partner who advised her on messaging, pushed her to think hard about how to *deliver* the punch. It would take precious time on the debate stage just to set up the story of Biden fighting busing in the Senate and a little girl riding to a newly desegregated school. She had to get the language of the whole thing just right. It had to make viewers feel something about her—and about Biden.

"That little girl was *me*," she finally said from her podium at the Fontainebleau.

For some of her aides, the bite was too strong. The part about her was fine, but they worried about her casting Biden as racist. Even for Democratic primary voters who agreed with her, there was a difference between Biden's insensitivity and what they saw as out-and-out racism from Trump. Even more important, Democratic voters were looking to give Biden leeway. He might be their best shot to defeat Trump, and Harris had to be careful. Voters could both disagree with Biden's position on the issue and decide to punish her for pointing it out. One of her aides suggested that she start off with a preface saying she didn't perceive Biden as racist.

As they discussed this tension, Harris could see the problem. There was a split on her war council. The more aggressive set didn't think she needed to take the sting out of the attack. But others pressed to add the preface.

"If you don't say it, then for the next forty-eight hours people are going to ask you 'Do you think he's a racist?'" Harris's top Senate aide, Rohini Kosoglu, offered.

I don't want to call him a racist, Harris thought. *He's not a bad guy. And voters don't think he is, either.* The possibility that the whole thing might turn into a media frenzy about whether she had called him racist or not made the decision to preempt those questions easier. It was settled. She would add the words. Besides, the line had the dual value of giving her semi-plausible deniability while she more or less called him a recovering racist.

She had crossed over from weighing a hit on Biden to precision-tuning it, hoping to do the most damage to him without blowing herself up in the process.

Only two variables—a big X and a bigger Y—remained.

"Would there be an opportunity to raise something like this?" said one Harris adviser. "And how would Biden respond?"

Elizabeth Warren opened up the Democratic Party's *Hunger Games* version of presidential debates by raising the stakes for Biden, Harris, and the rest of the field. Faced with the calamity of more than two dozen hopefuls entering the race, party leaders decided to winnow the field for the debate stage by establishing qualifying criteria. A candidate had to collect contributions from sixty-five thousand donors, including at least two hundred donors in at least twenty different states, or poll at 1 percent in at least three national polls or surveys in each of the first four states on the primary calendar to get in. The result was a twenty-candidate crowd for the opening debate, and the Democratic National Committee split the group into two sets of ten to square off—or decagon off—on back-to-back nights. Lots were drawn to determine which candidates debated each night.

Warren drew the ace of a spot in the first heat at the Adrienne Arsht Center for the Performing Arts in Miami on June 26, 2019. Up against an ensemble cast of also-rans, she wiped the floor with her competition.

It was the second night, though, that the Democratic universe—and Twitter-happy Donald Trump—were waiting for. By virtue of their standing as the front-runners, Biden and Sanders would stand at podiums in the middle of the stage, with Harris to Sanders's left and Pete Buttigieg, the suddenly relevant South Bend surprise, to Biden's right. The positioning was no small matter to the candidates themselves because they knew viewers and moderators would give less credence to contestants standing near the exits. There were other optics to consider, too.

I want to be onstage with Biden, Buttigieg thought when the two-night debate format had first been announced. *But I don't want to be right next to him.*

The advantage to being onstage with Biden, he reasoned, was that they occupied some of the same emotional space for Democratic voters. They were both trying to appeal to Democrats who believed in the Obama-esque mantra that there aren't blue states or red states but a United States—the kind of stuff white midwestern moderates lapped up.

Buttigieg liked the direct contrast opportunity—perhaps voters might take a candidate not too unlike Joe but at the beginning of his career and with a vision of the future rather than a call to turn back the clock four years. But he didn't like their physical differences.

He's a lot taller than I am, Pete thought, chuckling to himself at what drives voting preference. *You refine your position on the Intermediate-Range Nuclear Forces Treaty and then you just have to worry about which candidates are which height.*

At nine P.M. eastern time, on June 27, the first moment of truth arrived for four of the five candidates who had spent the previous six months positioning themselves as the legitimate contenders for the Democratic nomination. Just before NBC's Lester Holt welcomed the at-home audience into the theater, Biden glanced down at his podium. He had rested his notepad there. Buttigieg, standing at the next podium over, saw Biden looking down and followed the former vice president's eyes to the pad. It had just three phrases written on it. Actually, one phrase repeated three times.

Middle class
Middle class
Middle class

Biden used his cheat sheet to attack Trump and Sanders in his first answer of the night. "Donald Trump thinks Wall Street built America; ordinary middle-class Americans built America," he said before aiming his fire at Sanders's Medicare for All plan. "Too many people who are in the middle class and poor have had the bottom fall out under this proposal." Then he trailed off into talking about clean air and other topics that weren't even tangential to the question he'd been asked. By the first commercial break, Biden had used all of his notes. He'd said "middle class" exactly three times.

Looking past Sanders at Biden, Harris wondered if and when she would get her chance to strike. *Why hasn't this come up yet?* she thought. For nearly two weeks, her advisers had assured her that Biden's record on race would be a hot topic. They were ready to build a public relations blitz around her talking about riding the bus as a schoolgirl. *This is in the water already. It's all over the news,* she thought. *Why is it being avoided?*

After nearly an hour, Savannah Guthrie asked Buttigieg why he had not improved the representation of African Americans on the South Bend police force in his time as mayor.

They're finally asking a question about race and they're asking a white guy about policing in South Bend? some Harris allies thought.

"Because I couldn't get it done," Buttigieg said. He went on to talk about the convulsions in his community over the officer-involved shooting of a Black man. Former Colorado governor John Hickenlooper, who is white, scolded Buttigieg for not having done more earlier to address systemic policing issues. California representative Eric Swalwell, who is white, said Buttigieg should have immediately fired the city's police chief. Marianne Williamson, a spiritual adviser to celebrities who is also white, said the whole discussion was a reminder that "the Democratic Party should be on the side of reparations for slavery."

Biden indicated to the moderators that he wanted to speak on the subject.

"Vice President Biden, we're going to get to you," NBC's Chuck Todd said.

Now! Harris thought.

"As the only Black person onstage," she said against the din of crosstalk, "I would like to speak on the issue of race."

The crowd in the small theater erupted in cheers. Told she had thirty seconds, Harris half-smiled.

"OK," she said. Her engine revved as she recalled neighborhood children not being allowed to play with her and her sister because of their skin color. The preamble bought her time to locate her target and recall, with prosecutorial clarity, the case she had been preparing for weeks—the one she had practiced reciting earlier that day in the air-conditioned conference room at the Fontainebleau. If there was one characteristic that distinguished Harris from her rivals, it was her ability to deliver a payload on cue. She knew she could land this one. The only question was whether it would blow up Biden, backfire on her, or take them both out.

"I'm going to now direct this at Vice President Biden," she said. "I do not believe you are a racist."

She let that hang in the air for a moment, just enough time to let it sink in with the home-viewing audience that the next words out of her mouth would all but tattoo "racist" on Biden's forehead. Sanders stood motionless and silent between them, the corners of his mouth drawn down like the ends of an upside-down "U" as he stared forward. His expression said a thousand words that could be boiled down to a single thought: *Better him than me.*

Biden gave a quick glance in Harris's direction, but he refused to look her in the eye as she unloaded.

"I also believe, and it's personal—I was actually very—it was hurtful to hear you talk about the reputations of two United States senators who built their reputations and career on segregation of race in this country," she said. "And it was not only that, but you also worked with them to oppose busing. And you know, there was a little girl in California who was part of the second class to integrate her public schools, and she was bused to school every day. And that little girl was me."

Biden was gobsmacked.

Kamala? Are you kidding me? We're friends, he thought, steaming inside.

He shot her a fleeting look of disdain as she wrapped up. Both Biden and Harris had played up the friendship she had developed with his son Beau when they were attorneys general of their respective states. She and Beau spoke often, and when he died of brain cancer in 2015, she was at his memorial alongside the vice president and his family.

Biden forgot what he was supposed to say. Some of his younger aides watched with fright as he fumbled around for his prescripted comeback. This was premeditated murder, one of the aides thought. He wasn't nimble enough to just react in the moment and he couldn't quite find his bearings. His answer included some of the points, but it was word salad with a finely garbled dressing.

He's overprepared, one of them thought.

Biden told Harris that her busing plan had been put in place at the local level and that he only opposed the federal government intervening to force busing.

"That's why we have the Voting Rights Act and the Civil Rights Act," she said to applause. "That's why we need to pass the Equality Act. That's why we need to pass the ERA—because there are moments in history where states fail to preserve the civil rights of all people," she said.

Biden picked up on the ERA—the never-ratified Equal Rights Amendment—and noted that he had been a supporter of it. He was missing the point. Finally, he just gave up.

"My time is up," he said. "I'm sorry."

He just got knocked out, a second adviser concluded.

Inside Harris's greenroom, backstage, the unfolding drama took aides a little by surprise. *That was crisp!* one adviser thought as it played out on TV. Harris hadn't delivered her lines with quite the same swagger in the prep sessions. She'd held back her best for game time.

For Biden, the minutes until the next break passed like an eternity. He was pissed. She had painted a picture: Harris was the little Black girl exercising the long-denied rights of an entire race, and Biden was the white guy standing on the Senate floor in Washington blocking others from the same equality of educational opportunity. America had changed a lot in Joe Biden's time in the public eye. But whether or not any of that struck him, what did hit him in the gut was his feeling of betrayal. When the moderators went to a commercial break, his frustration bubbled over as his jaw set and he turned to his right to look Buttigieg square in the eye. He thought Harris was full of malarkey, but that's not what he said.

"This is just a bunch of bullshit!" Biden muttered.

While Biden stewed, Harris tweeted—or, at least, her account did. At 10:11 P.M., right after she'd said the words, her Twitter account posted a photo of her as a child with the caption "There was a little girl in California who was bussed to school. That little girl was me. #DemDebate." Within hours, her campaign began marketing "That little girl was me" T-shirts for thirty dollars apiece. Harris had needed a political jolt, perhaps a bolt of lightning, and she had created one for herself. At the end of what had been a lousy fundraising quarter, donations began pouring in.

For Biden, it was a double blow. He had come into the debate just hoping not to have a debacle. His team wasn't so worried about the politics of the busing issue as it was his inability to cope with the attack. They didn't think he would lose any voters over a position he had held since Nixon was in office. But he had appeared weak, befuddled, and definitely angry. If voters concluded that he couldn't fend off Harris, what would they think about his capacity to go up against Trump? If he couldn't defend himself, how could he defend anyone else? Harris had exposed the weakness of the party's front-runner, just as she had planned, and it struck fear in the hearts of the majority of Democrats who saw him either as their favorite or their first fallback option.

For many of them, Biden's profile was the right one for the challenge of winning back Rust Belt states. He was a white guy who talked about the working class becoming the middle class. In theory, he was the best bet to do just a little bit better than Clinton with the key voters in those crucial swing states. *In theory*. Less-educated voters also tended to look for robust demonstrations of strength in their leaders. Biden had just shown the opposite.

He had planned to leave the debate and celebrate with supporters at a packed watch party at the Estefan Kitchen, a landmark in the city's upscale Design District, run by the singer Gloria Estefan and her husband. But the restaurant cleared out quickly after the debate. No one would be there to greet him. Donors and political allies texted and called his aides with messages of frustration. One aide described the reaction as a "meltdown." These supporters weren't ready to bail on him; it was still early in the process. And many of them were pissed at Harris. But that was just another way of pointing out that she had gotten the better of Biden. Collectively, they were downtrodden, and their discontent settled over the campaign. The most pronounced visible effect in real time was on the commodity Biden needed most: cash. It was the most brutally honest measure of party loyalists' assessment of his performance. Contributors held back, just as Harris's coffers were being flooded.

It was clear to Biden's team that the ship had to be righted, quickly.

On a three-hour flight from Miami to Chicago the next morning, Biden's mood bounced between despondent and downright shitty. Sullen, quiet, almost depressed, he was lost in his own thoughts. He had been warned that a presidential campaign could be embarrassing, that bad moments could strip some of the bark off the reputation he had carefully cultivated over decades. He knew he was going to be the main target at the first debate, but he'd expected to be afforded more respect. He didn't have to take this shit from anyone—especially not Kamala, the so-called friend of his dead son. He wanted revenge.

As Biden arrived in Chicago, his aides called an emergency meeting at a Washington office the campaign had opened up before its planned move to Philadelphia. They were in a tailspin—a "break glass" moment, as one adviser described the post-debate scramble to set Joe right—and they needed to find a way to reassure donors and voters that the candidate wasn't too far past his prime to carry the Democratic standard against Trump.

They were consumed by a single question articulated by one adviser: *What the fuck do we do?*

Schultz, Donilon, Symone Sanders, Cristóbal Alex, Dunn, and pollsters John Anzalone and Celinda Lake brainstormed an approach. Over sandwiches, Donilon piped up with at least a partial solution—cling to Obama.

The VP wants to explain everything, and he got lost in the weeds, Donilon said. There is a better way to shift the discussion to better ground. When issues like busing come up, Donilon continued, he should just talk about the first Black president picking him for vice president. That way he could reverse the energy of any attack on a bill he'd written, a position he'd taken, or a remark he'd made involving race issues without addressing the particulars. Biden had alluded to Obama in his busing answer, but he hadn't framed his record with the Obama lens. Since Obama had picked him, the logic went, he must not have a racist bone in his body. Never mind that the real reason Obama chose him, above all others, was that the centrist senator from the mid-Atlantic would balance the ticket, not double down on Obama's progressiveness on matters of race. Biden was the front-runner for the 2020 nomination *because* he appealed to middle-of-the-road whites better than most modern-day Democrats.

For Biden to find his feet, he would need to show he was still well-liked among Black voters and demonstrate that he could hit back effectively, even if not in the moment. The best approach, they decided, was for Biden to give a speech.

His aides quickly let the media know he'd taken offense at Harris going after him because of the relationship she'd had with his son and criticized her behind the scenes for selling T-shirts commemorating the moment. Her chances of being picked as Biden's VP were now nil, some of them said, in what amounted to a shot across her bow. Whether that was true or not, the perception that her ambitions were at risk might put a check on her as the campaign evolved. His aides also rushed him to South Carolina to deliver a speech on his ties to Obama.

"I was vetted by him and selected by him," Biden said. "I will take his judgment of my record, my character, and my ability to handle the job over anyone else's." Biden said his rivals liked to pretend that his public service spanned only his time in the Senate, excluding his work as Obama's wingman. And he apologized, not for any of his actions as a public servant but for creating the "mis-

conception" that he intended to praise segregationists "who I opposed time and again." The line reiterated the misconception that
he had fought them on the right of federal courts and the administration to use their powers to force schools to integrate. It was a
clever use of the truth—that he often battled those same senators
on other matters—to distort the reality of his record on busing.

As Harris strode quickly and quietly through the narrow hallway
to her dressing room following the debate, she wasn't sure how she
had fared. Inside the room, her team waited patiently for her to ar-
rive. The backstage area was tight, and advisers had not wanted to
celebrate in front of the other candidates and their aides. They
were nearly bursting at the seams by the time she appeared in the
doorway.

"What do you think?" she asked. "What went well? What are
people talking about?"

They assured her she'd knocked the busing moment out of the
park and otherwise nailed her debate performance. In a campaign
defined to that point by breakout moments, the made-for-viral-clip
quips landed in televised town hall meetings and at campaign
launch events, this was Harris's time. She had been confused by
Biden's tack in his reply to her. While defending himself on segregation, he had argued that the federal government didn't have the
right to intervene. It was at odds with Democratic orthodoxy of
several generations.

"Never in a million years did I think he would give up his time
and never in a million years did I think he would start with an argument about states' rights," said one of Harris's senior aides. "They
handled it by complaining. In the aftermath it was that she was
unfair or that she was being mean, and that's an excuse that no
other candidate would be willing to use."

For that reason, Harris would be surprised by the vitriol of the
Biden team's pushback afterward. But perhaps even more unantici-
pated was how her salvo attracted return fire from all corners. With
Biden weakened, other candidates chose to go after Harris. Their
aides quietly told reporters they, too, were shocked—shocked!—
that Harris would go after the former vice president so audaciously.
Many of them perceived her as a greater threat to them in the mo-

ment. If she took off, they would be left behind. So, the incentive for her rivals to make her look bad far outweighed the incentive to pile on a wounded Biden. They were all competing with her for primacy in the space between Biden and Sanders. Most of them believed Biden would eventually implode on his own. Six months into the campaign, some of them wondered how that hadn't happened yet.

It was Harris, though, who would trip over her own feet. In the days after the debate, she was asked whether Congress should write local busing plans now. Harris said no, putting her in the same position as Biden—or so it seemed.

"She gave a technical answer to a values question," one aide lamented.

Harris hadn't adequately prepared for the aftermath of her big moment onstage. She could have pointed out that the legal landscape on the issue had shifted. It wasn't ever about Congress writing busing plans. It was about whether courts should have the power to write them. Harris believed courts had the right and responsibility to enforce desegregation policies. Biden believed Congress had the right and responsibility to stop courts from imposing busing plans on state and local governments. But the details were complex. And in answering a question based on the misconception that Congress might write busing plans, it appeared that she didn't have a difference of opinion with Biden on the policy at all.

Harris saw a sharp rise in her polling numbers in the two weeks following the debate, and she briefly moved into second place, behind Biden, in the average of national surveys. In Iowa, she said the debate showed her strength. "I know how to fight," she said on the campaign trail. It took a little while longer—about a month—but she jumped into second place there. By that time, though, her national standing had taken a beating from Biden and the other campaigns.

Her failure to follow through on the Biden attack, while he pushed back off the debate stage, combined with her inability to explain her support for Sanders's Medicare for All plan, contributed to a fall as swift as her rise. Harris struggled with healthcare questions, at one point insisting that Medicare for All would not end private insurance—even though that was the primary objective of the policy. In late July, she rolled out her own version of a single-payer universal health insurance system that one aide described as an effort by her staff to "nail her feet to the ground" on the topic. But her version, which included a ten-year phase-in, took criticism from the left and the right. There was no good middle ground on healthcare policy in the Democratic primary. Sanders would clobber anyone who strayed from Medicare for All, Biden would do the same to anyone who embraced any version of it, and all the other candidates looked for every opportunity to ream one another.

The lesson most of the other candidates drew from the first debate, to their own detriment, was that voters didn't want to see blood spilled. That was good for Biden. His shaky performance was not.

CHAPTER 5

•

"You Forgot Biden"

Barack Obama had an open mind about the 2020 Democratic nomination fight—for the most part. He didn't want Bernie Sanders to win, and he didn't think Joe Biden would be a good candidate. He suspected most of the hopefuls would flame out long before Iowans met at caucus sites in February 2020. In other words, he was just like most ordinary Democratic primary voters.

Unlike the rest, though, the forty-fourth president of the United States fielded countless requests to meet one-on-one with candidates who planned to run. They came to his downtown office in the West End of Washington, D.C., to show deference to the putative leader of their party—often in the ritual act of seeking his counsel—and in hopes of perhaps winning his favor down the line. Obama would have preferred to be playing golf, or at least watching hoops on television.

When Pete Buttigieg came to visit in March 2019, he found the former leader of the free world relaxed, with an open collar, watching the NCAA men's basketball tournament on his office flat-screen. Buttigieg wasn't much of a basketball fan—he had come only to kiss the ring—but Obama kept the game on. "Mayor Pete" was generating some buzz among media types and Democratic donors. Obama didn't think much of his chances. The two men had met once before, in the fall of 2017, to talk about the future of the party after Buttigieg had run for, and dropped out of, a race for Democratic National Committee chairman. At that time, few voters could have picked the hyper-kempt Buttigieg out of a lineup of business consultants.

"Axe"—longtime Obama adviser David Axelrod—liked the thirty-seven-year-old kid, whom he'd seen speak at Harvard in 2015. One of Axe's protégés, communications strategist and former Obama campaign aide Lis Smith, was in the process of turning Buttigieg from an anonymous small-city mayor into the darling of the salon set of Democratic insiders. At the same time, Smith introduced him to voters by cajoling and bullying the media with Lyndon Johnson–like flair—and the four-letter vernacular to match—into giving Buttigieg airtime and digital ink.

The rising profile and the connections to Obama's political family were enough to gain Buttigieg an audience with the former president. They weren't enough to bridge the many experience gaps between the two men.

Buttigieg didn't show up with a polished apple, but it was obvious to Obama that he was overly awed. A Harvard graduate, Buttigieg had taken leave from his job at the consulting firm McKinsey and Company to volunteer in Iowa for Obama's first campaign in 2008. He planned to model his campaign after Obama's, placing a huge bet on overperforming in Iowa. Buttigieg's rhetoric echoed Obama's and even his speech patterns sounded like they had been practiced into a mirror in which Buttigieg saw Obama's reflection looking back at him.

Nervously, Buttigieg worked himself up to ask Obama for advice about identity on the campaign trail. Obama was the only Black president, and Buttigieg would be the first openly gay candidate. To Pete, that made his sexual orientation similar to Obama's race.

Obviously, Obama's race was one of the most compelling aspects of his candidacy and one of the most important things about his emergence, Pete thought, but he couldn't let it endanger the whole project. And Obama had figured out a way to kind of live in it without ever showing any flicker of resentment around it. *That takes unbelievable discipline,* Pete surmised, *which is a really good template for someone like me.*

"How," he asked Obama, "did you maintain your discipline?"

Obama didn't have to think long about what it was like to be openly Black. And it was not hard for him to see that Buttigieg might run into problems appealing to Black voters if he drew such a direct parallel between his orientation and race. The media might like him. Donors might write checks. Heck, Iowa might even hand him the caucuses. But good luck working Black churches with that in South Carolina, Pete.

Before he left, Buttigieg asked Obama for a favor.

"Would you be willing to put Chasten in touch with Mrs. Obama?" Buttigieg asked, explaining that his husband might benefit from the guidance of Michelle Obama, whom he regarded as an unusually visible and capable spouse on the campaign trail. Obama readily agreed to the ask, which fell so far below a request for an endorsement in the hierarchy of political favors that it was impossible to reject.

As Buttigieg walked out of Obama's office that day, he was being heralded by the news media as the hottest candidate in the race. His first big national television breakout had come earlier in the month during a round of CNN town hall interviews with Democratic hopefuls in conjunction with the South by Southwest festival in Austin, Texas. Preternaturally cautious by nature, Buttigieg believed that he would have to take some calculated risks to distinguish himself quickly in a jam-packed field of better-known candidates. Onstage, CNN's Jake Tapper teed him up perfectly by asking whether Vice President Mike Pence, the former governor of Buttigieg's home state, would make for a better or worse president than Trump. It was an obvious line of inquiry given that Buttigieg had worked with Pence. The Trump-Pence line he'd worked on with his advisers was that he had more military experience than the president and more executive experience than the vice president. But Buttigieg had been playing around with an alternative, and he bought a few seconds to make a choice. Then he rolled the dice.

Pence has a different view of the Bible than I do—one that places priority on sexuality and rectitude over protecting the meek, he said. Even still, Buttigieg asked, "How would he allow himself to become the cheerleader of the porn star presidency? Is it that he stopped believing in Scripture when he started believing in Donald Trump?"

Nailed it, Pete thought as he felt the audience come alive. Backstage, a CNN producer keeping track of viewership and online engagement numbers had already noticed a massive spike from the previous two hours, when Representatives Tulsi Gabbard and John Delany had been onstage. Mike Schmuhl, Buttigieg's campaign manager, looked at a graph on the producer's iPad showing a flat line and then what looked like the sketch of a fast-rising mountain. Pete walked offstage and gave Schmuhl a fist bump. In a matter of minutes, his phone started buzzing. It didn't stop. He couldn't keep up with all the congratulatory text messages coming in. One of them was a 312 number from Chicago that he didn't recognize. He looked a little closer.

Holy shit, he thought. *It's Oprah.*

Buttigieg's ascendance reflected an emerging dynamic. In the first election since Trump's victory, the first choice of a thin majority of Democratic voters was a straight white man—Biden or Sanders. But there was enough hunger for an alternative—someone with a fresher feel than the septuagenarians—to create an arena-like competition for dollars, airtime, and votes among a handful of hopefuls from the largest and most diverse field ever assembled. It appeared to these candidates—Buttigieg, Harris, Warren, and a couple of others—that a plausible path to the nomination involved either winning a plurality of delegates to the convention or converting voters from the camps of one or both of the front-runners.

This led to quite a bit of speculation about the possibility of a long, drawn-out primary battle and a brokered convention in which a nominee was chosen through horse-trading or after multiple ballots. Biden and Sanders were ideological polar opposites within the primary lineup and the larger party. But polls also showed that even with most Democrats still uncertain about whom they would ultimately choose, Sanders was the second choice of most Biden voters and Biden was the second choice of most Sanders voters. On some level, that spoke to the instant name recognition for the two top contenders. Harris and Warren were household names to twenty-four-hour cable news junkies, but most voters couldn't name their own senators—much less lawmakers from other states.

Buttigieg burst onto the political scene and then began to build out his Iowa-focused operation. Harris laid her bet on the big debate moment. Warren, who was mocked by other campaigns' operatives for a series of unorthodox early strategic and tactical decisions, spent the spring and early summer of 2019 laying the groundwork for a sustained campaign against the front-runners. Spurned by heavy-hitting donors afraid of her desire to tax the wealthy, she swore off high-dollar fundraising events. She spent down her war chest fast, hiring staff in the early states, and at her Boston headquarters in an old book-binding plant in the hard-scrabble Charlestown section of the city. And while her rivals spit on Trump, she spit out a ream of policy proposals designed to give her ownership of the seldom-sought mantle of substance queen— all while posing for an endless series of pinkie-promise "selfies" that allowed her to show she was a woman without talking about it.

While Harris had taken off like a rocket in the two weeks after the first set of debates, Warren simply continued a long steady ascent. On July 12, Warren, Harris, and Sanders sat tied at 15 percent in the Real Clear Politics average of national polls, trailing Biden by 12 points. Warren was gaining ground fast in Iowa, too, where she was less than 3 points behind Sanders for second. No one was more alarmed by the turn of events than Sanders. He left the campaign trail and told just a few of his most trusted advisers to drop everything and get their asses to Burlington pronto for what one of them described as "super-secret" meetings.

Just off a leafy section of Van Patten Parkway in Vermont's Queen City, inside the four-bedroom, two-and-a-half bathroom house he and Jane had lived in for the past fifteen years, Sanders looked around the living room at his war council—campaign manager Faiz Shakir, deputy campaign manager Ari Rabin-Havt, Ben Cohen of Ben & Jerry's ice cream fame, and senior advisers Weaver and Rocha. He was losing, not just to Biden and the establishment, but, unexpectedly, to a pair of bridge-the-gap senators who combined for twice as much support as he had. These men had been assembled to assess the damage and plot a comeback.

The polls don't look good, Sanders said.

This, the advisers knew. It was why they had been dragged to Vermont on a gorgeous summer weekend.

What are we going to do to change that? he asked.

It's hard to tell the candidate—the person without whom the campaign wouldn't exist—that his habits are part of the problem. But Sanders refused to commit to schedules more than a week or two at a time, which made it difficult for his team to roll out new policies with the kind of strategic precision that drove news cycles and brought positive attention to the candidate. Warren had mastered that art. Sanders was also loath to spend money on anything, including staff, but his advisers wanted better management of his communications effort and more boots on the ground in the early states.

Shakir needed to be able to execute the campaign without the candidate questioning every decision. Sanders's insistence on making decisions himself—and his reluctance to make them—were giving an advantage to the other candidates, his advisers believed. They were all frustrated by the bottleneck, which would have been familiar to Biden's aides.

"Things are only going to get more chaotic as the campaign heats up," Shakir told Sanders. "How is it best to streamline these decisions?"

Sanders never liked the idea of hiring more staff. Ironically for someone so often accused of being an out-and-out communist, he reflexively disliked big bureaucracies. *They're morasses that produce bad outcomes,* he thought.

Weaver and Rocha, who were basically in charge of advertising, knew that the same issues would be problematic once it came time to buy airtime. They had Shakir's back on this.

Faced with a united front of his advisers, Sanders pushed for more justification and clarification of his team's plans. But over the weekend at Bernie's, as they noshed bagels and lox, he accepted the frame that he really only needed to make a series of minor adjustments that would have outsized effects on his ability to compete effectively. He would have to let go of some of his control—and some of Jane Sanders's control—to get the result he wanted.

Jane Sanders, who could be a source of tension within Bernieworld, agreed with his advisers. He trusted no one more than his wife, and he listened to no one more than his wife. Ultimately, he was in charge of campaign decisions, but her influence was hard to overstate. During his early campaigns for office, she had often been what amounted to an all-purpose aide. She'd been through the fires with him, and he had been surprisingly successful with her at his side. The professionals regarded her as a dilettante, but she was now working on her second presidential campaign. And she'd been there for a string of wins for municipal and federal offices dating back to the 1980s.

Sanders was worried enough about his position in the polls to bring his team to Vermont. But with more than six months left to go before the Iowa caucuses, he wasn't focused solely on the mechanics of his operation. It was important to him to use some of the time to build stronger bonds at the top of the operation. In their early fifties, Weaver and Rocha were relative graybeards in campaign circles, with their own political networks inside and outside Sanders's movement. Shakir, who barely looked old enough to shave at thirty-nine, hadn't come in with those ties or a strong relationship with the candidate. It was important to Sanders that they all use some of their time together to get better acquainted with one another. For all the Republican talk of Sanders's affinity for socialism—and ultimately the not-so-subtle charge that he was somehow un-American—he sure seemed to revel in iconic national traditions like playing baseball, flipping burgers in the afternoon sun, and enjoying ice cream with his friends on a warm summer day.

During one break in the planning sessions, the seventy-seven-year-old hopeful grabbed a classic "Big Ox" wooden softball bat and stood in front of a backyard backstop installed for his grandkids. Shakir, the former Harvard second baseman, stood fifty feet away and lobbed a baseball toward home plate. An orange-billed ball cap on his head, the right-handed-hitting Sanders leaned his weight back on his long, skinny right leg and then sprung forward with a compact swing. He sent the ball in the air toward shallow right center field, where a fully outstretched Rocha snagged it and tumbled to the turf.

"Highlight of the week!" Sanders called out like the color commentator on a sportscast. Given where he stood in the race at that moment, it probably was.

Until the second pair of Democratic debates at the Fox Theatre in Detroit at the tail end of July, Warren enjoyed a ride fairly free of friction. Trump occasionally taunted her with the nickname Pocahontas, and rival campaigns anonymously sniped at the "I have a plan" slogan she had developed to highlight her substance. They, too, were putting out policy ideas—if not at the rate or the depth Warren was. Most other politicians regarded Warren the way they would anyone who liked to brag about being a better student. They thought she was extremely bright, but not to the exclusion of everyone else. This made her less street-smart in the political world than she was book-smart outside of it.

"There were a lot of hard eye rolls on our campaign every time the Warren campaign released another policy," said a top aide to Amy Klobuchar, a Minnesota centrist who put long hours in reading briefing books and was having trouble getting the same kind of attention Warren did. "Everyone's doing the same thing on this campaign, and somehow she's the only one with substance?"

Warren's dynamic with Sanders was different, more textured. Even if their constituencies didn't overlap much yet, either one would eventually need part of the other's base to win the nomination. She already had come a long way in rising to meet him in national polling as his numbers flagged. In the world of progressive elites, they shared allies who would be pleased if either one of them advanced. There were any number of reasons for them to be cordial to each other, but, most of all, it was strategically imperative not to alienate each other's voters. Despite their proximity in the polls, neither their friendship nor their quiet alliance had been seriously tested. Their aides were quoted in stories leading up to the debate saying that they wouldn't go after each other. But that didn't mean they weren't trying to win.

Warren had a plan for that.

Before the debate, longtime adviser Dan Geldon gave Warren advice on how to approach Sanders. Now in his late thirties, with thinning black hair and the unweathered face of a quiz bowl contestant, Geldon had worked for Warren dating back to her days setting up the Consumer Financial Protection Bureau for Obama. He spoke in a soft, hushed tone but reflected and incited Warren's pugnacious approach to reforming the nation's economic and political systems. Jaws had dropped in Washington when she had parted ways with A-level consultants Mandy Grunwald and Mindy Myers at the start of her campaign and given Geldon more power as a strategist. But she trusted him, and that decision appeared to be paying off.

The rest of the debaters, all of whom were to her political right and none of whom she considered to be serious contenders, didn't seem to require as much thought as Sanders. The way to make yourself look good and Sanders look bad is to do a better job of making the case for a progressive worldview, Geldon counseled. He's got a handful of shopworn talking points, you've got, well, you. Show voters that you are the better messenger, he said.

In her first debate, Warren had pushed out what she wanted to get across to voters early and then sat back and watched much of the rest of the show. She had benefited from Biden, Sanders, Harris, and Buttigieg—all of her main rivals—sharing the stage the night after her debate. In that way, she had coasted to victory over them, and her absence from their debate spared Biden the possibility of a pile-on. She had said almost nothing in that first debate. This time, though, she would have a real contender in the mix with her. Bernie likes to dominate the airtime, Geldon said. You can't outshine him if there's a total eclipse.

Warren took the admonition to heart. When Sanders spoke, she interjected. If he tried to make a point, she said it better. She wasn't just trying to outperform him, she was trying to get under his skin. But Sanders wouldn't give her the satisfaction of losing his cool.

What she didn't fully appreciate, while she focused on Sanders, was the damage she sustained from lesser-known centrists. Former representative John Delaney of Maryland and Representative Tim Ryan of Ohio made for an effective centrist goon squad. Delaney was pissing away a significant chunk of his personal fortune on a vanity bid that had netted him a few more than zero supporters, and Ryan, a former college quarterback who once ran an ill-advised campaign against Nancy Pelosi to head the Democratic Caucus in the House, was a much younger version of Biden with an affable manner and a working-class constituency in Youngstown. Ryan liked to throw footballs out to supporters at campaign events, which would have been an expensive habit had he proved more popular.

In his opening statement, Delaney accused Warren and Sanders of running on "bad policies like Medicare for All" and "impossible promises."

Later, during an exchange with Delaney, Warren hit back. "I don't understand why anybody goes to all the trouble of running for president of the United States just to talk about what we really can't do and shouldn't fight for," she said.

In the moment, Delaney was knocked back. Warren had re-pelled his attack with force—but not before he could deliver a small cut. Delaney represented a business-friendly view that the Sanders Medicare for All plan, which Warren was now set on defending bet-ter than its author, would dismantle an entire insurance industry that was vital to the economy. Ryan jumped in, too, taking up for union workers who worried that they would end up with higher taxes and less coverage than they got under plans negotiated by their leaders.

Neither Sanders nor Warren, both of whom would need sup-port from labor, had an answer for that, but both were more pol-ished debaters than Ryan and Delaney. Sanders showed off his agility when Ryan said Sanders didn't know whether union workers would end up with better coverage under his plan.

"I do know it," Sanders said. "I wrote the damn bill!"

Few seemed to notice at the time the extent to which the also-rans had exposed a major vulnerability without fully exploiting it. Sanders did, but Warren didn't. She had drawn attention to herself as an advocate of Sanders's signature proposal. That's just where Biden wanted her.

Since rocketing up past 40 percent right after his launch, Biden had floated down toward the pack in the late spring and early sum-mer. "There was no buzzworthiness around him," one donor close to the campaign said. "No one was paying attention." His first de-bate performance had been just plain bad. In addition to crumpling when Harris hit him, he had dodged yes-or-no questions. He was the only one of twenty candidates who saw his favorability rating drop more than a percentage point after the June set of debates. The more voters saw of him, the less they saw him as the guy to take on Trump. That was all he was running on, it was what most of the voters cared about exclusively, and he was still losing sup-port. But every voter could identify him, and he retained broad approval among them. His favorability drop, according to FiveThir-tyEight and Morning Consult, was from 76.5 percent to 74.4 per-cent. Most of the other candidates weren't even recognizable to that much of the electorate. Only Sanders, at 75.4 percent, had a higher favorability rating after the first round of debates.

In early August, Warren, Harris, and other candidates pulled off the early-state campaign trail to woo party elites on Martha's

Vineyard, the East Coast summer retreat of rich and powerful liberals. The ninety-six-square-mile island south of Cape Cod is
smaller than Queens County, New York, and far less densely populated. For one month every four years, it is the hottest Democratic
political turf in the world, and it's where Obama spent his summer
vacation playing golf with NBA MVP Stephen Curry, former Boston Celtics star Ray Allen, and a handful of close friends from the
worlds of finance and politics. One pal who spoke to him said the
former president didn't see a winner in the field yet.

"He's disappointed," the friend said, explaining that Obama
didn't yet see anyone who was ready to take control of the primary
and beat Trump. "A lot of his question is, who has excitement
around them? The answer to that is Elizabeth Warren. But he's always been mixed on her, at best."

From a distance, Warren was on fire. She was widely hailed by
the media as the big winner of the debate, her second such victory
in a row. Her operation was ramping up around the country, mir-
roring the increasing attention the media and Democratic insiders
were paying her as a candidate on the move. Now, her decision to
dump cash into hiring a bunch of staff in the first four states—and
even in some other key locations on the map—looked prescient
rather than foolish. Money poured into her campaign coffers as
fast as her finance team in Charlestown could count it. She would
soon report having raised a little more than $19 million in the sec-
ond quarter—less than Sanders and Buttigieg, who both came
close to $25 million, and Biden, who brought in $21.5 million, but
about triple her first-quarter haul.

She was the only candidate riding a long rise, and she saw the
second debate as an inflection point claiming new turf. In her mind,
she had distinguished herself as the giant on the progressive side of
the field. Ironically, the woman with the plans was unconcerned
about the thorny details of Medicare for All. Voters, she believed,
wouldn't care too much about them, and no one who had worked
on legislation thought Sanders's bill would actually make it into
law as it had been introduced. Of course it would be changed.

Elections are about values, she thought, *and my support for this
is more about showing where my values are than it is about whether
Bernie's plan can pass Congress in its current form.*

For her, the debates, like town hall meetings and other national events, were opportunities to seize a news cycle and show progressive Democrats she stood with them. But some of Warren's supporters thought she was sending exactly the wrong signals. They worried that stapling herself to a plan without a funding mechanism—and one that bore Bernie Sanders's fingerprints—would alienate a lot of the electorate and create a permanent stain for her within the establishment.

She and Geldon, her alter ego, ignored the concern. Polls suggested she was making all the right moves. Between mid-June and early October, she went from a little bit over 7 percent in the national survey averages to more than 26 percent. She rose well past Sanders, sucking up Harris's dwindling support.

The sugar high of Biden's launch had worn off in May, and shaky performances in the first couple of debates drained him. But he and his team recognized the same target of opportunity in Warren that Ryan and Delaney had failed to truly exploit. By jumping in front of Sanders during the Detroit debate, Warren had, at least for the moment, made herself the most ardent defender of his plan.

Biden still wasn't sharp on the stage when he, Warren, and Sanders first debated one another directly on a sweltering night in Houston on September 12, 2019. But he hit his mark on one topic.

"How are you going to pay for it?" he asked Warren about Medicare for All. "I want to hear that tonight. My distinguished friend, the senator on my left, has not indicated how she pays for it." Warren refused to say whether middle-class taxes would be raised to cover the costs. Sanders, who already had acknowledged taxes would go up as premiums evaporated, chose to attack Biden's plan as too skimpy. In August, with union leaders bearing down on Medicare for All, Sanders had announced a tweak to his proposal requiring companies to apply savings reaped from a single-payer government insurance system to wages and benefits for workers. Now, Warren was the only candidate who supported his original bill without the fix for unions, and, despite her proclamation that she had a plan for everything, she wouldn't or couldn't say how the figures added up on the issue that was dominating debates.

One irony of all the infighting was that none of their plans—from Medicare for All to Biden's Obamacare-plus proposal—stood any chance of becoming law without Democrats winning the presidency and control of the Senate and then eliminating that chamber's filibuster. Not only was that a pretty tall order, but senators from small states, like Biden and Sanders, had historically been the most reliant on Senate rules allowing a minority to block legislation. They all knew that the practical challenges to any of the plans were enormous, and they attacked one another with abandon.

Now, it was Warren's turn in the barrel. She hadn't thought the issue would matter at all, and suddenly it was consuming her campaign. Buttigieg went on television and called her "evasive." The most dangerous narrative for any candidate, and particularly for a woman, was starting to take hold—that she was deceptive. And yet her numbers were rising, not dropping.

Warren had some unorthodox theories about what could drive her to the presidency. She was a natural risk-taker and she took comfort from the fact that the political world had laughed at some of her early strategic decisions only to be proven wrong by her robust fundraising and rise in the polls. Most of her tactics seemed to be paying off, even when—especially when—the smart set in Washington said they were dumb. And she believed her campaign should show voters what her presidency would be like, which meant pushing hard for significant change.

The country is on fire, and Washington is ossified, she thought. *I have to have a high tolerance for risk because new ways of doing things are the only means to take urgent action.*

So far, her risks had been nearly perfectly calculated. In early August, she pushed past Sanders and a fast-falling Harris into second place in Iowa. In late September, she overtook Biden for the lead. She had deployed an army of organizers in the state who used a model of voter contact that emphasized building personal relationships over long periods of time through phone calls and text messages. Other campaigns' operatives uniformly described her operation as a juggernaut.

But Warren was concerned about Sanders. His aides and his supporters were becoming nastier toward her and her team. It wasn't just online harassment, either. She didn't like that his backers heckled her organizers at county fairs and on college campuses. It wasn't polite. Now she was in a position of strength, but she worried that it would be difficult to put together a coalition later if the toxicity continued.

She called him to hash it out.

"Your people have been going after me very aggressively," she said. "I'm worried how this is going to play out."

"No, it's your people who are attacking me," Sanders replied gruffly.

Shakir awoke to the sound of his cellphone ringing. A little disoriented, he could tell it was late at night, and he wondered briefly why anyone would be calling him at that time. He groped for his phone and looked down at the screen, his stomach tightening in an instant as his brain registered the name Ari Rabin-Havt.

"I think he's sick," said Rabin-Havt, the top aide traveling with Bernie Sanders in Nevada. "We're going to take him to the hospital."

"Okay," said Shakir, who was the calmest presence at the center of the Sanders whirlwind. "Please keep me updated." He booked the first available morning flight from Washington to Las Vegas and spent much of the rest of the night on the phone with Rabin-Havt, Jane Sanders, and Jeff Weaver. Then, with the sun not yet risen over his townhouse on Capitol Hill on October 2, he set out on the ten-minute ride to Reagan National Airport to find out whether his boss and the campaign were going to survive.

Sanders had suffered a heart attack while talking to supporters at a restaurant in Las Vegas.

"Ari, can you do me a favor?" Sanders had asked. "Where's Ari? Get me a chair up here for a moment."

Always hyper-attuned to changes in Sanders's mood and behavior, Rabin-Havt thought it was highly unusual for the peripatetic senator to want to sit. There was something really wrong with Bernie. Sanders was having chest pains. He'd been feeling them for a while, and they were now more intense.

His aides debated the pros and cons of whether to seek medical attention—and, if so, where to go. He might receive better care at a major hospital, but it might take longer to get there and the risk of being seen would go up. At his age, a hospital trip—no matter the diagnosis—could be devastating politically. Rabin-Havt insisted on getting him to a doctor. He went with Sanders to the urgent care clinic next to the MGM Grand hotel about five miles away, and he called Shakir.

"Ari saved his life," said one colleague. "He may not make eye contact, but he's hyper-perceptive and he knows Bernie, and it was Ari that was like 'We've got to do this.'"

When Rocha got a call from Weaver at five-thirty that morning, he was in the locker room at his gym. He assumed Weaver, who typically didn't dial in to the campaign until nine or ten A.M., had punched somebody and needed bail money.

"Bernie's had a health scare," Weaver said. "They've taken him to the hospital."

Rocha felt a lump form in the back of his throat. He sat down on a wooden bench to keep his bearings.

"They think it's his heart," Weaver said. "It's not good. I don't know how bad it is."

Rocha wanted more information, but Weaver didn't have anything to give.

"Let's be real, here," Weaver said. "It's just a matter of time before the press realizes that our guy is down and that he's at the hospital."

Weaver didn't have to read out the potential political ramifications of a heart attack. Even if Sanders wasn't going to die, it was hard to see how he could keep running a presidential campaign. Rocha, who would be the top-ranking aide at the campaign's headquarters in Washington, asked Weaver what he wanted done.

"Put everything on hold," Weaver said. "Get to the office and shelter in place. Don't spend any more money. Just hold what we've got."

The adults on Sanders's campaign weren't certain that it was over. But they weren't sure it would continue, either. They had just determined to close it down for the moment. Rocha thought it was more likely than not that Sanders's four-year-plus quest for the presidency was going to go bust in Las Vegas.

Rocha headed for the D.C. office and set up a war room on the sixth floor. With bleary eyes and coffee cups in hand, senior aides began to filter in that morning. The press team began fielding calls from reporters almost immediately—*Is he alive? Will the campaign go on? What's happening?* It was going to leak out. The campaign would eventually put out a statement in which Weaver described Sanders's condition as "chest discomfort," which only led to more questions—and distrust—from reporters hungry to find out whether Sanders had suffered a heart attack.

Rocha spoke by phone with Rabin-Havt, who was in a room at Desert Springs Hospital Medical Center, where Sanders had been moved during the night. When doctors forced Sanders to give up his wedding ring, Rabin-Havt had put it on his own finger for safekeeping.

"He's alert," Rabin-Havt said. "He can do things." There had been a blockage in one of Sanders's arteries, and surgeons had put in two stents to circumvent them. But there wasn't a full prognosis to read out yet.

We're fixing to have three hundred young staffers show up upstairs at the office and somebody's going to report their guy just had a heart attack, Rocha thought. *We've got to pull these people together and let them know he's OK.* Rocha didn't know if he could hold his shit together. He didn't know if Bernie was kinda OK or really OK. He didn't know if the campaign was going to go on. But it was on him to lead at headquarters. There was no one else to do it.

"He's not dead," Rocha told the staff when they assembled in a conference room. "You're going to see reports, but we're going to find out what it is. It's going to be fine. Let's all just support each other."

His voice cracked toward the end. He was going to lose it, right there, in front of the whole staff. He got up from his seat at the conference table and walked out through the doorway. *They're going to think you're not telling the truth if you just walk out,* he thought. Rocha turned on his heel. He stood in the doorway and shook hands or hugged each aide as a procession left the meeting. Some members of the staff started sending résumés to friends to see if they could find work on other campaigns.

Shakir headed to the hospital once he landed in Vegas. *I don't even know what I'm going to be walking into,* he thought on the drive. *The first thing to keep in mind is the senator's health, then everything else. This is a human event, not a political event.*

The truth was Shakir wasn't all that close to Sanders personally—not like Weaver or Rocha or Rabin-Havt. Just a couple of months ago, it had taken the force of the former two to help him coax Sanders into making adjustments to the campaign during the weekend retreat. They were getting to know each other better and becoming more comfortable with each other, but they didn't know each other on an intimate level. That was about to change.

When Shakir walked into the hospital room, Sanders was resting.

"Faiz!" Sanders exclaimed. He propped himself up in bed, grabbed his glasses from a side table, and affixed them to his face. "Let's talk about the campaign."

Shakir was a little taken aback. Of all the scenarios that had played out in his mind during the flight and the drive to the hospital, this was not one of them. He had expected to find out more about his boss's physical health, and maybe—maybe—get a sense of how Sanders was thinking about whether to continue campaigning or not. Even for Sanders, this felt oddly direct.

"Are you sure you want to talk about the campaign?" Shakir asked. "How are you doing?"

For fuck's sake, Bernie thought, *don't ask me how I'm doing.* It was written all over his face. "I'm great," Sanders said. It had been only half a day and already he was tired of that question. Now he was alone with the one person who should be focused entirely on the political equation. "Let's talk about the campaign," he repeated.

He's showing me that he has no intention of pulling out, Shakir thought. *He's demonstrating his conviction to me so that we never have to discuss that alternative. He's saying, "We are going forward."*

Shakir still hadn't gotten a full report on Sanders's medical status.

"All right," he said, "if you want to talk about the campaign, I'm here for you."

Shakir recommended that the campaign pull back its advertising temporarily. He framed it as a strategic retreat rather than a holding pattern. "When you're able to walk out of here, we put it back on the air," he said. "Nothing could send a more powerful message than walking out of the hospital and being strong on the air in Iowa and sending messages that we're guns blazing."

Sanders liked the cadence. Pull back and then explode onto the scene again. Reclined partway in the hospital bed, he gave his assent.

Not even the shadow of the Grim Reaper could stop Sanders from pursuing the presidency. If he died on the campaign trail, so be it.

By the time the Democratic candidates met for the fourth time on a stage at Otterbein College in Westerville, Ohio, on October 15, their numbers had been culled to a dozen qualifiers debating on a single night. Collectively, they were a battered crew—among the real contenders, none more so than Biden.

The national front-runner had bumbled through his first three debate performances, and his numbers nationally and in Iowa trended downward in the kind of steady descent that signaled voters had gradually lost interest, confidence, or both. Donors sent that message, too. In early October, Biden's campaign reported raising $15 million from July through September, a precipitous drop from the more than $21 million he had collected in the shorter window of his April 25 launch through the end of June. The numbers were supposed to be going in the other direction. His campaign's "burn rate"—the percentage of its funds that it already had spent—was hovering around the 75 percent mark. Sanders, who had raised about twice as much money as Biden since the start of the campaign, was closer to 55 percent. At this point, advertising and hiring staff could break Biden's campaign. He was down to $9 million in the bank more than three months out from the Iowa caucuses. His bet on centrism—and on big-dollar fundraising events—looked particularly ill-advised when juxtaposed against the energy progressive grassroots voters and donors had for Sanders and Warren.

Biden couldn't really afford his own polling, but there was at least one silver-lining data point that consistently showed up in other surveys. Between Becca Siegel, Biden's chief analytics officer, pollsters John Anzalone and Celinda Lake, and manager Greg Schultz, the campaign's view of the electorate had begun to evolve over the summer. Voters weren't bound by ideological tests. If Sanders dropped out, a good chunk of his support would go to Biden rather than Warren. If Warren dropped out, her base would split between Biden and Sanders. If Biden dropped out, his base would fragment, with much of the white working-class piece of it going to Sanders. Buttigieg's voters could break in unexpected ways, too.

These revelations were important because they provided a plausible explanation for how Biden could come back—eventually, maybe, possibly.

Schultz started incorporating it into his political meetings with party elites and donors. Those check-ins intensified once CNBC reported, the day before the debate, that Michael Bloomberg, the billionaire former New York mayor, was looking to run if Biden faltered. Bloomberg had publicly considered and decided against a bid earlier in the year. Now, he saw Biden as weak enough to topple. Putatively, Bloomberg's newfound interest was a response to Warren moving up. He hated her anti–Wall Street rhetoric and the regulations she would implement if she won power. But he had always longed to run for president. Biden's slide, he believed, gave him an opening. There were a lot of influential Democrats who were uncertain of what to do if Bloomberg moved forward.

Hold on, Schultz would tell them, things aren't as bad as they look. "Iowa is as white a state as you can get, and New Hampshire isn't too far behind," one top Biden ally said, echoing Schultz's approach behind closed doors. "Joe Biden has historically done well in states that are racially diverse and look more like America." It was true that Biden had won in a racially diverse state in the past: over and over again in Senate races in Delaware. The less-tested proposition was that he could win anywhere else. He had never actually won a caucus or primary in any state, regardless of the racial makeup. What Schultz was saying and what he was doing were out of sync: If things weren't that bad, the campaign manager to the former vice president would not be traveling the country several months before the Iowa caucuses to reassure party powerbrokers that there was a path to victory.

While Schultz tried to reassure top Democrats outside the campaign, the upper echelon of Biden's brain trust began to discuss whether, when, and how to get rid of him. The brutal fundraising quarter acted as a catalyst, as did the perception that Schultz hadn't allocated the right amount of money to the Iowa operation. There were differences of opinion within the group about whether the campaign should be putting more or less into Iowa. Valerie Biden Owens, Ricchetti, Donilon, Klain, and Dunn were in on these discussions, according to a person familiar with them.

"A lot of people in leadership did not think Greg had what it takes to run a presidential campaign," this person said. "They did not think the vice president was served very well."

Of course, the main driver of campaign donations was candidate performance. That was something Schultz couldn't entirely control. It might have been true that the Iowa operation was a mess—or even that Schultz's skills weren't suited to running a presidential campaign—but the money crunch wasn't his fault.

Over time, the idea of moving Schultz out percolated up to Biden, who listened to the criticism but wasn't yet inclined to make such a public move. Firing or demoting his campaign manager would be read as a sign of panic when he needed to calm nervous allies. Besides, he didn't have a replacement at hand. For better or worse, Biden didn't like to be pressured into major decisions, and he didn't like to move until he could see a clear route to a destination. It didn't make sense to him to act for the purpose of taking action.

Biden wasn't alone in leaving doubt with Democrats. Sanders was coming off a heart attack. Harris had seen her peak in July. Only Warren was on an upward trajectory nationally, and she was getting hit relentlessly by her opponents and in the media for dodging questions about Medicare for All.

All of this created an opportunity for Minnesota senator Amy Klobuchar.

She had launched her campaign outdoors in February in Minneapolis, which is idiotic—unless it happens to snow. Klobuchar had delivered her speech that bone-cold day with soft white pellets cascading onto her hair and shoulders. She'd looked tough enough to survive a winter on the plains. But since then, she'd disappeared like an overnight frost. She had barely qualified for the October debate, and she was running low on funds. Without a breakout moment, she would be eliminated from the next debate, and that would be the end of her campaign.

She was going to have to hit somebody hard enough to make her cash register ring. There were only a few options for a worthwhile target. She would never go after Biden. Klobuchar believed he was the best candidate to become president—perhaps aside from herself—and people who knew both of them told her she might make for a sensible vice presidential pick if he won the nomination. She wasn't going to blow that chance just to keep her campaign alive. She couldn't go after Sanders, either. The guy had walked out of a hospital ten days earlier. There would be no sympathy for the devil who attacked him. Besides, she and Sanders were friendly in the Senate—so far at odds within their own party on many topics that it was easy to get along personally.

Warren made for an ideal quarry. On October 8, Warren overtook Biden in the average of national polls by tenths of a percentage point, marking the first time he'd fallen to second place. He would recover within twenty-four hours, but Warren was on the march. That meant the media and voters would notice if Klobuchar knocked her back. And Klobuchar didn't like Warren—not even a little bit.

"They were true rivals," explained one Klobuchar aide. "They both rubbed each other the wrong way often." It wasn't ever clear that Warren had given Klobuchar much thought, which is probably what rubbed Klobuchar the wrong way. What Klobuchar said on the debate stage that night was more than a rough rub.

"At least Bernie is being honest here and saying how he's going to pay for this and that taxes are going to go up," Klobuchar said with as much "Minnesota nice" as she could muster. "I'm sorry, Elizabeth, but you have not said that. And I think we owe the American people, to tell them where we will send the invoice."

It was the pleasant way of calling Warren dishonest while praising Sanders—a line that could appeal to the centrists Klobuchar was after, including white working-class men, and further divide progressives.

For almost four months, Warren held hard to her position defending Medicare for All and declining to specify whether she would have to raise taxes on the middle and lower classes to pay for it. All along, she stuck with two assumptions. The first was believing criticism was evidence she was on the right path politically. The second was believing that the issue would disappear as the next election-year controversy surfaced. One reason she didn't abandon those assumptions is that the incoming fire didn't arrest her rise until mid-October.

———

Four days after the debate, twenty-five thousand of Sanders's friends came out to greet him at Queensbridge Park in New York for his first rally since the heart attack. One of those friends mattered a little more than the rest as Sanders hoped to announce his resurgence with authority on a patch of home turf. Standing against the backdrop of housing projects and the smokestacks of the Ravenswood power plant, Representative Alexandria Ocasio-Cortez endorsed Sanders and embraced him like a favorite member of her family.

"He's my *tío*," she told the crowd, using the Spanish word for uncle.

But just a few weeks earlier—before the heart attack—it wasn't at all clear that he could win the support of the twenty-nine-year-old superstar of the progressive movement.

She had been an organizer for his 2016 campaign, but he had not backed her primary victory over veteran Representative Joe Crowley, a moderate member of the House Democratic leadership, in 2018. Since then, Ocasio-Cortez had become the most recognizable young face in the progressive world, gracing magazine covers, taking up space rent-free in Donald Trump's mind-to-Twitter stream of consciousness, and occupying Republican ad makers who sought to tie all Democrats to her brand of "Democratic socialism."

Ideologically, the pair were a natural fit. But Ocasio-Cortez was interested in expanding her political turf beyond the boundaries of the hard left. Warren had been courting her heavily for months, through text messages and phone calls, and Warren was the candidate on the rise. For Sanders, who was relying on support from Latinos and who appealed far more to men than women, an endorsement from the young Latina progressive—who had, to some degree, transcended from the political realm to a plane of cultural significance—would be meaningful.

The last weekend in September, AOC agreed to visit Sanders in Burlington.

Over dinner at the Sanders house and breakfast the next morning at the city's popular Penny Cluse Cafe—Sanders couldn't resist the blueberry pancakes—they talked about common policy interests. Her endorsement, the reason she had been beckoned to Vermont, didn't come up. This was Sanders's version of wooing a fellow politician. But as Shakir drove her to the airport, Ocasio-Cortez made clear what was holding her back.

AOC explained that she still liked and respected the same things about Sanders that had led her to support him in 2016, when she wasn't even a candidate for office. But I still don't see your path to victory, she told Shakir. How are you going to win? What do you see as the challenges and what are your plans for overcoming them? she asked.

It was obvious that she didn't want to weaken her own standing by endorsing a loser. Warren's path looked clearer.

Shakir laid out the basics of a multi-candidate race in which Sanders had the strongest base of any of the contenders. He would win early states and build momentum. He would take his share of states on Super Tuesday and beyond, and he would walk into the party's convention in Milwaukee with more delegates than anyone else.

Ocasio-Cortez made no commitment before departing Burlington. She had told others that she wasn't planning to endorse Sanders. Shakir believed that she might stay out of the race entirely.

If she endorses no one, I won't be surprised, he thought. *If she endorses someone else, I'll be surprised.* He felt optimistic about the prospects of her joining up with Sanders on Saturday, September 28.

Three days later, Sanders's heart seized up. While Sanders was recuperating, and plotting an uncertain comeback from a hospital room in Vegas, Shakir's phone rang. He picked it up and instantly recognized the voice on the other end of the line.

"I'd like to talk to the senator," AOC said.

Shakir walked the phone over to his boss, who was sitting in a chair. Sanders didn't like lying in bed. He hated it. His own incapacity made him impatient.

"I want to get out of here," he'd yelled at one nurse. "I want to walk around."

Everyone was trying to keep him calm, but Sanders didn't have that setting. He'd received a lot of well-wishes from the well connected. Former Senate majority leader Harry Reid, who had ascertained the still-secret whereabouts of Sanders, even put in a call to a senior physician at the hospital to make sure it was clear that the patient was important to him. After a lifetime in politics and a few major health scares in his own family, Reid knew all the top doctors in the city.

But a call from Ocasio-Cortez was special because she could give Sanders something politically valuable. On walks through the hospital hallways, made late at night so that no one would see him or put a picture of him out on social media, Sanders had considered his return to the trail. During meetings in his hospital room, Shakir and Rabin-Havt advised him that he could best turn his heart attack into a rebound for the campaign if they could carefully fashion a rollout designed to draw maximum media attention. It would be a second chance to lean harder into his personal story—the one he'd drifted away from since his launch—to generate some momentum and, if the cards fell right, to highlight the support he was getting from women of color. AOC could be the key ingredient for all of that. No one else had her star power. Cameras would follow her, and so would young progressives.

Sanders took the phone from Shakir and lifted it to his cheek. The voice on the other end of the line instantly put him at ease for the first time in days. As she spoke, his mood shifted more noticeably. He smiled broadly. Then, as he began to realize where she was heading, his brown eyes lit up like a child's.

I'm going to endorse you, she said.

He pumped his fist in the air.

Now, in front of the big crowd in Queens with the country's most identifiable young progressive at his side, Sanders felt the energy coming back into a campaign that had been stuck before the heart attack. Beyond the excitement of the moment, AOC could help him with three subsets of the electorate: young progressives, Hispanics, and women. Two of AOC's closest allies in the House freshman class, Representatives Rashida Tlaib of Michigan and Ilhan Omar of Minnesota, would soon follow her endorsement of Sanders, putting a trifecta of the most prominent progressive women of color in his camp. The fourth member of their squad, Representative Ayanna Pressley, committed to Warren, a fellow member of the Massachusetts delegation to Congress.

But AOC was the big prize, and her endorsement moved numbers. Sanders's national polling average would never drop below the 15.2 percent it stood at on that day. He saw spikes in Iowa and New Hampshire as Warren tumbled backward. In January, Sanders would run into Larry David, the dead ringer for Sanders who played him in sketches on *Saturday Night Live*, at Rockefeller Center in New York. The famously neurotic comic, who wrote for *Seinfeld* and starred in HBO's *Curb Your Enthusiasm*, had one important question for Sanders as they greeted each other warmly in the *Today* show greenroom.

David leaned in close to Sanders. "So," he said, his Brooklyn accent and cadence indistinguishable from the senator's, "what's it like to have a heart attack?"

From a political perspective, it was a boon. The stents saved Sanders's life, but the heart attack saved his campaign.

Two days later, and eight and a half miles away from Sanders's Queensbridge Park rally, Barack Obama glided across the wood-planked floor of Yves, a trendy brasserie with low ceilings and French midcentury décor in the Tribeca section of New York. When the former president entered the candlelit eatery, known for its veal schnitzel, king salmon, and Burrata cremosa, he was at ease, tieless in a white dress shirt and black suit. He held a glass of vodka in hand as he greeted old friends.

Normally, Obama hated the glad-handing work of meeting donors, even on behalf of his foundation. But this Monday night confab with Black corporate power brokers huddled in the boutique eatery across from the Greenwich Hotel was a little bit different. Obama had a covert political mission to accomplish, a reminder that he could still play the old game he couldn't engage in publicly.

Flashing his familiar 135-million-vote smile, he saw what amounted to a Black all-star team of the corporate world: Ken Chenault, the former chairman of American Express, tech executive Charles Phillips, Merck CEO Kenneth Frazier, and Citigroup's Ray McGuire, among others.

By the time Obama circulated through the cozy confines of Yves, from which the tables and chairs had been removed to make more space, an Irishman of sorts had snuck in to join the group of Black luminaries. The actor Robert De Niro, who owned the Greenwich Hotel, where Obama had spent the day, wandered in late, after the prospective donors, and sat on one of the long permanent benches in the middle of the eatery.

Usually, Obama eschewed making substantive remarks at informal shindigs like this. A touch on the shoulder here, his classic "How are *you*?" there, a pat on the back, and out the door. But these were guys who liked him and guys he genuinely liked—a group with whom he intended to leave an important if subtle message about the election. Obama made his way back toward the door and delivered an announcement to the crowd of forty or so people.

"I'm gonna take a few questions," he said.

The session began with a fastball, a pitch down the middle for the issue Obama wanted to address. "If Joe Biden, Elizabeth Warren, Pete Buttigieg, and Kamala Harris asked for advice, what would you tell them?" a prominent executive queried.

"They all did!" he popped back, eliciting laughter from the crowd.

Obama paused for a moment, collecting himself before shocking the audience with the singular message that he had wanted to deliver. He embraced the prospect of a Warren presidency.

After nearly eleven months of campaigning, the race looked like it had stabilized with four truly competitive candidates: Joe, Bernie, Elizabeth, and Pete. Each had a claim to the advantage; no one was a prohibitive favorite. Until the past week or two, though, Warren had been rising steadily. The biggest obstacle to her success, it seemed, was convincing the establishment that she was truly different from Bernie, enough of a mainstream politician to be trusted with the reins of government. Now Obama was making that case for her.

Ignoring the other candidates, he launched a lawyerly argument, methodically ticking off the objections to Warren he knew existed in the minds of his corporate and financial friends. He knew Elizabeth, he said, very well. They had intersected during his time at Harvard, and then again during his time in the Senate where she often testified as an expert witness. He'd also "hired" her to stand up the Consumer Financial Protection Bureau. And while he didn't appreciate the smattering of attacks she'd made during his presidency, he said he was sure that she was a tough-as-nails campaigner who could get things done in Washington, should she succeed him as the next Democratic president.

After establishing himself as an authority on Warren, Obama

underscored that she had cleared his threshold for viability not only as a candidate but as president.

Standing before the crowd, he said he had encouraged all the candidates to ask themselves a three-question litmus test. "Why you?" Obama said. "Why now?" and "Is your family behind you?"

He expressed confidence in Warren, saying she had considered each question and had a satisfactory answer to all three.

"Many candidates like the idea of being president," he told the crowd. "But few really have a 'why,'" or a rationale for running.

Obama paused again, before making his final appeal, squarely addressing the elephant in the room, in a tone that was half-ribbing and half-reprimanding. "So what if she raises your taxes a little bit? Compare that to what we have now."

This was definitely not a time to sit on the sidelines, Obama said with some urgency. If Warren won the nomination, he said he would support her and stressed that he wanted Wall Street and corporate types to do the same. "Everyone in this room needs to pull their weight," he said.

Republicans, he continued, are winning cycle after cycle, up and down the ballot, because their donors care more than the Democrats' donors.

Like so many other Democrats, he saw Warren, who had taken the lead in Iowa from Biden in late September, barreling toward the nomination. It was time to start swinging folks in his coalition behind her. The persuasion effort among Black men would be as difficult as it was crucial. Hillary's loss could be attributed in part to insufficient support among Black men in major cities, and she had never had the support of elite Black men that she had among Black women. Things would have to be different for Warren. She would need the votes of Black men on the ground and the money of Black men in boardrooms—especially because she had forsworn buckraking with wealthy donors.

"Now, this is not an endorsement!" he said with a grin. His audience got the joke and laughed with him. He'd just given his seal of approval to Warren without using the "e" word.

"It was a ninety percent Warren sermon," said one donor in the room.

When he was asked to return to the original question on his advice, Obama said he liked Buttigieg, a rising talent who'd worked on his own campaign. But despite his affinity for the South Bend mayor, he rattled off a list of reasons why Buttigieg couldn't win.

"He's thirty-eight," Obama said, pausing for dramatic effect, "but he looks thirty."

The audience laughed.

Obama was on a roll, using the tone of light ridicule he sometimes pointed at himself—"big ears" and "a funny name," he'd said so many times before. Now, it was directed at Buttigieg.

"He's the mayor of a small town," the former president continued. "He's gay," Obama said, "and he's short."

More laughter.

Only months earlier, Buttigieg had sat in Obama's postpresidential office in Washington seeking counsel on how to maintain equanimity in the face of homophobia on the campaign trail. Now, behind his back, Obama was riffing on him to some of the wealthiest Black men in America at a time when Buttigieg had been dubbed "Mayo Pete" by critics who believed he couldn't connect with African American voters.

Obama kept going, acknowledging that he knew Kamala Harris but offering no further commentary.

But when he wrapped up, he had left someone out.

"You forgot Biden," one executive said, reminding him of his two-term vice president.

Obama seemed apprehensive, according to a source in the room.

"His support for Biden was tepid at best," the person said.

At that point, it didn't matter what he said about Biden. His silence spoke for him.

CHAPTER 6

•

Lucky Strike

"**Y**OU HAVE A FUCKING PROBLEM," LIS SMITH DECLARED, HER phone clutched in her hand and pinning strands of her jet-black bob to her face. "You cannot put this fucking poll out. You cannot."

Smith, half political savant and half tommy gun, had plotted Pete Buttigieg's rise in the media. Now she was warning CNN that there would be hell to pay if it didn't spike the gold-standard *Des Moines Register* poll. She was so worked up she couldn't focus. Standing in a hallway just off the lobby at the Des Moines Marriott, she handed her phone to senior campaign adviser Michael Halle.

"It's going to Zucker," CNN political director David Chalian told Halle, referring to the head of the network, Jeff Zucker.

At that moment, Smith knew something about the *Register* poll that the other campaigns didn't, something that threatened to torpedo the year of backbreaking work she'd spent getting her guy to this point. There was no way, if she still had breath in her lungs and a charge in her cellphone battery, she was going to let that happen. And though it wasn't her priority as she worked over CNN's politics team, she also knew something about Biden of which he and his team remained blissfully unaware—just how fucked he was in Iowa.

———

It was February 1, forty-eight hours before the caucuses. Just eighteen days earlier, the Real Clear Politics average of polls had put Biden atop the field in Iowa for the first time since October. His two main progressive rivals were tearing each other apart after months of self-enforced comity. It wasn't, so far as he and his campaign could tell, such a bad spot to be in, given that they never gave Biden much of a chance in the state in the first place.

From the campaign's earliest days, Biden's team would have preferred to start the race almost anywhere but the Hawkeye State. In the spring of 2019, in the basement of the McLean house, he and his advisers had tossed around the idea of skipping the state altogether. He'd gotten 1 percent there in 2008, and Iowa's overwhelmingly white Democratic electorate was trending hard left. In 2016, a survey found that 43 percent of the party's voters identified themselves as socialist, and a CNN/*Des Moines Register* poll in March of 2019 showed that 56 percent of them were very or mostly satisfied with the idea of a president who moved the United States in a more socialist direction. In addition to Biden's ill fit for the aggressively progressive electorate, Donilon and the others knew he could not—and would not—campaign as the fresh blood Iowa's Democrats would look for.

But he couldn't afford to sit it out, either. With the exceptions of 1988, when Dick Gephardt won with a plurality, and 1992, when favorite son Senator Tom Harkin ran away with the state, the winner of the Iowa caucuses had gone on to become the Democratic nominee in every election dating back to 1976. Jimmy Carter's campaign that year technically claimed victory in Iowa after coming in second to "uncommitted." Mike Donilon, whose brother, Tom, had worked for Carter, believed state Democrats were proud of the role they played in picking the next great hope for the national party. Perhaps their proudest moment had come when they chose Obama over John Edwards, Hillary Clinton, Biden, and other more familiar candidates in 2008.

Ultimately, the Bidenworld consensus on whether and how much to invest in Iowa came back to where Greg Schultz sat. "We should totally not do it," the soon-to-be campaign manager had told the vice president and his team. "But we have to."

They landed on a plan to survive the state and keep moving through New Hampshire toward more diverse and friendlier terrain in Nevada and South Carolina. Yet Biden knew all too well what a loss in the caucuses usually did to presidential campaigns. It was one thing to look past Iowa in a campaign memo; it was another to actually withstand a defeat there. He didn't necessarily have to win, but he couldn't get swamped.

The execution of the Biden Iowa campaign was hardly surgical. Instead, for most of 2019, it felt half-assed. His state director, Jake Braun, was often difficult to find, according to colleagues. And having entered the race late in April 2019, Biden had lost out on the top draft picks in terms of staff. Braun, for example, was a former Obama administration official whose last campaign credit was from 2008.

For the first several months of the campaign, Biden visited the state far fewer times than his main rivals. And when other candidates began filling the Iowa airwaves with ads, Biden held most of his small treasury in reserve. It was a minor miracle that there weren't MISSING posters with his likeness stuck to silver maple trees across the state.

The first wake-up call came in mid-September, when Warren pushed into first place in Iowa. Biden and his aides didn't like what they were seeing. It was one thing to lose to Sanders there. That was to be expected. But Warren looked increasingly like she might have the capacity to bridge the gap between progressives and moderates. An Iowa win could springboard her to the nomination; at the very least, it would bring in the kind of money and media attention required to wage a long campaign.

Buttigieg was on the move, too. By mid-November, the South Bend surprise had more than a hundred paid staff in the state, spread across nearly two dozen field offices. He had spent more than $2 million on TV ads. He took a lead in polling at that point and held it through the end of the year. Sanders, who had foundered in Iowa in the weeks following his heart attack, was suddenly coming back into the picture, too. A dark horse, Senator Amy Klobuchar from next-door-neighbor Minnesota, started to gain traction at the back of the pack. "Survival" in Biden's original estimation meant finishing in the money. Suddenly he was facing the prospect of getting out-organized by not just one candidate but three or four.

Biden had dropped into a third-place tie in Iowa by the night of

the Iowa Democratic Party's November 1 Liberty and Justice
Celebration—known as the Jefferson-Jackson dinner before Democrats decided that they didn't want to be associated with slave-
owning presidents. Biden had spoken at countless state-party
fundraising dinners over the years, but this one was the most important of his career. In 2008, Obama had packed the dinner and
roused the audience in what would become seen as a pivotal moment for his campaign.

Biden's aides in the state sent word that the Wells Fargo Arena
in Des Moines would be packed with supporters. And it was. Just
not Biden supporters. Buttigieg, for example, had to raise his voice
to be heard over the chants of his legion of fans. Biden followed,
and he was greeted with polite applause. Though he ripped Trump,
the object of every Democrat's ire, he never got much more than
that in response. Worse, he could see in the section reserved for his
supporters that the seats were mostly empty. He was furious. It was
his staff's job to put bodies in the arena. They had failed him, left
him humiliated. More than that, he felt deceived. He'd been told
everything was taken care of. It wasn't. He let the leaders of his
team on the ground, deputy campaign manager Pete Kavanaugh
and Iowa state director Jake Braun, know he was profoundly disappointed right after the dinner. It was worse than a tongue-lashing.

"This is not how you win a campaign," he said. "We don't look
strong. I mean, how could this happen?"

Biden stayed mad through that night and into the next morning.
Nothing was going right in Iowa or at the national level. Top advisers urged him to rein in Schultz and Kavanaugh. The pooh-bahs
wanted more control, even though they had signed off on every
major decision so far. Their response to the L-J dinner was to devote even more of Biden's time and more of the campaign's limited
treasury to Iowa. Something had to be done to put Biden on track.

"Alarm bells were ringing," one top aide said.

Enter Hillary.

In the first week of November, exactly three years after one of
the most painful days of her life—and in the history of the Democratic Party—Hillary Clinton began to give serious consideration
to jumping into the primary. Her calculus was simple, according to
one top adviser: "Biden was doing badly, and Bernie was soaring."

She had never seen a world-beater in the crowded field of candidates, but now she saw opportunity. A Fox News poll released that week showed Biden leading Trump 51 percent to 39 percent in a head-to-head matchup, and Sanders ahead of the president 49 percent to 41 percent. Hillary edged out Trump by a smaller 43 percent to 41 percent margin, but there was a silver lining in the survey for her. Two-thirds of Democrats said they would definitely vote for her or consider voting for her in a primary. Biden had lost altitude in national polls and in Iowa, where half his support had dried up since mid-September.

Hillary knew all too well that Sanders had a die-hard following, and she could see that he was building momentum. Less than two weeks earlier, Ocasio-Cortez had endorsed him at a crowded outdoor rally. A Trump-Sanders matchup was a lose-lose proposition for Hillary, and, she thought, for the country.

"It was natural to second guess your decision not to run," the adviser said.

Longtime Clinton advisers explored the logistics of launching a campaign—specifically whether there was enough time for her to meet filing deadlines in key states. The answer was that she could launch as late as mid-December and still get on the ballot in the right places to wage a protracted battle for the nomination. But the most important variables involved her ability to do a better job this time of explaining to voters why she should be president and whether she could win.

If I get in, what is the likelihood that I can consolidate the anti-Bernie vote rather than diluting it? she thought. There was a real risk that she could inadvertently help Sanders, and there was no guarantee that she could beat Trump in a rematch, even if she had replayed that scenario in her head at least once for each of the 77,736 votes that had separated her from Trump in the pivotal battleground states in 2016. Only one factor had changed in the eleven months since Huma Abedin had confided in a small set of fellow Clinton advisers that Hillary still saw herself as a potential 2020 candidate: the calendar. There was still no true favorite for the nomination.

Hillary wasn't the only prospective candidate taking a hard look at a late entry. Former New York mayor Michael Bloomberg and former Massachusetts governor Deval Patrick were already set to go, and another handful of has-been and never-will-be hopefuls were more quietly assessing their options. But none of them were as instantly recognizable, as popular within the Democratic Party, or as polarizing as the former first lady, New York senator, and 2016 Democratic presidential nominee. Only 40 percent of Democratic voters said they would at least consider backing a Bloomberg bid, and Patrick didn't have national name-recognition.

Hillary weighed the pros and cons for almost a month before coming to a conclusion around Thanksgiving: She *could* put together a campaign, but that didn't mean she *should*.

Exit Hillary.

Even as they plowed more money into Iowa, Biden's aides tried publicly to play down the state's importance to his chances of winning the nomination. "I think we're the only ones who don't have to win Iowa, honestly, because our strength is the fact that we have a broad and diverse coalition," Schultz told *The Wall Street Journal* for a November 4 story. Behind the scenes, too, that was his message to nervous donors and other political elites. In private sessions, he would talk to them about the strength of Biden's support in Black-majority congressional districts across the South. Just wait, he told them, the demographics will eventually favor us.

But in the late fall and early winter, as the possibility loomed of getting not just beat but embarrassed in Iowa, Biden and his top aides decided to go all-in. They knew the state was a sinkhole, but they threw their money and Biden's time into it anyway.

If I can just get some key endorsements, I can get traction and move the needle, Biden thought.

It was an old-school play, based on Biden's unshakable belief in the power of his own charms. The modern conventional wisdom held that endorsements didn't really help much. Biden got former Iowa governor Tom Vilsack and his well-liked wife, Christie, to back him publicly in late November. Vilsack, a former secretary of agriculture, had a strong relationship with Biden from their days in the Obama administration, and their politics aligned. Right after Thanksgiving, Biden set out on an eight-day "No Malarkey" bus tour of rural areas. He deployed two of his top lieutenants, deputy campaign manager Pete Kavanaugh and organizing director Kurt Bagley, to marshal the Iowa campaign. "We were basically throwing everything we had into Iowa, including our money, in an attempt to carve out a decent finish," said one top Biden aide.

The state Biden had long seen as political quicksand had become a battleground of necessity, but also possibly one of opportunity. With the candidates crunched so closely together, the smallest of margins could mean the difference between delivering a knockout punch with a victory and possibly taking one with an embarrassingly poor finish. The uncertainty drew Biden further in. If he managed to win Iowa, becoming the momentum candidate as well as the establishment front-runner, he might be able to lock down the nomination quickly.

Despite being strapped for cash, the campaign poured even more of its money into Iowa after the candidate complained about his poor showing at the Liberty and Justice dinner. The shift starved Biden's operations in the other early primary states, but the campaign would cross that slushy New Hampshire bridge when—if—Biden made it out of Iowa.

Partly because of the cash crunch, Biden also shifted his stance on super PACs in the fall and welcomed their help. Until his political career was on the line, he had made clear that he didn't want assistance from super PACs, which could raise and spend unlimited sums on behalf of the candidate—and shield donors' identities—so long as they technically didn't coordinate with a campaign. He finally signaled his assent in late September, and a group of his former aides began raising money to spend on ads in Iowa under the flag Unite the Country. The group sought out rainmakers like billionaire real estate investor George Marcus and Wall Street financiers Bernard Schwartz and Roger Altman to write six- and seven-figure checks to pay for ads backing Biden. When Biden was too low on cash to compete with the onslaught of ads from other campaigns, Unite the Country and a second group called Democratic Majority for Israel picked up some of the slack. The airtime, a stronger debate performance, and Biden's argument that Trump saw him as the toughest possible opponent combined to give the former vice president a lift of about 5 points in mid-January 2020—enough for him to retake a lead for almost two weeks.

Biden would benefit from, and suffer for, Trump's impeachment in Congress. In September, a government whistleblower had shed light on Trump's scheme to use $400 million in federal money to extort Ukraine into announcing an investigation into Biden and his son Hunter. The House impeached Trump for it on December 18.

The Senate trial opened on January 22. While the daily debate involving Hunter Biden's work for a Ukrainian energy company appeared to act as a drag on the former vice president over the final months of 2019, it may have created a rally-around-the-flag effect for him in January.

Biden took a polling lead in Iowa for the first time in four months on January 13, with impeachment in the news and just before the Senate began debating its rules for the trial. It was also a day before the Democratic debate in Iowa, which heavily featured foreign policy in its opening half hour. That was Biden's sweet spot. As a former chairman of the Senate Foreign Relations Committee, he was more at ease on that topic than any other. It showed. Biden deftly used Obama and Beau as shields to defend himself on his vote for the Iraq War. Calling his vote "a mistake," as he had done in 2007, Biden noted that "the man who also argued against that war, Barack Obama, picked me to be his vice president and . . . turned to me and asked me to end that war." And, referring to Beau's service, he told voters, "I know what it's like to send a son or daughter" to war, "and that's why I do it very, very reluctantly."

He recalled his involvement in the Iran nuclear deal that Trump reneged on, and he took a swipe at Warren when she called for the removal of all U.S. troops from the Middle East. "There's a difference between combat troops and leaving Special Forces in," he said. "That's how we were able to defeat and end the caliphate for ISIS." *We* was a particularly clever framing. The word made it sound like Obama, rather than Trump, had defeated ISIS. But his pronoun of choice could be defended as a reference to the United States. Not many Democratic voters would give Trump credit for picking up the Obama playbook on ISIS and executing it in a way that Obama hadn't. Fewer still would follow closely enough to make the distinction at all. Biden had just deftly taken credit for destroying ISIS and suggested that Warren was confused on national security. For once, he looked to be in his element on a debate stage.

A week after the debate, as Trump's impeachment trial began, Biden opened about a four-point lead in Iowa over second-place Sanders, 21 percent to 17.3 percent, in the Real Clear Politics average. Warren clocked in at 16.7 percent, Buttigieg had 16.3 percent, and Klobuchar, riding a small wave, pushed up past 8 percent. After months of trudging through Iowa, and deciding to pour more effort into a state his campaign had long predicted he would lose, there was suddenly reason for some in Biden's camp to believe he could win. That included Biden.

But the Iowa caucuses are hard to poll and even harder to predict. They are low-turnout affairs featuring the most committed activists, and they include two rounds. First, voters align with their top pick. If that candidate doesn't clear a 15 percent support threshold, the voters are free to realign with another candidate. Complicating matters, the Iowa Democratic Party planned to report three sets of numbers—the first-round numbers, the second-round totals, and the portion of "state delegate equivalents" won by each candidate from the second round. Based on a formula, the SDEs determined how many national delegates each candidate won.

The only poll that ever really mattered before caucus day was the *Des Moines Register* survey, which was done in conjunction with CNN. Conducted by J. Ann Selzer, the most-respected pollster in the state, the poll would set the final expectations two days before the vote. That was true both for the campaigns and for caucus-goers. The candidate who led in the survey could expect a winner's boost from headlines in the *Register* and wall-to-wall cable television coverage the day before the caucuses. Any candidate who underperformed could expect to lose supporters.

The political world waited to see how the *Register* poll would rank Biden, Sanders, Warren, and Buttigieg. Its findings could influence the decision-making of Iowa Democrats and create a domino effect of momentum far beyond the state. *Politico,* the insider news outlet for the politically obsessed, called it "the most consequential poll in politics." CNN planned to roll out the results live as a special event, complete with a *Brady Bunch* grid of political analysts.

Biden was about to get creamed. The *Register* poll didn't have him in front of the other three candidates; it had him behind. A train was bearing down on him and he didn't know it. Even if he had, there was nothing he could do to stop it. Fortunately for him, someone else was already ripping up the tracks.

Known only to a handful of people at the time, the survey put Sanders in first place with 22 percent, followed by Warren at 18 percent, and Buttigieg—Lis Smith's boss—in third with 16 percent. Biden registered at a lowly 13 percent.

Buttigieg's strategy for Iowa had exploded forward along with his national presence and his shockingly strong fundraising. Where he had once hoped just to make the cut of candidates who would survive the caucuses and move on to New Hampshire, only victory would do now. He could easily win the state and still lose the fight for the nomination. But with the cachet he had built, there was no way to see how he could lose the first contest and come back. He had pumped millions of dollars into broadcast ads and a field operation in the state to get to this point. He now had a real hope of winning the nomination, but the plan for that required him to stay hot in Iowa, take the caucuses, and catch fire in New Hampshire. If he could do that, he might spin into a virtuous cycle of more money and wider support—*if, could, might.*

The *Register* poll results were like a smoke-triggered sprinkler system. They threatened to drench what his team believed was growing momentum in the rural areas, where he was competing with Sanders. Sanders's clear lead would result in a bumper crop of positive stories predicting his imminent victory, setting up a self-fulfilling prophecy.

This poll is going to shape the whole race, Smith thought, as she tried to persuade CNN. *It can't come out.*

Smith had ammunition at hand, but she wasn't sure it would do the job. The previous day, Ben Halle, one of Pete's press aides and the brother of adviser Michael Halle, had learned that a campaign volunteer received a polling call in which Buttigieg's name was left off the list of choices. Ben Halle sent a Twitter direct message to Selzer and asked what had happened.

There was a minor problem at a call center. The type size of the candidates' names had been changed on one of the call center's computer screens, Selzer said. That had inadvertently obscured Buttigieg's name. It did not appear to be anything more than an isolated problem. But in an exchange of messages, and eventually on the phone, Selzer couldn't prove that the problem had not been more widespread. She also didn't have any evidence to suggest that it had affected more than the one call. As a professional data cruncher, Selzer was more given to delivering precise answers about what she knew and didn't know. There was no way to be 100 percent sure, in short order and without any other complaints lodged, whether the topline results had been tainted in any significant way. The order of candidates made enough sense, and their percentages weren't that far off from those in other surveys—with the exception of Biden, who had dropped like a rock.

The last part wasn't terribly surprising. Even friends who had been campaigning with him in Iowa saw a candidate who was lethargic and uninspiring on the stump and sometimes at a loss for the right words. With the impeachment trial hanging in the backdrop, the safe-bet candidate may have looked more risky. All that Trump's allies in Washington could talk about—including Iowa Republican senator Joni Ernst—was the unsubstantiated allegation that Biden and his son Hunter were corrupt. Could Ukraine be Biden's version of Hillary Clinton's email scandal—a gift to Trump that just gave and gave and gave in 2016? That was certainly a concern for some Democrats. But more ominous for Biden was the fact that he had not been able to take advantage of the absence from the state of several of his top rivals. With the senators in the race splitting time between Washington and Iowa during the impeachment trial, Biden and Buttigieg had the state almost to themselves. Buttigieg gained steam during that time. Biden slipped back. The more voters focused on him, the less they saw him as their first choice—or even their second choice.

When Buttigieg's brain trust first found out about the polling glitch, his top aides didn't know exactly what to do. That was largely because they didn't have the bottom-line results. But Michael Halle decided to plant a seed, just in case they wanted to try to pull the poll down. He got in touch with Matt Paul, an adviser to the Iowa Democratic Party with whom he'd worked on Hillary's 2016 campaign.

"Don't you think this is strange?" Halle asked. He suspected Paul would stir up just a little buzz in insider circles about the validity of the numbers.

Early Saturday, the day of the poll's release, Pete's aides went back and forth on whether they should try to spike the poll. If they actually knew the results, the decision would be easier.

By the middle of the afternoon, they decided to reserve their right to object. It was game time. They sent a memo to David Chalian with a series of questions about the methodology. They demanded answers by six P.M. central time, two hours before the network planned to go live with the results and its big special report from Drake University. They began telling reporters in the lobby off the record that there was something funky about the *Register* poll. In doing so, they were laying a marker so that if the survey was released they could later say they had raised a red flag before they knew the results.

"What we wanted to avoid was looking like sore losers," one Buttigieg staffer said. But they also knew off-the-record tips would lead to back-channel chatter between reporters from other outlets, CNN, *The Des Moines Register,* and possibly Selzer. Pressure would start to build. But they still needed to know what the poll actually said; it would be counterproductive to sink a survey if their guy was in the lead.

Right at the six o'clock deadline, Buttigieg's team cracked the case—he was in third place in the polls. "We got the results two hours in advance" of the CNN special, one Buttigieg aide said.

Now, with the poll showing Buttigieg in third, it wasn't a question of whether they would try to kill the poll but whether they could execute.

While Smith ran through her improvised playbook, Jeff Weaver and Chuck Rocha were drinking bourbon and chowing down on slabs of meat in a nearby restaurant. They were in a good mood. Sanders, they believed, was in a good position to win Iowa. It wasn't clear what the relative strength of the other campaigns would be. But if there was one thing Sanders had demonstrated in 2016, it was that his army of supporters would walk through a wall of fire to vote for him. That was forcing Warren to take new risks.

The day before the most recent debate, Sanders campaign manager Faiz Shakir awoke to a phone call from press guy Mike Casca.

"We got a problem," Casca said. "I got a little bit of a red alert here, unfortunately."

CNN was planning to report that Sanders had told Warren thirteen months earlier that a woman couldn't win the presidency.

"Oh, crap," Shakir said. "Give me a second. Tell them to hold off please on the story. We want to comment. But we have to talk to Senator Sanders first."

Shakir called Sanders and told him about the coming story.

"Are you serious?" Sanders asked. They agreed to meet in a conference room in their hotel, along with a few other campaign aides.

When Sanders arrived, he wore a pained look, almost like he was sick to his stomach. He sat down. He hung his head and stared down at the conference table.

"Senator Sanders, any part of this that has any ring of merit to it?" Shakir asked.

Sanders stiffened and lifted his head, bolt upright. He looked square at Shakir. Anger flashed in his eyes.

"Faiz," he said, "she invited me over to her house to discuss running for president of the United States. You think there is any chance in the world that I would tell her that she can't win and a woman can't be president of the United States?"

"No," Shakir said, plaintively. "I don't."

Sanders sighed. He bowed his head again. "All right," he said, staring back at the table, "that's all I needed to hear."

Shakir decided the campaign should challenge Warren to back up the claims of the anonymously sourced CNN story. That would give her an out to shoot it down. Sanders publicly denied the allegation. Warren doubled down. "I thought a woman could win; he disagreed," she said in a statement released by her campaign.

The feud spilled over into the debate.

"Bernie is my friend, and I'm not here to try to fight with Bernie," Warren said when asked about their 2018 meeting. But that's exactly what she was trying to do. She said she was the only candidate on the stage who had beaten an incumbent over the past thirty years.

Sanders first quarreled with her on that. They debated for twenty seconds over whether his 1990 defeat of a Republican candidate was within the previous thirty years. It went downhill from there. When the debate came to a close, Warren crossed a podium to confront Sanders, who had said "anybody in their right mind" believed a woman could win.

"I think you called me a liar on national TV," Warren charged, her hands clasped in front of her.

Tom Steyer, the billionaire California investor and presidential candidate, stood awkwardly behind them as he waited to get a moment with Sanders.

"What?" Sanders said to Warren.

"I think you called me a liar on national TV," she repeated, with more gusto.

Both of them knew they were still under the spotlight, still wearing microphones and still within the visual range of television cameras.

"Let's not do this right now," Sanders said, putting his hands out toward Warren as if to calm her. "You want to have this discussion, we'll have this discussion."

"Anytime," she offered.

Sanders briefly let his anger get the better of him. He pointed his index finger at Warren's chest.

"You called me a liar!" he said. "You called me—all right, let's not do this now." He turned away from her.

For more than a year, the two progressives had observed a tacit nonaggression pact. The idea was to strengthen the position of the left and hammer away at the more moderate candidates and Trump. To win the nomination, either one would have to rely on the other's supporters to form a coalition within the party. It had been easy before there were real stakes on the table.

Now, with three weeks to go before the caucuses, they were at each other's throats. Warren's national poll numbers had been dropping for three months. Part of that was her struggle with Medicare for All and part of it was the political energy Sanders had drawn from his heart attack. Many of the Sanders fans who were giving look-sees to other candidates, particularly Warren and her reform-over-revolution message, had come home after the heart attack. Just like Ocasio-Cortez. Warren was desperate for media attention and sympathy—and she firmly believed that Sanders had in fact mansplained to her why only a man could beat Trump.

Even before the meltdown, their relationship had begun to fray in the heat of the campaign. Afterward, it was nonexistent. That was as good for Biden as his own relatively strong debate performance. In politics, as in war, division is a predicate for conquest. But in the immediate contest, Warren's shot spoke to Sanders's standing in Iowa. He was in first. Everyone knew it. Weaver and Rocha, enjoying dinner and a drink, definitely knew it.

They were discussing the upcoming caucus when Weaver's cell rang and Smith's number popped up on his screen. Weaver and

Smith had formed a pretty good bond over two election cycles—Smith had been deputy campaign manager for Martin O'Malley's short-lived 2016 run when Weaver managed Sanders's bid. When they weren't in the middle of a live firefight, both of them were amiable and respectably irreverent about the ridiculousness of conventional politics. And they were both deeply loyal to their candidates. Weaver thought of Smith as a political soldier—his term of endearment for operatives with guts. He was about to watch the soldier in action.

"I'm getting reports," Smith said, pressing Weaver about what he might have picked up. She sent him the messages between Halle and Selzer. "It's a problem," she said.

Holy hell, Rocha thought as he listened to Weaver's end of the conversation. *Lis Smith might derail this whole fucking thing.*

Finally on the phone with CNN's David Chalian, Smith insinuated the network's reputation was on the line. It wasn't in her interests for him to kill the poll, she argued, her brown eyes growing wide. It was in *his* interests.

Chalian couldn't commit to anything. This was the crown jewel of polls, and CNN had spent big to promote it. "I don't see how we're going to go through with this," he said. But he told Halle that Zucker would be the one to decide.

CNN risked humiliation: Killing the poll would make the network look just as incompetent as releasing a tainted one. Either option could influence the outcome of the caucus. The main question was whether network executives were confident that the poll was valid, followed by the corollary question of whether it would be perceived that way. But Smith had added a major disincentive to releasing it. Even if the numbers were valid, at least one campaign—Buttigieg's—would surely say publicly that they weren't. Since only one candidate was in first place—Sanders—the other camps would have reason to join in the complaint. Who knew? Maybe Sanders, who liked to call out foul play, might be tempted to join in. The ground around his inner circle had already been seeded.

Smith retreated from the lobby to campaign manager Mike Schmuhl's room upstairs, where Schmuhl and another famished colleague wolfed down hotel buffalo wings and nursed beers. Bud Light in hand, Smith couldn't sit still.

She dialed Chalian's number over and over again seeking a verdict—or at least silently lobbying for one. When he didn't answer, she and one of her deputies started calling Mark Preston, one of Chalian's CNN colleagues. *They're stalling,* she thought. She would turn the pressure up just by robo-dialing them. Her message would be as clear as her number on their screens: There would be no putting this back in the box if it blew up.

For his part, Chalian was in a terrible spot. It wasn't clear that the poll was wrong. On the other hand, the entire political world was waiting for this last bit of caucus news the day before the Super Bowl, and he couldn't afford to put out a poll that was tainted—or one that would be painted that way by at least one campaign and a bunch of media outlets that had no reason to defend CNN.

When Smith finally got Chalian on the phone again, she maintained that the result wasn't bad for Pete—though it was—and that it was simply "the right thing to do" to prevent its release. She hoped the messages Selzer had sent to Ben Halle would cast enough doubt to outweigh CNN's reluctance to bring the whole thing down.

"It should be enough," she argued, adding that the last thing anyone needed was a new conspiracy theory about how a poll had been "rigged." It all amounted to one very big implicit threat to add a Democratic-flavored pile-on to Trump's politically calculated bashing of the network as "Fake News."

They went back and forth. "You've got to make a decision," she finally said. "You've got fifteen minutes."

"We're not going to be part of a poll that is dubious," he said. That wasn't the same thing as saying that it *was* dubious or that they wouldn't put it out. This kind of climactic moment was what political operatives lived for—or died from.

A few minutes later, the three aides huddled around the TV in Schmuhl's room as CNN announced live on the air that the poll was toast.

"We killed the Iowa poll!" Smith shouted.

"We killed the Iowa poll!" the others repeated with childlike glee. They all exclaimed the phrase over and over.

"It was like when you win a fucking Super Bowl," said one person who was in the room.

Buttigieg's aides would maintain that they had simply fought to preserve the integrity of the caucuses. And yet they had just robbed Bernie Sanders of forty-eight hours of media coverage of being the undisputed, No. 1–ranked candidate in Iowa. "I would have preferred if the poll came out," said one Sanders aide. "It would have been good for us." That was an understatement. If there was one thing all of the polling made clear, including the spiked survey, it was that the candidates were closely bunched enough that even a small windfall or setback could alter the outcome. Sanders's best bet for winning the nomination was reeling off wins in the first three states and building a big enough head of steam to power him through the rest of the country.

Still, Weaver admired Smith's handiwork. He sent her a congratulatory text.

For Buttigieg, the poll's abrupt death kept his campaign's momentum going at a crucial moment. He couldn't win the nomination without coming in first in Iowa, and the poll threatened to prevent that from happening.

"It could have fucked us," he told one close ally.

But Biden was the luckiest candidate. A poll showing him at 13 percent, just a couple of weeks after he had led the field with more than 20 percent, would have been absolutely devastating for him. It would have signaled to some of his supporters that it was time to abandon ship, and the political obituary writers in the press corps would have been fast at work pre-drafting copy for caucus night. Donors and potential endorsers would have been rattled—again!

He was spared all that, at least for a couple of days, by the obliteration of the poll. Still, having it spiked was only a temporary reprieve. The actual caucus results in two days would expose the degree to which Iowa Democrats had rejected him. There was no way he could stop that from happening.

CHAPTER 7

•

Panic! at the Caucus

O N THE MORNING BEFORE THE IOWA CAUCUSES, JOHN KERRY grabbed a seat in the back corner of the restaurant at the Savery Hotel, a 101-year-old steel-and-red-brick building that had played host to countless presidential candidates over the years.

Kerry had spent weeks campaigning for Biden, and he had come to a damning conclusion: He was convinced that his old Senate pal didn't have fire in his belly. *Joe's got a lot to work with,* Kerry thought, *but he doesn't seem to personally want it.*

That was a foreign concept to Kerry, a former secretary of state who had long imagined himself sitting behind the Resolute Desk in the Oval Office. Kerry wanted it. Sixteen years after he'd lost the 2004 election to George W. Bush, he still wanted it. He had decided against running in 2020 in large part because Biden jumped in.

Now, after getting a long, up-close look at Biden on the stump, he was having second thoughts. *He's good at it and then he's not good at it,* Kerry thought. *He sounds like he's trying to move the country backward; he needs to be the candidate of the future.* Most of the polls showed a close race, but Kerry could see that Biden wasn't connecting with Iowans. And like many fellow Democratic movers and shakers, Kerry worried that Sanders might take down the party if something wasn't done—and soon—to stop him.

He didn't have to look far to find the man he thought could do it—just into the nearest mirror.

No more than a hundred feet from where Biden's advisers were eating eggs and pancakes, Kerry popped AirPods into his ears and began to unspool his theory of the case to a friend.

"Bernie is taking off because young people in America are driven by a sense of hopelessness," he said. Student debt and healthcare are "real issues," he continued. "Bernie is real."

Big-time donors could be encouraged to get off the sidelines, he said, because "now they have the possibility of Bernie Sanders taking down the Democratic Party—down whole." For more than a year, many of Obama's top donors had either stayed out of the primary or given to multiple candidates. Without a cue from the former president, they were free to do as they pleased. One thing they hadn't done as a group was get behind Biden.

The other fear for Democratic insiders, if less terrifying than Sanders taking control of the race, was that a Biden swoon would give oxygen to Mike Bloomberg, the former Republican mayor of New York, who was planning to jump in after the first four states on the calendar. Bloomberg had booked a $10 million, sixty-second national TV ad that very night.

From Kerry's perspective, the field didn't look strong enough to take on Trump, a sentiment that permeated much of the Democratic intelligentsia. "No veteran, no prosecutor, no real government experience at a time when the world needs a president who is going to get something done." He didn't have to say to his friend that he'd just read lines from his own résumé.

"Maybe I'm fucking deluding myself here," Kerry said, as he began to play out the practical considerations of making a late bid for the presidency. "I'd have to give up Bank of America," where he sat on the board. "I'd have to give up my speaking." He'd just finished making payments on his house, he said, and would have "enough to live on"—a couple million bucks in the bank—to "be in a position to see if I'm working" on the trail. If he were to run, it would be with an eye toward capturing the nomination at the convention after a protracted multi-candidate fight. Biden, he told his friend, didn't seem to have what it took to run the marathon.

Kerry quickly clicked off the phone as two Biden advisers approached his table in the back. He gave them some advice. Biden should talk for ten minutes and then take questions from the audience, he said. Long speeches were draining energy from Biden and from his supporters. When the advisers left, Kerry got up and paid his tab.

What Kerry had observed was also obvious within the campaign and to the national news media. Print and broadcast outlets were full of stories about the funereal nature of the final weeks of Biden's third and presumably final trek through Iowa. Part of the problem was that his advisers were at war over what to tell the candidate about his chances of winning, which made it impossible for Biden to get a real read on his own status. That made it harder for him to simultaneously tamp down expectations and pump up his base.

There were basically four camps: pooh-bah optimists, led by Ricchetti; pooh-bah pessimists, led by Donilon; the overly rosy Iowa ground team, led by state director Jake Braun; and the uncertain realists, led by Schultz and his deputy, Pete Kavanaugh, who had been dispatched to Iowa late in 2019 to redirect the operation. To some extent, Ricchetti and Donilon were just playing to form. Ricchetti, the ultra-successful lobbyist, looked at the bright side of everything. Donilon, the lovably gloomy Eeyore of the campaign, always wondered when other shoes would start raining down. He was reticent about giving his advice in front of other people, so much so that colleagues often found out later that he had been on senior-level conference calls without saying a word. Frequently, he was the only one sitting with Biden, wherever the candidate was.

But the real tension point was between Ricchetti and Schultz. The campaign manager walked the same difficult tightrope as many of his predecessors: He had to try to balance the competing demands of a state team that always wanted more money and more candidate time, a headquarters team that saw Iowa as a total but necessary waste, a council of graybeards with a spectrum of opinions, and a candidate who wanted to win—or at least come close to it—but was such a bad advocate for himself on the campaign trail that Kerry, his loyal old Senate pal, was openly musing about launching his own bid. Ricchetti, who was traveling with Biden in the final days before the caucuses, told Biden that he could win. It's what the candidate wanted to hear. Braun, the state director, told him the same thing. "We were trying to win Iowa," said an aide who was close to Biden during the caucuses. "We always thought we were playing to win Iowa."

Once again, just like on the night of the Liberty and Justice dinner, Biden's expectations were set at a level much higher than reality suggested they should be. It was an ongoing problem for Schultz that Biden's older advisers and his state staff were constantly playing for the candidate's approval. But more important, Schultz couldn't make decisions without the blessing of the older advisers, who were sometimes tactfully at odds with one another. He simply wasn't empowered, and he didn't take power, which meant two things: He wasn't effectively managing the campaign, and he was an easy scapegoat for problems—like lackluster fundraising and poor support among the electorate.

Schultz and Kavanaugh tried, without much success, to temper the sunny projections Biden was getting from Ricchetti and the state staff. "Ricchetti and Jake Braun were talking to each other and had their own model, which no data scientist had ever looked at, saying that we were going to win," said one miffed Biden adviser.

The truth was that the campaign's actual data crunchers couldn't get a good feel for what was going to happen in the caucuses. With the top four candidates so tightly packed in polling, and the game-theory nature of a two-round caucus, it was impossible to pinpoint an outcome. A point or two in polling could disproportionately affect delegate hauls. It wasn't even clear that the candidate who had the most supporters at the caucuses would actually win the second round or lead in delegates at the end of the night. Weaver, the Sanders adviser, had been pushing media outlets for weeks to focus on the raw vote at the caucuses, rather than the complicated delegate math, to declare a winner. He was frustrated to find out that he couldn't make strategic alliances with other campaigns to trade second-alignment supporters in order to harm common enemies. The stack of candidates was just too close for any of them to be sure how the voting would play out.

In the closing days of the campaign, Biden plugged into a senior-staff conference call from his bus, which had been chugging him through Iowa. The news he received differed from the rosy projections he'd been hearing. He was told by his polling and data teams that the numbers suggested the most likely scenario was a third-place finish, with an outside shot of second place. Biden did not react well to bad news. He took it in silently. But even the bad news sounded too rosy to Kavanaugh. "To be clear, sir," he said in his dry New England brogue, "we could also get fourth."

Like Schultz, Kavanaugh had become a lightning rod within the campaign, in part because he was willing to deliver truth to the candidate. He infuriated the pooh-bahs because he made little secret of his disdain for their old-school views on campaigning. Broadly, they felt like he looked at them as codgers playing a different game. Younger staffers said he could be too brusque. "He treated everyone like children," said one colleague, who believed he behaved like "an asshole." The list of people he'd ticked off included Donilon, who had so meticulously created Biden's message of competence, character, and compassion, only to find that Kavanaugh and Schultz weren't building advertising or fundraising pitches around it—or at least not ones that produced windfalls of cash and votes for the candidate. Donilon was the third-worst enemy anyone could make in Bidenworld, behind Joe and Jill Biden. There were professional differences between Biden's innermost circle and Schultz. With Kavanaugh, the friction was both professional and personal.

The night before the caucuses, Ricchetti was unusually nervous. He had given Biden hope that victory was at hand. But now, sitting at a booth in the Savery Hotel's bar, just a few feet away from Jill Biden, he worried aloud about his own predictions of success. "I just pray to God that we get third," he said.

Publicly, Biden hedged his bets. He was optimistic, but not totally unrealistic. More important, he'd been in politics long enough to know that setting low expectations for the media created a win-win dynamic, where the opposite was true of setting the bar high. Controlled expectations meant that if he won Iowa it would be treated as an upset—perhaps a checkmate for the nomination—and if he lost, he could write it off to never having believed that Iowa was important to his plans. To date, his entire campaign had been a painful exercise in trying to meet a low standard of performance for a former vice president.

He played down the value of the caucuses in an interview with NBC News in late January. "I think I have a real firewall in South

Carolina," Biden said. "And then we go into the Super Tuesday states that have a significant number of minorities and African Americans" where "I think I'm going to do fine." The paradox was not lost on the Iowa voters he courted. While he was asking for their support, he was telling the national media it was insignificant.

At the Savery that Sunday, hours before Ricchetti privately conceded that a third-place finish would be a godsend, Biden aides and surrogates floated in and out of the bar, picking at shared plates of food. Almost to a person, they looked listless. Representative Cedric Richmond of New Orleans, the national co-chairman of the campaign, was plainly in a bad mood. Normally quick with a quip, he wore a mask of intensity.

I should have pushed back harder on the campaign team, he thought. *We're just wasting our time and money in this state. New Hampshire is going to suck, too. There's no good reason to invest so much in states where we'll look more like a loser for having gone all in.*

Symone Sanders sat at a long table in the restaurant part of the bar, picking at a salad. She agreed with Richmond's point of view, and she was more than ready to get out of Iowa. A few feet away, Donilon sat calmly at the bar, emotionless. It wasn't clear whether his serenity stemmed from confidence that the campaign was going to bounce back or that it was dead. For the moment, the spiking of the *Register* poll had saved Biden some embarrassment, and probably the loss of at least a little bit of his flagging support. Even though numbers had leaked out, the media had focused far more on the oddity of the last major poll being killed than the rank order of the candidates.

Donilon said little as he sat alone at the bar, self-isolating from the main table where campaign aides and Biden friends had gathered. The coming days, he knew, would be brutal. A year earlier, at Biden's house in McLean, the prospect of dropping Iowa and rebounding by South Carolina seemed reasonable. On the ground in Iowa, deep in the muck, it wasn't clear that Biden could survive to South Carolina. On a calendar, weeks went by fast. In a difficult campaign, they were eternities unto themselves. And there were almost four full weeks between Iowa and South Carolina. The numbers in New Hampshire, next up on the primary calendar, were god-awful. The campaign was so cash-strapped that it was spending less on its advertising than its outside allies were. These next weeks would test Biden's resilience and the narrative they had drawn up together. If the former vice president aimed to be the calm force at the center of the country's political storm, he would first have to prove he could do that on his own campaign.

There was no way for Biden to know whether he would come back. Much of the Democratic Party's elite, like his old Senate buddy John Kerry, had already given up on him or was in the process of doing so. Iowa might be his Waterloo. But it could also just be an ugly bump in the road. His fate, he hoped, would rest not in the hands of party leaders or Iowa caucus-goers but in those of primary voters. For much of his life, he had believed in himself when others had not. He had overcome so much to rise to the vice presidency and now national front-runner status in the Democratic primary. As he closed his eyes that night in a suite at the Savery, Biden had reason to be confident in his own agency, even as the world told him he had lost it.

He would just need a little good fortune—or maybe a lot—to survive the next twenty-four hours.

Tucked away in the bedroom of his suite at the Holiday Inn next to the Des Moines airport, Bernie Sanders swiped back and forth on his iPad. He tapped the screen over and over again to refresh the *New York Times* website. It was a little after eight P.M.—an hour after the caucuses had opened in most locations—and the *Times* didn't have results. Sanders didn't like to watch TV, but he had the flat-screen in his room on so that he could follow the action. The cable networks didn't have results, either. Nor did the Iowa Democratic Party.

At the Iowa Events Center, five and a half miles north of the airport hotel, state and national party officials were just learning about a glitch in the app that precinct workers were using to report results. Down the hall from them, in a special boiler room, liaisons from each of the campaigns fidgeted with their own phones and laptops as they waited to hear something—anything—about why they didn't have any information from the party.

Sanders paced between the bedroom and the suite's living room, where members of his family had gathered around on comfortable faux-leather couches and chairs. They were there to celebrate a first-state win. Sanders had come so close to defeating Clinton here in 2016—close enough that he had decided in a room at the same hotel to call it a "virtual tie" at his post-caucus party that night—but had come up a hair short. Winning Iowa this time was key to his strategy for taking the nomination.

His impatience slowly turned to sullenness. He always carried with him the fatalistic sense that the fruits of his labor would turn sour at any minute. Inside the bedroom, he barely said a word. When he did, it was to curse the gods. "This is bullshit," he grumbled to no one in particular. Every few minutes he would ask Faiz Shakir, who was with him in the suite, whether there was anything to report. Shakir felt helpless, pained at the frustration and sinking despair evident in a man who had poured his soul into campaigning for the better part of five years.

"This is a fucking catastrophe," Sanders said. Then he started dialing Jeff Weaver in the nearby campaign headquarters—over and over again. The boiler room there was descending into chaos.

Bernie and his aides had never expected to be so in the dark. They had plowed money into building an internal reporting system that would give them their own results more quickly than the party's system. A month earlier, when Buttigieg's steady rise put him in the lead in polling, Weaver and Rocha had popped into Iowa to do a status check on preparations for the big first contest. In a small room at the Sanders campaign's headquarters, the one that would become the boiler room on caucus night, Bernie's Iowa team described its plan for reporting results. They would use their own designer app. Weaver was unimpressed. He didn't trust that it would work.

"If that's plan A, what's the backup plan?" he asked. There was no plan B. The emergency remedy was a phone tree.

But now plan A was tanking. Something had gone wrong with the campaign's app, and the party's app apparently wasn't working, either.

In the HQ boiler room, Sanders aides yelled at the television, and then started yelling at one another and into thin air. "This is not right," the campaign's pollster, Ben Tulchin, screamed. "What are we going to do?" His anxiety began spreading around the room. Weaver, the burly ex-Marine, took charge.

"Take a walk," he instructed Tulchin. "Get unfrazzled."

Desperate for information, Sanders's team had little choice but to fall back on a plan B. Top advisers scrambled to make Google sheets to send out to precinct captains so they could tally outcomes at their locations and send them back. It was the political equivalent of using a stick to draw up a new play in the dirt with time running out in the fourth quarter of the championship game.

Weaver couldn't concentrate amid the bedlam, and he periodically stepped into the hallway to take calls from Sanders, who was spinning his wheels back at the hotel. At first the calls were hourly. Then Sanders called three or four times an hour. As the night progressed, it began to feel like the boss was on the line every two minutes.

"What do you know?" Sanders would ask anxiously. Weaver didn't know much. After one call, he walked back into the boiler room and stood over the shoulders of number crunchers working on laptops.

"I need fucking something to tell the old man," he barked. "He's not going to quit calling me."

In Bernie Sanders's hotel room, minutes felt like hours. But inside the Iowa Democratic Party's war room, a different kind of time warp took hold. For the apparatchiks of the state and national party, those same minutes felt like seconds.

Top officials from both party organizations huddled together at the Events Center around eight-fifteen P.M. local, when they first confirmed that there was a technical problem with the reporting of results.

To track and calculate results from the many caucuses across the state, the Iowa Democratic Party was using an application developed by Shadow Inc., a relatively new firm in the political arena. The face of the company was Tara McGowan, a well-known digital operative and the wife of Buttigieg senior adviser Michael Halle. The party's use of a mobile-phone app was innovative, but it was also technologically more complex than necessary. The basic idea was for precinct chairs to enter in results from their locations, and they would be compiled by the national party for public reporting. Some of the precinct chairs immediately found that they had difficulty downloading the app and getting it to work.

Under normal circumstances, the atmosphere in the party war room on caucus night would be tense, especially given the narrow margins the campaigns were expecting in a closely fought contest among multiple candidates. But the relationship between the DNC and the Iowa Democratic Party was already sour. In September, the DNC had nixed the state party's plan to hold a series of virtual caucuses after the hacking of a DNC phone call, which had led some Iowa Democrats to believe the national party was trying to undermine the caucus system altogether. The two sides still had to work together, but the reservoir of trust was shallow after the DNC's decision.

"They sort of smile-fucked each other for the next five months," said one person who was in the war room that night.

Shortly after eight P.M., DNC officials had concluded that there was a bigger problem than the inability of some precinct chairs to use the app. DNC computers were not able to read the results that were coming in. Party officials concluded that it was a coding issue on their end, rather than a problem with the app. It would take only forty-five minutes to sort out, the DNC folks told their Iowa counterparts. Around the country, Democrats waited anxiously for numbers to appear on cable networks.

Down the hall from the party war room, representatives from each of the campaigns started to get antsy. For several hours, they had been sequestered together in a square subdivision of a gigantic conference room with five or six tables and half a dozen chairs around each table. But the aides were mostly hugging the walls, trying to use the electrical outlets to charge their phones and computers and occasionally joking with one another nervously as they awaited the seemingly inevitable precinct-by-precinct rollout of results. Between their connections to their own campaigns and the communal TV, they should have been getting a readout by now. But no information was coming in. They called Seth Cohen, the state party's caucus director, but he didn't have any answers to share.

That's because neither the Iowa party nor the DNC could figure out what the hell was going wrong. Within the hour, as the problem persisted, party officials began to examine whether they were dealing with an "export" problem—either a flaw in the app or a hack. For the campaigns, the technical aspect didn't matter as much as the fact that there was no reliable information.

"The app is fucking up," one campaign official said in a text message. "Can't trust the numbers coming in."

Democrats were botching their first presidential election night since their spirit-shattering, whole-world-is-lost defeat of November 2016. There wasn't a Russian hacker in sight.

The vibe in Buttigieg's election-night suite at the Des Moines Marriott couldn't have been more different from that of Bernie Sanders's. Sitting on a couch in the living room, surrounded by family, longtime friends, and a handful of his top aides, Pete took in the cacophony of the caucuses with all the kinetic frenzy of a frozen lake.

There was good reason for him to be less bothered than Sanders by the state party's inability to report results. Like Sanders, Buttigieg's team had also built an internal reporting system to feed results directly to staff so they wouldn't have to rely on the party. Unlike Sanders's system, Buttigieg's worked. They had developed a text-based system by which precinct captains could report results: The captain at each caucus site had a personal identification number and a lanyard with instructions for sending the outcome back to headquarters by tapping a few numbers into a phone. Buttigieg's aides started getting results as soon as caucuses across the state wrapped up, and the digits coming into rows and columns on spreadsheets in the campaign's boiler room at a Des Moines office park looked very good.

In a factory-like suite divided between a big open space for labor—dozens of volunteers working at a pop-up call center—and a suite of offices and cubicles, Buttigieg's top brass set up shop in a conference room. They wired up TVs so they could monitor MSNBC and CNN, and put a set of phones on cheap folding tables that had been pushed together to make one large square in the middle of the room. They used the phones to keep an open line with data analysts in the campaign's South Bend headquarters and their representative in the boiler room down the hall from the Iowa Democratic Party's space at the Events Center.

Earlier in the day, the team had gone over budget numbers and set up a plan for buying advertising in New Hampshire based on real-time fundraising data on caucus night. The expectation was that if Buttigieg had a good night, his coffers would fill up quickly and the new money could be instantly channeled into building his presence in the next state on the calendar.

But the state party app's foul-up created its own set of complications for Buttigieg's team. First, they didn't know for sure how their rivals were doing. They hadn't planned on their precinct captains having to report data for the other campaigns, too. That left an incomplete picture in which they could see Pete was hitting the marks they had projected for statewide victory, but they were unable to tell whether Sanders was outperforming them. More than that, the failure of the party and the news media to report results meant that donors weren't able to see that Pete was crushing it. They had planned on that excitement fueling contributions that could be poured into New Hampshire. They were learning the very lesson they had taught when they killed the CNN/*Des Moines Register* poll: A muddled outcome hurt the winners and helped the losers.

Around nine P.M., Halle left headquarters for the ten-minute drive to the Marriott so he could meet up with Pete and the handful of top aides who were in the election-night suite. On his way, he sent a message to Lis Smith, who was already in the suite, to say that he felt good about their chances of winning.

"I'm not going to say anything until you get here," she replied; that way they could deliver the good news to Pete together.

A series of nearly two thousand battles had taken place inside school gyms, churches, and municipal event centers across Iowa, and they had produced a neck-and-neck race for first place. But few outside of the campaigns knew that. Nor did the public know that Biden was getting absolutely crushed. It was like the broadcast of a World Series Game 7 had gone dark during the pregame show and never come back. What should have been a dramatic night for the party—an electrifying triumph for one candidate and a brutal defeat for the national front-runner—had turned into the equivalent of a rain delay for its voters. Rather than adding excitement, the confusion was draining energy from the caucuses. Only one candidate, Buttigieg, could be confident that he might do well enough to win. Sanders's team thought they were in position to win, based on anecdata—little bits of information they could pick up from caucus sites.

For example, Sanders had withstood a major push by some of the biggest muscle in organized labor to knock him out early. With nearly five hundred caucus-goers packed into the massive Buchanan Auditorium lecture hall at the University of Iowa's Pappajohn Business Building, the unions hoped to blunt the force of Sanders's Medicare for All pitch. The site choice had been a late change because there weren't many rooms big enough to accommodate the turnout of college kids and union workers, and the number actually ended up being about 100 more than the official occupancy of 387 people.

But the rank-and-file workers, gathered among the theater-tiered rows of gray seats with flip-up, school-style arm desks, weren't there to stop Medicare for All at all. Turning out union voters backfired on labor. Sanders got 160 votes in the first round, closely followed by Warren at 150. Buttigieg's team counted 76 heads, and Klobuchar had 71. That left Biden with 37, a little more than half of Klobuchar's total and a little less than twice businessman Andrew Yang's tally of 20. After a second alignment of caucus-goers, Biden was shut out of state delegate equivalents—the key measurement from each site used to tabulate the statewide winners. In a close race, though, Buttigieg and Klobuchar each picked up .405 SDEs to the 1.215 apiece earned by Sanders and Warren.

At the same time, Sanders's team had absolutely dominated the state's four Spanish-language caucus sites, as well as more than half a dozen English-language locations where a majority of caucus-goers were Hispanic. His early push to expand his base into the Latino community was paying off. Results like those at the college and in Latino-heavy caucuses heartened Sanders's team, which was still scrambling to get its precinct leaders to report as much information as possible.

"None of our shit was working," said one Sanders aide who was in the boiler room. "We were flying blind."

Buttigieg's decision to pour millions of dollars into staffing up in Iowa was paying off, too. He was viable—meaning he had enough support to win delegates—in nearly every precinct across the state. His performance in rural areas that Sanders had won in 2016 was particularly outstanding. That meant Buttigieg had local captains everywhere, giving him the fullest picture of the results at a time when most of the other campaigns had to guess.

A thousand miles away, across the street from city hall in the heart of Philadelphia, Biden's war room was ready to surrender.

His national team had gathered on the nineteenth floor of the "Scranton Exchange." That was their nickname for Biden's office space in one tower of Centre Square, a $300 million–plus complex known for the giant *Clothespin* sculpture out front. Like their corporate counterparts, modern campaign organizations like to give unique nicknames to everything in sight, and Biden's was no exception. "Scranton Exchange" nodded to his hometown. The conference room his team huddled in that night, "Champ," was named for one of the former vice president's two German shepherds. As they settled in, chomping on a smorgasbord of Mexican food from District Taco, it wouldn't take long for "Champ" to become an ironic twist on Biden's finish.

The campaign's top officials were split up between Philadelphia and Des Moines, where Ricchetti and Donilon accompanied Biden everywhere in the closing days before the caucuses. Schultz, Bedingfield, and Symone Sanders were also in Iowa. During the final few weeks, Dunn had become a more consistent and obvious presence in the Philly HQ. Having helped undermine Schultz from her perch on the pooh-bah council, she was quietly taking control of the day-to-day operations of the campaign. Schultz began to notice that he was left out of meetings and off of important email chains. "Greg was the first one to feel the change," said one high-ranking Biden adviser.

By a little bit after nine P.M. eastern—eight P.M. in Des Moines—they all knew the flip side of what Buttigieg's operation was seeing in the numbers. While Biden's headquarters team couldn't get much information from TVs tuned to CNN and MSNBC, allies on the ground were reporting back that the candidate was losing supporters between the first round of voting and the realignment for the second round. The team in the state was so poorly organized that they had sent Biden and several of his surrogates to precincts where he failed to meet the key 15 percent threshold. It was particularly annoying to his team that, by happenstance, the cable networks had stationed reporters inside caucus precincts where Biden was likely to do poorly. So, to the extent that there was anything to report, it wasn't good for Biden.

"We had a sense of where it was going," said one aide who was in the "Champ" conference room that night.

Their worst Iowa fears were being realized: Biden was going to lose. And it was going to be ugly. There was a chance he might drop to fifth, behind Amy Klobuchar, in what had been a four-horse race in Iowa and nationally for months. The state had sucked Biden and his team in like a vortex. On a consensus-driven campaign, no one had screamed and yelled to stop putting the candidate and his money into an unwinnable race. If anything, touring Iowa had given Biden false hope. So had Ricchetti and Braun. So while most of the campaign brass was prepared for a shellacking, the ultra-competitive Biden was not.

At nine P.M. central, ten P.M. on the East Coast, Brian Williams re-opened MSNBC's election HQ broadcast from a third-floor studio at 30 Rockefeller Center and kicked the coverage over to Steve Kornacki. Bespectacled and boyish-looking, the forty-year-old political junkie could make a race for county clerk feel like Armageddon. He stood in front of a video board that was supposed to show caucus results. It was empty.

"We expected this thing would be full," Kornacki said, noting that at the same time of night in 2016, two-thirds of the results had been reported, and that in the two election years prior to that, the winners had been declared. Instead of caucus numbers, the Iowa Democratic Party put out talking points. "They say they are doing 'quality control,'" Kornacki reported, "out of 'an abundance of caution.'" And, he added, the state party said "there is no ETA" for results.

Later that hour, with the whole political world watching, the Iowa Democratic Party circulated a dial-in number for the campaigns to jump on a conference call. At 9:51 p.m. in Des Moines, Kevin Geiken, the state party's executive director, announced on the call that there were "inconsistencies" in the numbers coming in and that it would take longer to report the results. The party was confident of two things at that moment, he said: The app didn't go down and there was no corruption of the numbers. Eventually, officials would be able to sort out who had won. When an aide for one campaign asked if Geiken might entertain a question, the line went dead.

"Did they just hang up?" one participant's voice crackled over the phone line.

Indeed, Geiken had hung up. He had read an official statement that would go out to the news media as soon as the call was over, and clicked off.

The problems only metastasized. The state party had a backup plan for the app, which had not been tested before caucus night. The state's plan B was essentially the same as Bernie's: a phone tree. The truth was, that's how Iowa caucus results had been reported within campaigns and to the state party for years. It was simple and it usually had been effective enough. There was just one problem: The number was easily discoverable and Trump supporters began flooding it. "The app is the issue and the hotline is smoked," Joe Galasso, a volunteer in charge of new registrations for Precinct 2 in Waukee, explained as it was happening.

Suddenly, reporting turned into a free-for-all. All over the state, Iowans who had pictures of caucus result cards took photos of them and posted them on social media or sent them to campaigns and the state party. That caused more confusion, not less, as the reports amounted to a patchwork of results that no one could use to quickly determine a winner.

This created a new problem for Biden: Since he was hardly taking any caucuses outright, the reporting of partial results figured to harm him the most. Without a clear winner, everyone might focus on the former vice president, who finished out of the money. With the state getting pressure to release any results, no matter how incomplete, his campaign moved fast to nip that idea in the bud. Dana Remus, one of Biden's lawyers, sent the state party a stiffly worded letter threatening to sue if partial results were reported.

At the White House, and inside Trump's northern Virginia campaign headquarters, it was popcorn time. Nothing could have delighted Donald Trump's team more than watching the chaos at the caucus play out like a disaster film. Trump was pulling through impeachment—the apex of the push to punish him for election interference in 2016 and 2020—and Democrats were screwing up this high-profile contest. Brad Parscale, Trump's tough-talking, barbarian-sized campaign manager—six foot eight and a muscular 250 pounds on a good day—tweeted out a taunt echoing the 2016 Sanders message about the Democratic establishment. "Quality control = rigged?" Parscale wrote, adding a deep-in-thought emoji.

Democrats had been waiting for this moment for 1,182 days, since that dark, brutal night when blue turned red on electoral maps, Barack Obama told Hillary Clinton that she needed to call Donald Trump to concede, and a depthless despair smothered the hope of making history again. Iowa was supposed to be the beginning of the comeback. For on this night, for the first time in more than three years, a Democrat would win a presidential election again. Or maybe not.

When Geiken abruptly hung up the phone, the major campaigns all came to the same instantaneous realization: The race wouldn't be called that night. It set off a mad scramble.

At the Savery, Biden huddled with Donilon, Ricchetti, and Bedingfield sprawled out in a mezzanine conference room, where, with a small legion of family and top aides, he had been watching the caucus nightmare unfold in slow motion on a projection screen. So far, the main event had been a frustrating metaphor for the entire Iowa experience for him: excruciatingly long, deeply disappointing, and impossible to skip. The senior staff kept reading and hearing reports about the technology fail. But even worse, they were now hearing that Biden simply wasn't viable in precincts where they'd assumed he would do well.

"We should just go out there. Let's go out there now!" Richmond told Biden and the team early in the night. "We're not going to know the outcome tonight. This will put us in a position of strength instead of going later," the congressman insisted.

But he was met with some hesitance from Biden and other advisers.

"I don't know," the former vice president said.

Ron Klain echoed Biden's skepticism. Time in the conference room stood still, but it was starting to dawn on them that Biden had somehow gotten lucky once again. The implosion of the caucuses meant there would be no immediate winner, but also no immediate loser. Just as the spiked CNN/*Des Moines Register* poll had concealed Biden's cratering in the polls, the crapped-out app would hide, at least in the short term, how badly he'd had his ass handed to him. That is, so long as none of the results were reported anytime soon.

Two hours later, with the scoreboard still blank and Geiken's abrupt signoff fresh in mind, Bedingfield had caught up with Richmond's urgency. "We need to go and we need to go now," she told her boss. "There's clearly not going to be a resolution tonight. We need to get you out there as fast as we can before others start doing the same." The fog of the caucus could be used as a smoke screen to let Biden address the nation without having been declared a loser. Then he could "turn the page" on Iowa, she said, and jump on a plane to New Hampshire.

Turn the page, Biden thought. *Good idea.* He agreed to the plan. But he didn't have quite the same urgency his staff did. One of his grandchildren wasn't ready to go, and that meant he wasn't ready to go. It was just a six-minute drive to his reception at Drake University, but there was no time to waste. Schultz, who was already at Drake, pressed the aides with Biden to put the family in separate cars. The grandkid didn't have to be on the air. When he was finally ready to go, Biden and his team jogged down the hallway to the stairs. As she moved, Bedingfield dialed Bill Russo, a deputy who was at the campaign's post-caucus reception.

"We are rushing to Drake right now," she said.

"Right now?" asked Russo, who would have to alert the media.

"Right now!" she said.

By then, Amy Klobuchar had arrived at her own election-night party at the Marriott. She'd talked to her campaign manager, Justin Buoen, after the party's conference call and immediately determined to be the first on air.

"I'm not going to wait," she said.

This is a scrappy way to get out there with my message, she thought, as her competitive edge flared. She didn't have the money to pay for big advertising campaigns, and going first would create a dual benefit. It wouldn't just guarantee she would get more eyeballs—and hopefully more donations—before viewers on the

East Coast turned in for the night. It would also allow her to claim some sort of victory and move on to New Hampshire. On a typical caucus night, Iowa would separate the wheat from the chaff, and political insiders frequently referred to the number of "tickets punched" to describe the set of candidates who were still viable after the contest. Klobuchar wanted to be sure that the number was at least five.

In other words, the shit show was good for her, too.

"We are punching above our weight," she said to supporters gathered at her watch-night party and a national television audience at 10:17 P.M. local time. "Somehow, some way, I'm going to get on a plane to New Hampshire, and we are bringing this ticket to New Hampshire."

Punch. Ticket. New Hampshire. The debacle had turned fifth-place Klobuchar into a pundit declaring that her campaign was alive and kicking, and there were no numbers to refute the audacious assertion. The Iowa caucuses had one job—to winnow the field—and it had failed.

Biden popped in front of a camera just after Klobuchar, saying, "We feel good about where we are." It was true only in the sense that he was in Iowa and his embarrassing defeat had not been revealed. From that perspective, he was a winner, too.

For Biden, the knowledge that he was going to finish fourth was crushing. There was a question of whether he would even clear the 15 percent threshold to take at least one delegate. At his Philadelphia headquarters, staffers wore the glum expressions of a losing team as they cleared the "Champ" war room of empty taco plates and beer. Cristóbal Alex sensed an opportunity to make a point about what had just happened—or not happened—out in Iowa.

"Everyone grab a drink," he said. "Let's toast to getting the fuck out of there." They lifted beers in the air and drank to the silver lining.

"This was a gift," one Biden aide later said of the caucus failure.

At the Holiday Inn, Sanders had given up on his iPad and the annoyingly uninformed punditry taking place on television amid the absence of an outcome. With aides and family members in the living room of his suite, he lay down in his bed and went to sleep.

He woke up from his nap to a debate over what he should say. It had been raging at his campaign headquarters. Most of the team wanted him to declare victory quickly. Weaver got on the phone with Sanders.

It would be close between him and Buttigieg in terms of the count of state delegate equivalents, but Sanders's aides were pretty certain that he would win the popular vote for the first and second rounds. All the candidates were making speeches. Bernie needed to say something, and the near-consensus of his team was that it should be to claim a win.

"You go out," Weaver told Sanders.

"We gotta be sure, we gotta be one hundred percent sure," Sanders said. "I don't want to go out there and say I won if I didn't win."

After his "virtual tie" pronouncement in 2016, he didn't want to be embarrassed this time around by a false declaration.

"No problem," Weaver told his boss. But it was important for Sanders to say something—anything—now that several other candidates had taken to the airwaves. It frustrated Weaver that there were three metrics for winning: first alignment, second alignment, and the delegate count. The media cared only about the delegate count, and that diminished the value of actually winning the most votes.

When Sanders hung up, he informed the team that there would be no victory speech without better information. "There wasn't enough data to know that you were going to be the winner," said one aide involved in the discussion who argued that Sanders should be bold about it anyway.

"If you win, you want to go out there as early as possible because then you capture the news cycle," said another senior Sanders aide. "You don't want to do it at two in the morning if you can avoid it, when everybody's asleep. But you also don't want to do it if you're not going to win."

The aides put together a brief speech for Sanders to deliver to the supporters at his "victory" party. "I have a good feeling we're going to be doing very, very well here in Iowa," he said in the Holiday Inn ballroom at 10:44 P.M. central time. Then he went back to bed. The next morning he would board a somber flight to New Hampshire. Buttigieg was on the rise there, too.

"We're heading into a state that's going to be a slugfest that we thought we were going to win pretty easily three weeks ago," said one of Sanders's aides. "Now it's going to be a dogfight."

Buttigieg was on the brink of winning the caucuses, and of becoming the first openly gay candidate ever to win a presidential primary contest, and yet his emotions were mixed as his aides argued over whether he should declare himself the winner. The victor in Iowa usually went on to take the party's nomination. He still had a long, uphill battle for that, but this didn't feel triumphant. He had been prepared to win or lose, not to sit in limbo.

Around him, there was a flurry of activity. Schmuhl, Smith, and the others pored over a draft of Buttigieg's remarks in the suite's bedroom while the candidate kept his post on the couch next to his husband, Chasten. When Klobuchar started speaking, Smith's and Schmuhl's phones began buzzing with texts from friends, fellow campaign aides, and political advisers pushing them to have Pete go out and call himself the winner.

Pete knew he had to say something sooner rather than later.

What we've done here—coming from nowhere to the pinnacle— is an extraordinary achievement, and it's historic, he thought. *It would be costly to let this linger and not say how I feel about that.*

Pete's internal debate was playing out at the same time among his top aides in the bedroom. They believed that if and when all the results were tabulated, he would eke out a narrow victory over Sanders. But if he said that, and it turned out to be wrong, he would never live it down.

Adman Larry Grisolano came up with an approach that split the baby. Just use the word "victorious," he said. It was a distinction without much of a difference—a sheer fig leaf—that would allow the candidate to say he was a winner without saying he won.

Buttigieg still wasn't sold on calling himself "victorious" when he jumped into an SUV to ride to his watch party at Drake. From trailing cars, Buttigieg's aides hopped on the phone with him.

Over time, his senior aides had developed a collegial manner for sorting out disagreements that reflected Buttigieg's bloodless approach to the world. Once a decision was made, they were all on board. As he listened, they urged him to say he had won.

"Yep," Pete said finally. "This is the way to go."

For the candidates, the shambolic caucus had come to a close. But as most of them sped to the airport to board planes, there was still work left to be done by their campaigns in sticking knives deep into a party that had failed so abjectly on such an important night.

On a second conference call, around one a.m. local, Weaver went off on party leaders. "This is bullshit," he fumed, channeling Bernie, after Iowa Democratic Party chairman Troy Price announced once and for all that there would be no outcome announced. The night had thrown into question "one hundred years" of Iowa caucuses, Weaver shouted.

Michael Halle, the Buttigieg adviser, pushed the party to report whatever numbers it could. Because Pete's team had captains in nearly all of the precincts, Halle knew that any data put out by the party would show that Pete was either leading or in close contention to win. It was never clear to the others on the line whether he knew what information his wife's app had actually reported to the national and state parties.

"Surely you guys have partial results," Halle said. "Please release some results."

That was a nonstarter for Price. We're not going to just pump out numbers until we make sure we have paper copies of the results to match what we have electronically, he explained.

"Do you have the paper copies?" asked Biden lawyer Dana Remus. "Do you have the preference cards? Are you counting the preference cards?" She was trying to get party officials to concede they didn't have any physical proof of who each caucus-goer had aligned with. The sophisticated operatives on the call knew that there was no way the actual cards would be submitted from caucus locations that night.

"Yes," Price said. "We're going to have preference cards matching results."

"So you're going to be able to guarantee that every caucus-goer matches a signed preference card?" Remus pressed.

"Yes," Price said.

No one believed him. Remus had made her point, and it was clear, given the letter she'd sent threatening legal action, that the Iowa Democratic Party was in no position to begin putting out partial results yet.

"It was very evident what they were up to," one person affiliated with the state party said of Biden's team. "They were having a bad night. They wanted to drive home this story of the problems with the results because they knew it was going to take away from him coming in fourth or fifth place."

Biden had come off the stage at Drake to thank a handful of Iowa allies before boarding a flight to New Hampshire. The toothy smile he'd just flashed for the television audience had disappeared. He closed his eyes and pursed his lips. Iowa had screwed him over yet again. He was more than ready to leave. He was done with the state. Schultz tried to lift his spirits.

"You gave the speech you needed to give, and it's on to the next one," the young campaign manager offered.

Biden, furious but constrained by the presence of others who might repeat anything he said, hung his head and shook it slowly from side to side.

CHAPTER 8

Circular Firing Squads

B IDEN REPLACED SCHULTZ RIGHT AFTER THE IOWA CAUCUSES without telling him.

Months in the making, the proximate cause was the Iowa failure. Schultz was the fall guy.

Biden had told Schultz before the caucuses he wanted to make some changes—but not that he planned to switch campaign managers.

"I want Anita to help more," the candidate said.

"Great," Schultz replied. "That's what I've been asking for."

He didn't fully realize that he was the target of a soft coup. In fact, he'd welcomed Anita Dunn's more consistent presence at the campaign's Philadelphia headquarters in late January. He spent as much of his time wrangling the pooh-bahs as he did on anything else, and he needed assistance with administrative tasks. Dunn had built a juggernaut of a public relations business in Washington, and Schultz knew she would be able to take on some of the day-to-day management duties that had been overwhelming him.

A few days after the caucuses, with Biden campaigning in New Hampshire, Schultz and Ricchetti sent an email to colleagues announcing that Dunn would be "working closely with us on campaign strategy and overall coordination on budget and personnel." It wasn't until *The New York Times* reported on the message, on February 7, that Schultz could see what was really happening. The story quoted anonymous sources saying that Dunn would have final say-so over the budget, not an advisory role. As she and Schultz both knew, that meant she was running the campaign.

Ever since the Liberty and Justice dinner debacle in November, Dunn had assumed more of a role in executing decisions, particularly when it came to money. The situation needed urgent management. Before the Iowa caucuses, the senior team had gathered in the "Champ" conference room at their campaign headquarters in Philadelphia for a budget presentation. "And that's where we find out we're poor," one senior Biden aide said.

"Why don't we have any money?" one top aide asked. The members of the budget team said they were bleeding cash on events, with each campaign stop costing $15,000. The campaign was also burning through money on advertising, a large staff, and merchandise. "We had the production level of a general election campaign but our budget did not match what our production was," said one aide. The campaign's leadership was stunned.

As a result, Dunn took the reins, overseeing the campaign's check writing and holding near-daily meetings on where the campaign was spending money. The financial situation was so dire that, as one aide put it, "It was, 'Can we approve Friday on Tuesday?' "

There was a consensus in both Biden's inner circle and outside it that Schultz was overwhelmed in the job. It had taken three months to convince the candidate. Whatever Schultz's managerial faults, he was also loyal to a fault. Now, not only was Biden demonstrating that the loyalty was a one-way street, he wasn't even showing common courtesy. He had been pressured for months to make a switch at the top and resisted. Then he just discarded Schultz like a frozen-dinner package—in the pages of the *Times*, no less. For Biden, the story amounted to an opportunity to signal to anxious voters that his campaign would improve. That was mostly necessary because Biden hadn't inspired Iowans or grassroots contributors. For Schultz, it was humiliating and grounding. Now, at least, he knew how little Biden valued him.

Schultz was well liked, and the way Biden treated him, in contrast to the compassionate profile the campaign was building, did not sit well with Schultz's friends.

"It didn't surprise me that they wanted to bring in someone with more broad-based experience than Greg," said one Biden donor, who was still surprised by Schultz's discourteous demotion.

"They handled it very poorly. Sometimes people don't handle situations like diplomats. How do you take someone who just worked with you for the past eight years and throw them under a bus like he was thrown under the bus?" In a particularly brutal twist, it was now up to Schultz to call and visit top Biden allies—as well as fence-sitters still deciding whether to come aboard—to reassure them and ask for money. Worse still, he had to sit next to his replacement at the Philadelphia headquarters. And Dunn was given the authority that Biden had never granted to Schultz. She didn't have to ask the other pooh-bahs for permission before she made a decision.

"Anita was empowered by the boss," said one aide who was close to Biden.

The change could be felt immediately. Dunn pulled Elizabeth Alexander, a longtime Biden aide, into one of the small offices adjacent to the big open bullpen of desks where all of the HQ staffers worked.

"We have no money for paid ads," Dunn said. "We need as much free media as we can get, and I need you to go on the road with the vice president to get it." Dunn said the campaign was looking at the equivalent of two Senate races in Nevada and South Carolina. "We have to put everything we have into those two states and not think about anything else," she said. "We can't worry about Super Tuesday." Bedingfield was given the same set of instructions, as was Symone Sanders, who packed up for South Carolina.

But Dunn was worried about losing supporters to someone who would be on the ballot on Super Tuesday: Mike Bloomberg. So was everyone else on the campaign. That's part of the reason Schultz was forced to beg for campaign money right after Biden had shoved him aside.

"Bloomberg's Super Tuesday strategy was basically to go after our voters," said one top Biden adviser. "We had a huge amount of concern." And it wasn't just the voters Bloomberg was after. It was some of the same political heavyweights that Schultz was calling on. They were in a hot war over the allegiance of influential Democrats.

A little more than three months earlier, on November 7, 2019, Mike Bloomberg had woken up before sunrise and headed into his office at Bloomberg LP. He was at his desk at Fifty-ninth Street and Lexington Avenue, the epicenter of his namesake business empire, by six-thirty a.m. But he waited until a more decent time—seven a.m.—to call Kevin Sheekey, his right-hand man for many years, to deliver a priority message. He decided he would run for president after all.

It wasn't exactly welcome news. Sheekey had advised him not to do it. So had Patti Harris, the CEO of Bloomberg Philanthropies, and Howard Wolfson, a veteran political operative. Sheekey, Harris, and Wolfson were all former deputy mayors of New York, and each had a strong enough sense of politics to see serious downsides for Bloomberg in running. The most important downside was that he would lose.

Bloomberg liked a good argument, but he liked being the person to make the decision even better. And, he told Sheekey, he had done just that.

I'm going to take a swing, Bloomberg thought, *and if it doesn't work out, no problem*. He didn't see any of the Democratic candidates as a world beater, and he relished the idea of going head-to-head with Trump.

In some ways, the two men—one a bona fide magnate and one who lost enough money on paper that he didn't usually pay any individual income tax—were polar opposites. Bloomberg grew up in a working-class family but was refined enough that his new money—a $10 million severance check for his work at a Wall Street firm turned into tens of billions of dollars from the company he built—felt like old money. Trump was a rich kid who bore his father's chip on his shoulder and failed to fit in with Manhattan's high society. Where Trump was bombastic and ideologically flexible, Bloomberg was moderate enough in tone and temperament to maintain a centrist profile despite a deeply liberal streak on gun control, climate change, and public health administration.

But there were also similarities between them, mostly in the area essential to any successful entrepreneur or presidential candidate: ego. Like Trump, Bloomberg often played the long side of odds and profited for it. They both understood there was almost always a gap between the consensus of conventional wisdom around a decision and the optimal choice. Whatever failures he had endured, Bloomberg had been successful in his biggest gambles, just like Trump.

To have a shot at the Democratic nomination, the centrist Bloomberg would need Biden to fail—and he intended to help that process along. He announced early that he wouldn't even compete in a primary until March, a sign that he believed the field would still be wide open after the first four contests. While Biden scrounged for cash in the cushions of the Democratic fundraising apparatus, Bloomberg launched a sophisticated modern political operation out of his philanthropic headquarters on the Upper East Side of Manhattan, where rows of barely-old-enough-to-vote analysts pored over data about the American electorate. The nerd farm eventually moved into the campaign's Midtown offices, but not before it had been effectively used as a backdrop to convince the elite operatives Mike was trying to recruit that he would invest heavily in the most data-driven outfit the Democratic Party had ever seen.

In January, he began working hard to cannibalize Biden's support. Late that month, he met with the House's New Democrat Coalition, a group of lawmakers with strong ties to the financial services industry, and leaders of the centrist Blue Dog Coalition. Bloomberg dialed up Democratic officials in big cities and sent top aides to meetings like one in Detroit in which his advisers met with leaders of the Black community to try to assuage concerns about his record on stop-and-frisk policing in New York. Bloomberg recognized the error of his ways, the aides told an audience of Black entertainment, business, and political luminaries at actor Hill Harper's house. Members of his team showed up in state capitols and at fundraising events for state legislators. The effect of all this activity was to remind elected officials, donors, and other high-profile validators that Bloomberg loomed over Biden's shoulder.

On Friday, February 7, 2020, four days before the New Hampshire primary, about thirty members of the House cast their last votes of the day and walked over to a Capitol Hill townhouse owned by Oracle for a secret meeting with Bloomberg's political team. The lawmakers, lured by the promise of lunch before their flights home, climbed up a spiral staircase to a big, open event space with hardwood floors and enough windows for bright sunlight to fill the room. There, they found Mike's advisers had hooked up computers to TV screens ready to deliver a strategy presentation.

Most of these lawmakers were ready to jump ship to Bloomberg if Biden tanked. "Everybody was worried that Biden wasn't going to get the nomination," said one person who was in the room. "It's not that we didn't like Biden, it's just that he didn't have any momentum."

The deeper fear was that Sanders would win the nomination. That was a worst-case scenario for centrist Democrats. It meant that either Sanders would lose the general election and take down-ballot Democrats with him—they predicted Trump would effectively hammer them all as extremists—or win and take over the party as well as the White House. These moderate Democratic officials, many of them very friendly to business, were as critical of socialism as any Republican. Bloomberg offered a well-funded alternative with a cutting-edge campaign operation. His aides met with the lawmakers just hours after the *Times* reported on Schultz's ouster. Anyone could see in public polling that Bloomberg was gaining traction at Biden's expense.

But there was one way in which Bloomberg inadvertently helped Biden. Because the former New York mayor had already created a shadow national campaign, his lurking presence froze the field. No one, not even a former nominee like John Kerry or Hillary Clinton, could put together the money, the bodies, or the paperwork for a competitive campaign in less than three weeks—particularly since many state candidacy-filing deadlines had passed. But Bloomberg wouldn't be on the ballot in New Hampshire, Nevada, or South Carolina. So, it was too early for him to take actual votes from Biden in those states and too late for anyone else to jump in. Bloomberg could try to deprive Biden of campaign money, elite endorsements, and airtime, but he couldn't win a state until at least March 3. The fact that influential Democrats were even considering a former Republican mayor as their last best hope was an indication of just how desperate they were to stop Sanders. So was their willingness to overlook Bloomberg's weaknesses as a candidate to concentrate on the potential strengths of his budding campaign operation.

Lawmakers who had met with Bloomberg personally in his visits to the New Democrat and Blue Dog caucuses had generally come away unimpressed by his pitch. He was as dry as vegan jerky, with none of the natural political skills prized by his audience of elected officials. But as his aides laid out the plans for his campaign at the Capitol Hill row house on February 7, some of the participants were awestruck by the sophistication.

Bloomberg's aides revealed their road map—a shock-and-awe campaign that would use Bloomberg's personal money, as much as $2 billion of it, and ultramodern data applications to identify voters, talk to them about the issues they cared about, and deliver them to the polls. One image showed a heat map of the United States highlighting which parts of the country cared the most about which issues. Florida Democrats, for example, were most energized by climate change. Another part of the pitch involved demonstrating that Bloomberg didn't have to win that many states to beat Bernie for the nomination. He could do well enough in enough congressional districts, along with statewide victories and some losses, to rack up delegates for the convention.

His approach to the primary was the polar opposite of Biden's. The former VP didn't have enough money to run a comprehensive polling operation. He repeated the basic tenets of his campaign— battle for the soul of the nation, character, and competence— wherever he went with little intentional variation. Biden could pander in the moment, just like any politician, but the core of his message was consistent and genuinely guided by his belief system. Conversely, Bloomberg would deliver different messages to various parts of the electorate based on the data his team had compiled on them.

"He was unimpressive to a lot of the members, but his operation was impressive," said a person who attended the Bloomberg team's briefing. "Data, resources, top talent in the Democratic Party was impressive. We thought that he was the only way to wrestle the nomination away from Bernie." Mainstream Democrats worried that, without a strong centrist, Sanders might cruise into the nomination. They needed someone who could at least stop him from walking into the convention with a majority of the delegates.

"The Democratic Party felt that we have to have a backstop that can definitely help force a contested convention," said one Biden loyalist who was committed to stopping Sanders and had not yet given up on Biden. For others, Bloomberg was simply the answer to Bernie, and Biden was not.

No one in the room had any illusions about the unvocalized request: Mike wanted these members to be ready to give him their support in case anything should happen to that nice Biden fellow.

Bloomberg had the money that Biden didn't and much more.

He was also rebranding himself, sometimes comically, with a set of memes designed to position him as more trendy. He tangled with Trump on Twitter. And he hired battalions of aides in key states across the country, equipping them with virtually unlimited budgets and technological support, from iPhones to advanced analytics. He paid them at rates of as much as $300,000 per year, underwrote moving expenses, and rented furnished corporate apartments for some of them. On the road, his aides and emissaries stayed at the finest hotels with unlimited incidentals—one person to a room—as they organized meetings to court the political elite in a network of cities where Bloomberg Philanthropies had long subsidized various programs. Bloomberg was going to money-whip the Democratic Party, and every detail of his operation down to the whims of the most junior aides screamed that the ATM was fully stocked.

If Biden's credit card was of the high-risk, high-interest-rate variety, Bloomberg's was the invite-only American Express Centurion. Alongside the cash, the former New York mayor's cachet enticed the children of well-to-do New York families to work for him, and brought the class of Democratic political heavyweights leery of any leftward movement to back him. It would also take a lot of money for Bloomberg to burnish his brand for the left. While he had made his fortune by building a business that served the financial markets, few voters would make a distinction between that and being a Wall Street investing tycoon. He had won the mayoralty of New York as a Republican after the 2001 election. He backed George W. Bush in 2004, and his counterterrorism and law enforcement policies bore far stronger resemblance to a GOP worldview than a Democratic one.

As Bloomberg bought up television airtime—he doubled his spending in the days after the Iowa caucuses—his poll numbers shot up. Bloomberg appealed to many of the same sets of voters that formed Biden's core support, including Black voters and moderate whites. On the day of the Iowa caucuses, he was in fourth place at 9 percent in the average of national polls, a mite above Buttigieg and still trailing first-place Biden at 28 percent, second-place Sanders at 23 percent, and Warren, who was just under 15 percent. By the eve of the New Hampshire primary a week later, Biden had slipped behind Sanders—only the second time he had trailed anyone in the national polling average—at 23 percent to 21 percent. Bloomberg jumped into a virtual tie with Warren at 14 percent, and Buttigieg spiked up to 10 percent. No one needed advanced algorithms to figure out that Biden voters were beginning to flee to Bloomberg.

Buttigieg landed in New Hampshire early on the morning of February 4 needing a win. He thought he'd gotten it in Iowa, but the state party there would take days to resolve the matter. He was certain that the debacle had cost him contributions he needed to replenish his coffers, and that made New Hampshire do-or-die. Both Buttigieg and Klobuchar saw Biden as a wounded frontrunner, and, for both, that opened up an opportunity to become the establishment-centrist favorite. Yes, Bloomberg was lurking in the background, but there would be three more contests for these two to make their mark before he got in.

Still, Buttigieg was stuck in a tightening vise. With Biden's strong support among Black voters—who had shown no inclination to vote for either the former South Bend mayor or the Minnesota senator—there just weren't enough white votes in other states to give either of them a chance if Biden remained a choice. But applying force to hasten Biden's departure could get hairy. Buttigieg had to figure out a way to help himself without harming his future in the Democratic Party. He couldn't afford to alienate Biden supporters, who he would need to court in order to win the nomination, and any direct assault on the former vice president would tick them off and probably hurt Buttigieg in the long run, too.

Though Pete's national polling numbers started to creep upward, his team was startled by his inability to get a bounce from the national media. Part of that was the brackish result in the caucuses. But Bloomberg was responsible for the rest. Suddenly, his name—praised and cursed—was on the lips of every commentator on television and in the online headlines of every major news outlet. Buttigieg's aides bought as much airtime as they could find available in New Hampshire, which was basically what was left on premium channels. But they were finding that, much as Buttigieg had benefited from a free ride of national media attention for most of his campaign, Bloomberg's status as the flavor of the week was worth more than all his money could buy.

The New Hampshire debate, held four days after the Iowa caucuses, would be Buttigieg's best opening to adjust the trajectory of the race and bring himself the attention he needed to introduce himself to the rest of the country. Senior adviser Michael Halle, who acted as a de facto campaign manager, closely monitored data that showed Buttigieg's fundraising and poll numbers spiked when he drove conflict, which led him and Buttigieg to argue for more combat on the debate stage. But they were more or less overruled by the rest of the team. They arrived at a consensus that it wasn't worth the risk of damaging his carefully built brand. Instead, if Buttigieg could show Democratic voters that he was ready for the presidency, it might be obvious that he was a better choice than the septuagenarian set.

That was his focus as he jammed abbreviated prep sessions into a whirlwind schedule packed with rallies and media appearances. He readied himself to parry attacks from his rivals, as he always did, but he didn't load up with ammunition to direct their way. Being able to rise above the fray was an intrinsic part of looking presidential. He would simply refuse to get in the muck with anyone. He focused primarily on his own performance, and he tried to recharge his internal batteries as best he could.

That's why he didn't give much thought to Amy Klobuchar. But she was thinking a lot about him.

It annoyed her that the former mayor of South Bend was instantaneously treated by the media and influential Democrats as a more serious candidate for the presidency than a third-term senator from a state Trump had nearly won in 2016. In an earlier debate, she had said he had every right to be on the debate stage but that a woman with his résumé would have been laughed off it. More important, and less personal, she had the same objectives as Buttigieg. She needed to make a splash to keep her campaign funded, she couldn't win unless Biden faltered, and she had no intention of taking shots at the former vice president.

She could go after Sanders and Warren all day long, but it wouldn't differentiate her much from Biden or Buttigieg, who were both ahead of her in the polls and appealed to some of the same voters who thought it would take a moderate to flip Trump states

into the Democratic column. Buttigieg was the obvious target. And
it wasn't hard to go after him because, as one Klobuchar aide put
it, "there wasn't a personal relationship" between them.

As she made her way to the debate stage at Saint Anselm College in Goffstown, just west of Manchester, Klobuchar was concerned with two things: delivering her own message and nailing
Buttigieg to the wall.

Buttigieg suspected Klobuchar might come after him. She'd
done it before. But he didn't recognize the haymaker she threw
until the back of his head landed with a thud on the canvas. He'd
humorously said in Iowa that he'd prefer to watch cartoons than
the impeachment trial in the Senate, carefully adding that it was
actually serious business. Klobuchar just grabbed on to the first
part. She wound up for the swing with a preamble about the "courage" shown by Alabama Democrat Doug Jones and Utah Republican Mitt Romney in voting to remove Trump from office despite
the potential political ramifications in their home states. The point
was a personal one, that it took little courage for Buttigieg to beat
up on people who were actually making tough decisions. She
looked right at him from across the debate stage. Buttigieg raised
his hand to reply. Then, Klobuchar unleashed the political kill
shot.

"I think this going after every single thing that people do, because it's popular to say and makes you look like a cool newcomer—I just don't think that's what people want right now," she
said. "We have a newcomer in the White House, and look where it
got us."

Buttigieg wasn't shocked by the angle of her attack, but he was
knocked back by its force. His game plan was to stay above the fray,
not to get into a sparring match with anyone—especially not someone like Klobuchar, who was below him in the polls. He tried to get
his bearings. *Just keep your cool and focus on getting your points
across through the rest of the debate,* he thought. No one really
paid much attention to the rest of the debate.

There are a lot of measurements of how a debate moment
scored, from the crush of questions in the media spin room afterward to the online donations that pile up. For Klobuchar, there was
one that stuck out in particular. As she bounced into the passenger
seat of her state director's SUV, she was fixated on Twitter. Giddily,

she interrupted the conversation her two top aides were having in the backseat.

"You guys," she exclaimed. "I got fifteen thousand new friends during the debate!"

"They're not your 'friends,'" her campaign manager, Justin Buoen, shot back.

More important, Klobuchar was gaining support among New Hampshire voters. At just the moment Buttigieg had determined he needed to appear presidential, she'd made him look small. As had been the case for the past year, most of the candidates had been competing to be the just-right alternative to overheated Sanders and too-cold Biden. The Goldilocks revolver had spun through Beto O'Rourke, Kamala Harris, Warren, and Buttigieg. Now, it was Klobuchar's turn in the chamber.

Her rise was most concerning to Buttigieg. For the last few weeks before the Iowa caucuses, his aides had watched her numbers creeping up. "People who were going to Klobuchar in Iowa were coming directly from us," one of his top advisers said. There was every reason to believe a bounce for her in New Hampshire would come at his expense. Klobuchar wasn't the only candidate who had Mayor Pete teed up.

The morning after the debate, Sanders roused Faiz Shakir for breakfast. It was unusually early for Bernie, before eight A.M.

"What's on your mind?" Bernie asked.

Shakir knew what his boss wanted to hear. The night before they had talked about Buttigieg moving up in the polls after Iowa, and Sanders relished going after Mayor Pete more than any of the other candidates. Like Klobuchar, he had relationships with the other top contenders. But he didn't really know Buttigieg. More important, he didn't really respect him. Like many of the candidates and their aides, he thought Buttigieg didn't have any deeply held convictions. And most important, he could draw a contrast with Buttigieg that would resonate with the working-class voters he was trying to reach.

Shakir went over the well-trod ground with his candidate about the threat a Buttigieg bump posed to their plans to win New Hampshire.

"What are we going to do about that?" Bernie asked.

Go after Pete, Shakir answered, and now.

They hammered out a few ideas. Sanders was set to make an appearance later in the morning at New Hampshire's renowned Politics and Eggs series of breakfast talks with candidates. Together, they decided how he could use the venue to make news.

With reporters packing the room, Sanders read off a list of headlines about Pete's ties to billionaire donors.

"I like Pete Buttigieg, nice guy," he hedged. "But we are in a moment where billionaires control not only our economy but our political life." It was a hit on Buttigieg—and on the lurking Bloomberg—and it launched a concentrated effort to depress Pete's support by portraying him as a candidate of elites.

The Iowa caucuses had robbed Sanders of momentum in New Hampshire. While Buttigieg seized some of that, the clouded result—in the middle of the week the Iowa state party finally declared him the winner by a nose—tempered his rise and his fundraising. After her debate performance, Klobuchar found the cold New Hampshire wind suddenly at her back. And anyone or anything that weighed down Buttigieg, Sanders, or both was a godsend for Biden.

The lights went out on Biden's campaign—literally—two days before the primary. Exhausted from a grueling staccato of campaign events in Iowa and New Hampshire over the previous several weeks, Biden was in the midst of another awful day on the trail. In the morning, he had made headlines by calling a young woman at a town hall event on the Seacoast a "lying dog-faced pony soldier." It wasn't the first time he'd insulted a member of the public or reached for a phrase that made him sound even older than his age, and many Democrats believed he was struggling, in part because he seemed agitated and out of touch.

As Biden boarded his campaign's "Soul of the Nation" tour bus, outfitted with a kitchenette, an office, and bunk beds, he was looking forward to some downtime that night. But on the short ride to the Nashua Radisson, his aides got word that the power was out at the hotel.

Suddenly, Biden had a very real feel for the difference between being vice president and the fourth-place finisher in the Iowa caucuses. The luxury of the campaign bus didn't compare to Air Force Two, and the Nashua Radisson, notable for the twin towers of its medieval castle facade, wasn't exactly the Ritz. What happened next was a one-two punch of apt motor coach clichés. First, the wheels came off the bus—or, at least, Biden's aides directed the driver to pull off to the side of the road. Then, Anthony Bernal, the top aide to Jill Biden, threw deputy campaign manager Pete Kavanaugh under the bus.

"I told Pete that was a shit hotel," Bernal complained loudly enough to be heard throughout the bus. The idea that Kavanaugh could have predicted an electrical problem was absurd, and in any case he wasn't the only person who signed off on decisions about where the vice president and his team would stay on a given night. The Biden team, never totally cohesive, was now in cannibal mode.

Rather than rolling with the punches, Bernal was using the moment to twist the knife in Kavanaugh's back. Kavanaugh hadn't been demoted like his ally Schultz, but he was wounded. To some, it looked like Bernal was trying to score points with the Bidens at the expense of the weakened Kavanaugh. Maybe it would only take one more push to drive him out of a position of influence.

We should be righting the ship instead of fighting one another to get closer to the Bidens, thought one aide who watched Bernal launch the diatribe behind Kavanaugh's back. Bernal, Ricchetti, and Dunn had spent several days piling on Schultz and Kavanaugh, according to the aide. "It was the whole week, and constantly looking for ways to do it, including ones that were nonsensical like the fucking lights going out at the hotel."

With no immediate plan to move the candidate and the campaign's leadership to a new hotel, the bus sat by the side of the road as tempers flared inside. The press began to report that the bus had broken down and uploaded pictures to social media sites. Despite the bus not having any mechanical failure, the images of it served as a fitting metaphor for the campaign. It was February 9, less than thirty-six hours before the first votes would be cast in Dixville Notch, and Biden was stuck on the side of the road.

This wasn't even the end of what had been a savage stretch of sorrow. Biden was almost out of money. He hadn't just lost Iowa; he'd been humiliated. And now New Hampshire was shaping up to be just as bad, if not worse. Cedric Richmond, the campaign co-chair, had been in his ear about shaking up the strategy and the staff. So had Ricchetti and Dunn.

The campaign had a candidate problem, and no one dared to tell Biden that. The whiteness of Iowa was not the reason he couldn't raise money from donors across the country, nor was a lack of imagination in online appeals for cash. High- and low-dollar Democratic givers weren't impressed with Biden's performance. In Iowa, he had traveled extensively, and caucus-goers just weren't buying what they were seeing. When Biden and his senior aides realized in late 2019 that he wasn't getting much bang for the buck in the caucuses, the answer had been to throw good money after bad. Just getting the trimmings right for Biden—a luxury bus, choice venues, and broadcast-quality stages—had cost a small fortune. Moreover, Biden hadn't grown any fonder of dialing for dollars. He was the reason the campaign didn't have any money.

It was easy to put all of the blame for an organizational failure at Schultz's feet, or even lay it on Kavanaugh and the state teams. Surely, they had come up short, and few in the organization questioned the conclusion that Schultz's strengths weren't matched to the job. But the key decisions were born of consensus. The campaign manager didn't have autonomy. Biden had been lousy in debates and lackluster on the trail—where he was increasingly given to shouting at voters who criticized him. Those moments were raw and authentic, but they also displayed an inability or unwillingness to be gracious in the face of what he saw as disingenuous attacks. Many Democratic voters worried about how he might handle a tirade from Trump if he couldn't manage to get through a town hall meeting without insulting a voter, or beat lesser-known candidates in debates. Biden's entire brain trust knew that New Hampshire was going to be brutal. More money and more face time had not helped Biden in Iowa; there was no reason to think they would in New Hampshire.

Around the same time, Schultz and Kavanaugh started exchanging ideas on a wake-up call about the campaign's viability. Rather than committing the real message to paper in memo form, which could have leaked and further damaged Biden, Kavanaugh put options for slashing costs into a slide deck on the campaign's budget. Biden's senior advisers claimed to be surprised in January when regular budget meetings revealed that the operation was strapped for cash. Of course, reading the newspaper, or clicking onto the Federal Election Commission website, would have told them that. But the picture grew darker with each successive budget meeting. It was Kavanaugh's slide deck, which included options for keeping the campaign afloat as its treasury dwindled, that presented a reality check.

The worst morning was February 4, according to Biden aides. Biden was down to about $1.5 million in the bank—less than some candidates were spending in a single day at that point. There was a chance that he wouldn't be able to make payroll after the New Hampshire primary. He would have to scale back on his travel and events, and he might have to fire people or cut their salaries, if he couldn't raise cash fast. Top advisers went to the Bidens to review options. "There was a discussion about asking them to put in their own money," one campaign insider said, adding that "refinancing their home" was "on the table." The Bidens made clear that they didn't want to bankroll the campaign, let the operation go into debt, or fail to pay aides. Triage would be ugly, and there weren't many ways to do it that met Biden's proscriptions. "The fact that they were presented with options for financing meant that it got uncomfortably low," the insider said. The subtext was unmistakable: It might soon be time to wrap up the campaign.

Biden was determined to make it to South Carolina if he had to jump on a bicycle and ride there. The pooh-bahs sure as hell weren't going to tell him to give up on the dreams of half a century of political work. Biden was, at once, dejected and relentlessly confident in his own abilities. "Just hang on," he told Jill repeatedly. "Just hang on till we get to South Carolina."

If there was one thing Biden had a better feel for than most politicians, it was reading the mood of the people around him. "We'll be okay, but I have to figure out how to keep the staff engaged," he told one confidant at the time. He was down in the mouth, but he felt like he couldn't let it show or he would risk the total disintegration of the campaign. His staff reflected him in important ways: loyal and full of faith. But some of his aides had come to believe loyalty meant telling him when it was time to quit. And he knew the next couple of weeks would be worse, not better, for the campaign.

Bernie Sanders spent most of New Hampshire primary night in a jazzed-up gymnasium. His team had set up couches and television screens. He was surrounded by grandchildren and friends. To pass the time, he shot hoops, along with Shakir and the kids. As results started rolling in slowly, Bernie grew anxious and then excited and a little bit anxious again. He was up by several points for most of the night, but Buttigieg was closing the gap.

Finally, after what seemed like days waiting, the TV networks declared Sanders the winner late in the evening. He smiled broadly and wrapped his arms around Jane. He'd needed this win—a real, uncontested victory. The burdensome weight of Iowa lifted from his shoulders. In November, *The New York Times* had published a story asking whether New Hampshire had fallen out of love with him. At the time, it had given him great joy because he had hoped that he wouldn't be looked at as a front-runner too early. Underdog status had helped fuel his 2016 campaign, and it was central to his narrative as a candidate. Now, he thought back to that story with deep satisfaction.

But every candidate on the ballot, including Sanders, lost that night.

Sitting on the couch in his suite at the Nashua Marriott, Pete Buttigieg's emotionless state reflected a truth he understood all too well: The buzz of finishing in the money was intoxicating, but it wasn't enough to propel him to the nomination. He'd staked his hopes on winning both of the first two states to seize national attention and more campaign cash. He still wasn't known to most voters across the country. More than anyone, he needed to smell like a winner, not just an overperformer. He hadn't reached the end of the campaign trail yet, but his path was as narrow as his waist now. National polls put him in fifth place, with Bloomberg coming out of nowhere to seize third. Worse for Buttigieg, his numbers with Black voters—the set that had propelled Obama and Clinton to primary victories—barely registered in surveys. The road ahead would get only harder as the primaries became more diverse.

For the second straight time, Klobuchar did her best to turn the agony of defeat into the exhilaration of not getting slaughtered. She had finished ahead of both Warren and Biden, better than she had done in Iowa. The result was a boon for her fundraising, which would allow her to keep running. From the outside, it looked like Klobuchar and Buttigieg had a good night. Inside their campaigns, reality was creeping in.

Sanders was in perhaps the most conflicted position. Like most politicians, he exulted in the ecstasy of being called a winner, and his win was already exacerbating the fears of party leaders.

But Sanders's aides knew that he was suddenly running behind schedule. They thought he would win Iowa outright and perhaps take New Hampshire in a blowout. His strategy had been built around sweeping the first three states before Biden got a chance to make his case in South Carolina. Sanders had beaten Hillary by more than 20 points in New Hampshire in 2016, earning 60 percent of the vote. Four years later, he escaped as the victor with a 25.7 percent to 24.4 percent margin over Buttigieg. Klobuchar snagged 19.8 percent of the vote, while Warren came in fourth at 9.2 percent and Biden finished fifth at 8.4 percent.

Sanders received about twenty thousand fewer votes than Hillary had when she lost to him in the state. The numbers offered a harsh corrective to a Sanders article of faith, proving 2016 had not been about the appeal of Bernie Sanders, but about the rejection of Hillary Clinton. "It's just like somebody's puppy got run over," one of his top aides said.

To the outside world, Sanders looked like he was gaining strength. But in reality the fatal flaw of his campaign was revealed in all its truth by the outcomes in the first two states. His ceiling and his floor were basically the same number: 25 percent. That meant that three-quarters of the party was against him.

And though he needed to persuade only a third of that group to shift into his camp, he chose the night of the New Hampshire election to demand that they come to him rather than meet him partway. "Now our campaign is not just about beating Trump," he said at his victory party. "It's about transforming this country. It's about having the courage to take on Wall Street, the insurance companies, the drug companies, the fossil fuel industry, the military-industrial complex."

His words were an implicit assault on the centrist wing of the party, and they threatened to further alienate millions of Americans who worked in the industries he named as enemies of the public. Some of those voters would be necessary for Democrats to beat Trump. Sanders was still running a Trump-like campaign, based on the idea that energizing his most ardent supporters would allow him to win a plurality in states across the country and somehow seize the nomination at the party's convention. A candidate shouldn't reach out "until you have crushed your opponent on the battlefield," one Sanders campaign insider explained. "Otherwise, it's a sign of weakness."

Sanders was still in war mode, and he still planned to take the party as his prisoner so that he could negotiate the surrender of his rivals. But to do so he would have to have stronger finishes going forward. If the field remained at roughly the same size, there was a good chance the candidates to his political right would continue to split the non-Sanders vote. That would position him well both to win states by plurality and to pick up extra delegates, because some of the other candidates' support would be reallocated to him in states and congressional districts where they didn't hit the magic 15 percent threshold.

But it all relied on a basic concept that Sanders would be the first among relative equals—a concept that wouldn't hold if candidates started dropping out. The real question wasn't whether the rest of the Democratic Party would gang up on him, it was when.

Over the course of countless debates and now two primary contests, the Democratic field had become a circular firing squad. More than a dozen candidates were casualties, along with the CNN/*Des Moines Register* poll and the Iowa caucuses. Sanders cast his rivals as a bunch of apostates, no matter their proximity to him on the ideological spectrum. In turns, Harris, Warren, and Buttigieg rose up as middle-path alternatives to the ideological poles of Sanders and Biden, only to be brought down by the rest of the pack. The latest example came from Klobuchar and Sanders whacking Buttigieg from both sides. Meanwhile, Biden's campaign was deeply engaged in its own circular-fire exercises.

The morning of the primary, Kate Bedingfield sat on the floor of the DoubleTree hotel in Manchester and dialed in to a strategy call with the senior leadership of the campaign. A few feet away, Biden fielded questions from local reporters on "radio row," the alliterative nickname for the space on the second level of the hotel where broadcasters and podcasters set up tables to interview candidates and surrogates during the week of the primary.

Bedingfield listened closely as Cedric Richmond, Donilon, Ricchetti, Dunn, and Symone Sanders batted around the question of whether Biden should ghost the Live-Free-Or-Die state before the results were in that night and speak, instead, from South Carolina.

For a couple of days, Richmond had been running a campaign within the campaign to make a hard turn away from the states where Biden would surely lose and toward South Carolina, where he was losing steam and could still do something about it. A youthful-looking forty-six, with close-cropped hair and brown eyes that burned with the intensity of an impatient man, Richmond had become close to Biden during the 2018 midterm election campaign when they both worked to help Democrats win control of the House of Representatives. During that campaign, Richmond worked with House majority leader Jim Clyburn's super PAC to mobilize Black voters in highly competitive districts across the country. While those swing districts are typically overwhelmingly white, many of them have a significant enough minority population for a boost in turnout to make a difference in the outcome. A number of the Democrats running in those majority-white districts were men and women of color. Richmond asked Biden to appear on behalf of candidates or record endorsement messages for them, and Biden always found a way to help.

When Biden prepared his presidential bid, he told Richmond he wouldn't run unless Richmond agreed to serve as co-chairman of the campaign. For most of 2019, that meant acting as a surrogate for Biden with political contacts and the media. But as Richmond watched the campaign evolve, he became ever more frustrated at the decision to pour limited money and candidate time into all-white states where there was little Biden could do to avoid getting crushed.

He was upset with Schultz and Kavanaugh, and with the coterie of old white advisers who were more than a decade detached from their last on-the-ground campaign experience, but he was mostly pissed at himself.

I should have pushed harder to focus on South Carolina, he thought.

He wouldn't make the same mistake again.

Earlier that week, after Iowa, Richmond had come to a strategic conclusion: Fight on your best turf. With that in mind, he made the case to Biden and the rest of the team to bolt New Hampshire for South Carolina before the results were in.

Our narrative is that we will turn this thing around when Black voters get a chance to render their judgments, Richmond said to his colleagues. "Why don't we just take that narrative and literally, physically put him in South Carolina." Richmond's spark eventually caught fire with the rest of the senior leadership on the campaign, but Biden was a harder sell.

"When we took it to him, he was not on board," said one senior campaign aide. Biden told his team that he didn't want to abandon his allies in New Hampshire.

"I don't want to send the message that just because I'm not doing well here that I don't care about them," he said. In a series of conference calls and in-person lobbying efforts by top campaign aides, Biden vacillated. It was no, then yes, then no. Richmond lobbied him. Symone Sanders lobbied him. Ricchetti and Dunn did, too.

By the time Bedingfield was sitting on the floor, plugged into the campaign call while she kept watch on Biden, a final decision had to be rendered immediately. We have to pull the trigger on this, Dunn said. It needs to be a yes if we're going to get everyone down to South Carolina and organize an event there.

It wasn't a move without risks. When word spread that Biden was leaving the state early, before the polls had even closed, his supporters might flock to other candidates and push him into a worse finish than he would have had otherwise. And throwing a giant middle finger at a swing state that could be pivotal in a general election—Hillary had won New Hampshire by less than four-tenths of a percentage point in 2016—was less than ideal. But for Biden, who had run his primary campaign with the goal of doing nothing to hurt his general election hopes, it was time to concentrate on winning a nomination that appeared to be slipping through his fingers.

By the time Bedingfield hung up, the consensus had lined up behind Richmond's tactic. Bedingfield shepherded Biden toward the campaign bus, where she and the other Kate B.—fellow communications aide Kate Berner—sat down to tell the boss where his top aides stood.

Biden repeated his concerns. But he agreed to the plan, conditionally.

I don't want the people who have been busting their asses for me in this state to think I've taken them for granted or that I'm abandoning them, he said. I want to talk to former governor John Lynch about it first. He dispatched a couple of aides to find Lynch inside the DoubleTree and bring him out to the bus. Biden laid out the plan to depart early.

"This is what I'm considering," he told Lynch. "I only want to do it if you're comfortable with it."

The moment was pure Biden. He wanted his close ally to feel some agency in a decision that was so far along toward final that Biden's inner circle was already scrambling to book flights. Relationships mattered to Biden, and he wanted to make sure that he wasn't going to create a rift with Lynch.

"Absolutely," Lynch said. "It's the right decision."

An email was circulated to staff and close allies informing them of Biden's impending exit. Before noon, Biden popped into a Dunkin' in Manchester to pick up sweet parting gifts for supporters and to talk with the press. Biden referred to the workingman's doughnut frequently on the campaign trail and was photographed during Obama's 2012 reelection campaign bringing boxes of the company's product to campaign volunteers.

Biden was asked if he regretted all the time he'd spent in New Hampshire.

"No!" he said. "We've got to win this state in a general election, and I think we're going to be able to do that." In other words, there wasn't much point in him being there as far as the primary was concerned.

Part of Richmond's urgency stemmed from his feel for South Carolina. It was the best state for Biden, but it didn't look as good as it had before the caucuses. With Biden getting pummeled in Iowa and then New Hampshire, he was losing altitude in South Carolina. Richmond still believed Biden would win the state if he made it to the February 29 primary. But it wasn't clear at all whether he could politically survive the next eighteen grueling days, including the Nevada caucuses on February 22, to get there. On top of that, he would need a decisive win in South Carolina, not a narrow plurality, to breathe life back into his campaign. Biden's brutal reception in Iowa and New Hampshire was so bad—so much worse than anyone had anticipated—that it was threatening to destroy his chance to make it to the South Carolina primary as a serious contender. If he didn't move to solidify his support among Black voters now, there was less of a chance that he could get the bounce he needed.

The campaign's emphasis on Iowa and New Hampshire meant that Biden hadn't been to the Palmetto State often. His poll numbers there weren't as strong as he would have liked. Bloomberg, who wouldn't even be on the ballot until after the South Carolina primary, was eating into his African American backing across the country. Billionaire Tom Steyer, an also-ran in the first two states, had staked his chances on an upset in South Carolina, where he, too, was focused on Black voters. If there was one unifying theme for the Black electorate in the primary, it was finding a candidate who could beat Trump. The billionaires might serve that purpose. And Sanders's appeal to the younger set crossed racial lines.

"We had to retreat to our base," one Biden aide said. "That was South Carolina."

"Retreat" was the right word. Biden had no money, no wins, and no organization to speak of in Super Tuesday states. Even if he won in Nevada, South Carolina, or both, there was no guarantee that he would be able to quickly stand up teams to take advantage of new momentum.

But his team had hope that Democratic primary voters, particularly Black voters, would mobilize themselves on Super Tuesday if Biden could just turn things around. Schultz, Kavanaugh, and Becca Siegel, the campaign's chief data analytics officer, had long looked at districts like Alabama's Seventh as places where Biden didn't need to spend much money or knock on many doors to win big. Represented by Terri Sewell, the state's first Black congresswoman, the district covered western Alabama's "Black Belt"—named for the rich soil—and took in parts of Montgomery and Birmingham. Nearly two-thirds of the voters there are Black, and many of the whites are more Democratic leaning than their exurban and rural counterparts in the state.

Sanders and Buttigieg would each win nine delegates in New

Hampshire. Biden's team thought he could pull eight out of just the one district in Alabama. The same was true for two dozen or so Black-majority and Black-plurality districts across the country. Those districts tended to have more delegates in play because Democratic Party rules disproportionately awarded delegates to districts based on their propensity to support the party's candidates. Black-majority districts produced a lot of votes for Democratic presidential candidates and, as a result, were given more power in the nominating process. A candidate who received 85 percent or more of the primary vote in a congressional district got all of the district's delegates, a feat known as "thresholding" rivals.

It was frustrating to Biden and his team that he was being judged on poor performances in states where he had expected to lose since at least 2015. But the losses had been ugly—fourth place in Iowa, less than 10 percent of the vote in New Hampshire—and his demeanor on the trail alternated between tired and agitated. He repeatedly mocked voters at events. His strategy for winning the nomination remained more plausible on paper than those of any of his rivals, but the real-life Biden wasn't living up to the résumé version.

Richmond's audible, routing Biden to friendlier turf, spoke volumes about the need to energize the candidate, as well as the campaign. "Bailing on New Hampshire was not in the strategy memos," one Biden confidant said.

As Biden climbed aboard a jet bound for South Carolina, his aides scrambled to find him a venue and a crowd to speak to once he arrived. There was no time to put up a riser in the back so that TV cameras would have a clear line to his podium over the heads of his supporters. When Biden stepped to the microphone, he spoke not of the death by thousands of votes he was suffering in New Hampshire, but of resurrection. "When I die," he said, "I want to be reborn in Charleston."

He was in Columbia.

"Two states!" he said in describing his fourth- and fifth-place finishes. "Up till now, we haven't heard from the most committed constituency in the Democratic Party, the African American community."

Biden may have sounded upbeat, but his campaign was downtrodden. One top party donor with close ties to Joe said he'd "had his legs cut out" from under him, between the piss-poor performances, fellow Democrats looking for a new hero, and Bloomberg ready to pounce.

"That was the low point," said one adviser.

Late that night, Biden senior adviser Cristóbal Alex received a call from former Miami mayor Manny Diaz, a Bloomberg backer and onetime lawyer who had represented Cuban child refugee Elián González's family in one of the most explosive legal and political fights of the previous two decades. Diaz was in a jubilant mood.

"Listen, man, I'm thinking about you," he said to Alex. "I'm having a cigar and some scotch."

He picks now to call, Alex thought. *The darkest moment!*

Diaz didn't have to say what he wanted. It was obvious. This was a soft recruitment call. Long ago, Diaz had promised to be with Biden unless Bloomberg got in the race. Now, Bloomberg was moving forward at full steam. He had all the momentum, much of it thunder stolen from Biden, and Biden had just limped to the finish in New Hampshire in a brutally honest fifth place. Diaz was asking Alex to leave the losing team and join a winner.

For months, Bloomberg had been working personally and through his allies to flip donors and politicians previously loyal to Biden, and that had ramped up significantly in the eight days between Iowa and New Hampshire. But this—opening the door for one of Biden's top aides when Biden was insisting he would stay in the race—was a sign of just how bad the rest of the world thought Biden was doing. The outlook was even worse from inside the campaign. Biden had described Iowa as a "gut punch." The New Hampshire result landed a little lower.

The Democratic Party establishment lost in New Hampshire. Biden, Buttigieg, and Warren limped out. Klobuchar was doing better, but, like Buttigieg, she registered no significant support outside of whites.

Bloomberg, who wasn't on the ballot, won. That was the point of Diaz's call to Cristóbal Alex that night. If there was ever a time to jump off Biden's bus by the side of the road and onto one of Bloomberg's private jets, it was now.

CHAPTER 9

•

"None of Us Knew
If There Was Going to
Be a Campaign"

BIDEN WAS NO LONGER TRYING TO WIN A STATE. HE WAS OUT OF money. He had dumped his campaign manager. His aides were at one another's throats. Bloomberg was trying to suffocate him by recruiting his donors, his political endorsers, and his staff. The financial outlook was so bad that the campaign asked volunteers to drive Biden signs from state to state because they couldn't afford to buy new ones.

For almost four months, Biden, Dunn, and other senior campaign aides had been trying to get Beto O'Rourke's campaign manager, Jennifer O'Malley Dillon, to come run the show. For a variety of reasons, including her father's recent cancer diagnosis and the strain on her husband and children, she had not committed to an operation that was losing altitude. Dunn, a highly capable strategist, was an interim fix as the campaign's chief, but she didn't have the expertise—or the ego—to think she could run state-by-state political operations. There was one hope left: Biden had to finish at least second in Nevada—probably a strong second—and blow everyone else out in South Carolina. If he made it that far, it would be easier to find a campaign pro willing to take over the day-to-day duties.

So, when Biden retreated to South Carolina on February 11, Dunn pushed Biden's remaining chips into Nevada.

"We made the strategic decision that we were going to defund Super Tuesday totally—100 percent," said one Biden insider. "Because there wasn't going to be a Super Tuesday if we didn't figure out how we were going to come in second in Nevada and win South Carolina by enough of a margin."

The trouble with Nevada, though, is that it didn't line up well for Biden. While it is more diverse than Iowa and New Hampshire—nearly every state is—the younger and more heavily Latino electorate leaned hard toward Sanders. Plus, the nature of the caucus, as opposed to a primary, meant that the contest would be dominated by progressive activists.

Biden needed a wedge. Dunn picked through the cushions of the campaign couch and found enough cash for a poll of Nevada voters. Campaign pollster John Anzalone had worked for Hillary Clinton when she stopped polling several weeks before the 2016 election. He still had PTSD from that experience. On this campaign, Anzo had been arguing into the wind about Biden's "Soul of the Nation" message. While many voters reacted positively to the broad stroke, it wasn't particularly effective at swaying or mobilizing them in the primaries.

"It doesn't move the needle," Anzo said, over and over again. "We've been pushing this message for almost a year now. No one knows what this 'soul of America' bullshit means. What are the substantive issues that line up behind it?" The Biden campaign had never been about issues. But Anzo believed Biden was leaving votes on the table by not talking to voters enough about concrete proposals to improve their lives. Many voters could recite Sanders's agenda without thinking about it: a political revolution that brings Medicare for All, a $15-an-hour minimum wage, and an end to the "endless" wars. It was easier to identify what Biden was against than what he was for.

Dunn acted with urgency. "One thing you can say about Anita, she fucking takes charge," said one person familiar with the internal campaign discussion. "We put a questionnaire together, we had a call, we had the fucker in the field. I mean she moved shit along in a campaign where that did not happen." What Anzo wanted to do ran against the basic theory of the campaign. Anzo thought Biden might not make it to Super Tuesday if he didn't find a way to connect his theme to more specific areas of contrast with Sanders. "Sanders is going to be our only competition," said one top Biden aide. "Sanders is the only one who has diverse votes besides us."

On the biggest fight with Sanders so far, over expanding health insurance, Sanders lined up more closely with the primary elector- ate. It made sense that Biden would benefit from running on an issue or two that highlighted where he agreed with more Demo- cratic voters, even if his overall message was about personal traits.

Anzalone's polling showed that Nevada Democrats, less than a year and a half after a Las Vegas gunman killed five dozen people and wounded more than four hundred others, were very open to Biden's proposal for curbing gun violence. He found that was par- ticularly true among Black voters and white seniors. Sanders, who also supported gun control measures, had voted in the past to pro- tect the gun-manufacturing industry from legal liability. Neither one of them had emphasized gun-safety issues in Iowa or New Hampshire, where a lot of Democratic voters own firearms. But Biden now had a reason to promote his past fights with the NRA and hammer Sanders on that old liability waiver, and a place to do so where he didn't risk a backlash from gun owners. He might also blunt Bloomberg's natural appeal to the heavily populated gun- safety community that Bloomberg had helped build with his own money. And, perhaps most important, Biden could use gun control to talk about the 1994 crime bill—which included a ten-year ban on "assault weapons"— in a way that helped him, instead of hurt him, with Black voters.

The inherent risk in the play was the possibility that he could drive away swing voters ahead of the general election. Guns were often dicey for Democrats. Many analysts had blamed Al Gore's 2000 defeat on his support for gun control measures, which was most evident in the firearms restrictions added into the very same crime bill that Biden had written in the Senate. Since reversing him- self on federal funding for abortion early on in the campaign, Biden had mostly refused to take positions that could help him win the nomination at the cost of his general election strategy. The most cautious candidate in either party had to choose whether to gamble just a little bit—and Dunn threw the dice for him.

Biden's senior staff put together a plan for him to promote his proposals—including a new ban on "assault weapons" and repeal- ing the liability waiver—in a speech at the Tropicana, a casino over- looking the site of the 2017 shooting massacre. In earlier months, with Schultz lacking the authority to make and execute decisions, it would have taken weeks or months to get Biden's inner circle of advisers to sign off on everything from the messaging detour to the venue. Inertia killed ideas bad and good in Bidenworld. No one could change the candidate's bias against action, but Dunn was more worried about helping Biden at this point than pleasing him. And he desperately needed help to pick up just a little more of the vote.

"There was finally an appetite to take some amount of risk," said one senior Biden aide. "There's a certain amount of freedom that comes from having nothing to lose."

Anzo, who had worked in Nevada before, thought campaigns paid too much attention to Latino voters and not enough to Black voters. The Latino population dwarfed the Black population, but was less likely to vote. Besides, said one high-ranking campaign official, "we weren't going to move many Latinos because of where Bernie was with them."

This strategy wasn't about winning. Biden's team was focused on coming in second. After fourth- and fifth-place finishes, they might be able to sell that as a comeback. Anything less would push donors and voters out the door. It would all be over fast.

The morning after he arrived in Nevada, Biden set out to meet Black voters. At one of his stops, a Black History Month festival at the Springs Preserve in Las Vegas, he found an oasis in the desert of his defeats. It was February 15, one week before the caucuses, and he couldn't move through the crowd to deliver his speech. Every few steps, supporters stopped him to offer encouragement. Some voters simply hugged him. It ended up taking almost forty-five minutes for Biden to move through the throng. Accustomed to meeting with small groups of mostly older and mostly white supporters in high school gyms across Iowa and New Hampshire, Biden now shook hands, flashed his toothy grin, and listened to stories of what the Obama-Biden administration had meant for the Black community. The warm environs of the nature preserve and the embrace of a younger, more diverse set of voters provided an obvious contrast for a campaign in need of fresh air and fresh bodies.

This doesn't feel like Iowa or New Hampshire, thought Yvanna Cancela, the thirty-two-year-old Nevada state senator who accompanied Biden. *This community is wrapping its arms around him.* At the same time, Bloomberg was squeezing hard.

Biden's aides could feel the billionaire's grasp as they tried to concentrate on beating Buttigieg, Klobuchar, and Warren. As Biden battled them on multiple fronts, Bloomberg was trying to starve him behind his own lines. Mayor Diaz's call to Cristóbal Alex was one of many—Bloomberg was a poacher, searching for opportunities. Bloomberg didn't even need Biden's donors—he was funding his own campaign—but moving them into his corner would starve the former vice president.

"Folks we had been working on for a year said we're going to stay on the sidelines or go with Bloomberg," said one top Biden aide. "It was annoying."

It was also an existential threat.

As Elizabeth Warren stepped to the podium that day in Nevada, there were two thoughts on her mind: *I need to hit someone hard, and that someone is Mike Bloomberg.*

Warren had lost almost everything: Iowa, New Hampshire, and now her voice. She stood in a roomy casino hotel suite big enough to fit six podiums along with the Bellagio's modern-luxury bed and plush furniture. Through the window on the back side of the hotel, facing away from the bustle of the Las Vegas Strip, she could see the sun setting over the Spring Mountains.

Over time, her debate prep sessions had moved away from full mocks and into more of a set of drills with her aides. But if practice had become less cumbersome, it was becoming more important. Warren had all but faded out of the Democratic primary over the past several months, and this could be one of her last chances to fight her way back into the conversation. Mike Bloomberg was the perfect target. He was surging in the polls, and, more than anything, Warren loathed the very idea of his candidacy.

Of course, she detested his faith in Wall Street and major corporations. But there were a lot of people who disagreed with her reform agenda. What really rankled was the idea that a billionaire could buy the Democratic nomination. That would put both parties in the thrall of plutocrats—leaving voters with no choice but to elect one of them. She had felt that way from the moment he started talking about running.

There was a personal element, too: He had thrown an elbow at her during a gun safety event in a way that she thought under-scored his view of wealth as a virtue. Bloomberg, the sponsor of the Des Moines event in the summer of 2019, told the audience that he had just talked to Warren backstage. "Let me just remind you that if my company hadn't been successful, we wouldn't be here today," he said. "So, enough with this stuff." He wasn't spe-cific about what he meant by "stuff," but it was pretty clear he meant her highly charged rhetoric about the greed of financial and industrial titans.

Bloomberg's plan to skip the four early states made her mad, too. *What would it mean if a billionaire bought his way in, not just self-funded but isolating himself from the democratic process?* she thought. *He didn't get the same kind of vetting. He didn't even pretend to engage in democracy. This is a huge part of what I'm running against.*

But the final straw came in late January when the Democratic National Committee changed its rules to allow Bloomberg to qual-ify for the upcoming Nevada debate without demonstrating sup-port among grassroots donors. That really pissed her off. She asked her aides to start compiling a dossier on Bloomberg. She knew she'd read some unflattering profiles and recalled that some of them involved the treatment of women who worked for him. She wanted the details, line by line. *Holy crap!* she thought as she read news clips. There were full buckets of issues she could raise: non-disclosure agreements with women; his assertion that people who lost their homes during the 2008 financial crisis were at fault; and the stop-and-frisk policy that disproportionately affected Black and brown communities. *It's just one thing after another,* she thought. *He thinks he can run for president?*

The trick for Warren was not finding lines of attack against Bloomberg but narrowing them down. She wanted to hit him on stop and frisk because she thought he was disingenuous in portray-ing its effects on people of color as accidental. That was a feature, not a bug, of his policy, she thought. She could tie that in pretty easily to blaming homeowners for losing their houses during the crash—an area where there was also a disproportionate effect on Black and brown Americans. The NDAs, which Trump had also used to shield his personal and professional behavior, presented a way to connect the newly Democratic billionaire to the Republican one in the White House. The same went for Bloomberg's affinity for reducing his tax bill. *We're running against Donald Trump,* she thought. *What things do you think you can lay out against Donald Trump? Women, race, and you're the kind of sleazeball that doesn't pay your fair share of taxes.*

As an entry point for all of it, Warren homed in on the names he'd been accused of calling women—like "fat broads." The incidents were well documented. She found them appalling. And they made the comparison to Trump so easy to understand.

This guy shouldn't even be on the stage, she thought. *I can have that fight with Tom Perez or I can just take out Michael Bloomberg myself.*

Straining through a developing case of laryngitis—she had been barnstorming the country for more than fourteen months—Warren looked up from her practice podium.

"Horse-faced lesbian," she croaked. *This might be fun.*

Bloomberg, on the other hand, focused his mind on Sanders. Though he had been slated for the debate as a late qualifier under the DNC's arcane selection rules, he still wouldn't be on a ballot until after the Nevada caucuses and the South Carolina primary. For weeks, he'd been gradually preparing for the debate, his first since his third mayoral election in 2011. Shortly before the debate, his team rented out space in a warehouse so he could practice. Bloomberg was determined not to punch down. He and his aides joked about taking out Pete by pointing out that Mike's philanthropy had underwritten a good bit of the resurgence Pete claimed in South Bend. Biden was sinking on his own. Klobuchar and Warren were afterthoughts. Julie Wood, a former communications aide in his city hall office, played Warren in full mock debates. She was as aggressive as anyone dared to be in her playacting criticism of one of the wealthiest men on the planet.

In his own small world, Bloomberg was known as an inveterate debater. He was such a contrarian that he would take a point of view opposite his own just to keep his employees on their toes. But he was such an authoritarian that few survived getting in his face. And his debate style was more Talmudic than rap battle.

Before Bloomberg could get settled behind his podium in a ballroom at the Bellagio the night of February 19, Warren dropped the horse-faced-lesbian line on him. The crowd gasped. Biden's mouth opened just a bit as his lips formed a wincing smile. Debate-stage theatrics were more entertaining when he wasn't the target. Warren kept going, as Bloomberg, standing next to her, refused to meet her eyes.

"Democrats are not going to win if we have a nominee who has a history of hiding his tax returns, of harassing women, and of supporting racist policies like redlining and stop and frisk," she warned, rasping through her prepared hit. Minutes later, she pressed him to release women from nondisclosure agreements. Her aides watched with glee as she moved into the kind of Socratic badgering she'd been famous for at Harvard.

"We have a very few nondisclosure agreements," Bloomberg said.

"How many is that?" she shot back, getting under his skin.

Annoyed, Bloomberg told her to "let me finish" and then said, "Many of them didn't like a joke I told."

The audience let out another audible gasp.

Warren asked if he planned to keep women "muzzled" by NDAs or if he would free them from the obligation right there on national television.

The planned punches had landed, but this was all ad-lib.

"That was a total evisceration, literally limb by limb in front of millions of people, but good for us," said one top Biden aide who watched the exchange with slack-jawed amazement. "He was still going to be a major problem for us, but that changed things."

Bloomberg couldn't handle the substance or the speed of Warren's interrogation. He looked dazed. He couldn't get out complete sentences. It was hard for the other candidates to keep a straight face. She gutted him and buried him in the desert like a wayward mob lieutenant. No one would remember anything else about that debate. When it was over, Bloomberg found himself alone, standing next to a big curtain in the wings. Each candidate had a staff member assigned to escort him or her back to a holding room. No one immediately came to collect Bloomberg. He stood awkwardly alone and lost, just offstage.

Buttigieg stopped to offer a handshake and a warm greeting. Bloomberg, deep in thought, mumbled back a stifled "Hello."

A few days before the caucus, the Democratic establishment was back where it had started more than a year earlier: so many candidates, and not one looked capable of beating Sanders in a three-, four-, five-, or six-way race. Deep inside Biden's Philadelphia headquarters, though, there was a glimmer of optimism. The top brass thought that finishing lower than second in Nevada would crater them in terms of donors and key supporters, but they were so pressed up against that fact that it nearly overwhelmed a perhaps even more important question: Given the damage he'd already sustained, did Biden still have a realistic path with voters through the rest of the primary? Biden's chief analytics officer, Becca Siegel, believed that he did.

A veteran of Clinton's 2016 campaign, Siegel took an unusually honest approach to the work of applying data science to the art of presidential campaigns. Unlike many of her peers in the field, she didn't pretend that statistics could be used to precisely project outcomes. That was particularly true when it came to the first real multi-candidate slugfest of the information age. The whims of voters and donors could change on a dime, upsetting carefully constructed models. Siegel looked at the various scenarios and tried to figure out whether Biden could still pull off the nomination.

While his dismal performances had shrunk his lead in South Carolina, his numbers with Black voters remained strong enough for Siegel to see Biden winning a drawn-out fight for the nomination. The campaign's South Carolina director, Kendall Corley, kept reporting back that voters "still like us here."

Ultimately, Siegel found herself in agreement with the campaign leadership's blunt assessment—she wasn't sure Biden could withstand the damage of finishing third, fourth, or fifth in Nevada. South Carolina would be part bellwether and part influencer for Black voters in Super Tuesday states. Once the votes were tallied there, Siegel could develop a more informed projection for district-by-district delegate hauls on Super Tuesday. Biden had little doubt that he would win states with significant Black populations—he'd started doing that in Delaware in 1972—but the question was about margins.

The Silver State had been added to the roster of early primaries and caucuses a dozen years earlier as a way of giving Hispanic voters more power in the nomination process. They were the fastest-growing racial or ethnic group in the country. Democrats believed that growth favored them heavily—they won the Hispanic vote every four years—but were continually disappointed at their own failure to register and turn out Hispanic voters at the rates of white and Black voters.

That mission required levels of familiarity with various Latino communities. There were Hispanics whose families had lived in states since before they were admitted to the Union. Some Hispanic voters were new citizens. Many were of Mexican descent, but others had roots in every country in Central America and South America. Brazilian Americans were often considered Latino but not Hispanic, because Brazil is in South America but Portuguese is its official language. Moreover, Hispanic voters could identify strongly, or not at all, with nations of family origin.

In short, courting the "Hispanic community" required granular-level politics. Most politicians and operatives were terrible at it. Democrats were leaving votes on the table election cycle after election cycle. But there was a steep price to targeting Hispanic voters. Because they didn't vote with the same frequency as non-Hispanic voters, it cost more money and more time to get them to the polls. For many campaigns, it was a cold calculation that it wasn't worth the effort to recruit Hispanic voters. Biden, for example, had focused his campaign on Black voters and middle-income whites.

But Sanders, from the outset of his campaign, had viewed Hispanic voters as a key part of his strategy. For one thing, they skewed much younger than Black or white voters, which meant that, collectively, they were more likely to be attracted to his democratic-socialist agenda. Regardless of race or ethnicity, he did his best among younger voters. Beyond that, many of the older Hispanics had come from countries where his politics would have been viewed as more mainstream than they were in the United States. Whether on the right or left, populists flourished in Central and South America.

For more than a year, Sanders had been talking about building a diverse coalition. In Nevada, he intended to show that he had one. The Bernie Bros might still be a particularly boisterous set in his camp, but he knew that if he was going to win the nomination that would mean walking into a convention with a lead in delegates that included representatives from a diverse set of communities. Buttigieg and Klobuchar were already beginning to grasp the paradox of their own campaigns—the one that beset Sanders in 2016—which was that their successes in Iowa and New Hampshire highlighted the degree to which their own support bases were almost entirely white. The optics of a convention awarding the nomination to a candidate with little or no backing in communities of color were awfully ugly, at best, and both of them were in better position to bleed Biden's white support than to win in diverse states.

As much as anything, math drove Sanders's diversity strategy. Young, Democratic-leaning Hispanic voters represented a vast, largely untapped political resource. If Sanders had a ceiling with the existing voter pool, one way to raise that ceiling was to find more voters. Sanders left the details to Chuck Rocha, the operative who described himself as a "Mexican redneck."

A few days after the New Hampshire primary, Rocha landed in Las Vegas. It was up to him, he thought, to make up lost ground from the Iowa debacle and a less-than-impressive Sanders win in the Granite State. From the moment Rocha emerged into the sunlight at the airport, he could feel sweat under his trademark cowboy hat. It wasn't hot enough—with highs in the midsixties—for that to be a function of the weather. The whole campaign was now riding on a bet Rocha had placed early in 2019, and he wasn't at all sure that it would pay off.

His theory of turning Sanders into a superstar among caucusgoing Las Vegas Latinos revolved around his vision of the typical Latina housekeeper cleaning hotel rooms on the Strip. She was a member of the powerful culinary workers' union, known as the turnout machine in Sin City's casino industry. Sanders couldn't count on the leaders of her union to get behind him, but Rocha believed he could win the housekeeper by talking to her without the filter of the labor bosses. His Nevada strategy was born out of necessity.

In early 2019, just after announcing his campaign, Sanders met with members of UNITE HERE, the culinary workers' parent union. They told Sanders they loved most of what he stood for, but the move to Medicare for All was a bridge too far. Sanders had already identified the issue as the one that would force other candidates to choose which side they were on, a kind of death compactor for anyone who wasn't clearly for it or against it. It would crush Harris and Warren, who both signed on to it before releasing their own watered-down plans.

"I'm going to make this a litmus test for who's really for Medicare for All," he'd told top advisers about his campaign strategy early on. He had run into resistance from some of them, but Sanders was set on it. The message from UNITE HERE leaders didn't surprise Sanders, but it disappointed him. It was craven and self-interested, he thought.

Labor should be firmly for Medicare for All, he thought. *Workers will get paid more if employers don't have to pay the bill for health insurance.* It was the one area where he embraced the idea of trickle-down economics. But many labor leaders hated Medicare for All. When they ran for election within their own unions, they often pointed to concessions they had won on health plans, which were easier to obtain than pay raises. Instead of convincing him that he needed to adjust course, the meeting with UNITE HERE leaders cemented his belief that he should stake his campaign on Medicare for All.

Everyone's going to say they're for it until the pressure comes, he thought. *Then they will flip-flop.* He had been right about that. Harris and Warren both moved off his bill and paid a price for it.

Sanders could bear losing union endorsements, but he couldn't afford to alienate all the members. If he played his cards right, the members would follow him and pressure their leaders to endorse him, or at least stay on the sidelines. In Iowa, he had won the support of rank-and-file union members who crossed their leaders to caucus for him.

Now, in Nevada, the pan really met the fire. Before the votes were counted in New Hampshire, the Culinary Workers Union advised its members that it opposed Medicare for All. It wasn't a direct endorsement of Biden, but it was a surprisingly powerful rejection of Sanders delivered by the union that carried the most sway with Nevada Latinos. At the same time, Biden got a boost from the endorsement of Representative Steven Horsford, the only Black member of Congress from Nevada, and from former Senate majority leader Harry Reid, who had called Sanders's doctors in

October to make sure his old Senate colleague was getting the best possible care.

"Iowa and New Hampshire are not representative of the country," Reid said in an interview with the Associated Press, the outlet most likely to get picked up by other media. "He's going to do well in Nevada, he's going to do extremely well in South Carolina. So people should not be counting Joe Biden out of the race yet."

All of this made the Latina housekeeper that Rocha had conjured in his mind's eye all the more crucial to Sanders's hopes of winning the state. Rocha could see her turning down beds and cleaning bathrooms—all while she listened to the radio. He could recall returning to his own hotel room countless times to find that the radio was tuned to a Spanish-language station.

Months before the caucuses, he began buying up radio ad time in the state. In addition to providing a communications link for Sanders to speak directly to Latino voters, there was a sub-rosa benefit to the medium. Unlike TV ads, radio ads weren't tracked closely by other campaigns or the press. Besides, most political consultants—an overwhelmingly white set—bought into the conventional wisdom that no matter how much money they threw at Latino voters, turnout would always disappoint.

Where others saw waste, Rocha saw opportunity. In addition to the radio ads, he dumped millions of Sanders campaign dollars into direct mail, door-knocking operations, phone calls—he even sent a panel truck into Hispanic neighborhoods to blast Mexican music. The idea was that a surge of Latino voters for Sanders would change the universe of the electorate and deliver him a victory, even if he lost the white vote to more establishment candidates.

As the caucus approached, Rocha set up a war room in Las Vegas and tried, through his own anxiety, to keep Weaver and Sanders calm. That wasn't an easy task, because Sanders now needed a big win to compensate for the first two states. The campaign's top brass feared a repeat of the Iowa caucus debacle. Originally, Nevada Democrats had planned to use the app that had failed in Iowa. In its place, they strung together a reporting system that relied on officials to enter data into Google sheets. A close race could once again turn a win into a loss—or a brutal muddle.

In the final days before the caucuses, Weaver called Rocha constantly—several times a day at first and then seemingly on an hourly basis. Biden looked stronger. The union leaders were tacitly backing him and dumping on Sanders. Weaver wasn't sure that the money the campaign had spent to communicate directly to Latino voters would withstand the attacks. He pressed Rocha on the housekeepers and their families. His message was the same every time he called: "They gotta show up, Chuck, they gotta show up."

Biden didn't have enough money to court constituencies he couldn't be sure would turn out in numbers. Besides, by the time he'd launched his campaign and set up a Nevada organization in the spring and summer of 2019, Sanders's campaign was already embedded.

O'Malley Dillon, arguably the sharpest campaign operative in the Democratic Party, showed up in Las Vegas as a volunteer for Biden the week of the caucuses. Dunn had called to plead with her to pitch in. There was no money to offer.

"We just really need your help in Nevada," Dunn had said as the campaign was cratering in New Hampshire.

As the two women talked, it became clear to O'Malley Dillon that there were only two possible outcomes from a quick stint.

If he's going to end his campaign, I can help him do that with dignity, the former Obama deputy campaign manager thought. *If he does well, there might be a long-term plan to consider.* Either way, she was only donating a week of her time.

At forty-three, O'Malley Dillon had done more of the hands-on work of presidential campaigns than all of the old white guys around Biden combined. She got her start on Al Gore's 2000 campaign and had risen as high as deputy manager on Obama's reelection effort. In 2016, she lost out—or perhaps won out—when she was the runner-up to head Hillary Clinton's effort. Auburn-haired, freckled, and bespectacled, the Franklin, Massachusetts, native had been on Biden's radar ever since O'Rourke's campaign went belly-up on November 1. Two weeks later, Biden asked one of his advisers for her number while he was on a campaign swing through California and Nevada. He called her mid-flight to get a read on whether she'd be willing to join up.

You did a great job with O'Rourke, Biden told her, and I really like him.

O'Malley Dillon, who was already fielding calls from other campaigns, including those of Amy Klobuchar and former Massachusetts governor Deval Patrick, knew why the former vice president was calling. And it wasn't to re-live the O'Rourke campaign. Biden made his way to the point.

"We need help," he told her. "Whatever you might want to do, if you'd like to be part of the team, we'd love to talk about that."

There was no specific job offer dangling at the end of his thought. But it would be hard to imagine an operative of her caliber taking a secondary role on a presidential campaign again.

O'Malley Dillon wasn't ready to make her next move. They agreed to keep talking. Over the course of the following months, she talked to Dunn (with whom she had worked before), Donilon, and Biden repeatedly. In January, the discussions heated up. But O'Malley Dillon's father had been recently diagnosed with cancer, and she was helping him figure out a course of treatment and make appointments. Beyond that, she had three young kids at home, and the disruption another political campaign would cause for her family was not something she took lightly. And, of course, Biden was struggling on the trail.

When Dunn called to ask her to go to Nevada, O'Malley Dillon had already determined she wasn't going to work for anyone else. She supported Biden, but she still wasn't ready to sign on to a campaign that might have a short shelf life.

Even as Dunn had worked to replace Schultz, she sympathized with his troubles. She knew Biden reflexively didn't trust him enough with decision-making authority. That exacerbated a sluggish consensus-building process that hamstrung the campaign's operations. One Biden trait that could be counted as a strength and a weakness was his deliberate, Senate-style approach to reaching conclusions. But the campaign had to make better decisions faster, and that wasn't going to happen with a campaign manager who couldn't manage the candidate, the older advisers, and the build-out of operations at the same time. Some of Schultz's loyalists were angry with Dunn for moving him out, but she was trying to solve a problem that wouldn't resolve itself without action.

"Anita's been trying to take control for a long time," said one miffed Biden aide.

That created the opening to hire O'Malley Dillon. The biggest question was whether there would be a campaign to take over. Getting on the ground in Nevada would give O'Malley Dillon a chance to assess how the operation ran before making a decision.

When she took up residence in an office in the campaign's Las Vegas headquarters, she didn't have a title or an official role. Dunn assigned her to help organize the team's reporting system for caucus day and get a close look at how the campaign functioned. Seasoned campaign operatives in Bidenworld knew who O'Malley Dillon was, and immediately grasped that she might soon be their boss.

"It was a shit show," one Biden team member said of the Nevada operation. "Everybody was kind of doing their own thing and it wasn't really cohesive, and we were putting out fires every day. Jen was just quietly observing."

While Schultz was popular with his colleagues, even friends on the campaign acknowledged that he struggled to manage both the personalities of Biden's longtime advisers and a full-time presidential campaign operation. He had once ended a nine a.m. daily call with department heads—when everyone on the team would learn the message and strategy for the next twenty-four hours—in under three minutes. "This is outrageous," one of them said after Schultz hung up. It was a turning point for some of the veteran hands on the campaign.

When Schultz had to run every decision past a war council of Biden's longtime advisers—and then the candidate—he couldn't move quickly.

Dunn empowered O'Malley Dillon, who immediately demonstrated that she could snap into action without convening the equivalent of an international summit of the Biden for President Society first. When culinary workers went on strike outside one of the casinos, she tore up Biden's schedule to get him on the picket line. It was the kind of decisive action that kept Biden from looking unsupportive of—or out of touch with—a union that was doing heavy lifting to help him.

The move marked a sea change in the campaign. "Typically, with the way our scheduling process worked, we would have been the last candidate to confirm and it would have gone on the schedule for potential consideration and gone through eight rounds of deliberation," said one Biden aide who welcomed O'Malley Dillon's arrival at first but would later become one of her critics. "We confirmed that we were going to participate within ten minutes." That was a result of Dunn demanding greater urgency and O'Malley Dillon following through, the aide said.

O'Malley Dillon's mind and her elbows were equally sharp. She could play cutthroat politics with the best infighters in the business. If Biden survived Nevada, those traits might enable her to bring order to an undisciplined campaign—*if.*

"None of us knew if there was going to be a campaign," one of his top aides said.

There were some things O'Malley Dillon couldn't fix. When Biden looked out from his podium in the gym at Hyde Park Middle School the night before the caucus, he could see the floor—a lot of it. The combination of a small crowd and ample bleacher seating meant that there weren't enough people in the room to cover the empty space. Reporters tweeted pictures of the sparse crowd at the home of the Panthers, where a handful of championship banners hung on the wall behind an American flag and Biden campaign sign.

The truth was that the rally looked like any number of small-audience events Biden had held in Iowa and New Hampshire. School gyms were a staple for him. So were poorly attended rallies.

Five miles away, thousands of people packed themselves into the Las Vegas Convention Center to hear another 2020 contender— President Donald Trump. His rallies had become something of a Grateful Dead or Phish tour for the red-MAGA-hat crowd. Many of the same supporters showed up to rally after rally. Biden could only dream of that kind of devotion.

Leaning forward from behind his podium, Trump said the Democrats' Nevada caucus would fall victim to the same technical problems as their Iowa caucus, and that Russian president Vladimir Putin was pulling for Sanders to win the presidency.

"Wouldn't he rather have Bernie, who honeymooned in Moscow?" Trump said.

It was hard to miss the contrast between Trump's raucous rally and Biden's half-empty gym. The juxtaposition was just embarrassing. Afterward, Biden trip director Ashley Williams dressed down the political aides on hand in a way that made it clear her sentiments were shared, or would be shared, with the vice president and Jill Biden.

"I'm so angry I don't even want to talk to other staff," Williams said out of earshot of the vice president and his wife.

Her colleagues were taken aback by the blame-casting.

"You *are* staff," one of them replied. "What are we doing here?"

Williams was unmoved by the admonishment to work cooperatively.

"I could body-punch someone," Williams said in a construction so odd it lingered in the air.

Like Anthony Bernal, Ricchetti, and other aides who traveled with the Bidens, Williams was acting like a first-class passenger on a sinking ship. Instead of bailing water or helping lower a lifeboat, they pointed their fingers at the crew. It was hard for others to imagine the Bidens weren't thinking the same things Williams was saying. At the very least, she had the access to share her views with them.

Ironically, Biden had delivered one of his more passionate speeches to the sparse crowd in the gym. To the political operatives, he seemed to be digging deeper in a dark moment. He wasn't sure he would get the second-place finish he thought he needed.

"He thought this might be the end of the road," one aide said.

No place had made a bigger impression on Sanders's heart than Las Vegas—figuratively and literally.

Four months before the caucuses, doctors there had inserted stents that restored the flow of blood to his heart and his campaign. No other Democratic candidate would have been able to survive politically following a campaign-trail heart attack suffered in his late seventies. Sanders hadn't just survived the heart attack, he had turned it into a clarion call for working-class voters to put their shoulders, their small-dollar online donations, and their votes into his "revolution."

On caucus day, he flew back into the state from a California swing designed to pump up Latino voters in advance of Super Tuesday. Rocha camped out in the war room he'd set up and waited for numbers. He believed he'd done his job with Latinos. He just wasn't sure they were buying. The early entrance polls and data coming in slowly from the caucuses alarmed the Sanders team.

Outside, rain poured down on the Strip. That wasn't supposed to happen in Las Vegas in February—or really at any other time. Rain could easily dissuade people from showing up to the polls.

Inside the war room, Weaver couldn't understand why it looked like Bernie wasn't doing as well as he should be with Latinos. "Where are the Latinos?" he demanded of Rocha. "You spent three million dollars. Where are the Latinos?"

"You need to fucking relax," Rocha said, trying to hide his own anxiety. In truth, his sweat glands were working overtime. "I created the part of the universe that you can't cross-match against the data file." What he meant, essentially, was that they wouldn't be able to track a surge of new Latino voters in real time.

I hope he doesn't notice I'm making this shit up as I go along, Rocha thought.

At the same time, in the seven casinos where caucus sites were set up on Culinary Workers Union turf, Latinos poured in to vote. The decision to caucus for Sanders meant bucking the same shop stewards who negotiated contracts with management and influenced promotions, pay, and benefits for workers. The union's message was clear: anybody but Bernie. And, in a caucus, there was no secret ballot.

"Those workers get up in those rooms and walk to the Bernie side, or they raise their hands for Bernie, while the union is standing right there looking at them," said one senior member of the Sanders camp. That's what the vast majority of culinary workers did. Sanders won the Bellagio, Mandalay Bay, the Park MGM, Rio, and Wynn resorts. "It was just overwhelming," the Sanders aide said.

The casinos were a microcosm of what was happening across the state. In a head-to-head matchup with Clinton, Sanders won just over 50 percent of the Latino vote. Now, he was on track to win a hair less—exactly half of Latino voters—in a six-way race.

The effect of their votes was greater than their number for two reasons: the formula for allocating delegates rewarded candidates who could maximize their vote at certain caucus locations, and Sanders's larger campaign narrative relied on showing that his coalition was now broader than the working-class whites who backed him in 2016.

Sanders was on track to win the state—as he had expected. But he needed to add as much as possible to his momentum before the establishment struck back. Ideally, he would win close to a majority of the popular vote, at least on the second alignment. And the establishment candidates all had their eyes on second place. To come in even a distant second, Biden needed to rely heavily on Black voters and some share of the Hispanic union workers and moderate whites.

"First was not an option," said one Biden ally close to the campaign. "Would we be second amongst a busy field where Chuck Rocha had out-organized him and organized the Latino community better than anyone could possibly have imagined?"

Early in the night, with just 4 percent of precincts reporting, the Associated Press called the race for Sanders. In the first round of caucusing, he got more than 35,000 votes and increased his total to more than 41,000 when voters realigned for the second round. Because delegates were awarded disproportionately, he would end up claiming two-thirds of the available pool of thirty-six.

But for Biden and Buttigieg, who found themselves in a close race for second place, the caucus quickly—and then slowly—began to resemble its counterpart in Iowa. Results came in slowly, and Buttigieg's team said they didn't match up with the campaign's internal reporting. With the coveted second-place slot still up in the air, the Buttigieg campaign's top brass began sending smoke signals that their candidate had won—or, at least, he was going to come in second by a razor-thin margin.

The claim set off alarm bells in the Biden campaign's boiler room at an electrical workers' union hall in Las Vegas and at his Philadelphia headquarters. They had to obliterate that narrative right away. Biden was fighting for survival, and everyone knew the stakes. The perception that he would come in no higher than third represented an existential threat.

Siegel, Biden's chief analytics officer, called bullshit on a teleconference call.

"There's no way," she said. "He's absolutely not in second place."

"How strongly do you feel that we can say we came in second?" David Kieve, one of the aides in Nevada, asked.

Siegel, still in her late twenties, tended to be cautious about making major pronouncements. But as Sanders had nearly swept the Vegas Strip caucuses, Biden had won, tied for first, or come in second in all seven of them. More important, his focus on the Black electorate was paying off. He would finish with 38 percent among Black voters, well ahead of Sanders's 28 percent and billionaire California investor and philanthropist Tom Steyer's 17 percent. It was all enough to overcome any concern about being wrong.

"I feel confident," Siegel replied.

Biden's team pushed back hard against Buttigieg in the media, determined to prevent another Buttigieg public relations coup. It annoyed Biden's aides that Buttigieg was jumping the gun again, especially because they saw no path for him to win the party's nomination. It was already clear that Buttigieg had next to no support from people of color. Entrance polls showed him claiming 2 percent of the Black vote and about 11 percent of the Latino vote. Buttigieg was simply trying to prolong his campaign at their expense.

"The Buttigieg team did basically the same thing that they had done in Iowa," said one senior Biden aide.

Mayor Pete was bothersome in the moment, but the real importance of what Siegel said was that Biden had locked down second place. He had cleared the bar that the campaign set for him. All week, top advisers had been on the phone with Democratic elites asking them to hold off for just a little longer before abandoning the campaign. It was a desperate plea for a stay of execution.

"If we don't get second in Nevada, we're not going to get first in South Carolina," Schultz told one of the campaign's VIP supporters. "Then you can leave us. But hold on, give us until South Carolina."

It was a crappy second-place finish. Biden won less than 20 percent of the electorate. He'd gained only 755 votes in the second alignment, compared to 5,000-plus for Sanders and about 1,500 for Buttigieg. But Biden's support base was broad enough, geographically and ethnically, to deliver him 9 of the 36 available delegates. Sanders won 24, Buttigieg tallied only 3—despite finishing within 2 percentage points of Biden in the popular vote—and Warren, Klobuchar, and billionaire investor Tom Steyer were shut out. Against any other candidate than Sanders, Biden's slot would have been considered so distant as to warrant derision, not resurrection.

But for a campaign battered by the candidate's lackluster performance, roiled by the coup against Schultz, and devastated by its inability to break 20 percent of the popular vote in any state against Sanders and a roster of relative no-names, this was what winning looked like. Biden's aides were elated—and relieved.

But it sure didn't feel like winning to Biden. As he sped toward his "victory party" in a black Chevy Suburban, a couple of his grandkids distracted him from the gnawing concern that he hadn't finished well enough. He had to sell Nevada as the turning point for his campaign, the spark for a comeback. Sanders had put up the biggest numbers of the primary contest so far, and Bloomberg's billions loomed over Biden's shoulder.

"I ain't a socialist, and I ain't a plutocrat," Biden declared when he took the stage at International Brotherhood of Electrical Workers Local 357. "You know, the press is ready to declare people dead quickly, but we're alive and we're coming back and we're going to win."

Not everyone was buying it. "Biden Claims Comeback Despite Distant Second Finish to Sanders," *Politico*'s headline writers concluded. "Second is the new first for Joe Biden," the online publication for political insiders chided in its report on the caucuses.

I wanted an actual win, Biden thought. *This is good. But, shoot, it might not be enough.*

He caught up with Schultz in a hallway after his speech. Secret Service officers and Biden's family milled about. His shoulders, stiff for the performance onstage, had softened a bit. His chin dropped an inch or two. He'd been churning for months on end. Campaigning for president sapped his strength. He asked Schultz about the margin.

I wanted us to get second by about five points, Schultz told him, but this will work. Already, Biden's aides had begun checking in with major supporters. Schultz felt confident they would freeze in place until South Carolina.

He told his boss as much, adding that Biden still had to close the deal with South Carolina voters.

Biden took in the pablum impassively. But he understood fortune was shining on him, at least a little bit. Klobuchar had helped extinguish Buttigieg's flame, and she was dead in the water. Warren had torn a second hole in Bloomberg's ass, even as she continued to fade into oblivion. There was no telling what Bloomberg's money would mean on Super Tuesday, but he wouldn't be on the ballot in South Carolina. For the next week, it would be Biden vs. Sanders, and the fight was moving to Biden's home turf. He didn't know whether to feel lucky or unlucky. Besides, he didn't have any energy left for emotion.

At least he's not pissed, Schultz thought. That was a first for 2020.

CHAPTER 10

•

Firewall

JIM CLYBURN HAD HEARD ENOUGH—OR, REALLY, NOT ENOUGH. The House Democratic whip pushed himself out of his seat at Charleston's Gaillard Center concert hall. He dashed for the exit with the urgency that friends recognized as a seventy-nine-year-old man's hurry to find a restroom. But Clyburn didn't need to pee. He needed to find Joe Biden—and fast—before the end of a commercial break during the CBS News/Congressional Black Caucus Institute debate.

It was February 25, four days before the South Carolina primary, and Biden was blowing it again. Almost an hour and forty-five minutes had passed already, and Biden hadn't mentioned the one promise Clyburn had said would nail down Black votes in South Carolina, throughout the rest of the primary, and in the general election.

Clyburn was shocked, but not stunned. He made a beeline for the backstage area.

Pete Buttigieg approached to greet the most powerful Democrat in South Carolina politics. Clyburn brushed Mayor Pete aside. His eyes darted around, and he finally found Biden.

They huddled together out of earshot of the other candidates. There wasn't much time until Biden had to be back onstage for the final segment of the debate.

"You've had a couple of opportunities to mention naming a Black woman to the Supreme Court," Clyburn lectured his friend of nearly half a century, like a schoolteacher scolding a child. "I'm telling you, *don't you leave the stage tonight* without making it known that you will do that."

Biden had seemed to get it the night before, when Clyburn talked to him at a Congressional Black Caucus reception aboard the USS *Yorktown,* a decommissioned aircraft carrier that sat in Charleston Harbor as part of a naval museum. Along with Cedric Richmond and Representatives Bennie Thompson of Mississippi and Marcia Fudge of Ohio, Clyburn led Biden, Symone Sanders, and Valerie Biden Owens away from the mingling to a quiet food-preparation area. Biden was desperate to get Clyburn's endorsement and seemed eager to show respect to this group that had long sought a meeting with him.

Very few endorsements carry weight in modern politics. In South Carolina, though, a perception had built up that Clyburn's imprimatur meant everything. Voters believed it, the media believed it, and even most political insiders thought there was at least a good helping of truth in it. There was no Black political figure in the history of the state who had more influence with Black voters in South Carolina or across the Deep South.

When Clyburn first arrived in the House in 1993, he was the first Black member of Congress from South Carolina since George Washington Murray served two terms as the lone Black member of the House in the 1890s. He was the best inside player among a bumper crop of Black freshmen who won races in new Black-majority districts in the South created in the 1990 round of redistricting. Driven by then–House GOP whip Newt Gingrich, Republican legislatures had packed Black voters into super-majority districts to shrink the number of districts in the South represented by white Democrats. His plan helped Republicans win more seats overall and created safe districts for Black Democrats.

The reason this mattered for Clyburn was that the balance of power within the Congressional Black Caucus abruptly shifted from big-city northern power brokers like Charlie Rangel of New York and John Conyers of Detroit to a larger group of southern Black lawmakers. Clyburn was popular with the new set, and he won a seat on the House Appropriations Committee, where he accumulated power by allocating spending to the parochial and policy priorities of his colleagues. He won the chairmanship of the

Congressional Black Caucus in 1999. And, four years later, when it came time for Black lawmakers to help push one of their own into the leadership ranks of the Democratic Caucus, it was Clyburn who had the votes.

Over time, his constituency within the House spread from its original base among Black southern Democrats. But his alliances with that group made him a known figure in many majority-Black districts outside South Carolina, meaning that Clyburn's endorsement would ripple well beyond the Palmetto State. With many of those states' contests to follow on the heels of South Carolina, no imprimatur was more critical to Biden's path. Obama had more sway with Black Democrats than Clyburn, to be sure, but Obama's endorsement wasn't available. Clyburn was the big catch.

In mid-February, Cedric Richmond had made the plea directly to Clyburn as they sat down for lunch with Thompson and Fudge at the Hawk 'n' Dove, a restaurant and bar a few blocks from the Capitol. Richmond unburdened himself about his fears for the Biden campaign.

"Look, this campaign is going nowhere," Richmond confided. "You're going to have to endorse."

Clyburn wanted to endorse Biden. In fact, he had no intention of endorsing any other candidate. But he had promised the CBC Institute leaders that he wouldn't make a call until after the South Carolina debate. He didn't want to drain drama, and potentially the viewing interest of South Carolina voters, away from the institute's highest-profile event.

At the same time, he had left Biden with the impression that he would eventually endorse him. Clyburn's wife, Emily, had died in September, and he had talked with her about the various candidates. They had known Biden since at least the early 1970s, and Emily wanted Biden to win the nomination. Clyburn did, too. But he could also see how badly the wheels had come off Biden's campaign, and he was a savvy enough politician to know that there wasn't much point in endorsing someone who was going to lose. He also knew he would have more leverage with Biden before an endorsement than after one.

Clyburn told Richmond that he would wait until after the debate.

Richmond protested.

"He's going to have to win South Carolina to stay alive," Richmond said. "And he can't win South Carolina without your endorsement."

"Well," Clyburn replied, "I'll let you know."

By the time they gathered on the *Yorktown* the night before the debate, Biden was still waiting for the final word from Clyburn.

"I'm going to endorse you the morning after" the debate, Clyburn said. "But my endorsement ain't going to mean much, just to be frank, if you flame out in the debate."

The truth was, Clyburn already had gone so far as to film an ad for Biden. That afternoon, he'd quietly ducked into an elegantly reappointed nineteenth-century house on Water Street in Charleston's exclusive South of Broad neighborhood. A block and a half from one edge of the city's peninsula, the three-thousand-square-foot maze of hardwood floors and high ceilings belonged to former Obama drug czar Gil Kerlikowske, who had worked with Biden as the Justice Department's main man overseeing the 1994 crime bill's community-oriented policing program, COPS. The house was being used as a central gathering spot for a hodgepodge of Biden-affiliated political operatives during primary week.

As he recorded the ad for the pro-Biden super PAC Unite the Country, Clyburn hid his irritation at the fact that an anonymously sourced story in *Politico* the previous night had reported that he would endorse Biden. It was clear to Clyburn that Biden's campaign or its allies had leaked the details of the plan, down to the timing, even though Clyburn hadn't given his final approval. The congressman's aides were less reticent, as they chattered around the filming, letting everyone there know Clyburn was pissed.

The leak boxed Clyburn in. To the outside world, he would look duplicitous if, for some reason, he backed out of the endorsement. He had always said he would wait until after the debate, and he had added in recent days that he thought Biden would perform well. But no politician wants to endorse a candidate who then falls flat on his or her face. When that happens, two politicians look weak, not one. And Clyburn still wasn't sure that his endorsement would be enough of a lift for Biden. There were two questions hanging over Biden's head at that point: whether he would win the state and whether he would win by a margin large enough to signal to the rest of the country—and specifically to Black voters in the states voting three days later on Super Tuesday—that he was alive and kicking.

He and his top aides believed that he would, in fact, win. But there is always room for a surprise in electoral politics, and they still couldn't get a good handle on what a margin might look like.

"We were in jeopardy of it being too close," said one top Biden aide.

While the margin mattered for the number of delegates Biden would win, it mattered much more for the signal. In that way, South Carolina had proved pivotal to Obama in 2008 and Clinton in 2016 when they secured the ballots of more than 80 percent of Black voters.

On the *Yorktown* that night, Clyburn and his House colleagues offered Biden counsel and made what amounted to a political *ask*—the favor a politician requests in return when he is granting one. Biden, he thought, was getting tongue-tied on the trail because he was too scripted. The former vice president looked like he was trying to remember what he was supposed to say instead of just saying what he believed.

"I've been around you long enough," Clyburn said. "You know these issues, but you are not talking to the American people. You are just recalling words."

Biden, who had mostly been listening to the criticism, interjected to object. He thought he *was* talking to the American people.

"No," Clyburn said, cutting him off. "There are three things you need to do. Tell people what your presidency will do for them; tell them what it will do for their families; and tell them what it will do for their communities."

On the latter, Clyburn had a specific symbol in mind. Whether or not it was the key to winning over Black communities, it was something Clyburn wanted to get Biden to commit to before he made the endorsement public.

Biden should break ground on the Supreme Court in a way that Obama had not, Clyburn said. When Supreme Court justice Antonin Scalia died in 2016, Clyburn pressed the White House to name the dean of Howard University's law school, Danielle Holley-Walker, as his replacement. Clyburn expected Senate majority leader Mitch McConnell to block any nominee. But he believed

that if McConnell blocked a clearly qualified Black woman—
Holley-Walker held degrees from Yale and Harvard law and had
clerked for a judge at the second-highest level of the judiciary, a
federal circuit court—it would create a backlash among Black
women voters. Obama went in the opposite direction, politically,
by naming Merrick Garland, a white judge who previously had
been confirmed to the federal bench in an overwhelmingly bipartisan vote. It was a play for the middle designed to make McConnell
choose between confirming Obama's pick and blocking a milque-
toast nominee. McConnell never hesitated in refusing to even consider the nomination.

If Obama had gone with Holley-Walker, Clyburn thought,
*Black voters would have mobilized and Hillary Clinton would have
been elected president.*

Now Biden had a chance to make history just by making a
promise.

"Find a way to say that you were a part of picking the first Latina
woman member of the United States Supreme Court and you're
looking forward to making the first African American woman a
member of the United States Supreme Court," Clyburn instructed.

This wasn't offered as a condition of Clyburn's endorsement,
but it was an expectation. Clyburn believed, and there was good evidence to support his view, that a Supreme Court justice was worth
a lot more to the Black community than a vice president. Biden's
camp had talked about two Black women, Stacey Abrams and Kamala Harris—Abrams in positive terms, Harris in the negative—
as possible VP selections.

VPs come and go, Clyburn thought. *Al Gore was vice president.
Where is he now? But a Supreme Court seat: That's for life. No VP
ever did as much good for the Black community—or for justice, in
general—as Thurgood Marshall.*

"Naming a Black woman will bring the campaign forward,"
Clyburn told Biden.

Because CBC members had been pushing the idea behind the
scenes, Biden's aides had prepared him for this ask. When they had
discussed it privately, Biden's team urged him not to make a commitment.

"That's an interesting point on a Black woman for the Supreme
Court," Biden said.

Before wrapping up, he asked for assistance. "I don't know what you're going to do, but I need your support," Biden told the lawmakers.

Technically, none of the endorsements were conditioned on Biden saying he would name a Black woman to the high court. And Biden hadn't agreed to do it. But with Clyburn's ads still unreleased, his endorsement still ungiven, and his plain frustration over the leak, he could still pull back if he wanted to. He could also give a faint endorsement rather than a full-hearted one.

The meeting was fresh and front of mind for Biden the next day, as he prepared for that night's debate. He understood the difference between a narrow victory and a blowout: his margins with Black voters. If he committed to naming a Black woman to the Supreme Court, that might give him a lift. It would also help him with the CBC, meaning he could get a boost in delegate-loaded Black-majority districts across the country.

"I think I should do it," he told his advisers.

"Don't do it," Symone Sanders replied, speaking in concert with the group. If he wanted to do it at some point, his advisers agreed with one another, he should make a carefully considered plan around announcing that. It wasn't the kind of thing he should just throw out there on a debate stage. Besides, it might look like he was pandering and backfire. Biden was torn.

But Clyburn and his CBC colleagues believed their message had landed. And so, the next night, as Clyburn watched the debate unfold and didn't hear the words come out of Biden's mouth, he grew more and more frustrated. One opening, two, then three—Biden kept looking at flat, belt-high fastballs down the middle of the plate and leaving his bat on his shoulder. *Why won't he say it?* Clyburn asked himself. Finally, he took matters into his own hands at the commercial break.

Backstage, Biden looked his friend in the eye and nodded his assurance. Clyburn returned to his seat to watch the end of the debate. In his closing remarks, Biden fumbled out the promise.

"Everyone should be represented," he said in answer to a question about his personal motto and the biggest misconception about him. "The fact is, what we should be doing—we talked about the Supreme Court. I'm looking forward to making sure there's a Black woman on the Supreme Court, to make sure we in fact get every representation."

The crowd burst into applause.

"Not a joke," Biden said awkwardly. "I pushed very hard for that."

What? Clyburn thought. Biden hadn't already gotten a Black woman named to the court. He was supposed to say he had supported the nomination of the first Latina on the high court, Sonia Sotomayor, and then transition smoothly to promising to name the first Black woman. It wasn't that hard. Richmond was right. Biden was struggling on the campaign trail.

But it was good enough, Clyburn thought. The vow was now public, and there would be no easy way to go back on it. Even if Biden lost, pressure would mount on any other Democratic nominee to fulfill it.

Three days earlier, as Nevadans had gone to caucus, Biden's lead over Sanders in South Carolina narrowed from 23 percent to 21 percent—its tightest margin of the campaign—according to the Real Clear Politics average. Billionaire Tom Steyer, who saturated South Carolina with enough money to feed some nations for a year, had pushed his number up to 16 percent. Sanders's internal polls, a luxury that Biden couldn't afford, had the race within the margin of error at the top of the field.

Yet South Carolina looked like a trap to Sanders in the way Iowa had to Biden. He thought he would likely lose there, but he couldn't afford either to walk away from the first state where a heavy share of voters were Black, or to put in a weak effort certain to doom him to an embarrassing finish. The polls served as bait to his campaign to invest even more than he already had. He was three for three in winning the popular vote in the early contests, and, if he could somehow manage to take South Carolina, he might be unstoppable.

Sanders knew from experience that the winner in South Carolina often did far better than polls showed beforehand. Hillary Clinton had blown him completely out of the water despite surveys indicating a healthy but smaller margin of victory for her. Still, Sanders burned cash on ads. Even a strong second-place finish, he thought, could keep Biden in check as the race turned to Super Tuesday and a long slog to the convention. If Biden stumbled badly before voters went to the polls, Sanders's team concluded, there was an outside shot that their guy might win. Biden had shown a propensity to underperform already.

"Let's put the final push in, maybe we can pull this thing out," one of Sanders's top advisers said. Still, Sanders deployed most of his resources to other upcoming states. As aides made his schedule, they inked in travel out of South Carolina the week of the primary so that he could campaign up the East Coast in North Carolina and Virginia. Like everyone else, Sanders was uncertain about what the February 29 primary would do to the race.

The morning after the debate, Clyburn rose early and met up with Biden at Trident Technical College in North Charleston for a National Action Network breakfast. Technically, Clyburn was there to receive a leadership award from the NAN, a civil rights group founded by Al Sharpton. Sharpton had kept close tabs on the primary—and had met with many of the candidates since his January 2019 face-to-face with Biden—but he'd withheld his endorsement. Here, it was Clyburn's word that everyone was waiting for. Clyburn didn't know that the new NAN award had been named in honor of his late wife until he received it, and the tribute made him emotional. At the end of the breakfast, Clyburn, Biden, and various elected officials moved to an auditorium at the school. They walked in to the strains of Jackie Wilson's "(Your Love Keeps Lifting Me) Higher and Higher."

"Now, once, I was downhearted—disappointment was my closest friend," Wilson crooned. *"But then you came, and it soon departed. And you know, he never showed his face again."* The music stopped as Clyburn stepped up to a microphone bedecked with a Biden sign.

Six hundred fifty miles north on I-95, activity in Biden's Philadelphia headquarters came to a halt. All of the cable networks were carrying the announcement live. This was big. Staffers fixed their eyes on monitors around the office as Clyburn began to speak in North Charleston. Everyone knew Clyburn would endorse, but not what he would say. Would it be full-throated? Tepid? Even Clyburn's people weren't sure.

His voice cracking, Clyburn mentioned the award named for his wife. "There's nobody who Emily loved more in this country, as a leader, than she loved Joe Biden."

Then he unspooled a story about attending his accountant's funeral the previous Friday. A veteran of Black funerals, Clyburn had arrived half an hour early so he could kibbitz with fellow congregants. Like any community gathering, a funeral is a political event for a politician. An elderly woman, sitting in the front pew, beckoned to him with her index finger. She asked him to lean down, and he did. She told him the community needed to hear from him about who he intended to vote for.

"I decided right then and there that I would not stay silent," Clyburn said. "I want the public to know that I'm voting for Joe Biden. South Carolinians should vote for Joe Biden." Clyburn said his own challenge as a public servant is "making the greatness of this country accessible and affordable for all" and that no one he'd ever worked with was more committed to that than Biden. And then, with his voice breaking again, he introduced Biden by calling him "my late wife's great friend." Clyburn wrapped his arms around Biden—literally, as Biden would say—creating a picture-paints-a-thousand-words image for local and national media outlets.

"I knew he was going to endorse," one former Clyburn aide said. "I didn't know *how* he was going to endorse."

Sanders campaign manager Faiz Shakir, who had helped orchestrate AOC's "my *tío*" endorsement of Sanders following his heart attack, watched on television as Clyburn let his emotions show while speaking about his wife's feelings, and his own feelings, for Biden.

That's powerful, Shakir thought.

It was powerful enough to be felt back in Philadelphia, where Biden's headquarters team celebrated a new experience: an unmitigated public relations victory.

"That was a wall-to-wall coverage moment," said one Biden aide, who delighted with her colleagues as the endorsement news led broadcast after broadcast. "Clyburn endorsed in a way that had such moral authority that nobody could argue with it," said a second aide embedded at headquarters.

Inside Biden's campaign, there was a sense that, for the first time in ten months, the candidate had forward momentum. For all of the breaks that had gone Biden's way, there had been only sporadic interruptions in a firestorm of failure. He had survived getting in the race late, campaign infighting, pathetic fundraising, and finishing fourth, fifth, and a distant second in the first three states on the primary calendar. He had benefited from the spiking of the Iowa poll, the caucus debacle, debate-night drubbings of Buttigieg and Bloomberg in consecutive states, and so much more.

And yet the Clyburn endorsement was different from the rest: Biden had worked for it over the course of years—developing a relationship with Clyburn and his late wife, tending to a Charleston dredging project as vice president, and visiting the state for as long as he could remember. He had done what Clyburn asked him to do at the previous night's debate after they huddled backstage during a commercial break. He hoped that the endorsement would give him enough of a margin that the media, the donor class, and the reluctant party influencers would treat him like a real winner for the first time since his launch. It was impossible to know exactly where the line of demarcation for a "big enough" win sat, but he had three days left to work harder and, perhaps, get a little luckier.

CHAPTER 11

•

"The Old White Guy
Walks Away with the Prize"

O N THE MORNING OF THE SOUTH CAROLINA PRIMARY, BERNIE AND
Jane Sanders stopped in at an IHOP for breakfast, along with
top aides Faiz Shakir and Ari Rabin-Havt. They were accustomed
to having meals interrupted by a stream of people who wanted a
photograph or just a quick "hello" from the senator. Almost everywhere he went, there were fans. That was certainly true in Iowa and
New Hampshire, and his home state of Vermont. This place was
different. As Bernie looked around the joint, his eyes met a mosaic
of cartoonishly icy stares. The waitstaff was unusually curt—even
for a franchise pancake diner during the early shift on a Saturday.
He couldn't wait to get the hell out of there.

Pacing through the parking lot, he asked Shakir if he was imag-
ining things. "Seemed like a pretty hostile place," Sanders said.

"Yeah," Shakir confirmed. "It felt cold in there."

A foreboding feeling had taken root in the young campaign
manager's gut three days earlier during Clyburn's endorsement of
Biden, which included the prediction of a 15-point-or-better spread.
They must know something I don't, Shakir concluded about the
Biden team. His numbers showed a closer race.

Between the Nevada caucuses and Clyburn's endorsement four
days later, the margin of Biden's lead in the state had grown from a
couple of points to about a dozen. Several factors may have contributed to that, including Biden hitting the self-set mark of second
place in Nevada and the South Carolina electorate focusing more

on the race as primary day drew closer. The bump in Biden's stock didn't shock Sanders's team. But Clyburn's 15-point bar suggested that he had confidence the final number would be well north of that. If Biden won by a dozen points with just 35 percent of the electorate—the level at which he was polling—it would be interpreted as a sign of life but hardly confirmation that he was on fire. Clyburn was trying to define that line of demarcation for a "big enough" win at 15 points, and he wouldn't want to create expectations that Biden couldn't meet.

And yet even with Biden surging, Democratic elites preoccupied themselves with the fear of Sanders winning big in California and Texas three days after the South Carolina primary. Bloomberg's dramatic failure in the Nevada debate had rattled nerves. "A panic set in," said one party heavyweight. Neither Buttigieg nor Klobuchar had hit the 15 percent threshold to win statewide delegates in Nevada, and their problems with voters of color were clear. Other than Biden, that left Warren, who hadn't finished above third place in any of the first three contests. If all of the non-Sanders candidates stayed in the race, they would siphon support from one another and give Bernie an easier path to capturing large troves of delegates.

Together, California and Texas accounted for more than 750 delegates, compared to less than 200 for all four early states combined, and Sanders was positioned well to win both of them. And they weren't the only Super Tuesday states where Sanders figured to win or do well.

The delegates from each state were split into pots: one based on the share of the vote each candidate won statewide and one based on the share of the vote each candidate won in each congressional district. If Sanders hit the 15 percent mark statewide in a given state and no one else did, he would get the whole pot of statewide delegates.

Bloomberg's debate performance in South Carolina rated only a little better than his showing in Nevada—like the difference between a technical knockout and one of the stone-cold variety. Before Bloomberg's debate debacles, some insiders took his presence as calming. Most of these insiders were more opposed to Sanders than they were in love with Bloomberg, but they figured his billions and his national profile could stop Sanders from running away with the nomination. Now, though, Bloomberg looked less capable of carrying the establishment on his back. "You can't be the savior if you're a dud," one heavyweight Democratic donor said. Many unnerved Democratic establishment centrists weren't sure what they would do if it came down to Trump and Sanders in a general election. Founded or not, their fears of losing their party to socialism competed with their fears of Trump winning a second term.

But even with all the if-then factors lining up in Sanders's favor, there was a basic countervailing truth that escaped many of the fearful establishment Democrats: It wasn't just the party elites who didn't want Sanders. Most of the party's *voters* didn't want him, either. That made the probability that he would win the nomination as small as a mouse's molars. A more likely possibility was that it would take a long time for Sanders to be defeated, perhaps not until the summer convention. Of course a floor fight at the convention would hardly encourage the unity Democrats would need to beat Trump; but it might turn out to be the only way to stop Sanders.

As South Carolina voters filed into schools and churches to vote that Saturday morning, every Democratic candidate claimed to have a viable strategy for winning the nomination. But more than a year after the campaign started, not one of them had anything resembling a probable path. The flaws were plain: If Sanders won pluralities in state after state, he would surely still walk into a hostile convention with less than half the delegates and no allies. Buttigieg and Klobuchar couldn't compete with voters of color, and the idea that a nominee would emerge from a contested Democratic convention without support from Black and Hispanic voters wasn't serious enough to be laughable. Bloomberg had money, but no game. Warren had peaked in the fall.

And JoeBiden—one word to his aides—had underperformed even the low expectations his campaign had set for him. He'd stumbled through debates, lost the states where he'd campaigned the most, and burned through his money. Even if South Carolina put a strong wind at his back, he wasn't prepared to capture its force because he didn't have cash for TV ads or real campaign operations in Super Tuesday states.

As Buttigieg's aides looked at the Super Tuesday map, they could see that their candidate was on the bubble in state after state and district after district. These were not states and districts where he would win. They were places where a marginal change would put him over or under the 15 percent delegate threshold. Buttigieg senior campaign adviser Michael Halle thought Buttigieg's result in South Carolina would have an outsized influence on whether he could be competitive elsewhere. A disappointing finish would likely drain enthusiasm and keep him under the threshold in most states and districts. An unexpectedly strong showing in South Carolina could potentially give him just the boost he needed to capture delegates on Super Tuesday.

By the morning of the South Carolina primary, Buttigieg's aides had gamed out scenarios for keeping the campaign moving—or ending it—based on his performance that night. Among the dozens of public polls of South Carolina, there had been only one survey in which Buttigieg hit as high as 15 percent. He consistently trailed Biden, Sanders, and Steyer. Pete's aides weren't certain what he would want to do after a third consecutive loss in which each state was worse than the last. But they planned to present him with a clear view of his chances of rebounding, and his options, by the morning after the primary.

Clyburn thought Buttigieg would get blown out. One of his grandsons was working on the former mayor's campaign, and the congressman had trash-talked him in the days leading up to the vote. "When you were growing up, I never spanked you," Clyburn said. "But I'm going to give you a good spanking on this election day."

Biden spent much of his election day, a Saturday, in neighboring North Carolina, where he campaigned for votes in that state's upcoming Super Tuesday primary. Returning to South Carolina in the afternoon, he stopped in for an evening Mass at a Catholic church in Columbia. With the annual commemoration of "Bloody Sunday" in Alabama the following morning, Biden had worried that his participation in services at the Brown Chapel AME Church in Selma would preclude him from attending Mass in a Catholic church on Sunday. Riding in the back of a Suburban from church to his hotel, Biden received a call from Dunn, who was at the campaign's headquarters in Philadelphia. Exit polls had been released. They didn't predict the votes for each candidate, but they did show enough demographic data for campaign aides to start to get a good idea of how they would fare.

"You're going to win a very large victory based on the exit polls," Dunn reported.

Biden wasn't surprised, but a heavy weight lifted from his shoulders. For the first time in three presidential campaigns, he was going to win a primary, and there wouldn't be headlines about how he had underperformed expectations. For the first time, in this state, the vision he had for winning the Democratic nomination— back in the rental house in McLean in early 2019, at the Naval Observatory in 2015, and for the previous forty-plus years—matched up with reality on the ground.

In Philadelphia, Biden's headquarters team gathered in the "bullpen"—the open office space—to watch coverage of the primary on television. There was little need to be connected to the campaign's boiler room in the state, and the mood was light. His aides knew what the exit polls suggested, so scoreboard watching was all about measuring the rout.

That was one obvious sign this night would be different from all the others. The other was the Italian food they picked at while they waited for the first returns. On the nights of the first debate—when Harris had hammered Biden on school busing—and the Iowa caucuses, District Taco had been the fare of choice. Subsequently, Ricchetti declared that the restaurant was dead to the campaign. "It was a ban at HQ. You weren't allowed to eat District Taco," said one aide. "You couldn't go there for lunch. Ricchetti hated District Taco. It was a hard rule." There was also a prohibition on getting haircuts on election days. Biden's run of misfortune had been so profoundly dark as to engender superstitions around tacos and personal hygiene.

But before the pasta could get cold—one minute after the 7:00 P.M. poll-closing time—the Associated Press called the race for Biden. "We started drinking at 7:02 P.M.," said one source who was in the bullpen. Dunn walked around the office reminding people that they had to stay sharp because only Sunday and Monday stood between South Carolina and Super Tuesday. She was roundly ignored. "We had been at the lowest point," said one senior aide to the campaign. "We had been a front-runner, we had been a failure. We were the biggest losers, the biggest failure, and then we came back." And, channeling Nuke LaLoosh, the simpleminded pitching phenom in the classic baseball film *Bull Durham,* the aide said, "You know, winning is more fun than losing."

As Dunn had predicted to Biden, it was a big win. Exit polls showed he took first among Black voters with 61 percent and first among white voters with 33 percent. His share of the Black vote fell far short of Obama's 78 percent in 2008 and Clinton's 84 percent, according to exit polls. But the white share of the electorate would prove to be unusually high at more than 50 percent, according to Democratic operatives who later matched data to voter files. They attributed the dynamic in large part to Republicans, with no primary on their side, showing up to smack down Sanders and socialism. No one talked about the other way of looking at it: Biden was strong with the Black voters who showed up to the polls—given the number of candidates in the race—but he wasn't driving *more* Black voters to the polls. His overall vote total was more than 30,000 shy of Obama's 2008 tally, or about 11 percent less, in a three-way race that also featured Clinton and John Edwards.

But overall, Biden finished with 49 percent of the vote statewide, not so far behind Obama's 55.4 percent. Sanders came in second at 20 percent, Steyer took third with 11 percent, and Buttigieg cobbled together 8 percent. Warren placed fifth with 7 percent, and Klobuchar managed just 3 percent. In winning by almost 30 points, Biden performed best in the only majority-Black district in the state—Clyburn's Sixth District—where he got nearly 60 percent of the vote.

His data analysts believed that would foreshadow crushing his competition in majority-Black districts in Super Tuesday states, where a disproportionately high number of delegates were in play. It was a relief to win the "firewall" state, but it was also just the start of what promised to be a long fight to win the most delegates before the party's nominating convention.

"At least we were going to be able to compete," said one top Biden adviser, who noted that digital and radio ad buys in Super Tuesday states were "minuscule." There wasn't enough time to stand up new operations in those states, even as money started to flow back into the campaign's coffers in real time. How much value would the big victory have in terms of free media coverage substituting for advertising, voters seeing Biden as resurgent rather than recumbent, and Democratic insiders shifting toward Biden? All of that was unknowable.

Biden was beaming when he arrived at the Carolina Volleyball Center, where he would deliver brief and enthusiastic remarks on his comeback. Spotting Clyburn when he walked in, Biden made a beeline for his old friend.

"You put this campaign on your shoulders," Biden told him. It was true enough. Given Biden's margin—and the fact that he'd led all along in state polls—Clyburn didn't account for the difference between victory and defeat. But he could certainly claim credit for a good part of the decisive margin.

Biden went over his speech in a spacious holding room with low-bottomed chairs arranged around a conference table. In the room's mirrored wall, he could see the reflection of perseverance. He wasn't the first choice of most Democrats, but he aimed to be their last one.

Taking the stage at his victory rally, wearing his trademark navy blue suit and with a silver tie knotted tight at his collar, Biden punched the life-giving nature of his win. It wasn't just political resurrection he found in South Carolina. When he'd landed in the state the night of the New Hampshire primary, he'd been visibly weary and emotionally downtrodden. His ad hoc rally in Columbia that night, eighteen days before his primary win, had felt like a much-needed homecoming. He had maintained faith that the "firewall" state would turn things around for him, even on the most brutal days slogging through the first two states, but it was never real until it happened. One of Biden's aides described his feeling as "a place beyond happiness."

Now, sustained, he told a boisterous crowd that he would be able to keep fighting.

"Just days ago, the press and the pundits declared this candidacy dead," he said. "Now, thanks to all of you, the heart of the Democratic Party, we just won, and we won big because of you. And we are very much alive."

That night, Clyburn spoke to the grandson who worked for Buttigieg. The congressman gloated about his prediction that Biden would thrash the field.

"I knew I had it coming," his grandson said.

There was no question about the influence Clyburn had in energizing Biden's campaign, nor was there any question that Biden's success in South Carolina would translate into more support on Super Tuesday. Even the narrative of Clyburn rescuing the campaign was a good one for Super Tuesday—and for the general election—when Biden would need Black voters to take ownership of his fate. But it wasn't clear to anyone just how much or where Biden's numbers would jump over the next three days.

He wasn't in a position to maximize the good fortune. The campaign had made next to no investment in states beyond South Carolina because he'd blown his war chest on Iowa and New Hampshire. He had shifted staff out of Super Tuesday states into Nevada and South Carolina. All of this robbing Peter to pay Paul left him exposed to the vagaries of momentum. And Bloomberg, polling in double digits nationally, still had yet to appear on a ballot. With so many candidates in the race, Biden himself was not immune from the 15 percent threshold problem. A widely split vote threatened to drag him under in a long list of states and congressional districts, including the delegate mine of California.

That all added up to a long, drawn-out fight to the convention. For the anti-Sanders wing of the party, the best move was to coalesce behind a single candidate who could easily defeat him. But through four states, no candidate had won a majority of the vote. It was hard to see the incentive for any of them to drop out. At least, it was hard to see from outside the campaigns.

Within the political world, though, pressure could be applied—if you had the right leverage.

On the wall behind his desk, in a corner pod in the Philly HQ bullpen, Greg Schultz maintained a whiteboard of the names of Democratic elites who liked Biden but were supporting other candidates. These were the people who could be leaned on to lobby their own favorites to get out of the race at a crucial moment. It was such a secretive operation that Schultz, who was still a vital liaison for the campaign to big-timers in the political world, used his own shorthand on the color-coded chart so that fellow aides couldn't surmise what he was up to.

While Schultz would later tell others that he never got to the point where he asked these elites directly to put pressure on other candidates to exit the race, they were people with whom Biden campaign aides and allies had frequent ongoing contact. They all knew Biden's team believed their guy would win a one-on-one scrap with Sanders, but that he feared that Klobuchar, Buttigieg, Bloomberg, and Warren would just suck votes away from him in a protracted battle royale. An intraparty primary is like a small town—all the political players know one another—and Schultz had an up-to-date phone tree.

When Pete Buttigieg woke up early Sunday, March 1, 2020, at the Hampton Inn in Americus, Georgia, he had made up his mind. *This is going to be the last day,* he thought as he got out of bed.

He'd flown into the state for a quick meeting with former president Jimmy Carter later that morning on his way to Selma, Alabama, where he and other prominent politicians would join civil rights leaders and activists for the annual march commemorating the 1965 "Bloody Sunday" attack on peaceful voting-rights demonstrators at the Edmund Pettus Bridge. Before he'd shut his eyes Saturday night, Buttigieg had heard a unanimous recommendation from his people that it was time to pull the plug. His delegate projections for Super Tuesday based on the results in the first four contests looked bleak: He would need freakishly great outcomes in the coming states to have any path to the nomination, even through a party-splitting convention brawl. Halle had walked him through the math. His aides noted that it would be better for his future in Democratic politics if he ended the campaign without debilitating losses on Super Tuesday and in the interest of bringing the primary to a close. If he was perceived to be running a vanity project at the cost of defeating Sanders, many Democrats would never forgive him. *It is time to wrap it up,* he thought, as he got ready to meet the thirty-ninth president.

Jimmy Carter didn't seem like a hard-ass. The frail Georgian, now ninety-five, had come to define noble obligation for Democrats in the thirty-nine years since he'd handed the keys of the White House over to Ronald Reagan. He'd also developed a liking for Buttigieg, who had made a point of seeking out his wisdom over the course of the campaign. Though older at the time, Carter, too, had been a little-known politician from a relatively small corner of the country who banked his chances on Iowa—he came in a strong second to "undeclared" in the 1976 caucuses—and his ability to appeal to progressives and moderates who saw in him what they wanted to see.

Over breakfast at the Buffalo Café in Plains, the kind of folksy red-brick tavern where a former president could feel at home while dining out, Carter complimented Buttigieg. You've run a brilliant campaign, the oldest living president began, but . . .

Pete lost focus for a moment as he digested the "but." When they had first sat down, Buttigieg felt like he was taking part in a benediction. Now, he realized, Carter was delivering an elegy.

In his own guileless way, he's telling me to get out, Pete thought.

One state over, in Alabama, Klobuchar hoped to discuss the same topic with Buttigieg. Obama was trying to get in touch with her, but she hadn't connected with him yet. She was smart enough to know he wasn't calling to encourage her to fight for every last vote. She had heard Buttigieg was jetting in around the same time her flight landed, so she waited at the airport for his arrival.

We're in similar positions, and we need to figure out what we're going to do here, she thought. Two weeks after she had embarrassed him on a debate stage in New Hampshire, the pair shared a set of options.

A version of the same conversation Buttigieg was having with his top aides was going on in her camp. She simply didn't have a clear path to the nomination—or even really a murky one. Like Pete, she could hang on through a rough Super Tuesday—she thought she could win her own home state but little else—and hope to be the last establishment candidate standing at the end. But at what cost to the party and to her own reputation? And at what cost to Biden, who was ahead of her in delegates? She had always looked at herself as an alternative if Biden flamed out. Now, he was on fire.

But she wouldn't get the chance to talk it all over with Buttigieg. His flight was delayed, and she didn't want to be late to the Selma bridge crossing. Klobuchar left the airport for the Brown Chapel AME, where civil rights activists had prepared for their march in 1965. Sitting in the historic building, the first Black church in Alabama, Klobuchar began to make her peace with the end of her campaign.

What's the right thing to do for the country? she asked herself.

As is often the case for politicians, Klobuchar's answer to that question matched her own self-interest. Like Buttigieg, she could preserve her viability in a future race by getting behind Biden before getting slaughtered on Super Tuesday. More immediate, she envisioned herself on the short list of potential vice presidential picks for Biden. If she hurt him on Super Tuesday, that possibility might vanish. She called her husband and told him what she had decided.

On the bridge later that day, Buttigieg noticed that Biden and Sanders weren't there. Biden had spoken at the church service in the morning, as had Bloomberg, who watched as a number of congregants turned their backs on him in protest of his policing policies as New York mayor. It was Buttigieg, Warren, and Klobuchar who could afford to spend their time mingling with civil rights leaders and elected officials from all over the country two days before a primary in the state.

All of us are assessing our campaigns, he thought. *The others are running theirs.*

Obama's calculus had changed, too. For more than a year, he had stayed almost entirely out of the race publicly. Behind the scenes, he had offered counsel to Biden on occasion, but he had reacted to the twists and turns of the process-of-elimination primary like so many other Democrats. He had met with candidates. He liked most of them enough. He had gone through an O'Rourke phase, a Harris phase, and a Warren phase, according to people close to him. Or, as one friend put it, "He flirted a lot."

But now he could see the conundrum facing the party pretty clearly. The main alternatives to Biden were Sanders, who preferred being an "independent" democratic socialist to being a "Democrat," and the ultra-wealthy former Republican Bloomberg, who did not have the common touch of, say, a Donald Trump. The party was in danger of splitting off to one extreme or the other. The also-ran candidates only served to weaken Biden, with the possible exception of Warren, whose modest set of supporters might break evenly between Biden and Sanders if she dropped out.

Biden had become Obama's choice, even if he wouldn't say it publicly. The man had been his vice president—his "brother," Obama had said. Between Dunn and O'Malley Dillon, who was lined up to take over the campaign, Obama also had strong ties to the mechanics of the Biden operation. He was ready to get his hands a little dirtier on Biden's behalf, but he wasn't about to tell candidates when to get out. He had run twice himself. He knew that was a personal decision. But he would be helpful in other ways.

That Sunday night in South Bend, after announcing his withdrawal from the race, Buttigieg received calls from Biden and Obama.

Biden called first. I'd like your support, he said. Pete demurred. He wasn't ready to give up his last chip yet. He said he had just ended his campaign and wanted to think about it. Biden agreed to give him that space.

Obama's call was different, less plaintive, more tactical. As they spoke, Buttigieg's mind replayed their meeting at Obama's Washington office almost a year earlier.

You have to know who you are in politics, Obama had counseled then. A campaign can have a distorting effect on your compass. The media will fashion one version of you. Your rivals will have another. Even your supporters and aides will have ideas about who you are that differ from your own true north. *Know yourself,* Pete thought.

Obama played to Pete's ambition to press for a Biden endorsement.

Look, Pete, you will never have more clout than you do right now, Obama said.

Buttigieg understood. If he waited until after Super Tuesday—with fourteen states and American Samoa on the calendar—his endorsement wouldn't mean as much. Worse yet, if Sanders or Bloomberg won the nomination, Buttigieg might shoulder blame for continuing a quixotic campaign at the expense of the Democratic Party.

Buttigieg had run these calculations in his own mind before Obama called, and he had chosen not to endorse while he was dropping out. But the clock was ticking. Voters would go to the polls in Super Tuesday states in less than forty-eight hours. The mere fact that Obama said anything more than "Congratulations on a great campaign" pointed to the urgency of the Biden camp.

Biden hadn't closed the deal, but Obama now had his back. The former president made a round of calls to Biden's rivals after South

Carolina and before Super Tuesday. He never connected with Klobuchar, who was savvy enough to know why he was trying to reach her.

Early Monday morning, Rufus Gifford, Obama's former finance director, sent an email to Obama's list of top donors asking for their help. "We need you again," Gifford wrote. It was a sign to the moneyed set of Democrats that Obama wanted them to get behind Biden now.

That morning, Buttigieg and Klobuchar both sent word to Biden's team that they would endorse. Their exit would mean two fewer establishment candidates bleeding votes from Biden. This was a blessing that would help him clear the delegate threshold in more states and districts—and perhaps increase his margin in those he would win—as he battled Sanders.

Across the country, as media outlets reported on the force of the South Carolina victory and high-profile endorsements coming his way, support for Biden exploded. That was as much about Sanders as it was about Biden. "At that moment, Bernie was going to be our nominee from a delegate perspective," said one top strategist for another campaign. "Fuck, we were like 'This is going to happen.' California—first nail in the coffin."

But Democratic voters were paying close attention to the race, and they began to line up to stop Sanders at a speed that no one in politics could remember. Numbers moved so fast that the new army of data analysts working for Bloomberg, who had built his namesake company on relaying financial market fluctuations instantaneously to traders, had trouble keeping up. Bloomberg's data crunchers tried to pour new survey information into models designed to predict how many delegates each candidate might claim in Super Tuesday states. Biden's graph resembled a vertical line.

"It was moving so fast they couldn't price it into the models," said one senior Bloomberg adviser. "It was crazy to watch how fast the numbers were moving and what that did to the delegate count."

For months, Biden's chief data analytics officer, Becca Siegel, had been doubling as an internal sales representative, explaining to her colleagues why certain unconventional decisions were optimal. Not many people within the campaign fully understood why her data pointed to sending Biden to a certain location within a state, spending limited ad dollars in one media market instead of another, or focusing intently on one set of voters over another. But they all bought into her basic strategy: Compete to get at least 15 percent in every district and push to prevent rivals from winning delegates in Biden's best districts. The former, which depended on Biden performing well enough in predominantly white working-class and rural parts of the country, would be easier without competition from Klobuchar and Buttigieg. The latter relied on Black voters in other states repeating what their counterparts in South Carolina had done.

"Our strategy didn't change" before Super Tuesday, said one Biden aide. But now there was a new emphasis on running up the score—moving Biden's numbers up to the mark needed to win all of the delegates in districts where it looked like he was positioned to take a majority. "Now, it's like 'Let's just pound those districts,'" the aide said.

On Monday morning, as Biden's HQ team tried to keep up with the good news—instant polls showing surges across the map, donations pouring in, and long-sought endorsements getting locked down—his aides noticed a rancid smell. Thinking it was a gas leak, they scrambled out of the office and into the street. But the stench was inescapable. It permeated the air in Center City. For much of the Biden team, the long-awaited taste of victory was that of mercaptan—a chemical additive to natural gas that smells like rotten eggs—released from a refinery along the Delaware River.

Later that day, Biden met Buttigieg on a tarmac in Dallas. They climbed into the same Chevy Suburban so they could talk privately. As they rode toward the chicken joint where Buttigieg would officially offer his endorsement, Biden hinted that there would be a place in his administration for Buttigieg.

"I want to support the future generation of Democratic leaders," Biden said.

That was no small point for Biden to make. He had served as vice president to a man who'd wrested control of the party machinery from the Clintons and then let it atrophy. Between Obama and the two Clintons, there hadn't been enough sunlight for other Democrats to fully develop their talent and their profiles for years. Biden's return, thirty-two years after he'd first run for the presidency, was evidence of that in and of itself. To get vanquished rivals to give their all for him—especially those who might run in 2024 if he lost—Biden had to sell the idea that he would help rather than block them.

Pete listened closely as Biden talked about being a bridge to the next generation. Then, Biden paused for a moment. Take a look at my speech, he said, handing his notes to Buttigieg.

Pete, usually so unemotional, didn't get far before he felt a twinge in his throat. *"I look over at Pete during the debates, and I think, you know, that's a Beau,"* Biden planned to say in comparing the former mayor to his own late son. *"I promise you that over your lifetime, you're going to end up seeing a hell of a lot more of Pete than you are of me."*

I can't believe this, Pete thought. *There's nothing I can say to match the power of that.*

Biden's fortunes had turned over the course of two weeks. In that time, he'd gone from disappointing, broke failure back to front-runner for the Democratic nomination. Warren had erased the threat of Bloomberg. Biden had stumbled into second place in Nevada and soared in South Carolina. And now two of the rivals who ate up anti-Sanders vote share were urging their supporters to get behind him in advance of the most consequential election day of the primary calendar. One of them sat next to him, speechless. The other, Klobuchar, would join him at a rally later in the night that winked at the possibility she would become his running mate.

Biden had set a vision and a strategy for the campaign and stuck to them. They were his strengths, even when his skills as a campaigner were shaky. And they had put him in position to capitalize on good fortune. Or, as one top aide to another candidate put it, "Only in America can Jim Clyburn and Elizabeth Warren, the Black guy and the woman, do all the work and then the old white guy walks away with the prize."

CHAPTER 12

•

The Passenger

JOE BIDEN COULDN'T REALLY FEEL THE DEMOCRATIC PARTY RISING up to meet him until the morning of March 3, 2020, Super Tuesday. The night before, he'd accepted endorsements from three former rivals—Klobuchar, Buttigieg, and O'Rourke—in Texas. It was one thing for political adversaries to lay down their swords and pledge their loyalty. But that didn't mean voters would come with them. So it wasn't until he walked into Buttercup Diner in Oakland, California, the next morning—a little exhausted from a late-night Whataburger with O'Rourke and an early flight to the West Coast—that he started to understand the scale of the shift in his direction. Early-arriving voters crammed into the family-style restaurant, and late-comers pressed their faces to a picture window to get a look at the establishment favorite.

There was a crowd—a legitimate, diverse, somewhat excited crowd!—to see him. They weren't there for Bernie Sanders, or for the whole lot of Democratic candidates. Just Joe. It reminded him of being vice president, and it also reminded him of the lifeless days on the trail where he could see vast stretches of open space at sparsely attended rallies. Even if his campaign had stoked turnout for his visit on the most important day of the primary calendar, people had actually shown up. He could feel the energy surround him. That had not been true at the Liberty and Justice Celebration in Iowa in November, nor at his big speech the night before the Nevada caucuses. It hadn't been anywhere, really, until South Carolina, where he had spent so much time over the years. This was Oakland, a bastion of West Coast liberalism, where he was known mostly in name only. At seventy-seven, he was suddenly, finally, the "it" candidate of the Democratic Party and at just the right time—for him and for the party.

I love this, Biden thought. *This is what I thought the campaign would feel like.*

In a historic Capitol back room, several of Jim Clyburn's closest friends lined up election scorecards next to plates of chicken—Popeye's, and General Tso's from a nearby Chinese restaurant—as they sat around a giant conference table. Clyburn stood atop the political world, at least for the moment, and he had invited members of the Congressional Black Caucus to track Super Tuesday results with him in the Lincoln Room. Voters in fourteen states and American Samoa would render their verdicts on the Democratic candidates. Clyburn hoped that Biden would at least fight Sanders to a draw, but anticipation of a Biden romp touched every political nerve in his body. He predicted as much to the clutch of lawmakers who had joined him—Richmond, Thompson, Fudge, Lisa Blunt Rochester of Delaware, Steven Horsford of Nevada, Karen Bass of California, and a couple of others.

The scene served as a testament to the usually glacial pace of shifts in power in the United States. Clyburn controlled the Lincoln Room by virtue of his post as majority whip, the third-ranking job in the Democratic leadership. Originally the House post office, and later dedicated to Lincoln because he had sought solitude there during his brief tenure in the House, the suite shared a wall with the Capitol's famed Statuary Hall.

Outside that wall, where visitors trudged across the black and white marble floors each day, stood statues donated to the Capitol collection by each state. In 1931, at the height of the Jim Crow era, Mississippi had sent a stone memorial of Jefferson Davis, the president of the Confederate States of America. There were other Confederate statues in the hall and around the Capitol, but Davis's visage remained the building's most striking symbol of southern white resistance to abolition and equal rights for people of color. And yet on the inside of the Lincoln Room, descendants of slaves and sharecroppers now held power. The CBC had existed for less than half a century, but its ranks had grown more robust and its members more influential in Congress over the course of nearly five decades. That change had been so slow, so incremental, from the Emancipation Proclamation to the Voting Rights Act to modern battles over congressional redistricting and voter-identification laws. But the transformation of Biden's campaign had been effected in the blink of an eye by Black voters and a few key members of the CBC.

Richmond, the campaign's co-chairman, had insisted on getting Biden out of New Hampshire—and to the friendly confines of South Carolina—pushing the candidate and his fellow campaign advisers to shed the cloak of defeat as quickly as possible. Fudge and Thompson, influential in their own rights, lobbied Biden, along with Clyburn, to show more fight and to name a Black woman to the Supreme Court. Eddie Bernice Johnson, a Dallas Democrat, urged Clyburn to get behind Biden because she saw the former vice president as the party's best hope for winning the general election and helping down-ballot candidates in November. And then there was Clyburn, who had turbo-boosted Biden's campaign with a perfectly timed and perfectly toned endorsement in South Carolina.

More than that, the CBC members' districts, many of them majority-Black, held outsized influence in Democratic presidential nomination fights. On this night, they would find out if it would be enough to keep Biden viable or, perhaps, slingshot him to the front of the pack. They would not have to wait long.

Just after the first poll closings of the night, at seven P.M. eastern, the Associated Press called Virginia and North Carolina for Biden. Sanders had campaigned aggressively in both states, where roughly one-fifth of the population is Black. But the instantaneous calls indicated that Biden had won big. In Virginia, he carried 69 percent of the Black vote, and in North Carolina, he took 62 percent, according to exit polls. Biden also won the white vote, taking nearly half of it in Virginia and about one-third in North Carolina, with Sanders, Bloomberg, and Warren on the ballot alongside him. Biden was doing what Hillary Clinton had struggled to do nearly as well in the 2016 primary: beating Sanders with non-college-educated whites while trouncing him among Black voters. Exit polls in North Carolina showed a draw between the candidates among less-educated whites, while Biden won them 46 percent to 31 percent in Virginia. He also won a plurality of Hispanic voters in both states. But the Black voters in these states, who favored Biden by huge margins, held more value in the complex math of delegate allocation.

In North Carolina, Biden won 43 percent of the statewide vote and 56 percent of the delegates, mostly because of his strength in majority-Black areas. His best district across the two states was North Carolina's First, represented by G. K. Butterfield, who watched the call in the Lincoln Room. Biden took 5 delegates to Sanders's 1 there. And overall, North Carolina and Virginia provided him 135 delegates to Sanders's 68. Lawmakers in the Lincoln Room began filling out their scorecards with estimated delegates—and with deep satisfaction.

At the same time, Sanders won his home state of Vermont, but not as decisively as he would have hoped. Biden took more than 20 percent of the vote in the state, allowing Sanders only an 11 to 5 margin in delegates.

Inside the Lincoln Room, Clyburn began to loosen up. In the days since his endorsement of Biden, he had recorded automated calls to Black voters in several Super Tuesday states and campaigned for Biden in North Carolina. Friends around the country told him that his endorsement had lit a fuse for Biden among Black voters.

"I told you it was going to happen," he crowed to his colleagues as the results of the first batch of states were announced. Then he lifted a glass of Jack Daniel's and Diet Pepsi to his lips and took a healthy sip.

At eight P.M. eastern time, the Associated Press called Alabama for Biden. For months, Biden campaign data guru Becca Siegel had been obsessed in particular with the state's Seventh District. Like Clyburn's district, "Alabama Seven" is the only Black-majority district out of seven House districts in a state where Black residents make up more than a quarter of the population. When Siegel's team ran data through an algorithm used to prioritize the campaign's allocation of resources among the nation's 435 House districts, Alabama Seven routinely ranked No. 1 because it carried the most bang for the buck in terms of potential delegate haul. In the dark days before the Iowa caucuses, Schultz had tried to keep

Biden's heavy-hitting political allies and donors on board by pointing to the district as representative of a strategy that would gain
traction later in the year.

As it turned out, Biden won nearly two-thirds of the vote in the
district, which spans from Montgomery to Birmingham and takes
in the rich-soil counties of the central and western part of the state.
But because the other candidates split up the remaining third, none
of them reached the 15 percent threshold for delegates. Biden won
all eight of them—netting more in that single district than Sanders
had in the state of Vermont. Tellingly, Biden also won Alabama's
Second District, a swath of majority-white rural terrain in the
southeastern "wiregrass" region of the state, in similar fashion.
His dominance in Black-majority and conservative white areas in
Alabama helped him beat Sanders 44 to 8 in delegates—a net
greater than Sanders's edge over Biden in Iowa, New Hampshire,
and Nevada combined.

In other words, Alabama was a perfect showcase of the Biden
coalition's strengths in a Democratic primary fight. Save for Vermont, Biden was sweeping everything east of the Mississippi River.

At the Champlain Valley Exposition center in Essex Junction, just
outside of Burlington, Vermont, Bernie and his top aides watched
the results flash up on television from a holding room. The early
states were a gut punch. The campaign had stopped polling a few
days before Super Tuesday because it would be too late for results
to drive new strategies and ad buys. At the time, Bernie's internal
surveys showed him up in Maine, Massachusetts, and Oklahoma
and competitive in Virginia, North Carolina, and Minnesota. He
didn't expect to win all of those states, but he didn't plan on losing
all of them, either. He still held hope for Texas. His team's theory
was that Bloomberg's money would bring voters to the polls who
would pull the lever for Bernie, which would in turn give him a
boost in what looked like a very close race. It was the dynamic they
had seen play out with union leaders pushing voters to the polls to
thwart Sanders only to find that the boosted turnout benefited
him. Same thing with working-class whites in the 2016 election,
where Hillary's turnout efforts had sometimes provided new voters
for Sanders in the primary and Trump in the general election.

As Sanders watched in frustration while Biden racked up delegates in early-reporting states, he knew he couldn't afford to remain silent. Several states hadn't wrapped up voting yet. He didn't want his supporters to see the early returns and decide it wasn't worth the effort to vote for him. Sanders dispatched Faiz Shakir to speak to the faithful at the Essex Junction center and the media who would broadcast his message across the country. Just a few days earlier, Super Tuesday had looked like an opportunity for Sanders to bolt ahead of Biden and perhaps build a huge delegate lead. Now, the "victory" party had a somber cast. Biden's performance in South Carolina, Bloomberg's failure to gain traction, and the exits of Klobuchar and Buttigieg conspired to flip the script on Sanders. The results in the final few states could be the difference between a brutal night and a fatal one for his campaign.

"That's a sinking feeling," one top Bernie aide said of watching the early states roll in. "You start to sense a wave. It's starting to feel like 'Oh, shit, this is going to be a tough one.'"

Shakir, in a bit of a state of shock, told Sanders supporters that the night would only get better as polls closed in western states, a message that had the dual benefit of being true and of giving voters in western time zones a reason to continue showing up to the polls. But Shakir knew it was hollow in the most important sense: Sanders had been completely blindsided by the speed with which the party coalesced around Biden. In the states and districts where Biden wasn't blowing him out, the former vice president was at least meeting the threshold for delegates. It was a wipeout across the board.

Inside the Lincoln Room, apprehensive banter began to turn more lighthearted.

"Damn, Jim, you've got more stroke than we thought," one of Clyburn's colleagues called across the room.

"You ain't seen nothing yet," Clyburn crowed, taking another pull from his Jack and Diet.

Biden's South Carolina turnaround had carried into Super Tuesday. Even Biden's allies in the room—not everyone there had endorsed him—were shocked by what they were witnessing. None of them had ever seen such an abrupt reversal of fortune. Not in a political race with stakes these high. This luck, the potent residue of the campaign's diluted design, owed in large measure to Clyburn. He had turned Biden's South Carolina "firewall" into a Super Tuesday fireball.

Just how long it would burn into the night remained an open question. Texas counties started to report results, and California, the biggest prize, still loomed from the West Coast. With those states' large Latino populations, Sanders might still be able to salvage his night. He had been running neck and neck with Biden in polls leading up to Super Tuesday. If Biden could pull out Texas, he could withstand a sizable loss in California.

One of the lawmakers called Representative Eddie Bernice Johnson, whose district included the city of Dallas and some surrounding communities. Once connected, she was put on speakerphone.

"Dallas County is coming in big for Biden," Johnson reported. "He is going to win Texas." Cheers rang out in the Lincoln Room. The liquor flowed more conspicuously. The lawmakers grew more giddy. They joked about Bloomberg winning American Samoa. He had poured a billion dollars into his campaign, and the only thing he had to show for it was a territory that most Americans couldn't find on a map of the South Pacific.

It was hard to encapsulate the charmed existence Biden was now living. One of the lawmakers dubbed it "the Clyburn Effect," and the phrase immediately took root.

Late in the night, with the count of California's votes trickling in, Clyburn rushed over to Richmond to give him a message for Biden.

"Tell him yourself," Richmond said, thrusting his phone toward Clyburn. Biden was already on the line.

"You're going to win the fucking nomination," Clyburn exclaimed.

The next morning, still feeling the euphoria of the previous night, the seventy-nine-year-old minister's son would fight off the urge to have a Jack Daniel's breakfast with a splash of Diet Pepsi.

In the intervening days between the South Carolina primary and Super Tuesday, Bloomberg associates had advised him to drop out. With vote share from Buttigieg and Klobuchar swinging to Biden, there was more of a chance that Bloomberg would be embarrassed if he stayed in. He hadn't listened. He wanted to see votes on the board.

It was possible, he thought, that he could still capture enough delegates to make a run for the nomination as an alternative to Sanders and Biden. It was the same fool's gold that had shimmered for so many other candidates whose ambitions were then thrashed by the polar forces of the iconic rabble-rouser and the venerable establishment man. Bloomberg had just paid more than any of them to pan for it.

"There wasn't much to decide," one senior Bloomberg aide said of the former mayor's options. "That was it. There was no reason to continue on. We put all of our eggs into the Super Tuesday basket, and it didn't work. Mike is not somebody to sit around and cry over spilt milk."

By morning, he would be out of the race.

Sitting in Burlington, Shakir marveled at the unfolding devastation.

I know Biden has become the non-Bernie pick, but he didn't even campaign or buy TV ads in most of these states, he thought. Exit polls would show that Biden defeated Sanders 47 percent to 18 percent among voters who had made their decisions in the final few days—a cohort that accounted for 29 percent of the electorate in a combined survey that covered most of the Super Tuesday states.

The night before, Sanders had held a rally in St. Paul, Minnesota. He thought the state lined up well for him. Even Biden's team projected the former vice president winning zero delegates there as late as Monday morning. But as Sanders asked home-state senator Klobuchar's supporters to join his cause that night, she was 950 miles south on I-35 in Dallas at a nationally televised Biden rally. She asked her backers to switch over to Biden.

Biden had no campaign organization in Minnesota. He had spent no money on advertising there. Before the South Carolina primary, he was at 8 percent in the state in a *Star Tribune* poll that placed him fourth, behind Klobuchar, Sanders, and Warren. All Biden had was momentum and Klobuchar's endorsement.

But when the votes were counted, Biden took 39 percent to Sanders's 29 percent, with Warren finishing third at 15 percent. Zero delegates had turned into 38 delegates.

Credit Clyburn, Shakir thought, as Biden rolled over Sanders. It was a little more complicated than that, but not much.

Like any legend, the Clyburn Effect was a mix of truth and perception. Clyburn's endorsement explained a portion of Biden's margin in South Carolina. That had helped convince Buttigieg and Klobuchar to drop out, in part so they would not look like big losers on Super Tuesday. Their absence from the race, and their endorsements of Biden, signaled to establishment Democratic voters that it was time to rally around Biden as the anti-Sanders candidate—at least the voters who hadn't come to that conclusion on their own. Clyburn's endorsement was meaningful for Black voters and for white progressives as a validation that Biden could be trusted. It was the first and most forceful domino.

But it didn't explain how well Biden did with working-class white men on Super Tuesday. Another Sanders adviser pored over the exit polling and drew a conclusion about his candidate's vulnerability. In 2016, Sanders had been the clear favorite of white men. Now it was too obvious to ignore that many of them had been voting against Hillary, not for Sanders.

"Nobody could have imagined what happened on Super Tuesday with the momentum swing," said a top aide to Biden who watched in awe inside the Philadelphia war room as delegate totals racked up. "No one will ever be able to claim credit for that because that was just fucking crazy and weird."

Biden's romp was even more pronounced than the most optimistic expectations in his own camp. His top aides initially looked at Super Tuesday as a test of whether Biden could fight Sanders to a draw on tough terrain. They projected a dogfight for the nomination among several candidates that might last until the convention in June. Biden had hired a delegate-hunting specialist, David Huynh, in large part to deal with that contingency. But with Klobuchar and Buttigieg out, and Bloomberg going down in flames, they could feel the earth shifting under their feet. Biden wasn't going to be on an even plane with Sanders when the night was done. He would be standing atop Sanders. And his team believed that he would win a one-on-one fight. "It was going to be Sanders vs. everybody else's delegates," one senior Biden aide said. "And everybody else's delegates would go to Biden." Super Tuesday clarified that.

Biden had started the campaign with the lead, but his shaky performance had given a rotating set of alternatives the opportunity to claim the establishment mantle. Now, with Sanders threatening to rack up an "insurmountable lead" in delegates—the shorthand Democratic operatives used to indicate that the race was no longer competitive—the center of gravity in the party was moving toward the cautious fallback of Biden. Despite his struggles—and in part because of them—he had demonstrated a few key characteristics that augured well for a matchup against Trump. He was calm in the face of crisis, he could persevere, and he wouldn't go down without a fight. But he was assuredly not what most Democratic voters had envisioned as a Trumpslayer—not on his first day in the race and not after more than a year of campaigning.

Even for Biden, who spent the day stumping in California and watched the results in Los Angeles, it was hard to fully comprehend the meaning of what was happening. He took it all in soberly. He was pleased that he was doing well but not certain that he was in the midst of burying his competition.

Sanders had demonstrated in 2016 that he wasn't the type to bow out when he still had a platform. But for many of his top advisers, Super Tuesday immediately marked the beginning of the end. "It starts creeping in after Super Tuesday," one of them said. "It's not over, but you've taken a pretty big bullet to the upper chest."

Biden had won in states where Sanders spent months building infrastructure and Biden didn't have any organization on the ground. "He didn't have anything in Massachusetts, nothing in Minnesota. Nothing here, nothing there," said one outside adviser to the campaign. "He wasn't really ready for Super Tuesday."

If we can't compete against him and he didn't really campaign, one top Sanders adviser thought, *this thing is going to be a downward trajectory.*

Adding injury to insult, Sanders's strong victory in California on Super Tuesday would not be called that night—or the next day or the next or the next. Just days earlier, Biden had reason to fear that he would fail to make the 15 percent threshold in the state and lose out on a share of the statewide delegates. But Sanders's far-slimmer-than-expected 36 percent to 28 percent margin over the surging Biden yielded an overall delegate split of 225 for Sanders and 172 for Biden. That 53-delegate net for Sanders in the biggest state on the map was more than negated by the 67-delegate advantage Biden secured just in winning North Carolina and Virginia by large margins.

The final tallies wouldn't shake out for more than a week. But it was obvious by late in the night that Biden would not only emerge as the winner of Super Tuesday but would lead the overall race by roughly 75 delegates heading into the rest of the primary calendar. It wasn't an "insurmountable lead," but it was close to that. The map also favored Biden in the next set of primaries, meaning he would have a chance to extend his advantage toward that "insurmountable" territory. The one frustration in the mix: Bloomberg. He had performed well enough in enough places to hold down Biden's delegate count.

"We would have done a lot better in our delegate count had he not been on the ballot," said one senior Biden aide. "All of his votes were coming out of our pocket."

Still, most on Biden's team realized their campaign had gone from cursed to charmed virtually overnight. It was one thing to talk about getting skunked in the early states, rebounding in South Carolina, and getting a springboard on Super Tuesday. It was another thing entirely to live through it. Over four days, the party swung in fully behind a candidate who had all but run out of money a few weeks earlier.

"We didn't draw it up this way at all," said one senior Biden adviser. "The trajectory is not unlike what we were saying for five or six months, but the stuff that happened on Super Tuesday, and right before Super Tuesday, was nuts and incomparable to anything I've ever seen."

Biden was the passenger on his own thrill ride.

He didn't even get to see much of the route to his rout play out on election maps. He had a busy campaign schedule that day. When he left the Oakland diner, people formed a human tunnel, like NBA reserves awaiting the starters to rush out onto the court. He flew to Los Angeles for a couple of meet and greets with voters, including one at the legendary Roscoe's House of Chicken and Waffles, which has been featured in such films as *Jackie Brown* and *Soul Plane*. Everywhere he went, voters were excited to see him. This was new, and exhilarating.

As results came in on the East Coast, Biden heard a string of updates from his staff at Roscoe's. State by state, voters were pulling the lever for him at an unbelievable rate. Delegate hauls were being loaded on top of delegate hauls. *This is crazy*, he thought.

After the AP called Minnesota for Biden a little before seven P.M. Pacific, it was time for Biden to get moving toward cameras. East Coast voters would be going to bed soon. He headed to the Baldwin Hills neighborhood in South Los Angeles, an affluent enclave known for years as "the Black Beverly Hills," to deliver his first rousing victory speech of the campaign season. On his way, he called Klobuchar to thank her for helping with Minnesota.

Not everything changed in an instant. His campaign was still so broke that he had to deliver his remarks from a bowl built by his team in the park area of the Baldwin Hills Recreation Center. The makeshift stage was less than ideal for security, and, less threatening but still politically perilous, Biden's aides had received reports that protesters in the crowd might take off their shirts to call attention to their effort to bring down the dairy industry. Whatever image the campaign wanted for the night, the naked breasts of virulent cow defenders were not part of it. "There couldn't be anything worse than someone taking their shirt off," one aide said. "That would be awful, and the pictures would be awful." Biden would soon find out that toplessness wasn't the worst way for a protester to disrupt his remarks.

Before Biden took the stage, Mike Donilon and Bruce Reed hurriedly drafted a speech in a children's classroom at the recreation center. The two veteran aides sat on tiny chairs at tiny desks. Donilon was tapping on the keyboard of his laptop when Reed's cellphone rang.

"Mr. President," Reed said, putting the phone on speaker so Donilon could hear.

Bill Clinton's voice crackled into the air, listing states Biden was winning. "You look good in Massachusetts," he said. But the purpose of the call was to give some broad-stroke advice on what Biden should try to achieve with his victory speech. The former president said it was time for Biden to call for a unification of the party. Clinton well knew that coalescence benefited the front-runner. Donilon and Reed took in Clinton's suggestions, bounced some specific language off him, and wrapped up their writing. This was going to be fun for Biden.

For the first time in almost a year, he was fully pumped up. He felt a little cocky. And it showed. The press, he told the crowd from a small stage above them, had written him off. "We were told, well, when it got to Super Tuesday it would be over," Biden said with newfound swagger. "Well, it may be over for the other guy!" He suddenly had some mojo. Three minutes later, a protester rushed the stage yelling "Let dairy die!"

Jill Biden moved her body between the protester and her husband as a security guard leapt into action to remove the unwanted guest. "Move her off," Jill Biden instructed.

Standing to one side of the stage, Symone Sanders heard someone yell, "There's another one!" Sanders saw a woman climb up toward Biden. *What the fuck is going on?* she thought, as she sprung into action. A former track runner, Sanders scrambled onto the stage and bolted toward the protester, grabbing her and pulling her several feet away from Biden and back down into the crowd. Remi Yamamoto, Biden's traveling press secretary, helped Sanders hand the protester off to a security guard. His aides knew he had come too damn far to let a protester fuck up his big moment. But Sanders's jumping onstage was an act of loyalty that superseded politics.

They were loyal to him, but he also needed to be protected from his own frailties. Jill Biden, Sanders, and Yamamoto physically demonstrated the way the people closest to Biden had been shielding him on the campaign trail in the metaphorical sense.

After the speech, in a small holding area near the stage, Biden was unfazed by the interruptions. "It's fine," he told family and aides. "I'm winning!"

"Let's be clear," Sanders said with a smile. "The only people who jumped onstage are the women who work for you."

Inside the Biden bubble, the realization started to take hold that something big had changed in just a few days. There was a time when the extra bodies of protesters might have been welcome as crowd fillers. Now, for the first time, Biden felt like the front-runner he had been from the start of the campaign. For the first time, he looked like the presumptive Democratic nominee.

"People will tell you 'This was our plan all along,'" said one Biden aide. "But saying that out loud and believing it and then actually seeing how it all transpired, I don't think anyone could have planned on that happening."

The one thing Joe Biden could be sure he got right as the results came in on Super Tuesday was that the vast majority of Democrats just wanted Trump gone, and they weren't willing to take a chance on anyone whose lens was wider than that goal. Everything else, he'd gotten wrong. He'd run a lousy campaign, flubbed debates, spent so much money on Iowa and New Hampshire that he teetered on the edge of insolvency, lost three straight states to start the primary, and allowed himself to be defined by his frailties. And yet by the end of the night, he had clear command of the race.

Biden was on the verge of winning with a bland message and a blank agenda. He offered no revolution, no reformation, and no fresh look. Factions of his party would want to superimpose their priorities on him because, on most issues, he was more reactive and cautious than his fellow Democrats. Amid a series of schisms in his party—the populists against the elites, the progressives against the centrists, and the next-generation leaders against the old guard—Biden had stood mostly to the side. Rather than a path forward, he proposed backtracking to the pre-Trump era. And despite a résumé as strong as any modern presidential contender and a lifetime of building political relationships, Democratic voters had vetted and rejected two dozen candidates before settling on him.

But with the help of his rivals, Clyburn, and those same Democratic voters, he now had a convincing lead.

Buttigieg had jammed Sanders in Iowa, winning in a mucked-up caucus. But his Obama-like talk of outsider-driven change did not meet a moment in which Democrats felt protective of institutions. Klobuchar flattened him as he was gaining steam in New Hampshire. Warren first took herself out, flailing on the issue that defined the most substantive dispute in the party: how to ensure that more Americans could obtain health insurance inexpensively. Then, she gutted Bloomberg, whose parallels to Trump—a billionaire who covered his tracks with nondisclosure agreements—were too much for most Democrats to swallow. Could they beat Trump with their own nominally Democratic, easy-to-rattle version of him? The answer was a clear no. For Harris and the other women who ran, there could be no doubt that the primary electorate preferred to counter Trump with a white man.

It was a politician who had not run, Clyburn, who delivered rocket fuel in South Carolina, pushing Buttigieg and Klobuchar from the race. And then, on Super Tuesday, Democratic Party voters rallied behind the only remaining hope for stopping Sanders in his tracks. Biden had been the first candidate to rise, and he was the last man standing. On one hand, he had polled better than anyone else throughout the race, and his coalition was well suited to winning a Democratic nomination. On the other, he was lucky as hell for the cosmic forces that held him in place and then propelled him to a commanding lead.

"Anyone who's being honest will say the stars aligned for Joe Biden," one longtime confidant said.

Fate would intervene again soon.

CHAPTER 13

•

"It's All Turning"

O N JANUARY 29, 2020, PRESIDENT DONALD TRUMP SAW HIS RE-
election clearly. That morning, he held a signing ceremony for
the U.S.-Mexico-Canada free trade agreement in the Rose Garden,
fulfilling a high-profile campaign promise that had won bipartisan
support in Congress and the approval of both business and labor
groups. The economy was growing, the monthly unemployment
rate had been no higher than 4 percent for almost two years, and
the field of Democrats hoping to challenge him still looked weak to
him. In particular, Trump felt vindicated by his party's united
defiance of Democrats' effort to impeach him. House Democratic
impeachment managers—the prosecutors—and Trump's defense
lawyers were making their closing arguments to the Senate that
very day, but it was clear already that the Republican-led Senate
would reject the charges. Only one Senate Republican, 2012 GOP
presidential nominee Mitt Romney, would vote to remove him from
office.

Trump attributed some of the Senate Republicans' resolve to
the actions of their counterparts in the House, who had held firm
in voting against all charges. Now, Trump had invited a group of
those House Republicans to lunch in the Cabinet Room as something of a reward for their loyalty in the crucible of impeachment
politics.

Seated in one of the two dozen or so high-backed, tan-leather
chairs around the historic room's long, oval conference table, Rep-

resentative Gary Palmer, who represented an Alabama district that hooked around Birmingham to take in white suburbs but none of the city, told the president a fresh war story from Capitol Hill. Democrats were looking into whether the president was improperly benefiting from the federal lease on the Trump International Hotel in Washington, and Palmer recounted, blow by blow, how he had defended the president.

Trump loved it. He remembered the fight to win the lease for the Old Post Office Building, which would be converted to the Trump luxury hotel, five blocks down Pennsylvania Avenue from where he and the lawmakers were now sitting. Trump reveled in the art of storytelling almost as much as the art of the deal, and he went on about the twists and turns of the bidding and negotiation for almost thirty minutes.

"I was surprised I got it," Trump said, "because I was so critical of Obama."

He thanked the lawmakers for standing by him during impeachment and said voters would reward Republicans at the polls for beating back what he saw as an overreach by Democrats. "He was getting his best numbers out of impeachment, and the party was pretty unified," said one person who was present. "It was a pretty upbeat occasion."

At the same time, White House domestic and national security policy officials were in the midst of a mini-campaign to get Trump to pay more attention to the spreading coronavirus. Eight days earlier, on January 21, Joe Grogan, a domestic policy aide at the White House, told colleagues that the first U.S. case had been confirmed in Washington State. The news ricocheted around the West Wing in minutes.

"It was chilling," one senior White House official said. "We've known it could be a problem. Now it's real. There was a lot of internal coordination going on already, but I don't think anyone really knew how to approach it. We didn't know how bad it would be."

Neither did the president. He often put less stock in the information and analysis he received from his own staff than he did from his circle of friends and the television hosts and pundits he watched all day long in a small study adjacent to the Oval Office, and deep into the night in the White House residence. If it wasn't on TV, it wasn't a problem. Cable networks were reporting on aspects of the disease, but it was hardly a fixation.

While some of Trump's aides could see the potential for an outbreak to harm public health and the president's reelection prospects, he was showing the Republican legislators that he was confident about his standing and theirs with the voters. One person in the room said that a lawmaker urged Trump to take a leading role in the U.S. response to the virus, citing the partisan division in Congress as the reason the president's voice was necessary.

"We're watching it," Trump said dismissively.

Later that day, Trump took the stairs down to a suite on the first level of the West Wing, walked past the big wooden door with a brass plaque, and into the main Situation Room. Around the table and on the back rows behind it sat members of his Cabinet, top White House aides, and a set of medical experts that included Dr. Anthony Fauci of the National Institute of Allergy and Infectious Diseases, and Dr. Robert Redfield, the head of the Centers for Disease Control and Prevention. They had all been summoned by Trump aides for the first meeting of a newly appointed White House coronavirus task force.

The Situation Room session was little more than a photo op. The panel's formation had been announced in a statement by the White House press secretary; it wasn't deemed important enough to warrant an official comment by the president. Two days later, as Bob Woodward would report in his book *Rage,* Trump sat in the Oval Office with Health and Human Services secretary Alex Azar, Fauci, and Redfield and asked very basic questions about the novel coronavirus—including whether it was "new"—while the three senior health officials advised the president to issue a ban on foreign nationals traveling from China to the United States as a means of preventing a domestic outbreak. When they left the Oval Office, Azar, Fauci, and Redfield announced the ban to the media in the White House briefing room. All three said the risk to Americans remained low.

"Until the COVID thing came, we were winning four hundred electoral votes," said a person familiar with the Trump team's internal figures at the end of February. That might have been too optimistic, but the campaign's models included the expectation that Trump would draw many new voters to the ballot box. For almost five years now, Trump had been building a definitive political brand that he believed would help him mobilize millions of people who didn't normally vote. He wasn't trying to shift Clinton voters into his column. There was little chance that would happen in large numbers. It was easier, he believed, to jack up the number of his die-hard voters and depress Democratic support. The strong economy and Trump's machismo appealed to many first-time voters, including some voters of color. At that moment, his data surveys and field polling showed that his focus-on-building-the-base strategy was working. "We were just crushing it and winning every poll," said the person familiar with the numbers.

But there was a caveat. On February 12, about two weeks before Trump's internal polling hit a new peak, his campaign manager, Brad Parscale, issued the president a warning. Speaking by phone to Trump and a small group of his White House aides, Parscale said the coronavirus was one thing that could derail the Trump train.

"This could take down your presidency," he said.

Trump dismissed that thought out of hand. What, he asked, does the virus have to do with politics?

On February 28, the night before the Democratic primary in South Carolina, Trump hopped aboard Air Force One for the short flight to Joint Base Charleston. When he arrived at the modest North Charleston Coliseum, where speakers blared familiar rock tunes from a past era, Trump wore a red tie with black stripes and the unmistakable air of vindication.

He had beaten impeachment, the economy was growing, and, while he was running the country, Democrats had shown they couldn't run a caucus. Biden, the rival he'd been most worried about, had lost his first three nominating contests, and Trump had narrowed the polling gap between them to single digits. For all the ridicule of his political strategy and tactics among the punditry, he felt good not only about where he stood but where the election was heading.

But already the virus was starting to become more than an annoyance he could simply wave away. What Trump knew and said behind the scenes was very different from his public posturing. He had told Woodward on February 7 that the disease was "more deadly" than "even your strenuous flu," and that it spread very easily.

Trump felt that it made little sense to scare people with the truth, but that decision would come to look troubling in retrospect. "It comes across as burying it," said one Trump White House official. But he'd also put a more prominent spotlight on the White House coronavirus task force by placing Vice President Mike Pence in charge of it on February 26. The idea was to streamline the federal response to the disease.

"It's all turning," he told a raucous crowd in North Charleston. "They lost. It's all turning." In the next breath, he compared the coronavirus to the Russia and Ukraine probes. "This is their new hoax," he said, arguing that Democrats were unfairly blaming him for the pandemic.

Trump often said publicly and privately that the virus would simply disappear on its own. He had gone from not caring much about it in January to privately acknowledging its lethality in early February to concluding that the best solution was to wish it away. He didn't have a clue what to do, according to his own advisers.

As the virus took hold of the nation, Trump thought about the disease as a parallel problem on essentially separate tracks: public health and the economy. On March 2, he held a Cabinet Room meeting with pharmaceutical industry leaders in which he secured their pledge to begin work on developing vaccines. His medical experts were increasingly concerned about trying to contain the spread of the virus and urged him to effectively shut down the country. But other White House aides, including his son-in-law, Jared Kushner, new chief of staff Mark Meadows, and Office of Management and Budget chief Russ Vought, were more focused on the economic effects of the growing crisis. Trump's reelection calling card was the economy. He viewed it that way, and he saw his greatest political risk as a prolonged downturn. There would be a clear challenge in running on having presided over "the greatest economy in history," while the stock market tanked, businesses closed, and workers lost their jobs.

Trump faced an ethical dilemma presented by the virus and a message challenge of his own making. He could choose to lean more heavily toward stopping the disease or more heavily toward keeping the economy on track, and each option would come at a human cost. What he couldn't afford to do was fail to show adequate sympathy for people hurt by the tack he chose. But Trump saw demonstrations of sympathy and empathy as signs of weakness. For Biden, they exhibited the strength of compassion.

By March 10, New York had more than one hundred confirmed cases. Governor Andrew Cuomo and NYC mayor Bill de Blasio, both Democrats, were initially reluctant to restrict New Yorkers' activities. That day, Trump met behind closed doors with Republican senators at their weekly luncheon on Capitol Hill. In the meeting, he bounced around various legislative ideas, including a stimulus package that would help lift the economy—particularly the airline and cruise industries—which had already taken a massive hit from the coronavirus. Before departing for the White House, he stopped to talk with reporters.

"We're prepared and we're doing a great job," Trump said, asserting that his actions had prevented a catastrophic spread of the disease. He pointed to the twenty-six U.S. deaths at the time and said it was a much smaller number than the eight thousand projected to die from the regular flu. "It will go away. Just stay calm," he said. "It will go away." He was talking about the pandemic the way presidents, senators, and Wall Street CEOs talked about contagion in a bear market, as though fending off panic could stop a pandemic.

Meanwhile, Trump's key measure for prosperity, the Dow Jones Industrial Average of major stock prices, fell more than 20 percent in a month. He tried to take control—the leadership role he had been advised to take by one of the House Republicans in the January meeting at the White House—with an address to the nation hastily written by aides Stephen Miller and Jared Kushner. Sitting behind the Resolute Desk in the Oval Office, Trump said he was taking action to prevent Europeans from entering the country. He blamed China for the disease. Much of what he said was untrue. But more than any individual claim, it was the tenor of the speech that seemed detached from reality. The virus was a clear and present danger to Americans. Trump said it affected only the elderly. He said that it would be defeated handily. And he said it would not cause much economic damage.

"This is not a financial crisis," he said, just hours after the Dow dropped about 1,500 points. "This is just a temporary moment of time that we will overcome together as a nation and a world."

Trump was forced to cancel several upcoming campaign trips late that night, joining Biden and Sanders in suspending rallies.

Trump wasn't the only public figure who failed to recognize the scale of the threat in January and February. But he was the only one who was president.

On March 10, Biden met with autoworkers in Detroit, part of a swing through key Rust Belt states ahead of the March 17 primaries. He loved talking with guys in hard hats, and he loved photos of those interactions just as much. To beat Trump, he had to reclaim "the blue wall" states—Michigan, Wisconsin, and Pennsylvania—that Trump had seized with protectionist policies and rhetoric in 2016. Biden hoped he could do the same in Ohio. He had been repeating the obvious to anyone who would listen: Hillary lost because she was disconnected from the working-class white men who surged to the polls in the Rust Belt to make sure she never returned to the White House residence. He believed he was a better fit for them.

Biden talked about the middle class in a way that somehow felt more sympathetic—more real—than the manner in which most of his Democratic peers did. He knew how fragile middle-class status could be for folks who had worked hard to get there or were still aspiring to do so. His family had moved from Scranton to Delaware when he was a kid so that his dad could find work. As he campaigned for the votes of white men in the Rust Belt, he said that the middle class was built on the backs of union labor. To the extent that Trump's "Make America Great Again" slogan recalled a distorted version of the 1950s of his youth, so, too, did Biden's nostalgic view of unions. For the most part, they were less prevalent, less white, and less focused on car making and mining than they had ever been. But for a share of the electorate—a crucial subset—his memory lined up with theirs. Biden felt like he could get "the connect" with lunch pail white guys if he could get in front of them.

But one-on-one interactions with voters came with a measure of unpredictability. As he stood surrounded by a small clutch of autoworkers in a factory in Detroit, one of them took issue with his policy on guns.

"You are actively trying to end our Second Amendment right and take away our guns," the man charged.

Biden had heard this before, and he was tired of it. *C'mon man,* he thought. *This is just bad faith. Take issue with my actual plan, but don't throw lies at me.* He felt the familiar flash of his Irish temper.

"You're full of shit!" he exclaimed, looking the worker dead in the eye. One of his aides tried to cut him off.

"Shush!" he commanded. Many of his advisers were uncomfortable with his willingness to fight with voters, especially those younger than himself, in a tone that suggested the superiority of wisdom and righteousness. But Biden didn't listen to them. They didn't know what they were talking about. He'd been doing this since before they were born. He believed it was better to have an honest confrontation with a voter than to let someone beat up on him unfairly.

Biden grew more self-righteous as the exchange continued, and wrapped up by calling the worker a "horse's ass."

So it was with a mix of urgency and relief that afternoon that Biden aides decided to cancel the rope-line segment of an evening event. It was Biden's favorite part of campaigning, but the coronavirus news looked bleak. More infections. More deaths. Biden was on the cusp of winning the party's nomination—making him the only force positioned to defeat Trump—and, as a septuagenarian, he was personally at risk. He had to be protected. For Democrats, the very existence of the republic depended on that. It was no longer good enough to distribute hand sanitizer to people he met and hope that he wouldn't be infected.

Biden had planned to hold a rally in Cleveland that night to cap off a swing through Michigan and Ohio, but his plane from Columbus was rerouted to Wilmington at the last minute. His aides called Ohio lawmakers who'd been scheduled to attend the rally to tell them not to board flights from Washington. Anita Dunn spoke to Jeff Weaver, the senior adviser to Bernie Sanders, to go over options for both remaining Democratic campaigns. The two of them had developed a rapport earlier in the primary season, at Weaver's urging. They agreed that it made sense to suspend rallies, and, while Biden was in the air, his team decided not to plan any new events. "It was clear this was going to cascade quickly," one of his advisers said.

Abruptly, just a week after Super Tuesday, the Democratic primary campaign screeched to a halt. The next day, the Democratic candidates' planned March 15 debate in Arizona was canceled. Instead, they would go up against each other in a CNN studio in Washington.

Biden gathered his debate prep team in the study of his house in Wilmington—which he called "The Lake"—on March 12. Valerie Biden Owens and press aide Elizabeth Alexander sat on a long leather couch in front of a bookcase. Ron Klain, Jen O'Malley Dillon, Symone Sanders, Kate Bedingfield, and a handful of other advisers fanned out in the spacious study, which featured a fireplace and a large U.S. Senate seal. Biden sat opposite the phone on his large wooden desk so he could hear Bob Bauer, who had dialed in to play Bernie Sanders. Dunn, who had recently had coffee with a reporter who had developed a cough, also joined the session by phone. Though Biden and his aides respected one another's distance, everyone in the room was barefaced.

Biden had been waiting for this kind of debate with Sanders for months. *For the first time,* he thought, *I can actually have a real contrast of visions without the distraction of other candidates jockeying for attention or trying to gang up on me. Voters will see me as the mainstream alternative to both Bernie and Trump.* Collectively, the group was worried that a cornered Bernie Sanders would go on the attack. The key was to keep Biden focused on a message of unification—for the party and the country. Because Biden held a good-sized delegate lead, he would be the beneficiary, as he already had been, of the party coalescing. After a season of wild debates, and the roller coaster that had now given him a commanding view of the nomination, Biden felt something approaching Zen. He could handle Sanders. There was just one headline he hoped to make at the debate—and he had decided on it long before this gathering.

In the CNN studio, Sanders made his points but hardly threw haymakers at Biden. It was damn near impossible for a trailing candidate to make up ground without hitting the front-runner, but Sanders knew that no one in the party was in the mood for blood sport in the midst of a scary public health and economic crisis. The coronavirus was speeding up the end of the primary.

It was Biden who succeeded in making news. "I commit that I will, in fact, pick a woman to be vice president," he declared.

From a historical standpoint, it was bold. Of course, no woman had been vice president. Geraldine Ferraro and Sarah Palin had endured brutal misogyny. Palin had clearly hurt John McCain's chances in 2008. Hillary Clinton, the only woman to lead a major-party ticket, had won a majority of the popular vote but lost states that would be pivotal for 2020—Pennsylvania, Michigan, and Wisconsin. Women didn't fare well in statewide elections in Pennsylvania. And yet this was the idea Biden had been so certain of since before he even entered the race. A more diverse ticket represented a huge nod in the direction of change for a candidate whose platform looked like a walk-back triangulation between Trump and Obama. Making sure women had one of their own in the No. 2 post in government was a way, in the midst of a campaign about returning to the old status quo, that he could inject freshness into his ticket.

Back in Wilmington, Biden consulted with his doctor and his council of medical experts. Biden got his personal medical care from Dr. Kevin O'Connor, an Army veteran who had been his physician since his days in the vice presidency. For policy, he turned to a clutch of medical experts that included Drs. Vivek Murthy, the former U.S. surgeon general; David Kessler, a former Food and Drug Administration commissioner; and Zeke Emanuel, an oncologist and bioethicist who had worked at the National Institutes of Health and the Office of Management and Budget. Biden's advisers had come to the same conclusion as White House officials and some congressional Republicans: Trump wasn't taking the coronavirus threat seriously enough. Biden was certain that the president should prepare for a worst-case scenario, but he wasn't sure that's what the country was facing. "Folks, we can beat this virus. We can keep it from being a pandemic," Biden had said on February 28. "But it takes a lot of work."

He talked to governors of his own party and he kept tabs on the response of Ohio governor Mike DeWine, a Republican with whom he had worked in the Senate. Biden didn't like what he saw and heard. The virus was getting ugly in Ohio and New York, and epidemiologists had no doubt it would get worse—much worse—

before it got better. He decided that he would sequester himself at home for the foreseeable future. He wasn't going to go anywhere if there was a threat to his life or the possibility that his trips could create a risk for anyone else.

"I'm not traveling," Biden told aides. "Period."

On Monday, March 16, Trump strode slowly into the White House briefing room, holding a black briefing book. His gait was halting, reluctant even, and he wore an unusually somber look. Behind him stood the medical experts—Fauci, White House coronavirus task force response coordinator Dr. Deborah Birx, and Surgeon General Jerome Adams—who had shared with him macabre models of death-toll projections. Reporters from major television and print outlets fanned out before him, separated by telltale empty seats. Trump approvingly noted the new formation in the small briefing room. Then he introduced federal guidelines for social distancing, intended to last for fifteen days. It was the first and last time for a long while that Trump would acknowledge the severity of the pandemic without lamenting its cost to the health of the economy—the main engine of his reelection campaign—or bragging audaciously and falsely that he had the disease under control.

"This is a bad one—this is a very bad one. This is bad in the sense that it's so contagious," he said in response to a question about a possible recession. "My focus is really on getting rid of this problem—this virus problem. Once we do that, everything else is going to fall into place."

He knew when he issued stay-at-home guidelines that he would wreak more havoc on businesses, retirement accounts, and paychecks. But for a brief moment in mid-March, he agreed with top scientists in his administration that he had to get the disease under control, or the entire system might collapse.

In the midst of the unfolding coronavirus crisis, Trump was looking to put in place a new team for the stretch run to the November election. When he'd tapped Parscale to run his campaign in February 2018, the first question establishment Republicans had asked was "Who will be the second campaign manager?" For months now, rumors had circulated in Washington that Trump would replace Parscale with one of Parscale's chief critics, White

House senior adviser Kellyanne Conway. She wanted out of the White House, but Trump liked her better as a television talking head than as a campaign manager. What Trump told Conway, according to a top White House official, is that he wanted her "in the foxhole" with him at 1600 Pennsylvania Avenue. But another source close to Trump said the president didn't see Conway as crucial to his reelection strategy or the execution of it. "She was never in any of the big campaign meetings," this source said. "Jared didn't even invite her." Either way, Conway would be aiming her fire from inside the White House.

That would be Trump's command center for the general election, anyway. Jared Kushner, who oversaw Parscale, worked in the White House. And Trump brought in a new, politically minded chief of staff, Representative Mark Meadows from North Carolina, on March 6.

Most of all, though, Trump's own presence in the White House made the federal building his de facto campaign nerve center.

"He's the axis on which all of Trumpworld turns," one adviser said from the White House during the early days of the pandemic. "He's only here."

Earlier that day, Jen O'Malley Dillon made her first appearance at Biden's Philadelphia headquarters as the campaign's new manager. It had been more than four months since Dunn started seeding the ground for her. So, even before O'Malley Dillon stepped off the Amtrak train at 30th Street Station, she knew the campaign needed a makeover. It was too small for a general election. It didn't have enough money. And it needed stronger managers for its departments. O'Malley Dillon also conducted an informal audit of the pooh-bahs and other players in Biden's orbit, trying to get a feel for all of the pain points in both the campaign organization and the world surrounding it. Over the next twenty-four hours or so, she would meet with all of the department directors to gauge their abilities and plans for the general election. But the meeting everyone would remember was an all-staff cattle call in which O'Malley Dillon introduced herself to the team and then announced that the headquarters was shutting down for the foreseeable future. She knew the bullet points of her existing reputation: an A-plus operative with a no-nonsense edge that could rub some subordinates the wrong way.

I'm coming in new, and I need to convince these people that I don't have five heads just as I'm telling them that we're going into lockdown and won't actually work together, she thought.

"I'm Jen," she told the group. "I have three kids. I love Peloton, and I'm good at it," she said. Reading the faces in the room, she could see uncertainty. *God, these younger people think I'm an old mom rambling on about Peloton,* she thought.

She would remain at the office for the next day or so trying to figure out not just the internal problems but the external. *How do we get the fuck out of this primary and get it to where we're in a good place with Bernie?* she wondered, knowing that Democrats had fears of 2016 intraparty divisions revisiting this cycle.

The next night, on March 17, Biden swept primaries in Florida, Illinois, and Arizona. Ohio had postponed its contest. Sanders was toast. Five-plus years of playing Don Quixote, shaking his sword at corporate windmills from the distance, had come to a backbreaking end. It was Biden, once ridiculed as the senator from MBNA for his support of the credit card industry, who had returned him to reality. Other than being white, male, and born about a year apart, they shared almost no common ground. Biden's side, the centrist side, the groomed side, the deal-is-more-important-than-the-details side, the winning-is-more-important-than-being-pure side, had crushed him with no remorse.

Biden looked into a camera and declared victory—from his basement. His lock on the nomination had tightened. He would be the champion of the anti-Trump coalition. He should be celebrating, taking a brief pause to drink in the affirmation of his party before barnstorming the nation for eight months in pursuit of the presidency. But there were no throngs jockeying to get close to him. There were no hands to shake or foreheads to kiss at his house. He wouldn't get to bask in the glory of a homecoming king.

Even the bottom-floor refuge in the main residence of his du Pont country mini-manor didn't quite feel like home. Lined with bookshelves and sketches by the longtime Wilmington *News Journal* cartoonist Jack Jurden, the main area of the "basement" was more of a second family room or the senator's version of a man cave than a subterranean shelter. Because the house sat on a hill, the bottom floor opened onto level ground outside, where Biden had put in a swimming pool. Beyond that sat the pond that gave the property its nickname: "The Lake." Biden could remember sitting with his elder son on a little dock behind the house before Beau died. But now, the basement had been converted into a makeshift TV studio, providing video only a little more sophisticated than the Skype calls cable networks were using to pipe in guests from their home offices.

Born in 1942, Biden was too young to remember the atrocities of Adolf Hitler and World War II, but he had lived through the Cold War, the Vietnam War—as a civilian—and the September 11, 2001, terrorist assault on the United States. He had also managed to survive personal tragedies and setbacks: the premature deaths of two of his children and his first wife, and his own battle with brain aneurysms. But the novel coronavirus was unlike anything he had seen. It was a mortal threat to him at age seventy-seven, a member of the most vulnerable set: the elderly. More broadly, he had never witnessed anything quite like this emergency shutdown of the country. Like Trump, Biden had said around that time that there was no reason to "panic" over the coronavirus. Unlike Trump, he said in the same breath that it needed to be taken seriously.

Dressed dandily as usual, in a blue suit with a white handkerchief jutting from his left breast pocket, Biden walked a few steps through his den to a podium as results from the March 17 primaries continued to roll in. He looked like the model of a U.S. senator. His white collar rode a little high around his neck, his starch-stiff green tie knotted meticulously at his throat. Like any of hundreds of senators and governors through time, Biden had practiced moments like this declaration of victory alone at home. But this time, it was for real.

And yet there was a hostage-video quality to the broadcast. It was cloudy and dark. The Lake house was closed off from the outside world; only a couple of Biden aides—his longtime right hand Annie Tomasini and Jill Biden's chief of staff Anthony Bernal—were allowed in regularly. Neither of them had their own families, which meant they could devote themselves entirely to the Bidens for the duration of the lockdown, and they wouldn't come in regular contact with spouses or kids who could be exposed to the virus. But Tomasini and Bernal were not television producers, and Biden's

Lake house was not wired for broadcast-quality video. Had Biden known how fast the coronavirus would spread in the United States, how it would kill people in numbers unseen in the country since the Spanish flu, and how it would shut down American society virtually overnight, surely someone on his staff would have retrofitted his house so he could broadcast from its confines. But it had snuck up on him, too.

As he spoke, there was an ever-so-slight time delay, putting Biden's words out of sync with the movements of his mouth. To many voters who had caved to the idea of Biden's inevitability, it was hardly a reassuring look. This was the guy who would send Donald Trump back to Mar-a-Lago for good?

"I cringed the entire time," said one Biden confidant who watched on television. "Who puts a podium in a basement rec room? It was awful. It just looked so bad. He looked like he didn't know what he was doing."

For much of the Democratic Party's elite, the moment was a metaphor for Joe's janky primary campaign. Like his political operation, his basement set wasn't ready for prime time. This was the era of hyper-personalized digital advertising. He would have to raise money online. The media moved in endless micro-cycles. Politics had marched into the social media battlefield. But there was another way of looking at it that got lost in the chorus of know-betterism. Just Joe—plain, simple, as unpolished as he looked polished—seemed to appeal to a lot of voters. They might not want to watch him talk from his basement, but they also weren't worried about what he was saying when they changed the channel.

Barack Obama fell into the former category. From his perspective, Joe's operation was like a little storm-battered ship that got lost in a fog and miraculously found its way to port. Obama had never expected Biden to get this far. He had worried that his friend would embarrass himself on the campaign trail. The former president had helped guide the ship the last few nautical miles by providing counsel and placing a few well-timed calls between the South Carolina primary and Super Tuesday. But Joe's campaign wasn't worthy of the raging seas of a general election against Trump, especially given Joe's deficiencies as a candidate.

As Biden locked down the nomination, he turned to Obama for help. For Obama, that would mean raising money and helping bring along Bernie Sanders, with whom the former president had truly unique influence. But it also meant that Obama had periodic chats with O'Malley Dillon, offering assistance to his former aide. She had been the operations chief on his reelection campaign, and he thought highly of her capabilities as a manager. "Jen, how can I be helpful to you? What else can we do?" he would say during their conversations. *He's a good partner,* Biden's new campaign manager thought. *He's heavily leaned in here.*

A clear priority was updating Biden's broadcast capabilities so he didn't look like he was transmitting from a bunker. The campaign decided to outfit his house with new television-network-grade fiber-optic cable.

But if Biden had to build a real studio in his house, O'Malley Dillon had to build a whole modern-day campaign. "What she inherited was not a campaign," one veteran Democratic operative who worked on several presidential bids said when O'Malley Dillon took over. "She's faced with a build, not a rebuild. Biden didn't have a campaign, and they are lying to you if they said they did. They did a disservice to the vice president of the United States."

O'Malley Dillon held as articles of evidence and experience, not faith, that a campaign needed a structured hierarchy to be successful, and that data should be used to inform strategy rather than dictate it. She had made that pitch when she interviewed to be Hillary Clinton's campaign manager, and she had lost out on that job. If she didn't feel vindicated by the 2016 outcome, it was only because the result meant Donald Trump was president.

As campaign manager, part of her job was to merge all the factions, to fuse the little-Biden-campaign-that-could with the legion of party and outside organizations that had eyed Biden warily enough to avoid endorsing him when the primary was competitive. The Obama people. The women's groups. The African American community. Hispanic-rights activists. Champions of LGBTQ rights. The unions. Not so much the Clinton people.

"There are things that needed to change," one veteran of the primary campaign said shortly after O'Malley Dillon took over. "She obviously came out of the Obama campaign operation and felt a lot of loyalty to those folks, and to remake parts of the campaign in the 2012 model, which she's familiar with, and some of that's good and some of it doesn't fit Joe Biden."

When O'Malley Dillon arrived on the scene, with her strong reputation among political operatives, there was a general sense inside the campaign that the operation was being taken over by a professional. But there was also latent mistrust around the fact that she hadn't officially joined up with Joe until he'd all but clinched the nomination. The rest of the team had just seen him through a primary fight, and she had initially picked another horse. Like many Obama veterans, she had looked past Biden and put her money on Beto O'Rourke as the best vessel for the Democratic Party.

The Obama people had not believed in Joe Biden. Barack Obama had not believed in Joe Biden. The Joe-firsters, the folks who referred to him as "JoeBiden," knew that. Like Biden, they'd watched their political friends and family rally around a new flavor every month for more than a year. The loudest voices in the party had grown more liberal and more combative since the last election, and the class of political professionals spawned by the Obama presidency had moved along with them. O'Malley Dillon might be the harbinger of an ill-fitting Obamaworld takeover.

But for all their hesitations, Biden's operatives knew O'Malley Dillon's reputation for capable management was sterling. She might be able to tighten the operation and scale it up for the general election. Because of the prospects for the latter, and because Biden himself had chosen to outsource the job after locking down the nomination, the Joe-firsters would try to give her latitude.

One of O'Malley Dillon's first moves was to make Rufus Gifford, a veteran of Obama's fundraising machine, a deputy campaign manager. Gifford had endorsed Biden in January and provided some assists during the primaries. After Super Tuesday, as Obama began to weave the party back together, Gifford had sent out an email to the eight hundred members of Obama's national finance team, asking them to begin rounding up money for Biden. Without demoting anyone else, O'Malley Dillon put him in charge of Biden's finance office, a move known in professional political circles as "layering" a new hire over an existing manager. There would soon be more new layers.

But no one other than Greg Schultz would lose their official rank. Biden had learned a lesson from stripping Schultz of his duties and title. It had been ugly and ignominious. Schultz's many sympathizers within the ranks of the campaign and in the donor class found themselves disgusted enough with Biden's humiliating treatment of a trusted adviser that they let him know he had fucked up.

Biden had gotten the message. He talked to Greg.

"Look," the former vice president said, "the next time I'm doing an event, I want you standing right next to me. I want everybody to know how much I appreciate you and the good work you do."

And, he added, "I'm really sorry about how this was handled."

Biden, who had so much difficulty acknowledging that past statements or positions had been wrong, was quick to offer personal apologies to people who felt harmed by him. It was endemic to his personality and an attractive feature of his political persona to moderate voters who dreamed of a more collaborative and less-polarized government. Biden, as always, was in the business of addition, not subtraction. O'Malley Dillon worked with Biden to find a new role for Schultz that would utilize his skills through the general election.

Biden sat at the nexus of a clash between the Democratic Party's elite and the campaign team that had, however precariously, gotten him through the primary. The sentiment that permeated the Democratic Party was that Biden was the nominee despite his campaign team, not because of it. Biden and the party machinery that had passed on him were now married. He might have been the second-to-last choice of many Democratic elites, but when it got down to him and Sanders, there was no hesitation.

By late March, Kate Bedingfield and her communications team had laid out a two-week plan for Biden's media appearances. It was already a given that Biden would operate from home. "We knew how he was feeling, and how adamantly he felt, about keeping safe, keeping the staff safe, modeling good behavior, and listening to science," said one Biden aide.

Most of Biden's health and political advisers supported the candidate's position. In addition to keeping him safe, it was consistent with advising Americans not to risk spreading the disease. That played well with the left. It made Joe look weak to the right, and there was no telling whether it would help him or hurt him in the long term with swing voters.

New to the team, O'Malley Dillon sided with her boss, his doctors, and a handful of advisers like Dunn who believed it benefited him to let Trump take center stage, even as prominent Democrats openly fretted that he was frittering the campaign away.

"Jen's empowerment of folks who are trying to do what he wants and are limiting his schedule and his engagement, that's a real negative outcome," one campaign aide complained. "I think things are good and I hope to God that we win this race. If we don't, I'm going to look back at this as a period of great missed opportunity when he should have been doing more."

Biden went on television a little bit during those early weeks of the pandemic, but it wasn't enough for some of his top advisers. Klain, in particular, wanted him to be more visible in countering Trump. Having served as the Obama administration's Ebola czar, Klain helped shape Biden's policy and messaging on conference calls. Klain argued adamantly that Biden couldn't stand on the sidelines while Trump was quarterbacking the federal response.

"Ron Klain was a huge advocate for needing to be out there every day," said one senior campaign official. Klain felt that letting Trump dominate the discussion of the disease—even if he was doing himself political harm—was an abdication. But getting media attention probably meant leaving the house, and Biden didn't want to do that. It put Klain in the awkward position of pressing Biden to get out of his comfort zone at a time when he wasn't just politically vulnerable but physically vulnerable.

Obama's allies were generally pleased with the O'Malley Dillon selection when it was made, but many began to second-guess the strategy when Biden disappeared from the campaign trail. "You put your dumb uncle in the basement," one Biden associate said at the time.

When it came to the coronavirus, there was an advantage in being the challenger. No matter what Trump did, Biden could say it wasn't enough. The downside risk to Biden was limited. He wasn't responsible for the outcome. If Trump handled the disease smoothly, it wouldn't matter what Biden had said. Trump would be able to add pandemic-wrangler to a list of accomplishments and use that to build momentum for his reelection effort. But Biden had little faith that Trump would respond to the coronavirus competently.

While Biden faded into the backdrop, Trump elevated himself. Every day, on live television, he presented himself as the nation's schizophrenic epidemiologist in chief. Almost as soon as he issued stay-at-home guidelines, he began talking about when he would lift them.

The stock market plunged. Companies large and small laid off workers. In late March, he signed the CARES Act, which pumped more than $2 trillion into the economy and empowered the Treasury Department and Federal Reserve to inject trillions more through policy and regulatory actions. He bragged about the supposed successes of the White House coronavirus task force, which took over whole swaths of the federal bureaucracy and spent wildly on countermeasures. Its main units were overseen by Kushner, who tapped friends to take power inside government entities like the Federal Emergency Management Agency and the Health and Human Services Department. They cornered the market on personal protective equipment and ventilators, forcing states to beg Trump for help.

Trump was taking action. But he kept playing down the disease, even as it killed thousands, then tens of thousands, then more than one hundred thousand Americans. He played it down even as it crippled the economy. He called himself a "cheerleader" for the country when he was asked why he ignored the hardships to communicate a sunny message. He sounded out of touch with the reality millions of Americans faced with the dual threat of the virus and economic collapse.

"Naturally, if people are losing their jobs, people are going to get disheartened," said one top Trump adviser. "The over-response, having those multi-hour press conferences and just not looking like he fully understood everything that was going on, hurt him." In April, Trump got caught between the fight to combat the disease and the battle to save the economy. Even though he had once said one was dependent on the other, he treated the two as separate problems. That led him to be slow to shut down commerce in the country and quick to pressure states to reopen for business. He couldn't take the medicine of stay-at-home guidelines that were crushing economic output.

"He should have picked one route or the other," the adviser said. "Leave it open and go all economy, or close it all and just protect people and reopen as quickly as possible." Trump was torn. No option was appealing. What he didn't fully take into account was how much worse things could have been for him politically. Polls showed that Americans didn't blame him for the coronavirus or the economic downturn. He was being given latitude by voters.

Both Trump and Biden were comfortable with the stylistic and substantive contrasts of their respective early responses to the coronavirus. Trump led loudly. Biden calmly said Trump misled.

While it was hard for Biden to look presidential from his basement, Trump, despite the power and trappings of the White House, looked more and more unpresidential by the day. This was Trump's first real crisis, and he couldn't manage it. Perhaps no one could, but Trump kept saying he had it all under control. That was at odds with the evidence. The coronavirus—its brutal and unpredictable effects on the human body, its capacity to spread quickly and slowly, its death toll, and the mortal blow it dealt to the economy—was all too real. More than ten million Americans filed for unemployment in March—and by the end of April the total number of new jobless claims in a six-week period would jump to thirty million.

When Trump announced stay-at-home guidelines in mid-March, his team was convinced that he was on track to win. For most Democrats, Biden's marginal lead in polling was too thin for comfort.

But inside the campaign, the sentiment was different. Dunn told one associate what campaign officials believed but would never say in public about the disease's effect on Biden's fortunes.

"COVID is the best thing that ever happened to him," she said.

CHAPTER 14

•

Law and Disorder

J EN O'MALLEY DILLON ARRIVED ON THE SCENE TO CONDEMN THE Biden primary campaign and build a completely different structure on top of it. But she would soon find out there were hard limits to what she could change—including Biden—and how fast.

She was hamstrung in the early weeks by the onset of the coronavirus, the national lockdown, and uncertainty about what a COVID-19-era campaign would look like. She also took over at a time when Biden didn't have enough money in the bank—or enough confidence about how to fundraise effectively during the pandemic—to make commitments to pay a slew of new staffers through November. Biden's debt rule still applied: There would be none of that on his campaign. O'Malley Dillon also wanted to sign off on new faces in each department. For all these reasons, she instituted a hiring freeze during her first several weeks on the job.

So it was peculiar to veterans of the primary campaign that O'Malley Dillon didn't seem to use the unexpected free time to figure out what had worked before she got there. She just assumed the operation was a shit show, several aides who worked on the primary said. "The fundamental thing is understanding what needed to change and what didn't," said one Biden adviser. "Jen did not spend much time taking stock of why the campaign was successful in the primary. She came in with an attitude of 'I'm going to overhaul this whole thing.' That ruffled a lot of feathers."

She recruited a crew of lieutenants to "layer" the existing department heads and take charge of building out the staff for the general election. She wanted a hierarchy that more closely resembled the 2012 Obama campaign, for which she had served as deputy manager. By late April, that transition was under way. Rufus Gifford came on full-time to ride herd on the fundraising operation as another deputy campaign manager. She brought in Jake Sullivan, the former national security adviser to Biden and senior State Department official under Hillary Clinton, to help with policy.

Ashley Allison, who had been Valerie Jarrett's deputy in the White House, came in to manage relationships with constituent coalitions—activist groups and other organizations supportive of Biden. Natalie Quillian, the former adviser to Obama White House chief of staff Denis McDonough, took leave from Boston Consulting Group to become yet another deputy campaign manager, overseeing chief operating officer Maju Varghese. The deputy campaign manager title would also go to Obama administration veteran Julie Chavez Rodriguez, a granddaughter of migrant-workers' rights leader Cesar Chavez, who joined the campaign as a Latino outreach specialist. Much later, Mitch Stewart, the Obama battleground states expert and Bloomberg campaign strategist, would come in to help oversee battleground state operations.

Over the spring months, and with some struggle, O'Malley Dillon essentially layered the entire campaign with the Obama crowd. Some of the moves, like Sullivan's, were never announced. He just started showing up on key Zoom calls and advising Biden on economic policy and national security. In the coming months, he would be a key architect of Biden's "Build Back Better" economic plan and slogan.

The primary survivors felt a mixture of disrespect and humiliation, and they put up a wall of resistance to O'Malley Dillon and her new guard. "The resentment for the new people was palpable," said one of the new senior managers who had to contend with the shenanigans of what felt like two campaigns within one. "We wouldn't get our calls returned. We would be left out of meetings." At the same time, the primary veterans were infuriated that they weren't a part of O'Malley Dillon's daily nine P.M. senior staff calls, which merged her deputies with Dunn, Ricchetti, Donilon, and a revolving gallery of longtime Biden advisers. O'Malley Dillon quickly grasped that she could only hope to contain the

pooh-bahs—to manage up to the campaign's board of directors—
with the help of Dunn, who also acted informally as an overseer of
the communications department.

The younger set balked at new accountability standards
O'Malley Dillon laid out. She didn't like what she saw as a fly-by-
the-seat-of-your-pants approach to planning and execution of everything from media rollouts to building organizations in the
states. Her response to that, reflective of her experience in managing campaign efforts at the local level up to the operations of
Obama's reelection campaign, was to micromanage each department until she believed that it was functioning as it should without
a heavy hand. Usually, that meant until one of her lieutenants was
in place and settled.

O'Malley Dillon's first concern, above and affecting all others,
was fundraising. At the end of April, fresh off of two months in
which Biden had dominated the end of the primaries, and all of his
rivals, including Sanders, had dropped out, the campaign had $57
million in the bank—or a little more than half of Trump's $107
million.

When Biden had sewed up the nomination, his primary finance
team held a videoconference call with elite donors and money bun-
dlers. Running through slides on a PowerPoint presentation, one of
his aides noted with pride that Biden had won despite being outspent twenty to one by the other campaigns. One high-level Biden
ally watched and listened in shock. *You're saying that like it's a
positive thing*, the ally thought. *It's a really negative thing*. Biden
had won despite his campaign's failure to raise enough money to
operate in most of the Super Tuesday states. If not for pure name
recognition, he wouldn't have been able to get on the radar of most
voters.

Despite Gifford's best efforts to open the Obama donor spigot
into Biden's basin as an outside campaign adviser in early March,
money was still tight in April and May. The arrival of the coronavirus had conflicting effects. On the one hand, more donors were inspired to contribute to get rid of Trump. On the other, unemployment
and financial market instability created huge disincentives to giving. In all, Biden didn't get the windfall he expected from taking
control of the race for the nomination.

For Gifford, the challenge of running a virtual fundraising machine seemed daunting. He was accustomed to having enticements

to help loosen high-dollar donors' purse strings, but in 2020 these folks would definitely not be getting a photograph with the candidate or the chance to rub elbows at a fancy dinner with titans of industry, finance, and politics. It wasn't clear whether those events would resume in the fall or whether he would have to buckrake remotely through election day. The virtual element did have two silver linings: The check-collecting wouldn't be limited by travel time for Biden, his surrogates, or the contributors, and the cost of holding a fundraiser over Zoom was next to nothing. He just had to figure out how to get people to give.

Together, Gifford and O'Malley Dillon put together a plan to try to revive the emotional attachment donors had to Obama's campaigns. This had to make contributors feel like they were full participants in a mission much larger than themselves or Biden. They would come to find that the coronavirus made the creation and maintenance of a community—any community—easier than it had ever been before. Distanced from friends, relatives, and local groups, donors yearned to be connected to something. The campaign could establish itself as a virtual hub for Democrats, like mybarackobama.com had become a dozen years earlier. They weren't perfect parallels, but the concepts were similar.

The invasion of the Obama people gave a more professional cast to the Biden operation, even as it irked his primary-era loyalists. They fought back by clinging to the one aspect of the campaign they knew that O'Malley Dillon and an army of commissioned officers couldn't change: Biden. They beknighted themselves as guardians of his brand and portrayed O'Malley Dillon and her crew as outsiders whose instincts and maneuvers were a creeping threat to it.

There was nothing more politically valuable to Biden than having survived the Democratic primary as a centrist who had rejected the increasingly progressive impulses of his party. Even as his team negotiated an agenda with Sanders's aides, it was the Sanders side that was usually giving ground from the platform they had brokered with Hillary Clinton in 2016. The value of that agenda was that it sat between Trump and Obama on the political spectrum, didn't promise too much, and lacked ideology. Just like Biden. This, he believed, was the way to win the election: less change more gradually.

But Obamaworld veterans believed it wasn't just the campaign mechanics that needed updating. They thought Biden did, too. For two months, Trump, his campaign, and the Republican National Committee had chided Biden for "hiding in his basement." The taunts caused many Democrats to wet their beds. David Axelrod and David Plouffe, the masterminds of Obama's 2008 campaign, took to the pages of *The New York Times* to write a column criticizing Biden for failing to go toe to toe with Trump in the social media arena.

"Online speeches from his basement won't cut it," they wrote on May 4 as they encouraged Biden to at least use modern virtual tools to show up for the fight. "Mr. Biden can turn the tables on Mr. Trump," they added. "To do this, the challenger needs to behave more like an insurgent, building the capacity to wield facts, humor and mockery at lightning speed in those surreal moments of opportunity that Mr. Trump regularly provides."

The suggestions revealed the two political gurus' misunderstanding of the differences between Obama and Biden. Obama, who was elected president in an era of social media and around-the-clock cable news analysis, knew how to throw a punch. But Biden took pains to refrain from the caustic barbs of cruel sarcasm. He had grown up politically in the Senate in a different time, when lawmakers attacked one another's ideas but held back from personal insults. He had also been mercilessly teased as a child for his stutter, something he would occasionally discuss, and he leaned more toward empathy than mockery. More than that, he was running a campaign on his personal character, compassion, and competence. Few acts could be less authentic for Biden than filming a TikTok "burn" to respond to Trump on the controversy of the day.

There were also concerns that Biden couldn't energize white progressives and minority voters with an agenda and a persona so bland it made cardboard taste flavorful. In internal political and policy debates, the new managers were more likely to push Biden to the left, which created an opening for disaffected primary aides. For more than a year, they had bristled at bottlenecks and tried with futility to alter Biden's style and substance. Now, faced with incoming pressure on Biden from new staff, they were the most ardent adherents of the Biden Way that had been used by the pooh-bahs to explain to them why the boss wasn't going to tilt left or modulate his tone when he was talking to younger voters.

Before O'Malley Dillon's arrival, Biden's small team had sometimes been divided over strategy and tactics but had forged an abiding loyalty to his core message. They had stuck with it, and it had worked. Even if some of his younger advisers were more attuned to the modern Democratic Party's leanings, they understood Biden's innate centrism and the political value it held in the general election. They had been willing to sacrifice their own policy priorities, and, at times, their own wisdom and instincts about campaigning, to suit Biden. They knew he wasn't going to change, and they had bought into the idea that he'd set the right course for his campaign. The primary had not shaken their faith in that. It had strengthened their belief that the Biden Way—no matter how clunky—was the right way to win this election.

The internal battle to #KeepBidenBiden simmered throughout the spring. But another unforeseen moment in 2020's America was about to bring it to a boil.

On the morning of Memorial Day, mask in hand, Biden ventured out of his house for the first time since mid-March. He and Jill rode in a black Chevy Suburban to a nearby veterans memorial for a brief, solemn visit to commemorate members of the armed forces who had been killed in battle. Though Beau had died of brain cancer long after his tour in Iraq, the Bidens' attention to the holiday served as a reminder of their son's service to his country. The moment also spoke to the former vice president's long history of public service, showing him in the performance of a rite familiar to national leaders. In lieu of campaigning, or talking to the press, he signaled what was important to him: masks and the military. In the midst of so much death, it should not have been so striking for Americans to see a political leader conducting himself with solemnity and reverent purpose.

Seventy miles away, at Baltimore's Fort McHenry, Trump delivered a rousing speech comparing the battle against the "invisible enemy" of the coronavirus to the American victory in the War of 1812. In simple but graphic language, he retold the story of Francis Scott Key, whose witness to the British attack on the fort inspired "The Star-Spangled Banner." Trump then spent the rest of his day attacking Biden on Twitter for a "poor work ethic" and what he said was a "weaker" stance on China.

And then, at 8:19 P.M. that evening in Minneapolis, police officer Derek Chauvin put his knee on George Floyd's neck for more than eight minutes, killing a Black man who was only accused informally—not charged or convicted—of using a counterfeit bill at a corner market where he was a regular customer. Ghastly video of Floyd's final moments on earth, recorded by onlookers who pleaded with the cops to let up, circulated directly into the national consciousness.

The next day, May 26, hundreds of mostly peaceful protesters marched a couple of miles across the city from the place where Floyd died to a police station thought to be the home base of Chauvin and three other officers who'd stood by during the fatal confrontation. As day turned to night, more aggressive demonstrators smashed the windows of a police cruiser and sprayed graffiti. When they broke into the precinct's parking lot, officers pushed them back with force. By Wednesday, May 27, it was apparent to Trump that he had to say something. Initially, he expressed sympathy for Floyd and suggested the police had been in the wrong. Floyd's death was "very sad and tragic," he said that morning during a trip to Florida's Space Coast. Later in the day, he tweeted that "the FBI and the Department of Justice are already well into an investigation" of the killing "at my request."

It was an unusual tack for Trump, who often spoke of "law and order," frequently surrounded himself with men and women in uniform—generals, border patrol agents, and police—and had a long history of failing to distinguish between suspects and criminals. But he was genuinely torn. He was for law enforcement, but he didn't approve of what the video showed. There was a potential political opportunity in exhibiting empathy for Floyd—something he'd never shown regarding COVID-19—as he tried to cut into Biden's margins with people of color and educated white suburbanites.

Polling suggested that the Black Lives Matter movement was gaining social acceptance, but Trump didn't put much stock in those surveys. If anyone had a feel for America's hidden prejudices, it was Donald J. Trump. In Trump's mind, the hope for being rewarded for moderation always became subsumed by the fear of alienating his base. He ultimately didn't believe he could afford to appear less than sympathetic to cops, especially when he needed to jack up his base for the election. He ignored the polling, and the advice of some of his aides, and went with his gut instinct: side with the police and drive a wedge deeper into the body politic.

Trump denounced rioting and looting when they accompanied protests in Minneapolis and other cities over the following days. "When the looting starts, the shooting starts," he tweeted in the early morning hours of Friday, May 29. He urged governors and mayors to put down violence by activating National Guard troops. He fueled conflict and refused to help extinguish it—either by taking a serious stand against police killings or by sending in his own forces to quell unrest. The "law and order" president might not have started the fire, but he sure liked to watch it burn. For one thing, the protests were bumping his handling of the coronavirus out of the lead spot on cable broadcasts.

"It actually took away from the COVID stuff and helped us," said one high-level Trump campaign official.

But some conservative critics quickly began to drive home the point that Trump was in charge. It was hard to swallow the idea that he was both helpless to stop violence as president and suited for another four years in office because he would keep Americans safe. "The first requirement of leadership is that you watch over the people in your care," Tucker Carlson said on his Monday, June 1, Fox News show. "Donald Trump is the president. Presidents save countries, and that's their job and that's why we hire them. It's that simple."

Trump had already gotten the message and leaned hard into a violent show of federal force. Sunday night, nearby Saint John's Church, where presidents regularly attended services, had caught on fire during protests against police killings and systemic injustice. He tried to exert control on Monday. The White House pushed the public out of Lafayette Square and set up a guarded perimeter. During a day of peaceful protests, Trump amassed a force of hundreds of armed federal agents and D.C. National Guard troops in the park. Late in the day, as Mayor Muriel Bowser's citywide seven o'clock curfew neared, Trump announced that he would deliver remarks in the White House Rose Garden at six-thirty P.M. Attorney General Bill Barr emerged from the White House and walked through the lines of soldiers and agents like a commander reviewing troops before a major battle. Instructions for the crowd to disperse, amplified by loudspeakers, could not be heard clearly over the cacophony of a low-flying chopper and the protesters chanting at the federal force.

About half an hour before the curfew, and as Trump was supposed to begin his remarks, horse-mounted U.S. Park Police officers flanked the protesters from the east side of H Street Northwest, the road separating the park from Saint John's Church. Riding into the crowd and discharging loud flash-bang devices, rubber bullets, and tear gas, the federal cops drove the fleeing crowd up city streets and away from the park and the church. Trump was creating chaos just hundreds of yards from his heavily guarded house. The blasts were audible in the Rose Garden, where White House television correspondents affirmed for their producers that each percussion could be heard easily right where Trump was about to speak. He had timed the federal assault on peaceful protesters to coincide with his remarks.

"I am your president of law and order and an ally of all peaceful protesters," Trump said as George Orwell silently rolled over in his grave. "As we speak, I am dispatching thousands and thousands of heavily armed soldiers, military personnel, and law enforcement officers to stop the rioting, looting, vandalism, assaults, and the wanton destruction of property." Then, with a phalanx of armed troops having cleared his path, Trump marched across the park, with generals and family members in tow, to Saint John's. Ivanka Trump, who is Jewish, withdrew a Bible from her fifteen-hundred-dollar Max Mara purse and handed it to her father. He held it aloft as video and still cameras captured what he viewed as a moment of triumph. In at least one way it was that.

He had picked his base as the winner of an internal debate over how to handle the protests, knowing that there was little he could do to recapture the educated white voters who would be turned off by such shows of brawn or make inroads with Black voters who were petitioning for social and political change. "I don't want to say those groups were written off," said a top campaign official. "But we realized that we would be working to get them and that we needed to find votes elsewhere." Trump's escalations removed him from a political vise, according to campaign advisers.

"He had managed to put himself in a position where he pissed off everyone," said one Trump adviser. "He pissed off the lefties, the media, and the soft moderates by not being supportive enough

of the protests. But he also pissed off his base by not being supportive enough of the police. That's the worst place to be in as a
politician."

Now, he stood clearly with the MAGA crowd. They liked cops,
they hated protesters, and they loved shows of machismo from
Trump. James Mattis, who had served as Trump's first secretary of
defense, broke his public silence on the president two days later.
"Donald Trump is the first president in my lifetime who does not
try to unite the American people—does not even pretend to try.
Instead he tries to divide us," Mattis wrote in a statement to *The
Atlantic* that many Washington insiders saw as a powerful rebuke
of the commander-in-chief. "We are witnessing the consequences
of three years of this deliberate effort. We are witnessing the consequences of three years without mature leadership."

If Donald Trump wavered at first before quickly leaning into his
base, Joe Biden's response to the outcry over George Floyd's killing
required the most nimble positioning of his entire campaign. Biden
had won the primary as the candidate of conservative white Democrats and Black voters, many of whom believed that enough swing-
voting whites would pick him over Trump. Police killings and
violent protests drove a clear wedge between younger Black voters
and the swing-set whites. The pressure to pick a side, like Trump,
bore down on him. If he sided too much with his party's activists,
Trump could bludgeon him with moderate whites. If he ignored
the racial justice movement, or gave a blanket defense of cops, he
could reopen the wounds of the crime bill.

In the wake of Floyd's killing—which followed so many others
like it—liberal Democratic activists began to shorthand their calls
for criminal justice reform with the incendiary slogan "Defund the
Police."

That was a political gift to Trump—a cudgel he could use to
hammer the entire Democratic Party—and anathema to Biden's
way of thinking.

"What we didn't expect was there would be the overreaction
and that some of the well-meaning effort of people who were pushing for social change would get hijacked by radical elements who
want to defund the police," said one Trump adviser. "We realized

that Joe Biden was in a pickle because he had been so terrible to the Black community." In polling and in focus groups in June, Trump advisers found that "the anarchy, the unrest, the rioting" were "alarming to a lot of groups," said a top campaign official. That was particularly true among seniors, Latinos, and some of the educated whites that Trump had all but written off only weeks earlier, according to campaign aides.

"Protesting such brutality is right and necessary," Biden said in a statement issued late one night during the initial round of demonstrations. "But burning down communities and needless destruction is not. Violence that endangers lives is not."

Throughout his political career, Biden had tried to find a middle path on issues that inflamed racial tension. He had lived through the governor calling in the National Guard to put down rioting in Wilmington following the assassination of Martin Luther King, Jr., in 1968. In his first run for the Senate four years later, a local newspaper concluded that his position was "for and against" school busing.

By early June, Trump was using the moment to hit him from both sides. On the one hand, Trump presented himself as the candidate of law enforcement, and Biden as the candidate of lawlessness. On the other, Trump pointed to his own prison-reform law, and Biden's crime bill, to portray himself as a champion of the Black community and Biden as a poor choice for Black voters.

Biden found himself trapped between working-class white Rust Belt voters, who tended to favor law enforcement, and the Black, white, and Hispanic activists who called for defunding the police.

As American cities erupted, civil rights activists turned up the heat on Biden's campaign. Biden's most prominent Black advisers and aides, including Ashley Allison and Symone Sanders, could hardly pick up their phones without hearing or reading about the civil rights community's frustrations with their candidate. And then Biden wrote an op-ed in *USA Today* embracing both police and protesters. It set off a firestorm.

"There's all this backlash from everybody, from activists to Hollywood types," said one Biden aide. "Hollywood people are calling up and saying, 'Hey, my people in these circles are saying this ain't good.'"

The flames quickly spread outside the civil rights and celebrity communities. Big-time donors registered their criticism with Biden's fundraising team and his top counselors. "There was a sense that Joe Biden already lacked—that he needed to double down on his support for the Black community based on past votes, based on the crime bill and stuff like that," said a senior campaign aide.

It was June 10, and Biden was now in the midst of a touchstone political, cultural, and social crisis that pitted him against key segments of his voting base and tore at the patchwork fabric of his growing campaign team. To the extent that police violence against unarmed people of color was politically harmful to Trump, the aftermath of Floyd's killing imperiled Biden's coalition like no other issue.

Even before George Floyd became a household name, Biden's stance on criminal-justice issues had been a hot topic of discussion for a campaign that was staffing up with aides who were more progressive than their boss. The newbies came from Obamaworld, the camps of defeated rivals, and various corners of the Democratic activist universe. Shortly after she took over, O'Malley Dillon had opened up a series of conversations to try to figure out how Biden could engage and mobilize the Black electorate. Democrats had learned the hard way in 2016 that a nominee's success with Black voters in a primary did not necessarily translate to overwhelming Black turnout in crucial swing states in the general election.

"This was a long-standing, ongoing conversation just in terms of the primary narrative and positioning," said one senior Biden aide.

Just a few days before Floyd was killed, Biden touched a raw nerve when he told radio host Charlamagne Tha God that any Black person who voted against him "ain't Black," a comment that Trump backers circulated with glee.

It was already clear that Biden's record—and Trump's use of it—threatened to hold down Biden's numbers with Black voters in the general election. But when the national conversation turned suddenly away from coronavirus and toward issues of policing, protesting, rioting, and Trump's deployment of federal force, the discussions inside the Biden campaign became much more intense.

They became a staple of O'Malley Dillon's nine p.m. daily senior staff calls, a series of one-on-one conversations between high-ranking campaign aides, and video-conference calls linking Biden officials with leaders of activist groups. Activists wanted Biden to renounce his support for the crime bill, commit to policing reforms, and side with protesters over cops. Ashley Allison, who worked closely with civil rights groups, went to O'Malley Dillon to push for Biden to offer a public apology for the crime bill, according to several campaign officials. Ron Klain wanted Biden to embrace more of the Black Lives Matter agenda while distancing himself from the group's "defund the police" mantra. Anzo, the pollster, found 70 percent of the public understood that "defund the police" didn't mean abolishing law enforcement. Along with Allison and Sanders, he advocated for Biden to stop talking about putting more money into hiring COPS.

On the calls, Biden's views were represented by the original set of senior advisers—Donilon, Ricchetti, and Dunn—who were largely unmoved by appeals for changes in Biden's position. He would, and did, show support for victims of police violence in his remarks, in public appearances in places where he wouldn't create a disruption and where a family wanted his presence. But he wasn't going to tilt left in the general election after having maintained a centrist profile through a brutal primary. Besides, Biden and his older white counselors saw an advantage in the contrast with Trump, who was talking tough on crime but had sought to cut Justice Department funding for the COPS program.

O'Malley Dillon believed she was convening a dialogue that the campaign needed to have—no matter where it landed—to make sure that Biden's actions and remarks were consistent with his broader strategy and sensitive to the various parts of his coalition.

We have to make sure that we're speaking to the moment, and not approaching this from a historical standpoint, she thought. *The country is coming together in a different way than it has in the past—just look at the suburban moms protesting in their own communities—and we have to think about this in the context of the current environment.*

But some veterans of the primary campaign shook their heads silently at her approach, concluding that she was advocating for changes that would sabotage Biden's authenticity and his appeal to swing voters. Just giving a platform to the progressives, some of whom were her new hires, showed her hand, they thought.

Again, the campaign was divided along a set of deep fault lines mostly based on generation, race, ideology, and time in Biden-world. Most of that reflected the broader Democratic Party's internal conflict over how to solve problems of systemic racial injustice without clamping down on cops to the point that they couldn't defend themselves and the citizenry. The part that was unique to Biden's campaign was the increasingly raw relationship between O'Malley Dillon's squad and the high- and mid-level primary aides who now reported to them. One colleague later marveled at Allison complaining in these conversations that Black voters were unfamiliar with Biden's position on the legalization of marijuana—he was against making the drug legal but for decriminalizing its use. "The people don't know because the motherfuckers who work for him are not communicating," the colleague said of Allison.

Ultimately, there was no consensus to be had within the campaign on Biden's positions on criminal justice.

The escalating back-and-forth came to a head on a videoconference call in late July. Allison, O'Malley Dillon, and their allies were outgunned by the longtime advisers closest to Biden. "There was a lack of understanding of where he is flexible and where he is not," said one participant in the virtual meeting. "No one was going to make any traction saying that Biden shouldn't talk about the COPS program or telling him that he needed to straight-up apologize for the crime bill."

Still, some Biden aides felt it was important for their candidate to embrace the gathering movement precisely because a racial justice protester was not necessarily a Democratic voter. There was potential opportunity in terms of reaching out to new voters, and potential risk in alienating Black activists if Biden didn't stand with them. Black Lives Matter activists wanted Biden to adopt their proposal for "defunding the police"—which didn't actually mean zeroing out funding for local departments—and Allison pushed for Biden to at least commit to more of the hard proposals from activists.

The answer that came back from the pooh-bah chorus: The activists may be for defunding the police, but that's not where the majority of Black people in the country are. We're not going to push him to go there.

While Trump would try to depress support for Biden by attacking him from both sides on criminal justice issues—soft on crime and the engineer of mass incarceration all at once—he didn't seem to have any real intention of bringing centrist voters into his own column. For Biden, the eye of the storm was the safest spot.

"He's not willing to be on one side or the other," the aide added, "because for him it is not that clear-cut."

At the end of July, just a few days after the meeting, Biden unveiled his agenda for Black economic empowerment in a speech in Wilmington. He spoke about the country being "plagued" by systemic racial injustice, advocated for the reauthorization of the Voting Rights Act, and hit Trump for his response to the Floyd protests. "Every instinct Trump has is to add fuel to the fire," Biden said. "We need leadership that will calm the waters and lower the temperature."

What he didn't do is change his platform on criminal justice.

"Nothing changed from Day One to where he ended up, except he was a leader in the actions he took to speak out at that time and reference what was happening in the country and give remarks on it," said a top campaign official.

Few people in the world knew as much about the life cycle of social and political movements as John Lewis. The seventeenth-term congressman from Atlanta was the last living member of the Big Six civil rights activists. He had been a Freedom Rider, marched on Washington, and bled for voting rights at the Edmund Pettus Bridge in Selma. He had also watched a successful nonviolent movement lose political influence as more radical leaders took control of its message and tactics. He'd been ousted from his chairmanship of the Student Nonviolent Coordinating Committee by Stokely Carmichael, whose advocacy for "Black Power" alienated some white supporters of civil and voting rights. Battling terminal cancer in the spring of 2020, Lewis watched the escalating battle over systemic injustice, police killings, and reform efforts with deep concern.

On the House floor one day in June, Lewis sat with Jim Clyburn, whom he'd known since 1960, when they met as student activists working with Martin Luther King, Jr. Already frail from his illness, Lewis settled in on the Democratic side of the ornate chamber. Clyburn could see the toll disease was taking on his friend. The swell of Lewis's full cheeks had flattened, and he had shed dozens of pounds from his once stocky frame. The man famous for marching peacefully into billy clubs now walked with the aid of a cane. Colleagues and aides kept a close guard around him in the Capitol so that he would not catch the coronavirus from a well-wisher hoping to shake his hand.

As the two men sat a few rows in front of the Speaker's rostrum on the House floor, in a section of seating unofficially claimed by the Congressional Black Caucus for decades, Clyburn asked Lewis for his thoughts on the direction of the Black Lives Matter movement.

Lewis replied with a parable about the civil rights movement of the 1960s that he knew Clyburn would understand. Back then, in their view, a successful nonviolent movement had been overtaken by a more extreme faction that pushed for violent confrontation. Lewis and Clyburn both believed their movement had been lost to the backlash engendered by extremism. Richard Nixon had been elected in 1968 on that "law and order" platform. This wasn't just a movie they had seen before. They had lived through the death of their nonviolent movement.

" 'Burn, baby, burn' killed us," Lewis, who had been beaten by police and arrested more than three dozen times, said to Clyburn. "And 'defund the police' will kill them."

Clyburn agreed. He thought that the words "defund the police" would undermine the reforms the activists were hoping to achieve. And, as the third-ranking House Democrat, responsible for raising money for the party's candidates, he worried that the left's slogan of the moment would cost Biden and Democratic House incumbents at the polls.

That same month, Lewis visited the newly baptized Black Lives Matter Plaza in Washington, D.C., which had been hastily named—and painted—by Mayor Muriel Bowser at the spot where federal forces had attacked protesters outside Lafayette Square. Wearing a mask, and standing with his arms crossed over his chest, Lewis embodied an iconic link between the past and the present. It was the last time he would be seen in public before he died the following month.

If anything, Biden was running like an incumbent president sitting on a lead. Trump, Biden believed, was his own worst enemy.

The more Trump talked, the better for Biden. Because he suddenly found himself at home, rather than on the campaign trail, he caught more of Trump on television than he would have normally. That included the daily White House briefings on the coronavirus. Biden would often shake his head and say, "I can't believe this guy," or "Can you believe this guy?"

In most presidential elections featuring an incumbent, the presumptive nominee of the other party finds himself awkwardly figuring out how to compete with the president for political oxygen before his party's summer convention. Biden's aides didn't want him to take the spotlight off Trump. They wanted him to follow an iron rule of politics: Never get in the way of an imploding rival. The coronavirus gave him a justification to lay low. This made Democrats, from Obama's campaign geniuses to donors and voters, very uncomfortable. But it infuriated Trump and his campaign aides, who tried mostly in vain to get the media to cover Biden's absence from the campaign trail. There were no Biden-basement clocks on banners at the bottom of cable news programs. Insets carried counts of the coronavirus death toll.

"They used coronavirus as an excuse to keep him in the basement, and it was smart," said one Trump adviser. "Biden was able to hide his biggest weakness, which is himself. And he did it with an excuse that sounded responsible."

Biden didn't travel from the time his campaign suspended events in mid-March until early June, when he flew to Houston to meet with members of George Floyd's family. By Independence Day, Biden's lead in the Real Clear Politics average of national polls increased to 49.6 percent from 40.1 percent, 3.1 percentage points better than on Memorial Day. In terms of the big four swing states—the three in the Rust Belt and Trump's new home state of Florida—the movement was in Biden's direction, from a statistically insignificant three-tenths of a point in Pennsylvania to 3.8 points in Wisconsin. The changes were relatively small, and they occurred in the midst of both the pandemic and the protests. That made it difficult to attribute them to any particular factor. But one thing was clear from those surveys and others: Trump had lost ground since Biden had pulled off the campaign trail, and a strong majority of Americans—about two-thirds of them, according to Gallup—did not view the president as honest and trustworthy.

For Trump to defeat Biden, he would have to make Biden more unacceptable to a greater share of the electorate, and that was difficult to do with Biden out of the picture. Interestingly, neither campaign trusted the public polling on the race. After winning in 2016 despite polls showing Clinton with leads in key swing states, and after three years in the presidency in which his approval rating typically sat well below where his team thought it was, Trump relied on his own set of pollsters and Parscale's digital surveys to gauge his standing.

Biden's pollster and his analytics team also believed Trump would do better than public surveys suggested. In June, Anzalone and Siegel talked about how to effectively bake in what Republicans referred to as the "hidden Trump vote." The analytics office's surveys were quick-and-dirty versions of more traditional polling, which was more time consuming and more costly. The advantage to traditional polls was that they could often do a better job of testing messages with voters, like the gun control themes Anzalone polled before the Nevada caucuses.

Siegel believed that public polls were oversampling college-educated voters, who were more likely to respond to surveys. She reweighted her models to reduce the share of college-educated voters. The broad result of that was internal campaign surveys that showed Biden faring worse than in public polling. The campaign's pollsters also rendered surveys with a tight race.

In the Trump era, there was a significant shift of less-educated voters toward the GOP and a nearly concomitant move of more-educated voters toward the Democratic Party. The trend was first observed in the 2016 election, and it was confirmed in 2018, when Democrats picked off dozens of House seats, and, in a more consequential outcome for the 2020 race, the governorships of Pennsylvania, Michigan, and Wisconsin. For years, Republicans held an advantage in midterm elections because highly educated voters were more likely to vote in lower-turnout elections. That advantage flipped to the Democrats in 2018.

What all of that amounted to was a race in which both campaigns could agree that Biden's lead was growing modestly as spring turned to summer, Trump dominated the airwaves and social media, and the nation grappled with coronavirus. But both sides also believed that lead was smaller than the public knew.

Trump tried to tie Biden to the "defund" slogan. His campaign made an ad in which no one picks up the phone at a police station. "You have reached the 9-1-1 police emergency line," a voice actor playing an outgoing dispatch recording said in the ad. "Due to the defunding of the police department, we're sorry, but no one is here to take your call. If you're calling to report a rape, please press one." The words "You won't be safe in Joe Biden's America" flashed on the screen.

Parscale constantly surveyed voters on the various messages the Trump campaign sent out through television and digital ads. In mid-July, around the time the tension inside the Biden campaign reached its peak, Parscale found that the "call" ad scored better than any of the others in swing states. It was particularly effective with undecided voters, an indication that "defund the police" could be used to disqualify Biden in key voters' minds if Trump could convince them that was Biden's position.

While Trump made small concessions to police reform ideas, his rhetoric was clearly in favor of police. The contrast in approaches highlighted yet again Biden's efforts to seek balance and Trump's preference for choosing sides. But the "defund the police" fight also pointed to a broader difference between the campaigns. Trump had been burned in the early days of the protests. "When the rioting started, he vacillated," said one Trump adviser. "There were people in his ear, looking at polling, saying you don't want to hurt all the work you've been doing with Black voters and suburban moms— missing the fact that, above all, suburban moms want to feel safe. He eventually got there. That was the most effective message he had."

With no end in sight to confrontations between authorities and citizens across the country—and new police killings adding to the intensity of the racial justice movement—Trump stayed on his course of escalation and recrimination. In July and early August, he would close the national polling gap back to less than 6.5 points.

Trump's campaign aides found that the president's sustained hot rhetoric was working with one key group in particular. "The one community where our numbers went up during the four to six weeks following the murder of George Floyd, and the resulting pro-tests, was Latinos," said one high-ranking campaign official.

Biden's "soul of the nation" theme promised to lower the temperature on political, social, and cultural divisions—when it came to policing and the full complement of other issues. Biden resisted the activists in his party and the new Obamaworld team that had taken control of the mechanics of his campaign. He could, would, and did push them away. He understood that both white suburban women and Black voters wanted to feel safe—the movement against systemic injustice was rooted in Black voters' desire to be protected. He understood the political peril of taking officers off the streets, which is why he liked to point to his proposal to increase funding for the COPS program and the Trump budgets that tried to cut it. Biden's message was consistent, if non-ideological. He offered a solution that demonstrated empathy for police and law-abiding citizens of all backgrounds who wanted to feel safe, even if it left something to be desired for everyone.

Trump, as he so often did, stuck with his base. It was an easy strategy and one that he had pinned himself into over five years as a candidate and president. "Numbers get baked in over time, especially so with this president, and baked-in really hard and really immovably," said one senior Trump campaign official. Some of his aides were surprised at the traction he was getting on the "law and order" message. Said a second official, "We were saying 'This is Joe Biden's America,' even though President Trump is the president."

CHAPTER 15

•

The Keys to Tulsa

DONALD TRUMP DIDN'T HAVE THE GUTS TO FIRE ANYONE FACE-TO-face, especially not his burly campaign manager.

It was one of the most telling ironies of the mismatch between Trump's macho persona and his innate fear that manifested itself in paranoia and narcissistic self-preservation. He had become a cultural icon by telling contestants on the hit television show *The Apprentice,* "You're fired!" In real life, he always sent hatchet men to do the dirty work.

In this case, as in many others, the task fell to Jared Kushner, the Bar Mitzvah–voiced son-in-law who served as Trump's senior adviser and fixer in the White House. In a mirror reflection of his father-in-law, Kushner appeared meek but wielded power with precision and personal ruthlessness.

One day in late June or early July, Kushner summoned the campaign manager, Brad Parscale, into his first-floor cubbyhole in the West Wing, just a few paces from the Oval Office. The two men had been working together on Trump's reelection since the moment the president was sworn in.

On the surface, they couldn't have been more different. Kushner, a tall, lanky thirty-nine-year-old, had been born into a New Jersey and New York real estate empire. He'd gone to Harvard, after his father, Charles Kushner, made a multimillion-dollar donation to the school. He was soft-spoken and meticulously kempt, like the heir to a fortune someone else built.

The forty-four-year-old Parscale looked like a bouncer at a Florida strip club, with a long, thick beard and thinning hair that was cropped Marine-style on the sides and back. He liked fast cars and boats. Growing up outside Topeka, Kansas, he'd torn up rural back roads, pedal to the metal, as he raced against friends in a beloved Eagle Talon. Sitting in the White House, the pinnacle of American power, brought him a mix of pride and self-consciousness about his roots. *It's fucking redneck,* he thought of his background.

Cars—specifically a Ferrari he'd picked up when his daughter had turned eighteen—were a big part of the reason his job was on the line. Parscale had figured out that he could lease a $240,000 car, pay only the depreciation, and spend about $30,000 over two years. That might sound like a lot of money to some people, he thought, but it wasn't the same thing as dropping a quarter of a million dollars on a ride.

But his rich-man's car kept popping up in news stories. Trump allies used it to try to convince the boss that Parscale was paying himself too much at the expense of the campaign. There was a twenty-some-odd-foot boat, too, that was invariably described as a yacht. And Parscale's houses—ones that he had sold and his nice place in Florida—always put the final brushstrokes on the portrait of a playboy living large on Trump's dime. The two unforgivable sins in Trumpworld were eye-catching self-enrichment and drawing attention away from the main guy. Parscale appeared to be two for two.

But all of that was a backdrop for the primary source of tension between Parscale and Kushner as they sat down in the cramped West Wing office. The president's return to the campaign trail—his first rally since the coronavirus shut down the country—had been an unmitigated disaster. Parscale had boasted that a million people were signed up to descend on Tulsa, Oklahoma, to welcome the president back. But when Trump took the stage on June 20, he saw the twenty-thousand-seat BOK Center arena was half-empty. He was getting crushed in the press, not just because members of his traveling team had contracted the coronavirus. It was worse than that. Trump was being ridiculed for his tiny crowd size, which Trump took as a measure of his manhood. Someone was going to take the fall for making him look like a fool, and it sure as fuck wasn't going to be Kushner.

Trump had never stopped campaigning for president, and, for him, that meant building his brand the way a developing company might. Pick fights with bigger names, divide the existing market share, and attract new customers by telling them he was the best. Parscale, who had worked on branding for Trump since 2010, was as natural a fit to run Trump's reelection operation as he was an unorthodox choice to the Republican establishment and many Trumpworld insiders. As the 2016 campaign's digital director, he had proved his loyalty and demonstrated a knack for conducting Trump's base. Moreover, Trump's adult sons, Don Jr. and Eric, liked him, as did Kushner. Trump named Parscale to the top job on the campaign in February 2018, almost nine months before that year's midterms and thirty-three months before the next presidential election. At the time, Kushner said Parscale would build a "best-in-class" campaign, a phrase borrowed from the business world. The one thing that Trump, Kushner, and Parscale had in common was a singular shared goal: the reelection of the forty-fifth president.

Shortly after Parscale was put in place, Trump embarked on what would be a series of more than three dozen "Make America Great Again" rallies in support of Republican candidates before the midterms. It turned out that, like Obama, Trump wasn't able to transfer his popularity to other candidates, and a "resistance"-fueled Democratic wave flipped control of the House and the Speaker's gavel into Nancy Pelosi's hands. Trump had warned his base voters on the campaign trail that a victory for Democrats would lead to his impeachment, and many of them stayed home anyway. But he was sure they still loved him, in part because of the response he got on the trail and in part because his approval ratings had been virtually inelastic for two years. No matter what he did, what he said, or who he pissed off, he couldn't fall much below 40 percent. On the other hand, he couldn't rise to 50 percent.

That helped inform the strategy that he, Kushner, and Parscale developed for the reelection campaign in early 2019. While they would make some effort to sway voters—Kushner believed the president could eat into Democratic margins with Black voters, in particular—it primarily rested on the idea that Trump could, and would, identify people who loved his brand but hadn't voted in 2016.

That was an unorthodox approach for an incumbent president. Usually incumbents tried to broaden their coalition in advance of a reelection campaign, not deepen it. But Trump didn't do anything by the book. "I fully expect that by July of this year it will be a well-oiled machine, similar to what you might expect of a traditional campaign, and yet he will do it in a nontraditional way," said future White House chief of staff Mark Meadows, who was then still representing North Carolina, in early 2019. "There is going to be nothing normal about the way this president campaigns."

Trump officially kicked off his reelection campaign with a rally in Orlando on a rainy June day in 2019. The flash downpour on a miserably hot and humid day soaked a crowd gathered outside the arena, which included a number of the "Proud Boys," a hate group that backed the president.

Trump had been watching the Democratic primary with interest, taking note of Kamala Harris's rollout, which he told aides he found impressive. In the summer of 2019, when Elizabeth Warren was surging, Trump discussed her rise with Kellyanne Conway.

"Who would you rather run against—Warren or Biden?" he asked.

"Well, I'd rather run against Elizabeth Warren, but I'd rather debate Joe Biden," Conway replied.

"Oh?" Trump said, prompting her to expound.

"She'd be brutal. She'd get up in your face and say, 'You are a sexist, you are a racist, a misogynist, a disgrace to the country, and I'm going to be the one who ends it.' She will say that."

Trump took it all in, but he always saw Biden as the most likely Democrat to win the nomination. His impeachment prediction had come true after he withheld $400 million in defense aid to Ukraine in an effort to get that country's government to announce an investigation into Biden and his son Hunter. That dirt-digging operation, quarterbacked by former New York mayor Rudy Giuliani, had begun in late 2018 and continued through the summer of 2019. When *The New York Times* published a story on the Obama-Biden relationship in August, Conway brought it to Trump's attention in the Oval Office. "It's crazy," she said. "It looks like Obama doesn't want Biden to run, and it doesn't look like he's going to get involved."

Trump still saw Biden as the Democrat with the strongest position in terms of a platform, but he was deeply unimpressed by the front-runner's abilities as a campaigner. For months, he had watched other Democrats jump into their primary, which he took as a sign that they didn't think Biden was such a tough customer. He told associates that he truly thought Biden was confused, and when the pandemic hit he was amazed that Biden thought he could run a campaign from his house.

Conway saw Biden's isolation for the advantage it was. "This actually benefits him," she told Trump in April 2020. "Voters see you all day long on social media, in your two-hour press briefings on COVID," she continued. "They don't see him at all, so voters can make Biden whatever they need him to be." It was a longer way of saying that the dynamics focused the race as a referendum on Trump, when the best course for Trump was to make it a choice. But Trump saw a replay of 2016. Biden had been in the Senate for thirty-six years and served as vice president for eight more. Trump had run against Clinton, a less-tenured Washington insider, four years earlier. "He never really had the respect for Biden," said one ally who spoke to him frequently. Washington insiders are "what he ran successfully against."

On May 26, 2020, as Trump got ready to announce a deal that would cap Medicare insulin costs at thirty-five dollars per month for seniors, he watched Biden sit for an interview with CNN's Dana Bash from the study next to the Oval Office. Biden, sitting far apart from Bash, called Trump an "absolute fool," a rejoinder to Trump mocking him for wearing a mask during his first public appearance in two months the day before. On the way out to the Rose Garden, Trump was still talking about the clip.

"What do you think?" he asked Conway as they walked out into the warm sun.

"I think if we lose to him, we are pathetic," she replied.

A smile breaking at the corners of his mouth, Trump let out an approving laugh. Just a month earlier, his internal poll numbers had hit rock bottom. At the same time, he saw Biden as a dog of a candidate and himself as an underdog.

"He never thinks things are easy. He thinks they can go one way or the other," said a senior White House official. "Joe Biden had all the king's horses, all the king's men, all their money, all their attention. Biden had plenty of people pushing for him to win, to push Trump out." No one appreciated that more than the president himself. While he found Conway's "pathetic" remark amusing and he didn't think much of Biden, he knew there was work to do to win.

That concern was half the reason he wanted to get back to his road show—he still called the confabs "MAGA" rallies even though they were technically now "Keep America Great" rallies. The other half was just to get an emotional lift after three months of focusing on the coronavirus from the White House. It was a brutal slog for everyone, the president included. "When can I do the rallies again?" he asked campaign and White House officials again and again. Parscale didn't believe they actually had as much political value as Trump thought. He had noticed that the same people were going to rally after rally, giving each one a diminishing marginal value to the campaign. But if it made Trump happy, no one could tell him no.

The risks of a big rally in the midst of a pandemic were, at a minimum, glaringly obvious. Trump could get sick. His staff could get sick. Rally-goers could get sick. The whole thing could turn into a superspreader event that killed his fans and became emblematic of fatal ineptitude. Just the difficulty of finding a place where he could gather people together in public without violating any laws or ordinances would be a nightmare.

But Trump was insistent. He saw the rallies—and their cultural significance—as fundamental to his presidency and his political viability. He could be out on the trail, campaigning for votes, while Biden sat around in his basement with a mask on. Besides, he was asking the country to open up again, and he could show that he was willing to be part of that.

"In the president's defense, it didn't seem too early," said one White House official. "We'd been working for over a hundred days, and we did what Fauci, Birx, and Azar asked us to do. A lot of these states felt like they had flattened their curve. April and May were nightmares for this country but June felt a little different."

When Trump started agitating to get back on the trail in May, Parscale brought him a plan to put together an open-air rally at the

Florida State Fairgrounds, a three-hundred-plus-acre expanse in Tampa, according to a person familiar with the details. Parscale figured that with folks distanced by six or ten feet, he could get as many as one hundred thousand people onto the property. The location made good political sense in that it was in a vote-rich part of a swing state crucial to Trump's plans to defend his electoral college majority. But Trump balked. He didn't want to have anything to do with a socially distanced outdoor rally. He wasn't about to give in to Biden and the Democrats by demonstrating that the pandemic was enough of a threat to alter his campaign events. Besides, central Florida was hot and muggy in June and a magnet for late-afternoon or early evening downpours. He hadn't forgotten the soggy campaign kickoff in Orlando a year earlier.

Parscale went back to the drawing board to come up with a set of options for Trump. His first impulse was to stick with an outdoor rally but move the event toward one of the beach towns, like Pensacola, and hold it at night. *The president will get a cool ocean breeze and lower the risk of getting soaked,* he thought.

Parscale also loaded up some indoor-arena options for Trump, including one in Tulsa. Vice President Mike Pence told Parscale that Oklahoma was probably the only place they could legally put thousands of people in one arena at the same time. But from Parscale's perspective, an outdoor coastal rally felt like a win-win for Trump and his base. Still, he needed to run some traps before he brought the Florida beach-town idea to the president. He dialed up Ron DeSantis, the state's Republican governor and a staunch Trump supporter, for his input.

On the call, Parscale got a thumbs-up from the swing-state governor, according to a person familiar with the discussion. But a short time later, after giving it some additional thought and looking at the surging COVID-19 numbers in the Sunshine State, the governor changed his mind and phoned the White House.

"I don't like it," DeSantis told Trump. "I don't need the political pressure. Can you please do it somewhere else?"

After that conversation, Trump called Parscale and ordered plan B—or plan F. "Let's do Oklahoma," he told his campaign manager.

Parscale pushed back a little. "Look, I don't think we should do it inside," he said.

There was no use in lobbying Trump. He was set. As one former senior White House official put it: "One of the Trump axiomatic rules is he has to do the opposite of what you recommend because it's part of his narcissism." Plans for the indoor rally moved forward quickly. Early signs suggested that there was a pent-up hunger for Trump's supporters to see him back in the heartland. Parscale's campaign team clocked 150,000 registrations in the first twenty-four hours after the June 10 announcement of the rally.

Amazing, Parscale thought. After a few days, the numbers kept soaring. Parscale was eager to share them with the president. His team had cross-checked the cellphone numbers of registrants against voter rolls to try to make sure Trump haters weren't overloading the system. Trump fans had caused mayhem during the Iowa Democratic Caucuses by flooding the party's hotline with calls, and he didn't want to be a victim of the same kind of shenanigans. Parscale could see how often verified registrants had voted in the last four elections. Those voter histories showed him that there were one hundred thousand registrants within a fifty-mile drive of Tulsa, which has a metropolitan population of just about one million. The sum was staggering, but, in Parscale's thinking, it checked out.

He dialed Trump.

"Mr. President, I've got valid registrations from at least three hundred thousand people across the United States," he said. "And the reason I know it is I got their cellphone numbers." He told Trump about the hundred thousand people within a fifty-mile radius. Even if only a quarter to a third of the valid registrants from across the country showed up—and Trump fans were known to sometimes drive long distances to see him speak—this would be a MAGA rally on steroids. It could easily draw between fifty thousand and one hundred thousand people, Parscale thought.

There were a couple of hitches, though. First, the rally had to be rescheduled from June 19 to June 20 so that Trump wouldn't cross voters commemorating Juneteenth, the anniversary of the date on which Union soldiers arrived in Galveston, Texas, with news that the Civil War had ended and all formerly enslaved people were free. It was an unusual show of racial sensitivity from Trump amid national unrest over police killings of Black people and systemic racial injustice. But the alternative was eclipsing the coverage of his own rally with stories about his insensitivity.

The more consequential problem cropped up as Parscale continued to watch the registration numbers skyrocket. Users of Tik-Tok, a social media platform, were signing up for the rally to try to fool the campaign into overstating the likely turnout. On June 15, five days before the rally, Parscale tweeted that one million people had signed up for tickets. Oklahoma governor Kevin Stitt, who was seeing a spike in COVID-19 cases in his home state, went public with his desire to see the event moved to an outdoor space. The following morning, on *Fox & Friends,* Pence said the campaign was looking at the possibility of a hybrid indoor-outdoor rally. Outside the BOK Center, there would be something of a cultural bazaar for Trump enthusiasts who had been on lockdown. Trump loved the juxtaposition. He was about to reenter the campaign arena to a sea of adoring fans, while Biden was almost invisible to the public.

The night before the rally, Trump told the news site *Axios* that Tulsa should brace for a "wild evening." And he threatened that critics would receive harsh treatment from law enforcement, lumping peaceful demonstrators in with criminals. Less than a month into a social movement for reforms in the wake of the police killing of George Floyd, Trump chose to fan the flames of unrest. "Any protesters, anarchists, agitators, looters or lowlifes who are going to Oklahoma," he tweeted, "please understand that you will not be treated like you have been in New York, Seattle, or Minneapolis. It will be a much different scene!"

He was instigating conflict, raising tension, and trying to make sure that the world would be watching his gigantic rally. By now, such tactical plays were fitting for an all-about-that-base strategy that emphasized reinforcing his brand to would-be voters and trying to depress support for Biden.

A year earlier, in the spring of 2019, he had been blunt about the tactic of racial division in a conversation with former White House communications director Anthony Scaramucci. "The Mooch," as the Wall Street investment firm chief was known, had been fired by a Trump emissary in 2017, just eleven days into his job in the West Wing. Despite the abrupt separation, the Mooch kept in touch with his old boss and defended him on television. But Trump was upset that Scaramucci had criticized him for telling members of "The Squad" to go back to their countries. The four freshman House members, all women of color, were American citizens—three of them were born in the United States—and Scaramucci, the grandson of an Italian immigrant, didn't like the aspersions cast on immigrants and their families.

When Trump called, the Mooch told him it didn't make sense to attack immigrants and people of color. He didn't think Trump was racist, but he did think the president was tilting pretty hard in that direction. Beyond alienating people of color, most of whom wouldn't vote for him, Trump ran the risk of turning off white voters who found his commentary offensive. Scaramucci, who grew up in a middle-class neighborhood on Long Island, was one of them.

"Aren't you trying to attract the independents and moderates?" the Mooch asked.

"No," Trump replied matter-of-factly. "I'm worried about the base. If I take care of the base, everything else will take care of itself."

That's how Trump had won in 2016, by racking up about five million more votes than Mitt Romney had in 2012, many of them concentrated in the rural areas of the key swing states that had handed him the presidency. Additionally, the small set of swing voters who were still undecided in the closing weeks of the 2016 election broke hard toward Trump. But by now, the universe of undecided voters was minuscule. People felt strongly about Trump, and the election would be a referendum on him, he thought. He just needed to find the ones who liked him, stir them up, and mobilize them to the polls.

The idea of expanding the voting universe was not an Einsteinian breakthrough. Nearly half the country didn't vote for president. Obama had drawn new voters into the political system in 2008, and that was part of how Sanders had given Clinton a run for her money in 2016. There were millions of Trumpsters out there who just hadn't voted for him yet. Lobbing rhetorical bombs at Democrats—calling them names and threatening to meet them with force—fed into that theory. Additionally, if Biden took up for looters and rioters, or congresswomen who identified with socialism, Trump could use that response to dampen support for the Democratic candidate among the white suburbanites who'd left the GOP in the midterms.

His speech to the throngs in Tulsa would touch heavily on hot-button issues that invigorated elements of his base, including efforts to take down monuments to Confederate soldiers, liberal calls to "defund the police," and, of course, the pandemic disease that he referred to as "Kung Flu" as part of a broader attempt to attack China.

But before Trump could take to the stage in Oklahoma, it quickly became apparent to the campaign that he would not be greeted by the masses. The police announced much of downtown would be closed to traffic. Only ticket holders would be allowed to walk on the roads in the immediate vicinity of the BOK Center. Trump's warnings of protests and violence had piqued tension in the city, and local officials responded by circumscribing his event. The vast majority of the people Parscale expected to attend would not have tickets to get into the arena. They wouldn't be able to get anywhere near the rally. Trump and Pence were scheduled to address the outdoor group from a riser on the perimeter of the arena, but there would be almost no one there to greet them.

This was going to be a disaster. Trump was told aboard Air Force One to expect a small crowd. The outdoor speeches were canceled. Still, when he got backstage, he couldn't believe the empty spaces in the arena. He hadn't accounted for the fear some supporters would have of an indoor gathering, or local authorities clamping down on foot traffic, or anything other than the idea that some decent proportion of the million people he had been promised would show up. He barked at aides, and then he sucked it up and went out to greet the adoring fans who had survived the maze to get inside the arena.

He gamely praised them as "warriors." Inside, he fumed about the embarrassment of speaking to such a small crowd. It was a calamity. But he summoned the energy to deliver what amounted to his first campaign speech of the 2020 general election. He mentioned Joe Biden by name forty-one times. He built an argument that an angry "left-wing mob" was bent on destroying America. But like so many of Trump's hypotheses, it was diminished by the acknowledgment of a contradictory kernel.

"Joe Biden is not the leader of his party," Trump said. "Joe Biden is a helpless puppet of the radical left—and he's not radical left." It was June of the election year and Trump had just conceded that even he didn't view his rival as an extremist. To buy his narrative, one had to believe that Biden was in control of neither his agenda nor his faculties. "I don't think he knows what he is anymorc, but he was never radical left," Trump continued. "But he's controlled by the radical left."

Biden's absence from the campaign trail—interrupted by a Memorial Day appearance—fed into Trump's story line. Republicans said he was in hiding. But Trump was opening himself up to a potentially devastating weakness in his case. All Biden had to show was that he cleared the low bar of competence and leadership that Trump had set for him.

More immediate, though, Trump stumbled badly in telling the sparse crowd that he was sick of coronavirus tests. "Testing is a double-edged sword," he told the Oklahoma crowd. "When you do testing to that extent, you're going to find more people, you're going to find more cases. So, I said to my people, slow the testing down, please." Here was the president of the United States, with more than one hundred thousand of his fellow Americans dead from a pandemic disease, flouting the advice of epidemiologists by holding an indoor rally and revealing that he was ordering administration officials to reduce the rate of testing. Of course, more testing produces more positive results only if the disease is spreading. He didn't get that. He didn't get that, outside his base, millions upon millions of American voters took the counsel of medical experts seriously. Most important, he didn't seem to understand that just a little compassion for the dead—and just a tiny bit of humility about his own self-taught expertise in science—might go a long way.

Always the showman, Trump put on his political game face for the ride back to Washington on Air Force One, where he entertained members of Oklahoma's congressional delegation and Senator Tom Cotton, the Arkansas Republican who had designs on becoming the main passenger on the plane in the not-too-distant future.

Trump showed his jocular side to his guests, according to one traveler. "I wasn't running for president then, but I talked about the birther issue," he told the lawmakers. Trump had reluctantly acknowledged during his 2016 campaign that Barack Obama had, in fact, been born in the United States after years of fomenting the false conspiracy theory that Obama couldn't produce proof of his origin. Now, Trump joked, he still wasn't sure. "I might have been right about that," he said with a smile.

News coverage of the rally was split between outlets that focused on the attendance debacle and those that zeroed in on the idea that the president wanted to curb testing so that statistics on the number of infections would be smaller. None of it was good for Trump. By the time he arrived back in Washington, at Joint Base Andrews, he was deflated. Though it was the lawmakers who'd sampled the aircraft's bourbon, the teetotal president looked like he had just woken up from a bender. He held a MAGA hat in one hand. The girthy collar of his white dress shirt was open. One end of his unknotted extra-long red tie ran down his side, past his belly to his thigh. He was the very picture of disappointment.

Parscale saw lean-and-hungry looks all around him. Trumpworld's long knives—the really, really sharp, so-big-you-wouldn't-believe-it long knives—had been out for the campaign manager for years. And now it was stabbing time.

Less than ten days before the Tulsa rally, the *New York Post* reported that Trump advisers were telling the president to get rid of Parscale. That was the setup for a post-Tulsa ambush. During the coronavirus crisis, Parscale had retreated to Florida, where, like many Americans, he worked from home. That had not won him any favor in Trump's clique. He was acting as if there was a pandemic disease ripping through the country. The existing bill of particulars against Parscale, which had been read out in anonymous conversations with reporters for years, started and ended with what appeared to be his lavish lifestyle. The not-so-subtle hint to Trump was that Parscale was getting rich off the president's campaign—at the expense of the campaign.

None of that really mattered to Trump. He knew the details of payments to Parscale, who had set up lines of credit for the campaign with his personal account, said one person familiar with the arrangement. Besides, said one White House aide, "Brad didn't do anything without Jared's permission, if not direction."

Trump kept hearing about Parscale's big spending, both personally and with the campaign's money. It was true that the campaign blew through dough. By the end of June, Parscale had shoveled more than a quarter of a billion dollars out the door. The disparity of money coming in made it more concerning. In May, Biden had outraised Trump, $81 million to $74 million. That was a leading indicator that donors from across the Democratic ideological spectrum—and those who placed bets on which candidate would be the next president—were starting to open their wallets to defeat Trump. When the June numbers came in, Biden would show $141 million to Trump's $131 million.

What did matter to the president, and what Parscale's many critics began to harp on behind closed doors, was the humiliation of the Tulsa rally. Trump didn't actually say much about it, according to one senior White House official. "It was almost a quiet fury," the official said.

Advisers who had never before cited *The New York Times* or *The Washington Post* were suddenly chattering about the media hit the president was taking—because, they said, of Parscale. Some Democrats mocked the president for the small crowd size, while others lambasted him for exposing his own fans to the disease. In late May, the Lincoln Project, a political committee launched by anti-Trump Republicans, had cut an ad trashing Parscale. The theme was that he had gone from "dead broke" to "rich" while working for Trump. "Shhhh. Don't tell Trump," the ad said. One of the Lincoln Project's cofounders was George Conway, husband of Trump counselor Kellyanne Conway. To Parscale, it looked like he was being set up by a couple that was publicly at war over Trump. The ad included a mention of his "gorgeous" Ferrari. The Conways had net assets of at least $39 million when Kellyanne started work at the White House in 2017.

It was no secret that Kellyanne, who had been Trump's final campaign manager in 2016, was frustrated that she was boxed into a White House job that limited her opportunities to work on the reelection campaign and her ability to make money running an outside Trump-supporting super PAC. It was unusual, to say the least, that the Lincoln Project spent time and money trying to get Trump's campaign manager fired. If he was as bad at his job as the ad suggested, the Lincoln Project should have been happy to have him stay in place. But Kellyanne's husband had been trying to get Parscale fired, publicly, for over a month by the time of the Tulsa rally.

Kushner and Ivanka Trump aired their supposed disgust in the days immediately following, even though Kushner was Parscale's boss, the president had insisted on the specific location of the event, and Kushner had endorsed the whole thing. But what Trump and Kushner had not counted on was Parscale, a reputed digital mastermind, blowing the call on how many people would attend. Part of the problem was how Parscale had hyped the event. If several thousand people showed up at a political rally in the midst of COVID-19 without all the hullabaloo surrounding Parscale's million-person promise, there would have been little media attention to the size of the crowd. Trump was always annoyed that reporters didn't give more play to the numbers at his rallies.

The rally had quickly become a touchstone for a laundry list of complaints about Parscale within Trumpworld, from profligate campaign spending to questions about his capacity to manage a massive organization to victory. The flashy car, the small crowd, and the work-from-home situation were points that Trump insiders knew would land with the president. But the real thrust was that Tulsa had been emblematic of a campaign spiraling out of control.

Almost two weeks later, the repercussions were still being felt within the campaign. It was a brutal moment for the president. Biden's lead in the polls had expanded from less than 6 points to about 10 points over two-plus months. The grace period voters had given Trump when the disease first arrived—no one blamed him for the fact that it had entered the United States—was long over. During that time, Trump had been front and center as spokesman in chief on the pandemic and had stoked tension between law enforcement and racial justice protesters. The more voters saw of Trump, and the less they saw of Biden, the more difficult Trump's path to reelection became. He didn't believe that Biden had a 10-point lead, but he could see that the numbers were moving away from him. Many of his allies and donors wanted Parscale gone, and the Tulsa rally had given them a ready justification.

That's where things stood when Kushner and Parscale sat down in the West Wing.

"Do you think you could go back to being digital director?" Kushner asked. It was the job Parscale had held on the 2016 campaign. Trump didn't want to cast Parscale out—he liked his campaign manager and he knew that it was better to keep him inside the tent than to turn him loose. Kushner's offer amounted to a softer landing than an outright dismissal, but a humiliating demotion all the same.

"Look," Parscale replied. "That's a fuck me from you."

He let his words sink in for a moment.

"You know this isn't my fault," Parscale added. "What have I actually done wrong?"

Kushner, who had been bashing Parscale internally, sounded sympathetic. Despite the differences in their backgrounds, they had a shared love of data and digital innovation, and both men were committed to reelecting the president.

"You actually haven't done anything wrong," he said.

Kushner had floated a trial balloon, and Parscale shot it down. He would shelter in place and try to survive the cyclone. It might blow past. Trump might get distracted. But Parscale had a lot of enemies in Trumpworld and the larger orbit of Republican politics. He wasn't of the political arena. He wasn't like them. *These fucking people resent me because I'm sitting at the table,* he thought. *Kellyanne and Corey Lewandowski want to preserve their access to the president. She's completely obsessed with killing me. The consultants and TV ad buyers know they're frozen out because of me.* He saw enemies everywhere, and he wasn't wrong. The mushrooming fallout from Tulsa was evidence of it.

It was hard for anyone to look at the campaign and conclude that Trump hadn't taken a small but significant hit from the post-primary unification of the Democratic Party and his response to the coronavirus. "He's talking himself out of the presidency," said one Democratic strategist who thought Trump still had a good chance of winning.

In one Oval Office meeting with pollsters and campaign officials in late June, Trump was lobbied to make small changes that would have an outsized effect on his political outlook. The pollsters told him he should be more empathetic. Parscale agreed with them. Trump looked around the room.

"You know what?" he said. "That's not what I want to do. I want to do it my way. And if I don't win, I'll get out of here."

Parscale, weary of arguing with the president, threw his hands up in the air.

"OK," he said.

In short, Trump was responsible for his poor standing, and for the loss of faith from donors. But he was getting a lot of pressure to get rid of Parscale. Effectively, the decision had been made. But he didn't have a ready replacement. He talked to a series of potential campaign chiefs, and Karl Rove, who had played that role for George W. Bush, was a hot name in the rumor mill. But no one in their right mind would have come in from the outside to lead the floundering campaign. It was a no-win situation for any established campaign operative. If things turned around, Trump would seize all the credit. If they didn't, Trump would blame whoever was sitting in the top job. That's how he did things. That's how nearly every politician did things. In politics, loyalty is a one-way street.

In mid-July, Trump settled on a replacement for Parscale. Bill Stepien, a key figure in the New Jersey "Bridgegate" scandal, was one of a long line of aides Trump had picked up off the scrapheap of politics and given a second chance. Stepien worked as an operative on the 2016 campaign and then as political director in the White House before joining the reelection operation as a senior adviser. The forty-two-year-old former aide to then New Jersey governor Chris Christie couldn't have been more different from Parscale—in tone, management style, or physical stature. And despite, or perhaps because of, Bridgegate, Stepien had no desire to be in the spotlight. Trump, so obsessed with size, was ready to supplant his colorful six-foot-eight-inch Viking of a campaign manager with the five-foot-eight-inch adult version of an establishment-blessed college Republican.

On July 14, Trump called Stepien and Kushner into the study next to the Oval Office. All three men knew that Trump had hit new lows in his polling over the previous three weeks; he stood at 40.2 percent in the Real Clear Politics average at that very moment. Trump wasn't pleased at all with the direction of the campaign. But it wasn't just the poll numbers. His outfit was spending more than it was taking in. Parscale had become a distraction, calling more attention to himself than the candidate or the campaign. And Trump felt like the base wasn't jazzed-up enough.

For all these things to come together, Trump told Stepien, the culture at the top of the campaign has to change. Stepien was a known commodity to Trump, someone he'd met with weekly earlier in his administration and with whom he was comfortable.

"Do you want the job?" Trump asked.

"I'd be happy to do it," Stepien said, adding that his first move would be to cut his own salary from $15,000 per month to $10,000 per month as a demonstration of his personal commitment to sacrificing for the president's cause. With just less than four months left until the election, that amounted to about a $20,000 hit, but Stepien believed it was an important symbolic gesture as he took the reins of an operation that was going to have to spend less. Trump lit up at the show of loyalty. He offered little in the way of instruction, and the whole conversation lasted no more than ten minutes.

The following day, Kushner came to the campaign headquarters in northern Virginia to talk with Parscale. He walked into Parscale's office and sat down.

"I think it's time," Kushner said. "We've got to make this move."

Parscale was disappointed but not shocked. He'd heard that Trump was particularly infuriated when Conway pointed out that she was in the White House while Parscale was working poolside in Florida. *Where else should I be?* he thought. *The campaign office shut down for two months because of COVID. Should I work out of the Oval? Would they give me an office there? That's against the law. This is a fucking catch-22.*

It didn't matter. This conversation wasn't like the first one. He wasn't being asked about moving to another position; he was being told his run as campaign chief was over.

"I just want to think about how I want to deal with this," Parscale said.

"I think the smartest thing to say is you're staying on," Kushner offered.

If I quit, Parscale thought, *the whole campaign will go down. I could turn out the lights, the websites, the email system, the whole fucking infrastructure, down to the way data transfers between the campaign and the RNC.* It was all built on his Amazon server. The accounts were tied to his credit card. He wanted some time to assess his options.

Parscale called Rove, who had been advising him informally for a few months. "I think you're one of the smartest guys," he told Rove. "What do you think I should do? Do I walk? Or do I just say I'm here to help?"

For the outgoing campaign manager, the political calculus was the mirror opposite from that of an outsider considering coming in to run the outfit.

"Has Trump said what you should do?" Rove asked.

"No," Parscale replied.

"Then I think you welcome the new guy and go do your work," Rove said. "It kind of puts you in a win-win. Because if they lose, they shouldn't have gotten rid of you, and if they win, you're still doing all the work and you made the right decision to make sure he wins."

"All right," Parscale said. At one point in their conversations, Kushner had told Parscale he could keep control of the digital operation—basically continue working on his strength—and just do it without a title. Maybe that could work, he thought.

Before they hung up, Rove added another incentive.

"If you quit, it looks like you turned on your guy," Rove said.

When Trump announced Stepien's promotion, Parscale decided to remain on the campaign staff but hightail it back to Florida.

Stepien walked into the new job on July 15 concerned about the poll numbers, the president's standing with key demographic groups, the amount the campaign was spending, and a lack of co-ordination among campaign officials. *The president's in a bad place,* he thought.

He immediately tasked his new deputy campaign manager, Justin Clark, with reviewing the campaign's budget and pulled down television ads. He tried to professionalize the work environment, at a time when aides were moving back into the glass cubicles at the Rosslyn, Virginia, headquarters. Regular all-staff meetings were added to the calendar, Stepien required aides to be at their desks early and leave late—he sometimes slept in his office—and he put up a sign next to the elevator showing the number of days left until the election.

Parscale had looked at Trump's politics as a brand-building mission. *You have to spend to keep reminding voters of why they like Trump,* Parscale thought. *And this election isn't going to be held on one day. With all the early and mail-in voting, they will be making their decisions and casting their ballots for weeks.* Stepien favored nursing the money in the campaign treasury so that it wouldn't run out. He estimated that if he didn't tighten the purse strings, the campaign was on course to spend its last dollar by mid-September and go $150 million into debt by election day. Besides, Trump's megaphone was big enough for him to get free media coverage for anything he said. The question was whether he could pick the right message and stick to it.

Biden's top campaign operatives agreed with Parscale's approach to early and continuous spending. They were already starting to shove pallets of Biden's cash into TV and digital ads. Biden had a steadier stream of money coming in.

"The dysfunction of the campaign really can't be discounted," one GOP operative said of the pre-Stepien era. Ultimately, this operative said, Parscale wasn't qualified to be campaign manager in the first place, but the constant jockeying for power within Trump's orbit and a total absence of coordination were even larger problems.

That was Trump's culture, the operative said. "Nobody trusted each other in the foxhole."

CHAPTER 16

•

Head or Heart

BIDEN COULDN'T DECIDE. IT WAS AUGUST 9, 2020, AND HE AL-ready had blown through his own self-imposed deadline to pick a vice presidential running mate. He had known he would be the Democratic nominee for almost five months, and he had set up such a long and arduous vetting process that a war had broken out among the camps of the various hopefuls. Kamala Harris polled best, but he was still uncertain.

He called Clyburn for counsel—maybe for permission.

"I'm having a real battle between my head and my heart," Biden confided. He was down to the wire and he would be making his announcement in just a couple of days. His head told him that Harris was the smart pick. She had a national profile and could appeal to two overlapping sets of voters vital to his coalition: Black voters and suburban women. He had infuriated some Black activists with his response to police violence in the wake of George Floyd's killing, and a Black running mate might help offset that. But he was enamored of several other candidates. Former national security adviser Susan Rice was close to Biden but also a lightning rod. Michigan governor Gretchen Whitmer, the favorite of several of his closest advisers, was a politician whose profile matched up well with Biden's.

Clyburn could see the conundrum in Washington's absurdist version of a final rose ceremony. His late wife, Emily, had liked Harris. In fact, many of his constituents had been clamoring for a

Biden-Harris ticket for more than a year. He'd heard about that when Biden and Harris were among the candidates who attended his annual fish fry in 2019. But Clyburn also had been early out of the gate to suggest Rice as a potential vice president. He had known her father's family in Florence, South Carolina, and she had been his closest ally in the Obama administration. He'd even called Rice before he floated her name to make sure that was all right with her. She had no objection to being considered.

As usual, Clyburn rendered his advice in terms of the pros and cons of each candidate, rather than as explicit advocacy for one over the other. He had said publicly what he'd previously told Biden privately—it didn't have to be a Black woman but that would be a "plus" for the ticket.

"That's a battle you need to reconcile," Clyburn said. "Do it alone. And whatever is in your head, let your heart take a look before you make the decision."

If anything, Biden probably assigned more weight to the vice presidential pick than most nominees. After all, he believed he was a big part of Obama's 2008 victory. He knew the hopes of the anti-Trump universe rested on his shoulders, and the wrong choice could dash them. Only Biden could make this decision. It was eating him up inside.

Stacey Abrams didn't expect the framing of the question. Not from Chris Dodd, the seventy-six-year-old former Senate Banking Committee chairman. Born into the Senate—his father served before him—Dodd seemed like a central-casting version of the backslapping, dealmaking, old-white-guy status quo. He had been Ted Kennedy's drinking buddy back in the days when waitresses in Washington knew not to walk too close to their table. And he had left the Senate a decade earlier to land one of the cushiest lobbying jobs in the country as chairman of the Motion Picture Association of America. In other words, as a Biden VP selection committee co-chair, he seemed to represent the don't-rock-the-boat establishment. And then he spoke.

"Don't let a good crisis go to waste," Dodd said. "What would you do in the first one hundred days to achieve as much as possible?"

Abrams had an answer ready. She had answers ready for every-thing: her background, her worldview, and her policy priorities. But Dodd asking about the opportunity of crisis surprised her. Maybe it was him, maybe it was the contrast with Biden's passive, risk-averse campaign. She could think about that later. She needed to respond.

"Number one, democracy," Abrams said. Voter suppression must be countered by a new federal law, she explained. "Number two, COVID recovery." The federal response had to be attuned bet-ter to how state, county, and local governments deploy resources, she said, noting that federal dollars don't get to the people who need them most. "Number three, rebuilding our international pos-ture," Abrams concluded, arguing that it was imperative for the United States not only to restore marquee alliances but to under-stand the damage she believed Trump had done in empowering au-thoritarians worldwide.

She paused for a moment, recalibrating her mental sketch of Dodd. *I didn't take him for a fundamental-change guy,* she thought. She could say the same of Biden.

But the establishment man asking how she planned to tear things up if she ended up as vice president still counted as one of the less-unusual aspects of this job interview. At forty-six, Abrams had exactly zero credentials that matched the existing profile of a vice president of the United States. She hadn't served in Congress, lived in a governor's mansion, or run a federal agency. A former minority leader in the Georgia House of Representatives, she had lost her only statewide race. She was a woman. A Black woman. And she was sitting in the dining room of her Atlanta townhouse, talking into a camera perched on a chair. On the wall behind her hung one piece of a rotating set of artworks. Surely, this wasn't how Al Gore had interviewed for the job.

On the other hand, Abrams was so obvious a candidate for the job that she had been fielding questions about her credentials for more than a year. Thirteen months earlier, Biden had paid her a visit, and then his staff leaked that he was considering her as a running mate. He hadn't even entered the race yet. It was a testa-ment to two dynamics: Biden's search for validators in the Black community and Abrams's status as the hottest political force in the Democratic Party. She'd lost her race for governor in 2018—

by a hair—but only after a fight with Republican Brian Kemp over voter-suppression tactics. Had she won, she would have been the first Black woman governor in American history. Even in defeat, she sat at the nexus of politics and voting rights. It was a powerful intersection for Democrats across the country, and she raised gobs of cash for the Fair Fight operation she launched in its aftermath.

A Spelman- and Yale-educated lawyer, and the daughter of ministers, Abrams represented an intriguing option for Biden. She could rally the base. She could inject raw adrenaline into his moribund campaign. She had an outsider's feel for electoral warfare and an insider's understanding of when and how to compromise in the interest of governance. But she might violate the most time-honored rule in vice presidential selection: Do no harm. Biden's old Senate pal John McCain had done that, and it had helped elect Obama and Biden.

Abrams felt that she had to achieve two goals to land herself on the ticket. She had to get Biden to reimagine a job he had held and to envision her in it. She had made no secret of her interest. She had said publicly that she wanted it.

When given a position or a platform you have got to use it, because you don't know if it is ever going to come around again, she thought, *but you also have the responsibility to transform what people expect when you're there.*

Her answer to Dodd highlighted her ability to recruit new voters, the value state government experience might have as a complement to Biden in governing, and her handle on international affairs. It wasn't just that she believed she could do the job. As one of the first Black women seriously considered for the job, she felt a burden both to raise her hand and to follow through with distinction.

Biden had known all along that his popularity with older and more conservative Black voters fell off precipitously with their younger and more liberal children and grandchildren. He had also known since at least that plane ride coming back home from a midterm campaign swing in 2018 that he wanted to pick a woman to be his running mate. The only news he made in his March debate with Sanders, held the day before the country shut down, was that he would lock himself into choosing a woman.

Abrams was not a first among equals. Kamala Harris was the

choice of much of the Democratic elite. She was a senator. She had shown the gumption to run for president. She knew how to land a punch—almost too well. Turned against Donald Trump, she could be a valuable weapon for Biden. In the primary, her base had been a multicultural mix of highly educated women. If she hadn't attacked Biden on busing in the summer of the previous year—or perhaps if she had chosen to endorse him when the primary race was still competitive—the selection process might have been a total formality.

But Biden was considering a wider spectrum of women. Amy Klobuchar's politics lined up well with his, and she held appeal for working-class whites and Republicans. She had not hesitated to drop out and endorse him at the key moment in the primary. Loyalty mattered more to Biden than he ever let on publicly. If he wanted to double down on pursuing Rust Belt votes, the Minnesota senator, who knew her way around the state's Iron Range, made the most sense.

If he thought he needed to line up white progressive votes, he could turn to Elizabeth Warren. Maybe. She was the woman with the plans. He respected her intellect. Biden had coveted Warren's support enough in 2015 to float to her the idea of being his running mate, but she had chosen not to commit her support to him back then. More recently, she'd waited several weeks after dropping out of the 2020 race to endorse him. Moreover, pulling Warren from the Senate had risks: Republican governor Charlie Baker would get to pick her replacement if she jumped to a new administration.

The list went on and on: Senator Tammy Duckworth, Representatives Karen Bass and Val Demings, Atlanta mayor Keisha Lance Bottoms, Rice, and Whitmer, among others. But Harris was, at once, the most plausible and most controversial option inside Bidenworld.

I do not believe you are a racist. But . . . "I didn't think Kamala was going to come at me that way," Biden had said privately after the first Democratic debate. It was still a sticking point. It wasn't so much a matter of retribution for Biden, but he needed to know how she would handle the topic of their very public disagreement if it came up again. He also had to feel comfortable that he could trust her to take marching orders as a running mate. For senior aides, her failure to endorse Biden when it mattered was a sticking point. The campaign made overtures to her before the Nevada caucus. She declined. It wasn't until several days after Super Tuesday that she threw her support to Biden.

"She so screwed herself," one top Biden aide said to another about the endorsement flap.

These loyalty questions didn't disqualify Harris, but they helped open up the field in unusual fashion. They also hung over the already tortuous selection process Biden created. He was afraid of botching the biggest call a candidate can make.

For her part, Harris was stung by her primary defeat. It had been five months since the donors dried up, staff infighting boiled over, and the roar of the crowd died. It was hard to get the same juice from the Senate that coursed through her veins on the campaign trail. She focused her energy on the response to the coronavirus, but the policy end of that was mostly being led by Speaker Nancy Pelosi and Treasury secretary Steven Mnuchin. She could smack Trump around a little from her platform as a senator, and suggest how the response might be better. That didn't feel powerful. The chamber was all but dead from a legislative perspective. Majority Leader McConnell concentrated primarily on confirming federal judges nominated by Trump. So, like generations of senators who had run for president, lost, and returned to the marble-lined corridors of the Capitol—one of one hundred instead of the only one—Harris moped around like a college kid sent back to high school. Biden had felt that disappointment himself—twice.

The process he set up for what TV producers liked to call "the Veep's Veep" was brutal. Harris started it within a few days of Biden announcing his vetting team of Dodd, Representative Lisa Blunt Rochester of Delaware, Los Angeles mayor Eric Garcetti, and former Biden aide Cynthia Hogan. The vetters set up videoconference calls with each hopeful, with Dodd and Rochester forming one team and Garcetti and Hogan another. Both teams would get to talk to each candidate.

Harris didn't prepare well enough for her first meeting, with Dodd and Rochester. She thought it was a formality, an exchange of pleasantries. She didn't realize she was going to be interviewed for the job. Nor did she expect that the contents of the exchange would be leaked to the press. All of the hopefuls promised not to divulge the details of the vetting process. The vetters didn't all feel the same burden.

Dodd asked her what she had to say about the busing attack on Biden.

It was fair game, she thought, throwing off a time-buying laugh at the question.

What happened next would become the source of controversy over the ensuing months.

Harris maintained privately that she said something along the lines of "It was a debate. We were there to debate."

Dodd said she had answered, "That's politics," a longtime supporter and donor told *Politico* nearly three months later. The response had rankled Dodd, who supposedly found it offensive. What was offensive to much of the rest of the Democratic Party was an old white former senator leaking details of a private meeting in a way that would hurt the chances of a Black woman who was considered the front-runner for the job.

Neither Dodd nor Harris commented for the *Politico* story. He called her to smooth things over. It didn't matter. For one thing, the gap between her version and Dodd's was a distinction without a difference. What she was really saying, either way, is that she didn't have a substantive disagreement with Biden. She didn't think he was morally inferior. She was willing to defend him at the expense of looking craven herself. More important, she didn't run to the press to fight it out with Dodd. She showed discipline in letting herself take a hit rather than putting Biden in the middle of a war between his selection team and his leading contender. That was how Biden was running his campaign: staid, stable, stoic.

Beyond that, Harris didn't have to rise to her own defense. The Twitterati did that for her. If anything, the flap created a pro-Harris backlash. Black women and their political allies simply weren't having Chris Dodd's genteel sensibilities. And, by now, they were well organized.

In early April, when vice presidential fever hit Washington, and before Biden had even named his vetting team, a group of politically influential Black women got on the phone to discuss their concerns about the upcoming selection. Abrams's out-front acknowledgment that she was interested in the job had been met by much of the white political cognoscenti with questions about her credentials. Since Biden had limited himself to picking a woman, there was a good chance he might choose a Black woman.

This influential group—which included Democratic stalwarts Melanie Campbell, Donna Brazile, Minyon Moore, Leah Daughtry, and Karen Finney—wanted to make sure that Black women who came under consideration had a fair shot. None of the potential contenders would have the same six-terms-in-the-Senate-style credentials that Biden had when he was put on Obama's ticket, because the pathways to power for Black women had not yet been fortified and expanded. Harris, four years into her first term in the Senate, came the closest.

"Fair shot" was not what they saw for Abrams, who was experiencing a kind of double bind.

"On the one hand it's 'Know your place, don't be too uppity, don't be too mouthy,'" said one of the women who was on the phone call. "On the other hand, 'If I don't fight for myself no one is going to fight for me.'"

Abrams had opted to fight for herself, and for Black women more broadly, and now she was being told, in essence, that she wasn't qualified. "If a white man did that, he would be called bold," said the woman on the call, who noted that Harris was not treated that way. "The other thing that plays out is Stacey is a dark Black woman and Kamala is lighter skinned."

The group was initially divided over which of several candidates to support, but it was unified in two respects. First, the women wanted to pressure Biden to pick a Black woman. Second, they knew they had to show him that it made sense for him to do so from an electoral standpoint. That is, he had to believe that he had a better chance of winning with one of the Black women on his wing than with anyone else. They decided to tap their own networks of professional Black women to sign on to a letter to Biden advocating for the selection of a Black woman. Within twenty-four hours, they had two hundred signatures. *The Washington Post* wrote a story about the effort, effectively turning it into an open letter. Hundreds more women signed it.

The group of women asked Biden's team for a meeting, and specifically requested that it include O'Malley Dillon, Ricchetti, and Dunn, in addition to Symone Sanders. In the end, Biden joined with his aides to meet with the group. Scheduled for twenty minutes, he stayed on for about twice that long. The women decided beforehand that they would have to put a time limit on Brazile. Each of them would get a few minutes to speak, but they wanted to get to the point.

In rapid fire, they told him that they had research and had done their own analysis showing the electoral value of a Black woman. Beyond that, they said, motivated Black women would make phone calls for the campaign and bring their families out to the polls. And they had put together charts matching up the credentials of Black women against white candidates.

Biden listened, and he talked. What he said wasn't much different from his public posture.

"I won't commit to nominating a Black woman because I'm committed to the process," he said. The hopefuls had to be vetted. He also emphasized the importance, to him, of having a personal bond with a governing partner.

When Barack closed the door and I gave him advice one-on-one, Biden said, he knew he wasn't going to read about it in the paper. Having that kind of trust with his No. 2 mattered to him. It was something he said he believed could be built from a foundation, even if it wasn't preexisting.

Biden wasn't committed to nominating a Black woman, and O'Malley Dillon and Dunn were a little resistant, according to sources on the call. Dunn said the data they looked at suggested that none of the Black women candidates were likely to give Biden a real boost in the polls. O'Malley Dillon asserted that Black voters would come along either way to defeat Trump.

Before the end of the call, the Black women pressed Biden's aides on their plan to turn voters out to the polls if stay-at-home and social-distancing rules were still in place.

How do you win an election when there's no ground game? one of them asked.

O'Malley Dillon acknowledged that the campaign had not yet built up the infrastructure for political outreach to various communities in the Democratic coalition. Truth be told, it wasn't fully clear yet whether there would be any traditional voter-canvassing effort. O'Malley Dillon was creating plans for a fully digital get-out-the-vote effort on the fly. No campaign manager had ever faced this task. But there was an important subtext to the push and pull: "walking-around money."

In the old days, Democratic presidential campaigns paid consultants and pastors to distribute cash to canvassers. It wasn't a linear equation, but more money tended to produce votes. And no money tended to produce no votes. If there was no ground game, there would be no walking-around money. That could hurt the effort to turn out Black voters in major cities in swing states. Picking a Black woman for the ticket, on the other hand, could help juice turnout with or without putting money into canvassing efforts.

O'Malley Dillon added that the policy shop was still under construction. Jake Sullivan, who had run policy and strategy for Hillary in 2016, was silently being installed as a key architect of one policy. Biden's policies largely reflected the weight he gave to them in the campaign: not much. They were reactive triangulations between the Republican Party and the left wing of the Democratic Party.

Biden's entire theory of the case for his candidacy rested on having the message do the work for him in binding together the anti-Trump forces. He wasn't about to promise to do anything, on substance or politics, that would alienate any part of his fragile coalition. But the integrity of that coalition was about to be tested mightily by circumstances beyond his control.

The killing of George Floyd on Memorial Day permanently altered the dynamics of the vice presidential search. With Minneapolis aflame, home-state senator Amy Klobuchar could read the graffiti on the wall. There was zero chance Biden would pick a white former prosecutor from the county where Floyd's breath was stolen from him. Like any prosecutor, the former Hennepin County district attorney had a tough-on-crime record that would not help Biden secure the support of young minority voters. That record was being trotted out by her detractors. It could hurt him—probably *would* hurt him—if he chose her. Whether she made the call or Biden did, Klobuchar realized that she was being swept away by a political force much larger than herself.

It was disappointing. She had run her primary in a much different way than most of the candidates. She'd refused to attack Biden. She could win if he fell under his own weight, she thought, but she wasn't going to push. People close to her said that the vice presidential nod was on her mind, even as she ran for the top of the ticket. She had dropped out of the presidential race at the right moment, endorsed Biden immediately, and helped him win her home state in the primary. Since then, she had worked to raise money for him. There was no point in going through the vetting process when she knew she wouldn't be picked. Even before Floyd's killing and the ensuing unrest across the country, Harris was thought to be the front-runner. Klobuchar did what any savvy pol would have done: She found a way to both make herself appear selfless and appeal to a new constituency.

After nearly a month of protests and violent clashes between law enforcement and demonstrators across the country, Klobuchar spoke to Biden. The Democrats couldn't put two white moderates on the ticket in the midst of a racial justice movement.

You should pick a woman of color, she told him.

Then, the next day, she said the same thing on national television. It was a sharp elbow in Warren's ribs. On the trail, Klobuchar hadn't gained enough traction with voters of color to avoid slipping into the bottomless pit of defeated hopefuls. The least she could do was turn her deferred dream into an opportunity for political outreach.

Klobuchar's departure from the veepstakes ostensibly left Harris and Warren as the top contenders.

Warren was the veteran of the group. In 2016, she was the runner-up to Tim Kaine for the second slot on Hillary's ticket. Ultimately, Clinton wasn't sure that the notoriously independent-minded Warren would be a team player as vice president. Warren was close to former Obama adviser Valerie Jarrett, but most of the rest of that White House crew viewed her as a troublemaker because she had fought Obama on nominations and some policies.

Warren found Biden's labyrinthine vetting system much more rigorous than Hillary's. After initial meetings with the separate pairs of vetting team co-chairs, each hopeful had to submit reams of files to one of a series of legal teams assigned to the candidates. Then the lawyers would bring in the candidates, some in person and some by teleconference, to grill them about their backgrounds and even their politics. Warren was shown a video of her debate-stage reaction to Biden taking credit for securing the votes to establish the Consumer Financial Protection Bureau. Warren had built the agency. In the debate, she refused to look at Biden as he spoke.

Then, when she was asked about Biden's role, she thanked Barack Obama for his work on establishing the bureau. The vetters wanted to know how she would handle a question from the press about that moment.

They went through the companies she had represented as a lawyer, her erroneous claim that she had significant Native American heritage, and tax breaks she had claimed. Those questions drilled down to deductions worth a couple of hundred bucks.

We don't vet our presidents like this, Warren thought with amusement as she met repeatedly with teams of lawyers. *Donald Trump never could have been vice president.*

As the candidates battled through the painful vetting in the summer—one of them called it "an intellectual enema"—the Black women's group ran an aggressive behind-the-scenes campaign to turn the discussion exclusively to Biden picking a Black woman for his running mate. They amounted to a major force against Warren, who seemed to be the leading non-Black contender.

"There's no ambiguity to it," said one insider who was on the receiving end of lobbying calls. "They're trying to influence everybody who might be an influencer."

The pitch would start with the case for why Biden needed to pick a Black woman—an informal version of what Biden saw—and end with a not-so-subtle sandbagging of non-Black candidates, according to the insider. "Will somebody who's been a professor her whole life know how to do things as a team?" one of the women said of Warren while lobbying an influencer close to the Biden team. Biden had said he wanted a partner who could slide into the role he played as a counselor and loyal soldier for Obama. "Maybe she should be Treasury secretary."

The calls didn't stop when Klobuchar dropped out. But her exit was symbolic of a shift in the dynamics of the VP search. Over the ensuing weeks, two things would become much clearer: It was Harris's to lose, and Biden wanted to look at other options. By nature, he came to decisions at a pace that only a badly wounded slug would envy. By and large, this was a set of contenders that needed careful vetting. Many of them had never been subjected to any real scrutiny from the national press or an opposing presidential campaign. The Democratic Party couldn't afford for Biden to make a bad pick. It made sense for him to be deliberate. But Biden's abiding caution made him look indecisive, and it opened the process to warfare among the candidates' proxies.

In late July, just before Dodd's thoughts on Harris were published, a new name moved up the short list of candidates. Susan Rice, who had served with Biden as national security adviser and as U.S. ambassador to the United Nations under Obama, had the right friends in the former vice president's foreign-policy-heavy inner circle. Notably, she was close to Tony Blinken, who had been her deputy at the White House and Biden's staff director on the Senate Foreign Relations Committee. More important, Biden knew her well and liked her a lot.

But, like Abrams, her résumé was nontraditional. Rice, who grew up in Washington, D.C., was once a wunderkind in Democratic foreign policy and national security circles. Now fifty-five, she had climbed all the ladders available to a lifelong staffer and was well regarded enough by Obama that he appointed her to two jobs in his administration. She could have a hard edge, but most people who worked with and for her appreciated her bluntness. There wasn't usually much mystery to how she felt about a topic or a colleague. But she was also a partisan lightning rod. She had gone out on television to defend the Obama administration in the aftermath of the terrorist attack on U.S. facilities in Benghazi, Libya, in 2012. A few months later, she toured Capitol Hill trying to convince Republican senators to support her bid for secretary of state. That was a nonstarter. She withdrew from consideration, leading to John Kerry's nomination and confirmation. The tougher hurdle for Rice: She had never held, or even run for, elective office.

At first, Rice didn't really take the prospects of being named to Biden's ticket very seriously. She thought her name was on the list to pad the number of Black women Biden was considering. Her selection might excite the base of Washington foreign policy think-tankers and a handful of diplomats around the world. But most Americans had never heard of her. For the relative few who had, her name was synonymous with Benghazi. But three months into the process, Biden was looking for alternatives to Harris. Obama-world figures, Biden campaign advisers, and donors got into his ear to tell him that Rice could be counted on to be a team player. Cly burn recommended that Biden take a long look at her.

Rice could carry his message and absorb incoming fire for him. Harris, argued Rice supporters, would use the vice presidency to try to corner the market on the next available Democratic presidential nomination. That could potentially put her interests in conflict with those of the administration. Rice, who had toyed with running for office before, was less likely to run for president if she served in the No. 2 job. Or so the argument went.

All of this presented a conundrum for Biden. Fundamentally, his campaign was trying to balance mobilizing Black voters and appealing to moderate suburban whites. Already, he had promised to name a Black woman to the Supreme Court should a vacancy arise on his watch. Ideally, he would find a woman to run with him who scored well with both college-educated and non-college-educated white suburbanites. The most obvious path for winning the presidency ran through the three Rust Belt states that had flipped into Trump's column in 2016. All three had voted for Democratic governors in the 2018 midterms. Only one of them was a woman: Whitmer.

But George Floyd's death and the ensuing racial justice movement had scrambled the politics of his choice. If he picked a white woman, he risked disappointing a key faction in his coalition. His entire strategy rested on avoiding such missteps. The coalition had to hold in order for him to win.

"There's a bunch of folks that are trying to think 'Who's the African American person who's not Harris?'" one former Obama administration official said at the time. "It's down to Harris, Warren, and whomever wins the 'anyone-but-Harris-African-American sweepstakes.'" Those "sweepstakes" were less like a lottery and more like an espionage war.

Warren's allies boasted that she was the best to tackle domestic policy from the vice presidency—but they did it in ways that rubbed the Black candidates the wrong way. Rice didn't like Harris. Harris and Karen Bass didn't like each other. Hell, most of the Congressional Black Caucus was lukewarm, at best, on Harris. She was a member of the group, but only eleven of her CBC colleagues had endorsed her presidential campaign. Only seven of the forty-plus members of the California Democratic delegation endorsed her.

Harris was bright, and fast on her feet. Anyone who had watched a Senate Judiciary Committee hearing could see her play to audiences with prosecutorial flair. Witnesses had to make sure they didn't ease back after senior senators were done with them, because Harris could light them up and create viral social media moments toward the end of a daylong tribunal. She had energy on the stump and a billion-dollar smile.

But she wasn't perceived as a team player. She had landed the first punch on Biden in the primary when he was the front-runner for the nomination. Then she had showboated about it. Democrats still talked about the "merch"—T-shirts with a picture of her as a young girl—that her team had pumped out in the aftermath of the debate moment. She had made Biden look like a southern segregationist. Biden! The guy who had left her a sweet voicemail when she and her husband, Doug Emhoff, had decided to marry.

"I'm literally sitting at home crying because you got engaged," the then vice president had said.

Harris's reputation stretched beyond Washington. Over decades in politics in San Francisco and Sacramento, she'd cultivated more enemies and adversaries than friends in home-state political circles. "She never built out a network of people who were at her level," said one former aide. "She hated being in Sacramento. We had to drag her out kicking and screaming to do any networking. She would send out other people to manage those relationships."

She was demanding of staff, and often demeaning to them. That was particularly true when it came to young women. Some valued the harsh treatment as a sign that Harris trusted them and took an interest in their professional development. But she churned through aides like a wood chipper. "There's something to be said about Biden people sticking around," said one woman who worked for Harris. "Kamala's longest-serving aide is Rohini Kosoglu from the Senate. They are clearly different approaches."

There's no doubt that women in power are judged by a higher standard when it comes to how they treat their staff, but Harris's reputation stood out. It was the kind of thing that might matter to Biden, who often spoke of the need to treat everyone with dignity and who was known to apologize to his aides after letting loose his own temper. The hits on Harris were clearly taking a toll on her hopes and her reputation within Biden's inner circle. Dodd's umbrage over Harris's blasé attitude toward her attack on Biden was just one flash point. There were others.

Most candidates for the No. 2 slot understood that they were likely to do more damage than good to their own chances by campaigning hard for the post. Most presidential candidates didn't want to be lobbied, and Biden was no exception. It was one thing for a high-ranking official to casually mention a favored candidate when asked; it was another for an active campaign to take root.

But Harris had swept into action early in the process. She worked her phone incessantly, speed-dialing officials and donors close to Biden to make clear how much she wanted it. In a reprise of her days in California, most of the work was done by her advisers.

They would call people close to Biden and tick off a list of reasons why Harris should be the choice.

"If you talk to the press, put in a good word," one adviser told a Democratic donor. "If you talk to Bidenworld, put in a good word."

Biden didn't take well to Harris's full-on campaign for the job. It was the opposite of what he had done, keeping his head down during Obama's selection process.

While the Black women's group didn't endorse Harris, many of its members favored her. And its very existence served to bolster the hopes of the only Black woman in statewide elected office among the contenders. Some of the women clapped back to influential Democrats after one hundred liberals signed a letter backing Warren. The Massachusetts senator "has proven herself most prepared to be president if the occasion arises and deeply expert on the overlapping emergencies now plaguing America—COVID-19, Economic Insecurity, Racial Injustice and Climate Change," the letter, headlined by the signature of Hollywood royal Jane Fonda, read.

The idea that Warren would be better suited to deal with racial injustice than a Black woman was hard for some Democrats to swallow. "That Warren letter had so much backlash," said one member of the Black women's group. "At this moment in time, a Black woman is what this country needs."

Still, Harris grew increasingly concerned about her standing, not only for the veepstakes but more broadly as time went on. Even if Biden decided he needed a Black woman to run with him, it might not be her. He was clearly serious about looking for an alternative.

She worried aloud about her chances, asking friends and acquaintances what she could do to head off the surge of other Black women candidates. In particular, she fretted about Karen Bass, the fellow Californian. If she lost out to a House member from her own delegation—a lowly House member!—it would look bad. That could hurt her own future prospects of a presidential bid or even her hopes of winning reelection to the Senate. Her team believed Garcetti was behind an eighteen-page opposition-research dossier designed to point out her flaws.

"What do you think of my chances?" she asked officials and donors. "What can I do better?"

When negative stories about Harris's competition began to appear in the press, Biden insiders attributed it to Harris's allies. Bass got hammered at the end of July with a double whammy: She had praised the late communist Cuban dictator Fidel Castro and spoken at a Church of Scientology event. With Biden hoping to win Florida, any softness on Castro was impossible to tolerate.

The circular firing squad annoyed Biden. But he was also in part responsible for it. He had set up a process guaranteed to take many months. If nothing else, it allowed him to measure how each of the candidates handled the pressure.

Cedric Richmond kept a line of communication open with Harris's team. In that way, he suggested that he was at least open to her, if not pushing for her. He told her camp that her campaign for the job was backfiring. That message could be read two ways: as an earnest effort to help Harris or as a means of getting her to cut out an effective effort that was hurting her rivals.

"Stop it," he said, according to one Harris aide.

"We're not doing it," he was told in reply. That depended on the definition of "we."

Biden was taking too long. For veterans of his circle, that was unsurprising. He didn't like to make decisions on anyone's timetable, not even his own. But the Democratic convention, scheduled for August 17 through August 20, was rapidly approaching. There simply wasn't much time left for him to pick.

Whitmer had flown into Wilmington to sit down with him personally on Sunday, August 2, making her the only candidate to get a face-to-face meeting with Biden. She had former Obama White House chief of staff and Chicago mayor Rahm Emanuel, Donilon, and Anzalone in her corner. The interest in her reflected a desire to focus on pumping up Biden's chances with white swing voters in the Rust Belt. Public attention to her in-person interview gave Biden a chance to gauge the response to Whitmer from Democratic allies. It resulted in what one Biden aide called a "gnashing of teeth" among "Black organizational elites" over the next week. He "understood the sensitivities," said a second senior Biden aide. His polling showed most Democrats had never heard of the vast majority of his potential choices, while Harris was well known and well liked by party voters.

Biden made a final round of calls to the contenders the weekend of August 8 and 9.

He connected with Abrams through the magic of FaceTime. As he had back in early 2019, Biden thought Abrams was impressive. She was a political force unto herself. But his concerns about putting her on the ticket were significant.

"Stacey, you have tremendous capacity," he told her, "but you're not a governor or a senator." Voters would be looking for someone who had won high-level elections. "And you don't have the national name recognition of Kamala Harris or Elizabeth Warren, or even Susan Rice." With pollster Celinda Lake having conducted surveys on the pool of VP hopefuls, Biden had a precise measurement of that. Abrams pressed her case, even though she suspected he would not be moved by it.

"I've never run nationwide," she said. "But I was the most Googled politician in 2018, and I've got pretty good name recognition for someone who's never actually done anything to get it."

Abrams told Biden why she thought the whole frame of the vice presidential selection process was flawed. If it came down to who had won the most elections, or who had the highest name recognition, Black women were going to be at a disadvantage for some time. Harris was one of only two Black women ever to serve in the U.S. Senate, and, as Abrams knew all too well, no Black woman had ever been elected governor in the United States.

"I understand," Biden said. The fact that he had put together a list of candidates that included Abrams and Rice, as well as two Black women from the House, spoke to that. "It's a legitimate critique."

"Look, my hesitation is not about your ability to do the job," he said. "It's about this political moment." Democrats couldn't afford to take any chances with the prospect of Trump winning another four years. Biden couldn't gamble on an unknown quantity. If he did and lost, Trump would get a second term and he would never be forgiven. "You just bring up more questions than the others," he said, meaning that she would be perceived as more risky than some of the others.

Before coronavirus and police killings dominated the national conversation, Abrams thought, *Biden wanted to explore his options. Now, he wants to do the safest thing he can within the universe of limitations he's given himself.*

Biden did not tell Abrams what he planned to do with his pick—or that she was out—but it was clear to her from the conversation that it was highly unlikely to be her. Instead, she saw a process that had begun with Harris and would likely end there.

Biden hopped on videoconference calls with other candidates, too, that weekend, including Harris and Warren.

When he reached Warren, they talked casually about the parts of the American system that she believed were fundamentally broken and what Democrats could do to fix them if Biden won.

This is much more relaxed, Warren thought. *The first rounds were like riding in a speedboat. This is more like sitting in a canoe with Joe.*

Biden talked about his love of the Senate. "Why would you leave the Senate and become vice president?" he asked.

On one level, it was a natural segue into hearing her talk about what she thought could be done with the vice presidency. On another, it might have been an indication to Warren that he thought she should stay put. It would take only a couple of days for that to become clear.

Biden's staff connected him with Warren again on Tuesday, August 11.

"I've decided to go in a different direction," Biden told her by phone.

When Hillary Clinton had delivered a similar message four

years earlier, Warren had spoken too freely in response. "I hope you picked Sherrod Brown or Tom Perez," Warren had said, not knowing the answer.

"Well, Tim Kaine is—" Hillary started, defending her choice. Kaine had been Obama's "heart" option when he used his "head" to tap Biden for his ticket.

"I'm worried you need more energy, Hillary," Warren stated. "And I don't think Tim Kaine's going to bring it for you."

Warren had since learned that presidential nominees don't like having their selection parades rained on by their allies. Biden didn't tell her who he was going to choose, and Warren didn't offer any opinions.

Harris didn't think she would be Biden's choice. Her own disappointment in the presidential campaign had given her a pessimistic outlook about her political fortunes. *If I treat this like it's not going to happen,* she told herself, *I'll feel less burned if it doesn't.*

When Biden started calling candidates, one by one, to tell them they weren't his pick that Tuesday, Harris was waiting in her Washington apartment to depart for a flight to California.

Around one-thirty P.M. Harris was on the phone with top adviser Rohini Kosoglu when Biden sent word through Anita Dunn that he wanted to talk to her. A phone call was set up for two o'clock. Harris hadn't heard much from Biden directly through the process, and she and her team hadn't received many signals from inside Biden's camp either way. The first one came at 1:50 P.M.: The phone call was suddenly changed to a Zoom call.

Harris and Kosoglu conferred to figure out what it meant. On the surface, the answer was obvious: Face-to-face meant it was her. But Harris was skeptical.

We know each other, she thought. *He might want to let me down easy, and respectfully, by saying it to my face.*

At two P.M. Biden tried to connect with Harris. It didn't work. There were technical issues. It wasn't clear which side was having the problem. Biden had to wait a moment while his team figured it out.

"All right," he said, sitting down in the chair behind his desk at home in Wilmington.

"Hi. Hi. Hi. Hi. I'm sorry to keep you waiting," Harris said.

"That's all right," Biden said, taking off the surgical mask he was wearing to protect himself and others from the coronavirus. "Are you ready to go to work?"

"Oh my God," Harris said, processing that she might be vice president. "I am *so* ready to go to work."

She had survived the process of elimination, just like Biden had done in the primary. Her job now was to make history without making news. The Biden campaign was an exercise in sitting on a lead in the polls. Sure, Harris might be able to help energize Black voters or appeal to highly educated suburban women. But she had been chosen to avoid harm more than give help. First and foremost, she had been handed the responsibility of making Biden look prudent. That meant not fucking up. If she could handle that, she might just become the highest-ranking woman in the history of American government. Not bad for a little girl who rode the bus to integrate her school.

For Biden, who often talked about gut feelings, fate, and emotion, the biggest political decision of his life had come down to that choice between his heart and his head. Going with the latter was a no-brainer.

CHAPTER 17

•

Unconventional Summer

JOE BIDEN COULDN'T BELIEVE THE *WASHINGTON POST* HEADLINE he was reading: "How Jennifer O'Malley Dillon Transformed Joe Biden's Campaign." O'Malley Dillon had even posed for a feature-style photo, hands on hips in a plaid, sleeveless V-neck dress in front of her house. The picture was worth a thousand words, none of them good for Biden. At a time when he had barely emerged from his own home and hardly talked to the press— when Trump was accusing him of hiding in his basement—here was his campaign manager drawing attention to his absence with a profile of herself. Besides, Biden lived by the old Capitol Hill maxim that "staff ink stinks," which means that an aide is never supposed to distract attention from the boss.

More important, the whole column was about how O'Malley Dillon had saved him from his campaign. It didn't really matter if that was true. The narrative made her look good at the expense of Biden and his primary staffers. He never much liked being treated like the captain of the B-team in the Obama White House or when he first launched his campaign. Now O'Malley Dillon had just branded herself the A-team.

The profile landed like the mother of all bombs in the civil war between the Obama veterans and Biden's primary crew. Biden was running on a message of unifying the country, but the story was proof that his campaign was still badly divided. And the person responsible for keeping the peace had just publicly chosen sides. It was one thing for outsiders to conclude O'Malley Dillon was on a rescue mission; it was another thing for her to endorse the idea.

For Biden's primary aides, the story encapsulated everything they despised about O'Malley Dillon. They saw her as dismissive of what they had accomplished in the primary, of their capabilities, and of Biden's capacity to win without her. Biden's communications team, which had begun trashing O'Malley Dillon in conversations with authors of postelection books during the campaign's fight over policing policy in July, took the profile especially hard. She hadn't given them a heads-up that there was anything coming, they said.

But she was their boss, and Dunn had encouraged her to talk to *Post* columnist Karen Tumulty. Dunn and O'Malley Dillon thought the piece would be written with or without their participation, and both thought it was best to cooperate with the writer.

When the profile posted online just before eight P.M. on Friday, August 14, Biden had just wrapped up a successful rollout of Harris as his VP choice and was three days out from the start of the party's nominating convention. There was never a good moment for a divisive news story to land, but this one was particularly ill-timed. Primary aides quickly circulated the story to one another and reporters that night. Bedingfield complained directly to Biden about O'Malley Dillon, arguing that the story was not helpful to his campaign.

O'Malley Dillon was surprised by the tenor of the piece and the immediate backlash. *I've never shit on these folks publicly,* she thought, *and this makes it look like I'm doing that.* She called Biden to explain that it hadn't come out the way she had intended.

Biden was frustrated about reporting on Obama influencing his general election campaign—really about any stories that took the focus away from his message to voters. He told her he didn't like "process" stories, a term Bedingfield often used to describe media pieces about the palace intrigue of a campaign. O'Malley Dillon got the message.

She went into damage-control mode, calling several of the aides from the primary campaign who still had important roles in the general election effort to apologize for the way their effort had been portrayed. The long call list included Donilon, Ricchetti, Kavanaugh, Symone Sanders, policy guru Stef Feldman, Annie Tomasini, and Anthony Bernal. O'Malley Dillon didn't reach out to Schultz, but she got an earful from Bedingfield.

The communications director was upset about what she saw as the diminishment of her own role. O'Malley Dillon's oversight of Bedingfield's department, including weighing into the candidate's media strategy and tactics, had rubbed Bedingfield the wrong way from the start. Now, O'Malley Dillon had done a profile with a major newspaper—one that Biden didn't like—without looping in Bedingfield and the rest of the communications team.

It was hard for O'Malley Dillon to separate Bedingfield's proximate complaint about the story from the broader sense that Bedingfield had always viewed her as an interloper in Bidenworld. Was Kate genuinely mad about the story or did it just confirm her bias against O'Malley Dillon? That didn't really matter. The high road—the adult choice—was for O'Malley Dillon to apologize. "I'm very sorry about this piece and the way that it was framed," O'Malley Dillon said. "I never said these things, but I understand how they're really hurtful."

Still emotionally charged up, but grateful for the show of respect, Bedingfield thanked O'Malley Dillon for apologizing. Their relationship would improve but never fully mend.

In the summer of 2020, O'Malley Dillon had a lot of fires to put out, or at least contain. Most of them entailed figuring out how to win over voters and get them to the polls. But she also set her mind to winning a popularity contest within the campaign, which made the *Post* profile all the more head-scratching for Biden insiders.

The staffers who had raised their hands to work for Biden in the primary, who envisioned themselves in senior roles in the general election and later at the White House, didn't like having a new boss—or, at least, not one this bare-knuckled in her approach to getting things done. They had withheld information from her top deputies in the spring and early summer. They had balked at being managed. They complained to one another about decisions she made. O'Malley had worked on enough presidential campaigns to know that toxins could spread quickly and infect an entire organization. She launched a mini-campaign to promote herself internally—to try to position herself as the leader of a cohesive team—but she couldn't get most of the Biden-firsters to buy in. They ridiculed her behind her back.

She held all-staff weekly meetings over videoconference that her internal critics derided as "Jen rallies," in which she sometimes invited celebrity guests to speak. On one call in early August, when some of Biden's primary aides were still upset about the effort to get him to play down his support for police, *One Tree Hill*'s Sophia Bush told his team, "I hope you all veer left." O'Malley Dillon's children would frequently pop up on-screen while she spoke during meetings. "They'll come in like it's spontaneous, but it happens so much that it kind of feels like it's a little bit staged," griped one male campaign aide who did not have children. She mailed out stickers to staffers with the phrase "We can do hard things" on them.

She was failing to do the hard thing of bringing two sides together, but one side—much of the primary staff—wasn't interested in making peace. For O'Malley Dillon, the management challenge was enormous. Aside from having to develop virtual campaign strategies from scratch, she had to manage hundreds of people whom she had never met.

By necessity, her first moves had been to install professionals she trusted to handle major operations of the campaign, which she knew would ruffle some feathers. Without the camaraderie of a physical campaign foxhole, she couldn't use the typical tools to win favor with a hybrid team of primary staffers, Obamaworld managers, and specialists brought in from defeated primary rivals. She couldn't gather people in a room for a pep talk or an organizing cheer. She couldn't have her deputies take their teams out for burgers and beer. So, she did what she could to humanize herself from a remote location.

O'Malley Dillon also had to learn her new boss and his coterie of pooh-bahs. "She talked to people who are influential with him," said one person close to Biden. "She got buy-in on decisions, which builds trust, and with trust you don't have to go to everyone all the time." Figuring out how to please Biden, his family, and his top advisers helped her get "a lot of autonomy and a lot of leeway," said one high-level Biden aide. But the younger set of aides and advisers saw that politicking as brownnosing. She didn't *really* know Biden or what he stood for, they said. And yet he had chosen her to run a campaign that led an incumbent president by a healthy margin in national polls and in the key battleground states Democrats needed to win.

For Biden, the frustration over the *Post* column was fleeting. But for his original campaign staff, it was an aggravating factor in the case against O'Malley Dillon. Tumulty wrote that the new chief had turned around an "underfinanced, undisciplined and dysfunctional" campaign. The last word stuck particularly hard in the craw of Biden's primary-season squad.

They already used a back channel—a chain on the encrypted app Signal—to air complaints about O'Malley Dillon to one another. After the column, they named it "The Dysfunctionals." It had a ring reminiscent of what Hillary Clinton called half of Trump voters: "The Deplorables." O'Malley Dillon's own staff was growing more divided at just the moment the Democratic Party needed to come together.

"Shit!" Bill Clinton exclaimed, his cheeks reddening and his nostrils flaring. *Five seconds.* The forty-second president of the United States sat in his living room in Chappaqua, New York, trying to condense what he thought was an eight-minute argument for Joe Biden's economic plan into five minutes. At first, it had taken him five and a half minutes to run through the script for his Democratic National Convention speech. He tried it again, like a North Arkansas auctioneer reeling off cattle bids. *Four minutes and thirty seconds.* Denied his cherished cigars, Clinton now crunched on hard candies in between takes. He was sure he could nail the time slot if he took one more run. But he came in at five minutes, five seconds. He knew he had a reputation for going long on convention speeches, one that was first earned when he unspooled a stem-winder that cleared the hall in 1988. In fact, on one pretaping conference call, he had mused sarcastically that "I have never gone over my speaking time at a Democratic convention—never." He was going to get this one under budget.

Bill Clinton voluntarily limiting his own speaking time in the service of another politician was a pretty good early sign that this was going to be a convention like no one in the country had ever seen before.

It wasn't even a given that the former president would have a speaking role at the first-ever virtual national political convention. He had been in the news for his relationship with Jeffrey Epstein, the wealthy rapist of underage girls, and, more broadly, his reputation had not aged well in the #MeToo era. Clinton's mere virtual presence also threatened to remind viewers of Biden's work on the crime bill, welfare reform, and other bipartisan deals that didn't sit well with the party's left flank. Some younger Biden aides argued against including him. They didn't remember his presidency or understand that his history of bipartisan dealmaking was a feature not a bug for this convention. Biden, still sensitive to the party choosing Hillary Clinton as Obama's heir in 2016, was said, politely, to be "agnostic" about Bill Clinton speaking on his behalf. The risk, it seemed, outweighed the potential reward, and Biden was nothing if not cautious.

But there were Clinton alumni in Bidenworld, and time had been allotted for the former president to vouch for Biden's competence to handle the economy and hit Trump for the paycheck pain felt by millions of voters. Clinton took up the task with determination, glad to avoid the embarrassment of not being invited to speak at a party convention for the first time in decades. So did a full complement of Democratic power brokers, who were asked to keep their remarks short and on point. Hillary Clinton would go live on the third night of the convention. No one was waiting to deliver an I-told-you-so moment more than Hillary, and she started out that way. She hit Trump repeatedly, but then transitioned quickly to making the case for Biden and Harris. Things would get worse if Trump were reelected, she said. "That's why we need unity now more than ever." She added that there were many reasons to "vote for" the Democratic ticket. At her taping, House Speaker Nancy Pelosi joked that, as the "Speaker," she wasn't accustomed to time limits on her remarks. They all understood the potential for chaos and the consequences of division.

This solidarity of purpose was unusual for a Democratic convention. Often, the quadrennial confabs turned into an airing of the grievances of various factions of the party, like a group-therapy session with flamethrowers and no leader. "We fight over the platform. We fight over the credentials. We fight over who sits where," said one longtime delegate. "This convention had the potential to be very explosive, very dangerous." On an issue-by-issue basis, most of the party wasn't as centrist as Biden, and an in-person convention could foreseeably highlight embarrassing and politically fraught splits over planks in his platform. In that way, the virtual convention was a gift to Biden.

Still, it was disappointing that he wouldn't get the hero's welcome afforded a newly nominated standard-bearer. He wouldn't feel the energy of thousands of Democrats cheering for him and chanting his name. He had waited for that his whole life. He'd gotten an up-close look at it in Denver and Charlotte when he had been Obama's running mate, and, from farther away, at conventions dating back long before most of his voters were born. Missing out on that was a particularly cruel indignity during a campaign in which he hadn't been treated by the media, donors, his rivals, or even the Obama network with the respect he thought he deserved.

"Everything that happened in this unprecedented year, the process began with a slow, daunting acceptance that none of this is going to happen the way Biden envisioned it," said one person involved with the planning. "And that includes the convention."

When Biden appointed Mary Beth Cahill to take over as interim chief executive officer of the Democratic National Committee in April, the former aide to Senators Ted Kennedy and John Kerry hired one of her protégés, former Obama deputy campaign manager Stephanie Cutter, as the program executive for the convention. That put Cutter in charge of content, a role that her ex-boyfriend, Democratic strategist Erik Smith, had filled in the three previous Democratic conventions, and it robbed the program's leaders of some institutional memory. Cutter was not going to turn to Smith for any trips down any memory lanes. "They dated," said one mutual acquaintance. "They are not friends."

While Smith had produced a series of special events during the Obama administration, in addition to heading up the program for both of Obama's conventions and Hillary Clinton's, Cutter was fairly open with her team about not having experience in the realm of making television. But she ran a business—a political consulting firm called Precision Strategies—and was regarded as one of the party's strongest communications operatives. Her team included Ricky Kirshner, a Hollywood producer known for Super Bowl halftime shows and Democratic conventions; Jeff Nussbaum, a partner at West Wing Writers, a boutique speechwriting shop in Washington that was home to a roster of former White House wordsmiths; Rod O'Connor, a former Energy Department chief of staff who was in a relationship with Biden's niece, Missy Owens; and Zeppa Kreager, the chief of staff on the Biden campaign, who was an instant liaison to O'Malley Dillon.

Like any convention, this one presented its own unique blend of messaging and talent-management challenges. Biden's centrism, for example, created friction with efforts to unify a Democratic Party that didn't fully agree with him on policy. "There was a little bit of schizophrenia about that in an ongoing way," said one person who worked on the program.

The flaming shit show Biden's team worried about was more of the technological variety. No one in politics had ever attempted such an audacious mix of live and taped programming from so many remote locations in succession. But the virtual convention played into the don't-blow-it ethos of his campaign and the party two and a half months out from election day. Many of the speeches would be pretaped, and they would all be boxed into tight time frames. That limited the potential for damaging off-script moments.

The twin goals of pulling off a remote convention and delivering the right messages almost immediately came into conflict for convention planners. Early on, they discussed using a map with lights to show where various speakers were broadcasting from—or had taped their remarks from. The idea was to show the geographical diversity of the Democratic Party, countering the Republican narrative that Democrats were just a bunch of coastal elites. But, as it turned out, their leaders were just that. Barack Obama was on Martha's Vineyard with Michelle Obama. John Kerry lived there. And Maya and Meena Harris, the sister and niece of Kamala Harris, who were set to introduce the vice presidential nominee, were on the small, exclusive island off the coast of Cape Cod, too. Biden didn't need to pick up votes from the Martha's Vineyard set; he needed the Boone's Farm crowd. When they noticed that the wealthy East Coast enclave would be the brightest light on their map, convention aides scrapped that plan.

Just figuring out the schedule for the top luminaries was a headache. Through Dunn and Donilon, Biden had sent word that the author Jon Meacham, who was helping with his speechwriting, should be given five minutes on the final night of the convention as part of the lead-up to the nominee's acceptance. The request was treated with the urgency of those for the Obamas, Harris, and Jill Biden.

Lin-Manuel Miranda was asked to write and record a new song for the convention in the rap style of his Tony and Pulitzer Prize–winning musical *Hamilton*. The request was miscommunicated, or misunderstood, and Miranda wrote an instrumental piece that he played on piano. The convention's creative team couldn't find a good place to fit it into the program, and it was lost to history—and to an email inbox now worth a small fortune.

Originally, Cutter wanted Barack Obama to speak last on the third night. He would be a draw, people would stay tuned to wait for him to speak, and he could be counted on to knock the ball out of the park. But typically, that Wednesday night slot—August 19 in 2020—was reserved for the vice presidential nominee. How would it look for the Democrats to play down the importance of the party's first woman of color on a national ticket by letting someone else, even the former president, bat cleanup? Not good. The victim of that decision was the very person who it was supposed to help: Harris. Instead of speaking before Obama, she would have to follow him.

By Monday, August 17, everything was pretty much set—except for Andrew Cuomo's speech. Every four years, Democrats asked themselves the same question about the New York governor and former Housing and Urban Development secretary: "How is Andrew Cuomo going to fuck us this time?" In 2016, he spoke for double his allotted time, and his team routinely declined to participate in fact- and message-checking discussions with convention organizers. In 2020, the Cuomo team didn't deliver his recording until the day of the speech. He was supposed to use his credibility to explain why Biden had the best plan for dealing with the pandemic. Instead, he had recorded something of a tribute to himself. "We climbed the impossible mountain and, right now, we are on the other side," he said of his leadership of New York during the onset of the coronavirus. About four minutes and fifty seconds into a five-minute speech, he finally said "Joe Biden."

The convention's speechwriting squad watched in disbelief. They asked Cuomo's aides to refilm it. The answer came back: No. "They put his speech on our doorstep, lit it on fire, rang the doorbell, and then ran away," said one person involved in the content production. Cuomo was much more of a headache for Democrats than any of the four Republicans who spoke on the first night—former Ohio governor John Kasich, former New Jersey governor Christine Todd Whitman, former New York representative Susan Molinari, and former Hewlett-Packard CEO Meg Whitman—as a demonstration that some moderate Republican Party stalwarts were rejecting Trump and embracing Biden.

Before they spoke, though, and before Kamala Harris had been picked for the No. 2 role, Michelle Obama had smuggled herself into a closed restaurant in Martha's Vineyard to record her remarks. The featured speaker for the Monday-night opening session, the former first lady appeared before a backdrop that looked like a living room, with a standing bookshelf containing a family photo, a plant, and a Biden sign behind her. But her purse—or someone's purse—sat on a telltale round café table in one corner of the frame. By the time her recording played, most of the first night of the convention had gone off without a hitch. The overall themes of the evening—the pandemic, the economy, and racial justice—were no-brainers for the convention team. If they hadn't touched heavily on those subjects, they believed, they would spend the rest of the week explaining why. Michelle Obama, whose location was not revealed on-screen, punched the three main points. Then, she turned to Trump.

"Donald Trump is the wrong president for our country," she said. "He has had more than enough time to prove that he can do the job, but he is clearly in over his head. He cannot meet this moment. He simply cannot be what we need him to be for us." And then, with the knife twist of quoting Trump on the coronavirus death toll, she added, "It is what it is." While Michelle Obama praised Biden, the unifying aspect of her speech was a reminder to Democratic voters of the one thing they all agreed on: Trump had to go.

Kerry Washington, best known for her role as crisis fixer Olivia Pope on the Emmy Award–winning show *Scandal,* was lined up to host the third night of the convention from a Los Angeles studio. Originally, she had been slated for the final night, but it had occurred to someone that she'd played Anita Hill in the HBO film *Confirmation* and that it might be better to have someone else emcee the festivities before Biden's Thursday night acceptance speech. The conflict led to a switcheroo in which Julia Louis-Dreyfus, the star of HBO's *Veep*, moved from Wednesday to Thursday. But Washington almost missed out entirely on hosting.

Hours before the start of the Wednesday night program, someone on the L.A. studio staff tested positive for COVID-19. Washington sat in her car outside the studio, waiting to see if a second test could be done before she was set to go live. The only available option for a substitute was Democratic National Committee chairman Tom Perez. Nussbaum's speechwriters went to work drafting a new script for him as Washington waited for word on the retest. But the person tested positive again, according to a person familiar with the episode. "There was a chance people were going to tune in and see Tom Perez." No one else at the L.A. studio had tested positive, and Washington ultimately decided to go in.

Back in Massachusetts, Barack Obama boarded a private jet parked at the Vineyard's only airport. The sun had set and the convention was already under way as his plane taxied down the runway. Obama had little time to spare on his way to the Museum of the American Revolution in the Old City neighborhood of Philadelphia, about half a mile from the site of his memorable 2008 campaign speech on race. Obama's team had discussed several options with the Biden folks, who originally wanted him to go to Wisconsin. But it was impossible to miss the symbolic value of Obama returning to Philadelphia to play his rhetorical instrument for Biden. No state was more crucial in the general election than Pennsylvania. To win it, many Democrats believed, Biden needed two things from Black voters in Philadelphia and its suburbs: show up to the polls and vote for him. But he also needed the same thing from college-educated white voters in the metropolitan area. Obama had been so masterful at inspiring Black voters across the socioeconomic spectrum while also appealing to suburban whites. That's what Biden seemed to need in and around Detroit and Milwaukee, too, the big cities in the other two blue wall states Trump had flipped in 2016.

In part, that meant making sure Trump's claims that he would be better for Black communities—had been better, given historically low unemployment and his prison-reform law versus Biden's crime bill—would be dismissed. It also meant fending off Trump's false assertions that Biden planned to "defund the police" and "abolish the suburbs." The latter attack was rooted in an Obama administration rule that tied federal funding for local housing agencies to their plans for desegregating their communities.

It wasn't that Biden feared Black voters would suddenly vote for Trump en masse. But in a close election, Trump winning over a small share, or depressing turnout for Biden, could be politically fatal. Obama could deliver a beatdown to Trump that made him less attractive to voters of all colors.

That is, if he got to the museum on time. While he was in the air, a crowd began to gather outside the Museum of the American Revolution. Some Democrats would prefer not to keep a social distance if they could get close to the former president.

If Obama was worried about getting to the museum punctually, his travel schedule didn't suggest it. His plane took off at 8:16 P.M. and touched down in Philly at 9:04 P.M.—less than ninety minutes before he was due to speak.

Obama made it on time, which was very good for Biden, because no one in the party could fill the president's shoes. He took his place behind a podium and in front of a wall bearing the words "Writing the Constitution" as a highlight reel of his presidency played for the home audience. Wearing a well-tailored suit and a blue tie, Obama still held the lean, dignified bearing familiar from his presidency—plus a few more gray hairs that lent an éminence-grise quality to his look. He began his remarks in presidential style, too, talking about the Constitution, its imperfections, and the hard work it had taken generations of people to right the wrongs of slavery, segregation, and discrimination at the polls. If you think you have it tough now, Obama was saying to the next generation of Democrats, think about the folks like John Lewis who paid for your rights with their blood. Professor Obama had come to give a civics lesson.

But what came next was decidedly unusual for a former president. For four years, Obama had judiciously picked his spots to tackle Trump. He was frustrated by Trump, but he knew that an appearance on a Sunday talk show or a few sharp-tongued tweets would diminish rather than elevate rebuttals. He looked for moments where he felt he could have a real effect. This was one of them, and he had decided, as he worked on his speech, that he was going to let it all out.

"I have sat in the Oval Office with both of the men who are running for president," he said. "Donald Trump hasn't grown into the job because he can't. And the consequences of that failure are severe. A hundred and seventy thousand Americans dead. Millions of jobs gone while those at the top take in more than ever. Our worst impulses unleashed, our proud reputation around the world badly diminished, and our democratic institutions threatened like never before."

Over the course of a nearly twenty-minute speech, he validated Biden as "a brother." But it was his takedown of Trump that caught the attention of headline writers. "Obama torches Trump like American democracy depends on it," *Politico* blared on its website. All at once, he had gone high and low—from the tenets of the Constitution to Trump's competence.

And he had stolen Kamala Harris's thunder.

There was no way for the vice presidential nominee to compete with Obama. But her speech was a mess long before she delivered it. Inside her inner circle, a battle for power was brewing, and it spilled over into the production of her introduction as Biden's running mate. Biden had named Karine Jean-Pierre, one of his senior advisers and a veteran television commentator, as Harris's chief of staff when he selected her. But Harris had felt burned by staff in her primary run, and Jean-Pierre had not yet earned her trust. They clashed. Harris was demanding; Jean-Pierre was agreeable. "Those were two personalities that didn't mesh well," said one person who observed them together. More important for the speech, it was unclear to convention organizers whether Jean-Pierre or Harris's longtime aide Rohini Kosoglu spoke for the VP nominee.

The first set of writers for Harris's speech didn't include a woman of color. Sarada Peri, a former Obama speechwriter, was added to the team, along with a couple of hands from the West Wing Writers group who had worked on Harris's pre-campaign book. Drafts were circulated and rewritten, litigated and watered down, fretted over and torn up. It was like a battlefield operation when such a historic moment called for a well-planned surgery. The result was a speech by committee, pasted together at the last minute because Harris had been chosen less than a week earlier.

The order of speakers and the speechwriting process had failed Harris. Now, as she strode to a podium in the cavernous Chase

Center in Wilmington, Delaware, the camera-shot selection was about to fail her. The opening frame was a wide shot from a distance that gradually focused in on the first woman of color ever nominated for the ticket of a major political party. It was the opposite of intimate. Throughout her remarks, cutaway shots showed the empty room where she spoke. It looked like a diorama of a convention hall. There were poles with each of the states stationed in rows and columns, but no delegates seated around them.

Where others had validated Biden, she was left to validate herself. She told the story of growing up in movement politics and her relationship with Biden—through his late son Beau. She namechecked suffragists, leaders of the civil rights movement, and Black victims of police violence. Obama had enumerated the 170,000 dead from the coronavirus and the millions of workers who had lost jobs during the pandemic. Harris's version was less evocative: "Donald Trump's failure of leadership has cost lives and livelihoods." His recollections about Biden were those of a "brother"; hers were rooted in knowing his son.

Harris closed the third night of the convention, but Obama had already put the lights out. The oddly capacious shots of her were so distracting that Biden's team insisted on rearranging the room overnight so that his speech wouldn't suffer from the same distance from the viewing audience. Aides worked into the wee hours moving equipment around and rethinking the next night's direction so that he would appear closer to living rooms around the country.

That would be nothing like the scramble to tone down Julia Louis-Dreyfus's act.

About an hour before Dreyfus was set to go live from the L.A. studio Thursday night, Stephanie Cutter sent word to David Mandel, the *Veep* showrunner and veteran of *Seinfeld, Curb Your Enthusiasm,* and *Saturday Night Live,* that she wanted to talk about the script. Mandel, sitting in a dining room converted to a home office, surrounded by memorabilia from *The Harvard Lampoon* and *Veep,* and cue cards from an appearance on *Late Night with Seth Meyers,* dialed Cutter from a landline.

Already, there had been some tension between Cutter's team and Dreyfus's writers. Dreyfus thought she could land some body blows on Trump, with a big smile on her face, because, as a comedian and someone outside the political realm, there were things she could say that wouldn't wear as well on a politician. The political speechwriters were a little annoyed that she insisted on having her *Veep* writers draft her script. Now, Cutter had finally read the jokes, and she was not amused. One of them, in particular, was totally out of bounds.

Dreyfus planned to say that Biden understood hard work and struggle, while "the only time Donald Trump has struggled is walking down a ramp and trying to drink a glass of water." Her writers had been told it didn't fit in the spot they wanted to use it. So they had slotted it in at another point in the script.

Mandel was asked to call Cutter.

When Cutter picked up her cellphone, she demanded to know why the joke had been reinserted in a new place.

"You told us it didn't work in the other spot," Mandel said.

"Well, you can't do it anywhere," Cutter snapped back.

"Just tell us that!" Mandel said, trying to remain calm. *Assholes,* he thought. "What's your problem with the joke?"

"We're not opening the dementia thing," Cutter screamed, meaning that ridiculing Trump's faculties could remind viewers that Trump portrayed Biden as senile.

"You not opening the dementia thing is not going to prevent the Republicans from doing it till the end of time," Mandel tried to explain. If anything, preempting that GOP line of attack before the Republican convention the following week would be helpful to Biden, he thought.

They were shouting past each other. That wasn't the only joke Cutter wanted to cut. Mandel could have backed off because the stakes of the election were so high, or simply because there wasn't much time before the script had to be set. Instead, he surrendered to the archnemesis of all comedy writers: maturity. The younger version of him would have kept fighting for the joke with a studio executive. The seasoned veteran accepted the power dynamics. *I'm not going to win this,* he thought.

"Just tell me what you want," Mandel said, exasperated. "Dictate it."

The substitute: "Donald Trump thinks 'self made' means inheriting only half a billion dollars from your dad."

Cutter didn't care if it was funny. It was her job to make sure that nothing distracted from the blandness of the convention. In that way, Biden's close to the convention resembled his broader campaign goal: Don't fuck up. One-half of his low bar for success had been set by Trump, who told the public that Biden was an enabler of socialism and crime who couldn't speak English in complete sentences. The other half came from an anti-Trump coalition that would forgive almost any Biden misstep. It was nearly impossible to fail, particularly with a scripted speech drafted in part by Jon Meacham, one of the country's most gifted writers.

Many politicians would be tempted by the moment to try to expand their capabilities. Not Biden, whose campaign mantra might well have been the one on the wall of the tortoise's locker room: Slow and steady wins the race. His message was standard Democratic fare—hope over fear—along with lines specialized to highlight the character, competence, and compassion he hoped to contrast with Trump. And there were a few twists designed to bring in disaffected Republicans by affirming his own beliefs in God and country. The theme of the speech, a contrast of "light" and "darkness," is deeply woven into the Bible, from God creating light in the first words of Genesis to the final battle between good and evil in Revelations. He even included "one nation under God" in the final run of his speech, an implicit rejection of both Trump and Democrats who jeered when the word "God" and a plank acknowledging Jerusalem as the capital of Israel were amended into the party platform at the 2012 convention.

"Let us begin, you and I together, one nation under God, united in our love for America, united in our love for each other, for love is more powerful than hate," he said.

Aside from the Obamas—and a virtual roll call of the states that featured a round-the-country tour of delegates giving Biden their states' votes—it simply wasn't a very memorable convention. "The convention was as successful as could have been hoped for," said one of the organizers. "A lot of that had to do with the technical production, more than content." In other words, the show was more competent than compelling—just the message Biden needed to project.

The coronavirus, with an assist from Trump's own Tulsa rally, set off a chain of events in the summer that led to the cancellation of

Trump's plans to give a renomination speech to a packed hall. On June 2, a few weeks before the Tulsa rally, Trump concluded a feud with North Carolina governor Roy Cooper by announcing he would not accept his nomination in Charlotte. Cooper, citing the spread of the pandemic, had refused to bend the state's social-distancing regulations to accommodate Trump's desire to fill the city's Spectrum Center for his acceptance remarks. Instead, Trump said, he would leave many of the administrative functions of the convention in Charlotte but speak from Jacksonville, Florida—a swing state where the governor, Ron DeSantis, was an ally.

But by July, with the death toll continuing to rise, the backlash from the Tulsa rally still in effect—some blamed the COVID-19-related death of former Republican presidential candidate Herman Cain on his presence in Tulsa—and public health officials in Florida and Washington worried about a surge in cases in the state, Trump began to change his tune on the disease again. His poll numbers had taken a hit in the days after the rally, with Biden opening what had been a pretty steady 5- to 8-point lead into a 10-point edge. On July 11, a few days before he assigned Kushner to fire Parscale, Trump wore a mask in public for the first time while visiting a military hospital. It was also starting to become clear to Florida officials that the convention would be poorly attended, which meant that the cost of putting it on would not be worth the economic benefit. DeSantis, who would be up for reelection himself in 2022, urged Trump not to come.

Inside Trump's campaign, and at the White House, he had been getting pushed by aides to start showing that he was taking the pandemic seriously. Wearing a mask had been part of that. So, too, were revamped press briefings in which he was a little more disciplined about not improvising medical advice for the public. All in all, there was little upside to Jacksonville, which Trump already felt was going to be a second-class convention because it wouldn't have the feel of a packed arena. Finally, on July 23, a month and a day before the opening of the convention, the president canceled on Florida.

"I looked at my team, and I said, 'The timing for this event is not right. It's just not right with what's happened recently—the flare-up in Florida—to have a big convention. It's not the right time,'" Trump said. "It's really something that, for me—I have to protect the American people. . . . That's what I've always done. That's what I always will do. That's what I'm about."

The truth was that DeSantis and Trump's team had prevailed on the president to avoid turning his convention into a superspreader event. "Word got back that it would be a problem, and it could backfire if he did a gathering there," said one Trump adviser.

The next morning, Justin Clark, Jason Miller, former White House and Treasury official Tony Sayegh, and Lara Trump gathered at the campaign's Rosslyn offices to plan a convention on the fly. They knew they had little time and even less money to spend. The aides put their challenges in three buckets: finding out what the networks would air; how to produce live events and recorded speeches for broadcast; and the logistics of which venues they could use in and around Washington. They quickly tapped a former *Apprentice* producer, Sadoux Kim, to handle the production aspect. Miller and Sayegh worked with the networks; and the team identified the Andrew W. Mellon Auditorium, a few blocks from the White House and right next to the Trump International Hotel, as a main staging area for speeches. That wouldn't do for the president's acceptance remarks, though.

Clark urged the group not to overthink the staging. *We don't have months to do this—the Democrats knew they were going virtual a long time ago—so ours needs to be less glossy and more gritty,* he thought. "We're going to get our ass kicked if we try to outdo them in production value," he warned.

Miller agreed. "They're going to have celebrities," he said. "We're going to have working people, real people, real American stories. In all this stuff, build up to that concept that we can't out-Hollywood them, so let's not try."

It was a scramble to find speakers—and speechwriters. Cliff Sims, who had been banished from Trumpworld after writing the book *Team of Vipers* in January 2019, was called into a rescue mission to draft remarks for an eclectic cast of characters. On August 5, less than three weeks before the start of the convention, Trump told reporters he was thinking about accepting the nomination on the South Lawn of the White House.

In meetings in the Oval Office and the White House residence, Trump sat and reviewed a series of options with his convention team. The first two were Gettysburg, the site of the turning-point battle in the Civil War and Lincoln's eponymous address, and Fort McHenry, where Trump had spoken on Memorial Day. The White House was the third option. Trump loved that idea, but the convention planners did not. Still, they couldn't work out the logistics of Gettysburg, which would have required extensive wiring to power a stage on the battlefield. Besides, the backup option for rain at Gettysburg wasn't as good as the White House, and Trump could be left out in the elements of a stiflingly hot and humid—or even rain-soaked—night.

"The high reward did not outweigh the high risk," said a person involved in the discussions.

Trump had always twined his politics with the official business of the president more than his recent predecessors, but a political convention at the White House seemed out of bounds even to some of his supporters. "Is that even legal?" Senator John Thune, a South Dakota Republican, asked when he was first told of the plan.

The Hatch Act prohibits most federal employees, but not the president or vice president, from engaging in political work while they are on the clock for taxpayers. But beyond the question of whether any law would be broken, Trump was reinforcing two powerful messages: The rules didn't apply to him, and there was no line separating the people's business from his personal political interests. His coronavirus response had followed that pattern. He directed the supply of ventilators to the states of Republican senators in tough reelection races, and he more broadly gave or withheld assistance to governors of both parties based on the degree to which they praised or criticized him. His campaign used footage of Democratic governors lauding his efforts—sucking up to him because their constituents needed his help—in digital ads implying bipartisan agreement that his response was strong.

But his nods to bipartisanship were usually fleeting. For the entirety of the campaign, Trump had trailed Biden in national polls, as well as in most surveys in the Rust Belt states that had been pivotal in his 2016 victory. And yet he showed little interest in altering a strategy that relied chiefly on identifying supporters and turning them out to the polls. The one exception: He believed he could cut into Democratic margins with voters of color based on his criminal justice reform law, what had been robust employment for Black and Hispanic workers, and Biden's own stumbles—such as telling radio host Charlamagne Tha God that any Black person who voted for Trump "ain't Black." Even when the polls looked their worst in the spring, Trump had never wavered from the belief that he would beat Biden. "Trump got godlike," said one senior campaign official. "He thought he was invincible."

But in the summer, he ran into a cash crunch. Though he out-raised Biden in July by $25 million, reversing the trend of the previous two months, Trump was still spending much more than he was taking in. By the end of the month, when new Trump campaign manager Bill Stepien froze TV advertising, Trump's $300 million treasury was only $6 million fatter than Biden's, according to figures released by the two campaigns. Stepien had announced when he took over the campaign in mid-July that he was conducting an audit of the books. What was evident was that there was simply less money available than Republican officials would have liked.

Trump might not have realized he was on the ropes heading into the convention, but some in his inner circle were worried. "Biden had a huge advantage," said one top Trump adviser. "The convention was important for equalizing the field." Indeed, as his campaign went almost completely dark on television in late July and in August, Trump relied on the free and abundant media attention surrounding the convention to deliver his message straight to voters. Democrats had focused much of their convention on bashing Trump, and he would return the favor. He would use members of his family and people who had been helped by his policies to counter the portrait of heartless self-interest Democrats had painted of him.

His advisers never stopped worrying about the Democratic convention until it unfolded in front of them. Biden, they believed, had undershot in terms of glamour and buried the diversity of the Democratic Party as much as possible on the first night. "Everyone's butthole like unclenched the moment the Democrats started their convention," said one GOP convention planner. Republicans saw Democrats clamoring for racial justice in ways that were disconsonant with Biden's own pronouncement that "most cops are good."

White House officials, campaign aides, and Republican Party bigwigs felt that the Democratic convention had been a lackluster bust for Biden and that the GOP version was highlighting the best of the president and the party. Of course, part of that stemmed from the same benefit that accrued to the Democrats the week before: It was all completely scripted.

Since the divisive 1976 convention that had barely nominated President Gerald Ford over Ronald Reagan, Republicans had usually fallen in line, if not in love, with their nominees. They had a more distant past of division than the Democrats—but also a more painful one fresh in the minds of the politically attentive. In 2016, Republican senator Ted Cruz, who had lost to Trump in the primary, shocked the convention floor when he told delegates to "vote your conscience" in a direct shot at Trump's fitness for the presidency. The virtual nature of the Republican convention prevented any surprise denouncements of a president who had alienated a handful of his party's most prominent voices. And, despite the late move to Washington, the convention had gone off without any major technical difficulties.

So, as Trump strode onto a stage filled with American flags and decked with star-spangled red, white, and blue bunting in front of the famous South Portico of the White House on August 27, he could feel a warm wind at his back for the first time in months. He looked out at the crowd, seated close together in neat rows and columns on the South Lawn, and could see political allies and members of his cabinet, including Treasury secretary Steven Mnuchin right up front, gathered to celebrate him. Just offstage to his right, his adult children sat in the first row. Melania Trump, wearing a green dress, sat opposite them on Trump's left flank. The images streaming into homes across America were just what he had envisioned when he first talked about using the White House as his backdrop. The fact that Democrats were infuriated by his use of the venue for a political rally made it all the more satisfying.

He smiled broadly and basked in a chant of "four more years" before launching into a seventy-minute list of his accomplishments and his grievances with Biden and the Democratic Party. It was an effort, like his son's speech, to turn a referendum on him into a choice between the candidates and their parties. "This election will decide whether we will defend the American way of life or whether we will allow a radical movement to completely dismantle and destroy it," he asserted. Trump tried to tie Biden to his party's left wing, arguing that electing the Democrat would lead to defunding the police—despite Biden's rejection of that proposal. And he slammed Biden for failing to emphasize the components of his platform.

"Joe Biden may claim he is an 'ally of the light,' but when it comes to his agenda, Biden wants to keep us completely in the dark." Biden's decision to go light on specifics at his convention, and throughout his campaign, put Trump in the awkward position of running against policies supported by some Democrats but not the party's nominee. Even as he argued that "socialists" were pulling Biden's strings, the fact that he had to make that case pointed to the distance between Biden and the liberal wing of the Democratic Party. Still, Trump hammered away at Biden in no uncertain terms, calling him "weak," saying "no one will be safe in Joe Biden's America," and blasting the Democrat's long record of support for trade deals.

After Trump wrapped up to a standing ovation, closing the two weeks of party conventions, he got a small bounce in polling. Biden had held a 7.7-point lead going into the Democratic convention. Four days after the Republican convention ended, it had narrowed to 6 points, the closest it had been since the beginning of June. One hundred eighty-four thousand Americans had died of the coronavirus, the unemployment rate stood at 8.4 percent, and Trump was gaining ground. But the bump wasn't big. In a year of unbelievable disruption to American lives, no single event—especially not a political convention—seemed capable of quickly altering the basic state of the race.

CHAPTER 18

•

The Invisible Enemy

B IDEN ABSORBED BLOW AFTER BLOW.
His crime bill put Black people in prison. He was corrupt. Most painful, his fifty-year-old son Hunter was a "lowlife" and a druggie who, in just the past five years, had dated his dead brother's widow, had a kid with a second woman, and married a third woman six days after meeting her. He kept trading on his access to his dad—as an adviser to a shady-as-shit Ukrainian energy company, a Washington lobbyist, and, until he got kicked out for cocaine use, a public affairs officer in a special unit of the Navy Reserve for the well connected. The father had to answer for the sins of the son.

Could he keep his cool? Would he slam his own kid in pursuit of the presidency? Would he stumble over his own words in a moment of crisis?

That's what Bob Bauer was testing. Playing Donald Trump in the basement of the Lake house in Wilmington in September, the former White House counsel wanted to make sure Biden wasn't caught off guard by anything the president said or did during their first of three scheduled debates. A rangy lawyer, gray and balding up top with a white beard, Bauer had studied countless hours of Trump's MAGA rallies and debates to imbue himself with the president's rhetorical style. Over the years, Bauer had become an expert debate chameleon. Two decades earlier, he had portrayed Al Gore in primary debate sessions with New Jersey senator and former

NBA All-Star Bill Bradley, and, more recently, he'd played Bernie Sanders for Biden.

When Biden spoke, Bauer muttered acerbic rejoinders like Trump: "You're not very smart, Joe," he said. Or, "I don't know why you'd say that," and "That's dumb."

Trump's propensity to preview his own lines of attack gave pause to Biden's team. They weren't certain if that was a function of Trump's inability to contain himself or possibly an effort to rattle their candidate ahead of their meeting. Biden told his aides, as he had all along, that when it came to Hunter, he wouldn't distance himself from his son. He loved him, and there was no political upside to a father denigrating his child. Conversely, he discussed with his aides a tactical jujitsu move that might highlight the contrast to make with Trump on compassion. When Trump went after Hunter, Biden could talk about his kid's struggles with substance abuse. That was relatable. Biden could turn a shot at his family into a moment in which he displayed sympathy for the tough battles millions of American parents went through with the addictions of their own adult children.

Biden practiced for the debate—reading briefing books, jockeying with aides in focused sessions on race, and standing at a podium—in the very basement that Trump mocked him for retreating to. Nothing had changed in terms of Biden's vulnerability to the disease. Dr. Kevin O'Connor, his personal physician, was still strict about the protocols surrounding his ventures outside the house and the steps his aides had to take before visiting him. That dovetailed with what Biden wanted for debate prep anyway: privacy. There was no good that could come out of a broad set of aides listening to their boss get torn apart—and the smaller the number of people in the room, the less likely the details of the proceedings would leak into public view and give Trump added insight into Biden's plans or vulnerabilities. In other words, his tack was the opposite of Trump's tendency to air everything out before the debate.

Mostly, Biden's aides wanted Biden to be ready for Trump's behavior. "He's an erratic man," Symone Sanders told Biden while piped in on a conference call during one session. "He's not going to be normal. He's going to yell. He's just going to be annoying." The key, they believed, was for Biden to appear more presidential than the president. They also advised Biden to remember to look into the camera and talk directly to viewers instead of engaging with Trump. Keep responses short, they told him. And don't debate the particulars of his attacks on you and your family.

Trump tried to dodge his own debate rehearsals. After an August session at his Bedminster, New Jersey, golf club, the president found reason after reason to avoid meeting with his prep team. He was pissed that word had leaked to the press that he had brought in former New Jersey governor Chris Christie to "coach" him. That's not the way Trump saw it. He respected Christie's ability as a debater, often reminiscing about the time during a 2016 primary debate when Christie leveled Senator Marco Rubio—and then adding that it hadn't helped Christie in the polls. He wanted counsel from Christie and others, but he didn't think he needed to be "coached" by anyone, much less one of the politicians he'd dusted in that race. In September, Trump repeatedly called off plans for debate practice. It's too early, he said. As the day of the first debate drew closer, he shifted to telling aides he didn't need the workout.

Finally, several days before the September 29 debate at Cleveland's Case Western Reserve University, he sat down in the White House's Map Room with Christie, Stepien, Stephen Miller, Jason Miller, and Hope Hicks amid a sea of furniture upholstered in red. Jared Kushner would pop in and out of the space, once used by Franklin Roosevelt to track troop movements during World War II. Rudy Giuliani attended one session, and Kellyanne Conway, the White House counselor, was also present intermittently, according to White House and campaign officials.

Trump's advisers told him that the first thirty minutes of the debate would be the most important—many viewers would tune out after that, they believed—and it was imperative for him to be aggressive toward Biden early on. It was not difficult to convince Trump that was the right approach.

Create confusion and chaos on the stage, Christie counseled Trump. Hammer away at Biden. Interrupt him. He won't be able to handle it, he'll get angry, and he'll stutter. "Put him on his heels," Christie advised.

Conway thought that was a bad idea. "Let Biden speak," Conway told Trump. "He's not very good at it." Tire him out, she urged. "There's a legitimate question of whether ninety minutes is going to be tough on him, durability wise," Conway offered.

That argument dovetailed with the case Trump had been making against "Sleepy Joe" for the entirety of the campaign. But it was at odds with Trump's personality. He wanted to dominate the debate stage, get under his opponent's skin, and stay on offense at all times. That's what had worked for him in the scramble of the 2016 primaries and against Hillary Clinton. He had literally loomed over her shoulder at a town hall–style debate that year.

Trump bantered with his advisers as they tossed out questions.

"Joe and Jill Biden have a guest today. She's eighteen, but when she was fourteen, her uncle incested her, and because she's poor and couldn't travel out of state to get an abortion, she ended up with life-threatening complications," Conway started. "How do you defend wanting to outlaw abortion in cases of rape, incest, and a threat of death to the mother?"

Stepien worried that Trump might not be up to snuff on the details of policy, and the president wasn't the type to take a briefing book to bed with him. For better and worse, Trump didn't want to get into the weeds in a debate. In prep sessions, he didn't want to delve into his personal life—no questions about Stormy Daniels or his taxes—or defend himself against barrages like the ones Bauer was throwing at Biden.

"We did get to a point at the end where Christie would interrupt him or challenge him on an answer," said one of the participants. But Trump didn't fully acclimate himself to the give and take of a live-fire debate.

As the candidates tuned up for their debate in September, Trump gave Biden an invaluable assist in boosting Democratic turnout. Throughout his time in politics, Trump had claimed American elections were "rigged," systemically stacked against him and the GOP, and subject to massive voter fraud. In the spring of 2020, as many states made the ballot box more accessible to voters in response to the pandemic—expanding vote-by-mail and early in-person voting options—Trump fixated on making the case that the election system was becoming more susceptible to fraud. He attacked voting practices on Twitter, on the campaign stump, and on television programs. The assault continued throughout the summer and into the fall and included efforts to undermine the postal service and a quickly reversed late-June suggestion that the November 3 election should be delayed. At a White House press briefing on September 23, Trump declined to assure the public that there would be a peaceful transfer of power if he lost.

"I've been complaining very strongly about the ballots, and the ballots are a disaster," Trump said. "We want to have—get rid of the ballots and you'll have a very trans—we'll have a peaceful—there won't be a transfer, frankly; there'll be a continuation. The ballots are out of control."

Stepien feared that Trump's efforts to sow doubt about mail-in voting could backfire. The president had frightened some GOP voters about the security of their own mail-in ballots. Stepien tried to intervene with the president, but found himself getting nowhere. "Don't embrace mail-in voting," Stepien told Trump. "But you can't be scaring our people." The president didn't listen. Trump was painting himself and the entire Republican Party into a corner. His rants against mail-in and early voting exacerbated a partisan divide on the method of balloting in which Democrats were more likely to cast votes ahead of election day, and Republicans were more likely to show up to the polls on November 3. This split freaked out GOP officials, including Stepien. It meant Democrats would be voting in battleground states for weeks while Republicans put all their eggs in the election day basket. Trump was trailing in the polls. Even if he could close the gap with Biden late, millions of votes would already have been cast. Democrats would have time to harangue base voters who hadn't yet gone to the polls. The risk of political catastrophe for the entire GOP seemed to grow every time Trump mentioned the subject.

In late July, Stepien had turned to House minority leader Kevin McCarthy for help. "Kevin, you and I are on the same page here," Stepien said, inviting the Californian to an Oval Office meeting. "We've got to change the message on this." Indeed, McCarthy's House Republican candidates would be endangered if Republicans wary of mail-in balloting chose not to vote. Inside the Oval, McCarthy nudged Trump to tone down his attacks on voting systems. Trump had lost ground to Biden with seniors, the set both

most at risk for coronavirus complications and most likely to vote
by mail. Putting everything on election day could hurt down-ballot
Republicans, too. McCarthy generally had credibility with Trump
on the political needs of congressional Republicans, but Trump
was unmoved.

Beyond scaring Republican voters, Trump was effectively using
the biggest bully pulpit in the world to call Democratic voters' attention to new balloting methods and rules. The Biden campaign
and Democratic-leaning outside groups were dumping hundreds of
millions of dollars into educating their voters about how to prop-
erly request, fill out, and cast ballots. Trump was giving them invaluable free airtime. Democrats didn't believe Trump's fraud talk,
but they were constantly reminded that he wanted to invalidate
their votes. Operatives from both parties believed that couldn't
help but result in more Democrats participating.

"We knew that Democrats were going to vote by mail, Republicans were going to vote in person," said one high-ranking campaign official. That put a lot of pressure on GOP operatives to turn
election day into a voting bonanza. "So much was left to chance on
one day," said a second top campaign official.

Of course, Democrats saw the same partisan split on voting
method and worried about getting people to the polls on election
day—and during early voting periods before it. For six months,
Democratic officials had been telling Americans to stay at home if
they could and keep their distance from others if they had to go
out. O'Malley Dillon had spent much of the summer building a
virtual get-out-the-vote effort based on the theory that it wouldn't
be feasible for campaign organizers and volunteers to knock on
doors in the middle of a pandemic, particularly with the candidate
observing such strict rules about his own interactions with other
people.

But the idea that Democrats wouldn't knock on doors—or meet
face-to-face with powerful political players—was ludicrous to
many party leaders, particularly those who represented minority
communities. Many of their constituents were hard to reach without person-to-person contacts and were going to their jobs every
day. Officially, Biden campaign workers weren't supposed to be out
in the community meeting with political leaders and voters. But in
practice, there was more flexibility for less-visible outreach to al-

lies. One Biden campaign official who held secret in person meetings with local labor leaders in early September got a wink and a nod from campaign higher-ups in the battleground state where he worked.

"I was told by leadership in the state 'You are doing this at your own peril. Don't tell anyone that you're doing it,'" said the official.

On a Zoom call in mid-September, as both parties ramped up their get-out-the-vote pushes for the fall election, veteran Democratic organizers challenged the Biden campaign on its plan to contact voters without knocking on doors. Caroline Grey, a Biden aide who'd cofounded the Democratic digital firm Civis Analytics, had just explained the phone-and-text program devised to allow the campaign's field teams to avoid actual in-person meetings.

The campaign was working with what it called a "distributed organizing" model, which it contrasted with "traditional organizing," according to officials. The old method involved heavy staff investment, relying on aides and volunteers in particular states, volunteers communicating with paid organizers through a hierarchical chain of command, and paid organizers taking time to plan door-knocking and phone-banking shifts for volunteers. The new model put the onus on volunteers to take their own initiative and sign themselves up for shifts. Because they were going all electronic, get-out-the-vote organizers didn't have to be in the same communities or states as the voters they contacted.

There was a slideshow, with lots of numbers. But the officials couldn't account for the troubling paradox facing the Biden campaign: At a time when Trump was publicly trying to discredit early voting and vote-by-mail programs in the states, and when Republicans said they had knocked on one hundred million doors already, Democrats were ceding the field to stay consistent with the party's message about the dangers of the coronavirus. That didn't sit well with everyone.

"If Biden loses, this will be his not-going-to-Wisconsin," said one former Obama administration aide, referring to Trump's victory in the Rust Belt state that Clinton steered clear of in 2016. Direct contact with voters was a staple of campaigning, and, for many outside organizers who worked in big cities, it was also a good source of income.

Inside the campaign, the door-knocking issue was just one of a series of interwoven conundrums that tested the creativity and wisdom of O'Malley Dillon and the Obamaworld lieutenants she had placed in top roles. They had come in with a blank slate in terms of rewriting the rules of running a presidential campaign to fit the COVID-19 era. The fundraising piece had been perhaps the easiest to resolve. While there weren't a lot of goodies to pass out to donors, it turned out that the community aspect of Zoom fundraising was pretty popular. Biden didn't have to travel in order to meet with donors who could give hundreds of thousands of dollars to him through a "victory" committee that distributed funds to the campaign, the Democratic National Committee, and state Democratic parties. That enabled the campaign to put together exponentially more donor cattle calls for Biden and his surrogates. Rufus Gifford found in the summer that the campaign could hold as many as twenty-five videoconference calls with donors on a single night at virtually no cost.

The success of that effort pointed to two realities: Many people wanted to give money to defeat Trump, no matter the venue or the personal reward, and Biden was benefiting from the new, more efficient paradigm necessitated by the pandemic.

"If it were not for coronavirus, we would not have the money that we need to be competitive," one person involved in the campaign's finance effort said in early August, a month during which 125 video fundraisers were planned. It worked, though. Biden and the national Democratic Party raised a record $365 million that month, outpacing Trump by more than $150 million. Harris's spot on the ticket and the convention had helped Biden's brand. Merchandise sales in the campaign's online store, which had been a deserted outlet mall of "Malarkey" buttons and T-shirts with Biden's sunglasses-wearing visage, skyrocketed when Harris gear hit the virtual shelves.

"All of the sudden, the campaign became buzzworthy—that speaks to something that is happening because the brand is changing," said one person who worked on the finance team. "We flipped the script, and it was Trump who couldn't figure out how to run a campaign responsibly."

The boost in fundraising gave O'Malley Dillon more credibility with Biden. So did Obama. Aware that she was taking fire internally, the former president laced praise for his onetime deputy campaign manager into his conversations with Biden. She knows what she's doing, Obama told Biden. He wasn't worried so much about O'Malley Dillon's underlings as he was about the pooh-bahs. "He talked to Joe a lot about how strong Jen is and how he should rely on her because it's a fucking cesspool in the old guard," said one person familiar with their discussions. "Jen might not be in your inner circle," Obama told Biden, "but she is to be trusted."

For the entire Democratic Party, the Biden campaign was an exercise in faith without evidence. Between the onset of the coronavirus and the Democratic convention, the candidate and his campaign had been all but invisible. And yet, he was still ahead in the polls and he had taken control of the money chase. Trump's campaign had gone dark on television in late July and August. It was sucking wind financially. Republican donors were turning their attention away from the presidential race and toward saving the GOP majority in the Senate.

As the Biden team bathed in cash, Stepien, deputy Trump campaign manager Justin Clark, and senior adviser Jason Miller sat around a conference room table in September at headquarters trying to figure out how to make budget through the end of the campaign. "We were having to cut spending and shave down costs on the advertising side," said one senior Trump campaign official.

But even these indicators were not enough to settle the soul of the Democratic Party. It was one thing to raise a bunch of money online and to maintain a lead in the polls—Hillary Clinton had done both of those things before losing to Trump in 2016—but it was quite another to propose winning battleground states without an army of troops knocking on doors.

O'Malley Dillon defended the decision in a call with reporters. "While you might hear our opponent spend a lot of time talking about millions of door knocks or attempts that they're making week to week, those metrics actually don't have any impact on reaching voters," she said. "Our metric of success, the numbers we look at and use, are conversations." The idea was that building relationships with voters through phone and text—and in some cases voter-to-voter letter-writing campaigns—had a greater effect than an in-person conversation. It didn't matter whether she believed that. Her hands were tied by the campaign's overall message on the coronavirus. How could she send thousands of organizers and vol-

unteers out into neighborhood streets while her candidate was literally staying at home and telling others to do the same? But her
comments, and the organizing videoconference call, lit a fuse inside the party, and the force of the ensuing explosion acted as a
wake-up call for Biden.

Jim Clyburn went to Cedric Richmond after he read about the
decision. "This is a horrible mistake," Clyburn said. "I would love
to see people going to neighborhoods, ringing doorbells, and wav-
ing at people with Biden-Harris signs and that kind of stuff. Whatever the program designed for canvassing with COVID-19 protocol,
we need to do that."

An undercurrent of racial tension within the party jostled the
dynamics of the door-knocking controversy. Wealthier voters didn't
need or want anyone knocking on their doors. They were high-
propensity voters, and they tended to be white. In big cities, with
high concentrations of less-educated, less-wealthy minority voters,
canvassing—and the "walking around money" paid to party operatives to execute get-out-the-vote operations—was regarded by
many political players as a crucial factor in turnout. The Biden
campaign was proposing to cut that out of its campaign plan, giving organizers of color reason to worry about the impact both in
terms of turnout and their own bottom lines. At a time when
Biden's response to the George Floyd protests had left something to
be desired among civil rights activists, and with Trump making
clear inroads with subsets of the Latino community, the absence of
a real field campaign threatened to hurt his ability to counter
Trump's hits on him.

Internally, O'Malley Dillon had told staff repeatedly, "There's a
chance we will not knock on another door." Black and brown operatives on the campaign thought that was crazy and pushed back
carefully. "Black people don't get on Zoom," Sanders told her. But
it had been a sign of her growing power both that she made such a
decision and that the challenge to her plan was limited.

"We always wanted to canvass," said one person who worked
closely with O'Malley Dillon. "But we weren't going to do it unless
knockers were safe and voters were safe. For all we knew, this thing
was going to take off again." The campaign manager spoke regularly to Biden about strategic and budget decisions, and around the
time of the convention, she had explained the virtual field opera-

tions to him. He had asked about yard signs, but was not upset by the idea that voter contact would be done primarily over phone and text. That is, until he felt pushback from within the party. Once he was alerted to the concerns, the decision was reversed—at least on the surface. There would be physical canvassing of some kind in some places. But he basically stuck with O'Malley Dillon's analysis that the more critical parts of the get-out-the-vote operation were conversations of any kind and educating voters on how to make sure their mail-in ballots and early in-person votes were valid and counted.

The balance would continue to be a sore point well into the fall, as organizers in key battleground states believed they were being short-changed on the tools they needed to move voters to the polls. In an election that could be decided by small margins in a few states, they said, a second straight failure to mobilize voters of color—or a loss of a significant share to Trump—could be politically fatal.

Air Force One touched down at Cleveland's Hopkins International Airport at 3:31 P.M. on Tuesday, September 29, just thirty-five days before the election. Trump's traveling crew included Melania, his adult children; Representative Jim Jordan of Ohio; national security adviser Robert O'Brien; campaign aides Stepien, Clark, and Miller; and White House public relations maven Hope Hicks. Nearly an hour later, the president's motorcade pulled up to the Sheila and Eric Samson Pavilion at Case Western Reserve University. The president conducted a walk-through of the stage—Biden would have a separate chance to get a feel for the venue when Trump was done—without a mask. Neither candidate nor debate moderator Chris Wallace of Fox News was required to wear one. But audience members were, and Trump's kids ignored a request from a Cleveland Clinic doctor on site to put theirs on.

As the nine P.M. start time drew near, Biden's aides gathered in a conference room right behind the stage. Carpeted, with long tables and a television screen, it was stocked with orange Gatorade and Diet Coke—two Biden staples. Trump's advisers huddled in a matching holding space on the other side of the stage. Both parties were warned to keep their patter down because they were close enough that their voices could be picked up by microphones and broadcast to the entire country. Both camps wondered which version of Trump they were about to see.

It didn't take long to find out that it was full-on alpha Trump.

God, this guy's irritating, Biden thought. Every time he spoke, Trump cut him off. Every time moderator Chris Wallace started to ask a question, Trump cut him off. Less than ten minutes into the first presidential debate of 2020, Trump wouldn't let anyone else get in a word edgewise, sidewise, or otherwise. Biden had actually interrupted Trump a few times at the very beginning of the debate, and now it was Trump who seemed to have lost his cool. But inside Trump's staff holding room, the moment was playing out just as planned. The aggressiveness felt right, and Biden was plainly annoyed.

Biden had been prepared for Trump to behave unusually, but this, he thought, is disgraceful. Biden had just said the *Roe v. Wade* abortion ruling would be on the ballot—shorthanding the president's powers to appoint Supreme Court justices and sign laws that limit or expand abortion rights.

Trump interjected to say Biden didn't know what was on the ballot. A few feet behind him, in the holding room, his aides clapped.

Biden, refusing to look at Trump, put up his right hand, with the palm facing toward the president.

"Donald, would you just be quiet for a minute," he said.

That didn't slow Trump down a bit. A few minutes later, Trump lit back into him.

"If Pocahontas would have left two days earlier, you would have lost every primary," Trump said, suggesting that Bernie Sanders would have beaten Biden if Warren hadn't siphoned progressive votes away on Super Tuesday. Trump's aides laughed.

"All he knows how to do—" Biden started.

"On Super Tuesday, you got very lucky," Trump said.

"Look, here's the deal: I got very lucky," Biden agreed. "I'm going to get very lucky tonight as well."

A few minutes later, Biden was on the ropes. Wallace asked him whether he agreed with fellow Democrats who called for an expansion and packing of the Supreme Court. It was an issue that divided Democrats. Republicans were uniformly against Democrats sticking more liberal judges on the bench. Biden said he wouldn't answer the question because either way he would make a headline that would turn into a political headache.

Trump jumped in, in place of Wallace, as the interrogator. He repeatedly asked Biden why he wouldn't answer. Then he gave his own response.

"You want to put a lot of new Supreme Court justices. Radical left," Trump said.

Exasperated, Biden let loose.

"Will you just shut up, man?" he said, squeezing his eyes closed as if pained by Trump's conduct. Biden shook his head slowly back and forth. "This is so unpresidential," he added as an afterthought. This is what Trump had been counseled to do—hammer away at Biden.

But, inexplicably, he had stopped Wallace—the neutral party—from bearing down on his opponent. Like so much of the campaign, this was not the way Biden had envisioned his bid for the presidency. And yet, once again, an unpredictable moment—an unbelievable moment—favored him.

Behind the stage, Biden's aides watched the Trump show on a large television screen on the wall. No one touched the individually wrapped snacks. They were too rapt by the American carnage playing out on national television.

"This is hard to watch," Symone Sanders blurted out. No, she corrected herself, "This is fucking crazy!"

"Such a low moment," Bedingfield agreed. But the exchanges were short. Mostly, Biden's aides watched in silence—stunned, yet compelled to watch.

Biden and Trump weren't even a quarter of the way through a ninety-minute debate. By the thirty-minute mark, much of Trump's team felt the boss was delivering. But a few of his aides thought he was over the top. He kept interrupting, quarreling with Biden and Wallace, making a spectacle of himself and the process. There was a fine line between irreverence for sacred cows and boorishness. Trump had crossed it. *This is getting old,* thought one aide behind the stage. *It's getting old for everyone. I'm glad he started out aggressive, but he's staying too aggressive.*

Even when he wasn't interrupting, Trump was missing easy escape routes from tough questions. Wallace asked him to condemn white supremacists. Biden joined in that.

"Give me a name, give me a name," Trump said as he argued with both of them. "Who do you want me to condemn?"

"Proud Boys," Biden said, referring to the racist, misogynistic, and violent group that attended Trump rallies.

"Proud Boys, stand back and stand by," Trump said. It sounded like he was telling them to be ready for a fight.

Stepien had been right to worry about Trump's depth on his own policy wins. Both candidates were asked to explain why they thought they would be better at handling race-related issues than their opponent. Biden cruised into the comfort zone of talking about Charlottesville, his original contrast with Trump.

"Close your eyes, remember what those people look like coming out of the fields, carrying torches, their veins bulging, just spewing anti-Semitic bile and accompanied by the Ku Klux Klan," Biden said. "He said there were very fine people on both sides. No president's ever said anything like that."

That wasn't exactly true. Woodrow Wilson had screened the pro-Klan film *Birth of a Nation* at the White House, for example. But it got under Trump's skin. The president forgot—or ignored— the advice Conway had given him in debate-prep sessions. Someone else—maybe Rudy or Christie—must have circled back and gotten in her ear, she concluded.

Conway had counseled Trump to enumerate policies that benefited people of color, from the economic gains of his first three years in office to his criminal justice reform law, as well as popping Biden on the crime bill. But Trump was going completely negative; there was no real articulation of the high points of his record. He erroneously accused Biden of calling Black gang members "superpredators" and charged that Biden was unwilling to say "law enforcement."

This is not the debate we prepped for, Conway thought as she watched on television. The president is missing opportunities. He said nothing about Clarence Thomas, the Republican-appointed Black Supreme Court justice whose confirmation hearings Biden had run as chairman of the Senate Judiciary Committee. More broadly, she kept hoping he would course correct, a sentiment shared by many Republicans. That didn't happen.

Later, Biden saw an opening he'd been waiting for since the early summer, when he had resisted calls from some of his new aides to lean away from his plan to spend more federal dollars on the COPS program. "I'm totally opposed to defunding the police offices," he said. "His budget calls for a $400 million cut in local law enforcement assistance."

When Biden went after Trump as "Putin's puppy," a reference to the kid-gloves approach the president had taken to Russian president Vladimir Putin, Trump unleashed an unverified allegation that Hunter had received $3.5 million from the wife of the mayor of Moscow.

"Well, your son got $3.5 million," Trump jabbed.

Biden turned it around once, referring in his next answer to Beau.

"I don't know Beau," Trump fired back. "I know Hunter. Hunter got thrown out of the military," he continued, saying Hunter had been dishonorably discharged.

It wasn't "dishonorable," Biden clarified.

"For cocaine use," Trump snarled. "And he didn't have a job until you became vice president."

"None of that is true," Biden said, even though Hunter had been spared the indignity of a "dishonorable discharge" with the slightly less brutal "administrative discharge" after testing positive for cocaine.

Biden turned Trump's line around again. He was ready for this.

Looking directly into the camera, he said, "My son, like a lot of people at home, had a drug problem. He's overtaking it. He's fixed it. He's worked on it. And I'm proud of him. I'm proud of my son." If Trump was going to ridicule addiction, Biden was going to show empathy.

At the seventy-five-minute mark, Dunn convened a Zoom call with top staff and consultants to go over postdebate messaging. The first to speak was pollster David Binder, who was conducting dial tests to gauge the real-time reactions of forty to fifty Florida voters in Orlando. He gave a readout of what his focus group thought: Voters were not responding well to Trump. Then Dunn gave instructions on the message: "Trump is a chaotic mess; we need a president."

Another aide offered that Biden had handled the race question better than Trump.

"Good, but let's not get into the weeds," Dunn replied. "Trump is a mess. Period."

When it was all over, Biden joined his wife, his sister, Donilon, Klain, Symone Sanders, Bedingfield, and Biden spokesman T. J. Ducklo in the holding room across from his greenroom. He thought Trump looked like a jerk, but he wasn't sure whether that had translated to viewers.

"That was embarrassing for the country," Biden said. "He was all over the place. I couldn't get a word in." He was frustrated, and he was worried about how voters would perceive the debate debacle. "How is it playing?"

"The contrast between your leadership styles could not have been more on display," Bedingfield told him as she and Sanders gave him a readout on the takes of various journalists and commentators. There was really only one view: Trump had sandbagged himself. Biden had looked more presidential than the president, a nearly impossible feat for a challenger. Still, Biden had to be convinced that the whole exercise had been good for anyone, including him.

Most of Trump's traveling party on Air Force One assured him that he had won the debate and that he was on course to win the election. The fact that media outlets were calling Biden the winner was not a surprise to the president. If anything, he believed, the more the coverage blasted him, the more likely it was that he had prevailed.

The next morning, he called Conway to get her thoughts. There were two debates left on the schedule, and he wanted a performance review. He was a little surprised to hear her say it hadn't gone well.

"Next time, you are going to have an opportunity to say a couple of things that you didn't say this time," she said. "I hope your people are pulling together the fact that Biden interrupted you a lot at the beginning."

Trump was receptive, but he told her there was no reason to worry.

"It was fine," he said.

The day after the debate, Trump hopped back aboard Air Force One at Joint Base Andrews in the Maryland suburbs outside Washington. Destination: Duluth, Minnesota. For four years, Trump had been talking about how narrowly he had lost the state to Hillary—about forty-five thousand votes, or 1.5 percentage points—and how he would win it this time around.

It was a rare Trump campaign trip to a state he had lost. For the most part, he was playing defense on the electoral college map. It was much more likely that he would lose states from the 306-electoral-college-vote set he had put together in 2016, and his travel schedule for the final months of the campaign made that abundantly clear. Only Minnesota and Nevada, with a combined 16 electoral votes, offered any possibility of adding to his coalition. Trump would also go to New Hampshire and Virginia—two states that he was sure to lose again. But almost all of his trips were to states that had been in his column: Florida, Pennsylvania, Michigan, Wisconsin, and Arizona. Three of his adult children—Donald Jr., Ivanka, and Eric Trump—crisscrossed the country to campaign for their father, too, as did Eric's wife, Lara. At the Trump campaign headquarters in northern Virginia, battleground states director Nick Trainer kept track of planned campaign stops for the president, the vice president, Trump family members, and a "Women for Trump" bus tour on a gigantic whiteboard.

The idea was to have a marquee campaign surrogate in battleground states' designated market areas—"DMAs" to political ad buyers—as often as possible. Don Jr., for example, asked to be sent to "all the tier-two DMAs, all the Podunk, rural DMAs" when he sat down at headquarters in the late summer, said one campaign official. Thinking his siblings and his sister-in-law wouldn't want to stray outside the comforts of big cities too often, he "didn't have an ego about having to be in them," the official said. But Lara Trump, eager to test the waters for her own career in politics, also volunteered to go to smaller markets in her home state of North Carolina, Florida, Pennsylvania, and other states.

There were reasons to think that Trump might pull it off, despite public polling that had never wavered from a solid Biden lead. Biden's team had readjusted its survey methodology in the summer to account for what it expected to be better performance for Trump among less-educated white voters. Their internal polling always showed a closer race than independent surveys—a fact that Biden's aides repeated throughout the summer and fall, only to be ignored by much of the punditry. One hundred and forty-six electoral votes came from states considered by one or both campaigns to be in play or potentially in play: Florida (29); Pennsylvania (20); Ohio (18); Michigan and Georgia (16 apiece); Arizona (11); Wisconsin and Minnesota (10 apiece); Iowa and Nevada (6 apiece); and New Hampshire (4).

Then there was Nebraska's Second Congressional District, based in Omaha. In the entire country, there was no metropolitan area more closely representative of the country as a whole than Omaha's in terms of racial breakdown, income, and political competitiveness. Obama had won there in 2008 but not 2012. Democrats had flipped the House seat in 2014, only to lose it back to Republicans in 2016 amid Trump's victory there. In Nebraska, unlike in forty-eight other states, the electoral college votes were divided: The statewide winner got two electors, and the other three electors were decided by the outcome in each of the three congressional districts. That is, there was a chance Democrats could win a single electoral vote from the Second District even as Trump won a landslide statewide. Biden aides particularly liked their chances because they viewed the district as politically similar to one massive, well-educated suburb. If their calculations were right about a shift among college-educated whites, the Omaha-based district could prove the theory.

Trump had won 127 of the 147 electoral votes from these in-play places, including the Nebraska district, and he could afford to lose 37 from his column and still win the presidency with 269 electoral votes. That's because he had an asymmetric advantage over Biden, who had to win 270 to take the presidency. In a 269–269 electoral college tie, the election would be thrown to the U.S. House, where each state delegation would get a single vote. Republicans held majorities in more delegations than Democrats. In theory, that edge could be upended by a massive Democratic sweep in congressional elections, but it was hard to dream up a scenario in which Democrats fared that well down ballot while Trump won half the electoral votes. With Biden leading in most of the battleground states, the trick for Trump was to repeat what he had done in 2016—focus narrowly on a handful of states that would get him to the magic number.

For Biden, the decision-making and prioritization also mirrored the last presidential race. His team looked at a variety of "paths" to 270 electoral votes based on algorithms incorporating countless data points on the electorate in each state and how they correlated to one another. "We're gaming out all these different pathways and running Monte Carlo simulations," said one senior Biden aide who was involved in decisions about the allocation of resources among battleground states. Those "Monte Carlo" simulations try to project ranges of potential results by accounting for unpredictable variables. "Thousands of election simulations, plotting it out on a graph and figuring out the most likely outcomes," the aide said.

"We built a lot of uncertainty into how our data fed into strategy," said a second senior aide. "'Here are the ways we think the toplines might be fucked up. Here's what the new strategy would be.'" Their data science wasn't rocket science, but Biden's team—wary of a repeat of 2016, when Trump shocked Clinton by outperforming expectations in key swing states—wanted to make sure it could see the broadest possible set of outcomes. The idea was to account for the worst-case election projection and make modifications in real time. Ultimately, that meant pursuing multiple paths.

The best-case scenario started with winning Florida, which would be an indication of strength almost certain to reflect a significant electoral college victory for Biden. Another rested on a Sun Belt spike in which Biden won Arizona, Georgia, and North Carolina. But the most intense focus was on the states that had convinced Biden he could win the presidency in the first place: Pennsylvania, Michigan, and Wisconsin. He had always believed he was a better candidate for the Rust Belt than Clinton—a more appealing choice for the working-class white voters who had helped push Trump to victory—and that is where he was going to lay his biggest bets. It was also what Democratic primary voters had, collectively—eventually—seen in him. For moderate whites and Black voters across the ideological spectrum—and ultimately many progressive-leaning Democrats—Biden's argument that he could take it to Trump in the industrial heartland had won the day in the primary.

Now, as voters began to cast their ballots by mail and show up at polling stations to make an early choice, Biden just had to prove it. But first, fate would inject another major uncertainty into the campaign.

———

Sitting at home in the wee hours of Friday, October 2, Justin Clark saw the news that Trump and the first lady had tested positive for COVID-19. "Aw, shit!" the deputy campaign manager shouted to himself. The previous afternoon, Clark had gotten a call from Sean Conley, the president's personal physician. Conley told Clark that it was possible Clark had shared a ride with someone who had come back with a positive result, and he should self-quarantine for a couple of days. Within hours, Clark would find out that it was Hope Hicks who had the virus. Clark had been manifested to ride in a van with her after the Cleveland debate but had stayed behind. He believed he was in the clear.

But now his candidate, the president, was sick. On a six A.M. conference call, Trump's campaign advisers made three quick decisions: They would keep their ads running, they would scale back their digital fundraising effort, and they would cancel Trump's upcoming rallies. It made sense to keep advertising—to keep Trump in voters' minds—and suspend rallies, but not to stop raising money. Cash was a huge problem for the campaign already.

Trump had tweeted the news out about one A.M. When he did, Biden aides quickly exchanged a flurry of text, Signal, and email messages to share the revelation and begin preparing the campaign's response. But they couldn't reach O'Malley Dillon. She had fallen asleep around midnight, and her iPhone was inadvertently on a do-not-disturb setting. Finally, after a couple of hours, someone from the campaign called her husband, Patrick, to alert her to the situation.

O'Malley Dillon wanted to strike a balance. The first instinct was to point out that Trump was sick because he didn't take the disease seriously, but she didn't want to blame people who got COVID-19. *This is a fine line,* she thought. *There are good people who do all the right things and end up with COVID and it's not their fault. It's also not good for anyone when the president is sick.*

Bedingfield waited for a more decent hour of the morning and sent Biden a message about what had happened. When they convened on an eight A.M. conference call with the rest of the senior staff, Biden said he wanted to send out a release or a tweet wishing the president and first lady well, and he wanted to consider pausing the campaign.

"Look," he told his aides, "this is not good for the country. It is a potentially destabilizing moment. The president is sick; he could be very sick. I don't want us to do anything that looks like campaigning or profiting from this."

Taking down the campaign entirely was a complicated proposition and one that would likely fail to be executed. Ultimately, Biden was persuaded that the best course was to suspend negative ads. If he was going to score political points, it would be for passing up an opportunity to hit Trump, who never seemed to show that kind of restraint or generosity to political rivals. Trump had repeatedly attacked the late Arizona Republican senator John McCain, a friend of Biden's, after McCain's August 2018 death.

O'Malley Dillon worried that with thousands of staff and volunteers, any stray tweet could be hung around Biden's neck at a time when he believed it was best to back off of Trump. She emailed the entire staff to ensure that no one undermined Biden's approach by gloating about the president's condition. "As this situation continues to unfold, we ask that you refrain from posting about the situation on social media unless otherwise directed by your manager," she wrote.

Biden campaign aides who had attended the debate began to freak out. They had taken note of the Trump crew's defiance of mask protocol at Case Western Reserve University, and now many of them worried that Biden could have been exposed, or that they, themselves, might have caught the slow-developing disease. The first sign of trouble had come when Hicks had been diagnosed the day before.

Already, Biden's senior staff were in the midst of discussions about how to push the Commission on Presidential Debates to enforce more stringent safety rules to protect Biden, his staff, and his guests. Biden and the aides who'd attended the debate quickly got tested, and the campaign launched a contact-tracing exercise to try to determine whether anyone might have been exposed. It turned out that no one had gotten close enough to Trump or his aides to trigger an alarm. Biden had stood far apart from Trump on the debate stage, and the rooms used by the respective campaign staffs were on opposite ends of the backstage area. Then the Biden camp started fielding calls from guests at the debate, who had been on the floor of the auditorium. They were worried about their own safety. The campaign hastily arranged coronavirus tests for its guests.

That was strike two against the debate commission in the eyes of Biden's senior aides. The first had been what one top adviser called the "train wreck" of Trump commandeering the stage for ninety minutes. Something had to be done to protect Biden, and something had to be done to protect the integrity of the next two scheduled debates, as well as the upcoming vice presidential debate.

Trump's struggle with the disease worsened Friday, and rumors about his condition pinballed through the political and media ecosystem. Inside Trump headquarters, the diagnosis hit like a spiked brick. For more than six months, the president had been publicly playing down the threat of the virus. Though Trump was the most heavily protected person in the country, it had found its way into his system. Campaign officials had long believed that the pandemic robbed Trump of a clear path to reelection. That was debatable, but the potential for political catastrophe was not. His campaign aides didn't need anyone else to spell out the problem for them.

Welp, he can't protect himself, one senior campaign official thought while he watched the story developing. *This is a dose of reality in a reality show.* Campaign advisers contacted friends in the White House to try to get a feel for what was going on. There were reports that Trump was sicker than he had suggested in his middle-of-the-night tweet. There was even talk that Vice President Pence might have to step up temporarily if Trump got too ill. The situation was chaotic and the president's future—both in terms of his campaign and his personal health—was suddenly uncertain. In the afternoon, the White House announced that Trump would be going to Walter Reed National Military Medical Center to get treatment.

"That was the real low point of the campaign," said one top campaign aide. "It's depressing. You're sad, you're worried about him, it's dominating the news, we're not doing events, we're not raising money."

Sitting in the home office of his house in Concord, Massachusetts, a birthplace of the American Revolution, Rufus Gifford stared at his computer screen in disbelief. He had lived through the bumpy ups and downs of electoral and global politics—and had pictures with Obama, Biden, and European royalty to prove it—but nothing in recent memory caused as much anxiety as Trump's bout with COVID-19. It wasn't his concern for the president that troubled him. It was the hit that Biden's fundraising numbers were taking.

Gifford was humble enough to know that, whatever his talents, much of the cash was coming in organically because of the urgent desire of many donors—Democrats, along with some Republicans and independents—to see Trump defeated. But now, in the time it took for the president to take Marine One less than ten miles from the White House to Walter Reed, the spigot choked off. On a good day, the campaign and its Democratic National Committee partnership took in about $15 million, a large portion of it in response to the kind of negative advertising Biden had put the kibosh on.

Beyond the absence of negative ads, there was one obvious explanation for the drop-off in donations: With the president battling a potentially fatal disease, the level of intensity to get rid of him politically had subsided. There was no telling whether it would return—or when. And even though Biden was outraising and outspending Trump by multiples, the uncertainty the data team built into its forecasting required the Democrats to pump cash into a long list of expensive states. Put simply, Biden had to flip at least 37 electoral votes, and his aides couldn't be sure which states they would come from. That required going in heavy all over the map. The sudden loss of expected income mattered because the campaign couldn't predict precisely how much had to be spent in each state to win. Ideally, it would be able to spend with an inefficiency that correlated to the uncertainty of the electorate in each state. A smaller bankroll reduced the margin for error.

This is so uncertain, Gifford thought. *We could lose tens of millions of dollars. We have to rewrite our budget.*

On Saturday, October 3, Trump called Stepien and Jason Miller from Walter Reed. He was in a good mood, but he was exhausted.

"I'm feeling great, much better than I thought I would," Trump said. He joked with his aides about leaving the hospital in a Superman shirt. He asked about how the news was playing and what it meant for him politically. It was too early to tell. Trump said he understood that he would have to be down for at least a couple of days, but he didn't want to miss many beats on the campaign trail. Stepien, Miller, Clark, and battleground states director Nick

Trainer would later ask his family members to double up on their duties as surrogates as part of a program they called "Operation MAGA."

Stepien got off the phone thinking the illness would give Trump an opening to show a softer side to the public. He'd been getting hammered for lacking sympathy. After recovering, he could pivot to empathy. He'd had the disease. He knew how brutal it could be. Stepien advised Trump to pivot to that softer side. He framed the argument around seniors, a key constituency for Republicans that had been moving away from Trump during the pandemic. "They're afraid, and they'll think 'Hell, if the president could get it, I could get it, and I don't have anywhere near the health coverage,'" Stepien told Trump. The president sounded receptive, but he didn't act that way.

Instead, Trump played true to form, beating his chest. After returning to the White House on Marine One, without a mask, on October 5, he released a video message to the nation about the coronavirus. "Don't let it dominate you," he said. "Don't be afraid of it. You're going to beat it."

With less than a month to go until the election, Trump had just come off a debate performance in which he'd managed to make the challenger look more presidential, he was low on cash, he was discouraging Republicans from voting by mail, he had contracted a disease that had killed more than two hundred thousand of his fellow Americans, and he was ignoring advice to show just an ounce of humanity. He couldn't even see that he was hurting himself.

Trump was his own invisible enemy.

CHAPTER 19

•

Do No Harm

*W*HAT DO I DO? KAMALA HARRIS THOUGHT. *IF I MOTION TO HIM, he might think I'm messing with him.*

During the course of the primary season, and in just the past few days, Harris had rehearsed every imaginable scenario. Like any adult, she had real-life memories of the internal conflict over whether to tell a proud and powerful man that his fly was down. What Harris's lived experience didn't cover—what she couldn't possibly have prepared for in two full mock rehearsals with Pete Buttigieg playing her foil—was the question coursing through her mind now: *Do I let the vice president know there's a fly on his head?*

The usually dignified Mike Pence, so dry and even-tempered, so perfectly groomed at all times, looked clownish with a Halloween-sized black fly juxtaposed against the feathery cloud of his snow-white hair.

Harris had one job: Get through the vice presidential debate—one of her few public appearances before a broad national audience—without diverting attention from the referendum on Trump. In picking her, Biden had made a bet that the telegenic senator with the penchant for snap moments could modulate herself in service of the ticket and its mission of defeating Trump. Harris had the rare ability to deliver vicious attacks with a smile on her face and a good-humored chuckle—a skill she sometimes turned on her own aides—and she had a quick wit. It was tempting, after having listened to Pence gaslight the country about Trump's record and Biden's plans, to gently mock the vice president. But that would be at odds with the campaign's strategy for the night—and Biden's own discomfort with the rhetorical tool of ridicule. That was too risky. She had some time to think about it because the fly was comfortable—or perhaps stuck in Pence's hair product—at the eleven o'clock position on his head for almost two full minutes.

In a subterranean holding room offstage, Harris's aides watched with growing fascination. "What the fuck? We're in a basement. How is there a fly here?" Rohini Kosoglu, the staffer closest to family status with Harris, said to her colleagues. One of the aides tried to brush the fly off the television screen. *Oh my God*, Kosoglu thought when the fly remained on screen. *This is really happening.*

Harris's team watched closely for her reaction. She could be unpredictable in the best and worst ways.

The fly's timing was especially bad for Pence, in no small part because it directly undermined his articulation of the main contrast his ticket wanted to draw with Biden and Harris over the closing weeks of the campaign.

"This presumption that you hear consistently from Joe Biden and Kamala Harris that America is systemically racist, that as Joe Biden said, he believes that law enforcement has an implicit bias against minorities, is a great insult to the men and women who serve in law enforcement," Pence said just as the fly dropped straight down onto his head. "I want everyone to know who puts on the uniform of law enforcement every day, that President Trump and I stand with you."

Harris, who had been listening with her eyes down in front of her, looked over at Pence and saw the fly. Her eyes widened almost imperceptibly. *If I say something about it,* Harris thought, *I will become part of this story line.* In the basement, members of her team wondered what would come out of her mouth next. She left the elephant-sized fly in the room unmentioned.

"I will not sit here and be lectured by the vice president on what it means to enforce the laws of this country," Harris said, launching into a list of the types of crime she had prosecuted over her career as San Francisco's district attorney and California's attorney general.

When moderator Susan Page said good night, Harris had succeeded in doing no harm. The content of the debate was lost to the fly and to a second visual aid that played into the hands of the Democratic ticket. Pence and Harris were not only seated body lengths apart, but their tables were separated by plexiglass barriers that served as symbols of the failure of Trump—and of Pence, as the head of the White House coronavirus task force—to contain or kill COVID-19. With Trump having emerged from the hospital two days earlier, the plexiglass was also a reminder that he had not been able to defend himself against the disease despite all the protective trappings of the presidency. He had been given cutting-edge treatments not available to most Americans to fend off his own infection.

Some campaign officials worried that Trump had once again gone too far in proclaiming the disease defeatable based on his unique experience. On October 10, Trump emerged from isolation and delivered remarks from a White House balcony, asserting that he was "feeling great."

"It's bizarre," said one Trump campaign aide, who added that voters are sitting at home thinking, *I haven't been able to see my grandkids in months and this guy is declaring victory.*

Trump couldn't get out of his own way for long enough to allow a positive narrative—like the president recovering from a potentially fatal disease—to take root before he burned it down. His tendency to embellish even good stories to the point that he seemed dishonest hurt him. After his disastrous early COVID-19 press conferences—where he played what one campaign official derisively referred to as "Doctor Trump"—he had lost credibility with the public, even among many Republicans who would vote for him.

In a poll conducted before the first presidential debate and Trump's COVID-19 diagnosis, 52 percent of Americans told Gallup they found Biden honest and trustworthy, compared to 40 percent for Trump. Worse for Trump, two-thirds of Americans, including 40 percent of Republicans, found Biden likable. Only 68 percent of Republicans said Trump was likable, compared to the 90 percent of Democrats who felt that way about Biden.

Trump was failing to disqualify Biden or even make the election about a choice between the two of them. But Trump campaign officials believed that the message Pence was pushing when the fly alighted on his head might shift the dynamics away from a referendum on Trump. Maybe.

Over the long spring and summer months, as the nation battled the coronavirus and neighbors fought one another over police violence, protests, and rioting, officials in both campaigns came to a sobering conclusion: Almost nothing shifted voters from one side to the other in the presidential race. For the chattering classes, cable television producers, and columnists, everything mattered. For the electorate, nothing mattered.

Rufus Gifford was still on edge after the debate. Harris had performed well, he thought, but the campaign still wasn't raising money the way he had expected. Aside from a little pick-me-up from sales of branded "Truth over Flies" flyswatters, cash flow from the debate didn't approach the kind of spikes he had seen around Harris's selection for vice president or the Democratic convention in late August. The Democratic campaign relied heavily on event-driven fundraising and planned its budgets partly around the anticipated windfalls. Though Biden was still in a much better financial position than Trump, the free media attention associated with the presidency—combined with Biden's strategic decision to mostly stay out of the news—meant that it would cost the Biden campaign a lot more to promote the candidate to voters.

Though it wasn't public information yet, Trump's finance team saw a small windfall around the time he left Walter Reed. The faithful poured $8 million into his campaign coffers the day of his release from the hospital, compared with $4.7 million total during Trump's two-day stay.

Normally, Gifford didn't pay much attention to the bed wetters in the Democratic Party, the folks who were always anxious about everything. Many of his friends and political contacts obsessively watched MSNBC and were constantly texting him about what the campaign should do to right a ship that he believed was sailing on a true course at a safe speed. But this was different. *Thank goodness the media doesn't see our fundraising numbers until the twentieth of the month,* he thought. By then, maybe, the campaign could make up some of the loss. But for now, he had to figure out how to change expectations around how much money would be available to spend. He found himself on the phone with O'Malley Dillon, Multani, and Ricchetti seemingly every half hour as projections dwindled.

The campaign was also missing one of its most valuable surrogates, Michelle Obama, at grassroots fundraisers and on the campaign trail in general. The former first lady's absence was noticeable to Democrats who expected her to be out on the stump, or at the very least headlining events to help fill Biden's coffers.

"I know there's a pandemic but surrogates are out on the campaign trail and she is our best surrogate, with the exception of her husband," one Democrat close to the campaign said.

In the final months of the campaign, Biden aides said there were multiple requests made for the former first lady at events and fundraisers. "This was not about a lack of desire for Michelle," one senior Biden aide said, adding that the process to get her involved was "excruciating."

"She was not easy to get," the campaign aide said, a sentiment that was backed by others on the team. "For whatever reason, she just didn't want to do it."

Nursing what they believed was a small but substantial lead, Biden's advisers looked at the next two debates as risky because they offered Trump opportunities to gain ground. That's not because the advisers were sure Trump would win them—his behavior in the first debate had been an act of immolation—but because it was possible that he could. In a race they wanted to remain a referendum on Trump, debates inherently presented a choice between two candidates. Beyond that, Trump might have been contagious at the first debate, and, with his doctors treating his medical information like a state secret, there was no telling whether he or anyone in his camp posed a threat of spreading the coronavirus to Biden and his aides. The worst-case scenarios for Biden were all far more nightmarish than a fly landing on his head.

The morning after the Harris-Pence contest, the Commission on Presidential Debates announced that it would take a foolproof safety precaution for the next presidential forum, scheduled for October 15, after Biden's team had complained about the Trump camp flouting protocols at the Cleveland debate. The candidates' meeting at the Adrienne Arsht Center for the Performing Arts— site of Harris's busing attack on Biden—would be turned into a virtual debate. The candidates would participate remotely while moderator Steve Scully and an audience sat together at the art hall in Miami. Trump was being kicked out of the venue on the basis that he or a member of his team might infect others with the virus.

Trump was infuriated. A "virtual" debate? That might make him look weak, too sick to stand a dozen feet apart from Biden without spreading the contagion. In an interview with Fox Business's Maria Bartiromo, he declared that he wouldn't participate from a remote location.

Biden aides couldn't believe their luck. Trump, down a field goal or two, had just taken a knee in his own territory. It was Biden's strategy to run out the clock, to make no mistakes that opened the door for a Trump comeback. That's what the former vice president had been doing throughout the spring and summer when he faded out of public view. He was pursuing the lowest-risk strategy imaginable. Trump kept helping him do that. Taking a debate off the table—and giving Biden another week without a direct contrast—was political malpractice.

It was also a no-brainer for them to pull out of the debate. Trump had given them the perfect excuse. "When it could be virtual, we were happy to do that," said a top Biden campaign official involved in the decision. "But we were not going to put ourselves or anybody else in harm's way. When he refused the virtual stuff, we were like, 'There's no way we can trust the commission on this because they weren't able to control it before. Trump is not going to be a good-faith actor and so we are just not doing that.'"

Trump's campaign quickly offered a fix: Keep the third scheduled debate on October 22 and move the next one from October 15 to October 29. But Biden's team took advantage of the opening offered by Trump, booking its candidate for an ABC News town hall on October 15, ending negotiations before they could begin. "They're losing, we're winning," one senior Biden aide said. "Status quo means we win."

Becca Siegel had a reaction opposite to Rufus Gifford's as she scanned survey data on her laptop. Her data analytics team ran a quick and dirty electronic version of traditional polls to gauge the horse race numbers between the two candidates. Trump's illness had coincided with a bump in Biden's internal numbers. Siegel couldn't believe it—not in terms of being pleasantly surprised but in terms of not finding the data credible. *When people are sad, they are less responsive to polls,* she thought. *This data surely has a non-response bias.* Basically, she concluded, more Trump voters than usual were choosing not to answer surveys because they were demoralized about him contracting COVID-19. She told colleagues that the better numbers for Biden were just "noise" that they shouldn't pay attention to.

The trick was homing in on the right numbers to pay attention to. Every pollster and data scientist had a different model for the electorate. That was true of Biden's data shop and his traditional polling team of John Anzalone and Celinda Lake. Those variations partially accounted for the range of results that voters could see in who was leading the head-to-head matchup. But pollsters also differed in their analysis of the meaning of data.

Anzalone and Lake, Biden's pollsters, found that voters' perceptions of a candidate's honesty and favorability had greater significance—if still marginal in a very close contest—than they normally did.

"Movement in underlying traits was crucial more in this election than others," said one person familiar with their conclusions. "Usually people just hate everyone." That wasn't true with Biden. Trump's attacks, which had run the gamut from accusing his rival of senility to portraying him as an avatar of socialism, anarchy, and crime, could gain only so much traction against the steady, centrist image Biden leaned into at every turn. That helped explain why Trump and his allies focused so heavily on Hunter Biden. If they could portray Hunter as corrupt—and his father as an abettor or simply deceitful about it—the Democratic nominee's honesty ratings might take a hit.

There were twenty-seven days between the VP debate and election day, donor enthusiasm was pointing south, and internal campaign surveys appeared to be showing a false spike for Biden. Public polling reflected that surge for Biden, too, as his lead over Trump rose from 7.2 percentage points in the Real Clear Politics average on September 30 to 10.3 percentage points on October 11.

Biden's improving poll numbers in early, and mid-October may also have been a function of a lag from the late September debate.

"Whenever there was movement in Biden or Trump favorability, two or three weeks later, it would show up in the topline"—the basic horse race margin between the two candidates—said one Biden aide who followed the numbers closely.

For much of the country, it looked like Biden was poised to walk into the presidency. And yet, at the same time, millions of Americans couldn't help but feel a sense of déjà vu. For many Republicans, memories of the 2016 election—when Trump had broken polling models and won—were a compelling reason not to get too panicked about Biden's lead. Fear had signed a four-year lease on the back corner of the Democratic Party's brain. That included members of Biden's camp.

Anzalone had watched that year in horror as Clinton's team stopped him from polling several weeks before the election in favor of cheaper instant surveys from its data analytics squad. The data polls were reasonably good at tabulating a snapshot of the race, but they didn't go as deep in testing the candidates' messages or voter sentiments. O'Malley Dillon wasn't going to make the same mistake. She kept commissioning traditional polls through most of October.

The analytics team's numbers always looked better for Biden than the pollsters' figures, which created confusion for the campaign's leaders on the ground in various states. They would often complain to Julia Kennedy, the chief of staff for the polling operation. She repeatedly heard slightly varying versions of the same refrain: "Your number says this and analytics number says this, what the fuck is it?" As Klobuchar's deputy campaign manager in the primaries, Kennedy had developed a reputation for running a tight ship, and O'Malley Dillon had brought her in to manage Biden's traditional polling outfit. That put Kennedy in the position of trying to explain why the pollsters' numbers were different—and less bullish—than those from the data analytics team, and in the uncomfortable spot of knowing her answers were never going to be satisfactory.

"Run the race like it's even," Kennedy always told state-level campaign officials.

Anzalone wanted to keep polling as close as possible to election day and pressed O'Malley Dillon to keep commissioning his surveys right up until then. But the closer November 3 drew, especially with so many voters casting early ballots, the less value there was to thinking about how to alter messaging. Anzo accepted the decision to cut off traditional polling about a week before the election, but he was not happy about it. "He had so much PTSD from 2016," said one ally on the campaign. That made him the typical Democrat.

Marginal spikes and drops in voter attitudes in October mattered more in 2020 than they did in any previous election because voters were already casting their ballots in some of the crucial swing states. In Pennsylvania and Michigan, for example, the window for early voting had opened in late September. The perception that Trump was falling too far behind could depress his support, and negative reactions to him could spur some voters to cast ballots for Biden that they couldn't retrieve if they changed their minds. In a way, this was an asymmetric advantage for the Democrat. Trump's strategy rested in part on dissuading low-propensity Biden voters from casting ballots. Biden's camp had time to counter that and persuade them to vote.

Still, Gifford was right to be worried about the slowdown in incoming cash—Biden raised only $140 million in the first two weeks of October. In most campaigns, that would be an insanely high number, but it was off the pace Biden had been raising in the summer. Still, he had a huge edge over Trump, outspending the president at a two-to-one clip in the first half of the month.

The combination of a deep campaign war chest, Biden's strong favorability ratings, and the ability to take time to persuade "soft" Bidens—the voters who leaned toward him but weren't sure to vote—allowed his campaign to saturate television markets in battleground states with positive ads or those that drew contrasts with Trump in genteel terms. In Arizona, for example, it was a spot featuring Cindy McCain, the wife of the late Republican senator and frequent target of Trump derision John McCain, talking straight into the camera about Biden supporting American troops and saying, "Now more than ever, we need a president who will put service over self." In Georgia, another state where the Biden campaign was increasingly confident it could compete, Biden ran an ad featuring young Black men sitting in a barbershop with masks on, talking about Harris. "When Black women are lifted up, they lift everyone else up," one of the men said. Another likened Harris to his mother, getting things done.

Siegel, one of the few top operatives to keep control of her department from the primary through the general, boarded a flight from Colorado to Philadelphia in early October so that she could quarantine for two weeks, get tested for the coronavirus, and set up a modified data-team war room at the campaign's Scranton Exchange HQ.

For months, her team had been running election simulations based on voter data in fifteen states and two congressional districts—Maine's First and Nebraska's Second—where a candidate could pick up an electoral vote by winning the congressional district despite losing statewide. But as September turned to October, the picture of the electorate was coming more into focus, and Siegel felt that the simulations were getting more accurate. She ran what she thought of as doomsday scenarios to determine what could go wrong. For example, she tested what would happen if Black turnout fell short of expectations, if Trump managed to overperform with suburban voters, and if there was an error in polling.

In the data, she found a concerning trend. She shot a note to O'Malley Dillon.

If polling is off enough for us to lose Michigan, Wisconsin, and Pennsylvania, she wrote, we lose Florida and North Carolina, too. The same did not hold for two other sizable states that, respectively, were pet favorites of the two women. Siegel thought Biden could become the first Democrat to win Georgia since Bill Clinton in 1992, and O'Malley Dillon loved Arizona, where the Republican presidential nominee had won sixteen of the past seventeen elections.

It came as no surprise to Siegel or O'Malley Dillon that the three Rust Belt states that had secured the presidency for Trump in 2016 were tightly tied together. They had been the Democratic Party's focus for four years, in part because past data showed a strong correlation among Pennsylvania, Michigan, and Wisconsin voters. The states weren't perfectly synchronized, but a move in either candidate's direction in one of them likely reflected a similar shift in the other two.

Back in 2016, Clinton's campaign team had seen a correlation between Florida and the Rust Belt states—her rout among working class white voters in the Sunshine State had been an early election-night harbinger of the industrial states' flip into the GOP column—and Siegel's data suggested that was also true of North Carolina. Those five states were all top-tier targets for Biden as he looked to swipe at least 37 electoral votes from Trump.

But Georgia and Arizona, which accounted for a total of 27 electoral votes, didn't correlate with the others in the same way. This realization informed the campaign's increasingly solidified view that there were three paths for Biden to win: the three Rust Belt states; Florida and North Carolina; or Georgia, Arizona, and any one of the other five states. Because so many scenarios involved an extraordinarily close vote in the electoral college, and because the area lined up particularly well for Biden's coalition, the campaign also focused heavily on the single electoral vote in Nebraska's Second Congressional District, as well as its cousin, Maine's First Congressional District.

Biden also had to defend two states Trump had targeted as potential pickups: Nevada and Minnesota, which had a combined 16 electoral votes. Both campaigns invested in other states—Biden played in Texas, Iowa, and Ohio, for example, while Trump popped into New Hampshire at one point—but most of the battle would be fought in seven states, all of which Trump won in 2016 and four of which had Democratic governors. With new information constantly pouring in, including which voters had already cast ballots and which had requested but not sent in votes by mail, the data analytics team reported frequently to O'Malley Dillon on how to optimally prioritize spending for advertising, canvassing, candidate and surrogate visits to the states, and a whole host of other tranches among the states and within them. It was the same kind of operation that had led Biden's campaign to prioritize efforts in Alabama's Seventh District in the primary.

Usually, O'Malley Dillon followed the recommendations of the analytics team, but not always. There were political considerations to weigh, as well. When New York's Chuck Schumer, the Senate minority leader, picked up his flip phone to harangue Mike Donilon about putting more into Texas, it was impossible to ignore the ask. O'Malley Dillon knew Biden wasn't going to win Texas, and she knew the Democratic Senate nominee, MJ Hegar, was going to get blown out by incumbent Republican John Cornyn. Still, she arranged for Harris to travel to Fort Worth, McAllen, and Houston, even though the trip had no chance of flipping Texas for the Biden campaign.

O'Malley Dillon, who considered herself immune from pressure to change tactics from both inside and outside the campaign, hoped that putting a footprint in Texas would force Trump's aides to spend some of their limited dollars to defend the state.

At the same time as the VP debate, the campaign's field operatives were wrapping up their first week of door knocking in the general election, trying to make up for time lost to COVID-19 protocols. "The rural areas were getting a lot of attention from the Republicans," said one campaign aide who was on the ground in Pennsylvania. "They never stopped registering voters and knocking on doors. We weren't doing anything." The state, with its 20 electoral votes and its importance to Trump's electoral college coalition, was ground zero for Biden's campaign. If he lost Pennsylvania, he would almost certainly lose the election.

The decision to knock on doors, in the middle of a pandemic that had kept the candidate in his house for months at a time, had come on the heels of continued pressure from Democrats who worried that the absence of a physical presence would lead to a loss.

Labor unions, whose members were already working during the pandemic, had started their on-the-ground organizing in Pennsylvania right after Labor Day. Biden's campaign eventually followed suit. "The campaign didn't sign off on doing real shit until October 1," one Pennsylvania aide said.

In other states, tension between Democrats in the state and campaign officials reached boiling points in October. On call after call with the Biden campaign's Florida team, members of the state's Democratic congressional delegation pressed for more spending to counteract Trump's appeals to young Black and Hispanic men. The latter group was most concerning because it constituted a significant share of the electorate in a state where, historically, as few as 537 votes could tilt the outcome. In Florida, his new home state, Trump tied Biden to Bernie Sanders and socialism, an ideology that had been espoused by strongmen in Latin American countries where many Floridians had roots. Biden still rejected socialism, but polls showed that Trump's message was getting traction all the same.

O'Malley Dillon was not a fan of Florida. It was the state that always seemed to kick Democrats in the ass. She was well aware that Obama had won it twice, but she was just as schooled in the many ways in which every other Democrat in recent years had blown tons of money in the state only to lose by a relatively small margin. The state had two Republican senators and a Republican governor—two of them elected in a midterm 2018 election in which Democrats had thought they had a good chance to win—and Clinton's election night had first turned sour in Florida.

But there were reasons she couldn't afford to skip the state. For one thing, neglecting such a diverse state would send a terrible message to Democrats in other parts of the country, both about the state of the campaign and its ability to connect with its base. Plus, regardless of who won, the margins would end up being close enough to second-guess any decision to stay out. But most important, with 29 electoral votes, Florida represented a chance to put Trump away early—it was always among the first batch of states to report its results.

"You can't ignore Florida, because it's the knockout punch," said a senior campaign official who worked closely with O'Malley Dillon. "If you're in for a penny, you're in for a pound." In that way, Florida was the general election version of Iowa for the Biden campaign. Biden could compete there, and if he won, it would be indicative of a rout. But O'Malley Dillon thought it was more likely to be a money pit.

What she did become increasingly convinced about was the viability of Georgia. Shortly after the Democratic convention, Stacey Abrams connected with the campaign's leaders to pitch them on making a heavier investment in the state. At the time, it was considered a "tier two" priority for Biden's brain trust. That is, the campaign would put some money and time into the state, but not the concentrated firepower that went into Pennsylvania, Florida, Michigan, Wisconsin, North Carolina, and Arizona—the big six "first tier" states. Abrams had made the same case to Hillary Clinton's team to no avail.

But what Abrams was seeing—and doing—on the ground convinced her that Georgia deserved more of O'Malley Dillon's attention and Biden's resources. She and the CEO of her Fair Fight group, Lauren Groh-Wargo, had witnessed a dramatic increase in

Black participation in the Atlanta metropolitan area from 2014 through 2016 and 2018. Running for governor in 2018, Abrams had won one hundred thousand more raw votes, in an off-year election, than Hillary had in the 2016 presidential race in Georgia. Abrams believed in keeping voters engaged no matter the date on the calendar, so they didn't feel like politicians were asking them for a vote every two or four years just to then disappear until the next election. Metro Atlanta, with a population of six million people that were collectively more educated and less white than the rest of the country, had been a treasure trove for Kamala Harris when she was raising money in her own presidential bid. Though she didn't stick around to compete in the state's primary, the region was full of folks who liked her style and substance: suburban women of all colors, college graduates, and Black voters, regardless of geography and education level.

Even in a time of deeply polarized politics, the near-total absence of a swing-voting set was stark. There were Trump voters and anti-Trump voters. Trump had prepared for this. He believed that he could win an election by courting new voters who would become increasingly motivated to vote for him as he communicated with them more and more, and by trashing his rival badly enough to depress the Democratic vote. It was a belief born of experience. In the last war, he had shocked the country by turning out record numbers of voters and convincing many Democrats that Clinton should not be president. In all but a handful of swing counties in swing states, the difference would be which side could turn out more of its voters rather than which candidate could steal support from the other side.

This led O'Malley Dillon to rethink the art of persuasion. Modern campaigns use data analytics to assign two scores to individual voters, one reflecting the likelihood that someone will cast a ballot and another reflecting the probability that the vote will go to the campaign's candidate. Television and digital advertising, the candidate's travel schedule, and usually his or her messaging is tightly aimed at either winning over likely voters (persuasion) or getting out the vote (turning out people who already agree with the candidate).

Spurred on by the data Siegel was collecting, and the massive education campaign required to get Democrats to mail in ballots or vote early in person, O'Malley Dillon and her deputies began to think about persuasion and turnout as overlapping, according to a senior campaign official. Biden had held a lead over Trump for the entirety of the race. To win, they believed, he mostly had to stave off defections. That required convincing "soft" Democrats to love Biden and hate Trump—and to actually vote—while paying less attention to the unicorn-like swing voter.

"The trick was to include what would traditionally be get-out-the-vote targets in a persuasion universe," the official said. "There was definitely susceptibility in a lot of these voters." In plain English, that meant that Trump was having success in damaging Biden with Democratic-leaning voters who were less likely to vote. That had been a huge issue for Clinton in 2016. "It wasn't that there wasn't enough of a get-out-the-vote effort in '16," the aide said. "The issue was there was a big support problem." In the post-Obama era, the variable of Black turnout had become a conundrum for Democratic presidential campaigns. Clinton had not been able to sustain the numbers Obama had seen in 2008 or even 2012. That was part of the story, along with Trump's domination of working-class whites, of her defeat.

Trump and Biden would meet again on a debate stage on October 22 in Nashville, Tennessee. In the second round of debate prep, Trump's advisers concentrated on getting him to tone down his behavior. On one hand, he couldn't afford a repeat of the first debate. On the other, he had set a pretty high bar for outlandish conduct in a presidential debate. It wasn't hard, then, for him to find a middle ground.

Biden's aides prepared him to work his debate performance into the larger strategy of the campaign. Since Trump had focused so much energy on trying to portray Biden as mentally unfit, Biden's goal was simply to show that he knew what he was talking about. Most of Biden's ads had his face and his voice, a decision his team had made to give voters confidence that he was delivering his own message—not that of some hidden liberal cabal. For the debate, his aides wanted him to look into the camera a lot and speak directly to viewers.

Both candidates were largely able to stick to their plans, almost talking past each other. But Biden did give Trump what Republicans saw as a major opening with working-class voters. In discussing his plans to address climate change—including targets for reducing emissions over the next several decades—Biden said he would "transition away from the oil industry." Throughout the campaign, Republicans had argued that Biden would kill jobs—a message that was complicated by workers being laid off by the millions during the early months of the coronavirus crisis.

Trump was pumped up when he walked off the stage.

"You did a great job," Stepien told him.

Trump marveled at Biden's remark on oil as they walked toward the president's motorcade.

But compared to the spectacle of the first debate, there wasn't much to write home about, save for the appearance of Kid Rock in support of Trump. "He took the advice we gave him for the first debate and applied it in the second debate," one Trump adviser said, still lamenting the lost opportunity of the earlier matchup with Biden.

Before Trump returned to the campaign trail on October 12, he had given his advisers the instruction that they could not book him for too many rallies. He wanted to show voters he was working hard for their support, while Biden was holding more sporadic public events with a relative handful of people. The Tulsa rally, and social-distancing regulations in battleground states, forced his team to rethink the format for his stump speeches. Before he got sick, and after, Trump flew Air Force One into airports and spoke in hangars.

By October, Stepien felt confident that Trump's operation was running a better campaign than Biden's in a traditional sense. Trump's operatives were contacting voters directly and in person. The president was traveling the country, as were his children and other surrogates, and would hold almost four dozen hangar rallies over the final three weeks of the campaign. Despite being outspent, Trump hadn't been blown out. This would be a close finish if Republican voters showed up to the polls on election day.

Internal polling and focus group responses showed Trump aides that the president's "law and order" message was making a dent in Biden's backing and shifting some key Democratic base demographics a little more toward Trump. For starters, the connection between defunding the police and insecurity landed well with many Latino voters, they found.

"Black Lives Matter and defund the police efforts absolutely killed Democrats with Latino voters," said one high-ranking Trump campaign aide. "There's a reason why anyone who has a halfway decent house has gates around their house. The Latino community cares more about public safety and that component; it's such an integral part of the American dream."

Trump's team also saw an opening with young Black men, many of whom were turned off by Biden's crime bill and his positioning during the campaign. In late September, Trump went to Atlanta to unveil a program he called "The Platinum Plan," which he said would invest $500 billion in Black communities. Rapper and actor Ice Cube had worked on the plan with Trump advisers, and Lil Wayne would go on to support it, giving Trump high-profile validation. Ice Cube, who had once released a song called "Fuck Tha Police," took a barrage of criticism from Black Democrats and was forced to defend his work with the Trump team. He said Trump was willing to collaborate on the Contract with Black America that Ice Cube had worked on, while Biden's campaign was not.

Inside the campaign, this created more consternation around the politics of race. Top officials' biggest fears revolved around the possible failure to mobilize "soft" Biden voters among the subsets of young Black men and suburban whites. In different ways, Trump offered reasons for members of each group to vote for him or simply stay home. He was getting an assist from GOP allies. Down-ballot Republicans across the country had followed Trump's lead in accusing all Democrats of wanting to "defund the police" and linking them to the "radical left." Ads from the Trump campaign and from GOP congressional challengers featured burning cities, references to socialism, and the underlying message that a vote for Democrats was a vote for anarchy.

Polls conducted by candidates in congressional and state legislative races often showed voters saying they backed both Black

Lives Matter and the police, which led operatives in both campaigns to conclude that some people who said they supported Black Lives Matter weren't telling the truth. Never mind that Biden's position was to support both the goals of the BLM movement and police. Greg Schultz, who had been shifted into a role coordinating among the campaign, the DNC, and state parties, pleaded with the campaign's senior leadership to run ads on rural radio stations to make clear that Biden wanted more funding for cops, not less. He and his allies on the campaign thought that less-educated Democratic voters of all colors were susceptible to Trump's message. "There was an acknowledgment by a lot of us that this 'defund the police' thing was catching on in a more real way," said one person who agreed with the approach. "We finally ran some ads in battleground states, but it was probably three weeks after a number of us felt we were in a dangerous spot."

The feeling was that Biden was his own best messenger, this person said, because "Joe Biden is closer to the average voter than anybody in the Democratic Party. He will say you shouldn't shoot unarmed Black people and you shouldn't shoot a cop. Those aren't crazy statements, but somehow in our polarized environments they both are."

One of the loudest sources of complaints in October came from the Florida congressional delegation. The campaign wasn't spending money on paid canvassing in the state, which Black and Hispanic lawmakers said was necessary to drive the kind of turnout required to win. Early voting totals were coming up short of where they thought Biden needed to be to win, and that would also affect down-ballot races. They lit up his state team on a series of weekly phone calls in October, according to participants.

Yet the deeper Biden's team got into the general, the more they felt affirmed that Florida was the Iowa caucuses all over again. Even a massive advertising campaign, as well as sending Biden, Harris, and Barack Obama to the state, wasn't pushing Biden's numbers up. After the final weekend of early voting in Florida, Biden's team could see that not enough of their voters had made it to the polls. They discussed the various tools they might have to stage a turnout comeback, but believed they were doing the right things and getting nowhere. "There was nothing that we weren't doing that we could do."

Biden didn't have to win Florida if he could take Pennsylvania. It was the Keystone State, the one that bordered his home state of Delaware, that was central to the reclaim-the-Rust-Belt theory of the case that had informed his entire campaign. The campaign's focus on Pennsylvania was evident in the decision to deploy all four principals—Joe Biden, Jill Biden, Kamala Harris, and Doug Emhoff, to the state—for the final day of campaigning, Monday, November 2.

That night, on a call with senior staff, Siegel rendered her final pre-election projections for the electoral college. For the first time that week, her team predicted a loss for Biden in Florida. That wasn't a shock to the many Biden campaign aides who always thought Florida was unlikely to flip in 2020, but it did show that Trump was gaining steam in a key battleground state that had a strong correlation to several of the other states. Still, Siegel's squad believed Biden would most likely win Pennsylvania, Michigan, Wisconsin, Georgia, Arizona, and North Carolina—without surrendering any states Clinton had taken in 2016—for a total of 321 electoral votes.

If they were right, Biden would execute a near-clean sweep of the swing states, oust Trump from office, and finally fulfill his quest for the presidency. But, as one high-ranking official familiar with the campaign's internal polling and analytics said, the leads in the pivotal states were too close for certainty. "It's all a margin of error," the official said.

At Trump campaign headquarters, Stepien and his team pored over a series of data sets that included internal polling, public surveys, data analytics, and numbers from the Republican National Committee. *I don't know if we're going to win or lose,* Stepien thought. *I just know it's going to be close.* He said as much to his lieutenants. Most Trump campaign officials saw a narrow victory with 289 electoral votes. Stepien was even more bearish as he looked at a spreadsheet with all the various numbers. *There's not much slack here,* he thought. *Maybe we'll top 270 electoral votes with a few to spare. Maybe.*

CHAPTER 20

•

Black Clover

JIM CLYBURN HOPED FOR A LITTLE LUCK ON NOVEMBER 3, 2020. Before he left his house, he snagged a ball cap with a black clover on the front and the words "Live Lucky" stitched on the side. If luck ran his way, his daughter would win the school board seat she was running for, he would win his fifteenth term in the House of Representatives, Democrats would expand their majority in the House and take control of the Senate, and his friend Joe Biden— the man who had been resurrected by Clyburn's handiwork— would be elected president of the United States of America.

Later that day, an acquaintance pointed out the black four-leaf clover on Clyburn's hat and offered an observation about the House majority whip's career.

"You've been lucky," the acquaintance said.

"The harder I work, the luckier I get," Clyburn replied.

Joseph Robinette Biden, Jr., had worked hard in politics. And in just this election, his third bid for the presidency, he'd already reaped a lifetime's worth of good political fortune. From the *Des Moines Register* poll getting spiked to the chaos of the Iowa caucuses, from barely surviving the New Hampshire primary to the Clyburn Effect, and from a rival choking on crises to a political era so kinetic that it begged for moderation, Biden had been in the right place at the right time.

Much of that owed to his prescience in envisioning a framework for taking down Trump. But luck had been the residue of his design—a steady wingman. He knew it. He'd said it to Trump in their first debate. On this day, election day, he would find out if that luck had run out.

In 2016, Donald Trump won Pennsylvania by 44,284 votes, Wisconsin by 22,748 votes, and Michigan by 10,704 votes for a combined margin of 77,736. The biggest reason Biden and his campaign team had spent so much time, energy, and money on those blue wall states was the notion that it would not take much to flip them back into the Democratic column. All three had elected Democratic governors in the 2018 midterms, confirming for party loyalists that Republicans had not put a hammerlock on them. Data crunchers in both parties, and at independent news organizations, looked at Pennsylvania, with its 20 electoral votes and Trump's biggest margin of the three states, as the No. 1 battleground in the country.

As Pennsylvania went, they thought, so went the nation. But the Keystone State's rules for counting votes meant that it could take days, or even weeks, to get a final tally. In a particularly tight race, it might take that long to declare a winner. Several other swing states had similarly arduous vote-counting practices.

That uncertainty was at the front of Jen O'Malley Dillon's mind as she bounced back and forth between the Chase Center, a 92,000-square-foot conference hub along the banks of the Christina River in downtown Wilmington, and Biden's Lake house on election day. O'Malley Dillon, Donilon, Klain, and Dunn had kept Biden apprised of the chances of a "red mirage"—Trump looking like the winner early that night because election day votes would be counted immediately while it would take more time to report results from the mail-in ballots that had become a partisan calling card for coronavirus-wary Democrats.

Aides told Biden there were three scenarios for which he should be prepared. If he won Florida early in the night, it would be clear that he'd taken the election. The state had gotten very good at tabulating results quickly because of its history of electoral mishaps, a topic with which Klain, Al Gore's 2000 recount lawyer, was very familiar. There was also a chance that Biden could lose outright and that the data coming in from the states would show that early enough that he would have to give a concession speech that night. But the most probable outcome, his aides believed, was that he would be in a good position but not yet a clear victor. In any case, they advised, he should be ready to speak to the public that night.

For the last week or so, top Biden aides had been lobbying television networks to withhold a call on the race. They were worried that the red mirage would lead to premature calls in key states, giving the impression that Trump was winning when he wasn't. That could affect public perception—or, worse, result in Trump being named the winner before late-counted ballots would reverse the call—and give him fodder to contest a defeat.

If there was a watchword for the Biden campaign, it was "uncertainty." Public polls showed Biden winning handily, if not by huge margins. The analytics team projected a pretty close race in swing states, with Biden flipping Pennsylvania, Michigan, Wisconsin, North Carolina, Georgia, Arizona, and Nebraska's Second Congressional District to pick up 89 electoral votes. That amounted to a total of 321 electoral votes, but the projections were close enough to think there was a chance Trump could win in each of the states. Biden's pollsters were slightly more bearish. Anzalone thought Biden would win all the states the analytics team projected, except for North Carolina. Even though Biden held a slight lead in surveys over Trump there, he wasn't cracking 50 percent. Anzalone believed that Democrats had to have a majority of the electorate going into election day to win in southern states. His prediction was 306 electoral votes for Biden.

O'Malley Dillon hated election days, and, while this was her first one managing the campaign of a presidential nominee, it was no different from the others in that way. Early in the day, she started to get reports that Trump voters were showing up to the polls in droves. Democratic pollsters and analytics experts knew their own party's voters much better than the Republicans', and Trump's unique base added to the unpredictability. Of all the uncertainties that had defined the shattering 2016 loss for Democrats and could come back to bite them again, Trump turnout was at the top of the list. The election day lines looked long in many Democratic precincts, too, but the Trump surge was the first sign for O'Malley Dillon that the best-case scenario was unlikely to play out.

This won't be a landslide, she thought as she steeled herself for a long election night at the Chase Center.

———

In Philadelphia, at the "Scranton Exchange," Biden's data analytics team set up shop in desks at one end of the open bullpen space. On the other end, a medical team took temperatures. When Becca Siegel, the team's captain, had returned to the office for the first time since March a few days earlier, it looked like a stage set from a play about the primary. Printouts of ad-spending reports for the March 15 contests, delegate counts, and the like mixed with empty coffee cups and other trash.

Siegel liked to move around while she worked, toting her laptop until she had to stop back at her desk to recharge it. Her crew at HQ included about ten managers who were in charge of roughly 150 people working remotely on various ends of the extensive data operation: engineering, entry, and analysis. Siegel would be the star or the goat of intermittent Google Hangout calls with the senior leadership of the campaign, starting after the first polls closed. That's because she was the one with the numbers. She would be able to tell her colleagues whether they were on track for the easiest path to the presidency—a win in Florida—or the worst-case scenario of the bottom dropping out with less-educated white voters in the Rust Belt states.

She and her team had built a precinct-by-precinct system to analyze reported vote sums and project the unreported totals based on the probability that each uncounted vote was for Trump or Biden. That would allow her to estimate the growing or shrinking chances of a Biden win in each state as results trickled in. A big part of that calculation involved the correlation between voting method—by mail or in-person early versus casting a ballot on election day—and the likelihood of voting for Biden. For example, if a registered Democrat didn't vote early, he or she was considered to be less likely to vote for Biden on election day.

Siegel would be the messenger for the meaning of all the digits piling up in the campaign's computing systems—whether Biden was winning or losing. That could be a lonely role if her pre-election projections were off. As she got ready for the numbers to start rolling in, Siegel sipped coffee from Elixr, a small chain of boutique Philadelphia coffee shops that boasted of the "transformative" power of their light roasts. She didn't want a transformation, just an outcome that fell within the expected range.

On the other side of city hall, about a thousand feet away at street level, Greg Schultz, Pete Kavanaugh, and some of their friends convened a makeshift and socially distanced watch session in a conference room at the Residence Inn by Marriott. Schultz and Kavanaugh had come into town to share the moment with a core group that had started with Biden at the very beginning of the campaign. Kurt Bagley, the national organizing director, and Erin Wilson, the political director, huddled with them, along with Zeppa Kreager, who had been an unsung heroine of the canvassing program and the party's convention.

On prior weekends, they had participated in the campaign's dry runs of election night, and they were equipped to dial in to Google Hangouts calls, which were backed up by Zoom, Google Chats, Slack, conference call dial-ins, and the sundry other forms of instant communication that had proliferated in use during the coronavirus era.

Back in Wilmington, top Biden aides gathered in a ballroom at the Chase Center. When they'd first started filtering into Wilmington earlier in the week, safety protocols were so religiously observed that no food was allowed in the room. Plexiglass dividers had been installed to separate the desks, and Biden's aides wore masks.

O'Malley Dillon, Dunn, Bauer, Symone Sanders, Bedingfield, Kosoglu, and T. J. Ducklo were among the retinue of aides and advisers who settled into the ballroom Tuesday afternoon. Dana Remus's legal team could join virtually at any moment from Washington.

Trump paid a visit to his campaign headquarters in Rosslyn, Virginia, around midday and told staffers during an eleven-minute pep talk that he was not thinking about a concession speech. From there, he returned to the White House. Deputy campaign manager Justin Clark and battleground-states director Nick Trainer hopped a ride in the motorcade so they could bring the president to a political war room in the Old Executive Office Building, just across West Executive Avenue from the West Wing.

Then Clark and Trainer made their way toward the Map Room,

two floors beneath the residential floors of the White House. It would be the nerve center for top campaign and White House officials keeping tabs on the election throughout the night. When they reached their destination, an official from the White House medical unit told Trainer he had tested positive for coronavirus and had to leave. "He's like our battleground guy, our vote counter, and he's sidelined now for election night," said a colleague. "Nick was the guy we needed in the room."

Clark would be joined in the Map Room by Jason Miller, Stepien, data guru Matt Oczkowski and his numbers team, and White House Chief of Staff Mark Meadows for the crunch hours of poll closings and vote reporting.

On the biggest night of his political life, Biden sat in the big, open sunroom of the Lake house with Jill Biden, his children, and most of his grandchildren coming in and out from the adjacent dining room and kitchen. Donilon was in the house, too, working on various versions of an election night speech. They had all quarantined for two weeks so that they could be with Biden as he waited to find out if he would become the forty-sixth president of the United States. Election nights were usually family nights for Biden, which was a relief for his aides, who preferred the boss to be occupied and happy rather than engaged and anxiously asking questions. Harris was hidden away with her husband, Doug Emhoff, at a nearby home in Wilmington, ready to join Biden at the Chase Center whenever it was time for him to make a public statement.

With the TV on in the background, Biden fielded phone calls from folks with whom he'd formed relationships through a lifetime in the popularity business. Some of them called Hunter, who would obligingly hand his phone to his dad or put it on speaker. Close family friends piped in through FaceTime or were passed around the room, from one Biden to the next. When Biden wanted to make a call, Annie Tomasini would dial for him—the former Boston University basketball player's 617 area code popping up on the recipient's phone—and hand her cell to the boss.

"I love you," Biden kept telling friends who lent emotional support on a make-or-break night. He was surrounded and alone—the only person who could end Trump's run in the White House, with the hopes of tens of millions of Americans on his shoulders—all at once.

Biden had never lost a general election, from the time he won a seat on the New Castle County Council at twenty-seven in 1970. Two years later, he upset Republican incumbent Caleb Boggs to become one of the youngest senators in American history. He took that seat by 3,162 votes—or 1.4 percent of the nearly 230,000 cast—which he described as winning "narrowly" in a 2019 questionnaire filled out for TV producer Shonda Rhimes's website. Then he reeled off six more Senate victories, including one for a term he never served because he was simultaneously elected vice president. He won reelection with Obama in 2012. Ten runs, ten victories. Maybe, like he reminded younger staffers from time to time, he knew a little something about politics. Trump was one-for-one in elections, a perfect record at the highest level. One of them would leave this election with a blemished record and a heartbroken base.

Indiana and Kentucky, two states where Trump was sure to win, closed their polls first, at 6:00 P.M. eastern time, and the Biden analytics team in Philadelphia would be able to plug in vote totals from their precincts to get a better picture of what to expect the rest of the night. But neither state resembled one of the big swing states, and the real data would start to flow when Florida, Georgia, and Virginia, along with a handful of other states, began reporting results after 7:00 P.M. poll closings. Thirty minutes later, Ohio and North Carolina would be among the batch of 7:30 P.M. states.

At 7:13 P.M., Florida dropped 22 percent of its votes, and Biden led with 51 percent of them. These were early and mail-in votes. Within the hour, it would become clear to veteran vote watchers that Biden was in deep trouble in the Sunshine State. Miami-Dade County, home to Latino voters Trump had targeted with his economic appeals and warnings that Democrats would implement a socialist agenda, showed that Trump had increased his raw vote total by more than one hundred thousand over 2016 with 84 percent of the vote reported. Biden was ten thousand votes shy of Clinton's total.

Fuck, O'Malley Dillon thought, her mind racing to what

Trump's performance in Miami-Dade could mean for Latino voters in other parts of the country, like Arizona and Nevada, not to mention the potential in a super-close race to affect the Rust Belt. The responsibility of her job—to run the campaign that beat Trump—hit her like a sack of hammers. *What if we lose?* she thought. *Oh, my God.* She had expected to lose Florida, but the Miami-Dade numbers, where Biden was winning by a much smaller margin than he should have been, were just flat ugly. No one on her team had expected this. *Breathe.* Senior campaign officials jumped on a videoconference call. Miami-Dade was full of Cuban Americans and Venezuelan Americans who were more afraid of socialism than Hispanic voters in other parts of the country.

Speaking from the Philly HQ, Siegel told her colleagues that the results in South Florida could be isolated. Biden may have been bleeding Hispanics in Miami-Dade, but key information was flowing in from the other side of the state: Biden was doing well in big suburban counties on Florida's west coast. Those counties had been foreboding for Clinton's data analysts in 2016 because voters there had a surprisingly strong correlation to their counterparts in the Rust Belt. In many cases, midwesterners retired to the west coast of Florida, just like folks from New York and New Jersey flooded into Palm Beach, Broward, and Miami-Dade counties on the east coast. In other words, the most important bellwether for the rest of the night might not be Trump overperforming with Hispanic voters in Miami-Dade but Biden outperforming Clinton in Pinellas and Hillsborough counties in the Tampa-St. Petersburg area. In Pinellas, where Obama had won twice before Trump took it in 2016, Biden was ahead by about a point.

Trump was going to win Florida, cutting off Biden's path to a decisive early victory. The rest of the data was inconclusive beyond suggesting that the battleground states Biden needed to win would be very close. It was the next batch of states, including Virginia, that gave Kavanaugh, Schultz, and their crew a boost. Kavanaugh, who had worked as a field organizer in Virginia early in his career, had his eye on Chesterfield County, a longtime Republican stronghold that had elected Democratic representative Abigail Spanberger in the 2018 midterms. The county, nestled in suburbs south of Richmond, with wealthy, highly educated voters, was going Biden's way by several points. Moreover, he would end up getting about 26,000 more votes there than Clinton had. Trump's raw vote was up, too, but by only 8,000 votes. A 2-point loss for Democrats in Chesterfield in 2016 was turning into a 7-point win.

As the early-closing states slowly reported vote totals over the next couple of hours, it became clear that the rumored Trump surge was real. He was outperforming his 2016 numbers virtually everywhere that mattered, including in states that he was losing. Biden was still ahead of the nightmare scenario of a clear defeat, but no one could be sure that he was headed to victory, either. At 9:48 P.M., one Biden aide summed up the results so far by telling a reporter "It'll be a long time until I have fingernails again."

Sitting in the Map Room at the White House, watching the Florida results, Stepien was taken back to election night 2016, when he and Clark had set up a much less ornate and technologically impressive war room at Trump Tower in Manhattan. Stepien had been one of the campaign aides who told colleagues that the Florida numbers that year might foretell a victory. Now, as campaign aides sat around a square of tables in the White House, with stand-up TVs showing the various cable channels—the sound up on CNN, mostly—Stepien found himself throwing a wet blanket on the Sunshine State. The big win rolling in was exciting, but he worried that it might not be enough.

"The numbers are really, really, really good," Stepien told the room. "We need to understand that they are going to get less good as the night goes on, less good as the days go on." Both camps had expected Trump to win Florida going into the night—a different outcome would have meant a clear victory for Biden.

Still, the room was pumped up. "The fact that we were doing so well in Florida, particularly in Miami-Dade County, with our numbers of Latinos performing so well, that looked like an indicator of where things would go," one top campaign official said later. Trump would end up winning 46 percent of the vote in Miami-Dade, up from 34 percent in 2016. But it wasn't just Florida that looked good for the president. Trump held an early lead in North Carolina. Ohio and Iowa, two states Biden had visited, were far more Republican-red than most polls had suggested ahead of election day.

In other words, a few hours into election night, both campaigns saw a very tight race. *We're going to win it close if we're going to win it,* Stepien thought.

On video calls connecting the Biden campaign's boiler rooms, happening closer to every half hour than every hour, Siegel read out the numbers and her interpretation of them. Biden's senior aides had different feelings about what the closeness of the race meant based on their own experiences with, and expectations about, different states. "The size of the margin in Ohio was the first sign that we should have concerns about the other three midwestern states," said one top Biden adviser. "Suburban areas were slightly overperforming for us and not nearly the way rural parts were overperforming for them." The state would end up looking almost precisely the same as it had—save for some shifting in suburban and rural areas—as it did in 2016. "The underperformance in rural areas" was a surprise, said a second Biden campaign official. "We were projecting to do worse in some states but not to lose them."

North Carolina was coming in painfully slowly for both the campaign and Democrats outside it, who were watching the presidential contest and a key Senate race featuring challenger Cal Cunningham and Republican incumbent Thom Tillis. The North Carolina dynamic was similar to what was happening elsewhere on the map. Biden racked up bigger margins in Wake County and other heavily suburban areas while Trump increased his vote totals from 2016 by 2,000, 3,000 or 5,000 in rural county after rural county.

Campaign aides were getting bombarded with phone calls and text messages from freaked-out Democrats. "It was obvious we were not going to win our expansion states at that point," said one top campaign adviser. "People were going crazy. All of our friends, all of our supporters saying, 'It's just like 2016 again, just as we thought.'"

Biden was hearing from his network of friends, too. The early numbers from Pennsylvania—the most pivotal state for his strategy—showed Trump up big. He talked to aides in the Chase Center boiler room, who told him that Trump running up the score with election day results in early-reporting parts of the state was not unexpected. It took some calling around to contacts outside the campaign before he was sure his own team was right.

"His Pennsylvania political allies told him it was going to be fine. That was helpful," one adviser said. "What he was seeing was what everyone else was seeing, which was still a clearly divided country."

Clyburn was sitting with his daughter Angela at her victory party in Columbia, South Carolina, when his cellphone rang. He saw the telltale 617 area code of Tomasini's number and stepped outside to talk to Biden. Clyburn had kept one eye on the television screen at his daughter's party, and he didn't like the early returns in Pennsylvania.

"I don't know where this vote is coming from, but if any of this vote is coming from Pittsburgh or Philadelphia, we're in serious trouble," said Clyburn, his nervousness evident in his voice.

Now, it was Biden who played a reassuring role. After talking to his aides and friends, he knew where the vote had come in and where it hadn't, and, having lived a few miles from the Pennsylvania border for most of his life, he knew the state's politics almost as well as Delaware's. The big cities still had a lot of vote left to report, he calmly assured Clyburn.

More important than the location of votes: the method. Pennsylvania law banned counties from starting to tally mail-in ballots before election day. Because so many Democrats had voted by mail, it was going to take a long time to process all of their ballots. What Clyburn was seeing, Biden explained, was the red mirage.

While Biden wasn't on his team's videoconference calls, O'Malley Dillon and other aides were keeping him informed by phone. They had told him that it might be a long wait before there was any clarity. That was a double-edged sword. It meant that he wasn't winning big, but it also meant the bottom wasn't dropping out. There wasn't much he could do other than relay what he had heard to the congressman.

Clyburn was surprised by Biden's placid demeanor. It briefly made him feel marginally better. But the reports he was getting from House races around the country were not good, and the crushing margin of senator Lindsey Graham's victory over Clyburn protégé Jaime Harrison convinced him that Republicans' attacks on the "defund the police" movement were hurting the party's candidates—even those like Harrison who had rejected the slogan. Graham's Security Is Strength political action committee had accused Harrison of being "part of the liberal culture that wants to defund the police."

In Philadelphia, Siegel was having an experience different from that of most of the Democratic world. She could tell her party was panicking as the night wore on. *The Internet is silent,* she thought. For the Twitterati, that was a replay of 2016, too. Clinton campaign officials had practically disappeared from social media on election night that year.

For all intents and purposes, Siegel had as much actual information as anyone in the world. Members of her team were watching local television news and reading press releases from county election clerks to obtain more and more digits to feed into the analytics machine. She could understand why Democrats might be freaking out—Trump was winning Florida and North Carolina, Biden was trailing in Pennsylvania—but she didn't think the election was slipping away. It was supposed to be close.

There's a lot that could go wrong, she thought, *but I'm not seeing any of those things.*

In Atlanta, Stacey Abrams watched Georgia start to report its numbers from the couch in her living room, with a laptop balanced on her knees, and her phone—with a series of text-message threads—in her hand. She felt confident. She had pushed Biden's team to invest more in the state because she believed Trump could be defeated if Democrats ran a full campaign there. Before election day, Biden had been running up the score in absentee balloting, like he had in other states, and number crunchers had told Abrams that their conservative estimate for his performance showed Biden winning by about four thousand votes.

She had the *New York Times* website up on her laptop as votes came in. It was disappointing to see the paper's proprietary needle for North Carolina at the red end of its red-blue dashboard—an indicator used to project the likelihood of each party's candidate winning a state. But Georgia, which was pointed most of the way toward red, still had some wiggle room. That lined up with her expectations. The early numbers—election day votes—were for Trump but not enough to suggest Biden couldn't win. Still, she took comfort when the needle moved into blue territory.

She went to bed not too long after that, without the knot that had formed in her stomach on election nights in 2016 and 2018.

We're going to deliver Georgia, she thought.

But even if Biden won Georgia, and it would be close enough to preclude a call for some time, its 16 electoral votes alone would not secure him the presidency. The Rust Belt states were still in flux. Based on what had been reported and what was left outstanding in Pennsylvania, Biden officials believed they were in good shape. That could be confirmed only after more ballots were counted, which could be days. Michigan and Wisconsin were always a little harder to track because those states didn't release as much information about voters as their counterparts did.

So far, Trump hadn't lost a single state that was part of his 2016 electoral college coalition. Then, around 11:20 P.M. on the East Coast, Fox News called Arizona for Biden. *What?* Siegel thought. Biden was leading but not by enough to be confident. *Arizona is too close to call,* she thought.

For Democrats around the country, this was the first burst of really good news. Trump had won Arizona in 2016. That year, it was Fox that had presciently called Wisconsin before any other network, leading anchor Megyn Kelly to declare, "There goes her blue wall."

Stepien, Clark, Oczkowski, and Jason Miller rushed out of the Map Room and shuffled up the stairs to the residence to find their boss furious. The big win in Florida, and early results showing him ahead in other key swing states, had prompted friends to tell him he was on a glidepath to reelection. He had foiled the pollsters and the pundits again, they told him. Trump thought he was winning, but Arizona threw that into doubt for him.

"We feel good about where we are," Miller told the president. "We'd rather be in our shoes than their shoes."

Oczkowski walked Trump through the map. He was doing better in Philadelphia than he had four years ago, so Pennsylvania still looked good. Georgia was on a knife's edge. Wisconsin was super-close, too. Across the map, the data coming in tracked with a very tight outcome. But there was no reason to think that the election had slipped away—or that Fox had enough information to make a call on Arizona. The pace of vote counting was starting to slow down, Trump's aides told him, and there would be a lull in the coming hours.

But Trump fixated on Fox. If CNN or MSNBC had jumped the gun on a swing state, that would be one thing, he thought. But FOX? *How the hell can they do that?* he thought.

"Who is responsible for that?" he asked. "What can we do to fix it?"

His pointed questions prompted a round of calls from Trump family members and senior White House and campaign officials to members of the Murdoch family, which owned Fox, the cable network's executives, and some of its most prominent on-air talent.

Miller called Bill Sammon, a vice president at Fox and its managing editor in Washington, and Bill Hemmer, one of the network's hosts. Hope Hicks called Raj Shah, a former Trump White House spokesman and a senior vice president at Fox. Trumps called Murdochs, according to two people involved in the president's effort to get the call reversed. But the president couldn't reach Rupert Murdoch, who was in the United Kingdom, where it was very early in the morning, according to a third person briefed on the calls.

"We have our division of labor with strict guidelines and policies here," Hemmer told Miller. "Our decision desk makes the determination; we do the analysis." Like the decision desks at the other cable networks, Fox's was designed to be protected from outside influence—even from within the company. Arnon Mishkin, the decision desk director, was not going to be moved by anyone. Not even Fox's most powerful viewer.

It was time to put Biden in front of a camera. While it would seem foolish to actually declare victory, his chances looked good enough in the battleground states that he could credibly go out and position himself as the leader. Biden's aides didn't want to let Trump get out of the box first and either declare a win that wasn't there or cast doubt on the electoral process. They believed he would bend, break, or burn down any barrier in his path.

Biden rolled out from his house to the Chase Center and gave brief remarks from the stage there. They were the campaign's talking points. "We knew this was going to go long, but who knew we're going to go into maybe tomorrow morning, maybe longer," he said about 12:45 A.M. "But look, we feel good about where we are. We really do. I'm here to tell you tonight, we believe we're on track to win this election."

Trump retorted by tweet. "We are up BIG, but they are trying to STEAL the Election," he wrote. "We will never let them do it. Votes cannot be cast after the polls are closed." Trump, who had been at the White House all night, wouldn't go to the podium for another hour and a half.

After midnight, the ground-floor Map Room filled up with Trump-world luminaries: Rudy Giuliani, Jeanine Pirro, Laura Ingraham, and others. Wandering down the stairs from the stalled victory party in the East Room, the guests were in "various places of celebration"—having had a few more drinks than one too many—according to one person who was there. Raymond Arroyo, a host on the Catholic cable news station Eternal Word Television Network, popped in and began holding court.

Throughout the night, Trump, Jared Kushner, and other White House officials had dropped by periodically to have serious conversations about the election. These new interlopers were a distraction. Meadows, who spent much of the night working in the Map Room, helped the campaign aides by trying to clear the room. But the scene was no one's idea of a finely tuned machine on its way to victory.

"You didn't have that winning feeling at that moment," said a person who watched in disbelief as the Trumpworld celebrity reunion scene played out in the Map Room.

Meadows, Stepien, Clark, and Miller walked down the hall from the Map Room into the China Room to discuss what the president should say publicly. Giuliani joined them, standing between the fireplace on the room's west wall and shelves of presidential service pieces along the east wall that dated back more than two hundred years. Giuliani was the bull in the China Room.

"The president should just say he won," Giuliani said. He started talking about votes being "stolen" in crucial states. Trump wasn't present, but his aides worried about the influence Giuliani might have on him.

When Trump went to the East Room to address the nation after two A.M., he argued both that he was winning and that the election was fraudulent. But the telling line was his call for states to stop counting ballots. It would be the rare candidate who wanted to halt a tally he expected to win.

Wow, O'Malley Dillon thought as Trump claimed he was winning all over the map. *This is a complete fabrication.*

Biden, taking it all in from the Lake, was less surprised. This Trumpian behavior was one of the reasons he saw an opening for himself at the start of the race.

I can't believe it, he thought, *but I can believe it.*

Greg Schultz left the Residence Inn in Philadelphia and walked down a deserted South Broad Street on the way to his hotel. Police had blocked off streets downtown in anticipation of potential vio lence or out-of-hand celebration. A silver lining of the slow-motion result was that neither side had lost yet, which gave some time for the emotional angst of the buildup to election day to dissipate a little. Schultz had a moment of doubt on the lonely stroll.

What if we don't win these midwestern states? he thought. *The gap in Pennsylvania is still huge. I told everybody we were going to win these states for the last twenty months. What am I going to do for a living when three thousand of the most powerful people in the party feel like I lied to them?*

Biden campaign officials knew that the reporting of results in Pennsylvania was going to take days. Michigan was weaker than they had projected, but it still fell within the range that indicated a Biden victory there. And Milwaukee's county clerk had said that a batch of votes still being counted was likely to be reported some- time around four A.M. eastern. O'Malley Dillon set up a senior staff call for six A.M., went to her hotel, and showered. She couldn't sleep, but she wanted to give her team at least a small window to rest. By the time they got on that six A.M. call, both Wisconsin and Michigan had reported more numbers. They were in line with the campaign's modeling for a victory.

Later that morning, or maybe early afternoon—time had become a cloudy concept by that point—O'Malley Dillon drove over to Biden's Lake house to talk to him about the status of the race. For weeks, she had been telling him it was going to be close. Now, in the study of the Lake house, the one with the Senate seal, where there was enough room to have a socially distanced, masked-up meeting with Biden, Donilon, and Klain, her message changed.

"Sir, you're going to win," O'Malley Dillon said. More votes were in, they matched the models, and the campaign's teams on the ground were reporting back from their states that everything looked good. Trump might be in full meltdown—he'd tweeted repeatedly overnight—but it was a sign that reality was forcing him further into a corner of denial.

Biden was confident that his campaign manager was giving him her best analysis. But whether it was superstition or something else, he wouldn't be ready to tempt God, fate, or luck by believing he was going to be the president. It would be four long days before the networks declared him the winner. In the interim, Biden and his campaign aides gave daily updates to the country and the press about where the vote stood. He would end up winning 306 electoral votes, including those from Pennsylvania, Michigan, Wisconsin, Georgia, and Arizona. He'd lost Florida by about three and a half points, the largest spread for a Republican since George W. Bush's 2004 reelection campaign, and he'd lost North Carolina by almost a point and a half.

But what was striking was how close Trump had come to pulling off another upset. In 2016, Clinton had lost the three pivotal Rust Belt states by a total of 77,736 votes. Trump lost the three states that would have given him a victory—Wisconsin, Georgia, and Arizona—by a total of 42,918 votes. In Wisconsin, Biden wound up with a 20,682-vote margin, topping Trump by less than two-thirds of a percentage point. In Georgia, the number would be 11,779 votes, or less than a quarter of a percentage point. And in Arizona, where Fox had doubled down on its call for Biden despite pressure from the Trump camp, it would be 10,457 votes, or less than a third of a percentage point. To get Trump to a clear victory of 270 electoral votes—adding roughly 23,000 votes to flip Nebras-ka's Second Congressional District—it would still have taken fewer votes for him to win than his margin in 2016.

Publicly, Biden's team struck the posture that he had won a big victory. Privately, campaign officials acknowledged they had hung on by their fingernails.

"I expected it to be close," said one top Biden aide who had started before the launch. "I didn't expect it to be this fucking close."

As Clyburn watched the Democrats' House majority dwindle from 233 seats to 222 seats and their hopes of a Senate majority hang on two runoff elections in Georgia, he took stock of the dif-ference between where he had hoped four years of Trump would leave the country and where it actually stood.

This could have been a sound rejection of the politics of hate and division. The country could be healing right away, he thought. *Now we're going to have all kinds of contests over legislation, and Trump will still feel like he's got control of the Republican Party.*

It had been a good election for the GOP down ballot. The po-litical pendulum had swung back toward Republicans since the 2018 midterms, just not enough to carry the president across the line. With good planning, better than expected discipline as a can-didate, and a lot of luck, Biden had held Trump back. He knew how close he had come to defeat.

Said one source very close to Biden, "He didn't let himself be-lieve that he really had it in the bag until it was called."

The republic still stands. For that, Americans could feel lucky, if not fully reassured, by the 2020 election.

After a political battle fought in the midst of a maelstrom of pandemic disease, economic upheaval, and violent clashes over ra-cial justice, not that much had changed. Warnings that the out-come would lead to the entrenchment of an authoritarian right-wing regime or a socialist revolution did not come to pass. The country did not erupt into civil war. Power transferred peace-fully, more or less.

Partisans on both sides could point to successes: Biden captured the presidency for Democrats, while Trump pushed scores of down-

ballot Republicans to victory in the House, Senate, and state legislatures. Biden, separating himself from the orthodoxies of his
party's base, had no coattails. Even though Trump didn't acknowledge the legitimacy of the outcome, most of the key officials in his
party at the state and federal levels did.

And yet there were reasons for distress on both sides of the partisan aisle. After all, Democrats could see that more than 74 million people had voted for Trump, an increase of 17.8 percent over
his 2016 total. He had been right about his capacity to find new
voters who agreed with his substance and style, and were at least
tolerant of racism, sexism, and xenophobia. But Republicans could
calculate that the number of people who stood to be counted
against him grew even more, by 23.4 percent, to 81 million and
change. Troubling for the GOP, Democrats solidified their new advantage with educated white suburbanites, a subset of the electorate that had long formed a core of the GOP's voting and donor
base. Many establishment Republicans—including some who
worked for Trump—left the election unsettled by the success of his
use of the racial justice protests to foment fear.

"I think it really hurt the Republican Party," said one senior
Trump campaign official. "It certainly hurt members [of Congress]
among some of the groups that we struggle with—white college-
educated, white suburban, white female—all of those things
brought back Charlottesville, and I think not to our benefit."

Still, four years of Trump had brought a marginal shift in the
political landscape, not a decisive one. It had motivated greater
numbers of citizens to vote for and against him, with a relatively
small move in the direction of the latter on a percentage basis.
More people than ever before had voted—158,537,765 of them—
and the separation between the winner and loser was a little less
than 4.5 percentage points.

But between Trump's pernicious efforts to invalidate the results
by lying, intimidating state election officials, and inciting his followers to storm the Capitol, and Biden's incentive to portray the
outcome as a landslide, many voters didn't realize how close the
president had come to winning a second term. In a system based on
the electoral college, which can't be changed without two-thirds of
Congress and three-quarters of the states voting to alter it, the relatively close popular vote is a beauty contest. The real action is in

the accumulation of electoral votes in a handful of battleground states.

In two of the pivotal states—Arizona and Wisconsin—Trump lost despite taking a higher percentage of the overall vote than he had four years earlier, when third-party candidates were more of a factor. In the third, Georgia, Biden did not win any counties that Clinton lost in 2016. Instead, he took the state's 16 electoral votes by jacking up Democratic turnout in the metro Atlanta area. The most consequential flip for Democrats came in Maricopa County, Arizona, where Trump increased his vote total by 33.2 percent over 2016. Biden bumped the Democratic tally up by an unbelievable 48.1 percent, winning Phoenix's county by 45,109 votes out of nearly 2 million cast there, while he took the state by 10,457 votes overall.

But in cities in the Rust Belt, both nonwhite turnout and Trump cutting into Democratic margins were problematic for Biden. In Philadelphia, the Democrats' most reliable bastion in the most important bellwether for the election, Trump received 24,122 more votes than he did in 2016, compared to a 20,150 spike for the Democratic ticket. Overall, the Biden vote total of 604,175 in the city was just 3.4 percent higher than Clinton's mark four years earlier, and a small fraction of his national turnout surge. And while Democrats pointed to flipping Erie and Luzerne counties in Pennsylvania back into their column, the real story in Pennsylvania was something of a home field advantage for Biden. His performance in the three majority-white suburban Philadelphia counties closest to his home state of Delaware—Chester, Delaware, and Montgomery counties—accounted for the lion's share of his margin in the state.

In Detroit, Biden totaled 963 fewer votes than Clinton did in 2016, while Trump increased his small share of the city's roughly 245,000 votes by 4,972. It was the suburban part of Detroit's Wayne County, along with other close-in suburban counties, that delivered Biden's margin of a little more than 150,000 votes statewide. In the suburban part of Wayne, for example, Biden boosted the Democratic ticket's number by 78,689 votes, while Trump's total increased by just 30,588. The margin of Biden's increased performance in Michigan's Oakland County was a little bit higher.

A similar dynamic played out in Wisconsin. While Biden outperformed Clinton by about 9.9 percent in raw votes in Milwaukee

County, which is larger than the city itself, his biggest improvement over 2016 was in Madison's Dane County. The Democratic boost there was 42,424 votes, compared with 28,705 in Milwaukee County, which has almost twice the population. In the city of Milwaukee, turnout in Black-majority precincts was down from 2016, according to the *Journal Sentinel*.

The secret ballot means that it's impossible to know which voters picked which candidates, but turnout patterns and exit polls—which showed Trump winning 12 percent of Black voters and 32 percent of Latinos nationwide—strongly suggested two things about Democrats' standing with nonwhite voters: Biden generally wasn't able to turn out his Black and Hispanic supporters in key metropolitan areas in swing states the way he would have liked, and Trump bit into the Democratic edge in those demographics even after four years of casting aspersions on people of color.

This election was closer than prognosticators projected. From the electoral college perspective—the only one that matters in the selection of a president—it was closer than Trump's victory in 2016. Democrats had been optimistic, if not certain, that voters would deliver a beat-down to Trumpism. Many of them hoped that it was impossible for a president to rack up more votes after four years in which he spewed racist bile, separated immigrant children from their parents, extorted a foreign country to seek an investigation into his chief political rival, and tried to convince his fellow Americans that there was little danger from a pandemic disease that killed by the hundreds of thousands.

Those hopes were dashed.

In 2016, Trump had needed everything to go wrong for Hillary Clinton to win. This time, Biden caught every imaginable break. "If President Trump had just acknowledged there was a virus, even midway in August or September, acknowledged this is a fucked-up situation, and pivoted, we would have gotten crushed," said one longtime Biden aide and adviser. "But he pretended nothing was happening. People were just exhausted, and this guy has no sort of handle on reality. They see Joe Biden, and this guy's at least consistent."

The key to Biden's victory, more than anything else, was the consistency of his message about what he would do for voters—restore "the soul of this nation"—and why he was uniquely capable of delivering on that promise. Ridiculed for so long about his lack of discipline as a candidate, Biden stuck to his theory of the case during a brutal primary slog and in the face of pressure from his allies—even members of his own staff—to change his strategy and tactics in the general election.

Barack Obama had been wrong about him. So had Hillary Clinton, John Kerry, and Michael Bloomberg. And, of course, the two dozen other primary rivals and Trump had been wrong about him, too. This time, he had exactly what it took to win.

Knowing who he was, and where he wanted to be politically, allowed Biden's campaign to capitalize when luck ran his way—and it did, time and again. Trump, on the other hand, never came up with a way of explaining how he would use a second term to serve the public. That was a remarkable failure for a candidate whose "Make America Great Again" slogan had so nimbly encapsulated his message four years earlier.

Rather than rallying voters around a common purpose in fighting the coronavirus, Trump promised that it would go away. He never understood how to use the crisis to show Americans that he was suffering with them. Even after he contracted the coronavirus, he treated his recovery as evidence that the disease was weak. Along with Congress, he had spent trillions of dollars on emergency aid to people affected by the physical and economic devastation wrought by the coronavirus, and he had managed to get low marks for his handling of the situation anyway.

But some of his instincts about voters' attitudes proved to be savvy, if incendiary. He concentrated on the crime that accompanied protests for racial justice and sought to stoke it. The backlash, as he suggested so often with his echoes of Richard Nixon's "silent majority," would be good for him. It wasn't Biden shouting "defund the police"; it was Trump. He wanted voters to believe that electing the Democrat would lead to anarchy. And while that didn't work well enough against Biden—Trump had even said in Tulsa that Biden wasn't a radical—the president-elect came away convinced that the charge was brutal for Democrats.

"That's how they beat the living hell out of us across the country, saying that we're talking about defunding the police," Biden told civil rights activists after the election, according to an audio recording of the virtual meeting that was obtained by *The Inter-*

cept. Biden had resisted calls from within his own campaign to align more closely with activists and less closely with police. During the primaries, he had defended his crime bill, praised dead segregationists, and explained why he thought it wasn't the role of the federal government to stop de facto discrimination.

Trump had called Biden "Sleepy Joe." Unwoke Joe might have been more accurate. That was the ugly truth many Democrats had to face in the aftermath of the 2020 election: To beat Trump, they had to swallow their progressive values and push forward an old white man who simply promised to restore calm. Biden's victory was cause for relief among Democrats, but not a cease-fire in the party's civil war. That would rage on during the presidential transition period and the first days of the Biden presidency.

Biden's "brother," President Barack Obama, had not called him on election day, or the next day, or the next, or the next. In fact, according to a source close to the former president, Obama didn't call to congratulate Biden until Saturday, November 7, the day the networks had finally called the election. Over the years, Obama had watched the Tea Party and then Trump rise in resistance to him, and then the Democratic Party respond by nominating and electing a politician who had been picked to give establishment centrist ballast to his own ticket. The nation and the Democratic Party had moved away from Obama. While he had pitched in to try to save Biden and the party at key moments, he had to know that Biden's victory was a repudiation of the brands of hope and change that he sought.

Obama also called O'Malley Dillon that day to give her a virtual pat on the back. She had brought in the Obama squad to run the general election campaign and figured out how to scrape by in an election year unlike any other. She was grateful for the faith Obama had in her and the way he had validated her to Biden. In the days and weeks after the election, she had a better view of the postmortem than anyone. She knew just how tight it had been, and that disappointed her, too.

I would have loved a landslide, a complete rejection of Trump, she thought. But like many Democrats, she was relieved not to have relived 2016 after a brief scare on election night. *Our polling tools are so fucked up,* she thought. *That has to change if we're going to engage people in the right ways.*

For Republicans, who had abandoned long-held party tenets—from controlling spending to promoting free trade—Trump's defeat left them bereft of both principle and the power of the White House. But Trump remained the uniquely powerful force in the party—74 million people had voted for him—and defying him, even in his postpresidency, would come at a price.

Both parties were in transition. It just wasn't certain where either one was headed. One thing was clear, though: At the end of a brutal year, with so much seemingly at stake and with so many voters compelled to cast ballots, Biden's new Washington would be almost as evenly divided as possible. Twin January victories in Georgia Senate races would give Democrats 50 seats and control of the chamber—by virtue of Vice President Kamala Harris's tie-breaking vote. And in the House, Democrats held just 51 percent of the seats.

For the new president, there were many reasons to feel fortunate, but the most relevant was the one he often attributed to his father: "It is the lucky person who gets up in the morning, puts both feet on the floor, knows what they are about to do, and thinks it still matters."

ACKNOWLEDGMENTS

•

AFTER WE FINISHED OUR LAST BOOK, *SHATTERED,* OUR LITERARY agent Bridget Wagner Matzie, came to us with another idea: Do it again. The story of this election was always going to be one that had to be told, and she said we were best positioned to tell it. She couldn't have known all that would happen in 2020. She had faith in us. Bridget, we are so grateful and so fortunate to have you at our sides for a third time. You are an amazing advocate and we are constantly blown away by your instincts, attention to detail, and wisdom. Thank you for being there at every twist and turn.

We speak to our editor Kevin Doughten multiple times a day—sometimes more than our own family members—and that's no coincidence. Kevin is equal parts brilliant and demanding. He consistently sets the bar high, always asking the right questions, consistently wanting more explanation, while keeping his fingers on the pulse of the narrative the entire time. We couldn't ask for a better partner and friend and we're so lucky to have gone through this journey with you three times now.

We are indebted and beyond thankful to Sara Wilson and Abigail Goldberg-Zelizer, our talented and tireless researchers on this book, who never once complained about the amount of work being thrown at them or the speed at which it had to be completed. Even when they were inundated with assignments, they always asked for more, from transcribing hundreds of hours of audio to putting together detailed timelines in a dizzying year where the news cycles were relentless.

We'd also like to thank our team at Crown: David Drake, Annsley Rosner, Gillian Blake, Julie Cepler, Kathleen Quinlan, Dyana Messina, Gwyneth Stansfield, Christopher Brand, Lydia Morgan, Sally Franklin, Dennis Ambrose, Benjamin Dreyer, and Linnea Knollmueller.

But mostly, we are grateful to so many sources who agreed to talk to us knowing that we would, once again, chronicle perhaps the most important election in our lifetime.

—JA & AP

There are no words sufficient to express my gratitude for the sacrifices Stephanie, Asher, and Emma have made in service of three books. But in the year of COVID-19, protests for racial justice, economic uncertainty, and virtual learning, those sacrifices were all the more difficult to make and all the more meaningful. Thank you to the three blessings that mean more to me than life itself. I love you all so much it hurts.

Stephanie, you have held our family together through thick and thin, and for that you are a saint. Asher, I couldn't be more proud of your intellectual curiosity, your analytical abilities, or your innate kindness. I can remember you running around our house with a toy bat, shouting "home run"; now you run circles around me with your knowledge of Major League players and stats. Emma, my reader and rap battler, you light up every room you are in. I am proud that my daughter is so fierce and unafraid, so determined to knock down obstacles. I am certain that your respective talents will take both of you far in life, but you will never be far from my heart or my thoughts. In many ways, you have been asked to give up the most for this project—so much of our time together—and I am grateful for your forbearance.

Amie, it's hard to work with anyone else on a single story, much less three books. I have learned more from you than anyone in my professional career. You are an amazing reporter with unbelievable capacity to find the telling details, hear what a source isn't saying, and put everything together. More than that, you have become family. I love you.

Speaking of family, my sister, Amanda, has provided immeasurable support for this book and the others. My parents, Ira and Marin, have helped educate my children, taken them in, and given freely of their estimable counsel in how to report on and analyze this presidential election. My father-in-law, Bill Weintraub, and my mother-in-law, Ronnie Weintraub, welcomed our family for seven weeks when the pandemic hit, tactfully tolerating my odd behaviors—like smoking cigars in the morning. I am deeply grateful to my parents, my sister, and my in-laws for their encouragement and the sacrifices they have made for our family.

I want to thank Catherine Kim, David Firestone, Rebecca Sinderbrand, Gregg Birnbaum, Liz Johnstone, and all of my colleagues at NBCNews.com for giving me the support and space I needed to finish this book. I'd also like to recognize another writing partner—Stephanie Ruhle—who so often reminds me with her actions that talent and decency can and should occupy the same soul.

And, of course, a big shout-out to the family friends who have given me advice, simply lent their ears, or helped parent my kids during this time: Chris Pearson, Del Wilber, David Mortlock, Molly Jong-Fast, Dahlia Schweitzer, Greg Giroux, the Pearsons, the Bergmans, the Cohens, Janet Crowder, Hayley Alexander, Emma Morris, and Haley Wilson.

I have a small circle of smoking buddies who kept me company on the back patio during breaks in my work—you know who you are—and I am forever appreciative of your friendship. I am also thankful to the folks who work at Union Kitchen on Capitol Hill, W. Curtis Draper, Shelly's, and T.G.'s.

—JA

Working on a book in normal times is one of the toughest things to do. Working on a book during a pandemic is its own special kind of hell and I will be forever indebted to my family and friends for helping me get through this process in truly the darkest of times.

I can't possibly begin without a major nod to you, Jon. You're not only my coauthor and partner in crime. Eight years and three books later, you are family. While we've had our fair share of differences on each project, we've worked together so long and so close, we now see things in the same light—and sometimes even a little too similarly. I don't know anyone who works harder and is more efficient than you, Jallen. Thank you for your devotion to this book and to our ongoing partnership. It means so much.

I have the two best bosses in Bob Cusack and Ian Swanson, full stop. We've worked together at *The Hill* for almost a decade and, at this point, I see them both as my friends almost more than my editors. They've both been there for me in countless ways, offering encouragement, support, and counsel the entire time. I will never forget it.

This book, like the one before it, would not have gotten done without my mom, Esther Parnes, who constantly put her own needs and tutoring schedule aside to assist with babysitting and cooking while keeping an orderly home. As always, and now during high-pressure pandemic moments, she also consistently played the role of therapist, listening to the highs and lows of this journey while reassuring me even on the most stressful days at the end that it would all be okay. She provides tea and cookies along with love and moral support every day, and this book is as much hers as anyone's.

Thank you also to my sister, Sherry Parnes, who also offered her love and guidance, listened as I bounced ideas around during socially distant stoop sessions, and helped take my mind off the book with her understanding and humor when I needed it most.

Sending my love and much appreciation and gratitude to my dad, Henry Parnes, and to Abraham Zadi; Phillip and Magny Zadi; Tiffany, Jaron, and Alli Zadi; and Garri and Debbie Hendell. Sending more love and an endless amount of hugs to John and Cal, the greatest young men who have become fantastic role models, reading partners, and bunk bed companions to the youngest member of the family.

My best friends, the two people who have known me the longest outside of my family, were there every step along the way—even from a distance—to keep me in good spirits throughout this process. Jarah Greenfield, who used to field folded-up notes from me in seventh grade, is now the recipient of a constant stream of texts on a variety of topics. It's a good thing she's a rabbi. Simply put, I would be lost without her wisdom and her willingness to help. Craig Bode is my constant go-to when I want to celebrate or cry (and when I need emergency roofing advice, as was the case days before this book's deadline). No one knows me better, no one puts me more at ease, and when I ask for a second opinion, I know he knows the solution.

Thank you also to my dear friends Michael Collins, Lesley Clark, Bridget Petruczok, M. E. Sprengelmeyer, Niall Stanage,

Dolly Hernandez, Karin Tanabe, Jennifer Martinez, Kendra Marr Chaikind, Ben Tagoe, Jenn Grage, Chris Frates, Chris Donovan, Marni Tomljanovic, Libby Casey, Erika Bolstad, Sarah Hurwitz, Melissa Gross, Carlos Wolf, Keith Suthammanont, Jeremy Levine, Judy Kurtz, Sarah Courtney, Bethany Lesser, Becca Smith, Maria Underwood, and Mollie Bailey. I am beyond thankful to know each one of you and I hope I get to give you all a hug soon.

I send gratitude to the best neighbors and friends: David and Carolyn Sitler, Deborah Pearl Siegel, and Andy Burton and Katrina Spiratos, who are always there in a pinch and willing to lend a hand to make life a little easier. And I send my thanks to Claire Baldis-serotto, who stayed late and helped with childcare more times than I can count and is always amazing, patient, and creative.

And finally, once again, this book and everything else I do is for you, Remy Maddox. I tell you this all the time but here it is in print: You are the greatest thing that has ever happened to me.

—AP

NOTES
•

IN REPORTING THIS BOOK, WE SPOKE TO A WIDE VARIETY OF SOURCES with insight into the Biden, Trump, and unsuccessful Democratic primary campaigns, as well as other aspects of the 2020 election. We spoke to them almost exclusively on "background" so that they would feel comfortable revealing sensitive information and observations during the height of the race and so that they would not have to fear reprisals. In many cases, we describe what someone thought. Obviously, we are not able to read minds. Instead, the thinking is derived from interviews in which a source said he or she thought something, those in which sources described what someone else said about his or her own thinking, or documents that suggest what a person was thinking. Voting data came from uselectionatlas.org and state, county, and municipal elections boards, and, unless otherwise noted, polling averages came from Real Clear Politics.

CHAPTER 1: "YOU *KNOW* ME"

3 **He had run:** Jordyn Phelps, "What Happened 5 Other Times Joe Biden Was Deciding Whether to Run for President," ABC News, October 20, 2015, accessed November 24, 2020, abcnews.go.com/Politics/happened -times-joe-biden-deciding-run-president/story?id=34605046.

4 **he'd endured:** "Biden's Wife, Child Killed in Car Crash," *The New York Times*, December 19, 1972, accessed November 24, 2020, nytimes .com/1972/12/19/archives/bidens-wife-child-killed-in-car-crash.html.

4 **lost his eldest son:** Michael D. Shear, "Beau Biden, Vice President Joe Biden's Son, Dies at 46," *The New York Times,* May 30, 2015, accessed November 24, 2020, nytimes.com/2015/05/31/us/politics/joseph-r-biden-iii -vice-presidents-son-beau-dies-at-46.html.

4 **was broadly liked:** "2020 Democratic Presidential Nomination," Real Clear Politics, accessed November 24, 2020, realclearpolitics.com/epolls/2020 /president/us/2020_democratic_presidential_nomination-6730.html.

4 **like former New York mayor Rudy Giuliani:** Dan Janison, "Put a Pin in Your Trump Map to Mark Manhattan's Grand Havana Room Cigar Bar," *Newsday,* February 15, 2019, accessed November 24, 2020, newsday.com /long-island/columnists/dan-janison/trump-giuliani-manafort-russia-1 .27314079.

5 **had run for president himself in 2004:** "Sharpton Takes Step in Presidential Bid," *The New York Times,* January 22, 2003, accessed November 24, 2020, nytimes.com/2003/01/22/us/sharpton-takes-step-in-presidential-bid .html.

5 **half Sherpa and half flak jacket for Obama:** Glenn Thrush, "How Al Sharpton Became Obama's Go-To Man on Race," *Politico Magazine,* August 21, 2014, accessed November 24, 2020, politico.com/magazine/story /2014/08/al-sharpton-obama-race-110249.

5 **announced her bid that morning:** Astead W. Herndon, "Kamala Harris Declares Candidacy, Evoking King and Joining Diverse Field," *The New York Times,* January 21, 2019, accessed November 24, 2020, nytimes.com/2019 /01/21/us/politics/kamala-harris-2020-president.html.

6 **stocked America's prisons:** Sheryl Gay Stolberg and Astead W. Herndon, "'Lock the S.O.B.s Up': Joe Biden and the Era of Mass Incarceration," *The New York Times,* June 25, 2019, accessed November 24, 2020, nytimes.com /2019/06/25/us/joe-biden-crime-laws.html.

6 **ardent opposition to school busing in the 1970s:** Matt Viser, "Biden's Tough Talk on 1970s School Desegregation Plan Could Get New Scrutiny in Today's Democratic Party," *The Washington Post,* March 7, 2019, accessed November 26, 2020, washingtonpost.com/politics/bidens-tough-talk-on -1970s-school-desegregation-plan-could-get-new-scrutiny-in-todays -democratic-party/2019/03/07/9115583e-3eb2-11e9-a0d3-1210e58a94cf _story.html.

7 *Obama wasn't going to endorse him last time:* Michael Burke, "Obama Pushed Biden Not to Run in 2016: NY Times," *The Hill,* April 28, 2019, accessed November 26, 2020, thehill.com/homenews/campaign/441050 -obama-pushed-biden-not-to-run-in-2016-ny-times.

7 **declined to get on board with Biden early:** Brian Schwartz, "Billionaire GOP Donor and Trump Supporter Says He Rejected Joe Biden's Request for Fundraising Help," CNBC, June, 18, 2019, accessed November 26, 2020, cnbc.com/2019/06/18/billionaire-trump-donor-says-he-rejected-joe -bidens-request-for-fundraising-help.html.

8 **white supremacists gather with tiki torches:** Hawes Spencer and Sheryl Gay Stolberg, "White Nationalists March on University of Virginia," *The New York Times,* August 11, 2017, accessed November 26, 2020, nytimes.com /2017/08/11/us/white-nationalists-rally-charlottesville-virginia.html.

8 **"very fine people on both sides":** "Full Transcript and Video: Trump's News Conference in New York," *The New York Times,* August 15, 2017,

accessed November 26, 2020, nytimes.com/2017/08/15/us/politics/trump
-press-conference-transcript.html.

9 **registered a political action committee:** Alex Seitz-Wald, "Is New PAC Joe
Biden's Last Act in Politics or First Step Toward 2020?," NBC News, May,
31, 2017, accessed November 26, 2020, nbcnews.com/storyline/democrats
-vs-trump/new-pac-joe-biden-s-last-act-politics-or-first-n766891.

9 **he wrote in *The Atlantic* magazine:** Joe Biden, "'We Are Living Through a
Battle for the Soul of This Nation,'" *The Atlantic,* August 27, 2017, accessed November 26, 2020, theatlantic.com/politics/archive/2017/08/joe
-biden-after-charlottesville/538128/.

11 **took a job as a senior adviser:** Jack Torry, "Former Local Democratic
Leader Schultz Joins Biden's Staff," *The Columbus Dispatch,* December 16,
2013, accessed November 26, 2020, dispatch.com/article/20131216/NEWS
/312169764.

13 **leaked the news of her visit to the media:** Paul Kane, "Biden, Warren Huddle Amid 2016 Speculation," *The Washington Post,* August 23, 2015, accessed November 26, 2020, washingtonpost.com/news/post-politics/wp
/2015/08/22/biden-warren-huddle-amid-2016-speculation/.

13 **told *The Huffington Post*:** Howard Fineman, "Key Democrat's Advice for
Biden: Don't Run," *HuffPost,* October 19, 2015, accessed November 26,
2020, huffpost.com/entry/james-clyburn-joe-biden_n_562549f5e4b08589ef
486907.

13 **announce he wouldn't run:** "Transcript of Joe Biden's Remarks on Not
Running for President," *The New York Times,* October 21, 2015, accessed
November 26, 2020, nytimes.com/2015/10/22/us/politics/transcript-of-joe
-bidens-remarks-on-not-running-for-president.html.

17 **seemed to be enamored:** Matt Viser, "Beto O'Rourke, Who's Pondering a
2020 Presidential Bid, Met with Barack Obama," *The Washington Post,*
December 4, 2018, accessed November 26, 2020, washingtonpost.com
/politics/beto-orourke-met-with-barack-obama-as-he-ponders-a-2020
-presidential-campaign/2018/12/04/fa895cc8-f7fb-11e8-8d64-4e79db33382f
_story.html.

17 **Trump had won more than two hundred counties:** Jessica Taylor, "The
Counties That Flipped from Obama to Trump, in 3 Charts," NPR,
November 15, 2016, accessed November 26, 2020, npr.org/2016/11/15
/502032052/lots-of-people-voted-for-obama-and-trump-heres-where-in
-3-charts.

18 **to follow suit:** Sydney Ember and Astead W. Herndon, "How 'Abolish ICE'
Went from Social Media to Progressive Candidates' Rallying Cry," *The
New York Times,* June 29, 2018, accessed November 26, 2020, nytimes
.com/2018/06/29/us/politics/abolish-ice-midterms-immigration.html.

25 **razor-thin defeat in 2018:** Jessica Taylor, "Georgia's Stacey Abrams Admits
Defeat, Says Kemp Used 'Deliberate' Suppression to Win," NPR, November 16, 2018, accessed November 27, 2020, npr.org/2018/11/16/668753230
/democrat-stacey-abrams-ends-bid-for-georgia-governor-decrying-
suppression.

26 **his team leaked the idea:** Mike Allen, "Scoop: Biden Advisers Debate Stacey Abrams as Out-of-the-Gate VP Choice," *Axios,* March 21, 2019, accessed November 27, 2020, axios.com/2020-presidential-election-joe-biden
-stacey-abrams-vp-54472f8f-5bb2-4d1f-bc7c-0544a09ebba5.html.

CHAPTER 2: "WE AVOIDED THAT MISSTEP,
BUT NOT ALL OF THEM"

29 **hired some of the best talent in Iowa:** Thomas Beaumont, "Elizabeth Warren Makes Key 2020 Hires Ahead of 1st Iowa Trip," Associated Press, January 2, 2019, accessed November 27, 2020, apnews.com/article/82a9852e251 a42de9d89a2748d3a24fb.

29 **He'd gotten 1 percent there in 2008:** "Election 2008: Iowa Caucus Results," *The New York Times,* December 16, 2016, accessed November 27, 2020, nytimes.com/elections/2008/primaries/results/states/IA.html.

33 **revealed that "an awkward kiss changed how I saw Joe Biden":** Lucy Flores, "An Awkward Kiss Changed How I Saw Joe Biden," *New York* magazine, March 29, 2019, accessed November 27, 2020, nymag.com /intelligencer/2019/03/an-awkward-kiss-changed-how-i-saw-joe-biden.html.

34 **put out the statement:** Bill Russo, @BillR, Twitter, March 31, 2019, accessed November 27, 2020, twitter.com/BillR/status/1112339598699626501.

34 **awkwardly touching, hugging, or kissing other women:** Matthew Yglesias, "The Controversy Over Joe Biden's Treatment of Women, Explained," *Vox,* April 3, 2019, accessed November 27, 2020, vox.com/2019/4/2/18290345 /joe-biden-lucy-flores-amy-lappos.

34 **said publicly that they believed Flores:** Jasmine Wright, "Elizabeth Warren Says Joe Biden Needs to Give an Answer for Allegation of Inappropriate Touching," CNN, March 30, 2019, accessed November 27, 2020, cnn.com /2019/03/30/politics/elizabeth-warren-joe-biden-allegation-reaction/index .html.

35 **released a face-to-camera video:** Joe Biden, @JoeBiden, Twitter, April 3, 2019, accessed November 27, 2020, twitter.com/JoeBiden/status/1113515 882960052224.

35 **deliver a eulogy at former senator Fritz Hollings's funeral:** Jonathan Martin, "Biden, at Hollings Funeral, Talks About How 'People Can Change,'" *The New York Times,* April 16, 2019, accessed November 27, 2020, nytimes .com/2019/04/16/us/politics/biden-hollings-funeral.html.

35 **would host the first major fundraising event:** Andrew Seidman, "Joe Biden, at Philly Fund-Raiser Hosted by Comcast Exec, Says Trump Has 'Shredded' America's Moral Fabric," *The Philadelphia Inquirer,* April 25, 2019, accessed November 27, 2020, fusion.inquirer.com/news/joe-biden -philadelphia-comcast-fundraiser-david-l-cohen-2020-20190426.html.

35 **agreed to cohost a similar shindig:** Brian Slodysko, "AP Source: Biden Rakes in $750,000 at Hollywood Fundraiser," Associated Press, May 9, 2019, accessed November 27, 2020, apnews.com/article/000e903bf1bd4d179 e90612af75bd33d.

35 **he added Symone Sanders:** Julie Pace and Errin Haines Whack, "Biden Hires Strategist Symone Sanders, Adds Diversity to Bid," April 25, 2019, accessed November 27, 2020, apnews.com/article/2572f844ea074460a2f952 43c433f9bc.

35 **and Cristóbal Alex:** Alex Thompson, "Biden Nabs Big-Name Latino Operative in Latest Sign He's Running," *Politico,* March 6, 2019, accessed November 27, 2020, politico.com/story/2019/03/06/biden-2020-election-latinos -1206534.

38 **assemble for the She the People presidential forum:** Maggie Astor, "At She

the People Forum, 2020 Candidates Speak Directly to Women of Color,"
The New York Times, April 24, 2019, accessed November 27, 2020,
nytimes.com/2019/04/24/us/politics/she-the-people-forum-2020-women
.html.

CHAPTER 3: REFORM OR REVOLUTION?

42 **was a former Republican:** Alex Thompson, "'Liz Was a Diehard Conservative,'" *Politico Magazine,* April 12, 2019, accessed November 28, 2020,
politico.com/magazine/story/2019/04/12/elizabeth-warren-profile-young
-republican-2020-president-226613.

42 **had more support than Biden:** "2020 Democratic Presidential Nomination," Real Clear Politics, accessed November 28, 2020, realclearpolitics
.com/epolls/2020/president/us/2020_democratic_presidential_nomination
-6730.html.

43 **he had cited her absence:** Donovan Slack, "Why Bernie Sanders Decided to
Run for President," *USA Today,* February 15, 2016, accessed November 28,
2020, usatoday.com/story/news/politics/onpolitics/2016/02/15/bernie
-sanders-bill-press-2016-democratic-presidential-primary/80411020/.

44 **Trump had been taunting Warren:** Jonathan Allen, "Trump Challenges
'Pocahontas' Warren to DNA Test to Prove She's Native American," NBC
News, July 5, 2018, accessed November 28, 2020, nbcnews.com/politics
/politics-news/trump-challenges-pocahontas-warren-dna-test-prove-she-s
-native-n889206.

44 **releasing results of a DNA test:** Jonathan Martin, "Elizabeth Warren's
DNA Results Draw Rebuke from Trump and Raise Questions," *The New
York Times,* October 15, 2018, accessed November 28, 2020, nytimes.com
/2018/10/15/us/politics/elizabeth-warren-dna-ancestry.html.

44 **fought him tooth and nail:** Alex Seitz-Wald, "Ahead of Democratic Platform Meeting, Warren Urges Opposition to TPP Trade Deal," NBC News,
July 7, 2016, accessed November 28, 2020, nbcnews.com/politics/2016
-election/ahead-democratic-platform-meeting-warren-urges-opposition
-tpp-trade-deal-n605151.

44 **tanked one of his Treasury Department nominees:** Ben White, "Warren
Wins on Weiss Nomination," *Politico,* January 12, 2015, accessed November 28, 2020, politico.com/story/2015/01/antonio-weiss-pulls-out-treasury
-undersecretary-114191.

45 **she said on an April episode:** David Weigel, "Warren Says She 'Was Troubled' by Obama Speaking Gig," *The Washington Post,* April 27, 2017, accessed November 28, 2020, washingtonpost.com/news/powerpost/wp/2017
/04/27/warren-says-she-was-troubled-by-obama-speaking-gig/.

47 **once convicted of embezzling union money:** Brian Mahoney, "Sanders Adviser Was Convicted of Union Embezzling," *Politico,* February 1, 2016, accessed November 28, 2020, politico.com/story/2016/02/bernie-sanders
-union-embezzle-campaign-consultant-218567.

47 **recommended dramatically reducing:** Kevin Robillard, "DNC 'Unity'
Panel Recommends Huge Cut in Superdelegates," *Politico,* December 9,
2017, accessed November 28, 2020, politico.com/story/2017/12/09/dnc
-superdelegates-unity-commission-288634.

54 **won reelection handily in the 2018 midterms:** Steve LeBlanc and Bob Sals-

berg, "Sen. Warren Wins Re-Election, Promptly Rips into Trump," Associated Press, November 7, 2018, accessed November 28, 2020, apnews.com /article/7d7f1849c6b443dcbbfc08e87f032506.

54 **she took with little girls:** Abby K. Wood, "Elizabeth Warren's Selfie with My Daughter Went Viral Because Pinkie Promises Mean Something," NBC News, September 18, 2019, accessed November 28, 2020, nbcnews.com /think/opinion/elizabeth-warren-s-selfie-my-daughter-went-viral-because -pinkie-ncna1055561.

54 **husbanded about half the $21 million:** Shane Goldmacher, "How Elizabeth Warren Raised Big Money Before She Denounced Big Money," *The New York Times,* September 9, 2019, accessed November 28, 2020, nytimes.com /2019/09/09/us/politics/elizabeth-warren-2020.html.

55 **she called "big, structural changes":** Elizabeth Warren, "Big, Structural Change: We've Done It Before, and We Can Do It Again," *Medium,* May 23, 2019, accessed November 28, 2020, medium.com/@teamwarren/big -structural-change-weve-done-it-before-and-we-can-do-it-again-c9a042ed 8b59.

55 **was New Year's Eve 2018:** Astead W. Herndon and Alexander Burns, "Elizabeth Warren Announces Iowa Trip as She Starts Running for President in 2020," *The New York Times,* December 31, 2018, accessed November 28, 2020, nytimes.com/2018/12/31/us/politics/elizabeth-warren-2020-president -announcement.html.

55 **speaking to hundreds of Iowans:** Astead W. Herndon, "Elizabeth Warren Campaigns in Iowa: 'This Is How It Starts,'" *The New York Times,* January 4, 2019, accessed November 28, 2020, nytimes.com/2019/01/04/us /politics/elizabeth-warren-iowa.html.

56 **wrote a letter seeking a meeting:** Alex Thompson, "Bernie Alumni Seek Meeting to Address 'Sexual Violence' on '16 Campaign," *Politico,* December 30, 2018, accessed November 28, 2020, politico.com/story/2018/12/30 /bernie-sanders-campaign-harassment-1077014.

56 **was in court for pretrial hearings:** Adam Reiss and David K. Li, "Harvey Weinstein's Sexual Assault Case Moves Forward as Judge Declines to Toss Charges," NBC News, December 20, 2018, accessed November 28, 2020, nbcnews.com/news/us-news/harvey-weinstein-s-sexual-assault-case-moves -forward-judge-declines-n950321.

56 **issued a long statement:** David Weigel and Felicia Sonmez, "Bernie Sanders Apologizes, Says He Didn't Know About $30,000 Settlement of 2016 Campaign Staffer Accused of Sexual Harassment," *The Washington Post,* January 10, 2019, accessed November 28, 2020, washingtonpost.com/politics /bernie-sanders-apologizes-says-he-didnt-know-about-30000-settlement-of -2016-campaign-staffer-accused-of-sexual-harassment/2019/01/10/db2c061e -14fc-11e9-90a8-136fa44b80ba_story.html.

57 **hired Faiz Shakir:** Gregory Krieg, "Sanders Taps New Campaign Manager, Gets Endorsements From Top Vermont Lawmakers," CNN, February 19, 2019, accessed November 28, 2020, cnn.com/2019/02/19/politics/bernie -sanders-campaign-manager-endorsements-2020-primary/index.html.

57 **started with immigration:** Jason Horowitz, "Bernie Sanders's '100% Brooklyn' Roots Are as Unshakable as His Accent," *The New York Times,* July 24, 2015, accessed November 28, 2020, nytimes.com/2015/07/25/us /politics/bernie-sanderss-100-brooklyn-roots-show-beyond-his-accent.html.

58 **had called Mexicans rapists and murderers:** Suzanne Gamboa, "Donald

Trump Announces Presidential Bid by Trashing Mexico, Mexicans," NBC News, June 16, 2015, accessed November 28, 2020, nbcnews.com/news /latino/donald-trump-announces-presidential-bid-trashing-mexico -mexicans-n376521.

58 **tried to discourage illegal immigration:** Colleen Long and Jill Colvin, "Trump Suggests Family Separation Policy Deters Migrants," Associated Press, April 10, 2019, accessed November 28, 2020, apnews.com/article /2fd81e62756b4624a5ddc86acca8a19e.

59 **choosing a little patch of grass:** "Senator Bernie Sanders News Conference," C-SPAN, April 30, 2015, accessed November 28, 2020, c-span.org /video/?325700-1/senator-bernie-sanders-i-vt-news-conference.

60 **announcing in mid-February that he would run:** Sydney Ember, "Bernie Sanders, Once the Progressive Outlier, Joins a Crowded Presidential Field," *The New York Times,* February 19, 2019, accessed November 28, 2020, nytimes.com/2019/02/19/us/politics/bernie-sanders-2020.html.

60 **went to Brooklyn College:** Gregory Krieg, "'I Know Where I Came From!': Sanders Begins 2020 Campaign with Personal Speech in Brooklyn," CNN, March 2, 2019, accessed November 28, 2020, cnn.com/2019/03/02/politics /bernie-sanders-personal-brooklyn-speech-2020/index.html.

60 **routinely denied involvement in social media campaigns:** Katie Bernard and Gregory Krieg, "Bernie Sanders to Supporters: 'I Condemn Bullying and Harassment of Any Kind,'" CNN, February 24, 2019, accessed November 28, 2020, cnn.com/2019/02/24/politics/sanders-letter-to-surrogates/index .html.

60 **engaged in an all-out war:** Jonathan Allen and Alex Seitz-Wald, "Inside Bernie-World's War on Beto O'Rourke," NBC News, December 23, 2018, accessed November 28, 2020, nbcnews.com/politics/2020-election/inside -bernie-world-s-war-beto-o-rourke-n951018.

61 **sent a message to his supporters:** Katie Bernard and Gregory Krieg, "Bernie Sanders to Supporters: 'I Condemn Bullying and Harassment of Any Kind,'" CNN, February 24, 2019, accessed November 28, 2020, cnn.com /2019/02/24/politics/sanders-letter-to-surrogates/index.html.

61 **would hire the online warrior:** James Oliphant, "Bernie Sanders Hires Beto O'Rourke Critic as Top Aide in 2020 Race," *Reuters,* March 19, 2019, accessed November 28, 2020, https://www.reuters.com/article/us-usa-election -sanders-idUSKCN1R02GZ

61 **pay him more than $150,000 in campaign funds** authors' review of Federal Election Commission Disbursement Data, https://www.fec.gov/data /disbursements/?data_type=processed&recipient_name=David+Sirota &two_year_transaction_period=2020&min_date=01%2F01%2F2019 &max_date=12%2F31%2F2020

62 **gashed his forehead open:** Cleve R. Wootson Jr. and John Wagner, "Bernie Sanders Gets Seven Stitches on His Head, Maintains Campaign Schedule," *The Washington Post,* March 15, 2019, accessed November 28, 2020, washingtonpost.com/politics/bernie-sanders-gets-seven-stitches-on-his -head-maintains-campaign-schedule/2019/03/15/fc938d10-474a-11e9-aaf8 -4512a6fe3439_story.html.

62 **appeared at events:** Gregory Krieg, "Bernie Sanders Stays on the Stump After Receiving Stitches for Head Wound," CNN, March 16, 2019, accessed November 28, 2020, cnn.com/2019/03/15/politics/bernie-sanders-stitches -south-carolina/index.html.

CHAPTER 4: "THIS IS JUST A BUNCH OF BULLSHIT!"

64 **he'd gone head-to-head:** "Transcript And Audio: Vice Presidential Debate," NPR, October 11, 2012, accessed November 30, 2020, npr.org/2012/10/11 /162754053/transcript-biden-ryan-vice-presidential-debate.

64 **gone on an extended rant:** Katie Glueck and Annie Karni, "Trump and Biden Get Personal in Iowa Skirmish," *The New York Times,* June 11, 2019, accessed November 30, 2020, nytimes.com/2019/06/11/us/politics /iowa-trump-biden.html.

65 **joined the segregationists:** Derrick Bryson Taylor, Sheryl Gay Stolberg and Astead W. Herndon, "A Brief History of Joe Biden and School Busing," *The New York Times,* July 15, 2019, accessed November 30, 2020, nytimes .com/2019/07/15/us/joe-biden-busing-timeline.html.

66 **would have allowed schools:** "Antibusing Measure Approved in Senate," *The New York Times,* September 18, 1975, accessed November 30, 2020, nytimes.com/1975/09/18/archives/anti-busing-measure-approved-in-senate .html.

66 *The New York Times* **accused him:** "Undoing Justice," *The New York Times,* September 19, 1975, accessed December 29, 2020, https://times machine.nytimes.com/timesmachine/1975/09/19/80057347.html?page Number=36

66 **would note Biden's aggressive:** Byrd, Robert C., "Robert C. Byrd: Child of the Appalachian Coalfields," *West Virginia University Press,* 2005.

66 **agreed with him at the time:** Frank Newport, "Biden, Harris, Busing, Compromise and Public Opinion," Gallup, July 18, 2019, accessed November 30, 2020, gallup.com/opinion/polling-matters/259985/biden-harris -busing-compromise-public-opinion.aspx.

68 **waxed nostalgic about working:** Isaac Stanley-Becker, "'We Got Things Done': Biden Recalls 'Civility' with Segregationist Senators," *The Washington Post,* June 19, 2019, accessed November 30, 2020, washingtonpost .com/nation/2019/06/19/joe-biden-james-eastland-herman-talmadge -segregationists-civility/.

68 **called on Biden to apologize:** Scott Detrow, "Democrats Blast Biden for Recalling 'Civil' Relationship with Segregationists," NPR, June 19, 2019, accessed November 30, 2020, npr.org/2019/06/19/734103488/democrats-blast -biden-for-recalling-civil-relationship-with-segregationists.

69 **said in just the kind of ad hoc Capitol interaction:** Rebecca Klar, "Harris: 'Deeply' Concerned by Biden Segregationist Comments," *The Hill,* June 19, 2019, accessed November 30, 2020, thehill.com/homenews /campaign/449400-kamala-harris-deeply-concerned-by-biden-segregationist -comments.

69 **at about 12 percent by the end of February:** Harry Enten, "Kamala Harris Had a Very Good First Month of the 2020 Democratic Primary Campaign," CNN, February 9, 2019, accessed November 30, 2020, cnn.com /2019/02/09/politics/kamala-harris-first-good-month-poll-of-the-week /index.html.

69 **raised $1.5 million in her first twenty-four hours:** Christopher Cadelago, "Kamala Harris Raises $1.5 Million in First 24 Hours," *Politico,* January 22, 2019, accessed November 30, 2020, politico.com/story/2019/01/22 /kamala-harris-15-million-first-day-1119125.

70 **calling it "the best opening so far":** Peter Baker and Maggie Haberman, "Trump, in Interview, Calls Wall Talks 'Waste of Time' and Dismisses Investigations," *The New York Times,* January 31, 2019, accessed November 30, 2020, nytimes.com/2019/01/31/us/politics/trump-wall-investigations-interview.html.

70 **commissioned a poll:** Daniel Strauss, "Poll: Black Voters Favor Biden, Consumed by Pocketbook Issues Ahead of 2020," *Politico,* June 11, 2019, accessed November 30, 2020, politico.com/story/2019/06/11/biden-black-economic-alliance-poll-2020-1359082.

71 **asked her about her personal experience:** Veronica Rocha, Brian Ries, and Kyle Blaine, "Kamala Harris Takes Questions at CNN Town Hall," CNN, January 28, 2019, accessed November 30, 2020, cnn.com/politics/live-news/kamala-harris-town-hall-iowa/h_befa00377d7f6b5058e123fa752ae5c6.

71 **"Jamaica is not America":** Keka Araujo, "Don Lemon and April Ryan Debate Intensely Over Kamala Harris' 'Blackness,'" *DiversityInc,* February 14, 2019, accessed November 30, 2020, diversityinc.com/don-lemon-and-april-ryan-debate-kamala-harris-blackness/.

75 **winnow the field for the debate stage:** Reid J. Epstein, Lisa Lerer, and Matt Stevens, "The Democratic Debate Lineups Are Set. Here's What to Expect," *The New York Times,* June 14, 2019, accessed November 30, 2020, nytimes.com/2019/06/14/us/politics/democratic-debates-2020.html.

77 **attack Trump and Sanders:** "Transcript: Night 2 of the First Democratic Debate," *The Washington Post,* June 27, 2019, accessed November 30, 2020, washingtonpost.com/politics/2019/06/28/transcript-night-first-democratic-debate/.

78 **"I do not believe you are a racist":** Jonathan Allen, "Kamala Harris, Joe Biden in Tense Exchange on Busing at Democratic Debate," NBC News, June 27, 2019, accessed November 30, 2020, nbcnews.com/politics/2020-election/biden-harris-busing-integration-became-flashpoint-debate-stage-n1024216.

80 **Harris tweeted:** Kamala Harris, @KamalaHarris, "There was a little girl in California who was bussed to school. That little girl was me. #DemDebate," Twitter, June 27, 2019, accessed November 30, 2020, twitter.com/KamalaHarris/status/1144427976609734658.

80 **her campaign began marketing:** Rachel Frazin, "Harris Campaign Sells 'That Little Girl Was Me' Shirts After Debate Confrontation with Biden," *The Hill,* June 28, 2019, accessed November 30, 2020, thehill.com/homenews/campaign/450831-harris-campaign-sells-that-little-girl-was-me-shirts-after-debate-comments.

81 **Harris's coffers were being flooded:** Christopher Cadelago, "Kamala Harris Raises $2 Million in 24 Hours After Debate," *Politico,* June 29, 2019, accessed November 30, 2020, politico.com/story/2019/06/29/kamala-harris-biden-debate-1390512.

83 **deliver a speech on his ties to Obama:** Colby Itkowitz and Matt Viser, "Biden Says He Regrets Remarks About Working with Segregationists, but Stands by His Record on Issues of Race," *The Washington Post,* July 6, 2019, accessed November 30, 2020, washingtonpost.com/politics/joe-biden-will-deliver-a-speech-defending-his-record-on-issues-of-race/2019/07/06/da21d734-9ff9-11e9-9ed4-c9089972ad5a_story.html.

83 **Buttigieg calling Vice President Mike Pence:** Allan Smith, "2020 Candidate

Buttigieg Calls Pence 'Cheerleader of the Porn Star Presidency,'" NBC News, March 11, 2019, accessed November 30, 2020, nbcnews.com/politics /2020-election/2020-candidate-buttigieg-calls-pence-cheerleader-porn-star -presidency-n981661.

84 **Harris said no:** Alexandra Jaffe and Thomas Beaumont, "Harris Says Busing Should Be Considered, Not Mandated," Associated Press, July 3, 2019, accessed November 30, 2020, apnews.com/article/586b1e81cb684654b0cf68 9b9074c1cb.

84 **saw a sharp rise in her polling numbers:** Matt Stevens, "Kamala Harris Surges in 3 Polls After Strong Debate Performance," *The New York Times,* July 2, 2019, accessed November 30, 2020, nytimes.com/2019/07/02/us /politics/kamala-harris-polls.html.

84 **briefly moved into second place:** "2020 Democratic Presidential Nomination," Real Clear Politics, accessed November 30, 2020, realclearpolitics .com/epolls/2020/president/us/2020_democratic_presidential_nomination -6730.html.

84 **jumped into second place there:** Andrew Prokop, "A New Iowa Poll Shows Kamala Harris on the Rise," *Vox,* July 2, 2019, accessed November 30, 2020, vox.com/policy-and-politics/2019/7/2/20678960/poll-kamala-harris -biden-iowa.

84 **insisting that Medicare for All would not end private insurance:** Jeff Stein, "Kamala Harris Changes Answer on Abolishing Private Health Insurance, Saying She Misheard Debate Question," *The Washington Post,* June 28, 2019, accessed November 30, 2020, washingtonpost.com/politics/2019/06 /28/kamala-harris-reverses-answer-abolishing-private-health-insurance -saying-she-misheard-question/.

84 **rolled out her own version:** Abby Goodnough and Astead W. Herndon, "Kamala Harris Sets Up Debate Showdown on Health Care With New Plan," *The New York Times,* July 29, 2019, accessed November 30, 2020, nytimes.com/2019/07/29/us/politics/kamala-harris-medicare-for -all.html.

CHAPTER 5: "YOU FORGOT BIDEN"

87 **turning Buttigieg:** David Freedlander, "'I Want Him on Everything': Meet the Woman Behind the Buttigieg Media Frenzy," *Politico Magazine,* April 29, 2019, accessed December 1, 2020, politico.com/magazine/story/2019 /04/29/lis-smith-buttigieg-2020-president-campaign-manager-226756.

87 **volunteer in Iowa:** Holly Bailey, "What Pete Buttigieg Learned Organizing for Obama in Iowa: 'You Can Reach People.' And Wear Boots," *The Washington Post,* January 22, 2020, accessed December 1, 2020, washingtonpost .com/politics/2020/01/22/what-pete-buttigieg-learned-organizing-obama -iowa-you-can-reach-people-wear-boots/.

88 **had come earlier in the month:** Eric Bradner, "Pete Buttigieg Makes Star Turn in Town Hall Spotlight," CNN, March 11, 2019, accessed December 1, 2020, cnn.com/2019/03/11/politics/pete-buttigieg-star-turn-cnn-town -hall-2020-democratic-presidential-race/index.html.

89 **led to quite a bit of speculation:** Amber Phillips, "What's a Contested Convention, and What Would It Mean for the 2020 Race?," *The Washington Post,* March 4, 2020, accessed December 1, 2020, washingtonpost.com

/politics/2020/03/04/whats-contested-convention what does-it-mean-2020
-race/.

89 **polls also showed:** Phillip Bump, "A New National Poll Answers a Critical
Question: Who is the Second Choice of Democratic Voters?," *The Washington Post,* January 28, 2020, accessed December 1, 2020, washingtonpost
.com/politics/2020/01/28/new-national-poll-answers-critical-question-who
-is-second-choice-democratic-voters/.

90 **swore off high-dollar fundraising events:** Alex Thompson and Elena
Schneider, "Warren Swears Off High-Dollar Fundraisers in Potential General Election," *Politico,* October 9, 2019, accessed December 1, 2020,
politico.com/news/2019/10/09/warren-fundraisers-general-election-2020
-043127.

90 **spent down her war chest fast:** MJ Lee, "Elizabeth Warren Nabs Obama's
Chief Digital Strategist, Beefs Up National Staff," CNN, January 4, 2019,
accessed December 1, 2020, cnn.com/2019/01/04/politics/elizabeth-warren
-obama-digital-hire/index.html.

90 **sat tied at 15 percent:** "2020 Democratic Presidential Nomination," Real
Clear Politics, accessed December 1, 2020, realclearpolitics.com/epolls/2020
/president/us/2020_democratic_presidential_nomination-6730.html.

91 **what amounted to an all-purpose aide:** Stephen Braun, Wilson Ring, and
Steve Peoples, "Is Jane Sanders the Most Powerful Woman Not Running
in 2020?," Associated Press, March 17, 2019, accessed December 1, 2020,
apnews.com/article/bb512b6ff6174474bf7ae3ccfbead19b.

92 **at the tail end of July:** Sarah Ewall-Wice, "Democratic Debate: Lineup for
July Democratic Presidential Debates in Detroit Revealed," CBS News,
July 18, 2019, accessed December 1, 2020, cbsnews.com/news/cnn
-democratic-debate-lineup-for-july-democratic-presidential-debates-in
-detroit-revealed-today-2019-07-18/.

93 **rate or the depth Warren was:** Thomas Kaplan and Jim Tankersley, "Elizabeth Warren Has Lots of Plans. Together, They Would Remake the Economy," *The New York Times,* June 10, 2019, accessed December 1, 2020,
nytimes.com/2019/06/10/us/politics/elizabeth-warren-2020-policies
-platform.html.

93 **quoted in stories leading up to the debate:** Gregory Krieg, MJ Lee, and
Ryan Nobles, "Hoping for a Warren-Sanders Clash? Their Campaigns Say
Don't Hold Your Breath," CNN, July 28, 2019, accessed December 1, 2020,
cnn.com/2019/07/28/politics/bernie-sanders-elizabeth-warren-detroit
-debate-progressives/index.html.

93 **parted ways with A-level consultants:** Astead W. Herndon and Jonathan
Martin, "Elizabeth Warren Loses Finance Director as She Struggles in Early
Fund-Raising," *The New York Times,* March 31, 2019, accessed December 1, 2020, nytimes.com/2019/03/31/us/politics/elizabeth-warren
-fundraising.html.

94 **ran an ill-advised campaign:** Deirdre Walsh, "Who Is Tim Ryan? Meet the
Man Challenging Nancy Pelosi," CNN, November 22, 2016, accessed December 1, 2020, cnn.com/2016/11/22/politics/who-is-tim-ryan/index.html.

94 **accused Warren and Sanders:** "Transcript: The first Night of the Second
Democratic Debate," *The Washington Post,* July 30, 2019, accessed December 1, 2020, washingtonpost.com/politics/2019/07/31/transcript-first-night
-second-democratic-debate/.

94 **Warren hit back:** Thomas Kaplan, "Elizabeth Warren's Slam on John Delaney Was Called the Line of the Night. Here's What She Said," *The New York Times,* July 30, 2019, accessed December 1, 2020, nytimes.com/2019/07/30/us/politics/elizabeth-warren-debate.html.

95 **floated down toward the pack:** Aaron Blake, "It's Harris and Warren Up, Biden and the Men Down in First Post-Debate 2020 Democratic Poll," *The Washington Post,* July 1, 2019, accessed December 1, 2020, washingtonpost.com/politics/2019/07/01/its-harris-warren-up-biden-men-down-first-post-debate-democratic-poll/.

95 **saw his favorability rating drop:** Aaron Bycoffe and Julia Wolfe, "A Final Look at Who Won and Lost the First Democratic Debates," FiveThirtyEight, July 1, 2019, accessed December 1, 2020, projects.fivethirtyeight.com/democratic-debate-poll/.

95 **pulled off the early-state campaign trail:** Brian Schwartz, "Kamala Harris Raises Over $1 Million at Hamptons and Martha's Vineyard Fundraisers," CNBC, August 22, 2019, accessed December 1, 2020, cnbc.com/2019/08/22/kamala-harris-raises-1-million-at-hamptons-marthas-vineyard-fundraisers.html.

96 **report having raised:** Reid J. Epstein and Astead W. Herndon, "Elizabeth Warren's Fund-Raising: $19.1 Million in 3 Months, Outpacing Sanders," *The New York Times,* July 8, 2019, accessed December 1, 2020, nytimes.com/2019/07/08/us/politics/elizabeth-warren-fundraising.html.

97 **rose well past Sanders:** "2020 Democratic Presidential Nomination," Real Clear Politics, accessed December 1, 2020, realclearpolitics.com/epolls/2020/president/us/2020_democratic_presidential_nomination-6730.html.

97 **first debated one another directly:** Michael M. Grynbaum, "Houston to Host Third Democratic Debate on ABC," *The New York Times,* July 9, 2019, accessed December 1, 2020, nytimes.com/2019/07/09/business/media/democratic-debate-abc-houston.html.

97 **asked Warren about Medicare for All:** "Transcript: The Third Democratic Debate," *The Washington Post,* September 12, 2019, accessed December 1, 2020, washingtonpost.com/politics/2019/09/13/transcript-third-democratic-debate/.

97 **refused to say:** Danielle Kurtzleben, "Democratic Debate Exposes Deep Divides Among Candidates Over Health Care," NPR, September 13, 2019, accessed December 1, 2020, npr.org/2019/09/13/760364830/democratic-debate-exposes-deep-divides-among-candidates-over-health-care.

97 **announced a tweak:** Chelsea Janes, David Weigel, and Holly Bailey, "Sen. Bernie Sanders Changes How Medicare-for-All Plan Treats Union Contracts in Face of Opposition by Organized Labor," *The Washington Post,* August 21, 2019, accessed December 1, 2020, washingtonpost.com/politics/sen-bernie-sanders-changes-medicare-for-all-plan-in-face-of-opposition-by-organized-labor/2019/08/21/d8144e06-c423-11e9-9986-1fb3e4397be4_story.html.

98 **called her "evasive":** Thomas Beaumont, "Buttigieg Calls Warren 'Extremely Evasive' on Health Taxes," Associated Press, September 19, 2019, accessed December 1, 2020, apnews.com/article/c5153dd8ebe6483aa619d79689ebf562.

98 **she pushed past:** "Biden Holds Lead, Warren on the Chase," Monmouth University, August 8, 2019, accessed December 1, 2020, monmouth.edu/polling-institute/reports/monmouthpoll_ia_080819/.

98 **overtook Biden for the lead:** Reid J. Epstein and Lisa Lerer, "Warren Leads in New Iowa Poll with Biden Second," *The New York Times,* September 21, 2019, accessed December 1, 2020, nytimes.com/2019/09/21/us/politics/Iowa -biden-warren-.html.

99 **suffered a heart attack:** Sydney Ember, "Bernie Sanders Had Heart Attack, His Doctors Say as He Leaves Hospital," *The New York Times,* October 4, 2019, accessed December 1, 2020, nytimes.com/2019/10/04/us/politics /bernie-sanders-hospital.html.

100 **put out a statement:** Sydney Ember and Jonathan Martin, "Bernie Sanders Is Hospitalized, Raising Questions About His Candidacy," *The New York Times,* October 2, 2019, accessed December 1, 2020, nytimes.com/2019 /10/02/us/politics/bernie-sanders-health.html.

101 **on his own finger:** Ruby Cramer, "You Don't Know Bernie Sanders," BuzzFeed News, December 16, 2019, accessed January 16, 2021, https:// www.buzzfeednews.com/article/rubycramer/you-dont-know-bernie-sanders.

103 **met for the fourth time:** Maggie Astor, "The Times and CNN Will Host the Next Democratic Debate in Ohio," *The New York Times,* September 13, 2019, accessed December 1, 2020, nytimes.com/2019/09/13/us /politics/next-democratic-debate-october.html.

103 **reported raising:** Maggie Severns, "Biden Raises $15 Million During Third Quarter," *Politico,* October 3, 2019, accessed December 1, 2020, politico .com/news/2019/10/03/joe-biden-campaign-third-quarter-fundraising -026553.

103 **hovering around the 75 percent mark:** Marc Caputo and Natasha Korecki, "'They've Got No Margin for Error': Biden Cash Crunch Raises Alarms," *Politico,* October 16, 2019, accessed December 1, 2020, politico.com/news /2019/10/16/biden-fundraising-2020-049062.

103 **weren't bound by ideological tests:** Nathaniel Rakich, "Biden Supporters Used to Say Sanders Was Their Second Choice—Now They Say Warren," FiveThirtyEight, October 14, 2019, accessed December 1, 2020, fivethirtyeight.com/features/biden-supporters-used-to-say-sanders-was -their-second-choice-now-they-say-warren/.

104 **CNBC reported:** Mike Calia and Brian Schwartz, "Mike Bloomberg Is Pre- paring to Enter the Democratic Presidential Primary," CNBC, November 7, 2019, accessed December 1, 2020, cnbc.com/2019/11/07/mike-bloomberg -prepares-to-enter-at-least-one-democratic-primary-report.html.

104 **decided against:** Alexander Burns, "Michael Bloomberg Will Not Run for President in 2020," *The New York Times,* March 5, 2019, accessed Decem- ber 1, 2020, nytimes.com/2019/03/05/us/politics/michael-bloomberg-2020 .html.

105 **launched her campaign:** Dan Merica and Devan Cole, "Sen. Amy Klobu- char Enters Presidential Race," CNN, February 10, 2019, accessed Decem- ber 1, 2020, cnn.com/2019/02/10/politics/klobuchar-announcement-2020 -president/index.html.

105 **barely qualified:** Kevin Schaul, "Who Qualified for the Fourth Democratic Debate," *The Washington Post,* October 2, 2019, accessed December 1, 2020, washingtonpost.com/politics/2019/09/17/who-has-qualified-fourth -democratic-debate/?arc404=true.

105 **running low on funds:** Sarah Almukhtar, Troy Griggs, Thomas Kaplan, and Rachel Shorey, "Who's Up and Who's Down in 2020 Democratic Fund- Raising," *The New York Times,* October 16, 2019, accessed December 1,

2020, nytimes.com/interactive/2019/10/16/us/elections/democratic-q3
-fundraising.html.

106 **overtook Biden:** "2020 Democratic Presidential Nomination," Real Clear
Politics, accessed December 1, 2020, realclearpolitics.com/epolls/2020
/president/us/2020_democratic_presidential_nomination-6730.html.

106 **"At least Bernie is being honest":** "The October Democratic Debate Transcript," *The Washington Post,* October 15, 2019, accessed December 1,
2020, washingtonpost.com/politics/2019/10/15/october-democratic-debate
-transcript/.

107 **against the backdrop of housing projects:** Holly Otterbein, " 'I Am Back':
Sanders Tops Warren with Massive New York City Rally," *Politico,* October 19, 2019, accessed December 1, 2020, politico.com/news/2019/10/19
/bernie-sanders-ocasio-cortez-endorsement-rally-051491.

107 **endorsed Sanders:** Jenny Gathright and Michel Martin, "Alexandria Ocasio
-Cortez Endorses Bernie Sanders," NPR, October 19, 2019, accessed December 1, 2020, npr.org/2019/10/19/771596733/alexandria-ocasio-cortez
-says-bernie-sanders-heart-attack-was-a-gut-check-moment.

109 **putting a trifecta:** Gregory Krieg and Annie Grayer, "Rashida Tlaib Joins
Ocasio-Cortez, Omar in Endorsing Bernie Sanders," CNN, October 27,
2019, accessed December 1, 2020, cnn.com/2019/10/27/politics/rashida
-tlaib-endorses-bernie-sanders-aoc-omar/index.html.

109 **committed to Warren:** Astead W. Herndon, "Ayanna Pressley Endorses
Elizabeth Warren for President," *The New York Times,* November 6, 2019,
accessed December 1, 2020, nytimes.com/2019/11/06/us/politics/ayanna
-pressley-endorses-elizabeth-warren.html.

109 **never drop below:** "2020 Democratic Presidential Nomination," Real Clear
Politics, accessed December 1, 2020, realclearpolitics.com/epolls/2020
/president/us/2020_democratic_presidential_nomination-6730.html.

110 **played him in sketches:** Mary Papenfuss, "Larry David Kills as Bernie
Sanders in Spoof Town Hall on 'Saturday Night Live,'" *HuffPost,* September 29, 2019, accessed December 1, 2020, huffpost.com/entry/larry-david
-bernie-sanders-snl-democratic-presidential-forum-spoof_n_5d903870e4b0
e9e7604df8e8.

CHAPTER 6: LUCKY STRIKE

115 **In 2016, a survey:** Robin Opsahl and Brianne Pfannenstiel, "Iowa Poll:
Most Likely Democratic Caucusgoers Would Be Satisfied with a President
Candidate Who Leans Toward Socialism," *Des Moines Register,* March 10,
2019, accessed December 3, 2020, desmoinesregister.com/story/news
/elections/presidential/caucus/2019/03/10/election-2020-socialism-socialist
-democrat-caucus-iowa-sanders-aoc-green-new-deal-medicare-for-all/31138
09002/.

116 **a hundred paid staff:** Bill Ruthhart, "Inside Pete Buttigieg's Iowa Surge:
Loud Crowds, Strong Ground Game as He Emerges as Moderate Alternative to Joe Biden in 2020," *Chicago Tribune,* November 7, 2019, accessed
December 3, 2020, chicagotribune.com/politics/elections/ct-iowa-joe-biden
-pete-buttigieg-2020-presidential-race-moderates-20191107-qdqrz2fb3fd550
4xlkaq2ogzye-story.html.

116 **He took a lead:** "Iowa Democratic Presidential Caucus," Real Clear Poli-

tics, accessed December 3, 2020, realclearpolitics.com/epolls/2020/president
/ia/iowa_democratic_presidential_caucus-6731.html.

116 **dropped into a third-place tie:** "Latest Polls," FiveThirtyEight, Iowa, accessed December 1, 2020, projects.fivethirtyeight.com/polls/iowa/.

117 **the Jefferson-Jackson dinner:** Maura Barrett and Priscilla Thompson, "At
Iowa Dinner, 13 Democrat Presidential Hopefuls Try to Find a Breakout
Moment," NBC News, November 2, 2019, accessed December 1, 2020,
nbcnews.com/politics/2020-election/iowa-dinner-13-democrat-presidential
-hopefuls-try-find-breakout-moment-n1075591.

117 **seen as a pivotal moment:** Ryan Lizza, "The Relaunch," *The New Yorker,*
November 19, 2007, accessed December 1, 2020, newyorker.com/magazine
/2007/11/26/the-relaunch.

117 **had to raise his voice:** "Iowa Democratic Party Liberty and Justice Celebration," C-SPAN, November 1, 2019, accessed December 1, 2020, c-span.org
/video/?465865-1/democratic-presidential-candidates-speak-iowa-party
-dinner.

119 **Schultz told *The Wall Street Journal*:** Ken Thomas and Sabrina Siddiqui,
"Joe Biden Is Tested in Iowa as Rivals Gain Ground," *The Wall Street Journal,* November 3, 2019, accessed December 3, 2020, wsj.com/articles/joe
-biden-is-tested-in-iowa-as-rivals-gain-ground-11572821141.

119 **former Iowa governor Tom Vilsack:** Stephen Gruber-Miller, "Former Iowa
Gov. Tom Vilsack and wife Christie Vilsack endorse Joe Biden for president," *Des Moines Register,* November 23, 2019, accessed December 3,
2020, desmoinesregister.com/story/news/elections/presidential/caucus/2019
/11/23/tom-christie-vilsack-endorse-joe-biden-president-iowa-caucuses
-2020/4275737002/.

119 **"No Malarkey" bus tour:** Marianna Sotomayor, "Joe Biden Launches First
Bus Tour in Iowa," NBC News, accessed December 3, 2020, nbcnews.com
/politics/meet-the-press/blog/meet-press-blog-latest-news-analysis-data
-driving-political-discussion-n988541/ncrd1088531.

120 **signaled his assent:** Shane Goldmacher, "Biden Campaign Drops Opposition to Super PAC Support," *The New York Times,* October 24, 2019, accessed December 3, 2020, nytimes.com/2019/10/24/us/politics/joe-biden
-super-pac.html.

120 **sought out rainmakers like:** Federal Election Commission data, accessed
November 30, 2020, fec.gov.

121 **A week after the debate:** "Iowa Democratic Presidential Caucus," Real
Clear Politics, accessed December 3, 2020, realclearpolitics.com/epolls
/2020/president/ia/iowa_democratic_presidential_caucus-6731.html.

122 **"the most consequential poll":** Steven Shepard, "The Most Consequential
Poll in Politics Is About to Be Released," *Politico,* February 1, 2020,
accessed December 3, 2020, politico.com/news/2020/02/01/iowa-poll-2020
-110155.

122 **the survey put Sanders:** Alana Satlin, "Biden Comes in 4th in Unreleased
Gold-Standard Iowa Poll: Report," NBC News Live Blog, February 3, 2020,
accessed December 3, 2020, nbcnews.com/politics/2020-election/live-blog
/iowa-caucuses-live-updates-2020-democrats-make-their-final-pitches
-n1128596/ncrd1129276#liveBlogHeader.

CHAPTER 7: PANIC! AT THE CAUCUS

131 **lost the 2004 election to George W. Bush:** Floyd Norris, "Bush Wins 2nd Term by a Solid Margin: Kerry Failed to Connect on Economy," *The New York Times,* November 4, 2004, accessed November 27, 2020, nytimes .com/2004/11/04/news/bush-wins-2nd-term-by-a-solid-margin-kerry-failed -to-connect-on-economy.html.

132 **had booked a $10 million, sixty-second Super Bowl ad:** Nick Corasaniti, "Bloomberg and Trump Buy Super Bowl Ads at $10 Million Each," *The New York Times,* January 7, 2020, accessed November 27, 2020, nytimes .com/2020/01/07/us/politics/bloomberg-trump-super-bowl-ad.html.

134 **pushing media outlets for weeks:** Alexandra Jaffe, "New Iowa Caucus Rules Could Spark Clashing Claims of Victory," Associated Press, January 16, 2020, accessed November 27, 2020, apnews.com/article/43354ef7312 4d58d94ca434b9016b4a7.

134 **chugging him through Iowa:** Stephen Gruber-Miller, "Joe Biden Kicks Off 'No Malarkey' Bus Tour Across Iowa, with Focus on Rural Communities, Their Values," *Des Moines Register,* November 30, 2019, accessed November 27, 2020, desmoinesregister.com/story/news/elections/presidential /caucus/2019/11/30/joe-biden-no-malarkey-bus-tour-rural-iowa-council -bluffs-denison/4343082002/.

135 **"I think I have a real firewall in South Carolina":** Mike Memoli, "NBC News on the Bus with Joe Biden," NBC News, February 2, 2020, accessed November 27, 2020, nbcnews.com/video/nbc-news-on-the-bus-with-joe -biden-77997125565.

136 **spending less on its advertising:** Adam Brewster and Bo Erickson, "Super PAC Helps Biden Make Up Ad Spending Deficit in Iowa," CBS News, January 28, 2020, accessed November 27, 2020, cbsnews.com/news/super-pac -helps-biden-make-up-ad-spending-deficit-in-iowa/.

138 **so close to defeating Clinton:** Nick Gass, "Clinton Ekes Out Win in Iowa Against Sanders," *Politico,* February 1, 2016, accessed November 27, 2020, politico.com/story/2016/02/iowa-caucus-2016-donald-trump-bernie-sanders -218547.

138 **call it a "virtual tie" at his post-caucus party:** "Watch Bernie Sanders' Full Speech After Iowa Caucuses," *PBS NewsHour,* YouTube, February 1, 2016, accessed November 27, 2020, youtube.com/watch?v=RzxpYX4 TONo&t=1s.

139 **an application developed by Shadow Inc.:** Nick Corasaniti, Sheera Frenkel, and Nicole Perlroth, "App Used to Tabulate Votes Is Said to Have Been Inadequately Tested," *The New York Times,* February 3, 2020, accessed November 28, 2020, nytimes.com/2020/02/03/us/politics/iowa-caucus-app .html.

140 **DNC had nixed the state party's plan:** Reid J. Epstein, "Caucuses in Iowa Won't Include Absentee Participation, D.N.C. Says," August 30, 2019, accessed November 28, 2020, nytimes.com/2019/08/30/us/politics/dnc-iowa -virtual-caucus.html.

143 **Sanders got 160 votes:** Charlie Smart, Denise Lu, Matthew Bloch, and Ben Smithgall, "Results: The Most Detailed Map of the Iowa Democratic Caucus," *The New York Times,* accessed November 28, 2020, nytimes.com /interactive/2020/02/03/us/elections/results-iowa-caucus-precinct-map.html.

143 **had absolutely dominated:** Rafael Bernal, "Analysis: Sanders Ran the Table with Latinos in Iowa," *The Hill,* February 7, 2020, accessed November 28, 2020, thehill.com/latino/482030-analysis-sanders-ran-the-table-with -latinos-in-iowa.

145 **reopened MSNBC's election HQ broadcast:** "'Crash Course In Chaos: Steve Kornacki Explains the Iowa Caucuses | MSNBC," MSNBC, *YouTube,* February 3, 2020, accessed January 4, 2021, https://www.youtube.com /watch?v=IIuOxRBaZFA.

146 **would go out to the news media:** Daniel Arkin and Maura Barrett, "Results for Iowa Caucuses Delayed as State Democratic Party Finds 'Inconsisten-cies,'" NBC News, February 3, 2020, accessed November 28, 2020, nbcnews .com/politics/2020-election/iowa-caucus-results-much-slower-expected -state-democratic-party-quality-n1129431.

146 **Trump supporters began flooding it:** Ben Collins, Maura Barrett, and Vaughn Hillyard, "'Clog the Lines': Internet Trolls Deliberately Disrupted the Iowa Caucuses Hotline for Reporting Results," NBC News, February 6, 2020, accessed November 28, 2020, nbcnews.com/tech/security/clog-lines -iowa-caucus-hotline-posted-online-encouragement-disrupt-results -n1131521.

146 **sent the state party a stiffly worded letter:** John Bowden, "Biden Campaign Calls for Answers From Iowa Democrats After Delays in Caucus Results," *The Hill,* February 4, 2020, accessed November 28, 2020, thehill.com /homenews/campaign/481315-biden-campaign-calls-for-answers-from-iowa -dems-after-delays-in-caucus.

147 **tweeted out a taunt:** Brad Parscale, @parscale, "Quality control = rigged?," Twitter, February 3, 2020, accessed November 28, 2020, twitter .com/parscale/status/1224533010890002434.

149 **she said to supporters:** "Senator Amy Klobuchar in Des Moines, Iowa," C-SPAN, February 3, 2020, accessed November 28, 2020, c-span.org/video /?468887-1/senator-amy-klobuchar-addresses-supporters-des-moines-iowa.

149 **popped in front of a camera:** "Joe Biden in Des Moines, Iowa," C-SPAN, February 3, 2020, accessed November 28, 2020, c-span.org/video/?468891-1 /joe-biden-addresses-supporters-des-moines-iowa#.

150 **he said in the Holiday Inn ballroom:** "Senator Bernie Sanders in Des Moines, Iowa," C-SPAN, February 3, 2020, accessed November 28, 2020, c-span.org/video/?468889-1/senator-bernie-sanders-addresses-supporters -des-moines-iowa.

CHAPTER 8: CIRCULAR FIRING SQUADS

154 *The New York Times* **reported on the message:** Katie Glueck and Jonathan Martin, "Joe Biden Shakes Up Campaign Leadership, Elevating Anita Dunn," *The New York Times,* February 7, 2020, accessed November 23, 2020, nytimes.com/2020/02/07/us/politics/joe-biden-anita-dunn.html.

158 **wouldn't even compete in a primary:** Alexander Burns, "Michael Bloom-berg Will Not Run for President in 2020," *The New York Times,* March 5, 2019, accessed December 1, 2020, nytimes.com/2019/03/05/us/politics /michael-bloomberg-2020.html.

158 **data-driven outfit:** Edward-Isaac Dovere, "Michael Bloomberg's Secret Plans to Take Down Trump," *The Atlantic,* January 31, 2019, accessed No-

vember 23, 2020, theatlantic.com/politics/archive/2019/01/bloomberg
-building-data-organization-crush-trump/581710/.

158 **leaders of the centrist Blue Dog Coalition:** Lauren Egan, "As Democrats
Battle in Early States, Bloomberg Quietly Lays Groundwork Among Party
Leaders," NBC News, February 11, 2020, accessed November 23, 2020,
nbcnews.com/politics/2020-election/democrats-battle-early-states
-bloomberg-quietly-lays-groundwork-among-party-n1134651.

158 **at actor Hill Harper's house:** Ibid.

159 **couldn't win a state until at least March 3:** Dan Merica, Cristina Alesci,
and Jake Tapper, "Michael Bloomberg is the Latest 2020 Democratic Hopeful," CNN, November 24, 2019, accessed December 1, 2020, cnn.com/2019
/11/24/politics/michael-bloomberg-2020-election/index.html.

161 **the ATM was fully stocked:** Sally Goldenberg and Christopher Cadelago,
"$375,000 Salaries, Furnished Housing and a Lot of Sushi: Inside Bloom-
berg's Spending Spree," *Politico,* January 31, 2020, accessed November 23,
2020, politico.com/news/2020/01/31/michael-bloomberg-fec-spending
-spree-110144.

161 **backed George W. Bush in 2004:** Jennifer Steinhauer, "Bloomberg, Looking
to Convention, Restrains Cheer for Bush," *The New York Times,* January 29, 2004, accessed December 1, 2020, nytimes.com/2004/01/29/nyregion
/bloomberg-looking-to-convention-restrains-cheer-for-bush.html.

161 **doubled his spending:** Jennifer Medina and Alexander Burns, "Bloomberg
Plans to Double Ad Spending After Iowa Caucus Problem," *The New York
Times,* February 4, 2020, accessed November 23, 2020, nytimes.com/2020
/02/04/us/politics/michael-bloomberg-campaign-ads.html.

161 **he was in fourth place at 9 percent:** "2020 Democratic Presidential Nomination," Real Clear Politics, February 3, 2020, realclearpolitics.com/epolls
/2020/president/us/2020_democratic_presidential_nomination-6730.html.

161 **By the eve of the New Hampshire primary:** Ibid.

163 **a woman with his résumé:** *Los Angeles Times,* "Sen. Amy Klobuchar Says
We Can't Play a Game Called 'Name Your Favorite Woman President,'"
YouTube, November 20, 2019, youtube.com/watch?v=reVvTTgAEWk
&feature=youtu.be.

164 **prefer to watch cartoons than the impeachment trial:** NowThis News,
"Pete Buttigieg: Watching the Impeachment Coverage Makes You Want to
Watch Cartoons Instead," YouTube, February 7, 2020, youtube.com/watch
?v=UMQcsTtUDRA.

164 **Klobuchar unleashed the political kill shot:** NowThis News, "Amy Klobuchar Attacks Pete Buttigieg's Inexperience During NH Debate," YouTube,
February 7, 2020, youtube.com/watch?v=vCMae4WFz-8.

166 **"I like Pete Buttigieg":** "Politics and Eggs Breakfast with Senator Bernie
Sanders," C-SPAN, February 7, 2020, accessed November 23, 2020, c-span
.org/video/?469095-1/politics-eggs-breakfast-senator-bernie-sanders.

166 **Iowa state party finally declared him the winner:** Isaac Stanley-Becker,
"Iowa Democratic Party Projects Pete Buttigieg the Winner of the Delegate
Race, with Bernie Sanders Preparing a Challenge," *The Washington Post,*
February 9, 2020, accessed November 23, 2020, washingtonpost.com
/politics/iowa-democratic-party-projects-pete-buttigieg-the-winner-of-the
-delegate-race-with-bernie-sanders-preparing-a-challenge/2020/02/09/9d708
2e0-4b98-11ea-bf44-f5043eb3918a_story.html.

166 **"lying dog-faced pony soldier":** Cleve R. Wootson Jr., "Biden Jokingly

Calls Voter Who Asked About Iowa a 'Lying Dog-Faced Pony Soldier,'"
The Washington Post, February 9, 2020, accessed November 23, 2020,
washingtonpost.com/politics/biden-jokingly-calls-voter-who-asked-about
-iowa-a-lying-dog-faced-pony-soldier/2020/02/09/9e8da478-4b75-11ea-9b5c
-eac5b16dafaa_story.html.

167 **uploaded pictures to social media sites:** Katie Glueck, @katieglueck, "The
Biden bus pulls over after the press bus breaks down (we're now following
in staff vans)", Twitter, February 9, 2020, twitter.com/katieglueck/status
/1226595964426866689.

170 **TV networks declared Sanders the winner:** "CNN Projects Bernie Sanders
Wins New Hampshire Primary," CNN, February 12, 2020, cnn.com/videos
/politics/2020/02/12/bernie-sanders-new-hampshire-projection-win-vpx
.cnn.

170 **had fallen out of love with him:** Reid J. Epstein, "Did New Hampshire Fall
Out of Love with Bernie Sanders?," *The New York Times,* November 25,
2019, accessed November 23, 2020, nytimes.com/2019/11/25/us/politics
/bernie-sanders-new-hampshire-2020.html.

170 **National polls put him in fifth place:** "2020 Democratic Presidential Nomination," Real Clear Politics, February 11, 2020, realclearpolitics.com
/epolls/2020/president/us/2020_democratic_presidential_nomination-6730
.html.

171 **Sanders had beaten Hillary by more than 20 points:** "New Hampshire Primary Results," *The New York Times,* February 9, 2016, accessed December 1, 2020, nytimes.com/elections/2016/results/primaries/new-hampshire.

171 **he escaped as the victor with a 25.7 percent:** "2020 Primary Elections,
New Hampshire Results," February 14, 2020, accessed December 1, 2020,
nbcnews.com/politics/2020-primary-elections/new-hampshire-results.

171 **at his victory party:** CBS News, "Bernie Sanders Delivers Victory Speech in
New Hampshire," YouTube, February 11, 2020, youtube.com/watch?v=Po
UtnyhSEzU.

175 **photographed during Obama's 2012 reelection:** @rodneyhawkins, "Biden
walked into a FL field office with his aviators on, Dunkin Donuts coffee in
one hand, and boxes of donuts in the other," Instagram, October 20, 2012,
instagram.com/p/RAruBtmwwS/.

175 **Biden was asked:** Rebecca Shabad and Mike Memoli, "Biden Says He
Doesn't Regret Not Moving on to South Carolina Sooner," NBC News Live
Blog, updated February 12, 2020, accessed December 2, 2020, nbcnews
.com/politics/2020-election/live-blog/new-hampshire-primary-live-results
-democrats-make-final-push-n1134096/ncrd1135236#liveBlogHeader.

176 **eating into his African American backing:** Blair LM Kelley, "Why Mike
Bloomberg Could Win Black Voters' Support as Joe Biden's Candidacy
Falters," NBC News, February 14, 2020, accessed November 24, 2020,
nbcnews.com/think/opinion/why-mike-bloomberg-could-win-black-voters
-support-joe-biden-ncna11136766.

176 **Billionaire Tom Steyer:** Stephanie Saul and Nick Corasaniti, "Tom Steyer
Spends Millions in South Carolina. Black Voters Reap the Benefit," *The
New York Times,* January 25, 2020, accessed November 24, 2020, nytimes
.com/2020/01/25/us/politics/tom-steyer-millions-south-carolina.html.

177 **Black-majority districts:** Astead W. Herndon and Lauren Leatherby,
"How Black Voters Could Help Biden Win the Democratic Nomination,"
The New York Times, December 2, 2019, accessed November 24, 2020,

nytimes.com/interactive/2019/12/02/us/politics/2020-democratic-delegates
.html.

177 **When Biden stepped to the microphone:** "Joe Biden Delivers Primary
Remarks in Columbia, South Carolina," C-SPAN, February 29, 2020,
c-span.org/video/?469880-1/joe-biden-wins-south-carolina-democratic
-primary.

CHAPTER 9: "NONE OF US KNEW IF THERE WAS GOING
TO BE A CAMPAIGN"

181 **Las Vegas gunman:** Lynh Bui, Matt Zapotosky, Devlin Barrett, and Mark
Berman, "At Least 59 Killed in Las Vegas Shooting Rampage, More Than
500 Others Injured," *The Washington Post,* October 2, 2017, accessed November 24, 2020, washingtonpost.com/news/morning-mix/wp/2017/10/02
/police-shut-down-part-of-las-vegas-strip-due-to-shooting/.

181 **protect the gun-manufacturing industry:** Jonathan Topaz, "Bernie Sanders's Awkward History with Guns in America," *Politico,* June 18, 2015,
accessed November 24, 2020, politico.com/story/2015/06/bernie-sanders
-awkward-history-with-guns-in-america-119185.

183 **He had thrown an elbow at her during a gun safety event:** Mike Bloomberg, "Mike Bloomberg at the Presidential Gun Sense Forum in Iowa,"
YouTube, August 10, 2019, youtube.com/watch?v=v48_4-RknCE.

185 **he'd been accused of calling women:** Michael Kranish, "Mike Bloomberg for Years Has Battled Women's Allegations of Profane, Sexist Comments," *The Washington Post,* February 16, 2020, December 1, 2020,
washingtonpost.com/graphics/2020/politics/michael-bloomberg-women/.

186 **the night of February 19:** Maggie Astor, "Elizabeth Warren, Criticizing
Bloomberg, Sent a Message: She Won't Be Ignored," *The New York Times,*
February 19, 2020, accessed November 24, 2020, nytimes.com/2020/02/19
/us/politics/elizabeth-warren-debate.html.

190 **he had won the support of rank-and-file union members:** Gregory Krieg,
"Teamsters Kick Off Endorsement Process as 2020 Democrats Race for
Labor Support," CNN, October 11, 2019, accessed November 24, 2020,
cnn.com/2019/10/11/politics/teamsters-endorsement-process-2020/index
.html.

190 **Senate majority leader Harry Reid:** Rebecca Klar, "Harry Reid Endorses
Biden's White House Bid," *The Hill,* March 2, 2020, accessed November 24,
2020, thehill.com/homenews/campaign/485511-harry-reid-endorses-bidens
-white-house-bid.

191 **panel truck into Hispanic neighborhoods:** Kate Sullivan and Maeve Reston,
"Nevada Tests Bernie Sanders' Appeal to Latinos," CNN, February 19,
2020, accessed November 24, 2020, cnn.com/2020/02/19/politics/nevada
-latino-voters-2020-election/index.html.

195 **Five miles away:** Will Steakin and Quinn Owen, "Like Iowa, Trump Pre-
dicts 'A Lot of Problems' for Nevada Caucuses During Vegas Rally," ABC
News, February 21, 2020, accessed November 24, 2020, abcnews.go.com
/Politics/trump-continues-haunt-2020-democrats-vegas-rally-ahead/story
?id=69125584.

196 **had inserted stents:** William Wan, "How Serious is Bernie Sanders's
Heart Problem? This is the Stent Procedure His Doctors Just Performed,"

The Washington Post, October 2, 2019, accessed November 24, 2020, washingtonpost.com/health/2019/10/02/how-serious-is-bernie-sanders -heart-problem-this-is-stent-procedure-his-doctors-just-performed/.

197 **rain poured down on the Strip:** Jennifer Gray, "Nevada Rain and Snow on Caucus Day," CNN, February 22, 2020, accessed November 24, 2020, cnn .com/2020/02/22/weather/nevada-arizona-storm-forecast-saturday/index .html.

197 **caucus sites:** Dan Merica, "Nevada Democrats Increase Number of Critical Las Vegas Strip Caucus Sites," CNN, January 7, 2020, accessed November 24, 2020, cnn.com/2020/01/07/politics/nevada-democrats-strip-caucus -sites/index.html.

197 **In a head-to-head matchup with Clinton:** Amy Chozick, "Clinton Campaign Rebuffs Sanders on Latino Vote in Nevada," *The New York Times,* February 21, 2016, accessed November 24, 2020, nytimes.com/politics/first -draft/2016/02/21/clinton-campaign-enlists-polling-firm-to-try-and-rebut -sanders-claim-on-winning-latino-vote-in-nevada/.

197 **Sanders won just over 50 percent:** Charlie Smart, Denise Lu, Matthew Bloch, and Miles Watkins, "Results: The Most Detailed Map of the Nevada Democratic Caucus," *The New York Times,* Live Updates, accessed November 24, 2020, nytimes.com/interactive/2020/02/22/us/elections /results-nevada-caucus-precinct-map.html.

198 **Early in the night:** "Bernie Sanders Wins Democratic Presidential Caucuses in Nevada, Cementing Front-Runner Status," Associated Press, February 22, 2020, accessed November 25, 2020, apnews.com/article/2e944de69a 88cc87c4ec7de20501705b.

198 **Buttigieg's team said they didn't match up:** Zach Montellaro, "Buttigieg Claims Inconsistencies in Nevada Results," *Politico,* February 23, 2020, accessed December 1, 2020, politico.com/news/2020/02/23/buttigieg-claims -inconsistencies-nevada-results-116844.

199 **38 percent among Black voters:** Catherine Kim, "Joe Biden Was the Most Popular Candidate Among Black Voters in the Nevada Caucuses," *Vox,* February 23, 2020, accessed November 25, 2020, vox.com/policy -and-politics/2020/2/23/21149378/joe-biden-nevada-caucuses-black -voters.

199 **Biden's team pushed back:** Greg Schultz, @schultzohio, "Based on our internal data, Biden will come in a strong second tonight in Nevada. In the entrance polls, Biden won the Af-Am vote, voters over 65, voters who oppose Medicare for All. Make no mistake: The Biden comeback starts tonight in Nevada," Twitter, February 22, 2020, twitter.com/schultzohio /status/1231374998918418432.

199 **crappy second-place finish:** "Nevada Caucuses 2020: Live Election Results," *The New York Times,* Live Updates, accessed November 24, 2020, nytimes .com/interactive/2020/02/22/us/elections/results-nevada-caucus.html.

200 **he took the stage:** "Joe Biden Remarks Following Nevada Caucuses," C-SPAN, February 22, 2020, c-span.org/video/?469512-1/joe-biden-remarks -nevada-caucuses.

200 *Politico*'s **headline writers:** Marc Caputo, "Biden Claims Comeback Despite Distant Second Finish to Sanders," *Politico,* February 22, 2020, accessed November 25, 2020, politico.com/news/2020/02/22/joe-biden-claims -victory-nevada-116756.

CHAPTER 10: FIREWALL

203 **Clyburn first arrived in the House in 1993:** Biography of Congressman James E. Clyburn, clyburn.house.gov/about-me/full-biography.

204 **Obama's endorsement wasn't available:** John Fritze and David Jackson, "'Voters Themselves Must Pick': Why Barack Obama Isn't Endorsing Joe Biden or Anyone Else for President," *USA Today,* February 27, 2020, accessed November 26, 2020, usatoday.com/story/news/politics/elections /2020/02/27/why-obama-wont-endorse-biden-south-carolina-super-tuesday -nears/4890693002/.

204 **Clyburn's wife, Emily, had died:** Zach Budryk, "Emily Clyburn—Longtime Wife Rep. Jim Clyburn—Dies at 80," *The Hill,* September 19, 2019, accessed November 26, 2020, thehill.com/blogs/blog-briefing-room/news /462148-emily-clyburn-longtime-librarian-and-wife-of-democratic-whip.

205 **Unite the Country:** Unite the Country, "Rep. Jim Clyburn for Biden," YouTube, March 25, 2020, youtube.com/watch?v=ejs4B9cjeOo.

205 **anonymously sourced story in *Politico*:** Natasha Korecki, Heather Caygle, Marc Caputo, and Laura Barrón-López, "Clyburn Poised to Endorse Biden in Big Boost Before S.C. Primary," *Politico,* February 23, 2020, accessed November 26, 2020, politico.com/news/2020/02/23/clyburn-to-endorse-biden -south-carolina-116986.

206 **Obama in 2008:** Jeff Zeleny and Michael M. Grynbaum, "Obama Wins South Carolina Primary," *The New York Times,* January 26, 2008, accessed November 26, 2020, nytimes.com/2008/01/26/us/politics/26cnd-carolina .html.

206 **Clinton in 2016:** Gary Langer, Gregory Holyk, and Chad Kiewit De Jonge, "Black Voters Boost Hillary Clinton to South Carolina Primary Win," ABC News, February 27, 2016, accessed November 26, 2020, abcnews.go.com /Politics/live-south-carolina-democratic-primary-exit-poll-analysis/story ?id=37241467.

206 **Antonin Scalia died in 2016:** Robert Barnes, "Supreme Court Justice Antonin Scalia Dies at 79," *The Washington Post,* February 13, 2016, accessed November 26, 2020, washingtonpost.com/politics/supreme-court-justice -antonin-scalia-dies-at-79/2016/02/13/effe8184-a62f-11e3-a5fa-55f0c77bf 39c_story.html.

207 **Obama went in the opposite direction:** Juliet Eilperin and Mike DeBonis, "President Obama Nominates Merrick Garland to the Supreme Court," *The Washington Post,* March 16, 2016, accessed November 26, 2020, washingtonpost.com/world/national-security/president-obama-to- nominate-merrick-garland-to-the-supreme-court-sources-say/2016/03 /16/3bc90bc8-eb7c-11e5-a6f3-21ccdbc5f74e_story.html.

207 **Clyburn believed:** PBS NewsHour, "Clyburn Says More Important to Have Black Woman on Supreme Court Than as VP," YouTube, July 31, 2020, youtube.com/watch?v=urTtYJyraWE.

208 **Biden fumbled out the promise:** CBS News, "Democratic Debate in Charleston, South Carolina," February 20, 2020, cbsnews.com/video/cbs -news-democratic-debate-in-charleston-south-carolina-watch-in-full/#x.

209 **Biden's lead over Sanders in South Carolina narrowed:** Ibid.

209 **Sanders knew from experience:** "South Carolina Democratic Presidential Primary," Real Clear Politics, February 27, 2016, accessed November 27,

2020, realclearpolitics.com/epolls/2016/president/sc/south_carolina
_democratic_presidential_primary-4167.html.

210 **deployed most of his resources:** Jonathan Easley, "Sander's Zeroes-in on
Super Tuesday States," *The Hill*, February 28, 2020, accessed November 27,
thehill.com/homenews/campaign/485023-sanders-zeroes-in-on-super
-tuesday-states.

210 **Jackie Wilson's "(Your Love Keeps Lifting Me) Higher and Higher":**
"Representative Jim Clyburn Endorsement of Joe Biden," C-SPAN, February 26, 2020, accessed November 26, 2020, c-span.org/video/?469740-1
/representative-jim-clyburn-endorses-joe-biden.

211 **story about attending his pastor's funeral:** Chris Dixon, "Before the Clyburn Endorsement, an Elderly Church Usher with a Question," *The New
York Times,* March 8, 2020, accessed November 27, 2020, nytimes.com
/2020/03/08/us/clyburn-biden-endorsement.html.

212 **Charleston dredging project:** Tyrone Richardson, "Biden Pushes for Deep-
ening Charleston Harbor," *The Post and Courier,* September 15, 2013, accessed November 30, 2020, postandcourier.com/business/biden-pushes-for
-deepening-charleston-harbor/article_d9ce2388-4ef5-5fe0-b866-4dd902a
04ac3.html.

CHAPTER 11: "THE OLD WHITE GUY WALKS AWAY WITH THE PRIZE"

213 **margin of Biden's lead:** "South Carolina Democratic Presidential Primary,"
Real Clear Politics, February 29, 2020, accessed November 28, 2020,
realclearpolitics.com/epolls/2020/president/sc/south_carolina_democratic
_presidential_primary-6824.html.

214 **750 delegates:** Lauren Leatherby and Sarah Almukhtar, "Democratic Delegate Count and Primary Election Results 2020," *The New York Times,* updated September 14, 2020, accessed November 28, 2020, nytimes.com
/interactive/2020/us/elections/delegate-count-primary-results.html.

214 **Sanders figured to win or do well:** "California, Texas, N. Carolina, Virginia," Real Clear Politics, March 3, 2020, accessed November 28, 2020,
realclearpolitics.com/epolls/2020/president/SuperTuesday.html.

214 **Bloomberg's debate performance:** Niall Stanage, "Winners and Losers
From the South Carolina Debate," *The Hill,* February 26, 2020, accessed
November 28, 2020, thehill.com/homenews/the-memo/484661-winners
-and-losers-from-the-south-carolina-debate.

216 **one survey in which Buttigieg hit as high as 15 percent:** "South Carolina
Democratic Presidential Primary," Real Clear Politics, February 29, 2020,
accessed November 29, 2020, realclearpolitics.com/epolls/2020/president/sc
/south_carolina_democratic_presidential_primary-6824.html#polls.

217 **Associated Press called the race for Biden:** Steve Peoples, Meg Kinnard, and
Bill Barrow, "Biden Wins South Carolina, Aims for Super Tuesday Momentum," Associated Press, February 29, 2020, accessed November 29, 2020,
apnews.com/article/b9872b58b495fd17044f359338ab3f2a.

218 **he took first among Black voters with 61 percent:** Josh Boak and Hannah
Fingerhut, "AP VoteCast: Black Voters Carry Biden to His First Victory,"
Associated Press, March 1, 2020, accessed November 29, 2020, apnews.com
/article/ca32b175f2d249e5075bb057afa4748e.

218 **first among white voters with 33 percent:** "2020 South Carolina Democratic Presidential Primary," *The Washington Post,* last updated March 1, 2020, accessed November 29, 2020, washingtonpost.com/elections/election-results/2020-live-results-south-carolina-democratic-primary/.

218 **the white share of the electorate:** Peter Hamby, "Joe Biden's South Carolina Firewall Is Getting Whiter," *Vanity Fair,* February 27, 2020, accessed December 2, vanityfair.com/news/2020/02/can-joe-biden-survive-whitest-south-carolina-primary-in-a-decade-2020.

218 **overall vote total:** Max Greenwood, "5 Takeaways From the South Carolina Primary," *The Hill,* February 29, 2020, accessed November 29, 2020, thehill.com/homenews/campaign/485326-5-takeaways-from-the-south-carolina-primary.

218 **Biden finished with 49 percent of the vote:** "South Carolina 2020 Primary: Live Results," *The New York Times,* updated March 6, 2020, accessed November 29, 2020, nytimes.com/interactive/2020/02/29/us/elections/results-south-carolina-primary-election.html.

219 **wearing his trademark navy blue suit:** NBC News, "Watch Joe Biden's Full South Carolina Victory Speech," YouTube, March 1, 2020, youtube.com/watch?v=vzAPnjOPOCw.

219 **visibly weary and emotionally downtrodden:** *PBS NewsHour,* "WATCH: Joe Biden Speaks After New Hampshire Primary," YouTube, February 11, 2020, youtube.com/watch?v=-hv9TeLBYZU.

221 **annual march commemorating the 1965 "Bloody Sunday":** Astead W. Herndon, "'Bloody Sunday' Commemoration Draws Democratic Candidates to Selma," *The New York Times,* March 1, 2020, accessed November 29, 2020, nytimes.com/2020/03/01/us/politics/selma-bridge-march-2020-candidates.html.

222 **banked his chances on Iowa:** Steve Kornacki, "The Iowa Effect," NBC News, January 29, 2020, accessed November 29, 2020, nbcnews.com/politics/2020-election/why-iowa-matters-democratic-race-president-2020-n1122191.

223 **Biden had spoken at the church:** Jay Reeves, "Biden Warmly Welcomed in Selma as Dems Court Black Voters," ABC News, March 1, 2020, accessed November 29, 2020, abcnews.go.com/Politics/wireStory/democrats-gather-bloody-sunday-commemoration-selma-69321043.

223 **a number of congregants turned their backs on him in protest:** Aris Folley, "Churchgoers Turn Their Backs on Bloomberg in Protest During His Remarks at Service in Selma," March 1, 2020, accessed November 29, 2020, thehill.com/homenews/campaign/485384-churchgoers-turn-their-backs-on-bloomberg-in-protest-during-his-remarks-at.

225 **support for Biden exploded:** Matt Viser, "Democrats Embrace Biden as Sanders Hopes for a Big Super Tuesday Delegate Haul," *The Washington Post,* March 2, 2020, accessed November 29, 2020, washingtonpost.com/politics/democrats-embrace-biden-as-sanders-hopes-for-a-big-super-tuesday-delegate-haul/2020/03/02/db60234e-5cbe-11ea-b014-4fafa866bb81_story.html.

227 **Biden planned to say:** NBC News, "Joe Biden Thanks Pete Buttigieg for Endorsement: 'He Reminds Me of My Son Beau,'" YouTube, March 2, 2020, youtube.com/watch?v=9tbJ1wobGs4.

227 **would join him at a rally later in the night:** NBC News, "Biden Holds Rally

with Klobuchar on Eve of Super Tuesday | NBC News (Live Stream Recording)," YouTube, March 2, 2020, youtube.com/watch?v=nMu_8hoelms.

CHAPTER 12: THE PASSENGER

228 **late-comers pressed their faces:** Joe Garofoli, "Joe Biden Confident at Oakland Stop: 'I Think We're Going to Do Fine,'" *San Francisco Chronicle,* March 3, 2020, accessed November 30, 2020, sfchronicle.com/politics /article/Biden-makes-last-minute-Super-Tuesday-campaign-15101587.php.

229 **Originally the House post office:** United States Capitol Historical Society, "Congress Dedicates Lincoln Room," uschs.org/news-releases/congress -dedicates-lincoln-room/.

229 **Mississippi had sent a stone memorial of Jefferson Davis:** James Bikales, "Here Are the Confederate Statues in the Capitol," *The Hill,* June 12, 2020, accessed November 30, 2020, thehill.com/homenews/house/502521-here -are-the-confederate-statues-in-the-capitol.

230 **Associated Press called Virginia:** Alan Suderman, "Joe Biden Wins Virginia Democratic Presidential Primary," Associated Press, March 3, 2020, accessed November 30, 2020, apnews.com/article/ed2d494d28edb8c319f3495c 5c8d7740.

230 **North Carolina for Biden:** All Things Considered, "AP Projects Joe Biden Will Win North Carolina Primary on Super Tuesday," NPR, March 3, 2020, npr.org/2020/03/03/811844357/ap-projects-joe-biden-will-win-north -carolina-primary-on-super-tuesday.

230 **In Virginia, he carried 69 percent of the Black vote:** "Live Results: 2020 Virginia Democratic Presidential Primary," *The Washington Post,* last updated March 30, 2020, accessed November 30, 2020, washingtonpost.com /elections/election-results/virginia-democratic-primary-live-results/.

230 **in North Carolina, he took 62 percent:** "Live Results: 2020 North Carolina Democratic Presidential Primary," *The Washington Post,* last updated March 27, 2020, accessed November 30, 2020, washingtonpost.com /elections/election-results/north-carolina-democratic-primary-live-results/.

230 **Biden was doing what Hillary Clinton had struggled to do:** Aaron Zitner, Dante Chinni, and Brian McGill, "How Clinton Won: How Hillary Clinton Overcame the Challenge from Sen. Bernie Sanders," *The Wall Street Journal,* June 7, 2016, accessed November 30, 2020, graphics.wsj.com /elections/2016/how-clinton-won/.

230 **Exit polls in North Carolina:** "Exit Polls," North Carolina, CNN, cnn .com/election/2020/exit-polls/president/north-carolina.

231 **31 percent in Virginia:** "Virginia Exit Polls," CNN, cnn.com/election/2020 /primaries-caucuses/entrance-and-exit-polls/virginia/democratic.

231 **Biden won 43 percent of the statewide vote and 56 percent of the delegates:** "Live Results: 2020 North Carolina Democratic Presidential Primary," *The Washington Post,* last updated March 27, 2020, accessed November 30, 2020, washingtonpost.com/elections/election-results/north-carolina -democratic-primary-live-results/.

231 **His best district:** The Green Papers, thegreenpapers.com/P20/NC-D and thegreenpapers.com/P20/VA-D.

231 **Sanders won his home state of Vermont:** "Live Results: 2020 Vermont Democratic Presidential Primary," *The Washington Post,* last updated

March 30, 2020, accessed November 30, 2020, washingtonpost.com
/elections/election-results/vermont-democratic-primary-live-results/.

231 **Associated Press called Alabama for Biden:** "Joe Biden Wins Democratic
Presidential Primary in Alabama," Associated Press, March 3, 2020, accessed November 30, 2020, apnews.com/article/0d92d4ec59966e5a1cab6012
bfcfe795.

232 **dominance in Black-majority and conservative white areas:** Howard
Koplowitz, "Joe Biden Wins Alabama Democratic Primary," AL.com,
March 3, 2020, accessed November 30, 2020, al.com/news/2020/03/joe
-biden-wins-alabama-democratic-primary.html.

232 **beat Sanders 44 to 8 in delegates:** "Live Results: 2020 Alabama Democratic
Presidential Primary," *The Washington Post,* last update March 27, 2020,
accessed November 30, 2020, washingtonpost.com/elections/election
-results/alabama-democratic-primary-live-results/.

232 **Biden was sweeping everything:** "Super Tuesday: Live Primary Election Results," *The New York Times,* accessed November 30, 2020, nytimes.com
/interactive/2020/03/03/us/elections/results-super-tuesday-primary-election
.html.

234 **running neck and neck with Biden:** "California, Texas, N. Carolina, Virginia," Real Clear Politics, March 3, 2020, accessed November 28, 2020,
realclearpolitics.com/epolls/2020/president/SuperTuesday.html.

235 **voters who had made their decisions in the final few days:** Brittany Renee
Mayes, Leslie Shapiro, Kevin Schaul, Kevin Uhrmacher, Emily Guskin,
Scott Clement, and Dan Keating, "Exit Polls From the 2020: Democratic
Super Tuesday Contests," *The Washington Post,* last updated March 30,
2020, accessed November 30, washingtonpost.com/graphics/politics/exit
-polls-2020-super-tuesday-primary/.

235 **She asked her backers to switch over to Biden:** Nick Corasaniti and Alexander Burns, "Amy Klobuchar Drops Out of Presidential Race and Endorses
Biden," *The New York Times,* March 2, 2020, accessed November 30, 2020,
nytimes.com/2020/03/02/us/politics/amy-klobuchar-drops-out.html.

235 **8 percent in the state in a *Star Tribune* poll:** "Klobuchar, Sanders Lead
Democratic Field in Minnesota," *Star Tribune,* February 23, 2020, accessed
November 30, 2020, startribune.com/star-tribune-mpr-news-minnesota
-poll-results-democratic-primary-klobuchar-sanders-warren-buttigieg-biden
/567940781/.

235 **But when the votes were counted:** "Live Results: 2020 Minnesota Democratic Presidential Primary," *The Washington Post,* last updated March 28,
2020, accessed November 30, 2020, washingtonpost.com/elections/election
-results/minnesota-democratic-primary-live-results/.

237 **would not be called that night:** Meg Cunningham, "Sanders Projected to
Win the California Democratic Primary, 88% of the Vote Reporting," ABC
News, March 12, 2020, accessed November 30, 2020, abcnews.go.com
/Politics/sanders-projected-win-california-democratic-primary-88-vote
/story?id=69412137.

237 **Sanders's far-slimmer-than-expected 36 percent to 28 percent margin:**
"Live Results: 2020 California Democratic Presidential Primary," *The
Washington Post,* last updated May 20, 2020, accessed December 1, 2020,
washingtonpost.com/elections/election-results/california-democratic
-primary-live-results/.

238 **winner of Super Tuesday:** "Super Tuesday: Live Primary Election Results," *The New York Times,* accessed December 1, 2020, nytimes.com/inter active/2020/03/03/us/elections/results-super-tuesday-primary-election.html.

239 **AP called Minnesota for Biden:** Steve Karnowski, "Biden Defeats Sanders in Minnesota Super Tuesday Race," Associated Press, March 3, 2020, December 1, 2020, apnews.com/article/64876cb25df64241121cbab5e8f0050b.

239 **Baldwin Hills neighborhood in South Los Angeles:** Ariella Platcha, "Biden Stokes the Super Tuesday Crowd at South LA Rally," *Los Angeles Daily News,* March 3, 2020, accessed December 1, 2020, dailynews.com/2020/03 /03/biden-celebrates-early-lead-in-super-tuesday-results-at-south-l-a-rally/.

239 **he called Klobuchar:** Giovanni Russonello, "On Politics: Biden's Big Come-back," *The New York Times,* March 4, 2020, accessed December 2, 2020, nytimes.com/2020/03/04/us/politics/on-politics-biden-super-tuesday.html.

240 **He felt a little cocky. And it showed:** NBC News "Watch Joe Biden's Speech on Super Tuesday," YouTube, March 3, 2020, youtube.com/watch?v=YnE 9kKeOyTg.

CHAPTER 13: "IT'S ALL TURNING"

243 **signing ceremony for the U.S.-Mexico-Canada free trade agreement:** Ana Swanson and Emily Cochrane, "Trump Signs Trade Deal with Canada and Mexico," *New York Times,* January 29, 2020, accessed December 12, 2020, nytimes.com/2020/01/29/business/economy/usmca-trump.html.

243 **monthly unemployment rate:** U. S. Bureau of Labor Statistics, "The Em-ployment Situation—November 2020," US Department of Labor, December 4, 2020, https://www.bls.gov/news.release/pdf/empsit.pdf.

243 **Democrats' effort to impeach him:** Nicholas Fandos, "Nancy Pelosi An-nounces Formal Impeachment Inquiry of Trump," *The New York Times,* September 24, 2019, accessed December 12, 2020, nytimes.com/2019/09/24 /us/politics/democrats-impeachment-trump.html.

243 **Trump's defense lawyers were making their closing arguments:** "Trump Im-peachment Trial Live Coverage: The President's Defense Delivers Closing Arguments," NBC News Live Blog, updated January 29, 2020, accessed De-cember 12, 2020, nbcnews.com/politics/trump-impeachment-inquiry/live -blog/trump-impeachment-trial-live-coverage-president-s-defense-begins -day-n1123301.

244 **Alabama district that hooked around Birmingham:** "Alabama's 6th Con-gressional District," Ballotpedia, accessed December 12, 2020, ballotpedia .org/Alabama%27s_6th_Congressional_District.

244 **Old Post Office Building:** Jonathan O'Connell, "Trump to Turn Old Post Office Into Luxury Hotel," *The Washington Post,* February 7, 2012, ac cessed December 12, 2020, washingtonpost.com/business/capitalbusiness /trump-to-turn-old-post-office-into-luxury-hotel/2012/02/07/gIQAlS9gxQ _story.html.

245 **statement by the White House press secretary:** "Statement from the Press Secretary Regarding the President's Coronavirus Task Force," The White House, January 29, 2020, whitehouse.gov/briefings-statements/statement -press-secretary-regarding-presidents-coronavirus-task-force/.

245 **as Bob Woodward would report:** Bob Woodward, *Rage* (New York: Simon & Schuster, 2020.)

245 **announced the ban to the media:** "White House Briefing on Coronavirus Response," C-SPAN, January 31, 2020, c-span.org/video/?468862-1/white -house-declares-coronavirus-presents-public-health-emergency-us.

246 **North Charleston Coliseum:** "President Trump Campaign Event in North Charleston, South Carolina," C-SPAN, February 28, 2020, c-span.org /video/?469663-1/president-trump-campaign-event-north-charleston-south -carolina.

247 **"more deadly":** Robert Costa and Philip Rucker, "Woodward Book: Trump Says He Knew Coronavirus Was 'Deadly' and Worse Than the Flu While Intentionally Misleading Americans," *The Washington Post,* September 9, 2020, accessed December 12, 2020, washingtonpost.com/politics/bob -woodward-rage-book-trump/2020/09/09/0368fe3c-efd2-11ea-b4bc-3a2098f c73d4_story.html.

247 **placing Vice President Mike Pence in charge:** Michael D. Shear, Noah Weiland, and Katie Rogers, "Trump Names Mike Pence to Lead Coronavirus Response," *The New York Times,* February 26, 2020, accessed December 12, 2020, nytimes.com/2020/02/26/us/politics/trump-coronavirus-cdc .html.

247 **virus would simply disappear:** "40 Times Trump Said the Coronavirus Would Go Away," *The Washington Post,* November 2, 2020, accessed December, 12, 2020, washingtonpost.com/video/politics/40-times-trump-said -the-coronavirus-would-go-away/2020/04/30/d2593312-9593-4ec2-aff7 -72c1438fca0e_video.html.

248 **one hundred confirmed cases:** Associated Press, "Cuomo: More Than 100 Coronavirus Cases in New York State," U.S. News, March 8, 2020, accessed December 12, 2020, usnews.com/news/best-states/new-york/articles/2020 -03-08/cuomo-coronavirus-caseload-rises-to-105-in-new-york-state.

248 **stopped to talk with reporters:** "President Trump on U.S. Response to the Coronavirus Outbreak," C-SPAN, March 10, 2020, c-span.org/video /?470230-1/president-trump-speaks-meeting-senate-gop-coronavirus -response.

248 **Dow Jones Industrial Average:** Dow Jones Industrial Average, *The Wall Street Journal,* wsj.com/market-data/quotes/index/US/DJIA.

248 **Sitting behind the Resolute Desk:** "Presidential Address on the Coronavirus Outbreak," C-SPAN, March 11, 2020, c-span.org/video/?470284-1 /president-trump-travel-europe-us-suspended-30-days-uk.

249 **cancel several upcoming campaign trips:** Matthew Choi, "Trump Cancels Nevada, Colorado, Wisconsin Campaign Events as Coronavirus Spreads," *Politico,* March 11, 2020, accessed December 12, 2020, politico.com/news /2020/03/11/trump-cancel-campaign-events-coronavirus-126693.

249 **Biden met with autoworkers:** William Cummings, "'You're Full of S***': Joe Biden Gets in a Heated Gun Control Debate with Detroit Plant Worker," *USA Today,* March 10, 2020, accessed December 12, 2020, usatoday.com/story/news/politics/elections/2020/03/10/joe-biden-gun -control-exchange-auto-plant-worker/5011344002/.

249 **"the connect":** Richard Ben Cramer, *What It Takes: The Way to the White House* (New York: Random House, 1992).

250 **"You're full of shit":** Sarah Mucha and Devan Cole, "Biden Gets into Testy Exchange with Man Over Gun Rights," CNN, March 10, 2020, accessed December 12, 2020, cnn.com/2020/03/10/politics/joe-biden-testy-gun -exchange-michigan-worker/index.html.

250 **suspend rallies:** Sydney Ember, Annie Karni, and Maggie Haberman, "Sanders and Biden Cancel Events as Coronavirus Fears Upend Primary," *The New York Times,* March 10, 2020, accessed December 12, 2020, nytimes.com/2020/03/10/us/politics/sanders-biden-rally-coronavirus.html.

251 **debate in Arizona was canceled:** Reid J. Epstein and Sydney Ember, "Democrats Move Debate from Arizona to Washington Because of Virus Concerns," *The New York Times,* March 12, 2020, accessed December 12, 2020, nytimes.com/2020/03/12/us/politics/democratic-debate.html.

252 **"pick a woman to be vice president":** Matt Stevens, "Joe Biden Commits to Selecting a Woman as Vice President," *The New York Times,* March 15, 2020, accessed December 13, 2020, nytimes.com/2020/03/15/us/politics/joe-biden-female-vice-president.html.

252 **Palin had clearly hurt John McCain's chances:** Philip Bump, "Sarah Palin Cost John McCain 2 Million Votes in 2008, According to a Study," *The Washington Post,* January 19, 2016, accessed December 13, 2020, washingtonpost.com/news/the-fix/wp/2016/01/19/sarah-palin-cost-john-mccain-2-million-votes-in-2008/.

252 **Women didn't fare well:** Samantha Melamed and Anna Orso, "After Another 'Year of the Woman,' How Close Is Pa. to Gender Parity in Politics? (Not Very)," *The Philadelphia Inquirer,* updated December 27, 2018, accessed December 13, 2020, inquirer.com/news/women-pennsylvania-politics-year-of-the-woman-house-senate-congress-20181226.html.

252 **personal medical care from Dr. Kevin O'Connor:** Kevin O'Connor biography, New York Institute of Technology, nyit.edu/box/profiles/kevin_oconnor.

252 **he turned to a clutch of medical experts:** Yasmeen Abutaleb and Laurie McGinley, "Here's How Joe Biden Would Combat the Pandemic if He Wins the Election," *The Washington Post,* September 11, 2020, accessed December 12, 2020, washingtonpost.com/health/joe-biden-coronavirus-plan/2020/09/11/002b972c-eecc-11ea-99a1-71343d03bc29_story.html.

252 **"Folks, we can beat this virus":** WCNC, "Former Vice President Joe Biden Rallies Supporters in Sumter, SC," YouTube, February 28, 2020, youtube.com/watch?v=Se7JXwznnUk.

253 **Trump strode slowly into the White House:** "President Trump with Coronavirus Task Force Briefing," C-SPAN, March 16, 2020, accessed December 13, 2020, c-span.org/video/?470396-1/president-trump-coronavirus-task-force-issue-guidelines-public.

253 **"This is a bad one":** Nolan D. McCaskill, Joanne Kenen, and Adam Cancryn, "'This Is a Very Bad One': Trump Issues New Guidelines to Stem Coronavirus Spread," *Politico,* March 16, 2020, accessed December 13, 2020, politico.com/news/2020/03/16/trump-recommends-avoiding-gatherings-of-more-than-10-people-132323.

253 **he'd tapped Parscale:** Jessica Estepa, "President Trump Names Brad Parscale as Campaign Manager for 2020 Re-Election Bid," *USA Today,* February 27, 2018, accessed December 13, 2020, usatoday.com/story/news/politics/onpolitics/2018/02/27/president-trump-names-brad-parscale-campaign-manager-2020-re-election-bid/376680002/.

254 **politically minded chief of staff:** Seung Min Kim and Josh Dawsey, "Trump Picks Mark Meadows to Be New White House Chief of Staff," *The Washington Post,* March 6, 2020, accessed December 13, 2020, washingtonpost.com/politics/trump-picks-mark-meadows-as-new-white

-house-chief-of-staff/2020/03/06/c669d3fe-6010-11ea-8baf-519cedb6ccd9
_story.html.

255 **on March 17:** Reid J. Epstein, Lisa Lerer, and Thomas Kaplan, "Joe Biden Wins Primaries in Florida, Illinois and Arizona: Highlights," *The New York Times,* March 17, 2020, accessed December 13, 2020, nytimes.com /2020/03/17/us/politics/march-17-democratic-primary.html.

255 **Ohio had postponed its contest:** Nick Corasaniti and Stephanie Saul, "Ohio's Governor Postpones Primary as Health Emergency Is Declared Over Virus," *The New York Times,* March 16, 2020, accessed December 13, 2020, nytimes.com/2020/03/16/us/politics/virus-primary-2020-ohio.html.

255 **senator from MBNA:** Byron York, "The Senator from MBNA," *National Review,* August 23, 2008, accessed December 13, 2020, nationalreview.com /2008/08/senator-mbna-byron-york/.

255 **Biden looked into a camera and declared victory:** "Joe Biden Primary Night Remarks," C-SPAN, March 17, 2020, c-span.org/video/?470455-1/joe-biden -primary-night-remarks.

256 **most vulnerable set:** Veronique Greenwood, "How the Aging Immune System Makes Older People Vulnerable to Covid-19," *The New York Times,* September 8, 2020, accessed December 12, 2020, nytimes.com/2020/09/08 /health/covid-aging-immune-system.html.

256 **declaration of victory alone at home:** "Joe Biden Primary Night Remarks," C-SPAN, March 17, 2020, c-span.org/video/?470455-1/joe-biden-primary -night-remarks.

259 **picked another horse:** Jonathan Martin, "Beto O'Rourke Hires Former Obama Aide as Campaign Manager," *The New York Times,* March 25, 2019, accessed December 13, 2020, nytimes.com/2019/03/25/us/politics /beto-jennifer-malley-dillon.html.

259 **deputy campaign manager:** Michael Scherer, "Joe Biden Hired Rufus Gifford as New Deputy Campaign Manager," *The Washington Post,* April 29, 2020, accessed December 13, 2020, washingtonpost.com/politics/joe -biden-hires-rufus-gifford-as-new-deputy-campaign-manager/2020/04/29 /e76a44c0-8a32-11ea-9dfd-990f9dcc71fc_story.html.

262 **signed the CARES Act:** Erica Werner, Paul Kane, and Mike DeBonis, "Trump Signs $2 Trillion Coronavirus Bill Into Law as Companies and Households Brace for More Economic Pain," *The Washington Post,* March 27, 2020, accessed December 13, 2020, washingtonpost.com/us -policy/2020/03/27/congress-coronavirus-house-vote/.

262 **cornered the market:** Jonathan Allen, Phil McCausland, and Cyrus Farivar, "Want a Mask Contract or Some Ventilators? A White House Connection Helps," NBC News, April 24, 2020, accessed December 13, 2020, nbcnews .com/politics/white-house/political-influence-skews-trump-s-coronavirus -response-n1191236.

262 **called himself a "cheerleader":** John Avlon, "Trump Says He's a Cheerleader for USA. We Need a Quarterback," CNN, April 1, 2020, accessed December 13, 2020, cnn.com/2020/04/01/opinions/trump-coronavirus -hyper-partisan-opinion-avlon/index.html.

CHAPTER 14: LAW AND DISORDER

265 **resembled the 2012 Obama campaign:** Sean Sullivan, "Biden Campaign Staff Expands to Mimic Obama's Coalitions Effort in 2012," *The Washing-*

ton Post, May 27, 2020, accessed December 14, 2020, washingtonpost
.com/politics/biden-campaign-staff-expands-to-mimic-obamas-coalitions
-effort-in-2012/2020/05/27/480e1f06-9fad-11ea-b5c9-570a91917d8d_story
.html.

265 **came on full-time:** Michael Scherer, "Joe Biden Hires Rufus Gifford as New
Deputy Campaign Manager," *The Washington Post,* April 29, 2020, accessed December 14, 2020, washingtonpost.com/politics/joe-biden-hires
-rufus-gifford-as-new-deputy-campaign-manager/2020/04/29/e76a44c0
-8a32-11ea-9dfd-990f9dcc71fc_story.html.

265 **joined the campaign as a Latino outreach specialist:** María Peña, "Biden
Names Julie Chávez Rodríguez, César Chávez's Granddaughter, as Top Latina on Team," NBC News via Noticias Telemundo, May 19, 2020, accessed December 14, 2020, nbcnews.com/news/latino/biden-names-julie-ch
-vez-rodr-guez-c-sar-ch-n1210241.

266 **had $57 million in the bank:** Ken Thomas, "Biden Had Half as Much Cash
as Trump at End of April," *The Wall Street Journal*, May 15, 2020, accessed
December 14, 2020, wsj.com/articles/joe-biden-had-half-as-much-cash-as
-trump-at-end-of-april-11589576452.

268 **had chided Biden:** Donald J. Trump, @realDonaldTrump, "Sleepy Joe
Biden refuses to leave his basement "sanctuary" and tell his Radical Left
BOSSES that they are heading in the wrong direction. Tell them to get out
of Seattle now. Liberal Governor @JayInslee is looking "the fool". LAW &
ORDER!," Twitter, June 11, 2020, accessed December 15, 2020, twitter
.com/realDonaldTrump/status/1271080249623818242.

268 **took to the pages:** David Axelrod and David Plouffe, "What Joe Biden
Needs to Do to Beat Trump," *The New York Times,* May 4, 2020, accessed
December 15, 2020, nytimes.com/2020/05/04/opinion/axelrod-plouffe-joe
-biden.html.

269 **commemorate members of the armed forces:** Will Weissert, "Biden Marks
Memorial Day at Veterans Park Near Delaware Home," Associated Press,
May 26, 2020, accessed December 14, 2020, apnews.com/article/63bc4cbe6
62c1fe67878952209d737f4.

269 **delivered a rousing speech:** Matthew S. Schwartz, "Trump Praises Fallen
Soldiers In Memorial Day Ceremonies," NPR, May 25, 2020, accessed December 14, 2020, npr.org/sections/coronavirus-live-updates/2020/05/25
/861896865/trump-praises-fallen-soldiers-in-memorial-day-ceremonies.

269 **"invisible enemy":** "'It's the Invisible Enemy,' Trump Says of Coronavirus,"
The New York Times, March 18, 2020, nytimes.com/video/us/politics
/100000007040978/coronavirus-presser.html.

269 **"poor work ethic":** Donald J. Trump, @realDonaldTrump, ". . . 3 months
and, if I waited 3 years, they would do their usual "hit" pieces anyway.
They are sick with hatred and dishonesty. They are truly deranged! They
don't mention Sleepy Joe's poor work ethic, or all of the time Obama spent
on the golf course, often flying to . . . ," Twitter, May 25, 2020, twitter.com
/realDonaldTrump/status/1264912071898128384.

269 **"weaker" stance on China:** Donald J. Trump, @realDonaldTrump, "Nobody in 50 years has been WEAKER on China than Sleepy Joe Biden. He
was asleep at the wheel. He gave them EVERYTHING they wanted, including rip-off Trade Deals. I am getting it all back!," Twitter, May 25, 2020,
twitter.com/realDonaldTrump/status/1265011145879977985.

270 **put his knee on George Floyd's neck:** Christine Hauser, Derrick Bryson

Taylor, and Neil Vigdor, "'I Can't Breathe': 4 Minneapolis Officers Fired After Black Man Dies in Custody," *The New York Times,* May 26, 2020, accessed December 14, 2020, nytimes.com/2020/05/26/us/minneapolis -police-man-died.html?searchResultPosition=2.

270 **marched a couple of miles:** "Tear Gas, Chaos, Rain: Protests Rage After Man Dies in Mpls. Police Custody," MPR News, May 26, 2020, accessed December 14, 2020, mprnews.org/story/2020/05/26/protesters-rally-to-call -for-justice-for-man-who-died-in-mpls-police-incident.

270 **he said that morning:** Courtney Subramanian, "George Floyd: Trump to Receive 'Full Report' on Minneapolis Death, Calls It a 'Very Sad Event'," *USA Today,* May 27, 2020, accessed December 14, 2020, usatoday.com /story/news/politics/2020/05/27/george-floyd-trump-calls-minneapolis -death-very-sad-event/5267763002/.

270 **Later in the day, he tweeted:** Donald J. Trump, @realDonaldTrump, "At my request, the FBI and the Department of Justice are already well into an in-vestigation as to the very sad and tragic death in Minnesota of George Floyd . . . ," Twitter, May 27, 2020, twitter.com/realDonaldTrump/status /1265774767493148672.

270 **was gaining social acceptance:** Nate Cohn and Kevin Quealy, "How Public Opinion Has Moved on Black Lives Matter," *The New York Times,* June 10, 2020, accessed December 14, 2020, nytimes.com/interactive/2020 /06/10/upshot/black-lives-matter-attitudes.html.

271 **in the early morning hours of Friday, May 29:** Donald J. Trump, @realDonaldTrump, "These THUGS are dishonoring the memory of George Floyd, and I won't let that happen. Just spoke to Governor Tim Walz and told him that the Military is with him all the way. Any difficulty and we will assume control but, when the looting starts, the shooting starts. Thank you!," Twitter, May 29, 2020, twitter.com/realDonaldTrump /status/1266231100780744704.

271 **said on his Monday, June 1, Fox News show:** "Tucker Carlson Tonight," June 1, 2020, accessed December 14, 2020, video.foxnews.com/v/616104 8695001/#sp=show-clips.

271 **deliver remarks in the White House Rose Garden:** "President Trump Deliv-ers Remarks on Protests and Civil Unrest," C-SPAN, June 1, 2020, accessed December 14, 2020, c-span.org/video/?472684-1/president-deploy-military -states-halt-violent-protests.

272 **drove the fleeing crowd:** Katie Rogers, "Protesters Dispersed with Tear Gas So Trump Could Pose at Church," *The New York Times,* June 1, 2020, ac-cessed December 14, 2020, nytimes.com/2020/06/01/us/politics/trump-st -johns-church-bible.html.

272 **"I am your president of law and order":** "Statement by the President," The White House, June 1, 2020, accessed December 14, 2020, whitehouse.gov /briefings-statements/statement-by-the-president-39/.

272 **Trump marched across the park:** "President Trump Walks to St. John's Church," C-SPAN, June 1, 2020, accessed December 14, 2020, c-span.org /video/?472686-1/president-trump-walks-st-johns-church.

272 **withdrew a bible:** Bob Woodward, *Rage* (New York: Simon & Schuster, 2020).

273 **wrote in a statement:** Jeffrey Goldberg, "James Mattis Denounces President Trump, Describes Him as a Threat to the Constitution," *The Atlantic,*

June 3, 2020, accessed December 14, 2020, theatlantic.com/politics
/archive/2020/06/james-mattis-denounces-trump-protests-militarization
/612640/.

274 **"Protesting such brutality":** Joe Biden, "We Are a Nation Furious at Injustice," joebiden.com, accessed December 14, 2020, joebiden.com/2020/05/30
/we-are-a-nation-furious-at-injustice/.

274 **rioting in Wilmington:** Ben A. Franklin, "Armed Guardsmen Still Patrol
in Wilmington's Slums, 7 Months After Riot," *The New York Times,* November 17, 1968, accessed December 14, 2020, nytimes.com/1968/11/17
/archives/armed-guardsmen-still-patrol-in-wilmingtons-slums-7-months
-after.html.

274 **concluded that his position:** John Schmadeke, "Biden Gets Off to Flying
Start in Bid for Senate," *The Morning News,* March 21, 1972, accessed December 14, 2020, newspapers.com/clip/53784822/the-morning-news/.

274 **Biden wrote an op-ed in *USA Today*:** Joe Biden, "Biden: We Must Urgently
Root Out Systemic Racism, from Policing to Housing to Opportunity,"
USA Today, June 10, 2020, accessed December 14, 2020, usatoday.com
/story/opinion/2020/06/10/biden-root-out-systemic-racism-not-just-divisive
-trump-talk-column/5327631002/.

278 **was the last living member:** "John Lewis Biography," Biography.com, accessed December 15, 2020, biography.com/political-figure/john-lewis.

278 **Battling terminal cancer:** Emma Bowman, "Civil Rights Leader Rep. John
Lewis to Start Treatment for Pancreatic Cancer," NPR, December 29, 2019,
accessed December 15, 2020, npr.org/2019/12/29/792241464/civil-rights
-leader-rep-john-lewis-to-start-treatment-for-pancreatic-cancer.

279 **visited the newly baptized Black Lives Matter Plaza:** Jacob Knutson,
"Civil Rights Icon John Lewis Visits New Black Lives Matter Plaza in
D.C.," *Axios,* June 7, 2020, accessed December 15, 2020, axios.com/john
-lewis-black-lives-matter-plaza-da036fbe-0aef-46f4-b284-50ffe130aaf1
.html.

280 **meet with members of George Floyd's family:** Katie Glueck, "Joe Biden to
Meet with George Floyd's Family Ahead of Funeral," *The New York
Times,* June 7, 2020, accessed December 15, 2020, nytimes.com/2020/06/07
/us/politics/joe-biden-george-floyd-funeral.html.

280 **increased to 49.6 percent:** "General Election: Trump vs. Biden," Real Clear
Politics, accessed December 15, 2020, realclearpolitics.com/epolls
/2020/president/us/general_election_trump_vs_biden-6247.html.

280 **three-tenths of a point in Pennsylvania:** "Pennsylvania: Trump vs. Biden,"
Real Clear Politics, accessed December 15, 2020, realclearpolitics.com
/epolls/2020/president/pa/pennsylvania_trump_vs_biden-6861.html.

280 **3.8 points in Wisconsin:** "Wisconsin: Trump vs. Biden," Real Clear Politics,
accessed December 15, 2020, realclearpolitics.com/epolls/2020/president
/wi/wisconsin_trump_vs_biden-6849.html.

280 **did not view the president:** Megan Brenan, "Americans' Views of Trump's
Character Firmly Established," *Gallup,* June 18, 2020, accessed December 15, 2020, news.gallup.com/poll/312737/americans-views-trump
-character-firmly-established.aspx.

282 **made an ad:** Donald J. Trump, "Abolished," YouTube, July 2, 2020, accessed December 15, 2020, youtube.com/watch?v=AOOlOMLaFho
&feature=youtu.be.

CHAPTER 15: THE KEYS TO TULSA

284 **hit television show *The Apprentice*:** Emily Nussbaum, "The TV That Created Donald Trump," *The New Yorker,* July 24, 2017, accessed December 11, 2020, newyorker.com/magazine/2017/07/31/the-tv-that-created-donald-trump.

284 **soft-spoken and meticulously kempt:** Franklin Foer, "The Good Son," *The Atlantic,* August 13, 2020, accessed December 11, 2020, theatlantic.com/politics/archive/2020/08/how-jared-kushner-became-trumps-most-dangerous-enabler/615169/.

285 **popping up in news stories:** Jose Lambiet, "EXCLUSIVE: How Donald Trump's Campaign Manager Brad Parscale Went from Family Bankruptcy to Splashing Out Millions on Mansions, Condos and Luxury Cars Through His Companies That Get a Hefty Cut of the President's $57M Campaign Contributions," *Daily Mail,* August 22, 2019, accessed December 13, 2020, dailymail.co.uk/news/article-7375719/Brad-Parscale-fortune-companies-cut-Trumps-campaign-contributions.html.

285 **his first rally since the coronavirus:** Tom Lutz, "Brad Parscale Faces Trump 'Fury' After Tulsa Comeback Rally Flops," *The Guardian,* June 21, 2020, accessed December 13, 2020, theguardian.com/us-news/2020/jun/21/brad-parscale-donald-trump-tulsa-rally-covid-ivanka-kushner-rick-wilson.

286 **branding for Trump since 2010:** Deniz Çam, "From Web Designer to Trump's Digital Confidant: Brad Parscale," *Forbes,* December 6, 2017, accessed December 14, 2020, forbes.com/sites/denizcam/2017/12/06/from-web-designer-to-trumps-digital-confidant-brad-parscale/?sh=779521dd6e9e.

286 **Trump named Parscale to the top job:** David Nakamura and Anu Narayanswamy, "Trump Names Longtime Aide Brad Parscale as Campaign Manager for 2020 Reelection Effort," *The Washington Post,* February 27, 2018, accessed December 14, 2020, washingtonpost.com/news/post-politics/wp/2018/02/27/trump-names-longtime-aide-brad-parscale-as-campaign-manager-for-2020-reelection-effort/.

286 **"best-in-class":** Katie Rogers and Maggie Haberman, "Trump's 2020 Campaign Announcement Had a Very Trumpian Rollout," *The New York Times,* February 27, 2018, accessed December 14, 2020, nytimes.com/2018/02/27/us/politics/trump-2020-brad-parscale.html.

286 **rallies in support of Republican candidates:** John Fritze, "Trump Campaign Pledges 10 More Rallies Before Midterm Election," *USA Today,* October 23, 2018, accessed December 14, 2020, usatoday.com/story/news/politics/elections/2018/10/23/midterms-trump-campaign-rallies/1737613002/.

286 **Democratic wave flipped control of the House:** Jonathan Martin and Alexander Burns, "Democrats Capture Control of House; G.O.P. Holds Senate," *The New York Times,* November 6, 2018, accessed December 14, 2020, nytimes.com/2018/11/06/us/politics/midterm-elections-results.html.

286 **Trump had warned his base voters:** Jonathan Martin, "Republicans Seize on Impeachment for Edge in 2018 Midterm," *The New York Times,* April 8, 2018, accessed December 14, 2020, nytimes.com/2018/04/08/us/politics/trump-impeachment-midterms.html.

286 **had been virtually inelastic:** "Presidential Approval Ratings—Donald Trump," Gallup, accessed December 14, 2020, news.gallup.com/poll/203198/presidential-approval-ratings-donald-trump.aspx.

287 **"I fully expect that by July"**: Jonathan Allen, "Inside Trump's All-About-That-Base 2020 Strategy," NBC News, April 8, 2019, accessed December 14, 2020, nbcnews.com/politics/2020-election/inside-trump-s-all-about -base-2020-strategy-n991896.

287 **kicked off his reelection campaign**: Maggie Haberman, Annie Karni, and Michael D. Shear, "Trump at Rally in Florida, Kicks Off His 2020 Re-election Bid," *The New York Times,* June 18, 2019, accessed December 14, 2020, nytimes.com/2019/06/18/us/politics/donald-trump-rally-orlando .html.

287 **a number of the "Proud Boys"**: Christopher Mathias, "Trump's 2020 Campaign Kickoff Attracted Extremists to a City That Hates Trump," *HuffPost,* June 19, 2019, accessed December 14, 2020, huffpost.com/entry/donald -trump-orlando-proud-boys-qanon-infowars-extremists_n_5d0a2f14e4b0f7 b7442a11ca.

287 **$400 million in defense aid to Ukraine**: Maggie Haberman, Nicholas Fandos, Michael Crowley, and Kenneth P. Vogel, "Trump Said to Have Frozen Aid to Ukraine Before Call with Its Leader," *The New York Times,* September 23, 2019, accessed December 11, 2020, nytimes.com/2019/09/23/us /politics/trump-un-biden-ukraine.html.

287 **announce an investigation into Biden**: Aaron Blake, "The Bidens, Burisma and Impeachment, Explained," *The Washington Post,* January 27, 2020, accessed December 11, 2020, washingtonpost.com/politics/2020/01/25/hunter -biden-joe-biden-burisma-ukraine-impeachment/.

287 **Obama-Biden relationship**: Glenn Thrush, "Obama and Biden's Relationship Looks Rosy. It Wasn't Always That Simple," *The New York Times,* August 16, 2019, accessed December 14, 2020. nytimes.com/2019/08/16/us /politics/biden-obama-history.html.

288 **insulin costs at thirty-five dollars per month**: Kevin Liptak, Caroline Kelly, and Jacqueline Howard, "Trump Appeals to Seniors with Plan to Cap Insulin Costs at $35 for Medicare Enrollees," CNN, May 26, 2020, accessed December 14, 2020, cnn.com/2020/05/26/politics/white-house-insulin-cap -medicare/index.html.

288 **called Trump an "absolute fool"**: Eric Bradner, "Biden Blasts Trump for Mocking Face Masks," CNN, May 26, 2020, accessed December 14, 2020, cnn.com/2020/05/26/politics/joe-biden-cnn-interview-trump-face-masks /index.html.

291 **Trump fans had caused mayhem**: Kenya Evelyn, "Trump Fans Flooded Hotline to Disrupt Iowa Caucus Process, Democrats Say," *The Guardian,* February 6, 2020, accessed December 13, 2020, theguardian.com/us news /2020/feb/06/trump-fans-flooded-hotline-disrupt-iowa-caucus-process.

291 **the rally had to be rescheduled**: Peter Baker and Maggie Haberman, "Trump Moves Tulsa Rally Data 'Out of Respect' for Juneteenth," *The New York Times,* June 13, 2020, accessed December 13, 2020, nytimes.com /2020/06/12/us/politics/trump-tulsa-rally-juneteenth.html.

291 **commemorating Juneteenth**: Derrick Bryson Taylor, "So You Want to Learn About Juneteenth?," *The New York Times,* June 19, 2020, accessed December 13, 2020, nytimes.com/article/juneteenth-day-celebration.html.

292 **Users of TikTok**: Donie O'Sullivan, "Trump's Campaign Was Trolled by TikTok Users in Tulsa," CNN, June 21, 2020, accessed December 13, 2020, cnn.com/2020/06/21/politics/tiktok-trump-tulsa-rally/index.html.

292 **tweeted that one million people had signed up:** Donald J. Trump, @realDonaldTrump, "Almost One Million people request tickets for Saturday Night Rally in Tulsa, Oklahoma!," Twitter, June 15, 2020, twitter.com /realDonaldTrump/status/1272521253136498690.

292 **Oklahoma governor Kevin Stitt:** Sean Murphy, "Oklahoma Governor Seeks Larger Event for Trump's Tulsa Rally," Fox 46, June 15, 2020, accessed December 14, 2020, fox46.com/news/politics/election/oklahoma-governor -seeks-larger-event-for-trumps-tulsa-rally/.

292 **brace for a "wild evening":** Jonathan Swan, "Trump: Expect "Wild Evening" in Tulsa, Mask Optional," *Axios,* June 20, 2020, accessed December 13, 2020, axios.com/trump-axios-interview-tulsa-rally-31bd3a6f-b999 -45ea-af9a-e87649f9545f.html.

292 **"Any protesters, anarchists":** Donald J. Trump, @realDonaldTrump, "Any protesters, anarchists, agitators, looters or lowlifes who are going to Oklahoma please understand, you will not be treated like you have been in New York, Seattle, or Minneapolis. It will be a much different scene!," Twitter, June 19, 2020, twitter.com/realDonaldTrump/status/1273972301156016130.

292 **fired by a Trump emissary:** Michael D. Shear, Glenn Thrush, and Maggie Haberman, "John Kelly, Asserting Authority, Fires Anthony Scaramucci," *The New York Times,* July 31, 2017, accessed December 13, 2020, nytimes .com/2017/07/31/us/politics/trump-white-house-obamacare-health.html.

292 **go back to their countries:** Katie Rogers and Nicholas Fandos, "Trump Tells Congresswomen to 'Go Back' to the Countries They Came From," *The New York Times,* July 14, 2019, accessed December 13, 2020, nytimes .com/2019/07/14/us/politics/trump-twitter-squad-congress.html.

293 **how Trump had won in 2016:** Ronald Brownstein, "How Trump Won," *The Atlantic,* November 9, 2016, accessed December 13, 2020, theatlantic .com/politics/archive/2016/11/how-trump-won/507053/.

293 **Obama had drawn new voters:** Adam Nagourney, "Obama Wins Election," *The New York Times,* November 4, 2008, accessed December 14, 2020, nytimes.com/2008/11/05/us/politics/05campaign.html.

293 **His speech to the throngs in Tulsa:** *The Oklahoman,* "President Trump Rally in Tulsa," YouTube, June 21, 2020, youtube.com/watch?v=3kD7rp 3PEYE.

294 **downtown would be closed:** Hicham Raache, "Tulsa Police Release Map of Curfew and Road Closure Areas Because of Trump Rally," Oklahoma's News 4, June 18, 2020, accessed December 13, 2020, kfor.com/news/tulsa -police-release-map-of-curfew-and-road-closure-areas-because-of-trump -rally/.

294 **barked at aides:** Maggie Haberman and Annie Karni, "The President's Shock at the Rows of Empty Seats in Tulsa," *The New York Times,* June 21 2020, accessed December 26, 2020, nytimes.com/2020/06/21/us/politics /trump-tulsa-rally.html.

294 **"left-wing mob":** Kevin Freking and Jonathan Lemire, "Trump's Intended Show of Political Force Falls Short of Mark," Associated Press, June 21, 2020, accessed December 13, 2020, apnews.com/article/39c6f6230b51bda88 d6b61f49a281055.

294 **"puppet of the radical left":** Paul Waldman, "Why Trump Can't Convince Voters That Biden Is a 'Puppet of the Radical Left,'" *The Washington Post,* June 29, 2020, accessed December 13, 2020, washingtonpost.com/opinions

/2020/06/29/why-trump-cant-convince-voters-that-biden-is-puppet-radical
-left/.

295 **Memorial Day appearance:** Katie Glueck and Maggie Haberman, "Joe
Biden, Wearing Mask, Appears in Public at a Veterans Memorial," *The
New York Times,* May 25, 2020, accessed December 13, 2020, nytimes.com
/2020/05/25/us/politics/joe-biden-memorial-day.html.

295 **"slow the testing down, please":** Alicia Victoria Lozano, "Trump Tells
Tulsa Crowd He Wanted to 'Slow Down' COVID-19 Testing; White House
Says He Was Joking," NBC News, June 20, 2020, accessed December 13,
2020, nbcnews.com/politics/2020-election/trump-tells-tulsa-crowd-he
-wanted-slow-down-covid-19-n1231658.

295 **more than one hundred thousand of his fellow Americans dead:** "Four
Months After First Case, U.S. Death Toll Passes 100,000," *The New York
Times,* May 27, 2020, accessed December 13, 2020, nytimes.com/2020/05
/27/us/coronavirus-live-news-updates.html.

296 **very picture of disappointment:** Vanessa Friedman, "Trump, (Tie) Un-
done," *The New York Times,* June 22, 2020, accessed December 13, 2020,
nytimes.com/2020/06/22/style/trump-tulsa-tie.html.

296 *New York Post* **reported:** Ebony Bowden, "Trump Confidantes Push Him
to Drop Re-Election Campaign Manager Brad Parscale," *New York Post,*
June 11, 2020, accessed December 13, 2020, nypost.com/2020/06/11/trump
-confidantes-push-him-to-drop-campaign-manager-brad-parscale/.

296 **quarter of a billion dollars out the door:** Shane Goldmacher, "Trump Campaign Has Spent $325,000 on Facebook Ads Featuring Brad Parscale's
Page," *The New York Times,* June 30, 2020, accessed December 13, 2020,
nytimes.com/2020/06/30/us/politics/brad-parscale-trump.html.

296 **Biden had outraised Trump:** Elena Schneider and Zach Montellaro, "Biden
Outraises Trump with $80.8 Million in May," *Politico,* June 20, 2020, ac-
cessed December 13, 2020, politico.com/news/2020/06/20/biden-trump
-fundraising-330448.

297 **Biden would show $141 million:** Shane Goldmacher, "Biden Outraises
Trump for Second Straight Month, With $141 Million June Haul," *The
New York Times,* July 1, 2020, accessed December 13, 2020, nytimes.com
/2020/07/01/us/politics/trump-fundraising-2020.html.

297 **cut an ad trashing Parscale:** The Lincoln Project, "GOP Cribs," YouTube,
May 20, 2020, youtube.com/watch?v=mYpTJTngXE8.

297 **assets of at least $39 million:** Pat Ralph and Ellen Cranley, "Inside the
Marriage of Kellyanne and George Conway, Who Are Increasingly, Publicly
Facing Off Over Trump," *Business Insider,* October 14, 2020, accessed December 13, 2020, businessinsider.com/kellyanne-george-conway-marriage
-love-story-2018-8.

297 **Kushner and Ivanka Trump aired their supposed disgust:** Jim Acosta and
Sarah Westwood, "Jared Kushner and Ivanka Trump 'Pissed' at Trump
Campaign Manager Over His Rally Crowd Size Predictions, Source Says,"
CNN, June 21, 2020, accessed December 13, 2020, cnn.com/2020/06/21
/politics/jared-kushner-ivanka-trump-brad-parscale/index.html.

298 **Biden's lead in the polls had expanded:** "General Election: Trump vs.
Biden," Real Clear Politics, accessed December 13, 2020, realclearpolitics
.com/epolls/2020/president/us/general_election_trump_vs_biden-6247
.html.

300 **"Bridgegate" scandal:** Allyson Chiu, "Bill Stepien Was Ousted Over Bridge-gate. Now He's in Charge of Trump's Reelection Campaign," *The Washington Post,* July 16, 2020, accessed December 14, 2020, washingtonpost .com/nation/2020/07/16/trump-campaign-stepien-bridgegate/.

302 **Trump announced Stepien's promotion:** Maggie Haberman, "Trump Replaces Brad Parscale as Campaign Manager, Elevating Bill Stepien," *The New York Times,* July 15, 2020, accessed December 14, 2020, nytimes.com /2020/07/15/us/politics/trump-campaign-brad-parscale.html.

CHAPTER 16: HEAD OR HEART

304 **were among the candidates who attended:** Paul Kane, "Clyburn's Fish Fry Draws the Democratic Hopefuls and Illustrates a Concern," *The Washington Post,* June 22, 2019, accessed December 12, 2020, washingtonpost .com/powerpost/clyburns-fish-fry-draws-the-democratic-hopefuls-and -illustrates-a-concern/2019/06/22/014a280e-9468-11e9-aadb-74e6b2b46f6a _story.html.

305 **said publicly:** Mike Memoli, "A Black Woman is 'Not a Must' for Biden's Running Mate, Clyburn Says," NBC News, April 29, 2020, accessed December 12, 2020, nbcnews.com/politics/2020-election/black-woman-not -must-biden-s-running-mate-clyburn-says-n1194926.

305 **land one of the cushiest lobbying jobs:** Brooks Barnes, "M.P.A.A. and Christopher Dodd Said to Be Near Deal," *The New York Times,* February 20, 2011, accessed December 12, 2020, mediadecoder.blogs.nytimes .com/2011/02/20/m-p-a-a-and-christopher-dodd-said-to-be-near-deal/.

306 **lost her only statewide race:** Jessica Taylor, "Georgia's Stacey Abrams Admits Defeat, Says Kemp Used 'Deliberate' Suppression to Win," NPR, November 16, 2018, accessed December 12, 2020, npr.org/2018/11/16/6687 53230/democrat-stacey-abrams-ends-bid-for-georgia-governor-decrying -suppression.

306 **paid her a visit:** Bill Barrow, "Abrams, Biden Huddle Together as Both Look to 2020 Elections," Associated Press, March 14, 2019, accessed December 12, 2020, apnews.com/article/0f2e21e505ea4eb8bbcd1b2ded9c2b76.

307 **raised gobs of cash:** James Salzer, "Stacey Abrams Voting Rights Group Tops $32 Million Raised," *The Atlanta Journal-Constitution,* October 7, 2020, accessed December 12, 2020, ajc.com/politics/abrams-voting-rights -group-tops-32-million-raised/72KU2VSLORFKDC7IBPJHFOHPAE/.

307 **said publicly that she wanted it:** Astead W. Herndon, "Stacey Abrams Says She's Open to Being Vice President for Any Democratic Nominee," *The New York Times,* August 14, 2019, accessed December 12, 2020, nytimes .com/2019/08/14/us/politics/stacey-abrams-vice-president.html.

307 **would lock himself into choosing a woman:** Matt Stevens, "Joe Biden Commits to Selecting a Woman as Vice President," *The New York Times,* March 15, 2020, accessed December 12, 2020, nytimes.com/2020/03/15/us /politics/joe-biden-female-vice-president.html.

308 **dropping out of the 2020 race to endorse him:** Maggie Astor and Katie Glueck, "Elizabeth Warren Endorses Joe Biden: 'When You Disagree, He'll Listen,'" *The New York Times,* April 15, 2020, accessed December 12, 2020, nytimes.com/2020/04/15/us/politics/elizabeth-warren-endorse-biden .html.

309 **announcing his vetting team:** Bill Barrow, "Who's Who on the Committee Vetting Biden's Possible VPs," Associated Press, August 4, 2020, accessed December 12, 2020, apnews.com/article/joe-biden-jill-biden-atlanta-nancy-pelosi-donald-trump-2403396c8a83e3f8ad5fd2e041164b11.

310 **"That's politics":** Natasha Korecki, Christopher Cadelago, and Marc Caputo, "'She Had No Remorse': Why Kamala Harris Isn't a Lock for VP," *Politico,* July 27, 2020, accessed December 12, 2020, politico.com/news/2020/07/27/kamala-harris-biden-vp-381829.

310 **Twitterati did that for her:** Natasha Korecki and Christopher Cadelago, "Dodd Draws Fire—and Praise—as Biden VP vetter," *Politico,* July 30, 2020, accessed December 12, 2020, politico.com/news/2020/07/30/chris-dodd-biden-vp-387609.

311 **sign on to a letter:** Vanessa Williams, "More Than 200 Women Sign Letter Urging Biden to Pick a Black Woman as His Running Mate," *The Washington Post,* April 24, 2020, accessed December 12, 2020, washingtonpost.com/politics/2020/04/24/more-than-200-women-sign-letter-urging-biden-tap-black-woman-his-running-mate/.

313 **had a tough-on-crime record:** Nick Corasaniti and Katie Glueck, "Protests in Minnesota Renew Scrutiny of Klobuchar's Record as Prosecutor," *The New York Times,* May 29, 2020, accessed December 13, 2020, nytimes.com/2020/05/29/us/politics/klobuchar-minneapolis-george-floyd.html.

314 **she said the same thing:** Allyson Chiu, "Amy Klobuchar Withdraws From VP Consideration, Urges Biden to Pick a Woman of Color," *The Washington Post,* June 18, 2020, accessed December 13, 2020, washingtonpost.com/nation/2020/06/18/biden-klobuchar-election-vicepresident/.

314 **was the runner-up:** Andrew Prokop, "Elizabeth Warren Is Auditioning for VP on the Campaign Trail with Hillary Clinton," *Vox,* June 27, 2016, accessed December 13, 2020, vox.com/2016/6/13/11768224/elizabeth-warren-vice-president.

314 **Biden taking credit:** Rashaan Ayesh, "Warren Responds to Biden's Effort on Consumer Bureau: Thanks, Obama," *Axios,* October 16, 2019, accessed December 13, 2020, axios.com/2020-democratic-presidential-debate-biden-warren-68736505-e8b6-41db-8a16-84f52683c26f.html.

316 **moved up the short list:** Nahal Toosi, "'It's Absolutely Serious': Susan Rice Vaults to the Top of the VP Heap," *Politico,* July 27, 2020, accessed December 13, 2020, politico.com/news/2020/07/27/susan-rice-top-biden-vice-president-383026.

316 **gone out on television:** CBS News, "Rice: Libya Attacks Spontaneous," YouTube, September 16, 2012, accessed December 13, 2020, youtube.com/watch?v=60OxAyU8QwM.

316 **withdrew from consideration:** Mark Landler, "Rice Ends Bid for Secretary of State, and Fight with G.O.P.," *The New York Times,* December 13, 2012, accessed December 13, 2020, nytimes.com/2012/12/14/us/politics/rice-drops-bid-for-secretary-of-state-white-house-says.html.

317 **he had promised:** Harper Neidig, "Biden Pledges to Nominate Black Woman to Supreme Court," *The Hill,* February 25, 2020, accessed December 13, 2020, thehill.com/regulation/court-battles/484656-biden-pledges-to-nominate-black-woman-to-supreme-court.

319 **signed a letter:** Sean Sullivan, "Warren Allies Send Letter Urging Biden to Pick Her as Running Mate," *The Washington Post,* June 15, 2020, accessed

December 13, 2020, washingtonpost.com/politics/warren-allies-send-letter-urging-biden-to-pick-her-as-running-mate/2020/06/15/4d453762-ae75-11ea-b1e7-33e88fa24c71_story.html.

320 **praised the late communist:** Quint Forgey, "Karen Bass Walks Back Castro Comment Amid VP Vetting," *Politico*, July 27, 2020, accessed December 13, 2020, politico.com/news/2020/07/27/karen-bass-castro-comment-vp-vetting-382316.

320 **spoken at a Church of Scientology event:** Lauren Egan, "Rep. Karen Bass, Potential VP Pick, Addresses Her Past Praise of Scientology," NBC News, August 1, 2020, accessed December 13, 2020, nbcnews.com/politics/2020-election/rep-karen-bass-potential-vp-pick-addresses-her-past-praise-n1235589.

321 **Whitmer had flown into Wilmington:** Heidi Przybyla, Andrea Mitchell, and Kasie Hunt, "Michigan Gov. Whitmer Met with Biden as Running Mate Announcement Nears," NBC News, August 8, 2020, accessed December 13, 2020, nbcnews.com/politics/2020-election/michigan-gov-whitmer-met-biden-running-mate-announcement-nears-n1236213.

CHAPTER 17: UNCONVENTIONAL SUMMER

325 *Washington Post* **headline:** Karen Tumulty, "How Jennifer O'Malley Dillon Transformed Joe Biden's Campaign," *The Washington Post*, August 14, 2020, accessed December 13, 2020, washingtonpost.com/opinions/how-jennifer-omalley-dillon-transformed-joe-bidens-campaign/2020/08/14/d49de192-dbdd-11ea-8051-d5f887d73381_story.html.

329 **"The Deplorables":** Amy Chozick, "Hillary Clinton Calls Many Trump Backers 'Deplorables,' and G.O.P Pounces," *The New York Times,* September 10, 2016, accessed December 13, 2020, nytimes.com/2016/09/11/us/politics/hillary-clinton-basket-of-deplorables.html.

329 **unspooled a stem-winder:** "Dukakis Nomination as Presidential Candidate," C-SPAN, July 20, 1988, c-span.org/video/?3519-1/dukakis-nomination-presidential-candidate.

329 **relationship with Jeffrey Epstein:** Michael Gold, "Bill Clinton and Jeffrey Epstein: How Are They Connected?," *The New York Times,* July 9, 2019, accessed December 13, 2020, nytimes.com/2019/07/09/nyregion/bill-clinton-jeffrey-epstein.html.

331 **Biden appointed Mary Beth Cahill:** Reid J. Epstein and Shane Goldmacher, "Biden Will Fund-Raise with D.N.C. and His Appointee Will Lead the Committee," *The New York Times,* April 24, 2020, accessed December 14, 2020, nytimes.com/2020/04/24/us/politics/DNC-joe-biden-fundraising-mary-beth-cahill.html.

331 **Cutter in charge of content:** Michael Scherer, "Unconventional Democratic Convention Will Juggle Hundreds of Live Feeds to Re-Create the Feel of a Party Celebration," *The Washington Post,* August 16, 2020, accessed December 14, 2020, washingtonpost.com/politics/unconventional-democratic-convention-will-juggle-hundreds-of-live-feeds-to-re-create-the-feel-of-a-party-celebration/2020/08/15/02f887de-de60-11ea-809e-b8be57ba616e_story.html.

332 **speeches would be pretaped:** Astead W. Herndon and Reid J. Epstein, "It's Convention Time: 2-Minute Speeches, No Pomp, a Forlorn Milwaukee,"

The New York Times, August 16, 2020, accessed December 13, 2020, nytimes.com/2020/08/16/us/politics/democrats-convention-milwaukee -biden.html.

333 **a tribute to himself:** NBC News, "Watch Gov. Andrew Cuomo's Full Speech at the 2020 DNC," YouTube, August 17, 2020, youtube.com/watch?v=YKK IhowMoz4.

334 **backdrop that looked like a living room:** ABC News, "Michelle Obama's 2020 DNC Keynote Address," YouTube, August 17, 2020, youtube.com /watch?v=Linx1XLUbYo.

334 **lined up to host the third night:** Lauren Egan, "Kerry Washington Hosts Third Night of DNC," NBC News, August 26, 2020, accessed December 14, 2020, nbcnews.com/politics/2020-election/live-blog/dnc-live -updates-day-3-schedule-speakers-live-stream-n1237118/ncrd1237345 #blogHeader.

336 **Obama administration rule:** Emily Badger, "Obama Administration to Un-veil New Rules Targeting Segregation Across U.S.," *The Washington Post,* July 8, 2015, accessed December 13, 2020, washingtonpost.com/news /wonk/wp/2015/07/08/obama-administration-to-unveil-major-new-rules -targeting-segregation-across-u-s/.

336 **He took his place behind a podium:** ABC News, "Barack Obama Speaks at the 2020 DNC," YouTube, August 19, 2020, youtube.com/watch?v=ioR7LL BbDZg.

337 *Politico* **blared on its website:** Ryan Lizza, "Obama Torches Trump Like American Democracy Depends on It," *Politico,* August 20, 2020, accessed December 13, 2020, politico.com/news/2020/08/20/obama-torches-trump -like-american-democracy-depends-on-it-399108.

337 **Biden had named Karine Jean-Pierre:** Max Greenwood, "Biden Builds Out VP team Ahead of Running Mate Announcement," *The Hill,* August 11, 2020, accessed December 13, 2020, thehill.com/homenews/campaign /511490-biden-builds-out-vp-team-ahead-of-running-mate-announcement.

338 **The opening frame was a wide shot:** "Watch Sen. Kamala Harris' Full Speech at the 2020 DNC," NBC News, August 19, 2020, nbcnews.com /video/watch-sen-kamala-harris-full-remarks-at-the-2020-dnc-90344517727.

338 **Dreyfus was set to go live:** Sydney Ember and Lisa Lerer, "Julia Louis-Dreyfus Caps a Week of Starring Roles for 4 Actresses," *The New York Times,* August 20, 2020, accessed December 14, 2020, nytimes.com/2020/08 /20/us/politics/julia-louis-dreyfus-dnc.html.

340 **His message was standard Democratic fare:** C-SPAN, "Joe Biden Accep-tance Speech at 2020 Democratic National Convention," YouTube, Au gust 20, 2020, youtube.com/watch?v=pnmQroWfSvo.

340 **acknowledging Jerusalem as the capital:** Scott Wilson, "Democrats Restore Party Platform Language on Jerusalem, Following GOP Criticism," *The Washington Post,* September 5, 2012, accessed December 13, 2020, washingtonpost.com/politics/democrats-restore-to-party-platform -language-on-jerusalem-following-gop-criticism/2012/09/05/f023051a-f792 -11e1-8b93-c4f4ab1c8d13_story.html.

341 **Trump concluded a feud with North Carolina governor:** Annie Karni, "Re-publicans Will Move Trump Convention Speech Out of Charlotte," *The New York Times,* June 2, 2020, accessed December 13, 2020, nytimes .com/2020/06/02/us/politics/convention-charlotte-virus-republicans.html.

341 **speak from Jacksonville:** Dan Merica and Jeff Zeleny, "Trump to Accept Nomination in Jacksonville After Moving Most of Convention Out of Charlotte," CNN, June 11, 2020, accessed December 13, 2020, cnn.com /2020/06/11/politics/republican-convention-jacksonville/index.html.

341 **death of former Republican presidential candidate Herman Cain:** Aimee Ortiz and Katharine Q. Seelye, "Herman Cain, Former C.E.O. and Presidential Candidate, Dies at 74," *The New York Times,* July 30, 2020, accessed December 13, 2020, nytimes.com/2020/07/30/us/politics/herman -cain-dead.html.

341 **His poll numbers had taken a hit:** "General Election: Trump vs. Biden," Real Clear Politics, accessed December 13, 2020, realclearpolitics.com /epolls/2020/president/us/general_election_trump_vs_biden-6247.html.

341 **Trump wore a mask in public:** Jonathan Lemire, "Trump Wears Mask in Public for the First Time During Pandemic," *The Washington Post,* July 11, 2020, accessed December 13, 2020, washingtonpost.com/world/national -security/trump-wears-mask-in-public-for-first-time-during-pandemic /2020/07/11/f216cf76-c3bf-11ea-8908-68a2b9eae9e0_story.html.

341 **the president canceled on Florida:** David Smith, "Trump Cancels Republican National Convention Events in Jacksonville, Florida." *The Guardian,* July 23, 2020, accessed December 13, 2020, theguardian.com/us-news/2020 /jul/23/republican-national-convention-jacksonville-florida-donald-trump -cancel.

341 **"'The timing for this event is not right'":** C-SPAN, "President Trump Cancels Florida Component of Republican National Convention," YouTube, July 23, 2020, youtube.com/watch?v=nM_qBdlo1xQ.

342 **banished from Trumpworld:** Maggie Haberman and Annie Karni, "Cliff Sims, White House Tell-All Author, Sues Trump for Going After Him Over Book," *The New York Times,* February 11, 2019, accessed December 13, 2020, nytimes.com/2019/02/11/us/politics/cliff-sims-book-lawsuit.html.

343 **"Is that even legal?":** Alexander Bolton, "GOP Senator on Trump Accepting Nomination at White House: 'Is that even legal?' *The Hill,* August 5, 2020.

343 **His campaign used footage:** Donald J. Trump, "My Coronavirus Response is a Promise Made, Promise Kept," YouTube, April 29, 2020, youtube.com /watch?v=9hQqg7fIQGs&feature=youtube.

344 **Black person who voted for Trump "ain't Black":** Eric Bradner, Sarah Mucha, and Arlette Saenz, "Biden: 'If You Have a Problem Figuring Out Whether You're for Me or Trump, Then You Ain't Black,'" CNN, May 22, 2020, accessed December 13, 2020, cnn.com/2020/05/22/politics/biden -charlamagne-tha-god-you-aint-black/index.html.

344 **he outraised Biden in July:** Matthew Choi, "Trump Outraises Biden in July, Breaking Opponent's Short Streak," *Politico,* August 5, 2020, accessed December 14, 2020, politico.com/news/2020/08/05/trump-outraises-biden-in -july-breaking-short-biden-streak-392040.

344 **Bill Stepien froze TV advertising:** Nick Corasaniti, Annie Karni, and Shane Goldmacher, "Trump Halts TV Advertising as He Struggles in Polls Against Biden," *The New York Times,* July 31, 2020, accessed December 14, 2020, nytimes.com/2020/07/31/us/politics/trump-campaign-tv -advertising.html.

344 **conducting an audit of the books:** Nick Corasaniti and Stephanie Saul,

"Bill Stepien Takes Helm of Trump Campaign as a Data Obsessed Political Fighter," *The New York Times,* July 16, 2020, accessed December 14, 2020, nytimes.com/article/bill-stepien.html.

345 **divisive 1976 convention:** "1976: The Last Time Republicans Duked It Out to the Last, Heated Minute," NPR, March 13, 2016, npr.org/2016/03/13 /470271684/1976-the-last-time-republicans-duked-it-out-to-the-last-heated -minute.

345 **"vote your conscience":** Peter Schroeder, "No Trump Endorsement from Cruz: 'Vote Your Conscience,'" *The Hill,* July 20, 2016, accessed December 14, 2020, thehill.com/blogs/ballot-box/presidential-races/288607-no -trump-endorsement-from-cruz-who-tells-gop-vote-your.

345 **Trump strode onto a stage filled with American flags:** "President Trump Speaks at 2020 Republican National Convention," C-SPAN, August 27, 2020, c-span.org/video/?475004-5/president-trump-speaks-2020-republican -national-convention.

346 **small bounce in polling:** "General Election: Trump vs. Biden," Real Clear Politics, accessed December 13, 2020, realclearpolitics.com/epolls/2020 /president/us/general_election_trump_vs_biden-6247.html.

346 **One hundred eighty-four thousand:** Derek Hawkins, "U.S. Coronavirus Death Toll Approaches 180,000," *The Washington Post,* August 30, 2020, accessed December 14, 2020, washingtonpost.com/nation/2020/08/30 /coronavirus-covid-updates/.

346 **unemployment rate stood at 8.4 percent:** Megan Cassella, "U.S. Unemployment Rate Fell to 8.4 Percent in August," Politico, September 4, 2020, accessed December 14, 2020, politico.com/news/2020/09/04/august -unemployment-numbers-jobs-report-408825.

CHAPTER 18: THE INVISIBLE ENEMY

349 **Case Western Reserve University:** Isabella Grullón Paz, "What You Need to Know About the Upcoming Presidential Debates," *The New York Times,* September 28, 2020, accessed December 15, 2020, nytimes.com/2020/09/28 /us/politics/what-you-need-to-know-about-the-upcoming-presidential -debates.html.

350 **loomed over her shoulder:** Daniella Diaz, "Trump Looms Behind Clinton at the Debate," CNN, October 10, 2016, accessed December 15, 2020, cnn.com/2016/10/09/politics/donald-trump-looming-hillary-clinton -presidential-debate/index.html.

353 **phone-and-text program:** Amie Parnes and Jonathan Easley, "Democrats Worry Biden Playing It Too Safe," *The Hill,* September 14, 2020, accessed December 16, 2020, thehill.com/homenews/campaign/516394-democrats -worry-biden-playing-it-too-safe.

353 **one hundred million doors already:** Alex Thompson, "Trump's Campaign Knocks on a Million Doors a Week. Biden's Knocks on Zero," *Politico,* August 4, 2020, accessed December 15, 2020, politico.com/news/2020/08/04 /trump-joe-biden-campaign-door-knockers-391454.

353 **"If Biden loses":** Amie Parnes and Jonathan Easley, "Democrats Worry Biden Playing It Too Safe," *The Hill,* September 14, 2020, accessed December 16, 2020, thehill.com/homenews/campaign/516394-democrats-worry -biden-playing-it-too-safe.

353 **Clinton steered clear of in 2016:** Lisa Lerer and Reid J. Epstein, "These Are the Mistakes Democrats Don't Want to Repeat in 2020," *The New York Times,* July 18, 2019, accessed December 15, 2020, nytimes.com/2019/07/18/us/politics/2020-candidates-election-2016.html.

354 **record $365 million:** Marc Caputo, "Biden Posts Stunning Monthly Cash Haul: $365 Million," *Politico,* September 2, 2020, accessed December 15, 2020, politico.com/news/2020/09/02/biden-staggering-monthly-cash-haul-407712.

355 **still ahead in the polls:** "General Election: Trump vs. Biden," Real Clear Politics, accessed December 15, 2020, realclearpolitics.com/epolls/2020/president/us/general_election_trump_vs_biden-6247.html.

355 **saving the GOP majority in the Senate:** Shane Goldmacher, "As Trump Slumps, Republican Donors Look to Save the Senate," *The New York Times,* July 20, 2020, accessed December 15, 2020, nytimes.com/2020/07/20/us/politics/trump-polls-senate.html.

355 **O'Malley Dillon defended the decision:** Asma Khalid, "Republicans Are Knocking On Doors. Democrats Aren't. Biden Campaign Says That's OK," NPR, September 13, 2020, accessed December 15, 2020, npr.org/2020/09/13/911460651/republicans-are-knocking-on-doors-democrats-arent-biden-s-campaign-says-that-s-o.

357 **the decision was reversed:** Josh Dawsey and Matt Viser, "Biden Campaign to Begin Door Knocking After Criticizing the Trump Campaign for Doing the Same During the Pandemic," *The Washington Post,* October 1, 2020, accessed December 15, 2020, washingtonpost.com/politics/biden-canvas-trump-pandemic/2020/10/01/15775ba8-041a-11eb-8879-7663b816bfa5_story.html.

358 **Every time he spoke:** "First Presidential Debate," C-SPAN, September 29, 2020, c-span.org/debates/?debate=first.

359 **Biden said he wouldn't answer the question:** Dan Merica, "Joe Biden and Kamala Harris Don't Want to Talk About Changes to the Supreme Court," CNN, September 30, 2020, accessed December 15, 2020, cnn.com/2020/09/30/politics/joe-biden-court-packing/index.html.

360 **"Give me a name":** Associated Press, "Trump Tells Proud Boys: 'Stand Back and Stand by,'" YouTube, September 29, 2020, youtube.com/watch?v=qIHhB1ZMV_o.

360 *Birth of a Nation:* Allyson Hobbs, "A Hundred Years Later, 'The Birth of a Nation' Hasn't Gone Away," *The New Yorker,* December 13, 2015, accessed December 15, 2020, newyorker.com/culture/culture-desk/hundred-years-later-birth-nation-hasnt-gone-away.

361 **"I'm totally opposed":** Bloomberg Quicktake: "Now, 'Biden "Totally Opposed" to Defunding the Police,'" YouTube, September 29, 2020, youtube.com/watch?v=OKsVom6srTE.

361 **Trump unleashed an unverified allegation:** "Trump Goes After Hunter Biden," *The New York Times,* September 29, 2020, nytimes.com/video/us/elections/100000007368652/biden-trump-sons-debate-video-clip.html.

363 **how narrowly he had lost the state to Hillary:** "Minnesota Presidential Race Results: Hillary Clinton Wins," August 1, 2017, accessed December 15, 2020, nytimes.com/elections/2016/results/minnesota-president-clinton-trump.

364 **Nebraska's Second Congressional District:** Savannah Behrmann, "Nebraska and Maine's District Voting Method Could Be Crucial in This Elec-

tion. Here's Why," *USA Today*, November 4, 2020, accessed December 15, 2020, usatoday.com/story/news/politics/elections/2020/11/04/why-nebraska-maine-congressional-district-method-could-crucial/6073983002/.

364 **closely representative of the country:** "Nebraska's 2nd Congressional District," Ballotpia, ballotpedia.org/Nebraska%27s_2nd_Congressional_District.

364 **electoral college tie:** Elaine Kamarck, "What Happens If Trump and Biden Tie in the Electoral College," Brookings, October 21, 2020, accessed December 15, 2020, brookings.edu/blog/fixgov/2020/10/21/what-happens-if-trump-and-biden-tie-in-the-electoral-college/.

366 **tweeted the news out:** Donald J. Trump, @realDonaldTrump, "Tonight, @FLOTUS and I tested positive for COVID-19. We will begin our quarantine and recovery process immediately. We will get through this TOGETHER!," Twitter, October 2, 2020, twitter.com/realDonaldTrump/status/1311892190680014849.

367 **Trump had repeatedly attacked:** Michael Tackett, "Trump Renews Attacks on John McCain, Months After Senator's Death," *The New York Times*, March 17, 2019, accessed December 15, 2020, nytimes.com/2019/03/17/us/politics/trump-mccain-twitter.html.

367 **"As this situation continues to unfold":** Amie Parnes, "Biden Has No Plans to Scale Back Campaign," *The Hill*, October 2, 2020, accessed December 16, 2020, thehill.com/homenews/campaign/519331-biden-has-no-plans-to-scale-back-campaign.

367 **The first sign of trouble:** Maggie Haberman and Michael D. Shear, "Trump Says He'll Begin 'Quarantine Process' After Hope Hicks Tests Positive for Coronavirus," *The New York Times*, October 1, 2020, accessed December 15, 2020, nytimes.com/2020/10/01/us/politics/hope-hicks-coronavirus.html.

367 **hastily arranged coronavirus tests:** Natasha Korecki, Marc Caputo, and Caitlin Oprysko, "'There's No Joy in Being Right': Biden Makes Cautious Return to the Campaign Trail," *Politico*, October 2, 2020, accessed December 15, 2020, politico.com/news/2020/10/02/biden-campaign-debate-coronavirus-testing-425112.

368 **Walter Reed National Military Medical Center:** Peter Baker and Maggie Haberman, "Trump Hospitalized with Coronavirus," *The New York Times*, October 2, 2020, accessed December 15, 2020, nytimes.com/2020/10/02/us/politics/trump-hospitalized-with-coronavirus.html.

CHAPTER 19: DO NO HARM

371 **Halloween-sized black fly:** "Fly Lands on Mike Pence's Head During Debate," CNN, accessed December 16, 2020, cnn.com/videos/politics/2020/10/08/mike-pence-fly-on-head-debate-sot-vpx.cnn.

372 **Pence said just as the fly:** "Vice Presidential Debate," C-SPAN, October 7, 2020, accessed December 16, 2020, c-span.org/debates/?debate=vice.

373 **were separated by plexiglass barriers:** Kathleen Ronayne and J. David Ake, "In VP Debate, Plexiglass an Extra Participant on the Stage," Associated Press, October 8, 2020, accessed December 16, 2020, apnews.com/article/election-2020-virus-outbreak-joe-biden-donald-trump-utah-c42b91ff310a3867a300d556b39d5b37.

373 **emerged from the hospital:** Peter Baker and Maggie Haberman, "Trump

Leaves Hospital, Minimizing Virus and Urging Americans 'Don't Let It Dominate Your Lives,' " *The New York Times,* October 5, 2020, accessed December 16, 2020, nytimes.com/2020/10/05/us/politics/trump-leaves -hospital-coronavirus.html.

373 **delivered remarks from a White House balcony:** Caitlin Oprysko, "Trump Keeps Things Brief in First Public Address Since Hospitalization," *Politico,* October 10, 2020, accessed December 16, 2020, politico.com/news/2020/10 /10/trump-white-house-speech-coronavirus-428516.

373 **poll conducted:** Jeffrey M. Jones, "Americans View Biden as Likable, Honest; Trump, as Strong," *Gallup,* October 9, 2020, accessed December 16, 2020, news.gallup.com/poll/321695/americans-view-biden-likable-honest -trump-strong.aspx.

375 **turned into a virtual debate:** "CPD Announces Second Presidential Debate Will Be Virtual," Commission on Presidential Debates, October 8, 2020, accessed December 16, 2020, debates.org/2020/10/08/cpd-announces-second -presidential-debate-will-be-virtual/.

376 **he wouldn't participate from a remote location:** Krishnadev Calamur and Barbara Sprunt, "The Debate Over Debates: Trump Campaign Pushes for In-Person Debate Next Week," NPR, October 8, 2020, accessed December 16, 2020, npr.org/2020/10/08/921538492/second-presidential-debate-to -be-virtual-commission-says.

376 **booking its candidate:** Brett Samuels, "Biden to Participate in ABC Town Hall Oct. 15 in Lieu of Trump Debate," *The Hill,* October 8, 2020, accessed December 16, 2020, thehill.com/homenews/campaign/520244-biden -to-participate-in-abc-town-hall-oct-15-in-lieu-of-trump-debate.

377 **reflected that surge for Biden:** "General Election: Trump vs. Biden," Real Clear Politics, accessed December 16, 2020, realclearpolitics.com/epolls /2020/president/us/general_election_trump_vs_biden-6247.html.

379 **window for early voting had opened:** Anna Liz Nichols, "Early Voting Starts in Michigan Under New Rules," Associated Press, September 24, 2020, accessed December 16, 2020, apnews.com/article/election-2020-virus -outbreak-voting-voting-rights-michigan-2d74ffeda51e157b423097c2b7 6ea268.

379 **it was a spot featuring Cindy McCain:** Joe Biden, "Like John Did," YouTube, October 10, 2020, accessed December 16, 2020, youtube.com /watch?v=N0DMpKeH8bQ&feature=youtube.

379 **ran an ad featuring young Black men:** Joe Biden, "Shop Talk—Yes She Can," YouTube, September 21, 2020, accessed December 16, 2020, youtube .com/watch?v=8ilFf10OJOI&feature=youtube.

382 **Harris to travel to Fort Worth:** Lisa Lerer, " 'This Is No Time to Let Up,' Kamala Harris Tells Texas Democrats," *The New York Times,* October 30, 2020, accessed December 16, 2020, nytimes.com/2020/10/30/us/elections /this-is-no-time-to-let-up-kamala-harris-tells-texas-democrats.html.

384 **had won one hundred thousand more raw votes:** "Georgia Election Results," *The New York Times,* May 15, 2019, accessed December 16, 2020, nytimes.com/interactive/2018/11/06/us/elections/results-georgia-elections .html.

384 **Hillary had in the 2016 presidential race:** "2016 Georgia Results," *The New York Times,* accessed December 16, 2020, nytimes.com/elections/2016 /results/georgia.

385 would meet again on a debate stage: "Trump-Biden Second Debate,"
C-SPAN, October 22, 2020, accessed December 16, 2020, c-span.org/video
/?475796-1/trump-biden-debate&live.

CHAPTER 20: BLACK CLOVER

391 In 2016, Donald Trump had won: "2016 Presidential Election Results," *The New York Times,* August 9, 2017, accessed December 16, 2020, nytimes
.com/elections/2016/results/president.

391 2018 midterms: "2018 Midterm Election Results," *The New York Times,* updated November 27, 2018, accessed December 16, 2020, nytimes.com
/interactive/2018/us/elections/calendar-primary-results.html.

391 it could take days: Alison Durkee, "Here's Why Pennsylvania Ballots Will Take So Long to Count—And How Trump Could Challenge the Result," *Forbes,* October 29, 2020, accessed December 16, 2020, forbes.com/sites
/alisondurkee/2020/10/29/heres-why-pennsylvania-ballots-will-take-so-long
-to-count-and-how-trump-could-challenge-the-result/?sh=882f4186bff0.

391 "red mirage": David Wasserman, "Beware the 'Blue Mirage' and the 'Red Mirage' on Election Night," NBC News, November 3, 2020, accessed December 16, 2020, nbcnews.com/politics/2020-election/beware-blue-mirage
-red-mirage-election-night-n1245925.

396 Biden had never lost a general election: Katie Glueck, "Joe Biden," *The New York Times,* updated September 22, 2020, accessed December 16, 2020, nytimes.com/interactive/2020/us/elections/joe-biden.html.

396 Miami-Dade County: Steven Lemongello, "Trump Wins Florida Again, Bolstered by Miami-Dade Vote," *Orlando Sentinel,* November 4, 2020, accessed December 16, 2020, orlandosentinel.com/politics/2020-election
/os-ne-2020-general-election-florida-president-20201104-d6ny34gh7zg4rgf4
fet55ujway-htmlstory.html.

397 more afraid of socialism: Lizette Alvarez, "Trump's Gains with Florida Latinos Were Hiding in Plain Sight," *The Washington Post,* November 5, 2020, accessed December 16, 2020, washingtonpost.com/opinions/2020/11
/05/how-trump-won-florida-latinos-miami-dade-cuban-americans/.

397 Abigail Spanberger in the 2018 midterms: "Virginia's 7th House District Election Results: Dave Brat vs. Abigail Spanberger," *The New York Times,* January 28, 2019, accessed December 16, 2020, nytimes.com/elections
/results/virginia-house-district-7.

398 He was outperforming his 2016 numbers: Ford Fessenden, Lazaro Gamio, and Rich Harris, "Even in Defeat, Trump Found New Voters Across the U.S," *The New York Times,* November 16, 2020, accessed December 16, 2020, nytimes.com/interactive/2020/11/16/us/politics/election-turnout.html.

400 Clyburn protégé Jaime Harrison: "South Carolina U.S. Senate Election Results," *The New York Times,* updated November 24, 2020, accessed December 16, 2020, nytimes.com/interactive/2020/11/03/us/elections/results
-south-carolina-senate.html.

401 Security Is Strength political action committee: Security Is Strength PAC, accessed December 16, 2020, securityisstrengthpac.com/.

402 Fox News called Arizona for Biden: Michael M. Grynbaum and John Koblin, "Fox News Made a Big Call in Arizona, Buoying Biden and Angering Trump," *The New York Times,* November 4, 2020, accessed December 16,

2020, nytimes.com/2020/11/04/business/media/fox-news-arizona-trump
.html.

402 **Trump had won Arizona:** "Arizona Presidential Race Results: Donald J.
Trump Wins," *The New York Times,* August 1, 2017, accessed December 16, 2020, nytimes.com/elections/2016/results/arizona-president-clinton
-trump.

402 **"There goes her blue wall":** Fox News, "Fox News Projects: Donald Trump
Wins Wisconsin, Iowa," YouTube, November 8, 2016, youtube.com/watch
?v=JVBfaH-Qedw.

404 **gave brief remarks:** Joe Biden, "Joe Biden Speaks Live on Election Night
from Wilmington, Delaware," YouTube, November 3, 2020, youtube.com
/watch?v=4ph8dqqlsKI.

404 **Trump retorted by tweet:** Donald J. Trump, @realDonaldTrump, "We are
up BIG, but they are trying to STEAL the Election. We will never let them
do it. Votes cannot be cast after the Polls are closed!," Twitter, November 4,
2020, twitter.com/realDonaldTrump/status/1323864823680126977.

404 **go to the podium:** ABC News, "President Trump's Election Night Remarks," YouTube, November 4, 2020, youtube.com/watch?v=YlmaKd
bC6ZM.

406 **He would end up winning:** "Presidential Election Results: Biden Wins,"
The New York Times, accessed December 16, 2020, nytimes.com
/interactive/2020/11/03/us/elections/results-president.html.

407 **good election for the GOP down ballot:** Trip Gabriel, "How Democrats
Suffered Crushing Down-Ballot Losses Across America," *The New York
Times,* November 28, 2020, accessed December 16, 2020, nytimes.com/2020
/11/28/us/politics/democrats-republicans-state-legislatures.html.

INDEX

Key to abbreviations:

AOC = Alexandria Ocasio-Cortez
BLM = Black Lives Matter
CBC = Congressional Black Caucus
DNC = Democratic National Committee
Hillary = Hillary Clinton
VP = vice president

ABOUT THE AUTHORS

JONATHAN ALLEN is a senior political analyst with NBC News digital. A winner of the Dirksen and Hume awards for reporting, he was previously the White House bureau chief for *Politico* and the Washington bureau chief for Bloomberg News.

AMIE PARNES is a senior correspondent for *The Hill* newspaper in Washington, where she covers the Biden White House and national politics. She was previously a staff writer at *Politico*, where she covered the Senate, the 2008 presidential campaign, and the Obama White House.

ABOUT THE TYPE

This book was set in Sabon, a typeface designed by the well-known German typographer Jan Tschichold (1902–74). Sabon's design is based upon the original letter forms of sixteenth-century French type designer Claude Garamond and was created specifically to be used for three sources: foundry type for hand composition, Linotype, and Monotype. Tschichold named his typeface for the famous Frankfurt typefounder Jacques Sabon (c. 1520–80).